PROSLAVERY

*A History of the Defense
of Slavery in America,
1701–1840*

PROSLAVERY

A History of the Defense of Slavery in America, 1701–1840

LARRY E. TISE

THE UNIVERSITY OF GEORGIA PRESS

Athens and London

© 1987 by the University of Georgia Press
Athens, Georgia 30602
All rights reserved

Designed by Kathi L. Dailey
Set in Mergenthaler Baskerville
Typeset by The Composing Room
Printed and bound by Thomson-Shore, Inc.
The paper in this book meets the guidelines for
permanence and durability of the Committee on
Production Guidelines for Book Longevity of the Council
on Library Resources.

Printed in the United States of America

91 90 89 88 87   5 4 3 2 1

Library of Congress Cataloging in Publication Data

Tise, Larry E.
Proslavery: a history of the defense of slavery in
America, 1701–1840.

Revision of thesis (Ph.D.)—University of North Carolina,
1974.
Bibliography: p.
Includes index.
1. Slavery—United States—Historiography.
I. Title.
E337.5.T57   1987   973'.0496'0072   86-14671
ISBN 0-8203-0927-3 (alk. paper)

British Library Cataloging in Publication Data available

CONTENTS

ILLUSTRATIONS

TABLES

PREFACE

My study of proslavery literature and thought was first prompted as a personal interest and has remained ever since both a personal and a professional pursuit. The first kindling was sparked while I sat in an undergraduate history seminar under the wise counsel of Prof. Robert F. Durden at Duke University. As a small group of us read and argued about the history of the Old South in the seminar room, some of the last vestiges of that peculiar South began melting away all around us on the university campus, in the city of Durham, and throughout the South. Studying the Old South historically while we could literally watch the drama of one of the most wrenching changes to the South since the Civil War was perhaps the most stimulating and exhilarating experience possible for a serious student of history. Since additionally I derived from one of the backwaters of that South that was so badly in need of change and from generations of southern plain folk tinged in some manner by the burden of their own past, the study of proslavery became for me part of a process of learning and cleansing.

I began my study of proslavery literature and people with hopes of being able to understand and explain the causes of those overt expressions of racism contained in defenses of slavery. I wanted to know personally how a group of individuals in the Old South could have arrived at the ridiculous proposition that slavery could be good and beneficial both to the Negro and to American society. Unfortunately, while I found that I had been very well prepared morally for my encounter with proslavery (i.e., there was little chance that I would be persuaded by the arguments), I found that I was totally unprepared by what I had been taught about history. Almost none of the assumptions I took into the study worked even though they were taught to me by some of the finest and most enlightened historians of the nation. The more evidence I gathered the more I became convinced that historians from the time of the Civil War to the present had fallen into the unfortunate trap of treating proslavery morally rather than historically. And in making moral rather than historical judgments about proslavery, it is clear, at least to me, that we have thereby almost totally misunderstood the rich flow of American experience and social impulses between the American Revolution and the Civil War.

I found proslavery not to be any of those things historians said it would be. Beginning with the accepted notion that proslavery was an aberration in American history, I found instead that it was precisely one of the clearest possible indications of the nature and character of American society and its values—not merely in the Old South but throughout the nation. I also learned through my study that it would be very wise for historians to take a new look at the ebb and flow of American history between the American Revolution and the Civil War. While we have assumed that there was some progression in the growth of freedom and equalitarianism from the Revolution to the Civil War, I have found in my research on proslavery and the conservative ideology to which it became attached that the United States came dangerously close to losing its liberating and liberalizing tendencies in the first half of the nineteenth century. Given the depth of commitment Americans came to have for conservative republicanism, as I call it, and thereby for the institution of slavery, it is well that other factors and events eventually combined to bring the matter of slavery to a head in the midst of the Civil War. From my perspective, we are fortunate that the near national acquiescence with slavery as a morally acceptable institution, which conservative counterrevolutionaries North and South almost achieved, was finally shattered in the clash of sectional war.

Recognizing early in my study of proslavery the profound misconceptions on the subject perpetuated on nearly all sides, I recognized that if I were to interpret proslavery and all its implications properly I would have to pursue an extensive process of attempting to demythologize both popular perceptions of the defense of slavery and the misconceptions innocently perpetuated by historians. The first part of my study is, therefore, devoted to an analysis of some of the most popular myths about proslavery history and proslavery writers.

Since historical investigation should serve an architectonic as well as a critical function, I have attempted in the second part of the study to establish the outlines of an interpretation of proslavery history bereft of the myths. After demythologizing proslavery in line with the findings of my research, I was able to proceed to a new understanding of proslavery in American history by asking a very simple, yet crucial question: at what point and by what processes did Americans begin to reject the theory of natural rights and therefore the contagion of liberty inherited from their revolutionary experience? I believed and still maintain that the way one answers that question will determine the manner in which one must characterize proslavery history in America. The point at which American revolutionary ideology was supplanted with something else provides the clue to the launching of those cultural forces that led eventually to an open defense of slavery and the formation of a social philosophy that could hold both slavery and America intact for almost a century after the American Revolution.

From the outset I should make clear that my conception of proslavery ideology differs markedly from that of most historians. Far from being a body of prejudice entertained and expressed by a section of the nation, a group of one-dimensional racists, or even by a slaveholding class, I believe that proslavery ideology was a mode of thinking, a concatenation of ideas, and a system of symbols that expressed the social, cultural, and moral values of a large portion of the population of America in the first half of the nineteenth century.

I have adopted a straightforward dictionary definition for the term *proslavery*. By proslavery I mean quite simply the general attitude of favoring slavery, either "favoring the continuance of the institution of Negro slavery, or opposed to interference with it."[1] It should be noted that such a definition, without reference to racism, sectionalism, or class consciousness immediately brings into consideration a host of perspectives sometimes not associated with proslavery thought, including many expressed by those indirect upholders of slavery often classed as anti-abolitionists. By the definition I am using, a person could for reasons known only to himself denominate slavery an evil and yet argue that to tamper with the institution would be to court social, political, economic, or moral disaster. Hence, at least in my point of view, a proslavery thinker was anyone who urged the indefinite perpetuation of slavery for any reason whatsoever.

For purposes of clarification I have adopted a restricted definition of *abolitionist*. Because abolitionists were perceived by most Americans as radically different from their predecessors, I have maintained throughout a distinction between antislavery spokesmen before the arrival of Garrisonian Abolitionism in 1831, quite irrespective of the radicalism of their proposals, and those after 1831. Any antislavery proponent before 1831, even a would-be abolitionist, I denominate as an emancipator. Any person after 1831 who rallied to immediatism I call an abolitionist. And on the other side of the fence, even though their sometimes opposition to both slavery and abolition after 1831 is conceptually confused by the term, I have followed the usage of recent historians by calling these latter individuals *anti-abolitionists*.

Another crucial term that will be found on nearly every page of the following study is *ideology*. Although the term is often vague, it can be used in a very precise manner.[2] An ideology, in the words of one sociologist, is a society's "symbol-system" or a commonly adopted extrinsic source of information, values, and guidelines, "in terms of which human life can be patterned—extrapersonal mechanisms for the perception, understanding, judgment, and manipulation of the world." In addition to operating as a programmed "template or blueprint for the organization of social and psychological processes," an ideology is part of a cultural system, ever dynamic and fluid, embodying at any one point in time a contemporaneously meaningful symbol-system for both the society as a whole and the individual members thereof. Once launched, a society's ideology establishes a transcendent life of its own, forming opinions and shaping behavior until it is superseded or otherwise transmuted by a contemporaneously more meaningful system of symbols.[3]

In addition, I distinguish, after Franz Schurmann,[4] between "pure" and "practical" ideology. In the context of this study pure ideology refers to those symbol-systems or social philosophies that are in the process of formation, not yet fully articulated and not yet society-wide expressions of values and beliefs. Pure ideologies are, in every sense, spontaneous intellectual and psychological responses to disturbing events in society, separable from the propagandistic machinations of men. Practical ideologies, on the other hand, are more practiced bodies of thought, clearly defined, the content of propagandist literature. Pure ideologies in the process of evolution cannot function as propaganda even though their absorption by a citizenry may fulfill many of the same social and psychological tasks of a practical ideology. Once formed, however, pure ideology may become through adoption the ideational bulwark for upholding a derived set of values, attitudes, or beliefs. At that point pure ideology crosses the threshold of spontaneity and is transformed into practical ideology.

Methodologically I have attempted to blend together, as the occasion demanded, impressionistic, quantitative, and comparative history. While much of the study conforms to the traditional mold of narrative history,

I found it necessary at certain points to test some of my hypotheses by means of quantification or by way of comparison between American and other western societies. In fact, underlying the entire study is a multi-focal computer study that for convenience sake I have styled a "Pro-slavery Ideography." It consists of analyses of biographical data on defenders of slavery, information on published defenses, and ideas and arguments appearing in proslavery literature. It has been possible to report in the text only a small portion of the findings that contributed to my overall reassessment of proslavery history. Nevertheless, I have sometimes silently drawn data for my discussions of the parameters of proslavery arguments and American defenders of slavery from my Pro-slavery Ideography. I have tried everywhere possible to have my revision of proslavery rest on a more objective basis than past impressionistic studies.

A final note on my approach to the study of proslavery concerns my heavy emphasis on defenders of slavery. Although I have studied and include herein as appropriate every proslavery writing I could identify and every published defender of whom I am aware from politicians to planters, from scientists to novelists, and from ministers to lawyers, I found quite early in my research that the antebellum clergy provided essential social leadership in manners quite distinct from the patterns to which we are accustomed in the twentieth century. In the nineteenth century from the resurgence of religion during the Second Great Awakening until the Civil War, one could find among the ranks of the ministry some of the most superbly educated, socially aware, and power-fully stationed (both symbolically and actually) leaders America could boast. As educators, writers, reformers, orators, and spiritual leaders, clergymen constituted the largest, most vocal, and most readily accessi-ble national elite in American society. One measure of their significance is the fact that ministers wrote almost half of all defenses of slavery pub-lished in America.[5]

Perhaps as important as the social significance of clergymen as indi-viduals and as a conscious elite is the fact that their profession and Amer-ican religious life in general reflected the same social and ideological stresses out of which proslavery ideology sprang. Professionalization of the clergy, religious revivals, benevolent reforms, the missionary im-pulse, the rise of denominationalism, the infiltration of clergymen into educational institutions, and dozens of other currents in American re-ligious life paralleled and sometimes foreshadowed the course of proslavery history from the American Revolution to the Civil War. Since I believe that proslavery ideology was more a product of American than southern culture, more importantly a social than a political process, and more significantly an expression of national than sectional or class values, clergymen have served as the illuminating foci, although hardly exclusively, of my researches into and reevaluation of America's peculiar form of proslavery ideology.

This book is a revision and contraction of my doctoral dissertation at the University of North Carolina entitled "Proslavery Ideology: A Social and Intellectual History of the Defense of Slavery in America, 1790–1840," a project I completed happily in 1974. Those interested in more of the methodology of the study and especially in further documentation of the historiography of proslavery, of proslavery literature from 1840 to the period of the Civil War, in far more statistical tabulations than could be printed here, and in the most extensive bibliography available on historic proslavery literature should consult the dissertation directly.

A great many people are responsible for both the dissertation and this book. The dissertation itself, and thereby the book, is an expansion of a number of papers written under the inspiration and the wise critique of several historians at Duke University and the University of North Carolina at Chapel Hill: Robert F. Durden and John Alden at Duke; Stuart Henry, Frank Baker, and Ray Petry of the Duke Divinity School; and Frank W. Klingberg, Hugh T. Lefler, John K. Nelson, Donald G. Mathews, and Joel Williamson at Chapel Hill. Both Mathews and Williamson provided helpful criticisms of a number of chapters as the dissertation was evolving.

Because of a great many factors the study sat on the shelf for ten years needing to be revised and prepared for publication. During those years I spent most of my time first directing the North Carolina Division of Archives and History and thereafter serving as State Historian for the Commonwealth of Pennsylvania and as Executive Director of the Pennsylvania Historical and Museum Commission. That the dissertation finally became a book is directly attributable to the reading and criticism of the manuscript as well as the constant pestering of William S. Price, Jr., Jeffrey J. Crow, and Brent D. Glass, colleagues at Archives and History in North Carolina; to Malcolm Call, formerly of the University of North Carolina Press, who urged that I get on with the necessary revisions; to Bertram Wyatt-Brown, then at Case Western Reserve University, who demanded that I make a number of changes to get the proper actor with the right cause; and, especially, to Suellen Hoy, formerly of the American Public Works Association and presently of the North Carolina Division of Archives and History, who read, absorbed, and corrected much of the manuscript and made it everywhere better. Without the encouragement of each of these, nothing would have happened with the old manuscript.

When I finally got seriously into the process of revision, several colleagues and associates proved of tremendous assistance. Jeffrey Crow, my faithful co-editor on several projects, read and corrected many errors of style, expression, and notably of tone. Robert Grant Crist, a historian associate in Pennsylvania, generously proofread and significantly helped improve the final version. Eugene Genovese, who has done much to stimulate a resurgence of interest in the study of proslavery, attempted fruitlessly to persuade me to adopt his special perspective on what he believes to be the unique outlook of the slaveholders of the South. I am hereby returning the proselytizing favor in the following pages. The several versions I have gone through in the last couple of years have all been word processed faithfully and cheerfully in the shadow of Three Mile Island by Carol F. Teufel of New Cumberland, Pa. My dauntless and hereby thanked proofreaders were Linda Ellsworth, Susan Rosenfeld Falb, Nancy Kolb, and Nellie Longsworth.

On a totally different level I am indebted to a number of other individuals, particularly those who have had to listen endlessly to my expressions of desire to get the book completed. Among those who have actively encouraged, even rooted and cheered from time to time have been Alice, Larry, Jr., and Nicholas; the patient staff members at the North Carolina Division of Archives and History and at the Pennsylvania Historical and Museum Commission; but also my close friends and associates who have pricked my conscience or filled me with happiness from time to time—especially Myrle Fields, Freda Brittain, Betsy Buford, Kathleen McCarter, Betty Doak Elder, June Britt, Nellie Longsworth, Kathleen Gray, Ruth Strack, Cheryl Klipa, and Nancy Kolb. These dear inspirators had to bear for years with this and other frustrations. But still the project would not have been completed if my boss and chair of the Historical and Museum Commission, Vivian W. Piasecki, had not insisted that I take the time from my administrative chores to complete the manuscript. For that special act of inspiration, encouragement, and command I will be ever grateful.

PART ONE

The Mythology
of Proslavery History

ONE

Beyond Racism and the "Positive Good" Argument

Traditional approaches to proslavery literature and thought in the United States frequently have caused historians to misinterpret their evidence and to draw curious conclusions. One well-informed historian quite innocently selected "an unusually good statement of the hierarchical social theory" to demonstrate how South Carolina's proslavery nullifiers supposedly exemplified the racist thinking of southerners in the 1830s. In fact the statement was written by a Massachusetts-born, Harvard-educated opponent of nullification who had only recently emigrated to the South from a Congregational pulpit in his native state. Contending that in the face of the abolition movement southerners rejected both the social values of the American Revolution and of the entire Age of Reason, the historian declared the anonymous New Englander's writing perhaps the clearest exposition of the southern ideological retreat to "the medieval, Aristotelian concepts of hierarchy, rank, and order" that proceeded from the South's "Great Reaction" to radical antislavery. The unknown defender's argument that "the basis of civilization is order, which implies distinctions and differences of condition," must have seemed evidence enough that a southern proslavery thinker was at work weaving together uniquely southern notions.[1]

The ready ascription of proslavery writings and, as a consequence, proslavery ideas to southerners and particularly to southern sectionalists has blinded historians to the actualities of proslavery history. That a serious student of proslavery could assume without question that a particular defense of slavery derived necessarily from the mind of a peculiar type of American—a nullifying South Carolinian—is indicative of the blurred vision through which many historians have traditionally seen the defense of slavery. In the conventional wisdom that has grown up about proslavery it is assumed that southern slaveholders were in the vanguard of those who leaped to the defense of slavery in the nineteenth century, that most other Americans (especially in the North) openly or privately denounced both slavery and slaveholders, and that statesmen of the slaveholding South made proslavery the cause célèbre of defiant sectionalism.

The convention extends much further to assess ideas and motives. According to this line of reasoning, southern proslavery thought was an aberrant form of social thinking limited in time and space to the Old South. In the continuum of American history, so the story goes, proslavery thinkers turned away from the libertarian heritage of the American Revolution, of Jefferson, and of the Enlightenment to adopt social values alien to America. In defiance of the liberating tendencies of the Western world, southerners broke rank with those who viewed slavery as a social evil, or at best a necessary evil, by upholding the institution quite uniquely as "positive good." And southerners responded to racist impulses by pleading for the right to keep social control in the hands of a master race. Although there are variant notions as to the prime movers behind proslavery, such telling phrases as "slave power conspiracy," "ideology of the master class," and "fire-eating aristocrats" have perpetually applied a theory of self-interest to southern slaveholders in order to allocate historical blame for proslavery propaganda. Acutely aware of their economic interests, openly racist, and stodgily sectional, southern leaders discovered a macabre love of human bondage, created a social philosophy to uphold it, and went about building a unique culture that could glorify it.

While historians might differ on finer points, these seem to be, at least in outline, beliefs about proslavery that have been shared by most twentieth-century historians. Whether in the course of discussing the defense of slavery or a host of related topics from abolitionism to southern culture, from racism to political economy, or from sectional politics to comparative cultures, historians have borne and perpetuated the image of proslavery as a uniquely southern phenomenon, a scorned rivulet outside the mainstream of American history interrupting the even growth of the nation's social and political democracy. Discounting proslavery propagandists as few in number and deviously inclined toward the disruption of the American union and ascribing their thought to the baser nature of man, historians have been generally content either to

ignore proslavery or to repeat scathing criticisms first verbalized by abolitionists. Although a few historians have raised searching questions
about the nature of America's slavery experience, the conventional picture of proslavery as an aberrant body of thought remains largely
unchanged.

Despite such assumptions, proslavery is one of the great unexamined
topics in American history. Whereas successive schools of historians have
studied exhaustively and have frequently revised interpretations of such
closely related subjects as abolitionism, Civil War causation, and the economics of slavery, few historians until recent years have been attracted to
research in the field of proslavery literature and thought. Only one general history of proslavery and one fairly generalized evaluation of the
nature of proslavery thought have been produced. Aside from those two
studies, historians have seen fit to examine only minor facets of the topic,
rarely adding to or detracting from conventional interpretations.[2]

Now overlooked in some quarters, William Sumner Jenkins's *Pro-slavery Thought in the Old South* (1935) remains the only full-length analysis of
proslavery literature and thought in the United States. Jenkins's ahistor-
ical catalogue of proslavery writings and arguments from the Old South
has hampered rather than aided historians in their understanding of the
development of proslavery history in the United States. Although the
book offers a reliable portrayal of various proslavery arguments, its
sweeping chronicle on the rise of proslavery in the Old South is misleading. Historians and others who consult the book have gotten a mistaken
view of proslavery history that the historical record will not sustain.

Jenkins argued that a great revolution in proslavery occurred during
the 1820s in the Old South. Because of the Missouri debates, the Denmark Vesey plot, the activity of the American Colonization Society, and
the "increased propaganda of the abolitionist groups," Jenkins believed
that southerners began spewing forth a raft of proslavery pamphlets
that "manifested the awakened spirit in defense of slavery." In addition
to preceding Garrisonian abolitionism by more than a decade with an
aggressive defense of slavery, Jenkins thought he also saw in the 1820s
the emergence of what he called the "positive good theory" of slavery,
i.e., that slaveholding, far from being an evil, was positively good in and
of itself and was viewed by southerners as "the cornerstone of our republican edifice." Although he left the impression that the Old South
teemed with such outpourings prior to the appearance of radical abolitionism, he provided only a few curious examples to prove the case.[3]

Despite the flaws and limitations of Jenkins's *Pro-Slavery in the Old South,* his assertions that the South developed an aggressive proslavery stance and that the chief characteristic of its witness was the positive value of slavery have endured and have been universally cited in almost all historical works making reference to proslavery in America. His simple explanation for the rise of proslavery in the Old South has constantly suited the purposes of almost any school of historical interpretation. From liberal antiracist historians of the 1930s and 1940s to recent students of American racism, the positive good theory merely confirmed the Old South's rampant racism.[4] Students of abolitionism could easily embrace his notion of an aggressive slavocracy.[5] In studies of comparative cultures, particularly in the Western world, the positive good theory set the Old South apart from all other slave societies.[6] Historians of race relations in the North could assume that proslavery and racial statements of northerners were unrelated to the even more peculiar views of southerners.[7] Even historians who viewed slavery as part of the "burden" or "travail" of southern history could use the positive good theory to suggest the lengths to which southerners went to convince themselves that slavery was an acceptable social institution.[8] And although at least one historian, Eugene D. Genovese, has taken a refreshing new look at proslavery as the ideology of the master class, particularly through the eyes of the Old South theoretician George Fitzhugh, he has not questioned the universal consensus that southern slaveholders created a unique proslavery stance in America, distinctively held slavery to be a positive good, and aggressively pushed those notions on a rapidly changing world.[9]

It was not until the appearance of Genovese's *World the Slaveholders Made* (1969) that historians began to show an interest in attempting to understand the history of proslavery. By 1971 some historians began calling for a reevaluation of proslavery in American history. David Donald suggested a fruitful new line of investigation when he urged historians to look at the biographies of slavery's defenders to determine if they were not individuals of lost stature who dreamed of "a return to the Golden Age when the South had been led by giants."[10] Within a few years a number of articles and books began to appear that associated proslavery with the intellectual elite of the Old South who were struggling for acceptance in a non-intellectual culture, with southern clergy who tried to build up through their proslavery writings visions of a new millennium arriving through the perfection of the Old South, and with all elements of the Old South's "ruling race."[11] Despite the expansiveness of this emerging new look at the people who defended slavery, still almost no one searched beyond the boundaries of the Old South or the patterns of culture contained therein to determine the potential national focus of proslavery.[12]

As a result of the new attention, a host of historians began filling in the gaps where proslavery's history previously had not been adequately documented. Despite the fact that most prior studies of proslavery had dealt with the period from 1830 until 1860, most of the new articles and books filled in periods from the middle of the eighteenth century up through the Virginia debates on slavery in 1831–32—almost all uncharted territory. The focus of greater attention throughout the period has been the colony and state of Virginia, ranging from Edmund Morgan's brilliant *American Slavery, American Freedom* (1975) on the colonial experience, down through three seminal and important studies of Virginia during the critical decade of the 1820s and early 1830s, including Robert Shalhope's study of Thomas Jefferson's latter day republicanism, Dickson Bruce's examination of conservatism in the Virginia convention of 1829–30, and Alison Goodyear Freehling's analysis of both republicanism and conservatism in Virginia's epochal slavery debates.[13] Other articles and books began to document little known or previously unknown and unrecognized proslavery literature from the 1780s until 1820.[14]

With a healthy spate of original research into particular facets of proslavery history and literature, many worn-out assumptions about proslavery now seem to attract less attention. More recent interpretations of the nature and essence of proslavery history have been suggestively informed by the quests of two historians who have attempted to understand the young nation's commitment to slavery despite all of the libertarian rhetoric and tendencies of the American Revolution. Both Duncan MacLeod in *Slavery, Race, and the American Revolution* (1974) and Edmund Morgan in *American Slavery, American Freedom* attempted to understand why the liberating influences of the Revolution did not rid the new nation of slavery. Although the ideology of the Revolution did cause Americans to pause and consider the implications of their practice of slavery, the force of rhetoric was not sufficient to rid all of the new states of slavery. Although both found an abundant ferment of thinking about the future of slavery throughout the colonies and in Virginia in particular, the necessity of getting on with the business of creating the new nation precluded any settlement of the slavery issue. Although their findings were hardly startling, they did in the process open up a major new area of discussion for proslavery history. MacLeod attempted to figure out how Americans came to terms with slavery while they were establishing notions and forms of republicanism. Morgan found that Virginians simply concluded that republicanism could best be perfected in the presence of slavery where all nonslaves could enjoy and be guaranteed equality.[15]

By looking at proslavery and the acceptance of slavery in this manner, MacLeod and Morgan became merely the first among many historians to ask substantive questions about the relationship between slavery along with its defense and the mainstream of American political, social, and cultural thought. A few historians have subsequently tried to understand how proslavery fits into the mainstream of American conservative thought, while others have tried to trace proslavery in the context of the elongated course of Jeffersonian republicanism, and still others have tried to determine if the movement to defend slavery may not have been one of the offshoots of the benevolent movement that characterized antebellum America.[16] Perhaps the quintessence of recently liberated questioning about proslavery history is the fact that one historian could conclude that there was very little difference between American proslavery ideas and those used in Russia during the same period of time to defend the perpetuation of serfdom.[17]

Despite such encouraging trends, none of the research that has gone into the history of proslavery to date has been able to illuminate sufficiently proslavery literature, people, and thought in the context of American history. Even the most recent studies still tend to confine research, thinking, and interpretations to the influence of the Old South. Despite ample evidence that proslavery arguments never changed from early American history (or even from Russian arguments), historians still assume that something uniquely culpable happened in the Old South. Proslavery writers and thinkers are still seen as pathetic figures either in southern or American society. And although some historians have now come to associate proslavery in some manner with conservative social and political thinking about the American republic, the relationship is still viewed as aberrational.[18]

More unexpected from the perspective of the findings of this study is a new tendency to explain proslavery away as the end result of some mental, psychological, or economic process occurring in the Old South set apart from the rest of the American nation, not to mention the Western world. Lewis Simpson, in *The Dispossessed Garden* (1975), an analysis of slavery in southern literature, finds slavery in southern thinking to be a bitter intrusion in the myth of America as a Garden of Eden that ultimately led southerners to develop a culture of alienation from the modern world. Much the same theme has recently been pursued by Eugene Genovese and Elizabeth Fox-Genovese, albeit in the context of economic theory through various individual essays and notably in their joint *Fruits of Merchant Capital* (1983). According to their version, southerners entered headlong into combat with rising capitalism, refusing to accept the economic realities of the modern world marketplace wherein labor could be secured more cheaply with wages than by ownership. Rather than face the realities, slaveholders developed and proclaimed a new notion of organic society built on slavery while their economy continued to stagnate.

By the same token, Kenneth Greenberg, in *Masters and Statesmen* (1985), provides some excellent new insights on proslavery, but ends up with the same theme of aberration. Through an analysis of the many ironies and contradictions in southern society wherein southerners frequently said one thing while meaning something entirely different, Greenberg concludes that southern slaveholders eventually persuaded themselves that they were actually opposed to slavery. What they were practicing in the Old South, they came to believe, bore no relation to other historical forms of slaveholding. By avoiding reality they could defend slavery making use of antislavery principles and rhetoric.[19]

While all of these new studies provide intriguing insights and compelling theories to explain how the anomaly of proslavery might have occurred, none have looked directly at the length and breadth of proslavery history including the people who defended slavery and the literature they produced. In the absence still of any in-depth investigation of proslavery history itself, the subject continues to be surrounded with a body of mythology that hides and distorts one of the most fascinating phenomena of the nation's rich heritage. Any effort to understand its history of necessity will be a process of demythologization to find the kernels of truth that lie behind the myths. Any new and objectively valid interpretation will be possible only when we have torn away the traditional myths, looked beyond recent partial and conjectural theories, and begun building upon a more objective and historically accurate base.

Among the myths in need of examination are assumptions that proslavery arguments in the United States sprang forth from the Old South
in the nineteenth century in a novel character for both slaveholders and
Americans. An examination of American proslavery literature from
1701 until the nineteenth century will suggest that Americans had a rich
and telling proslavery history throughout their colonial and revolutionary years prior to the emergence of the Old South.

A second myth is that America was bereft of any who defended slavery
during the early years of the nineteenth century. During those years
colonizers and emancipators were busy at work forming societies to rid
the nation of both slavery and the Negro and most slaveholders, out of
conscience, felt relatively comfortable with the efforts. Any analysis of
the period will indicate that proslavery sentiments were present in a multiplicity of national concerns, wherever people talked about the nature
and future shape of American society. Throughout the period most of
the defending of slavery was left to social critics far removed from the
scene of slaveholding.

A third myth for examination is the notion that proslavery arguments
in the Old South were somehow different, more heinous, and distinct
from the proslavery convictions of slaveholders in other societies. An
analysis of proslavery literature in Britain and the West Indies prior to
the heyday of the Old South will suggest that the proslavery argument or
rather arguments were virtually the same wherever one found slaveholding on the defensive.

Another myth is the belief that southerners rallied around a notion
that slavery was a positive good both for master and slave and such a
perspective made the Old South unique among slaveholding societies. A
close examination of the thesis and of pertinent related literature from
other periods and other lands will suggest that the thesis is without basis
in fact.

A final myth that must be torn away for a proper understanding of
proslavery history in the United States relates to who defended slavery.
The popular notion is that proslavery was a pursuit unique to southern
slaveholding Americans. A composite biographical study of nearly three
hundred individuals who published defenses of slavery in the United
States suggests that the pursuit was almost without geographical distinction. The same study reveals a number of other factors that provide the
basis for a totally new understanding of America's proslavery history.

Given the enormous misunderstanding surrounding the history of proslavery in the United States, the debunking of popular myths on the subject must be viewed as a cleansing process that will enable both historians and their publics to begin to look squarely and intelligently at one of the most troubling facets of the nation's history. As painful and tedious as the process may seem, the end result will be a clearer glimpse at the essence and nature of American society and its fascinating course of development.

TWO

Origins of Proslavery in America, 1701–1808

One of the most difficult problems in charting the history of an idea is finding significant distinctions to indicate shifts of emphasis or trans-mutations of meaning. Unlike the life of a person, an idea usually has no definite date of birth or death and few stages of development as easily recognizable as childhood, adolescence, and adulthood. An idea, often shaped out of materials at hand and meaningful only in relation to other notions or thought patterns, is frequently amorphous and changing, al-ways difficult to categorize.

Such is the case with proslavery. By attaching simplistic definitions to slavery's defense, crucial shifts and changes in proslavery thought, par-ticularly during the American Civil War, are sometimes misunderstood or misinterpreted. In *White Over Black* (1968), for example, Winthrop Jordan discussed proslavery literature with which he was familiar and occasionally made reference to what he understood as proslavery thought. Seeking only to reveal "the attitudes of white men toward Negroes during the first two centuries of European and African settle-ment in what became the United States of America," Jordan treated pro-slavery in a manner reminiscent of traditionally antiracist historians. Proslavery became the product of growing racism and the concrete mani-festation of rampant devaluations of the Negro character, and its history proved identical with the development of anti-Negro thought.[1]

Despite its constant connection with the perpetuation of Negro slavery in America, proslavery thought served many purposes and frequently ranged conceptually far beyond the realm of mere discussions of race or other simple qualities. It was not necessary to denigrate the Negro race to defend slavery; nor was it essential to be critical of free labor to maintain slavery's necessity. In simplest terms, a member of a slave society could state a desire to preserve the status quo, registering a fear of social change, and thereby qualify as a proponent of slavery.

If proslavery ideology is seen without reference to racism, class consciousness, sectionalism, or some other factor that prejudges the issue, the problem of periodization becomes simpler. If equated with racism, perceived alterations in proslavery history would end with the rise of race consciousness in the early colonial period. If identified as class oriented, proslavery history would reach fruition with the rise of class consciousness in the middle of the nineteenth century. If connected with sectionalism, proslavery history would begin and terminate with the rise of southern consciousness in the 1820s or 1830s. But, if proslavery is viewed as merely one strand of social thought with various emphases at different points in American history, its history can be traced as that independent mode of thought distinct, if not entirely separable, from the movements with which it became associated.

Understood as mere social thought, proslavery has had a checkered career. In the early colonial period it was used, in addition to its perennial application as a defense of slavery, to uphold property rights, define the meaning of race, examine the relationship between heathen and Christian, establish the governance of religion over the duties of individuals, and expand the practice of slaveholding. On the eve of the American Revolution, proslavery was employed by loyalists and social conservatives to refute the theory of natural rights. During and following the Revolution, it served as a tool to slow the contagion of liberty unleashed by the War for Independence. In the early years of the nineteenth century, nationalists employed the same ideology to respond to foreign criticisms of American society. Proslavery then fell into the hands of colonizationists who sought to launch a mass migration of Christianized blacks to Africa. At nearly the same time proslavery served to quell the anxiety of slaveholders who feared that their slaves might organize a mass slaughter of the white populace. Before the rise of abolitionism, proslavery thought also aided early political economists as they assessed the value of the American labor force, slave and free.

Although proslavery ideology proved useful on numerous occasions prior to the emergence of abolitionism, its history enjoyed a new beginning with the radicalization of antislavery. Between the appearance of William Lloyd Garrison's *Liberator* in January 1831 and the national abolition crisis of July 1835, proslavery thought entered into its most typical, although least remembered, role in American history. In the hands of northern anti-abolitionists and social conservatives, ideologized proslavery became a weapon for fending off all forms of social radicalism. Seeing themselves as the conservators of nationalism and social harmony, the same individuals used proslavery to restore confidence in American government and society. Only after northern conservatives latched onto proslavery as a vehicle for instilling nationalism did the same body of thought begin to serve southerners bent on preserving their conception of a blameless slaveholding culture as an ideology of sectionalism. But even as some southerners made their proslavery case, others employed proslavery arguments to bolster national harmony. Finally, during the Civil War when proslavery became the ideology of the Confederacy, other non-Confederates continued to appeal to proslavery as a means of undermining Pres. Abraham Lincoln and the Radical Republicans and of reuniting the severed nation.

In order to understand how proslavery could have meant so many things to so many people, it is necessary to distinguish between the constant and the discontinuous in proslavery history. Added to the underlying racist presumption that the Negro should remain indefinitely in slavery was the belief that slavery was a valuable conservator of the American social organism, which could not subsist without keeping at least a part of its laboring force in total bondage. Also constant were those arguments, no matter how bland or heinous, which from colonial times until the end of the Civil War upheld the institution of slavery.[2]

If the conviction that slavery was necessary and the arguments to prove it persisted throughout proslavery history, its course can only be charted by referring to the uses to which it was put and the effects it had. From the perspective of racism, proslavery has no real history; from that of class consciousness, it had none until the 1850s. Only as social thought, with a variety of purposes and results, can the strange wanderings of proslavery history be traced and its frequent centrality in the mainstream of American thought be properly appreciated.

As products of European culture, early Americans were well acquainted with human bondage and with forms of thought that urged its perpetuation. Although Americans had to learn to equate slavery with the Negro, they did not have to forge an understanding of the concept of slavery from their experiences in the New World. Even though the institution of slavery had disappeared from many parts of Europe during the Middle Ages, the idea of slavery and many of its moral and legal implications had been kept alive by philosophers, theologians, and other writers. Moreover, colonial Americans were familiar with various forms of social bondage that remained in their homelands as well as with the slavery that had never entirely vanished from the Mediterranean world.[3]

Because of their European heritage and New World conditions, English settlers in North America were able to establish a system of bondage that eventually extended throughout the British colonies. Few seem to have opposed the process, although those who codified slave laws and who helped edge perpetual servitude ever closer to an identity with black skin certainly must have given serious thought to their work. For as they laid the groundwork for a social system with slavery as an essential ingredient they made it virtually impossible to construct a colonial society without it. Whatever evils early Americans may have associated with slavery as a result of their European heritage were quietly erased. As they built a slave society with which they could be content, they also erected the psychological and philosophical foundations on which to defend their social organism. But since no one criticized the system, none had to defend it.

Little was written or published about slavery in seventeenth- and eighteenth-century America. What was available appeared largely in the form of descriptions of slavery in various colonies. Only about a dozen defenses were printed before the American Revolution, and they were in response to a similar number of antislavery tracts. There were, however, occasional local discussions of slavery within individual colonies.[4] The forces that gave rise to nascent antislavery did not become apparent until the last third of the eighteenth century when events and ideas associated with the American Revolution began to challenge the future of slavery on a massive scale.

Nevertheless in the early eighteenth century, there was enough proslavery literature to indicate that colonial Americans and other English subjects could easily defend slavery when necessary. From 1700, when two judges of the Massachusetts provincial court exchanged opinions on the advisability of holding slaves, until the early 1770s when America's revolutionary rhetoric forced a brief international debate, a small number of Englishmen proved they had little difficulty borrowing from and perpetuating proslavery notions already ingrained in European and Western thought. Even though early defenders wrote in isolation from and without reliance upon other proslavery thinkers, all of them shared a cultural heritage that could easily buttress various forms of human bondage, including slavery.

Since they appropriated an established proslavery tradition, it is not surprising that in their isolation they held common assumptions and set forth similar arguments. Nor should it be considered strange that the earliest known written defense of slavery in America encompassed as great a variety of proslavery arguments as many full-blown writings from the nineteenth-century Old South. Moreover, in the limited number of eighteenth-century proslavery writings can be found examples of nearly every literary form used by successive defenders of slavery to express their views: staid formal defenses, instructive literature for slaves, sermons and orations on the reciprocal duties of masters and slaves, treatises on ethnology, discussions on political economy, and transcribed debates on slaveholding. Thus, the paucity of early American proslavery literature resulted neither from the absence of proslavery notions nor from any indisposition toward upholding slavery. What was missing was the need to defend an institution that nearly everyone took for granted.

Lacking any widespread opposition to slavery, its defense was usually sporadic and local. Throughout the eighteenth and nineteenth centuries, published defenses almost always appeared in direct response to specific antislavery tracts and for all practical purposes ended the debate. Not until the decade before the American Revolution did anything like an extended intercolonial and international debate on slavery get under way. Impelled by the widely circulating writings of a small coterie of Quaker emancipationists led by Anthony Benezet in Philadelphia, various colonial thinkers used proslavery ideas to counter the first major attack on slavery in the new world.

A brief dialogue between Samuel Sewall and John Saffin, fellow justices of the Massachusetts provincial court, at the opening of the eighteenth century exemplified the character of early American discussions on slavery. Although Sewall and Saffin, authors respectively of the earliest antislavery and proslavery tracts published in colonial America, scuffled briefly with little lasting significance, they did so at a time before anyone had seriously criticized the colonists' slave society. Uneasy about the rapid increase of Massachusetts's slave population and its possible social consequences, Sewall issued a short tract entitled *The Selling of Joseph: A Memorial* (1700). Equating slavery with manstealing, the wealthy merchant and longtime member of the governor's council penned a general condemnation of slaveholding. Taking Sewall's pamphlet as a personal affront, Saffin, a slaveholder who had recently presided unwisely over a case contesting his claims to a slave, answered Sewall's charges in *A Brief and Candid Answer to a Late Printed Sheet, Entituled, The Selling of Joseph* (1701). Irritated with the epithet *manstealer*, Saffin defended his behavior in the disputed case and lodged a general defense of slaveholding.[5]

After upholding his right of ownership of the slave in question, Saffin appealed directly to biblical sanction and the example set by the Hebrew patriarchs. Since Abraham owned slaves, "our Imitation of him in this his Moral Action, is as warrantable as that of [adopting] his Faith." Not choosing to argue that "Blackamores are of the Posterity of Cham, and therefore under the Curse of Slavery," Saffin held that "any lawful Captives of Other Heathen Nations may be made Bond men." But "Tis unlawful," he admitted, "for Christians to Buy and Sell one another for slaves."[6]

Saffin then turned to the rights of man and challenged Sewall's notion that the sons of Adam "have equal right to Liberty, and all other Comforts of Life." By no means an equalitarian, Saffin argued that God had intentionally "set different Orders and Degrees of Men in the World" and that any push toward equality would be "to invert the Order that God had set." Phrasing a statement that was repeated endlessly in proslavery literature on the eve of the Civil War, Saffin wrote that God had ordained "some to be High and Honourable, some to be Low and Despicable; some to be Monarchs, Kings, Princes and Governours, Masters and Commanders, others to be Subjects, and to be Commanded; Servants of sundry sorts and degrees, bound to obey; yea, some to be born Slaves, and so to remain during their lives."[7]

Besides upholding slavery as a blameless and natural social institution, Saffin had separate barbs for the Negro. He agreed with Sewall that Massachusetts would have been better served by importing white instead of black servants, since the latter produced "inconveniences." He also conceded that if someone could persuade the Massachusetts General Court that masters should "be Reimbursed out of the Public Treasury" for their property, quite a few would be willing to give up their Negroes. But one "would find it a hard talk to bring the Country to consent thereto; for then the Negroes must be all sent out of the Country, or else the remedy would be worse than the Disease." As for free Negroes, "if there be not some strict course taken with them by Authority," Saffin continued, "they will be a plague to this Country." Judging from the Negro past of dark paganism and perpetual war, however, blacks were better off as American slaves: "it is no Evil thing to bring them out of their own Heathenish Country, [to] where they may have the knowledge of the One True God, be Converted and Eternally saved." Uttering arguments long considered uniquely southern, Saffin's last would have vied as a "positive good argument" if he had issued it as a representative of South Carolina in Congress in the 1830s.[8]

Nor did Saffin eschew an opportunity to degrade the Negro by reference to innate shortcomings in the black race. In a poem of his own composition, "the Negroes Character," Saffin wrote:

> Cowardly and Cruel are those *Blacks* Innate,
> Prone to Revenge, Imp of inveterate hate.
> He that exasperates them, soon espies
> Mischief and Murder in their very eyes.
> Libidinous, Deceitful, False and Rude,
> The Spume Issue of Ingratitude.

Having confirmed his case with a cruel portrayal of racial deficiencies, Saffin hardly needed to add, "we may keep Bond men, and use them in our Services still; yet with all candour, moderation and Christian prudence, according to their state and condition consonant to the Word of God."[9]

In a few pages and more than a century before the flowering of proslavery ideology in America, Saffin produced arguments in twenty of the twenty-six general areas found in typical proslavery literature prior to the Civil War. Although there were nuances of meaning and defensive mechanisms that would await the rise of a different social and legal context, almost four-fifths of the arguments used by nineteenth-century proslavery advocates were cited by the first public defender of slavery in America.[10] Saffin stood not at the portal but in the center of proslavery history and articulated observations on slavery and the Negro that were a part of his culture. He reflected the values of his society and sustained an ongoing, lively proslavery tradition.

Like Saffin, proslavery writers would always depend upon biblical, religious, and historical sanctions. They would deny that the basic rights of man extended to either the Negro or the lower orders of society, and they would point out the inherent dangers in unleashing a servile, alien population. They would claim endlessly that slavery was a boon to the

Negro as an acculturating mechanism in European and Christian values and, depending on the circumstances, would argue that slavery was beneficial to America's white population. Although it often remained unspoken, proslavery writers sometimes depicted the Negro as cowardly, libidinous, or hateful. And, finally, they were not beyond arguing that slavery was a positive good.

Proslavery history is not an endless and inevitable progression from Saffin to positive good argumentation in the Old South. There were changes introduced into slavery's defenses that were brought about by the varying social circumstances that prompted proslavery writings. In the case of Sewall and Saffin, the discussion of slavery was impelled by the fear of unknown consequences of a sudden upsurge of slave importation and the inability of provincial courts to deal with the knotty problem of slave ownership. In the midst of a perceived social crisis, Saffin borrowed from the heritage of proslavery thought and offered what he deemed a convincing solution: keep libidinous and deceitful Negro slaves under control by perpetuating slavery and ban further importations, but legitimize the institution by inculcating Christian principles in both masters and slaves.[11]

Although proslavery arguments occasionally appeared in such fugitive pieces as Hugh Jones's promotional tract *The Present State of Virginia* (1742),[12] they were usually introduced when social dilemmas had to be resolved. One of the longest-lived and persistently nagging problems for certain colonials was the establishment of a proper relationship between Christianity and servitude. In terms of sheer quantity, more proslavery writing appeared in the context of resolving that dilemma than in any other before the rise of Quaker antislavery activity at the onset of the American Revolution. Frequently bearing the specter of reform, from the seventeenth century forward, Anglican clerics called masters to their duties, taught slaves obedience, and buttressed the institution of slavery with the sanction of religion.

As a result of his experiences in Virginia and the West Indies, Morgan Godwyn published *The Negro's & Indians Advocate* (1680), perhaps the first essay on masters' duties written in the English colonies. Angered by a Quaker tract that charged the Anglican clergy with neglecting the religious instruction of slaves, Godwyn penned a lengthy volume that curiously blended favorable views of the Negro's character and an earnest plea for the promotion of religion among slaves with defenses of slavery. While arguing that "the Negro's (both Slaves and others) have naturally an equal Right with other men to the Exercise and Privileges of Religion," he also attested to the compatibility of Christianity and slavery by suggesting that religious instruction, far from creating discontent among slaves, would make them better servants. In far away Massachusetts, less than a generation later, Cotton Mather was preaching the same message to Puritan masters.[13]

One of the most thoughtful formulations of the compatibility of religion and servitude appeared in a sermon of Stephen Hales, a reform-minded Anglican clergyman, before the trustees of the colony of Georgia in 1734. Hales thought that "our excellent Religion would inspire us with a generous and extensive Love to all Mankind" and "make us look upon the most rude and barbarous People as our Friends and Countrymen." One end of humane religion, despite "the Coldness and Indifference of some Planters," was the conversion of Negroes on British plantations. Countering the popular notion that Christianization produced inferior slaves, Hales contended: "So far from that, that it binds the Obligations to Duty more strongly upon us; for the Gospel Institution most strictly enjoins Obedience; it requires all not to be slothful in Business, and commands Servants to be obedient to them that are their Masters, according to the Flesh, with Fear and Trembling, in Singleness of Heart." Hence, if for no other reason, "out of a Principle of Self-Interest they [planters] should desire the Conversion of their Slaves."[14]

The sentiments of Godwyn, Mather, and Hales found their most concrete expression in the work of Thomas Bacon, another Anglican clergyman and wealthy government functionary in the Proprietary of Maryland. In four separate publications between 1749 and 1763, Bacon spelled out in practical lessons responsibilities of masters and slaves. Arguing before both black and white parishioners that clergymen must teach the Gospel "to the poorest slave, as well as the richest and most powerful," Bacon translated theory into practice by publishing tracts on the duties of masters and instructional literature on the obligations of slaves. Against the will of slaveholders he also struggled to maintain an integrated school for orphans, children of the indigent, and young slaves. Believing that "the industry and good morals of the lower sort are the strength and sinews of the state or society they belong to," Bacon envisaged a well-ordered society in which master and slave clung obediently to the tenets of their religion. Although his school failed and his life ended unhappily, the two-dozen-odd sermons that he prepared provided basic patterns for two genres of eminently practical proslavery literature frequently reprinted and imitated by nineteenth-century defenders of slavery.[15]

Two Anglican evangelicals who urged masters to execute their duties and who promoted religious instruction for slaves found grounds other than the compatibility of religion and servitude for the projection of proslavery notions well before the American Revolution. In the crucible of the Georgia Trusteeship, George Whitefield, the "great awakener," and William Knox, an Anglican lay theologian, learned to argue, as would some nineteenth-century southerners, for the expansion of slavery. Georgia was established as a philanthropic enterprise to provide a haven for British debtors and a bulwark against Spanish colonies to the south, but Georgia's trustees forbade the introduction of slaves from the beginning. However, by the end of the first decade of settling, certain of Georgia's leaders began clamoring for slavery. William Stephens, the colony's secretary, his son Thomas Whitefield, and his business manager James Habersham were the most vocal; Knox, for the time being, was an innocent bystander. In 1743 Thomas Stephens stated the case for proslavery Georgians as a whole when he wrote of the colony's retarded development: "In Spight of all Endeavours to disguise this Point, it is clear as Light itself, that Negroes are as essentially necessary to the Cultivation of Georgia, as Axes, Hoes, or any other Utensil of Agriculture."[16]

Although earlier Whitefield had paraded as a reformer of slavery, by 1747 he was convinced that Georgia could not subsist without slaves. In 1740 he had written slaveholders in the southern colonies that "I think God has a quarrel with you, for your abuse of and cruelty to the poor negroes." The day after he stated those sentiments, Whitefield took possession of the land on which he would build Bethesda Orphanage. Committed to making the orphanage a self-sustaining financial operation, he soon joined the chorus of those who sought to introduce slavery into Georgia. In 1748 he warned the colony's trustees that "Georgia never can or will be a flourishing province without negroes are allowed." By the time the trustees gave in to the wishes of Georgians, Whitefield was upholding slavery, like Saffin before him, as a "positive good" and arguing that he would consider himself "highly favored" if he could "purchase a good number of them [slaves], in order to make their lives comfortable, and lay a foundation for breeding up their posterity in the nurture and admonition of the Lord."[17]

Knox, a provost-marshal of Georgia from 1756 to 1762, built up his

American property holdings to include 8,400 acres of rice plantations and 122 slaves with the help of Whitefield and Habersham. Having acquired their proslavery perspective as well as land and slaves, it was only natural that the Society for Propagation of the Gospel (SPG), of which Knox was a prominent member, should ask him to respond to an antislavery letter sent to the society by the Philadelphia Quaker emancipator Anthony Benezet. In a pamphlet entitled *Three Tracts Respecting the Conversion and Instruction of the Free Indians and Negroe Slaves in the Colonies* (1768), Knox clearly stated his position that slavery was a moral institution and that it could be sanctified by religion and extended in the colonies. Like nineteenth-century evangelicals of the Benevolent Empire, Knox saw slavery as a means of acculturating and evangelizing the entire Negro race both in America and Africa. Basing his defense largely on the fact that most Africans knew nothing other than slavery, Knox proceeded to outline "a humane and christian system, for the civil government and religious instruction of those unhappy people." No one in antebellum America, neither New England reformers nor southern divines, would project a more lofty image of the perfected slave society.[18]

Knox's SPG response to Benezet constituted the first wave of reaction to the most formidable crisis encountered by Anglo-American proponents of slavery. During the decade that preceded the issuance of the Declaration of Independence and the onset of hostilities between America and Britain, antislavery ideas became entangled in Revolutionary rhetoric. In the 1760s as Quaker leaders John Woolman and Benezet (and later a Presbyterian physician, Benjamin Rush) began protesting the colonists' trade and their treatment of slaves, they were soon joined by Thomas Clarkson, Granville Sharpe, and John Wesley in England. When in 1772 British Chief Justice Lord Mansfield ruled in the case of the Negro slave, James Somersett, that slavery was illegal in England, this tiny coterie of emancipators realized their initial triumph in what would prove to be a century-long struggle against human bondage.[19]

Far more important than the rise of emancipation was the conceptual confluence of early antislavery thought with the ideology of the American Revolution. The emphasis on liberty and the rights of man in the rhetoric of discontented colonials quickly surpassed the mere realm of politics and began to affect then current notions of the proper social organism. Although revolutionary leaders entered the struggle with Britain as conservative constitutionalists, their political rhetoric forced

Four Early Proponents of American Slavery

George Whitefield, 1714–1770
*Great awakener, itinerant evangelist,
promoter of slavery for Georgia*

William Knox, 1732–1810
*Georgia colonialist, slavery proponent,
moralist*

Jonathan Boucher, 1737/8–1804
Virginia social conservative and Loyalist

John Drayton, 1766–1822
South Carolina governor and philosopher

Americans for the first time to consider the nature of the society in which they lived and to envision the type of society they wished to create if their independence were won. Among the social institutions that were most deeply affected was slavery. American pamphleteers who once clamored only for the rights of Englishmen for themselves soon doubled as critics of slaveholding, condemning all forms of human bondage whether political or social.

Even though natural rights theory posed the first major challenge to proslavery thought in America, advocates of slavery were not left defenseless. The period between the colonials' outspoken discontent with Great Britain and the rise of abolitionism in the 1830s witnessed an outpouring of antislavery and libertarian dogma that stimulated the promulgation of an equal amount of proslavery literature. In Virginia, Pennsylvania, Massachusetts, and England, proslavery writers countered the tide of antislavery propaganda and Revolutionary rhetoric by attempting to come to grips with natural rights theory. Each found his own appropriate solution to the dilemma and in the process provided a basis for proslavery ideology in the nineteenth century.

Among the first to understand the course of events was Virginia loyalist Jonathan Boucher. An articulate and informed political thinker whose ideas on all but a few issues closely approximated those of American constitutional conservatives, Boucher was incensed in 1767 by the antislavery views of fellow Virginian Arthur Lee. In a discourse ostensibly delivered to his parishioners in Hanover Parish but not published until 1797, Boucher scored Lee's natural rights arguments. Calling Lee "a mere rhetorician" unqualified to evaluate slavery, Boucher wrote that he had "no disposition to question either it's [*sic*] lawfulness, nor it's [*sic*] humanity," for the blamelessness of slavery "has again and again been clearly proved." Boucher's rebuttal to natural rights theory was racist in nature. In America, he observed, slavery "never can end," because an African could never be "quite on terms of equality with a free white man." To natural rights theoreticians, Boucher pointed out that "Nature has placed insuperable barriers in his [the Negro's] way." A convict could erase his wrong by suffering society's penalty, but not even a mulatto could erase the stigma of his color.[20]

As antislavery thought and Revolutionary ideology coalesced in the immediate years before the signing of the Declaration of Independence, so did proslavery. Between 1772 and 1775 five major defenses of slavery appeared under the signatures of American colonials, all of them bent on turning back the tide of emancipation and natural rights. Taken together with the writings they were intended to answer, they mark the arrival of the first phase of an intense trans-Atlantic debate on slavery that continued in cyclical intervals until the second half of the nineteenth century. Although proslavery ideas in the era of the American Revolution were overshadowed by the rhetoric of liberty and emancipation and their expression was minuscule compared to the massive outpouring of proslavery literature in the nineteenth century, the outlines of a distinctive proslavery critique were clearly present.

The circle of associates who promoted the program of the Anglican SPG were also active proponents of proslavery ideology. Whereas Knox and Boucher had earlier expressed the essentially proslavery perspective of the society, in 1772 one of its most famous members, Thomas Thompson, argued in favor of the slave trade. In *The African Trade for Negro Slaves, Shown to be Consistent with Principles of Humanity, and with the Laws of Revealed Religion,* which drew the public denouncement of Granville Sharpe in England and the silent contempt of Benezet in America, Thompson called upon his widely known experience as an SPG missionary in America and Africa to place the slave trade in a most unusual light. Since he profoundly respected native Africans and their civilization, Thompson could not cast aspersions, as had Boucher, on the Negro character. He admitted, in fact, that there was "something very affecting, and disagreeable, in the appearance and notion of human creatures, even the lowest of such, being treated like mere beasts or cattle."[21]

Refusing to use race as a justification for the slave trade and slavery, Thompson met equal rights proponents on the grounds of social and economic realities. "Absolute freedom," he argued, "is incompatible with civil establishments." All people are limited in some degree by laws and constitutions "designed and enacted for the public weal." Some individuals, therefore, had to serve others and were thereby less free than others. That fact alone accounted for slavery but not slave trading.

After investigating the moral laws of trade in general, Thompson concluded that neither the buying and selling of humans nor the activities of African slave traders were reprehensible. From his African sojourn at the very center of the slave trade, he could attest that all aspects of the trade were "conducted upon true mercantile principles." Africans taken in the slave trade were already slaves beforehand and, if not sold for the American market, would have been sent to some other. Denying the validity of arguments that presumed African barbarity and savagery as a

The condition of a flave, and that of a free fervant, differ chiefly in thefe refpeets ; the latter has a power to chufe whom he will ferve, which the other has not. And a free fervant has wages ; a flave, none. But the ferving without *see below* wages, is not ferving for nothing ; for there is his keeping, and *all neceffaries found him.

The ftate of fervitude, fimply confidered, is nothing fhocking, though circumftances too often make it fo. The ftrefs of labour that is endured by many, the mean diet, and *fcantinefs of their provi- fions ; the feverity inflicted on them for their faults and offences ; and other hard ufage with which they *serving for nothing,"* are

"and— "all nece=saries found— him." Is not this worse than a mere

---

Thomas Thompson's proslavery and pro–slave trade pamphlet, *The African Slave Trade*, 1772, drew the antislavery rage of Philadelphia Quaker Anthony Benezet whose script responses appear in the margins (pages 22–23).

are often treated : these miseries arise not from the nature of their case, considered merely as slaves, but from the injustice and cruelty of their owners. The proper work of slaves is nothing above their strength; and every real hardship that is imposed on them is an abuse of power.

No preten necessity of commerce can ballance these avowed evils.

Therefore no man should be allowed such power

By the law of nature, all persons are free. But absolute freedom is incompatible with civil establishments. Every man's liberty is restricted by national laws, and natural priviledge does rightly yield to legal constitutions; which are designed and enacted for the public weal.

Absolute freedom is not incompatible with civil establishments: because absolute freedom can only consist in restraining Evil Doers by just & equitable Laws, that the Weak & Poor, may be as free as the Rich & Strong, for all men ought to be absolutely free to do good according to their ability; & if they are not free to do evil, it is not to be accounted a restraint upon liberty; but a restraint only upon Tyranny; so that the Author

The

as manifestly conforms the one term for the other

justification for enslavement, Thompson told equalitarians that economic and social necessities proved both slavery and the slave trade "not contrary to the law of nature."[22]

While Thompson and Sharpe exchanged arguments in England, other Americans were preparing to answer the antislavery opinions of Woolman, Benezet, and Rush. Three proslavery writers who had quietly watched the growth of Quaker antislavery in Philadelphia were forced into print when Rush joined the emancipationist chorus with *An Address to the Inhabitants of the British Settlements in America, upon Slave-Keeping* (1773). The three proslavery rejoinders merit some scrutiny because they constitute the most acute formulations of traditional proslavery thought prior to the nineteenth century. Better than most eighteenth-century proslavery writers in their attempt to deal with aggressive antislavery arguments and natural rights theory, they based their positions on ideological nuances that would become commonplace in nineteenth-century America.

The first of them, Richard Nisbet, a transplanted West Indian who arrived in Philadelphia in the early 1770s, reacted strongly to Rush's "most malevolent slander" against West Indian planters. Determined to expose Rush's errors, Nisbet opened his *Slavery Not Forbidden by Scripture* (1773) with the charge that "abuse levelled at an entire body of people, seems so contrary to reason, and every charitable maxim, that a man who undertakes it, though of the first rate genius, lays himself open to be refuted by every school boy." After presenting West Indian slavery in its "true" light, Nisbet cited most of the standard arguments. Near the end of the tract, however, he broached the topic that made his proslavery views distinctive—a comparison of the Negro in the West Indies with other laboring classes in the world.

The Negro, who led an unenviable life in Africa, found his existence much improved when transferred to the West Indies. According to Nisbet, the Negro slave had "fewer cares, and less reason to be anxious about tomorrow, than any other individual of our species." In the vein of nineteenth-century political economics, Nisbet argued that, in fact, the West Indian slave

enjoys the singular advantage, over his brother in freedom of being attended with care during sickness, and of having the same provision in old age, as in the days of his youth. Instead of being oppressed to feed a large family, like the labourer in Europe, the more children he has, the richer he becomes; for the moment a child is born, the parents receive the same quantity of food for its support, as if it were a grown person; and in case of their own death, if they have any reflection, they will quit the world with the certainty, of their children being brought up with the same care they formerly experienced themselves. They may be pronounced happier than the common people of many of the arbitrary governments in Europe, and even several, of the peasants in Scotland and Ireland.[23]

Nisbet's perspective was not an early critique of free society or of capitalism. Rather it was an integral part of traditional proslavery thought called forth by natural rights theory. Those arguments that historians have frequently singled out as unique flanges of the ideology of the Old South's master class were a part of traditional proslavery thought long before the nineteenth century.

Nisbet's tract caused Rush to publish *A Vindication of the Address, to the Inhabitants of the British Settlements* (1773), which before the end of the year drew the fire of another proslavery Philadelphian, the anonymous author of *Personal Slavery Established* (1773). Applauding Nisbet's efforts, the writer took on not only Rush's *Vindication,* but also Philadelphia's entire antislavery community. As he reviewed each of the "late publications on the subject of personal Slavery," two aspects of his argument stood out in bold relief. First was his evaluation of the slave trade as a positive good. Far from manstealing, the slave trade was a "generous disinterested exertion of benevolence and philanthropy, which has been the principal means of heaping wealth and honours on Europeans and Americans, and [of] rescuing many millions of Africans, *as brands from the fire,* and even compelling them to the enjoyment of a more refined state of happiness, than the partiality of fate has assigned them in their native state." No nineteenth-century southerner would value the transfer of Africans to America any more highly. A second striking point in this pamphlet was the manner in which the unknown author labeled emancipationists. In his mind they were *visionary, fanatical, enthusiastical, ignorant, distempered,* and *designing*—all terms that became entrenched in the proslavery glossary of overworked epithets well before the rise of radical abolitionism in the nineteenth century.[24]

The third response to the Philadelphia emancipationists was the least distinguished. Written by Bernard Romans, a widely traveled adventurer, and included in his *Concise Natural History of East and West Florida* (1775), it merely demonstrates the varied literary reactions to the work of American emancipationists in the era of the American Revolution.

Arriving in New York in 1773 to complete the manuscript of his early guide to Florida, Romans joined the American Philosophical Society of Philadelphia where he met Rush and entered into the ongoing debate on slavery. Taking his cue perhaps from the anonymous author of *Personal Slavery Established,* Romans couched a stinging rebuke of Rush in the long narrative of his *Concise Natural History.* Calling Rush a "Rhapsodiest" and his pamphlets "silly" and "enthusiastical," Romans thought the emancipationist's attempts to "restrain us from properly using this naturally subjected species of mankind" would only "procure a greater number of vagabonds than we are already pestered with." Romans savagely attacked the Negro, whom he believed incapable of living as a free man and argued that his emancipation would limit the freedom of poor whites by curtailing their rights to seek property.[25]

While the Philadelphia debate continued, another erupted in New England which revealed even more clearly the effect of the collision of proslavery thought and Revolutionary ideology. In 1773 two Harvard seniors, Theodore Parsons and Eliphalet Pearson, decided to make slavery the subject of their commencement presentation, afterward published as *A Forensic Dispute on the Legality of Enslaving the Africans* (1773). Far from being an abstract exchange of ideas between college chums, the evidence suggests that the debate was a public airing of an ongoing private feud. Just before the commencement young Parsons's father, a Congregational clergyman at Byfield, Massachusetts, had come under the fire of his parishioners for holding slaves. An emancipationist deacon called the elder Parsons a mansteater, setting off a congregational feud that resulted in the deacon's suspension and the vindication of Parsons's right to own slaves.[26]

When the younger Parsons chose to defend slavery, therefore, he took up the cause of his father as well as that of other Massachusetts slaveholders. His address challenged the validity of natural rights theory and was perhaps the most astute proslavery refutation of Revolutionary ideology in the late eighteenth century. Seeing as his primary task the combating of the "principle of natural equality, which is so zealously contended for by the advocates of universal Liberty," he argued as had Saffin, Boucher, and Nisbet that the nature of society prohibited the enjoyment of perfect freedom by anyone. "That Liberty to all is sweet I freely own," Parsons began; but he counseled that "the nature of society . . . requires various degrees of authority and subordination; and while the universal rule of right, the happiness of the whole, allows greater

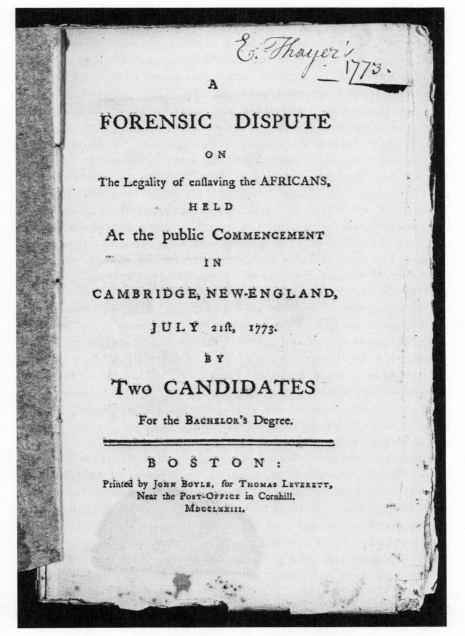

A

FORENSIC DISPUTE

O N

The Legality of enſlaving the AFRICANS,

H E L D

At the public COMMENCEMENT

I N

CAMBRIDGE, NEW-ENGLAND,

J U L Y 21ſt, 1773.

B Y

Two CANDIDATES

For the BACHELOR's Degree.

B O S T O N :

Printed by JOHN BOYLE, for THOMAS LEVERETT,
Near the POST-OFFICE in Cornhill.
MDCCLXXIII.

Published version of the 1773 debate on slavery between Harvard graduating
seniors Theodore Parsons and Eliphalet Pearson

degrees of Liberty to some, the same immutable law suffers it to be enjoyed only in less degrees by others." Africans, like all others, were entitled to liberty, but to no more than "concomitant circumstances being
considered tends *to happiness on the whole.*"[27]

If Americans acknowledged the principle of authority in social rela-
tionships—a governor's right to rule a state or a father's to oversee his
family—then, Parsons asserted, involuntary slavery can be justified as
natural and reasonable. Observing a "vast inequality" between "different
individuals of the human species, in point of qualification for the proper
direction of conduct," Parsons argued that "some are actually found so
far to excell others both in respect to wisdom and benevolence, both in
the knowledge of the principles of propriety, and a disposition to practice such principles, that the general end, happiness, would be better
promoted by the exercise of authority in the former, though necessarily
involving subordination of the latter, than by the enjoyment of equal
Liberty in each." Parsons emphasized the Negro's racial inferiority and
the backwardness of African culture to uphold American slavery as a
positive good. Because of the subjection of the African slave "to the ty-
rannizing power of lust and passion," Parsons held that "his removal to
America is to be esteemed a favor." The act of bringing Africans "from
the state of brutality, wretchedness, and misery . . . to this land of light,
humanity, and christian knowledge, is to them so great a blessing."[28]

Parsons's contention that American slavery was a blessing to degraded
Africans and a necessary feature of the social organism represented the
quintessence, the very heart of American proslavery thought whether
colonial or antebellum. Not all proslavery writers stated their case as
crisply and clearly as did Parsons, but neither did many find it necessary
to meet natural rights theory on philosophical grounds. Although Parsons's predecessors combated various social crises with their proslavery
arguments, they were not confronted with the potentially socially disor-
ganizing tendencies of equalitarianism as were the proslavery advocates
of the Revolutionary epoch. Hence, while they used traditional proslavery arguments to buttress their social outlook, they did not find it
necessary to conclude that a society of law, order, and carefully chan-
neled authority could not operate without firm control over the lesser
sorts.

The Revolution was the first major crisis that challenged the social and
moral values of a slave society. In their attempts to deal with equalitarianism, early American proslavery writers used, along with conten-

tions drawn from traditional proslavery thought, almost all of the catch-words and affirmations that would be heard in nineteenth-century America. Not only did they view the circumstances of the American slave as preferable to that of the African slave, but they also considered the position of the American slave as superior to that of the European peasant, the English factory worker, and the free Negro in America. Emancipators who thought otherwise became *visionaries, enthusiasts,* and *fanatics*—terms of utmost derision in the eighteenth century. Thus, for a brief period in the 1770s, it was possible to experience firsthand convulsions similar to what would occur in American society in the nineteenth century.

With the appearance of Romans's *Concise Natural History of East and West Florida* only six days after the battles of Lexington and Concord, the airing of proslavery notions in pamphlet and book literature came to a conclusion and was not revived until the nineteenth century. From 1775 until the first decade of the nineteenth century, when a small cluster of chagrined nationalists began to react to foreign sneers about slavery in the United States, Americans kept whatever proslavery ideas they entertained largely to themselves. Except for occasional outbursts in local newspapers, periodic essays on racial qualities and servitude, and sporadic defenses in Congress, the period of the "first emancipation"[29] was practically devoid of any public expressions on the benefits of slavery and of slave society.

Given some of the circumstances of the period, an absence of significant proslavery literature seems strange. In England and the West Indies cyclical debates on slavery continued in the 1770s, 1790s, and 1820s while Americans were unusually silent. In the British Empire each new wave of emancipationism was greeted with ever more strident defenses. In the United States a process of gradual emancipation was set in motion that for thirty years put slavery on the road to extinction in half of the nation. The nightmares of proslavery enthusiasts of the Revolutionary era were rapidly becoming realities. And yet the proslavery tradition that they had helped refashion and perpetuate seemed dead.

The liberating influence of the ideology of the American Revolution was powerful in the extreme, hushing in its wake any need of viewing society from the proslavery perspective of a Saffin, Nisbet, or Parsons. Americans were committed to building a nation on the foundation of freedom they had created in their late War for Independence. Whereas talk of liberty and equality had been alarming to some before the war, in the exultation of victory nothing seemed more appropriate than the institutionalization of freedom in American society. And most Americans came to believe that slavery was one of the imperfections that had to be gradually extinguished. Despite the steady march of emancipation from New England southward, therefore, not a single proslavery voice of the stature of a Boucher, Bacon, or Whitefield arose to resist the trend. Even in Congress, the new national forum for grievances and ills, following a flurry of tentative disputation during its initial session in 1790, no one scored emancipationism with fulminations from the well-stocked arsenal of traditional proslavery.[30] In an era captivated by a countervailing system of thought, a proslavery perspective had no place.

In spite of the ascendancy of Revolutionary ideology the first emancipation did not proceed without staunch opposition. In fact, from 1776 to 1808 wherever individuals argued against slavery others arose to defend it. As products of European civilization and as former slaveholding colonials, Americans inherited a proslavery tradition that could not be completely hushed. As irritants mounted with the loss of property, the overturning of a system of labor that sometimes proved its economic worth, and the unleashing of a race still considered alien, isolated citizens registered their complaints. Although no one challenged the basic Revolutionary ideology that guided the young nation, proslavery ideas continued to surface occasionally as a critique of the manner and speed with which the policy of liberation was being implemented.

As emancipationists discussed the means of manumission in each state, their plans were hounded with local and often anonymous proslavery opposition. When Pennsylvania began consideration of an abolition law in 1779, the legislature was petitioned by proslavery backcountry Presbyterians who disliked Quaker dominance and who feared the consequences of emancipation in wartime. When the bill became law, an anonymous newspaper writer correctly captured an American impulse by observing that "Some are prejudiced against perpetual servitude, from a maxim they have received, that *all mankind are born alike free*. Oh flattering language! but not true, unless taken in a very restricted sense." Suggestions that a similar law should be enacted in New Jersey in 1780 triggered an extensive newspaper debate on slavery among a half-dozen anonymous writers, some of them reciting arguments not heard in America since 1773.[31]

In Massachusetts and New York as well anonymous proslavery advocates criticized the emancipation process. In the former a correspondent of the *Boston Evening-Post* railed against the mistaken notion of equal rights and compared the method of abolishing slavery in Massachusetts to the recent high-handed tactics of British tyranny. A New Yorker meanwhile pointed out "the danger of taking too deep hold of *principles* [equal Rights]" and "making the slaves know the extent of their rights." But only in New Jersey where emancipationists waged their longest and hardest battle was the expression of proslavery sentiments more than sporadic. In that state the extended newspaper debate and the flood of proslavery petitions continued until 1805 when the last hope of perpetuating slavery had been lost. Although the struggle had been long and sometimes savage in several locales, by 1804 every state from Pennsylvania and New Jersey to the north had at least put legalized slavery on the gradual road to extinction.[32]

While the northern states of the young republic completed the first emancipation with occasional outbursts of bristling debate on slavery, the southern states were practically devoid of any public discussions. Although the southern colonies had shared in the formation of Revolutionary ideology and had similarly experienced the "contagion of liberty," the impulse toward freedom did not extend there to a massive crusade against slavery. Nor did the tendency toward self-scrutiny engendered by national independence cause southerners to apologize for the system of bondage they maintained. Indeed in their eagerness to get on with the building of state and national governments that could respond to their economic needs, they found little need to debate the issue or any parties ready to take up the debate. And if they were put to the test they likely would have responded obliquely that the presence of slavery controlling the lower portions of society made it possible for all freemen to live in the laps of equality. But the tests did not come at this time.[33]

Instead, as partakers of the Revolutionary heritage, southern leaders, in their contacts with the outside world and their private correspondence, generally condemned slavery as an evil that could be removed as soon as possible. While no southerner advanced a practical proposal for eliminating slavery, southern statesmen did discuss, largely in the confines of their drawing rooms, various schemes for removal. If the force of the Revolution did not cause them to move energetically against slavery, it at least required them to admit the evil of bondage and to speculate about a means of eradication.

The fact that during this period whenever southerners mentioned

slavery they called it an "evil" or at best a "necessary evil" has led historians to accept the hypothesis that a positive good theory emerged in the
South in the nineteenth century. Since the presumed transition of the
southern perception from slavery as an evil to a good has formed an
essential ingredient in historians' interpretations of southern history, it is
important to note that ascription of evil, like that of positive good, originated neither in the South nor in the post-Revolutionary era as frequently assumed. It was as old as the heritage of proslavery itself. From
slavery's earliest colonial defender to the last Confederate, depending on
the format of the argument, the attachment of evil to slavery was commonplace.

Although no proslavery thinker in the Old South from Saffin to
Fitzhugh claimed that there was no evil in slavery, they agreed with Parsons that the enslavement of Africans in America "is to be esteemed a
favor." For example, William Harper, one of the seminal thinkers of the
Old South's so-called positive good school, admitted that slavery was essentially evil. But he was quick to add that "the condition of our whole
existence is but to struggle with evils—to compare them—to choose between them, and so far as we can, to mitigate them." Fitzhugh himself,
despite his semantic sensationalism about "taking higher ground in defense of slavery," occasionally admitted that the entire thrust of his researches was "to compare the evils of domestic slavery with the evils of
liberty without property." No matter how the proslavery thinker chose to
state his case, in the final tally he had to admit that slavery from certain
perspectives was an evil.[34]

To overcome interpretive problems created by the belief that there
was an extreme swing from evil to positive good in southern proslavery
thought in the nineteenth century, it is more accurate to conclude that
evil and good were always juxtaposed in any thorough defense of slavery. The Revolution forced Americans to admit the evils of slavery even
as they defended it. As the Revolutionary heritage waned and other ideologies—economic, social, and political—began to supplant natural
rights theory, it became increasingly unnecessary to mention those aspects of slavery that everyone recognized as evil. In the period of transition, therefore, a strange situation held in which defenders blended into
their writings, in nearly equal portions, the negative and positive aspects
of slavery. From the perspective of Revolutionary ideology, slavery was
an evil; from that of perceived social needs, it was good. Hence, there
arose the concept of slavery as a necessary evil.[35]

Typical of the southern outlook on slavery during this period was the work of Devereaux Jarratt who published the closest approximation to a defense of slavery in the South between the beginning of the American Revolution and the nineteenth century. An Anglican priest who long cooperated with Methodist evangelicals, Jarratt blanched when his Methodist coworkers adopted a rule against slaveholding in 1784. Following a confrontation in 1785 with Thomas Coke, a Methodist bishop, in which he criticized Jarratt's retention of twenty-four slaves, Jarratt was alienated from the antislavery evangelicals. Angered at the unkind treatment he received from former intimates, he began writing letters condemning the Methodist practice of placing slaveholders "upon a level, . . . with *Horsethieves, & Hogstealers,* Knaves &c; . . . [and] with the obvious Name of *Oppressors, Rogues,* & Men destitute of even *heathen honesty.*" Although he upheld slavery using biblical sanctions, he concluded his letters with a reservation forced by Revolutionary thought: "I hope you wont understand that I am writing to you to prove the innocency or lawfulness of Slavery. No . . . I stand neuter, I neither persuade nor dessuade [*sic*] any one to this, or that in the Case."[36]

Jarratt carried his indecisiveness into another series of letters that he wrote for publication in 1790. He was then "well pleased that a spirit of liberation is prevailing" and that slavery would become extinct "as soon as it may be consistent with public and private utility." Dwelling on the evils of slavery, he admitted that "slavery, as it is practiced in general is most abhorrent to my mind. I wish its abolition." Yet, in the next breath, he asked rhetorically "whether slavery in itself, [can] *be inconsistent with the dictates of reason and religion,*" and answered, "I dare not pronounce it inconsistent, lest I should reproach my maker." For the time being, Jarratt remained "neuter" and left the issue to the wisdom of the legislature.[37] Although Jarratt would continue to defend slavery with traditional arguments under the brunt of the Revolutionary dispensation he bowed to antislavery social ideology, establishing a pattern of proslavery negativism that would continue into the nineteenth century and that would cause historians to see actual defenders of slavery as enemies of human bondage.[38] So long as Americans revered the Revolution and its ideology, slavery was inseparable from evil. It was only when they thought of slavery outside the perspective of Revolutionary ideology that they ascribed good to it.

Even before the conclusion of the first emancipation, the outlook on slavery as an unsavory institution began to shift. During the emancipation debates in the North, anonymous defenders of slavery began snipping away at natural rights theory.[39] In the South as well, at the turn of the century, certain thinkers sought to demonstrate that while they accepted the indictment of slavery implicit in Revolutionary thought, they could find other bases on which to establish the less reprehensible features of slaveholding. For example, in *A View of South Carolina, as Respects Her Natural and Civil Concerns* (1802), Gov. John Drayton called up a vision of society not expressed in proslavery literature since the Harvard debates of 1773. Writing in imitation of and in response to Thomas Jefferson's *Essay on the Causes of the Variety of Complexion and Figure in the Human Species* (1787), Drayton rehearsed the lessons of the Revolution before upholding slavery as an essential, natural institution in a hierarchical society. Like Parsons before him and Harper and Fitzhugh afterward, Drayton saw life as "continually chequered with good and evil, happiness and misery" and noted that "Nature, governed by unerring laws which command the oak to be stronger than the willow . . . has at the same time imposed on mankind certain restrictions, which can never be overcome." Some individuals, therefore, must by nature be slaves, while others will be free.[40] Even though he expressed faith in the Revolution, Drayton's momentary concern with hierarchy was the first indication of a new departure from egalitarianism to hierarchism in proslavery literature, harking back to pre-Revolutionary images.

The same tensions between Revolutionary ideology and hierarchism apparent in Drayton's *View of South Carolina* appeared even more strongly in an unpublished defense of slavery written by another South Carolinian four years later. Richard Furman, a Baptist clergyman whose *Exposition of the Views of Baptists, Relative to the Coloured Population of the United States* (1823) would be seen by historians as among the first indications of resurgent proslavery in the South in the 1820s, found himself in the center of an acrimonious debate on slavery at the turn of the century. As a slaveholder and uncrowned head of South Carolina Baptists from the 1790s, Furman had ample opportunity to consider and express his proslavery views. From its inception in 1779 the Charleston Baptist Association, of which he was a leader, frequently dispensed opinions on various moral and social problems involving slavery. On more than one occasion Furman had urged masters and slaves to carry out their respective social duties and encouraged various reforms of the institution.[41]

In 1800, probably in response to a violent reaction to the antislavery activities of Methodists in Charleston,[42] South Carolina Baptists began debating slavery. That year one of Furman's fellow ministers published a defense of slavery in a Savannah newspaper "intended to prove . . . that Christians have a right to perpetually enslave Africans." In his circular letter of the same year to Charleston Baptists, Furman attacked the "libertinism and infidelity which abound in this age," scolded emancipationists, and defended slaveholding. Without reference to either the Declaration of Independence or the Methodist emancipators, Furman counseled Baptists: "Rather, therefore, than advocate the speculative, abstract opinions, or attempt the innovations in practice, which on the subject have been advanced and planned by others; let us adhere to these scriptural principles, and perform these duties, so clearly laid down in the volumes of inspiration. On these we may and ought to insist." Under Furman's leadership South Carolina Baptists opted to continue reforming slavery instead of joining hands with emancipators.[43]

Nevertheless, some malcontents decided to pester Furman. In 1807, at a meeting of the association, an unknown assailant, identified by Furman only as "Rev. W. Mg." attacked Furman as a slaveholder and as a dealer in the slave trade. A bitter exchange occurred, following which Furman defended himself and slavery in a thirty-eight-page private letter.[44] Despite the strained circumstances under which he wrote and the private medium of his response, Furman declared his unaltered fidelity to Revolutionary ideology by appealing to characteristic proslavery negativism. To the assailant's query, "Is *Slavery* an Evil of any kind; if so of what kinds?" Furman wrote that "It is undoubtedly an Evil; and, as I conceive a Natural or Political evil; but frequently combined with Moral evil or Sin." To another question that struck at the heart of the issue, "Is it [slavery] consistent with the principles of the American Revolution?" Furman responded that "it does not appear to be consistent with the letter of one article in the Declaration of Independence; but however the expressions in the article may be apparently unlimited, it is certain they were designed to be understood in a restricted sense: For it cannot be conceived that they were designed to declare that children, idiots, lunatics, or criminals should enjoy equal privileges of Society with the rest of the community." Although he saw a limited social application of Revolutionary principles, Furman could not bring himself to overthrow its social ideology.

Like Drayton, Furman interspersed frequent concepts and assumptions relating to hierarchical society in his recital of traditional proslavery arguments. Describing society as the product of God's providence rather than of nature, Furman argued that "such is the order of providence that a considerable portion of the human race must necessarily move in a humble sphere and be generally at the disposal of their fellow men." Although he admitted that slavery was evil and those who trafficked in slaves were guilty of sin, he insisted that God's providence overruled the evil, for the Africans "have their situation bettered by being brought here & held as Slaves, when used as the Scriptures direct." According to Drayton, the task of Americans was not to wrench the nation apart with emancipation but to perfect the organic society by opposing "cruelty & oppression in the case of slaves . . . by impressing both them & their masters (to their mutual advantage) with a just sense of their respective duties; and, instead of convulsing our country with domestic commotion by these measures, to promote its peace & security: and all this with consistency & dignity of character." If there were tensions between the joint attribution of evil and good to slavery among its post-Revolutionary defenders, it was because Americans were beginning to divide their loyalties between Revolutionary social theory and countervailing patterns of social perception.

As indicated by the changing emphases of Drayton and Furman and their anonymous northern predecessors, the stranglehold that Revolutionary ideology exerted on the values and perceptions of American defenders of slavery began to deteriorate during the period of the first emancipation. No one dared question the correctness of natural rights theory, but disturbing cracks started to appear on the surface of social thinking spelling the eventual eradication of the libertarian ideal of the American Revolution. With the prospect of a change in values at the turn of the century, it seems fortunate that emancipation in the North had proceeded to the point of no return and that the founding fathers had had in the wake of the Revolution the foresight to bar the further introduction of slavery into the Old Northwest and to establish a date for ending the international slave trade. If these gains had not been won by 1800, they could have been lost in the subsequent transmutation of social values.

THREE

Proslavery's "Neglected Period," 1808–1832

Well before historians came to the faulty conclusion that a proslavery revolution occurred in the South in the 1820s, another historian, Alice Dana Adams, drew a far different picture of the South during the second and third decades of the nineteenth century. Adams unearthed evidence indicating that a host of local and state antislavery societies appeared in the South after 1808 and continued their work until the early 1830s. Since similar societies were conspicuously absent from the North during the same period, she concluded that the era from 1808 to 1831 constituted a "neglected period of antislavery in America" during which time "the South was indubitably the leader, and the larger force in the antislavery movement."[1] Adams documented what seemed to be the South's finest antislavery hour. It is thereby ironic that later historians would view the tail end of the same period as the time of a proslavery revolution in the South.

While one might justifiably ask how widespread and authentically emancipationist Adams's antislavery societies actually were, one facet of her findings should not be dismissed. She was not wrong in determining that the entire period from the ending of the slave trade in 1808 to the rise of radical abolition in the 1830s should be treated as a unified whole. Her antislavery societies were but one manifestation of a many-faceted process that transported Americans from obeisance to the heritage of their Revolution to their acceptance of far different social, economic, and political values in the nineteenth century. The process actually began before the end of the eighteenth century, but the by-products of what was perhaps one of the most far-reaching social revolutions in American history did not appear until after 1808. The ferment con-

tinued practically unabated until the 1830s when a novel nexus of institutions and values won the allegiance of Americans. Therefore, anyone who focuses primarily on the 1820s as a turning point in proslavery
history necessarily latches onto the conclusion of the process and will
miss the crucial formative influences that created the phenomena observed in that decade. Although historians have traditionally skipped
over the period from 1790 to 1820 in their overviews of proslavery in
America, it actually turns out to be the most important era for the shaping of American proslavery ideology.[2]

In the Colonial, Revolutionary, and post-Revolutionary periods, proslavery literature appeared in various crisis periods as a response to social disequilibration. What was true then was also true in the neglected
period. Between 1808 and 1831 proslavery arguments were employed in
as many instances as there were national or local crises in which either
the Negro or the institution of slavery was involved: from the definition
of nationalism to the purification of the nation's religious life; from the
disposition of unsettled territories to the establishment of a viable national economy; and from disturbing slave insurrections to the reform of
slave society. Proslavery argumentation played a role in each case and
contributed to the diminution of social and psychological tensions. Far
from being a period of quiescence followed by a proslavery revolution in
the South, the entire neglected period was one of intense, intercon-
nected social reevaluation.

Following the Revolution, proslavery did not suddenly make its first
extended reappearance in the South during the 1820s. On the contrary,
arguments in defense of slavery were actually revived in the North soon
after the closing of the international slave trade. Whereas in 1773 proslavery ideology was used to denigrate natural rights theory, in the
Jeffersonian era it served as a weapon for refuting foreign detractors of
the American character. Its defenders were neither slaveholders, southerners, nor Jeffersonians. They were instead northerners, predomi-
nantly New Englanders, promoting American nationalism in the face of
British imperialism. In the process of defining the national character
they began, almost unthinkingly, to associate slavery with American republicanism.

Many of these pronouncements on slavery came in the course of a
decade-long debate surrounding a seemingly innocent portrayal of
American society. In 1810 Charles Jared Ingersoll, grandson of a New

England loyalist and son of a Pennsylvania Federalist, published pseudo-nymously a booklet entitled *Inchiquin, the Jesuit's Letters, During a Late Residence in the United States of America.* The subtitle revealed the contents and purpose: "a favourable view of the manners, literature, and state of society, of the United States, and a refutation of many of the aspersions cast upon this country, by former residents and tourists." Written in the form of recently discovered letters from an unknown Irish Jesuit to one of his friends in Europe, *Inchiquin* defended American society against foreign criticisms of Americans' rustic manners and morals. Unlike many Americans brought up as Federalists, Ingersoll and others who adopted his views extolled every feature of American life—including slavery.

Ingersoll believed that the United States had created the only successful republic in the modern world. Whereas the French Revolution had discredited most democratic social and political experiments, American republicanism had grown out of virgin soil and had uniquely succeeded in eradicating peasantry, mobbism, and beggary. "Were it not for the slaves of the South," he noted, "there would be but one rank." Yet, the presence of Negro slaves was not to be lamented. Appealing to perspectives long since established by philosophers from Plutarch to Edmund Burke, Ingersoll claimed that there was nothing "in servitude militant with republicanism." Paraphrasing one of Burke's most famous statements about southern slaveholders, Ingersoll argued that they were more strongly attached to the spirit of liberty than northerners: "Such were all the ancient commonwealths; and such will be the masters of slaves, who are not slaves themselves." In slaveholders, he wrote, "the haughtiness of domination combines with the spirit of freedom, fortifies it, and renders it invincible."[3]

To the untrained eye Ingersoll's *Inchiquin* might seem an innocent enough exaltation of American values. But in terms of proslavery history, Ingersoll had opened a Pandora's box whose contents boded ill for slavery's future. Whereas other defenders since the American Revolution had never spoken of slavery without paying homage to natural rights theory, Ingersoll quietly introduced an alternate scheme of social and political values that by-passed and superseded the Revolutionary heritage. His standard of authority was conservative republicanism as mediated to Americans by Burke and other modern political thinkers, but Ingersoll changed the relationship between social thought and ac-

"The Land of Liberty," or the British view of American slavery.
Cartoon from *Punch, or the London Charivari*, 1847.

tion. Instead of proceeding from abstract theories about the rights of man to social action, Ingersoll urged acceptance of social reality, with action flowing only from present needs.

Ingersoll was hardly alone in his newly found appreciation of American slavery. In 1814 *Inchiquin* achieved a large measure of notoriety when a writer in the London *Quarterly Review* ridiculed Ingersoll's ploy of using letters from an Irish Jesuit to praise the American character and his attempts to make republicanism and slavery compatible.[4] This assault captured the attention of two other Americans who shared Ingersoll's values and who eagerly vindicated *Inchiquin.* Timothy Dwight, poet, clergyman, president of Yale University, and a pillar of New England Federalism, responded with *Remarks on the Review of Inchiquin's Letters.* James Kirke Paulding, a New Yorker who was making a name for himself as a novelist, followed suit with *The United States and England: Being a Reply to the Criticism on Inchiquin's Letters.* Both Dwight and Paulding reiterated and extended Ingersoll's novel assessment of slavery.

That Dwight should have defended slavery in 1815 was somewhat ironic. As a diehard Federalist who supported the Essex Junto and the measures of the Hartford Convention, his New England sectionalism was reaching its sharpest levels. Whereas in his early Revolutionary writings Dwight had identified himself as "an American, a republican, and a Presbyterian," in *Remarks on the Review of Inchiquin's Letters* he called himself tellingly "a federalist, a *New Englander;* a Yankee." Despite this intensive provincialism, Dwight could write that "The Southern Planter, who receives slaves from his parent by inheritance, certainly deserves no censure for holding them. He has no agency in procuring them; and that law does not permit him to set them free." If the master treats his slaves "with humanity, and faithfully endeavours to Christianize them," Dwight continued, "he fulfills his duty." Although he repeated his revolutionary condemnation of slavery, particularly that of the West Indies, which existed "in forms, and degrees, incomparably more horrid, than in the Southern *American* States," Dwight had now come to see that slavery in the United States was quite compatible with American republicanism.[5]

Paulding advanced much farther than either Ingersoll or Dwight. In three separate writings between 1814 and 1822, only one of which was directed toward the *Inchiquin* controversy, Paulding began to reflect the intense proslavery views that would make him a hero of slaveholders in the 1830s. Although Dwight had upheld slavery as it was practiced in the South, Paulding disliked the Yale president's disparaging comments on

southern society and culture. Even though he had never ventured for
long from his native New York, Paulding wrote that "For ourselves, we
know of no such discriminating patriotism as this; and however it may be
the fashion in that portion of the union [New England] to offer up their
breathren as sacrifices to their own interests, we do not admire it enough
to make it the object of our imitation." And in the remainder of *The
United States and England,* Paulding defended the manners and morals,
the literature and arts, the society and government of Americans, always
with a careful eye for achievements of individuals south of New England.[6]

But believing that no one should attempt to characterize southern
slavery without first having seen it, Paulding deferred any detailed defense of slavery until he could visit the South. Immediately upon publishing *The United States and England,* Paulding began making forays into
Virginia, spending four or five months on the road in the Old Dominion
during 1816. By 1817 he was ready to publish a two-volume defense of
the South and slavery entitled *Letters from the South.* For those who "are
accustomed to stigmatize Virginia and the more southern states, with the
imputed guilt of the system of slavery which yet subsists among them,"
Paulding finally had some answers. Prefacing his remarks with the negative expression, "Don't mistake, and suppose that I am the advocate of
slavery," Paulding offered a detailed defense. While finding that most
planters agreed that slavery was "a stain on the lustre of their freedom,"
he had little difficulty defending the institution. After cataloging his arguments, Paulding concluded that southern slaves were perfectly cared
for "and indeed enjoy, with a much keener zest than we, all those plea-
sures that spring from thoughtlessness of the past, and carelessness of
the future."[7]

Paulding's proslavery nationalism was more intense than that of any
other writer. His sensitivity to divisiveness within the republic caused
him to prophesy quite accurately in 1817 what in 1836 he would describe
in detail—the southern reaction to radical abolition:

> Whenever the misguided, or wilfully malignant zeal of the advocates of
> emancipation shall institute, as it one day doubtless will, a crusade against
> the constitutional rights of the slave owners, by sending among them fanati-
> cal agents, and fanatical tracts, calculated to render the slave disaffected,
> and the situation of the master and his family dangerous; when passions of
> these ignorant and easily excited blacks, calculated and intended to rouse
> their worst and most dangerous passions, and to place the very lives of their

masters, their wives and children, in the deepest peril; when societies are
formed in the sister states, for the avowed purpose of virtually destroying
the value of this principal item in the property of a southern planter; . . .
and when it is at length evident that nothing will preserve them but secession, then will certain of the stars of our beautiful constellation "start madly
from their spheres," and jostle the others in their wild career. There is no
dissenting voice in the south on this vital question, and the movement will
be unanimous. Let the fanatics be checked in time in their mad career, if the
union is worth preserving.[8]

But in addition to prophecy, Paulding's nationalism caused him to devote
much of his energy to upholding slavery. For example, when he traveled
to England in 1822, he penned another two-volume work, *Sketch of Old
England,* in which he described British abolitionists as misguided and
fanatical and detailed the condition of the English poor as much worse
than that of American slaves in a manner that would have done credit to
the Old South's George Fitzhugh.[9]

The trans-Atlantic *Inchiquin* controversy, which had already elicited
proslavery writings by three noted Americans by 1815, drew forth another in 1819. That year Robert Walsh, a renegade Federalist from
Maryland, issued *An Appeal from the Judgments of Great Britain Respecting
the United States of America,* which contained the longest and most extensive defense of slavery yet published in America. Unlike the random
comments of Ingersoll, Dwight, and Paulding, Walsh's *Appeal* was a systematic, well-researched volume that served for decades as the standard
one-volume history of the United States. Paulding was so envious of the
book, in fact, that he privately charged Walsh with stealing "the Idea and
plan which he merely expanded from a work of mine written during the
late War." James Madison, Thomas Jefferson, John Adams, and others
praised the work. Adams wrote that "it is the most able, the most
faithful, and the most ample apology for the United States," and further
that "indeed it is a Book after my own heart."[10]

Walsh's work shared a purpose with his predecessors, "to witness,—in
opposition to the false relations of the British travellers,—that the native
American is not backward." More than a third of the five hundred pages
was devoted to the proposition that the practice of slaveholding in the
United States made the nation neither socially retarded nor unre-
publican. He agreed with the critics that slavery was "the side on which
we appear most vulnerable, and against which the reviewers have directed their fiercest attacks." But Walsh responded to every antislavery

Defenders of American Slavery
Against British Attack

Robert Walsh, 1784–1859
First historian for and comprehensive
defender of American slavery in 1819

Samuel Stanhope Smith, 1750–1819
Princeton theologian and moralist
for slavery

assertion and articulated the most formidable defense of slavery prior to the rise of abolition. Borrowing heavily from colonial records, Parliamentary debates, and West Indian proslavery literature, he laid the blame for slavery in America directly upon British imperialists who continued to tamper with American affairs. Although he lamented the fact that slavery was not eradicated by the founding fathers during the Revolution or at the Constitutional Convention, he held that the federal government had neither the responsibility nor the power to touch slavery in the states.[11]

Walsh did not stop with historical and constitutional considerations. He appealed as well to the wide range of social, racial, and economic boons that had frequently caused proslavery writers to characterize slavery as a positive good. Freedom and slavery, he argued, could coexist, despite the ravings of British fanatics. "Their doctrine would deprive Greece and Rome of the distinction, upon which the admiration of mankind for those republics has been chiefly built." Negro slavery in America tended to place all whites on a level of equality, engendering in white masters "as much sensibility, justice and stedfastness, in all the domestic and social relations, as the European, of whatever country." Walsh struck soundly at the racial inferiority of blacks: "Their colour is a perpetual momento of their servile origin, and a double disgust is thus created. We will not, and ought not, expose ourselves to lose our identity as it were; to be stained in our blood, and disparaged in our relation of being towards the stock of our forefathers in Europe. This may be called prejudice; but it is one which no reasoning can overcome, and which we cannot wish to see extinguished." And he believed it was unadvisable to emancipate large numbers of Negroes who would perpetually pose the threat of servile insurrection and who could never be assimilated into America's white culture.[12]

One of the most significant features of Walsh's *Appeal* was the development of a perspective that historians would later associate only with late antebellum southern proslavery writers. He compared in detail American slave labor with European free labor. Using page after page of quotations and notes from the very reviews that dared condemn American slavery, Walsh showed that British manufacturers racked workers in pain and paid them too poorly to subsist. In his mind there was no resemblance between the lot of American slaves and British laborers: "The physical condition of the American negro is, on the whole, not comparatively alone, but *positively good*, and he is exempt from those racking

anxieties—the exacerbations of despair, to which the English manufacturer and peasant are subject to in the pursuit of their pittance." Not
only did Walsh characterize slavery as a positive good, he also considered
that abstract notion that has frequently been seen as a hybrid of the Old
South. Walsh charged that even "where the institution of slavery does
not exist, there are *other institutions* generating an hundred fold more
vice, misery, and debasement, than we have ever witnessed in the same
compass in America."[13]

Despite the fact that Walsh repeated the judgment that from the perspective of the Revolution slavery was an evil, his fervid defense of slavery illustrated for the first time since 1773 that Americans could openly
and fervently express proslavery views and win the approbation of living
founding fathers. Neither Jefferson, Madison, nor Adams protested this
obvious departure from Revolutionary ideology that overturned not
only natural rights theory but also the Revolutionary ideal of an eventual
democratic society in America. Perhaps the proslavery nationalists were
saved from the wrath of aged revolutionaries by the empty homage they
paid to the Revolution's assessment of slavery.

It should not be assumed that only writers in the *Inchiquin* controversy
rushed to the defense of slavery during this period. Others of like mind
shared their ideas on slavery at the same time.[14] For example, Samuel
Stanhope Smith, the clergyman-president of Princeton University, corroborated the proslavery opinions of his fellow Federalists in 1812 in his
Lectures on the Subjects of Moral and Political Philosophy. After paying deference to the Revolution in a lecture on the relation of master and servant,
Smith defended slavery on the grounds that Negroes, both in Africa
and America, knew no other condition. They had been "accommodated
to it from their infancy." In Smith's mind emancipation would have been
disastrous: "No event can be more dangerous to a community than the
sudden introduction into it of vast multitudes of persons, free in their
condition, but without property, and possessing only the habits and vices
of slavery." Although Smith did not by any means present the overt proslavery views of either Walsh or Paulding, his considered opinions were
unmistakably defensive of slavery.[15]

Hand in hand with the development of proslavery nationalism was the
flowering of the movement to return blacks to their African fatherland.
From the end of the Revolution, southerners, particularly Virginians,
inched toward African colonization as an alternative to emancipation, a
course of action necessitated by their reverence for Revolutionary ide-

ology and their general acceptance of the American slavery, which together posed a twin evil for society, that is, servitude (a denial of liberty)
and the Negro (an alien race). When southern leaders finally attempted
to deal with the problem of slavery after the turn of the century, they saw
that colonization could lead to the creation of an unflawed society. But at
the very moment they began rallying to this scheme, proslavery nationalists were arriving at much the same conclusion. The merging of
the two impulses, one from the South and the other largely from the
North, provided a second occasion for the expression of proslavery sentiments prior to the 1820s and the rise of abolitionism.

The conventional wisdom of historians notwithstanding, colonization
was not a new idea in nineteenth-century proslavery literature. From
John Saffin to Jonathan Boucher, colonization of the Negro outside
America had been regarded as the only possible alternative to the perpetuation of slavery. Colonization had often been mentioned during the
debates of the first emancipation in the North. It had even been suggested occasionally by proslavery writers in the West Indies. Historians
who have argued that "the project was supported only by men of genuine antislavery feeling" in the early nineteenth century are mistaken.
Proslavery advocates had always held and would continue to hold that in
colonization lay America's only hope to rid itself of both slavery and the
Negro. Even on the eve of the Civil War many of those who argued most
vociferously for the perpetuation of slavery frequently tantalized their
readers with the dream that America could one day rid itself of the twin
evil that divided the nation.[16]

After penning a vehement defense of slavery in which he discussed
defects of the Negro character, Walsh in his *Appeal* for nationalism described the one way in which the abolition of slavery could be achieved in
America: "*Colonization* is, in fact, the only reliance in this great question.
Without it, no plan of abolition can be effectual for the security of the
whites, or the good of the blacks; since the permanence of the latter, free
or enslaved, within the abode or the neighborhood, of the former, is the
main danger." As long as the Negro remained, whether as slave or free
man, America would have "a two-fold, or a motley nation; a perpetual,
wasting strife, or a degeneracy from the European standard of excellence both as to body and mind." After fortifying slavery with the bulwarks of traditional proslavery arguments, Walsh concluded that the real
evil in American society was not slavery but rather the presence of an
inferior and potentially volatile race of men. Between the War of 1812

and the rise of abolitionism in the 1830s most Americans came to agree with Walsh and with another proslavery writer who observed in 1822 that Negroes were "the '*Jacobins*' of the country, against whom we should always be upon our guard, and who . . . should be watched with an eye of steady and unremitted observation."[17]

Various individuals expressed their fear of Negro Jacobins in different ways. While Walsh dreaded either amalgamation or social disorder, many southerners were afraid of slave insurrections inspired by untutored free blacks. Some nationalists, such as Paulding, foresaw a growing wedge between North and South if slavery were not abandoned. In other quarters, clergymen caught up in the mission program of what became the Benevolent Empire began to combine America's growing apprehension about the Negro with the evangelical Protestants' desire to Christianize the African continent. Thus when Robert Finley, a New Jersey Presbyterian clergyman, published his *Thoughts on Colonization* (1816) proposing the formation of a national society to promote colonization and missions, he found a nation ready to expatriate the free Negro. To ensure the success of his proposal, Finley expanded upon a positive good proslavery argument as old as the African slave trade. Since free Negroes had had the opportunity to absorb Christian beliefs and civilized ways in America, he contended that they could become prime agents for bringing salvation and civilization to the dark continent. Put in those terms colonization became for Americans, to use Finley's phrase, "a happy and progressive" means of removing the nation's twofold evil.[18]

From the organizational meeting of the American Colonization Society in 1816 until the end of Finley's oversight of the institution in 1825, the society remained an innocuous body. But it did excite the imaginations of missionary-minded Protestants, win the confidence of most slaveholders, and gain the support of an impressive array of social and political leaders. And it successfully united, if only briefly, future abolitionists—William Lloyd Garrison, James G. Birney, and Gerrit Smith—and future proslavery advocates—Charles C. Pinckney, Christopher Gadsden, and Charles Hodge.

Early in 1825, however, events occurred that spelled doom for colonization and elicited a new round of proslavery writings. In June of that year Ralph Gurley became the new secretary of the American Colonization Society and proceeded with his plan to make colonization "a great national movement." Although Gurley shared Finley's desire to unite slaveholders and emancipators under the banner of colonization, everything he said and did renewed interest in the subject of slavery. He turned colonization into a moral crusade, united the society with other reformist agencies in the Benevolent Empire, and sought the support of New England. By sending colonization agents to New England churches and colleges in 1825, Gurley achieved all three objects as he ignited the enthusiasm of students, faculties, and clergymen whose energies were already being tapped by Congregational churches and colleges in support of other benevolent reforms.[19]

One by-product of the new excitement was the reopening of debate on slavery. At Winchester, Virginia, on July 4, 1825 William Meade, an agent of the society who would afterward become a loyal Confederate, joined with a plea to lessen the number of slaves the announcement that he was freeing some of his own slaves. Twenty days later in Newark, New Jersey, William T. Hamilton, who would soon become a vigorous proslavery spokesman in Mobile, Alabama, argued that the time had come to free "an entire people, who, though dwelling in the cradle of liberty, are shackled in the cruel bonds of slavery." At the same time debates among proslavery and antislavery correspondents of nationally known newspapers broke out in force. The pages of the *Boston Recorder,* for example, were filled with extended articles on slavery from June through December 1825. Letters poured into the *Recorder* from all sections of the country in such number that at the end of the year they were compiled into a hefty tome entitled *Essays on Slavery.* Meanwhile proslavery expostulations of "Caius Gracchus" against an antislavery colonizationist, "Opimius," filled the *Richmond Enquirer* for eight months. And in the *National Intelligencer* "Lycurgus the Younger" urged emancipation, as did "Philo Lycurgus the Younger" in the *National Journal.*[20]

As soon as the American Colonization Society's program was nationalized, the inherent contradictions in its scheme caused a schism in the ranks of colonization. Between 1825 and 1832 antislavery and proslavery critiques mounted until expatriation of the Negro faltered as a realistic and nationally acceptable solution to the problem of slavery. While future abolitionists such as William Lloyd Garrison expressed dissatisfaction with the slowness of colonization as a means of emancipation, anonymous defenders of slavery argued in newspapers throughout the country that the American Colonization Society should not be in the business of emancipating slaves at all. Sensing that the colonization program had lost its original purpose of removing the troublesome free black population, proslavery enthusiasts turned as angrily against the society as did abolitionists.

For all of the furor engendered by Gurley's vision for colonization, only one proslavery writer found it necessary to attack openly those emancipationists who threatened to convert colonization into a crusade against slavery. Disturbed by the tone of antislavery colonizationist writings in the *Boston Recorder, National Intelligencer,* and *National Journal* in the summer of 1825, Whitemarsh B. Seabrook, a South Carolina slaveholder and agricultural reformer, rushed his *Concise View of the Critical Situation* into print and offered an explanation of the emancipationists' tactics: "Under the specious plea of aiding the cause of the free coloured population, and of effecting a reformation of this portion of the community, the pulpit and the bar, the press and the legislative hall, have vied in the delineation of a picture, around which, like the cross of olden time, the modern crusaders will be invited to rally." Believing that certain American emancipationists had "declared interminable war" against slavery, Seabrook sought the conspiracy's fomenters. Behind the plot were British abolitionists, Hartford Conventioneers, and political malcontents who sought the destruction of the American republic. Like emancipators and proslavery nationalists, Seabrook hoped that slavery would some day end, but he could not believe that emancipators would "ever permit sectional feelings to betray them into the prosecution of measures, calculated to raze the foundation of our splendid political edifice."[21]

As indicated by the varied positions of Walsh, Smith, Finley, Pinckney, Meade, Hamilton, "Caius Gracchus," and Seabrook, the early nineteenth-century movement for African colonization encompassed proslavery ideas and individuals. Sensing the danger to America of the perpetual presence of both slavery and the Negro, proslavery nationalists, benevolent reformers, and southerners cooperated in an effort to make colonization a fact of national social policy, using proslavery arguments to promote the program of expatriating free Negroes. However, once colonization became "radicalized" by its close association with New England and the Benevolent Empire, others employed proslavery arguments as a means of stopping what seemed to be a rising tide of emancipationism. The reaction against colonization continued apace until the early 1830s when both abolitionists and political economists rejected expatriation as an immoral and impolitic solution to America's preeminent social problem.[22]

If proslavery arguments appeared in the writings and thoughts of nationalists and enemies of colonization, it also emerged in debates on the future of the nation's newly acquired territories. Arguments over the proper disposition of western territories that resulted in the Missouri Compromise have attracted such extended scholarly treatment that hardly anyone can miss the significance historians have traditionally attached to the "Missouri Question" as a causative factor in the rise of proslavery.[23] Contrary to the popular notion, however, the Missouri debates neither launched the discussion of slavery in connection with the territories nor sent southern slaveholders into furtive defense of the institution. Instead the Missouri debates were the most publicized exchanges in a struggle which continued almost without interruption from the Revolution to the Civil War and in which neither proslavery nor racial thought played a clear and decisive role. Nevertheless, during the neglected period, the territorial debates provided a third instance in which proslavery arguments seized the attention of the nation.

Neither the Constitution nor the Northwest Ordinance of 1787 abolished slavery in lands north of the Ohio River. The abolition of slavery in the area was to be decided by the individual states. In territories south of the Ohio, there was no legal encumbrance to affect either the introduction or perpetuation of slavery. Although Congress had oversight of these territories, it did not intervene to determine the future of slavery in any western territory until the Missouri debates. Hence, as an extension of the debates that occurred during the first emancipation in northeastern states, each state carved out of frontier lands argued the future of slavery. Between 1790 and 1820 fervid local debates on slavery occurred in Tennessee, Kentucky, Ohio, Indiana, and Illinois whenever constitutional questions arose. By the early 1820s after thirty years of sporadic struggles, slavery was finally abolished in the states north of the Ohio and firmly entrenched in those to the south.[24]

As long as doubts remained about slavery's future in the older states of the West, however, an occasional defense of slavery would appear. For example, in 1829 a clergyman of the Associate Reformed Church in Ohio demonstrated that although the future of slavery seemed permanently determined in the Northwest, the institution had not been forgotten as an important social issue. John Steele, a native of Pennsylvania, in speeches before his church synod and in a lengthy pamphlet argued that slavery was a blameless institution. While he admitted with proslavery nationalists and his southern contemporaries that slavery could not be

squared with the thrust of the Revolution, he also held, as had defenders
of slavery through the ages, that there was no conflict between Christianity and slavery. Steele's perspective was typical of proslavery argumentation which occurred frequently in the old West throughout the
neglected period.[25]

The Missouri controversy intervened in a long-lived and ongoing dispute about the admission of Negroes into the newer states and territories
and brought the debate for the first time to national attention. But instead of pitting North against South, antislavery against proslavery, and
egalitarian against racist, the Missouri debates rearranged and muddled
the traditional argument regarding the morality of slavery. Since the territorial problem cut madly across the ranks of slavery's friends and enemies in the first national dispute over the status of slavery in the territories, those whom some southern congressmen assailed as emancipators
were in fact men divided in their loyalties. While they wished to keep
slavery out of the Old Northwest and contiguous territories to the West,
they desired as strongly to bar the entrance of free Negroes. While they
attacked slavery as an improper institution for western territories, they
did not question either the right or the propriety of perpetual slavery in
the South. In much the same sense that racism, colonization, and the
endorsement of slavery in the South would become the ideological ingredients of America's greatest free soil organization—the Republican
party—on the eve of the Civil War, the free soilers of 1819 can hardly be
judged emancipators.[26]

Robert Walsh's extensive writings on slavery reflected better than those
of others the mood and values of the free soilers of 1819. Having written
the most important text of proslavery nationalism earlier in the year, by
the end of 1819 Walsh was again promulgating the doctrine of free soil.
In *Free Remarks on the Spirit of the Federal Constitution* Walsh amended his
encyclopedic treatment of American history to include the territorial dispute. Drawing upon his knowledge of the Revolution and his continued
correspondence with Madison and Jefferson, Walsh argued that the
founders of the republic had intended that slavery be restricted to where
it already existed. He noted too that, while they desired emancipation,
abolition was "not to be even attempted, until the federal empire . . .
should be consolidated, and the American nation not only secure in independence, but matured in strength and resources." Although Walsh
feared that his free soilism would "probably incur the displeasure of my
southern brethren," he believed nationalism could best be maintained by

not estranging "the majority of this [the middle states], and the eastern part of the Confederacy" with an endorsement of slavery extension.[27]

Aside from such free soil testimonies and the outcries of a few southern congressmen, the Missouri controversy of 1819–1820 did not elicit a single proslavery response. While congressmen from South Carolina in particular thought they saw a plot under way to make slaves dissatisfied and to disrupt the peace of southern society, they placed the blame not on a rising tide of emancipationism but on the disunifying machinations of diehard Federalist politicians who had not yet buried the hatchet from political reversals in 1800, the War of 1812, and the Hartford Convention. Few if any of them imagined as they would during the abolition crisis of 1835 that the nation was becoming sectionalized and that the northern section planned to wage war on slavery. Despite the melting away of slavery all about them, southerners had not yet, not even in South Carolina, become a conscious and sensitive sectional minority. Nor had they, as demonstrated by the paucity and temperateness of their proslavery responses, as yet decided to overthrow the heritage of the Revolution.

More important for understanding proslavery history than the rise of southern consciousness was the response of proslavery nationalists and colonizationists to the territorial debates. Along with their acceptance of slavery as an institution not necessarily incongruous with their new images of republicanism and the hierarchical society, northern proslavery nationalists added in 1819 a new article to their creed, which was as racist as it was antislavery. Not only did the Revolution no longer require them to foster equalitarianism, emancipate the slaves in the South, or incorporate the Negro in American society, their new reading of the intentions of the founders allowed them to bar both free and enslaved Negroes from certain sections of the nation wholly reserved for whites. Southerners had not yet even come to question the validity of the Revolutionary heritage.

Historians have often seen the closely connected outpouring of proslavery literature in South Carolina in the early 1820s as a direct response to emancipationist demands uttered in the course of the Missouri controversy. Southerners were certainly not unaware of Missouri when they issued their first spate of proslavery literature in 1822. But instead of responding to a rising tide of emancipationism with what some historians have seen as an "aggressive defense" and the "positive good theory," southern proslavery writers in the early 1820s reacted to a problem

that bothered nearly all Americans throughout the "neglected period"—
that of servile (i.e., Negro) insurrection. As in other instances in which
Americans invoked proslavery arguments before the rise of abolition,
the new breed of proslavery writers dealt with a perceived, intense social
crisis.

From the days of the Revolution when British commanders had attempted to alienate indentured servants and Negro slaves from their
masters, Americans from New Hampshire to Georgia were convinced
that in the case of foreign invasion Negro slaves posed the nation's greatest military liability. Particularly in the wake of the French Revolution
and slave convulsions in the West Indies, the specter of infiltration by
foreign radicals and Negro revolutionaries seemed most real. When the
Gabriel Prosser conspiracy occurred in Virginia in 1800, the possibility
of revolt from within was no longer mere apprehension. From that time
forward nearly all Americans shared the fear of slave insurrection. And
expressions of that fear appeared frequently in the speeches and writings of nearly everyone from Federalist to Jeffersonian and from the far-
removed New Englander to the slaveholder.[28]

Given the widespread fear of slave rebellion during the neglected period, the reaction of South Carolinians to the Denmark Vesey plot of
1822 becomes more understandable. The Gabriel conspiracy of 1800
occurred unexpectedly and without anticipation. The Vesey insurrection
took place in an atmosphere charged with more than two decades of
discussion about the liability of America's alien population and in the
midst of colonizationist harangues on the need to rid America of the
Negro. As the information provided by William Paul, a Negro house
servant, was unraveled by city authorities after May 30, 1822, what
Charlestonians had previously only dreaded became a nightmare. In the
weeks and months following the first revelations of a possible slave conspiracy, Charleston experienced perhaps its greatest siege of terror before the Civil War.

Instead of leaping to the defense of slavery as a perpetual institution
of southern society, Charleston's proslavery writers of 1822 and 1823
attempted to define an escape from an intense emotional crisis. With a
unanimous voice they urged, in the words of one writer, that "the whole
United States join in a Colonization Society, provide a place of emigration and means of transportation when necessary" to promote "the cause
of justice, of humanity, and of national safety." Another Charlestonian

affirmed that Americans saw slavery as "a common evil, and [all] are ready to unite in any just and honourable means to free the country of so unwelcome a burden." The same writer believed that expatriation of the Negro "would strengthen our union, and secure our liberties."[29]

Following the initial newspaper reaction, more serious writers undertook extended comments on the recent conspiracy of Charleston's slaves. The first was Edwin Clifford Holland, a native Charlestonian and editor of the *Charleston Times*. On October 29, 1822, he obtained a copyright on the first autonomous proslavery treatise written and published by a native southerner. Although he drew most of his arguments and evidence from Walsh's *Appeal* and did "not pretend to any thing very novel in his manner of treating the subject before him," he did promise to deal with "questions of the most profound and vital importance, affecting every one in all the different relations of life." Holland attested to southern doubts about the efficacy of slavery, arguing that southerners "had uniformly exhibited a disposition to restrict the extension of the evil— and have always manifested as cordial a disposition to ameliorate it as those of the Northern and Eastern divisions of our Empire." And he urged, with his fellows, the massive colonization of free blacks, "the greatest and most deplorable evil with which we are unhappily afflicted."

As for the crisis besetting Charleston, Holland placed blame in two quarters. Among the guilty instigators of rebellion were schismatic New Englanders who, while professing to be "members of the same great Republican family," sought to steal the wealth of southerners and disrupt the national union. Holland traced New England treachery back to the Hartford Convention—"that scorpion nest of sedition and intrigue; in which so many of the disturbed spirits of the Opposition exhibited such gigantic political effrontery." From that ill-fated convention, he argued New England Federalists proceeded to the Missouri controversy, the consummation of a design that nearly "ended in shaking the UNION to its centre." After Missouri came the missionaries, bearing tracts that "excited among our Negroes such a spirit of dissatisfaction and revolt, as has, in the end, brought down upon them the vengeance of offended humanity." And in the wake of the intended revolt followed the most infuriating insult of all, a "heartless indifference or selfish apathy with respect to the horrors we have escaped, and what is still worse, the gibes and jeers of the idle and unfeeling, or the foul rebuke of the 'humane' and the 'religious.'" Through political divisiveness, screaming attacks on the extension of slavery in the territories, misguided missionaries, and sneers at the subversion crisis, New England schismatics had indirectly caused the revolt and provoked the fears of Charlestonians.

Instead of proceeding to a portrayal of innocent and happy slaves disturbed by tampering outsiders as would southerners after 1835, Holland examined the most culpable Americans of all: "Our negroes . . . the '*Jacobins*' of the country, against whom we should always be upon our guard." Because of "their general inferiority in the gifts of nature" and the superior power of whites, Holland contended that it would be "utterly impossible for them to affect any revolution in the state and condition of society in which they stand"; but he warned that Negro slaves might succeed in disrupting American society. Underscoring his point, Holland cautioned: "Let it never be forgotten, that our NEGROES are truly the *Jacobins* of the country; that they are the *anarchists* and the *domestic enemy; the common enemy of civilized society*, and the barbarians who would, IF THEY COULD, become the DESTROYERS of our race." Despite all of his vituperation against the Negro, however, Holland made one surprising exception. Free mulattoes should be regarded as friends. Many of them owned slaves themselves or were "industrious, sober, hardworking mechanics." Particularly in the event of insurrection, Holland thought, free mulattoes form "a *barrier* between our own color and that of the black—and . . . are more likely to enlist themselves under the banners of the whites."[30]

Because of its many peculiarities, Holland's initial proslavery treatise cannot easily be associated with the type of proslavery literature that would proceed from the South beginning in 1835. In the first place, he upheld slavery only as a means of police control over an alien population, urging, along with his contemporaries in the North, that it would be unwise to unleash hordes of Negro slaves on the nation. In fact, he had hardly a kind word for the institution of slavery, not finding as did later southerners that it was a beneficent institution wholly compatible with American republicanism. Secondly, he did not lash out against emancipators as such. While he placed part of the blame for Charleston's crisis on New Englanders, he understood the enemy as political intriguers, not social revolutionaries. Thirdly, whereas later southerners would never admit dissatisfaction among their slaves, Holland located disaffection precisely among the Negro Jacobins of America. He indicated neither familiarity nor preference for an image of slave society as a smooth-working patriarchal hierarchy. Finally, and most importantly,

Holland was not attempting to defend slavery. His primary motive was to explain a social crisis and reduce its attendant tensions. In Holland's case the function of proslavery was to lessen critical community tensions. For the perceived social ills, he prescribed first the expatriation of free Negroes and then slaves. In the short run, he counseled watching the Negro "with an eye of steady and unremitted observation."

Another Charlestonian who published a defense of slavery in the wake of the Vesey conspiracy offered a slightly different prescription. Richard Furman, the city's leading Baptist clergyman since 1787, issued in December 1822 his *Exposition of the Views of the Baptists, Relative to the Coloured Population of the United States.* In the form of a letter to the governor requesting a "Day of Public Humiliation and Thanksgiving" for deliverance from the slave insurrection, Furman provided a religious version of Holland's largely political views. After reviewing events surrounding the near-insurrection and noting that only "divine interposition" had averted a catastrophe, Furman revived many of the arguments he had used to defend slavery in a private letter in 1807.

Following a brief defense of slavery Furman, like Holland, turned to social prescription and outlined tactics for preventing similar crises in the future. His guiding principle was Christian benevolence. It demanded not emancipation but rather the fulfillment of reciprocal duties between master and slave according to the dictates of Scripture and justice. Borrowing ideas associated with the benevolent movement in American religion, Furman presented an image of slave society wholly foreign to Holland's secular version. The master is "the guardian and even father of his slaves," Furman wrote. Slaves become "a part of his family, (the whole forming under him a little community) and the care of ordering it, and of providing for its welfare, devolves on him." True benevolence forbade the freeing of a people who "remain in the chains of ignorance and error, and under the dominion of tyrant lusts and passions." Since "a considerable part of the human race, whether they bear openly the character of slaves or are reputed free men, will continue in such circumstances, with mere shades of variation, while the world continues," Christians would have to content themselves with perfecting, not altering society. Because he was a clergyman and a leading southern proponent of benevolence, Furman's solution to servile insurrection was the acceptance of slavery as a necessity and the indoctrination of masters and slaves in the values of religious duties.[31]

Another Charleston clergyman, Frederick Dalcho, followed closely on the heels of Furman with a pamphlet that expanded on the necessity of slave instruction as a preventive measure. In *Practical Considerations Founded on the Scriptures, Relative to the Slave Population of South Carolina* (1823), Dalcho, an English-born son of a Prussian officer, shared with Furman the desire to perfect slave society through Christian benevolence. To those who drew lurid pictures of interfering outside missionaries, Dalcho wrote, "There is a chain which binds together the various orders of *our* community, which must not be broken. Some of its links may require to be polished; but this must only be attempted by a master workman, who perfectly understands of what materials the chain is composed." The "master workman" he had in mind was the properly trained clergyman. And for Dalcho, the only alternative to the reform of slave society was colonization. At one point he admitted with his fellow Charlestonians that if the federal government would purchase the plantations and slaves of the South and send the Negroes to Africa, "there would [not] be many Planters in South-Carolina, who would hesitate one moment, to get rid of both, even at something below their value." But he added that until that day arrived, "Manumission would produce nothing but evil."

Dalcho described in considerable detail the manner in which religion could be utilized to avert insurrectionary movements. From a religious text he preached social order and dutifulness; and in an extension he wrote: "God is the moral Governor of the universe; and the rulers of nations and communities, the fathers of families, and the owners of slaves, are, each in respective spheres, the head of a moral government, in subjection to God, for the good of society, the happiness of the people, and the glory and honour of God's name." Since Dalcho identified defective religious teaching as one of the causes of the Vesey conspiracy, he was determined to root out not only irresponsible workmen but also religious error. The pattern for a slave society bereft of discontentment and rebellion was the perfected Christian society.[32]

The first brief wave of proslavery literature in the South, therefore, was called forth by and attempted to deal with a particular servile insurrection. While Holland, Furman, and Dalcho borrowed heavily from traditional proslavery arguments to buttress the slave system, they took only scant notice of emancipationists and even less of the antislavery heritage of the American Revolution. Like America's earliest proslavery writers, they turned to defensive contentions as a means of dealing with a specific social crisis. They clearly held many of the views and judg-

Proslavery Analysts of Insurrection, Colonization, and Political Economy

Richard Furman, 1755–1825
Baptist proponent of the slaveholders'
duties to slaves

Frederick Dalcho, 1770–1836
Episcopal advocate of proper education
for slaves

Thomas Cooper, 1759–1839
Revolutionary, deist, and political
economist for slavery

Thomas Roderick Dew, 1802–1846
William and Mary president, political
economist, and enemy of colonization

ments of their northern contemporaries. Moreover, as in the cases of
Furman and Dalcho, they attempted to channel the benevolent impulse
in religion into a reformation of slave society, an unmistakable extension
of characteristically New England religious and social values. But unlike
their immediate northern predecessors and later southerners, they did
not challenge inherited libertarian values. And, finally, the proslavery
response was limited wholly to South Carolina and for all practical purposes to the City of Charleston. In brief, the proslavery response to servile insurrection in 1822 and following was but one rather isolated and
localized instance of the defense of slavery in the episodic career of proslavery during the neglected period.

The final great crisis during the 1820s that elicited an outpouring of
proslavery literature can be attributed to a major shift in the nation's
economy. With the "take off" of the economy under Jefferson's Embargo
of 1807 and the sudden growth of manufacturing, a new relationship
had to be established between manufacturing, agriculture, and government. Following the United States's escape from the British colonial system after 1815, new policies had to be formulated to foster economic
growth, protect nascent industry and marketing channels, and ensure
stable currency and the availability of credit. Characterized by periodic
booms and bursts, starts and stops, the nation's economy experienced a
long period of fantastic, if erratic growth.

While Americans continued to pay homage to the revered principles
of mercantilism well into the nineteenth century, during the 1820s
changes in the economy made sacred principles obsolete. The remainder of the nineteenth century became what historian William Appleman Williams has called "the age of *laissez nous faire*," and philosophers Adam Smith, David Ricardo, and Robert Thomas Malthus, among
others, became the new savants. Their earthshaking books—Smith's
Wealth of Nations (1776), Ricardo's *Principles of Political Economy and Taxa-
tion* (1817), and Malthus's *Principles of Political Economy* (1820)—were
adopted as the standards of authority. Theories of the marketplace, the
distribution of produce, and population growth overshadowed and replaced older discussions of profit and loss, forced and free migrations,
and the rights of man.

In the mid-1820s the science of political economy became a rage in
colleges and among the nation's most astute observers of economic
change. Thomas R. Dew introduced the subject at the College of William
and Mary and the former revolutionary, Thomas Cooper, at South Car-

olina College. George Friedrich List, Daniel Raymond, Williard Phillips, Hezekiah Niles, and Mathew Carey were a few of the young political economists whose writings began to influence economic thought. No sooner was the revolution under way when a host of political economists set about assessing the viability of slavery as a socio-economic institution, the relationship between slave and free labor in a laissez faire economy, and the profitability of slave labor in an agricultural economy.

New views on slavery were as varied as the political economists who expressed them. Among the first to apply the insights of the new science was Cooper, the scientist, deist, and agitator who became president of South Carolina College in 1820. His *Lectures on the Elements of Political Economy* (1826) was a pioneer textbook on the subject in America. Before coming to South Carolina, Cooper had endorsed Walsh's views on slavery as expressed in the *Appeal*. But in South Carolina Cooper quickly took distinctly palmetto positions on such issues as the tariff, state's rights, and the rights of slaveholders. Although a Jeffersonian and South Carolina constitutionalist, he held that slavery "is not anti republican, in as much as our republican Convention [1787] acknowledged, admitted, and allowed it." He also believed that Congress had no right to tamper with the institution in the states. But as a political economist Cooper had grave misgivings about slavery. In both his *Lectures* and *Two Essays* (1826) on government, he suggested that Americans were entertaining "a persuasion, by no means without foundation, that the prevalence of Slavery, depressed the industry, the growth and the improvement of the Southern States." By having to rear his own labor and care for them in sickness, infancy, and old age, the slaveholder expended more money for less work and less productivity than in any system of free labor. Slavery, Cooper believed, was unprofitable and expensive. But even though he concluded that "slave labour is entirely unprofitable," he still maintained the rights of states and slaveholders to employ slave labor if they wished.[33]

Cooper's initial assessment of slavery was followed between 1826 and 1830 by legions of others, some more kindly to the institution than Cooper had been. Since segments of South Carolina were experiencing the worst economic dislocation they had ever known, would-be political economists were particularly active in that state. About the time Cooper transformed his lecture notes into a textbook, a Charlestonian named Edward Brown published a brief pamphlet entitled *Notes on the Origin and Necessity of Slavery* written wholly from the great texts on political economy. Relying almost entirely on Smith's *Wealth of Nations*, Malthusian principles of population, and British proslavery writings, Brown argued that some form of enslavement, whether legal or economic, was as necessary to the creation and perpetuation of civilization as respect for law and order. Civilization in the New World or anywhere else, he contended, would have been impossible without slavery or "the division of mankind into grades." Gradation gave rise to "mutual dependence," the "very soul of civilization." Brown insisted that it was "the mutual dependence of one part of society on the other" that produced social "order and the courtesies of life." Whereas he held some form of control over labor as necessary, thereby drawing a somewhat different lesson from political economy than did Cooper, he agreed with Cooper and others of his generation who believed that where slavery exceeded the cost of free labor, slavery should be abandoned.[34]

Since the comparison of various forms of economy and systems of labor was one of the favored methodologies of these early nineteenth-century political economists, it was not surprising that another South Carolinian, Charles Cotesworth Pinckney, should measure the economic and social benefits of slave and free labor in 1829. In an address before the Agricultural Society of South Carolina, which has frequently been labeled incorrectly as a "positive good" defense, Pinckney drew together theory and evidence to demonstrate "that the situation of the slave labor of America will not suffer by comparison with the labouring classes of Europe, or perhaps of our own more favoured land." Wherever he looked, he found that societies necessarily contained poverty and a class of poor, but that none enjoyed better care and more constant welfare than the slaves of America. However, Pinckney never argued that slavery was a beneficent institution or that the situation of the American slave was the best of all possible conditions. Rather he suggested that among a host of conditions, American slavery was the least destructive.[35]

The ready application of political economy to slavery extended far beyond the boundaries of the palmetto state and provided conceptually useful arguments to both slaveholders and nonslaveholders. Zephaniah Kingsley, a Florida slaveholder and slave smuggler, made peculiar use of political economy in a pamphlet entitled *A Treatise on the Patriarchal, or Co-operative System of Society* (1828), which was a defense of slavery and an attack on racism. A man who openly practiced polygamy and miscegenation and who sometimes boasted about his four African wives, Kingsley thought slavery the best form of labor and the kindest condition of life enjoyed by any lower class in the western hemisphere. He insisted that Negro slaves were happier, more independent, and more industrious than "the common class of whites denominated free." In fact, "the slave or Patriarchal System of Society" was "better adapted for strength, durability and independence, than any other state of society hitherto adopted." But Kingsley held that Negroes, whether slave or free, were in many ways superior to poor whites: "under a just and prudent system of management, negroes are safe, permanent, productive and growing property, and easily governed; they are not naturally desirous of change but are sober, discreet, honest and obliging, or less troublesome, and possess a much better moral character than the ordinary class of corrupted whites of similar condition." Commenting on the Negro's industriousness, Kingsley rowed against the tide of national policy when he concluded that free Negroes not only should not be colonized, but instead should be given property and the opportunity to join the ranks of the free.[36]

If political economy proved useful in establishing the nonconformist racial views of Kingsley, it also informed the opinions of others more distant from the slaveholding South. For example, in 1827 James Raymond, a native of Connecticut and a recent graduate of Yale, wrote what he called a *Prize Essay, on the Comparative Economy of Free and Slave Labour* for the agricultural society of Frederick County, Maryland. In his study he made a point with which both Cooper and Dew, the South's preeminent political economists, agreed—that free labor was cheaper than slave labor. Raymond observed that "If we can convince him [the farmer] that free labour is the best, slavery, we hope, will in time be out of fashion, like an unhandy tool on the introduction of a new one upon an improved mode." But he also held, like Cooper and Dew, that "the period has not yet arrived, for the American public to give full credence to any part of the truth on the subject of slavery."[37]

During the same year Thomas P. Jones, a native Englishman currently serving as a professor of practical science in Philadelphia's Franklin Institute, used his knowledge of political economy to reach a conclusion that contradicted those of Raymond and southern thinkers. In a speech before the institute entitled *Address on the Progress of Manufacturers and Internal Improvement, in the United States,* Jones argued that Negro slaves could be used more profitably in manufacturing than in many phases of agriculture and that the Negro might prove a superior industrial laborer to the free white. Forbearing any consideration of "whether the negroes are absolutely inferior to the whites in intellect," Jones attempted to demonstrate that most manufacturing, particularly textile work, required only "the veriest dolts" as operatives. The Negro's ability to emulate others, find satisfaction in the completion of a simple operation, and be contented with minimal rewards made him a prime candidate for industrial work.[38]

As indicated by the dissimilarity of opinion between Jones and Raymond, Cooper and Pinckney, Brown and Kingsley, social thinking which paraded under the label of political economy in the latter half of the 1820s was as varied as its proponents. Despite the sudden penchant for appealing to political economy in discussions of slavery, there is little to suggest, as historians have frequently assumed, that studies in political economy marked the evolution of a new and distinctive proslavery tradition in the South. The fledgling political economists shared little in common other than the singular purpose of attempting to understand how slavery fit into the current system of economic values and practices in the United States. Since each individual read the emerging theories of political economy differently and sought to define his own theory, there was no consensus on the subject of slavery by the end of the 1820s either in the South or in the nation as a whole. While one slaveholder questioned the value of perpetual slavery, another thought permanent slavery absolutely necessary. While one slaveholder viewed slavery as an outmoded "unhandy tool," another saw in slavery the perfect solution to the boredom of industrial labor.

If anything of importance in the history of proslavery thought emerged from the ferment of political economy in the 1820s, it was the fact that for the first time since the American Revolution southerners began thinking about slavery in terms other than that of the rights of man. And in the North those who had long since devalued the heritage of the Revolution received a second infusion of social thought that made the Revolutionary and post-Revolutionary debates on slavery even more remote. The confrontation with political economy also taught southerners (as revealed particularly in the writings of Brown and Pinckney) a lesson that their northern contemporaries had already learned, that a republican society could and perhaps should be hierarchical to preserve order and the essential liberties of most citizens. By 1830 it had become apparent to some thinking southerners that every society had its poor, economically enslaved classes and that the Negro slave represented the southern version of that universal sociological fact. Nevertheless, there was nothing to suggest that southerners on the eve of the appearance of abolitionism had begun to shape that observation into anything approaching an ideology of proslavery.

The neglected period of proslavery was bounded on one end by the completion of the first emancipation and the ending of the international slave trade and on the other by the rise of abolitionism and proslavery. In a sense it was an interlude in the ongoing process of emancipation during which Americans doubted the wisdom of liberating the Negro and of attempting to incorporate him in American society. It was not, however, an interlude in the sense that at the end emancipationism picked up where it had left off in 1808. Even though abolitionists sought both emancipation and incorporation, they had little else in common with the kindly, dedicated emancipators who excited few as they guided America toward the fulfillment of its Revolutionary obligations. Whether they were or not, abolitionists who followed the dicta of Garrison, Weld, and Birney were perceived by the majority of Americans as radical revolutionaries bent on destroying the nation.

The perception of abolitionists as misguided fanatics was not the product of a warped southern mind, as historians have long assumed. Rather it was a logical extension of the national mood of the neglected period. For in addition to being an interlude in the process of emancipation, the neglected period was a time in which Americans fundamentally reoriented their outlook. The transition from Revolutionary ideals to proslavery nationalism, emancipationism to colonization, social incorporation of the Negro to free soilism, faith in egalitarian society to fear of insurrection, and mercantilism to "scientific" political economy were all part of a whole. Changing opinions on the question of slavery and the Negro were only visible indications of a more basic alteration in values that revolutionized the perspective of Americans on nearly every crucial social issue.

And yet, the neglected period was unique in its host of concerns, projects, and beliefs in reference to slavery and the Negro. But as the generation responsible for Jeffersonian America and its nationalism came to an end, its plans for American slavery shattered on the grounds of morality and practicality. At the beginning of the 1830s the blueprints for the extinction of slavery, painstakingly drawn in the early years of the neglected period and partially implemented in the 1820s, came under the scrutiny and attack of individuals who believed colonization cruel and impractical, had little patience with either free soilers or faint-hearted prophets of insurrection, and did not share the patriotism of proslavery nationalists. In 1832 the first signs of a generation gap surfaced in the writings of William Lloyd Garrison and Thomas Roderick Dew.

While Garrison and Dew have traditionally been viewed as the most significant early voices of abolition and proslavery respectively, the two men unknowingly joined forces in 1832 to kill America's favorite solution to slavery throughout the neglected period—colonization. In Garrison's *Thoughts on African Colonization* and Dew's *Review of the Debate in the Virginia Legislature of 1831 and 1832*, published within a month of each other, African colonization received its most damaging intellectual critiques. Although Garrison spoke for radical emancipators and Dew for slaveholders, their criticisms largely overlapped to constitute a stirring refutation of a generation of American social thought.

Garrison and Dew thought colonization cruel to blacks and whites, unworkable, and capable of destroying the American economy. Both believed that the Negro's long residence in America made conditions in Africa alien to his mind and body; both thought colonization proceeded from trumped up fears of miscegenation and racial warfare; and both held colonization to be the most economically unwise policy America could adopt in dealing with its slave population. And when they spoke of the economic effects of colonization, Garrison and Dew sounded a common theme:

> our interests must inevitably suffer by the removal of our colored population. Their labor is indispensably necessary and extremely valuable. By whom shall the plantations at the south be cultivated but by them? It is universally conceded that they can resist the intensity of a southern sun, and endure the fatigues attendant on the cultivation of rice, cotton, tobacco and sugar-cane, better than white laborers. . . . In a pecuniary point of view, the banishment of one-sixth of our population,—of those whom we specially need,—would be an act of suicide. The veriest smatterer in political economy cannot but perceive the ruinous tendency of such a measure.

Although these words expressed the central thrust of Dew's arguments, strange as it may seem, they derive from Garrison's *Thoughts on African Colonization*. While their purposes may have differed markedly, the two men shared a common revulsion of the misplaced values of a generation of Americans.[39]

The fact that Dew's *Review* was part of a bifocal attempt to discredit colonization should be borne in mind as one attempts to assess the effect on proslavery history of a writing that has long been seen as the crucial connecting link between southern apologies for slavery and the emergence of a positive good argument throughout the South. Despite a great deal of additional examination of proslavery literature in recent years, for reasons which are inexplicable, historians continue to assert that Dew's *Review* set the pace for all proslavery literature that would later appear in the Old South. Although Dew's *Review* would indeed be frequently cited, it was a unique perspective on slavery in America that would not be repeated and would not need replication.[40] To have been so widely adjudged a masterpiece of proslavery literature, Dew's *Review* contained a series of peculiar characteristics that linked it much more closely with the problems and concerns of the neglected period than with the type of proslavery ideology that became current in the South after the rise of abolitionism. Although written well after Garrison began his career of radical abolitionism, Dew seemed totally unaware of the rising storm and contented himself with criticizing the errors of the past.

Born and reared in Virginia in an atmosphere of affluence, Dew grew up reading Adam Smith's *Wealth of Nations* and made political economy the chief concern of his short life. Following acceptance of a position in 1827 at his alma mater, the College of William and Mary, Dew immediately challenged America's latter-day mercantilists and protectionists in his *Lectures on the Restrictive System* (1829). No proponent of autarky for the South as were later southern proslavery thinkers and believing that southern agriculture could best flourish in a world system of free trade, Dew preached a laissez faire doctrine. The same forces that led him to attack protectionism impelled him to write a deeply considered scoring of colonization. Penning his *Review* at a moment when all of the concerns of the neglected period funneled into Virginia and its legislature, Dew discredited colonization with the same methodical and theoretical precision that had informed his critique of protectionist economics. The legislative confrontation of slavery, preceded only a few months by the Nat Turner rebellion, the bloodiest slave revolt in American history, brought together the worst fears of Americans during the neglected period and a compelling reason to expel the Negro from America.[41]

With a storehouse of information gleaned from the best proslavery writers of the British West Indies, Dew in his *Review* considered in the greatest detail since Walsh's *Appeal* (1819) every aspect of slavery as it related to the economic, social, and political needs of Virginia. Using arguments and conclusions developed from the theoretical framework of political economy, Dew reversed the priorities of a whole generation of Americans. In his new order of things, colonization became the worst of all possible evils. Immediate emancipation was seen as a much lesser evil, but still impolitic. Dew recommended gradual emancipation with the retention of the Negro in America as the only ultimate solution to the twin evils of the neglected period. Despite the fact that he refuted the views of some emancipators, Dew's most important consideration was not the perpetuation of slavery but the continued presence of a cheap labor force in Virginia. Since he was convinced that neither Virginia nor America could survive without an abundant supply of cheap labor, he saw in colonization a severe threat to the political economy of the nation, one not even posed by immediate, universal abolition.

In Dew's scheme of thought morality played no role. The only evil he could imagine was that which destroyed the economy; the only good, economic growth. In a brief statement of his case wholly bereft of moral considerations, Dew wrote: "We have not formed our opinion lightly on this subject; we have given the vital question of abolition the most mature and intense consideration which we are capable of bestowing, and we have come to the conclusion—a conclusion which seems to be sustained by facts and reasoning as irresistible as the demonstration of the mathematician—that every plan of emancipation *and* deportation which we can possibly conceive, is *totally* impracticable." Equally indicative of his pragmatic thought was the fact that Dew considered the emigration of educated white farmers from Virginia an evil to be combated as vigorously as the colonization of Negroes outside Virginia. And whereas colonizationists frequently emphasized the "civilizing" influences of American slavery in making Negroes likely cultural and religious missionaries to Africa, to Dew civilizing the Negro meant "converting him into the agriculturist, and changing his slothfulness and aversion to labor into industry and economy, thereby rendering his labor more productive." While many historians (and among them notably Eugene Genovese) still insist that Dew launched proslavery in the South or laid the groundwork for what would become a distinctive southern proslavery voice, such is not clear in his *Review* or in his other writings during this formative period for proslavery. While in economic theory he may have generated ideas that would be helpful to other thinkers later, the only impact of the *Review* was to close off any notions of removing America's Negro population. Beyond this, his cumulative writings had very little direct influence on the ways in which southerners and Americans defended slavery.[42]

To illustrate the impracticality of colonization, Garrison appealed to moral as well as economic principles. But Dew relied almost entirely upon ironclad Malthusian principles of population, warning that "there is nothing more dangerous than too much tampering with the elastic and powerful spring of population." He also cautioned that the removal of some Negroes would certainly "stimulate the procreative powers of that very race which they [colonizationists] are aiming to diminish." As indicated by the European pattern of migrations and the laws of population, no plan of deportation "can ever effect the slightest diminution." Still relying on Malthus, Dew argued that since there was little possibility of expanding the "level of subsistence" in Africa, Negro colonists from America would either have to eradicate an equal number of Africans or be annihilated themselves.[43]

Compared to visionary schemes of colonization, Dew concluded that immediate emancipation was "much more practicable." But once again using political economy as the interpretive framework, he detailed the effects emancipation might have on the South's labor supply. Depending upon his West Indian sources, Dew argued that in no country where slave labor had been replaced by that of the free Negro had the economy been able to sustain the blow. "If an immediate emancipation of negroes were to take place," he supposed, "the whole southern country would be visited with an immediate general famine, from which the productive resources of all the other States of the Union could not deliver them." Without a redistribution of wealth, free Negroes "would still be virtually slaves." After calculating the social evils of slavery, which he readily admitted, Dew concluded that "we cannot get rid of slavery without producing a greater injury to both the masters and slaves." Locked into slavery by the laws of population and economy and by the force of circumstances, he grimly observed, "the time of emancipation has not yet arrived, and perhaps it never will."[44]

Although Dew made frequent reference to traditional proslavery arguments and criticized all schemes of emancipation, his *Review* should be recognized for what it actually was. In the words of one proslavery writer, "After President Dew, it is unnecessary to say a single word on the practicability of colonizing our slaves."[45] Dew was a doctrinaire political economist who happened to believe that the removal of any segment of a society's labor force would spell doom to its economy. Instilled with economic principles that were only beginning to dawn on other Americans, Dew spent himself combating what he conceived to be the height of economic folly. Totally unaware of the writings and work of abolitionists (by emancipators and abolitionists, he meant colonizationists), he was concerned solely with saving Virginia from a disastrous economic policy. And despite his severe criticism of the policies of the preceding generation, he shared with them a proslavery negativism that held slavery to be incompatible with American ideals. In brief, Dew's masterful essay looked wholly toward the economic and social errors of the past without anticipating the confrontation with abolition and his fellow anti-colonizationist, Garrison, just around the corner.

Although Garrison was already at war with slavery when he prepared *Thoughts on African Colonization* and although later proslavery writers would assume that Dew's *Review* had been directed against abolitionism, both writings were more logically the culminating blows against a generation of Americans who both Garrison and Dew believed had wandered curiously from the paths of the American Revolution and from the course of economic sanity. While Dew's perspective would prove useful to proslavery writers, the type of proslavery ideology that would capture the imagination and allegiance of Americans, despite the claims of some historians, cannot be found there. Nor did it appear, in its pure form, in any of the numerous proslavery writings that were published in the United States during the neglected period. The quest for a clear statement of proslavery ideology as it would emerge after the first national confrontation with abolition in 1835 must necessarily go awry if it is sought in the defenses of slavery of the 1820s. It simply was not there.

But this is not to suggest that the neglected period failed to influence later proslavery ideology. It definitely did. Elements of the social perspective that would become America's proslavery ideology were present in muted form in the writings of proslavery nationalists, colonizers and anti-colonizationists, free soilers and slavery expansionists, prophets of servile insurrection, and political economists. Nearly all of the beliefs and values that would constitute the core of America's distinctive proslavery ideology had in fact emerged during the neglected period. But only a crisis of the sort precipitated by radical abolitionists could blend those attitudes and traditional proslavery thought into a national proslavery ideology. Since those novel values appeared only tentatively and imperfectly on the pages of proslavery literature from 1808 to 1831, it is necessary to identify separately unique experiences that laid the groundwork for the rise of a national proslavery ideology in the 1830s.

FOUR

Proslavery Heritage of Britain and the West Indies, 1770–1833

Among the numerous myths perpetuated by traditional interpretations of proslavery history, none has stood on shakier ground or proved more misleading than the notion that, for all practical purposes, proslavery was a phenomenon that appeared only in the antebellum South. From the age of the abolitionist through recent historiography the impression has remained that the Old South alone deserved the dubious distinction of fostering proslavery thought and building a culture largely defined by its buttressing of slavery. The thesis of southern uniqueness and culpability has been argued by a generation of historians who have willingly assumed that southerners aggressively created a positive good theory of slavery even before the rise of abolitionism. And despite the fact that contemporary historians have undertaken comparative studies of slavery and racism in the Americas, the belief that the Old South took a peculiarly heinous position in defense of slavery remains stronger than ever.

What is most disturbing about the longevity of this thesis is the fact that in recent years historians have used the interpretation as a rationale for undertaking comparative studies of slavery in former slaveholding nations of the Western Hemisphere. In almost every case the questionable positive good notion has served as the essential point of departure. For example, in 1971, as a preface to his extensive comparative study of slavery and race in Brazil and the United States, Carl Degler wrote that "we must acknowledge that we can no longer assume that such a defense was a natural consequence of a slave society." Two years earlier Eugene Genovese had written, with less inclusiveness but with equal self-assurance, that "the Old South alone developed a serious positive-good proslavery argument, although hints and patches appeared everywhere that slavery existed." He continued his qualification by arguing that proslavery in the West Indies was "almost entirely negative and said no more than that slavery was making essential contributions to the economic life of the colony and metropolis," while in Brazil slavery was "defended as economically necessary and traditionally sanctioned, but no one argued with any discernible conviction, that it was a good thing in itself." Departing slightly from the position held by a long line of American historians, Genovese nevertheless concluded and has continued to argue in various essays, "The Old South came closest of all the New World slaveholding regimes to producing a genuine slave society. Accordingly, it alone could generate a reasonably comprehensive slaveholders' philosophy."

Degler, Genovese, and a host of other historians who have undertaken comparative analyses of slavery have apparently adopted a series of assumptions that flowed from what now seems a questionable thesis on the Old South's uniqueness. In the case of Genovese, of course, the thesis of uniqueness has been underscored with various theories about "slavery in the abstract." Still unexamined by historians is the validity of the traditional theory of a positive good argument that was somehow unique to the South. Nor has anyone sought to demonstrate precisely what non-American (let alone nonsouthern) defenders said about slavery and the Negro. Until that has been done, it is best not to generalize about the peculiar nature of American proslavery, assume that any one argument or set of arguments made the Old South unique, or attach a greater measure of guilt to southern racists than to any other group of slaveholders. That such an examination would surely be fruitful has already been suggested by a comparison of American proslavery arguments with Russian proserfdom arguments. The arguments were found to be almost identical except in the realm of race, which was not an issue in Russia.[1]

The most logical proslavery literature to study for the purpose of comparison including also the issue of race is that of Britain and the British West Indies, the metropolis and the colonial system of which the North American colonies had been a part. Although the West Indian colonies had always been economically, socially, and racially different from those in North America, their inhabitants shared with their fellows to the north the same language and national origin. And although a different sort of Englishman had settled in the West Indies, islanders and mainlanders alike had proceeded from and remained a part of the international English-speaking community, inheriting its culture, beliefs, and values. Whereas West Indian plantations became lucrative investments and profitable flanges of the empire, the North American plantations remained less important in the imperial economy. Hence, it was not surprising in 1776 when the British settlers in North America demanded independence that the West Indian planters chose to remain in the colonial system that had made them wealthy and on whose continued trade their fortunes depended. Aside from the greater degree of economic integration of the West Indies into the empire, however, British settlers in the Caribbean and in North America enjoyed a similar relation to the mother country.

As citizens of the same colonial system until 1776, West Indians and North Americans were equally interested whenever the question of slavery came under scrutiny in Britain. When a Briton attacked or defended slavery, his audience usually extended throughout the English-speaking colonies. By the same token, discussions of slavery by colonials regularly circulated in the metropolis. Because of the routine movement of men and literature within the empire, early American proslavery writings by Morgan Godwyn, Hugh Jones, Stephen Hales, Thomas Bacon, William Knox, George Whitefield, Thomas Thompson, and Richard Nisbet were not merely responses to other American colonials; they were also part of a much larger dispute on slavery throughout the British empire. And as the North American debate on slavery came to a head in the early 1770s, so did it in the empire as a whole.

If the contagion of liberty unleashed by Revolutionary ideology impelled American defenders into print between 1772 and 1775, a similar reaction with overtones for Britain and the West Indies followed in the wake of the Somerset case in 1772. Along with the reactions of Thomas Thompson and William Knox, both of whom had formed their opinions of slavery in North America, Edward Long, a former Jamaican planter, registered the response of West Indians. A native Briton who had spent twelve years in Jamaica before becoming a judge in the vice-admiralty court, Long published in 1774 a massive and influential three-volume *History of Jamaica*. Not content after the Somerset decision merely to trace events of the past, he set himself up as a philosopher, ethnologist, and psychologist to consider the Negro character and its adaptability to slavery. In his view Negroes were "a brutish ignorant, idle, crafty, treacherous, bloody, thievish, mistrustful, and superstitious people," a separate species vastly inferior to humans and more closely allied with apes and orangutans. And if anyone were to take the time, Long concluded, it might be found that apes could be taught as much of the "mechanical arts" as Negroes.[2]

Even though the *History of Jamaica* was frequently cited by American proslavery writers in the nineteenth century, Long's racial justification of slavery indicated the existence of a separate proslavery tradition in the British West Indies. His study also illustrated the extent to which West Indian propagandists would use perverse arguments to uphold the propriety of slaveholding. Adopting a manner similar to Long's, other Britons and West Indians waged an unrelenting battle with emancipationists from the conclusion of the Somerset case until the abolition of slavery in the West Indies in 1833.

In the course of the debate, which lasted more than six decades, British proslavery writers assumed every moral, philosophical, economic, and social position available to defenders of slavery in the English-speaking world. They not only declared slavery morally blameless and perfectly consistent with enlightened government; they also insisted that it was a positive good—that it civilized and Christianized degraded Africans and that it ensured the best possible relationship between capital and labor. Indeed the defenders of West Indian slavery can be held responsible for establishing a slaveholder's philosophy well before the first American southerner attempted to frame a response to radical abolitionism.[3]

In other ways, too, British and West Indian proslavery writers foreshadowed the nineteenth-century American debate on slavery. As in the United States, their publications appeared in the wake of various attacks on slavery and were clustered primarily in two periods of intense debate. After the brief spurt of proslavery responses that coincided with the American Revolution and the Somerset case, another major outpouring of defenses did not occur until 1788 when Parliamentary debates on the slave trade began. This flurry of proslavery literature continued until 1793 when fears engendered by the impact of the French Revolution silenced even the enemies of the slave trade. While the slave trade proved an explosive issue in England, the same question was handled quietly in the United States during the 1787 Constitutional Convention. When Parliament finally ended the slave trade in 1806, hardly a ripple occurred among West Indian slaveholders, reminiscent of the stillness that had greeted the same decision in America. Thus, British and West Indian defenders remained relatively silent from 1793 until 1823 when

British emancipationists organized for a death struggle with West Indian slavery. While the heyday of American proslavery activity followed the appearance of radical abolitionism in the 1830s, the debate on slavery reached the same height in Britain and the West Indies during the decade after 1823 until August 29, 1833, when Parliament abolished the institution in the West Indies.[4]

The introduction of a resolution in Parliament by William Wilberforce on May 9, 1788, which would have committed the House of Commons to a consideration of the slave trade in its next session, precipitated the first phase of the British exchange on slavery and the slave trade. Without waiting for the onset of Parliamentary debates, a host of merchants, gentlemen, West Indian planters, clergymen, and British West Indian sympathizers unleashed an outpouring of proslavery literature unparalleled in the English-speaking world. From the outset these defenders of slavery exhibited an intensity of argument, an awareness of crisis, and a comprehensiveness of logic which can only be compared to that of American proslavery writers after the appearance of abolitionism.

In vindictiveness and rhetoric none surpassed the first, Raymund Harris's *Scriptural Researches on the Licitness of the Slave-Trade* (1788). A dissenting clergyman later found to be a Spanish expatriate and ex-Jesuit priest, Harris (real name Don Raymondo Hormaza) relied on scriptural testimony to frame a case for slavery. Insisting that the Bible was the only infallible guide to truth, he argued that "whatever is declared in any part of the Scriptural Records to be intrinsically good or bad, licit or illicit, must be essentially so in its own nature, however contrary any such declaration may be to the received opinions of men." After studying the "Oracular decisions" of God, Harris came to a conclusion long associated with the Old South. God in his Holy Word "has positively declared that the Slave-Trade is intrinsically good and licit" and that the holding of slaves "is perfectly consonant to the principles of the Law of Nature, the Mosaic Dispensation, and the Christian Law." In a phrase that bursts the bubble of the "positive good" thesis in traditional historiography, Harris determined that slavery had "the positive sanction of God in its support."[5]

British and West Indian proslavery writers did not depend exclusively on the Bible in support of their contention that slavery and the slave trade were positive goods. In a lengthy defense entitled *A Short Essay on the Subject of Negro Slavery* issued also in 1788 by another clergyman, other grounds for slavery's benevolence were found. In a wide-ranging survey of traditional proslavery argumentation which relied heavily on Richard Nesbit's *Slavery Not Forbidden by Scripture* (1773), Henry Evans Holder, a native and resident cleric of Barbados, responded to "those who avow themselves the champions of liberty, but who may be found to be, the promoters of licentiousness." Calling more on theology and philosophy than on Scripture, Holder argued that "slavery may constitute a portion of the scheme of Divine government." Since ranks and orders were permitted in all societies by God's decree, the personal rights of individuals were "so far modified" that "no one common scale can be ascertained concerning them, to be applied indiscriminately to the whole race." And like chauvinistic proslavery Americans fifty years later, Holder believed that the slave trade was "a species of dispensation of Providence in their [the Africans'] favour, to bring them to a better state of civilization than they could attain in their domestic residence."

Moreover, a half-century before southern political economists began their careers, Holder held that slavery was a responsible welfare agency. Even though Negro slaves were "doomed" to labor for others, they "were at least certain of such a proportion of care and attention from their owner, as habit has made sufficient for their well-being." Holder stated further that the plight of the slave was no worse than that of any other poor laborer: "Look through Europe, and see whether it is not everywhere the case that the poor and indigent are destined to labour, more for the benefit of the rich and great, than for their own?" From his perspective emancipation was unthinkable "both on the score of its *injustice*, and of its *inexpedience*." It would not only result in financial loss to planter and empire, but it would also unleash a mass of degraded people incapable of caring for themselves. Emancipation would have the effect of destroying a productive and happy society, on the one hand, and of creating a state of idle, useless paupers on the other. Given the presence of an alien race, Holder might have added that slavery was the best possible relation between capital and labor.[6]

Other British and West Indian writers continued in the same manner by comparing in consummate detail the various benefits of free and slave societies. Three separate writers published works in 1789, 1790, and 1792 with extended comparisons of the conditions of slave and free labor. In a line-by-line proslavery commentary on Thomas Clarkson's *Essay on the Slavery and Commerce of the Human Species* (1786), Gilbert Francklyn, a Jamaican, wrote that "slavery has been, and, from the nature of man, must ever be, a very common and general situation of life." He observed that in all civilized societies "every man is restrained of some part of his natural liberty, and is consequently, in some degree, deprived of his freedom"; every deprivation, no matter how slight, "is a species of servitude or slavery." After traipsing through history to demonstrate his point, Francklyn asked Clarkson, "Do you conceive, Sir, any individual however highly honoured or distinguished, whatever knowledge or abilities he may possess, can possibly be justified in venturing to condemn, as *impious* customs and usages which have had the concurrence of people of all nations, and of all religions, throughout the world, from the remotest antiquity?" How could one condemn something, Francklyn asked, which was ancient, universal, and necessary in every society whether it be labeled wage or legal slavery?

Francklyn further held that every society, whether it be called slave or free, had its poor: "The poor people of every denomination, and every where, are truly and essentially those who bear, and ever must bear, burthens heavier or lighter, according as circumstances may occur." Slavery, after all, was but "a *genus* of the state of man, of which the different kinds of servitude are distinct species—that, as it is impossible totally to eradicate it . . . so the modification of the kind of servitude in usage in any country is not rashly to be attempted." In a sneer at nations that boasted liberty for all, Francklyn challenged, "Let any man of candour declare, whether the state of servitude and bondage, in which the poor are held both in France and England, does not merit the name of *slavery*, and justify the assertion of its *universal* existence at present, as well as the opinion of its having existed from the remotest antiquity, and that it ever must exist in the world."[7]

Another who argued the comparative innocence of slavery was William Knox, the old Georgia evangelical who had been a nemesis to emancipationists as far back as Anthony Benezet. Irate at the revival of emancipationism, Knox reissued his *Three Tracts* in 1789 and a year later published *A Letter from W. K., Esq. to W. Wilberforce, Esq.* In the latter Knox evaluated the circumstances of black slaves in the West Indies and white laborers in Britain. In his estimation the care given slave labor on West Indian plantations far exceeded the horrible plight of factory workers. And when the debate on slavery was carried from pamphleteering to the floor of Parliament, Knox led those in both Lords and Commons who made sure that the point of comparison was not forgotten.[8]

Jesse Foot, an ambitious surgeon who had spent three years on Nevis, underscored Francklyn and Knox's arguments in 1792 in a vastly popular book entitled *Defense of the Planters in the West Indies.* Published at the peak of the debate on the slave trade, Foot's volume ran through three large editions in as many weeks. In two brief essays he made his point. Foot argued that wherever there is wealth there must also be poverty, wherever shiny coins there must be those who dig up the ore, wherever clothing miserable weavers, and wherever soldiers and sailors broken families and degrading servitude. And "Whilst these are *necessary* gradations in a *civilised society,* and whilst it is found necessary that these various gradations in the conditions of men shall exist, so long will it be *necessary* for that society to consider how to apply its humanity—not with a *partial hand,* nor with an *unnatural* impulse, but with a general view to the conditions of the whole." Irritated that emancipationists should concern themselves with slaves a thousand miles from England while English laborers languished in poverty, Foot asked, "Are we not compelled by the force of reason to correct the desperate conditions of those in our own *state,* and *before our own noses,* before we are authorized in conscience to examine farther off?"

After challenging emancipationists to cast the mote out of their own eyes, Foot then turned to a comparative study of slavery. In his mind there were "many more positive conditions of *slavery* than that of one man being the property of another, and being subject to his will and dominion." Since he believed that ranks and orders, including enslavement, were necessary in the association of men, he maintained that the only duty of leaders *"is to make all occupations and all conditions of men as comfortable as the nature of their stations will admit."* As for West Indian slaves—in a statement that could have been written by George Fitzhugh—Foot argued that "their burthen of life is ever light, and their anxiety for their children is as short as that of a bird whilst its young are fledging." However, such was not the case of the English poor: "I am perfectly convinced, and therefore do not hesitate to declare the fact, that the peasantry of this country were *throughout* their lives a happier class of men—that they began and ended their days with less positive distress—and that they experienced fewer wants—when they were under the protection of the *Barons* than since that protection has been withdrawn."[9]

In addition to comparing the political economy of slavery, British and West Indian proslavery writers focused their attention on the antislavery radicalism that they associated with the French Revolution. In 1792 and

1793, the last years of the eighteenth-century debate on slavery, defenders of West Indian slavery increasingly utilized the widespread reaction against revolutionary France to discredit emancipationism. In a manner that would be instructive to American opponents of abolitionism, Foot opened the barrage in 1792 by equating emancipationism and French egalitarianism and by declaring that he intended his work to "extinguish a fire that was burning down a house or temple of worship." In the case of either social radicalism or emancipation, "when the passions are storming reason," he saw it "the duty of every social man to endeavour at least to stop their ravages."[10]

From the outset of the round of debates in the 1780s British proslavery writers, like their American counterparts fifty years later, portrayed emancipationists as radical revolutionaries. When James Tobin, a wealthy West Indian sugar merchant, responded between 1784 and 1788 to James Ramsay's antislavery pamphlets, the merchant-planter called Ramsay a traducer, ranter, and incendiary whose writing appeared "both in matter and style . . . much more like the impotent railing of an enraged old woman, than the manly resentment of a liberal mind." After Ramsay hired a detective to investigate Tobin's background, Tobin did some checking of his own. He found that, while Ramsay had served as a surgeon in charge of three thousand slaves in the West Indies, he had tried unsuccessfully to win an appointment to the King's Council. Tobin implied that, having failed, Ramsay sought vindication by attempting to steal the wealth of those whom he had wanted to join and by souring the minds of men to the institution of slavery.[11]

Suspicious about the intentions of British emancipationists already aroused, the French Revolution clearly played into the hands of proslavery writers. During the peak of the anti-French and anti-Revolutionary reaction, a Captain McCarty compiled a proslavery *Appeal to the Candour and Justice of the People of England* from the Parliamentary debates. In this appeal, he underscored the connections between emancipationism and the French Revolution and highlighted the subversive influences of each. He also reported that, while emancipationists would be content with "nothing less than the total desolation and destruction of the British West India Colonies," the West Indies were in fact "filled with emissaries and inflammatory publications by the friends of Abolition." McCarty even went so far as to insist that on some islands slaves were storing weapons for a planned armed rebellion.[12]

The fear of servile insurrection as an outgrowth of the French Revolution sealed the fate of the emancipationist schemes of British antislavery leaders in 1792. The most William Wilberforce could wriggle from Parliament that year was a tentative resolution that "the Slave Trade ought to be gradually abolished." As the excitement engendered by the Parliamentary debates died down at the end of 1792, two other proslavery advocates reiterated the arguments of the defenders of slavery. In an anonymous apology for voting against the immediate abolition of the slave trade, a man who styled himself "a country gentleman" repeated the frequently heard contention that the slave trade and West Indian slavery were missionary institutions that could only benefit Africans. With Englishmen, West Indians, and Americans, he held "that the condition of the African negroes and their progeny may be bettered, as well in respect to temporals as spirituals, by their removal to our colonies." "Thus, remove them . . . to an enlightened country, to teach them to know and worship the Supreme Being, and to open to them the sacred depositories of His will, and of the glorious rewards He has promised to confer on those who do it," the country gentleman continued, "is surely to benefit them." And judging the treatment the Negro had received in Africa, he concluded that both slavery and the slave trade were "positive goods."[13]

While the country gentleman perpetuated the notion of slavery as a positive good, another proslavery writer recorded deep-seated fears of the French Revolution. Bryan Edwards published two volumes entitled *The History of the British Colonies in the West Indies* in 1793 and four years later a third volume that detailed the history of St. Domingo and the circumstances that led to Negro rebellion on the island in 1791. Having spent much of his career as a West Indian merchant and planter with vast estates in Jamaica, Edwards had long been critical of British emancipators and served as one of their chief antagonists in Parliament in the early 1790s. It was, therefore, understandable that his mammoth *History* should reflect his intense proslavery sentiments and that his heavy anti-French pen, particularly in his treatment of St. Domingo, should continue to feed the ideological fires of British and American proslavery thought until the end of the Civil War.[14]

The response of British and West Indian proslavery writers and the confluence of the French Revolution effectively squelched British emancipationism for a period of thirty years. But in March 1807, Parliament outlawed slave trading in the British empire forever. For all of the rancor aroused in the 1780s and 1790s over the trade, Parliament's final action engendered little debate and hardly a dissenting vote. As in America at the same time, governmental action ended the trading without any measurable proslavery response either in legislative halls or in published materials. In both England and the United States, public officials were for the moment willing to abolish the slave trade.

From 1793 until 1823, the British Empire experienced a period of relative quietude on the subject of slavery corresponding in some ways to the "neglected period" in America. Whereas it is not difficult to find significant proslavery literature in Britain and the West Indies either before 1793 or after 1823, during the intervening period there was a marked absence of overt proslavery formulations. But the lack of defenses does not mean, as it did not in America during the same period, that slavery was no longer discussed or that British emancipationists awaited the proper moment to resume their quest of abolition. As in the United States, the evidence suggests that Britain's would-be emancipators had made a peace with slavery based on sociological and economic considerations that had been inoperative in the late eighteenth century and would be again in the 1820s.

While American emancipators decided during the neglected period to support colonization and to restrict slavery to the South on the grounds of public safety and political economy, their British counterparts chose to permit slavery in the West Indies for similar reasons. Henry Peter Brougham, a man chiefly remembered for his role as a leading abolitionist in Parliament after 1823, was ironically one of the few individuals who defended slavery in the British Empire between 1793 and 1823. A founder of the *Edinburgh Review* (1802), which would become a leading reform journal and repository of antislavery thought, Brougham used his knowledge of political economy and law to publish a massive two-volume *Inquiry into the Colonial Policy of the European Powers* (1803). In a consideration of the relationship between colonies and mother country, Brougham upheld slavery by appealing to some of the same concerns that caused his American contemporaries to defend the institution.

Acutely aware of the danger of servile insurrection and the effect of the St. Domingo rebellion on other plantation islands, Brougham argued that West Indian slaves "must be held in obedience" and that colonial policy required the restoration of slavery throughout the European colonies in the West Indies. He did not believe that free labor was a viable alternative since he was convinced that only Negroes could be used in hot climates and because he considered Negroes unfit "for becoming the subject[s] of a

Comparing the conditions of men: "Which Was Worse, British Poverty

peaceable and regular community." He, therefore, viewed emancipation as a scheme of "zealots" based on "inexcusable thoughtlessness," which would bring disaster to the entire colonial system. Applying the observations of Edwards and French proslavery advocate Pierre Victor Malouet, Brougham claimed the "distinction of race," a "radical difference of manners and character" between blacks and whites, and a "perpetual opposition of interests, as well as prejudices" as the leading grounds for racial slavery as opposed to free labor.[15]

Even though Brougham later became an abolitionist, his perspective on slavery in 1803 represented a social and economic resignation to the fact of slavery, paralleling a similar grudging acceptance by Americans during the neglected period. The type of mentality represented by Brougham during the years before the rise of British abolitionism was further revealed in the position his journal, the *Edinburgh Review,* took in reference to American slavery. When Robert Walsh published his *Appeal from the Judgments of Great Britain Respecting the United States of America* (1819), the *Review* took exception to Walsh's paradoxical condemnation of West Indian slavery and defense of American slavery. Although the reviewer called upon "the Americans themselves to wipe away this foul blot from their character" and scored Walsh for upholding the institution, he thought it "quite absurd to represent the difficulties of abolition as at all parallel in the case of America" and the West Indies. He continued:

> It seems to be pretty clearly made out, that, without slaves, those islands could not be maintained; and, independent of private interests, the trade of England cannot afford to part with them. But will any body pretend to say, that the great and comparatively temperate regions over which American Slavery extends, would be deserted, if all their inhabitants were free—or even that they would be permanently less populous or less productive? . . . it is a crime and a shame, that the freest nation on earth should keep a million and a half of fellow-creatures in chains, within the very territory and sanctuary of their freedom; and should see them multiplying, from day to day, without thinking of any provision for their ultimate liberation.

Defending West Indian slavery as a necessary evil on the grounds of safety and economics, the reviewer would not allow his contemporary Americans the luxury of the same argument.[16]

Both the neglected period of America and the similar interlude in the British empire were followed by the rise of abolitionism and the resurgence of overt proslavery argumentation. When in 1823 Wilberforce

Comparing the conditions of children: Children in British factories.
Cartoon from *The White Slaves of England*, 1853.

Comparing the conditions of women: "Slaves of the Needle."
Cartoon from *The White Slaves of England*, 1853.

and the British Anti-Slavery Society reopened their campaign against slavery by introducing antislavery petitions in Parliament, they once again put West Indian slaveholders on the defensive. From 1823 until 1833 West Indian slaveholders and their sympathizers, who were under constant pressure to make their case known to the world, quickly passed from kindly apologies to some of the most militant proslavery rhetoric ever articulated in the English-speaking world.[17] In fact, they upheld slavery with a furor and assertiveness never surpassed by even the Old South's greatest proslavery enthusiasts.

Proslavery's last phase in the British Empire resembled in nearly every respect the American proslavery response to abolitionism. Besides the intense rhetoric, the British and West Indians' common defense was based on fear of subversion, sound political economy, accepted evaluations of free and slave labor, and even assertions of the positive benefits of slavery. It can, therefore, be safely asserted that British and West Indian proslavery writers between 1823 and 1833 created an ideological defense of slavery heretofore seen as a distinctive product of the Old South. Two decades before southern intellectuals took their "higher ground" in defense of slavery, West Indian slaveholders had already exhausted all of the defensive mechanisms of political economy and the positive good argument.

A sampling of British and West Indian defenses after 1823 indicates the universal application of the aforementioned themes. Wilberforce's new *Appeal to the Religion, Justice, and Humanity of the Inhabitants of the British Empire* (1823) drew the immediate fire of George Wilson Bridges, a Jamaican clergyman. In *A Voice from Jamaica* issued the same year, Bridges offered a brief version of the proslavery negativism that characterized early American anti-abolitionists and then proceeded to a caustic attack on abolitionists and a defense of slavery from a comparative perspective. He showed that, whereas the West Indian slave had "a constant supply of all the necessaries of life" and no fears for the future, the English laborer's "o'er-wearied slumbers" were too often "broken by the agonizing thoughts of the future, or by vain attempts to soothe the heart-rending cries of hungry helpless children." In conclusion, Bridges stated that, while the English worker has no assurance of salaried work, "the advantages I have enumerated as possessed by the negro, ARE HIS OWN BY LAW."[18]

Another West Indian publication in the same year indicated that comparisons between free and slave labor had virtually become reflexive responses of British proslavery writers. According to S. P. Hurd in a *Letter to the Right Honourable the Earl of Liverpool,* the Negro was incapable of surviving in a system of free labor—"the ultimate aim of the abollitionists." Wilberforce, he argued, "might as well turn into the streets the children of the Foundling Hospital as the negro, unprepared by education for the exercise of his free will." Hurd, like Fitzhugh later, thought the problem for men of good will was the word "slavery," which had been "permitted to outlive the existence of the evil itself." According to Hurd, "the term prejudices every Englishman to the question, and he enters upon the consideration of the case with a bias on his mind." In a suggestion that would also later be made by Fitzhugh and Henry Hughes of the Old South, Hurd wrote: "Let the appellation slave be now changed to that of 'indentured servant for life,' and having stripped the subject of its unsightly garb, proceed to a comparison between the actual state of the English labouring freeman, and the indentured servant; and I doubt much, whether the balance will not be found equal, if indeed there exists no preponderance in favour of the latter."[19]

In 1825 James MacQueen, an eminent geographer, explorer, and one-time manager of a sugar plantation on Granada, made a notable addition to the growing body of proslavery literature with his *The West India Colonies.* Combining in one lengthy volume a general refutation of abolitionist writings by Thomas Clarkson, Thomas Cooper, James Cropper, and the editors of the *Edinburgh Review,* MacQueen offered a dizzying array of counter assertions, testimonials, and signed affidavits to undermine the credibility of his adversaries. While it is nearly impossible to extract a general perspective from MacQueen's piecemeal refutations, certain prominent features do emerge. Like Brougham, Bridges, and his American contemporaries, MacQueen employed a conventional formula of proslavery negativism, declaring that he was "an enemy to personal Slavery in the abstract." As with other practitioners of that tactic, he then turned the tables: "It is because I am an enemy to Slavery, that I would oppose the rash, unjust, and dangerous measures now proposed for the abolition of personal Slavery in the West Indies, measures which, whatever the authors of them intend, will make the *freeman* in these possessions *Slaves,* and give the rein to barbarism to trample down—to extirpate civilization." He proposed that "libertarians," "secret informers," and "anonymous writers" had misled Britons into believing emancipation just, when in fact it was a horrible act of injustice to both slave and master. Like American anti-abolitionists and southern defenders, Mac-

Queen thought people were "misled by the arts and calumnies of interested and designing men, of reforming politicians, who under the mask of liberty and humanity agitate, and disturb this country."[20]

With the same sense of the subverting influences of abolitionism shared by other West Indians and Americans who defended slavery, MacQueen ransacked the Bible, reports on the conditions of labor in Britain, and the literature of two generations of proslavery writers to uphold slavery and to support his major contention that abolitionism was but the front for a sinister conspiracy. According to MacQueen, abolition societies were filled not only with men who would destroy the empire, but with those who sought to overturn British government: "Whenever they do attain either political influence or authority, they rule with a rod of iron, and direct with the utmost virulence their engines against the establishment in church and state, and all who support and defend them." But whereas American proslavery writers pictured abolitionists as anarchists, infidels, and sons of the French Revolution, MacQueen presented a unique epithet of opprobrium: "they are busily employed in organizing that machinery, which if not broken up, will one day, and that not far distant, be employed to forge chains for both the mind and body, marching forward in the strength of their zeal till, like Cromwell, they engrave on the muzzles of their cannon—'Lord, open thou our lips, and our mouths will shew forth thy praise.' "[21]

In 1828 Alexander Barclay, a former Jamaican, reinvoked and extended MacQueen's anti-abolitionism in a popular proslavery publication. In *Practical View of the Present State of Slavery in the West Indies,* Barclay went far beyond a mere defense of slavery and condemnation of abolitionism by warning of a possible secession of the West Indian colonies from the British empire. After reviewing the writing of one abolitionist and declaring that he could "scarcely recognize a single feature of the community" in which he had "so long resided," Barclay admonished that "it was such language, more than the sword of Washington, that lost England her American colonies." Combining proslavery negativism with a traditional positive good assertion, he concluded his defense: "If slavery indeed could be justified in any state of man, it surely is where rude and ignorant pagans are advancing to civilization, under the government of an enlightened people, to whom they look up as so greatly their superiors, that subjection to their authority is scarcely felt as a hardship, and certainly not at all as a degradation."[22]

As proslavery Britons and West Indians became more insistent that abolitionists halt their ill-advised course, their defenses centered precisely on those themes that absorbed the interest of late antebellum American proslavery advocates. Since many American writers thought abolition a product of misguided philanthropy, Charles Edward Long's *Negro Emancipation No Philanthropy* written in 1830 is particularly instructive. In his pamphlet Long—grandson of the eminent Jamaican historian Edward Long, who had left an indelible mark on proslavery literature in the 1770s—presented views on philanthropy or benevolence that many Americans would soon come to share. He argued that philanthropy proceeded from an expansive, dangerous tendency that "encourages its votaries to navigate the Atlantic in quest of objects on which they may alleviate the ravening of their insatiable benevolence"; and that, because of its sentimentalism, it tended to overlook more immediate social problems and to range afar in search of objects for kind, but misguided deeds. What distant philanthropists could not know, Long insisted, was that the very bondage of Negroes "has raised them in the scale of creation; [whereas] giving them emancipation would at once restore them to their African habits."[23]

The comparison of free and slave labor reached fruition in the early 1830s as more proslavery writers affirmed the benevolence of slavery. Frederick W. N. Bayley, a poet and son of a British army officer in Barbados, wrote one of the best statements of the thesis in *Four Years' Residence in the West Indies* (1830). As "an Englishman and a lover of liberty" Bayley supposedly was "prompted by humanity to plead in behalf of those measures which four years' experience [*sic*] have convinced him would benefit the slave." After reading more than a hundred treatises on slavery and observing it in practice, he decided to come to its defense by stating unequivocally that free labor was impossible in the West Indies and that emancipation of the Negro "would be more dangerous than slavery in its existing state." Moreover, he insisted that "to say that the slaves in general are as happy as the lower class of poor in England, would be to fix upon them the stamp of misery." On the contrary, he found that West Indian slaves were among the happiest laborers in the world, "totally free from the cares, the troubles, the poverty, and even the labor and anxieties of the British poor."[24] Bayley's comparison proved so persuasive that in 1833 another writer extracted his arguments to form the basis of a new pamphlet, *The Condition of the West India Slave Contrasted with That of the Slave in Our English Factories*. The emphasis lay on the universal misery of free labor.[25]

None of the other grounds on which British and West Indian writers defended slavery had been abandoned on the eve of emancipation in 1833. As indicated by *Thoughts on Negro Slavery* (1833), an essay published by an English clergyman immediately before Parliament instituted gradual and compensated emancipation throughout the empire, no stone was left unturned in the battle to maintain slavery. Summarizing many of the arguments that had been bandied about in England, the West Indies, and America from the sixteenth to the nineteenth century, J. W. Wilkinson surveyed Scripture, history, and political economy only to find slavery blameless. "There can be no doubt," he wrote, "that the Negroes in our plantations enjoy a state of existence infinitely more desirable than that from which they, or their forefathers, have been taken." Despite their elevation in the West Indies, Wilkinson warned that the sudden emancipation of "8 or 900,000 barbarians from slavery to freedom would unhinge the frame of society in the colonies, paralyze the energies of the colonists, check, if not destroy, the cultivation of the soil, and, through a thousand channels, affect our manufactures and the revenues of the state."[26]

Wilkinson signed his statement on May 3, 1833. On August 29, after heated exchanges and effective maneuvering by abolitionists, the abolition bill became law in the British Empire. Although an occasional Briton came to the defense of American slavery, particularly during the Civil War, the long-lived debate in the British Empire concluded in 1833.[27] For more than a century Britons and British colonials had argued the merits and demerits of legalized human bondage from every possible angle. And even though it is difficult on the basis of a sampling of British and West Indian proslavery literature to determine if a logically connected and generally accepted proslavery ideology—a slaveholders' philosophy—ever emerged, it is clear that in their efforts to buttress the system of slavery on colonial plantations Britons and West Indians left no line of argumentation or rationalization to the imagination.

As a transatlantic antecedent, the British and West Indian slavery debate contributed directly to the form, content, and perspective of proslavery literature in the United States. Although the North American colonies had severed themselves from the British Empire at a moment when the question of slavery was reaching an early peak of excitement, the colonies' common origin and language with Britain continued to influence American social and cultural values. Despite the fact that from the American Revolution until well into the nineteenth century Americans were always wary of British influences, the United States remained in every sense a cultural province of the British Empire. American sensitivity to British values and opinions was clearly evident in the case of America's proslavery nationalists who, along with West Indians, lashed out against British critics of slavery throughout the neglected period and made full use of the insights, arguments, and information contained in British proslavery literature, particularly the more general works of Edwards and Long.

In addition to using British and West Indian proslavery writings as source material, nineteenth-century American proslavery thought was affected by the influx of individuals who grew up in the midst of the British debate. Among American proslavery writers one out of ten was born and spent his formative years either in Britain or the West Indies. Nearly half of those from the West Indies reached maturity at the time British emancipation occurred. William Harper, one of the early, influential writers who contributed immeasurably to the southern school of proslavery political economy, traced his origins to Antigua. Perhaps as a result of his experiences in the West Indies during the slavery debates of the 1790s, Harper relied heavily on British and West Indian proslavery writings. Until the 1830s when American proslavery arguments followed an independent course, Americans appropriated much of their ammunition from their British forerunners.[28]

It now seems obvious, moreover, that what Eugene Genovese has called "the logical outcome of the slaveholders' philosophy"—that proslavery ideology for which George Fitzhugh was perhaps the preeminent American spokesman—was, in fact, virtually a direct appropriation by Americans from British and West Indian proslavery literature and thought. In both America and the British Empire the comparison of free and slave labor was a common occurrence in proslavery writings from the seventeenth century forward. Most intelligent defenders who based their perspective on multiple arguments made at least a passing reference to the harsh conditions of labor in any form of society. It was not until the British debates on the slave trade in the 1780s and 1790s, however, that anyone began to systematize such comparisons. Between 1788 and 1792 Holder, Francklyn, Knox, Foot, and Edwards established the pattern for comparative studies of labor. In the early 1820s Bridges, Hurd, and MacQueen helped make the argument, with the help of political economists, a standard fare of British proslavery thought. And by

1833 British proslavery writers had arrived at those conclusions that have been mistakenly ascribed as unique to political economists of the Old South.

When Robert Walsh, Edward Brown, Thomas Cooper, Thomas P. Jones, Charles Cotesworth Pinckney, and other Americans began surveying slavery from the perspective of political economy in the 1820s, they simply latched on to a tradition whose source, in the English-speaking world, lay in Britain and her colonies. When Thomas Roderick Dew, William Harper, and William Gilmore Simms took what George Fitzhugh afterward called "a higher ground" in defense of slavery in the 1830s, they merely appropriated in their own contexts the conclusions that had been reached by political economists and proslavery writers in the British Empire. And when James Henry Hammond, George Fitzhugh, and Edmund Ruffin, among a host of other American intellectuals from both North and South, made such comparisons and concepts a chief medium of their proslavery views, they were only carrying forward a tradition that had already reached its logical, if not its final, outcome in the British Empire by 1833. In every sense of the word, American proslavery argumentation was but a tributary off a mainstream that lay elsewhere in the Western world.

But irrespective of the impact of British and West Indian proslavery thought on its American counterpart, a more fundamental consideration is the significance of a strong proslavery tradition in a non-American setting. If the British Empire offers any indication of the pressure and shape of proslavery thought elsewhere (and vast bodies of proslavery literature from other societies suggests that it does),[29] it is evident that any slaveholding society could meet criticism of its form of labor with essentially the same type of proslavery response that occurred in the Old South. While context and timing might cause variations in the intellectual or ideological framework of the response, proslavery writers in the Western world had available at nearly all times the same body of arguments. Because of the universality of those arguments, historians tread on thin ice when they attempt to determine uniqueness or to assign guilt on such a basis.

FIVE

The "Positive Good" Thesis and Proslavery Arguments in Britain and America, 1701–1861

The most misleading notion in traditional interpretations of proslavery history has been the belief that proslavery thought in the Old South progressed from a mild approval of slavery to a sort of heinous argumentation that showed no restraint in its efforts to prove slavery a positive benefit to blacks and to American society. Related to this view is one that depicts racist southerners creating de novo particularly reprehensible arguments in response to the sharp criticism of northern abolitionists. The single phrase that has come to symbolize the multiplication of arguments and the growth of intensity is the term coined by historians to denote the *positive good* theory of slavery. It has proved so appealing and expressive that one rarely encounters any mention of American proslavery in historical literature without a corresponding reference to the term *positive good*.

Despite the universal prevalence of the concept, it would appear that both the term and the concept behind it for interpreting a phenomenon in proslavery history was the fabrication of one historian, William Sumner Jenkins, as explained in his *Pro-slavery Thought in the Old South* (1935). Whereas the notion that slavery could be a positive good for slaves and slave society appears in proslavery literature of all nations and in nearly all eras, it was Jenkins who developed the still widely accepted thesis that proslavery writers in the Old South moved from a negative to a positive evaluation of slavery and thereby paved the way for the Garrisonian abolitionist response of the early 1830s.[1] Other historians accepted Jenkins's misguided assertions uncritically and added a corollary that cannot be found in Jenkins's writings, i.e., that the positive good argument was distinctively southern and thereby set the Old South apart from all other slaveholding societies in the Western world.

Contrary to the conventional wisdom of generations of historians, all parts of the positive good thesis are false and without foundation. Not only was the positive good argument in defense of slavery not unique to the Old South, but also Jenkins and other historians have erred in concluding that there was a significant shift in proslavery thinking in the Old South during the 1820s that represented a fundamental change in southern values and beliefs prior to the onset of abolitionism. Since the thesis has achieved such universal credence among historians and other students of American history, however, it will be instructive to focus in some detail on that data used by historians to postulate the thesis and on the types of arguments used in the Old South and elsewhere to buttress the institution of slavery.

A close look at the positive good arguments cited by Jenkins reveals the error of his hypothesis. His first example was taken from Charles Cotesworth Pinckney's 1829 *Address.* For comparison his statement appears first below, followed by similar proslavery statements of other writers.

Jenkins

Charles C. Pinckney, 1829: That slavery, as it exists here, is a greater or more unusual evil than befalls the poor in general, we are not prepared to admit.

Comparative Statements

Richard Nisbet, 1773: A Negro may be said to have fewer cares, and less reason to be anxious about tomorrow, than any other individual of our species. . . . They may be pronounced happier than the common people of many of the arbitrary governments in Europe. . . .

Captain McCarty, 1792: I consider the Negroes in the British West India Islands to be in as COMFORTABLE A STATE, AS THE LOWER ORDERS OF MANKIND IN ANY COUNTRY IN EUROPE.

Robert Walsh, 1819: The physical condition of the American negro is, on the whole, not comparatively alone, but *positively good,* and he is exempt from those racking anxieties—the exacerbations of despair, to which the English manufacturer and peasant are subject to in the pursuit of their pittance.[2]

Pinckney's defense was a comparison of American slavery with the labor conditions in Europe and in the northern United States. Despite Jenkins's

citation of the passage from Pinckney's *Address* as a positive good statement, it is obviously couched in negative language and does not even
claim that the American slave is in a more favored position than the poor
of other countries. At most, Pinckney held that the American slave's
condition was no worse. That is not the case in the statements of Richard
Nisbet and Robert Walsh, while the quotation from Captain McCarty's
defense is similar to Pinckney's assertion. If Jenkins had cited Walsh's
earlier statement (1819) which uses the phrase "positive good" apart from
any comparison, he would have been on firmer ground. Nevertheless, as
indicated by the parallel examples, comparative judgments on the goodness of slavery were not new in the 1820s despite the groundswell of
political economy. The Pinckney quotation is not, therefore, a unique and
novel positive good declaration.

Jenkins's second example, which has been generally accepted as a valid
positive good statement,[3] is the 1829 message of Gov. Stephen D. Miller
to the South Carolina legislature:

Jenkins

Stephen D. Miller, 1829: Slavery is not a national evil; on the contrary, it is a
national benefit. The agricultural wealth of the country is found in those
states owning slaves, and a great portion of the revenue of the government
is derived from the products of slave labor—Slavery exists in some form
everywhere, and it is not of much consequence in a philosophical point of
view, whether it be voluntary or involuntary. In a political point of view,
involuntary slavery had the advantage, since all who enjoy political liberty
are then in fact free. Wealth gives no influence at the polls; it goes where
white men perform the menial services which slaves do here. Upon this
subject it does not become us to speak in a whisper, betray fear, or feign
philanthropy.

Comparative Statements

Gilbert Francklyn, 1789: Slavery has been, and, from the nature of man,
must ever be, a very common and general situation of life. . . . It is certain
that, in civil society, every man is restrained of some part of his natural
liberty, and is consequently in some degree deprived of his freedom. Every
deprivation of freedom is a species of servitude *or slavery.*

Charles J. Ingersoll, 1810 (citing in part Edmund Burke): "The people of
the Southern colonies are much more strongly, and with a higher and more
stubborn spirit, attached to liberty than those of the northern. . . . such will
be the masters of slaves, who are not slaves themselves. In such a people the
haughtiness of domination combines with the spirit of freedom, fortifies it,

and renders it invincible." . . . Were it not for the slaves of the South, there
would be but one rank [of freemen in America].[4]

Miller's statement makes three assertions, two drawn from the insights of
political economy and one from Burkean conservative thought. He argues initially, as did many economists in the antebellum period, that the
plantation South, because of its massive export of agricultural produce,
created the true basis of wealth for America in the early years of the
nineteenth century. It is in that sense that Miller concluded slavery was a
national benefit. He suggested secondly that slavery exists everywhere in
some form, whether or not it is called slavery—a common assertion
made by proslavery writers and political thinkers from early in the eighteenth century. He argued finally that the separation of the lower class
from the rest of society by the mark of slavery made freemen equal and
instilled a greater love of freedom among them. Far from being novel,
Miller's argument was drawn from familiar sources of political economic
theory.

Jenkins's third example of a positive good statement derived from one
of the speeches made during the January 1832 Virginia debates. It is
based on the same insights alluded to by Governor Miller:

Jenkins

W. D. Sims, 1832: It [slavery] has existed and ever will exist, in all ages, in
some form, and some degree. I think slavery as much a correlative of liberty
as cold is of heat. History, experience, observation, and reason, have taught
me, that the torch of liberty has ever burnt brightest when surrounded by
the dark and filthy yet nutritious [influence] of slavery. Nor do I believe in
that [fanaticism] about the natural equality of man. I do not believe that all
men are by nature equal, or that it is in the power of human art to make
them so.

Comparative Statements

Jesse Foot, 1792: There are many more positive conditions of *slavery* than
that of one man being the property of another, and being subject to his will
and dominion: and if such positive conditions be *necessary* in every association of men, both under a civilized government as states but little removed
from that of nature—if various ranks and orders of men be necessary, that
the political wheel may go round, that the purposes of social life be more
completely fulfilled, . . . [let it be admitted].

Charles J. Ingersoll, 1810: Not that there is anything in inferior servitude
militant with republicanism.

Robert Walsh, 1819: The native citizen of the slave-holding state displays, specifically, as much sensibility, justice, and stedfastness, in all the domestic and social relations, as the European, of whatever country.[5]

Sims contended that slavery was an inescapable feature of human society, an argument long employed by defenders of slavery. And his belief in the compatibility of slavery and republicanism had its origin in Burkean and conservative political thought, which held that even Greek and Roman republicans built their free institutions in the presence of and upon the foundation of slavery.

All of Jenkins's positive good examples from 1833 and following are similar to those listed above, including one of the most famous—Gov. George McDuffie's 1835 assertion that slavery was "the cornerstone of our republican edifice." John C. Calhoun's equally famous declaration given in Congress in 1837 is often cited as the capstone of the movement toward a positive good theory:

Jenkins

John C. Calhoun, 1837: But let me not be understood as admitting, even by implication, that the existing relations between the races in the slaveholding states is an evil:—far otherwise; I hold it to be a good, as it has thus far proved itself to be to both, and will continue to prove so if not disturbed by the fell spirit of abolition.

We now believe it has been a great blessing to both of the races—the European and African, which, by a mysterious Providence, have been brought together in the Southern section of this Union. The one has greatly improved, and the other has not deteriorated; while in a political point of view, it has been the great stay of the Union and our free institutions, and one of the main sources of the unbounded prosperity of the whole.

Comparative Statements

Theodore Parsons, 1773: It is evident beyond all controversy, that the removal of the *Africans* from the state of brutality, wretchedness, and misery in which they are at home so deeply involved, to this land of light, humanity, and christian knowledge, is to them so great a blessing.

Personal Slavery Established, 1773: [Their removal compelled them] to the enjoyment of a more refined state of happiness, than the partiality of fate had assigned them in their native state.

Henry E. Holder, 1788: [Their removal was] a species of dispensation of Providence in their favour, to bring them to a better state of civilization than they could attain to in their domestic residence; and such it must undoubtedly prove in a very high degree, when it is their fortune to fall into the hands of rational and benevolent owners.[6]

The only feature in Calhoun's argument that had not already appeared in Jenkins's other examples was the boon of slavery for the enslaved. As indicated by the early American statements of Parsons, the author of *Personal Slavery Established,* and the West Indian clergyman Holder, the transportation of Africans to America had always been defended as a positive good for the enslaved.

There was, consequently, nothing unique about the defenses of slavery uttered in the South during the 1820s before Garrison. No one offered a single argument that had not already been used in substantially the same positive language in colonial America, in Britain, in the West Indies, or even in the northern United States early in the nineteenth century. The feature that made them appear novel was their greater dependence on the comparative aspects of political economy. However positive the arguments of southern proslavery writers, none was any more positive than those of other proslavery writers as early as the 1770s or as late as the 1810s. And those same arguments were also paralleled in Britain and the West Indies.

Nor were there any new arguments created by southern proslavery writers after the emergence of abolitionism. A systematic examination of proslavery arguments from 1701 through the Civil War in America, Britain, or the West Indies will further substantiate this somewhat startling conclusion and will demonstrate the amazing continuity in proslavery arguments wherever they appeared.

To study proslavery arguments quantitatively, ninety-one published defenses of slavery were chosen and subjected to a statistical argument analysis. The only rule of selection was that they be brief enough (twenty to sixty pages) to permit examination of every sentence. The selected defenses were then divided into six major groups reflecting chronological, geographical, and biographical variations. The groups and number of defenses studied are as follows: early American, 1701–1800 (twelve); British and West Indian, 1788–1833 (eighteen); American, 1800–1831 (twelve); Northern, 1831–1861, defenses written by natives of northern states while living in the North (fifteen); Northern in the South, 1831–1861, defenses written by native northerners living in the South (twelve); and Southern, 1831–1861, defenses written by native southerners living in the South (twenty-two).[7]

After listing arguments and devising schemes of organization, the arguments were arranged typologically around seven major headings: (1) *The Institution of Slavery*—arguments relating to definitions of slavery, its origin in society, and universally accepted legal foundations for its practice and perpetuation; (2) *The Negro*—arguments relating to the Negro's physiology, character, and past or to the nature of race; (3) *Slave Society*—arguments, whether comparative or not, relating to the political economy of slavery and slave society; (4) *American Slavery*—arguments relating to the peculiar history and character of slavery in the American colonies and the United States; (5) *Slavery in American Government*—arguments relating to the unique legal, constitutional, and ideological configurations in the United States; (6) *The Morality of Slavery*—arguments relating to Scripture, reason, tradition, theology, or ethics to prove the morality of slavery; and (7) *Master and Slave*—arguments relating to societal duties, including those of employers and employees and the obligations inherent in the two positions in slave society.[8]

The following analysis is not an exhaustive listing of all possible arguments. No systematic scheme could express every nuance of even most of the arguments used to defend slavery. However, the scheme adopted does test the frequency of appearance of the most common arguments in all of the periods and geographical areas under consideration. If the analysis cannot claim exhaustiveness, it can at least suggest the outlines of argument preferences in various areas at different times.

The Institution of Slavery

Among the possible definitions of slavery that a proslavery writer might select, three were most common in all six groups. Three-fourths of the defenses portrayed slavery either as a state in which man is governed without his consent, as the "slavery principle" implied by all government (for government to exist there must be some restraint placed on citizens), or as a status in society with corresponding rights and duties. Only a few writers (mainly West Indians) opted for the harsher choice of slavery as the absolute control of the master over a slave. It is interesting, however, that one West Indian author and one early writer in the North defined slavery as a system of "warranteeism," a notion later adopted by Henry Hughes in the Old South. Among the three major definitions there was an even distribution among all groups, except for northern proslavery men living in the South who revealed a nearly unanimous preference for

THE NEGRO AS HE WAS.

THE NEGRO AS HE IS.

Two popular arguments for slavery illustrated:
(*Left*) American slavery has civilized the barbaric black Africans.
(*Right*) Aged and infirm slaves are cared for by their masters,
but "wage slaves" face misery and ruin. Period cartoons
of unknown origin.

THE NORTHERN LABORER.

THE SOUTHERN LABORER.

the slavery principle of government.[9] Nevertheless, in general, the majority of writers in all groups preferred definitions devoid of a moral content that placed the guilt for slavery upon society or civilization. Yet, a large number selected the morally laden classical definition of a state in which man is governed without his consent.

When the authors of these defenses attempted to account for the origin of slavery, one-third revealed a desire to place the brunt of responsibility on society. They believed that slavery resulted naturally from the need of man to organize functioning societies. Two considerably less popular causes for slavery were God's curse on Ham and the inequality of men. While a third of the southern writers held that slavery resulted from inequality, numerous writers in each of the remaining six groups argued similarly. Few believed that slavery could trace its cause to manstealing by grasping whites (three), the fall of man in the Garden of Eden (four), war among nations (eight), armed conflict between African tribes (seven), or a decree from God that Israelites enslave their neighbors (two).

As to the legal foundation for making men into slaves and for embodying slavery in national law, the writers (with a single exception) could not agree on any one principle. In order of decreasing frequency they pointed to the following: racial inequality; the revealed will of God; utility—for the happiness of the greatest number; the right of the wise or superior to guide the ignorant or inferior; the natural custom or tradition of societies; and the fact that there are no natural rights guaranteed to men. Only two writers, both southerners, adopted Albert Taylor Bledsoe's principle that slaves forfeit their natural rights for the good of society. The exception mentioned above refers to the eleven of eighteen British and West Indian writers who argued that racial inequality could serve as a legal foundation for slavery.

The overwhelming majority of proslavery writers believed that slavery either should or would be a perpetual institution. More than half of them argued either that circumstances required an endless perpetuation or that the nature of society demanded the presence of slavery in some form. About one-third (most of them in the North or South after 1831) felt that slavery might some day be ended either at the will of masters, by the preparation of slaves for freedom, or through the removal of the Negro from American society. As in the case of other proslavery comments on the institution, at least a few representatives of each group supported these contentions. Since all groups shared a common heritage, however, it is not surprising that their general notions on slavery should be similar.

The Negro

Of the five categories of argument relating to the Negro and to the question of race, a significant number of proslavery writers chose to apply arguments from only two. Under the heading of Negro physiology only twenty-four of the ninety-one writers mentioned that blackness was a physiological mark of inferiority, that resistance to heat prepared the Negro for burdensome work in the tropics, or that immunity to certain diseases indicated a natural inclination for tropical toil. Similarly, only half of them appealed to ethnological arguments on racial unity or diversity. Thirty-five writers, evenly distributed among all six groups, argued that the Negro was an inferior species of man; but only one writer followed the American School of Ethnology, which became popular in the 1850s, in contending that the Negro was a separate species. The fact that only fourteen used arguments for racial unity (all except one were dated in the 1840s or 1850s) indicates that detailed questions about race did not become important until after the appearance of what most proslavery thinkers called an unbiblical doctrine of racial diversity.

However, about two-thirds of the writers used extensively two categories of arguments on the Negro. They related to the Negro past in Africa and the Negro character (see table 5.1). About half of all the writers (except northern-born in the South and West Indians) referred to the Negro past. If their arguments can be considered racist, then, British and West Indian writers reveal a tendency to appeal to racist arguments more often than any other group; while early American writers and those in the North tended to make less frequent references to race. Southern proslavery writers and writers in America between 1800 and 1831 fell into a median position. The fact that a considerable number paid no attention to the Negro past should not be forgotten. The absence of racial arguments, even though the subject was slavery, suggests that at least some proslavery literature and thought did not proceed on racist assumptions.

A similar nonracist pattern appears in the distribution of arguments on the Negro character (see table 5.2). Except for British and West Indian writers one-third to one-half of the writers in each group made no

THE VOICE
OF THE
CLERGY

Among the extraordinary incidents of the times is the fact that the Democratic State Central Committee has circulated through Pennsylvania, as a campaign document the Letter of BISHOP HOPKINS, of Vermont, in which it is maintained that Slavery, in the language of Judge WOODWARD, is an incalculable blessing. The sentiments of Bishop HOPKINS on this subject are so atrocious, and their adoption and promulgation by men professing to be Christians is so scandalous, that the Episcopal Clergy of Philadelphia have felt themselves constrained to define their position, as they have done, in the following manly and outspoken

PROTEST:

"The subscribers deeply regret that the fact of the extensive circulation through this diocese of a letter by

'John Henry Hopkins, Bishop of the Diocese of Vermont,'

in defence of Southern Slavery, compels them to make this public Protest. It is not their province to mix in any political canvass. But as Ministers of Christ, in the Protestant Episcopal Church, it becomes them to deny any complicity or sympathy with such a defence.

"This attempt not only to apologise for slavery in the abstract, but to advocate it as it exists in the Cotton States, and in States which sell men and women in the open market as their staple product, is, in their judgment, unworthy of any servant of Jesus Christ. As an effort to sustain, on Bible principles, the States in rebellion against the government, in the wicked attempt to establish by force of arms a tyranny under the name of a republic, whose 'corner stone' shall be the perpetual bondage of the African, it challenges their indignant reprobation.

PHILADELPHIA, SEPTEMBER, 1863.

ALONZO POTTER, D. D., L. L. D.,
  Bishop.
JOHN RODNEY,
  Rector of St. Mark's, Germantown.
E. A. WASHBURN, D. D.,
  Rector of St. Luke's.
WM. SUDDARDS, D. D.,
  Rector of Grace Church.
D. R. GOODWIN, D. D.,
  Provost of University of Pennsylvania.
G. EMLEN HARE, D. D.,
  Professor in the Divinity School, Philada.
M. A. DeW. HOWE, D. D.,
  Rector of St. Luke's.
W. W. SPEAR, D. D.,
  Philadelphia.
JACOB M. DOUGLASS,
  Philadelphia.
HENRY S. SPACKMAN,
  Chaplain U. S. Hospital, Chestnut Hill.
PETER VAN PELT, D. D.,
  Secretary of Board of Missions.
CHARLES D. COOPER,
  Rector of St. Philip's.
WILBUR F. PADDOCK,
  Rector of St. Andrew's.
RICHARD D. HALL,
  Philadelphia.
JOSEPH D. NEWLIN,
  Rector of the Church of the Incarnation.
B. W. MORRIS,
  Assist. Minister of St. Luke's Germantown.
D S. MILLER,
  Rector of St. Mark's, Frankford.
B. T. NOAKES,
  Rector of the Church of the Covenant.
R. A. CARDEN, D. D.,
  Rector of the Church of the Intercessor.
ROBERT C. MATLACK,
  Rector of the Church of the Nativity.
L. W. SMITH,
  Rector of St. Michael's, Germantown.
SAMUEL E. APPLETON,
  Rector of the Church of the Mediator.
PHILLIPS BROOKS,
  Rector of the Church of the Holy Trinity.
DANIEL WASHBURN,
  Rector of Trinity Church.
D. OTIS KELLOGG,
  Rector of St. Matthew's.
KINGSTON GODDARD, D. D.,
  Rector of St. Paul's.
J. L. HEYSINGER,
  Philadelphia.
RICHARD NEWTON, D. D.,
  Rector of the Church of the Epiphany.
C. A. MAISON,
  Chaplain U. S. Hospital, Philadelphia.
JOHN LONG,
  Rector of the Church of Our Saviour, Jenkintown.
ORMES B. KEITH,
  Rector of Christ Church, Germantown.
ADDISON B. ATKINS,
  Rector of St. Andrew's, Mantua.
SAMUEL E. SMITH,
  Rector of the Church of St. John the Baptist, Germantown.
HERMAN HOOKER,
  Philadelphia.
WILLIAM N. DIEHL,
  Rector of the Church of the Atonement.
BENJAMIN WATSON, D. D.,

C. W. QUICK,
  Rector of the Church of Our Saviour.
J. T. WALDEN,
  Rector of St. Clement's.
HORATIO P. WELLS,
  Principal of a Boys' School, Andalusia.
HENRY J. MORTON, D. D.,
  Rector of St. James'.
GEORGE LEEDS, D. D.,
  Rector of St. Peter's.
JOHN A. CHILDS,
  Secretary of Board of Missions.
THOMAS C. YARNALL,
  Rector of St. Mary's.
EDWARD LOUNSBERY,
  Rector of St. Jude's.
W. H. M. STEWART,
  Philadelphia.
J. G. MAXWELL,
  Rector of Emmanuel Church, Kensington.
J. A. VAUGHAN, D. D.,
  Professor in the Divinity School.
EDWARD S. WATSON,
  Rector of St. James the Less, Falls of Schuylkill.
SAMUEL EDWARDS,
  Rector of Christ Church, Media, Delaware County.
JOEL RUDDEROW,
  Rector of the Church of the Messiah, Port Richmond.
GEORGE A. DURBOROW,
  Rector of the Church of the Redemption.
ROBERT J. PARVIN,
  Rector of St. Paul's, Cheltenham, Montgomery County.
ARCHIBALD BEATTY,
  Philadelphia.
T. S. YOCUM,
  Minister of Christ Church, (Swedes) Upper Merion P. O., Bridgeport.
JOSEPH R. MOORE,
  Minister of the Church of the Crucifixion.
WM. J. ALSTON,
  Rector of St. Thomas' Church.
ALFRED ELWYN,
  Deacon, Church of the Mediator.
GUSTAVUS M. MURRAY,
  Philadelphia.
C. A. L. RICHARDS,
  Rector of the Church of the Saviour, West Philadelphia.
G. A. STRONG,
  Philadelphia.
JAMES W. ROBINS,
  Head Master of the Episcopal Academy
THOMAS B. BARKER,
  Deacon, Grace Church.
SAMUEL TWEEDALE,
  Assistant Rector of St. Mark's, Frankford.
M. A. TOLMAN,
  Deacon, Minister of St. Alban's, Roxboro.
GEORGE BRINGHURST,
  Rector of All Saints' Church.
G. W. SHINN,
  Deacon, Assistant Rector of St. Paul's.
C. W. DUANE,
  Minister of St. Luke's Miss. Church.
JOHN H. DRUMM,
  Rector of St. James the Greater, Bristol.
S. HALL,
  Philadelphia.
GEORGE B. ALLINSON,
  Deacon, Philadelphia.
SAMUEL DURBOROW,
  Rector of the Church of the Evangelists.

J. NEWTON SPEAR,
  Deacon, Philadelphia.
JOSEPH N. MULFORD,
  Assisting in Holy Trinity.
GEORGE G. FIELD,
  Rector of St. John's Free Church.
LOUIS C. NEWMAN,
  Missionary to the Jews.
REESE C. EVANS,
  Philadelphia.
E. C. JONES,
  Missionary at Blockley Almshouse.
J. DeW. PERRY,
  Philadelphia.
ROBERT G. CHASE,
  Rector of St. Matthias' Church.
T. G. CLEMSON,
  Rector of St. David's Church, Radnor.
H. W. DUCACHET, D. D.,
  Rector of St. Stephen's.
JEHU C. CLAY, D. D.,
  Rector of the Swedes Church, (Gloria Dei.)
E. W. HENING,
  Foreign Missionary Committee, Philada.
JAMES MAY, D. D.,
  Professor in the Divinity School.
EDWARD L. LYCETT,
  Rector of the Church of the Redeemer, Lower Merion.
J. S. STONE, D. D.,
  Professor in the Divinity School.
D. C. MILLETT,
  Rector of St. Thomas' Church, Whitemarsh.
RICHARDSON GRAHAM,
  Chaplain in U. S. Hospital, Chester.
BENJAMIN DORR, D. D.,
  Rector of Christ Church.
JOHN W. LEADENHAM,
  Philadelphia.
CHARLES M. DUPUY,
  Philadelphia.
FREDERICK W. BEASLEY,
  Rector of All Saints', Lower Dublin, and Christ Chapel, Oakgrove.
W. R. STOCKTON,
  Rector of St. Peter's, Phœnixville, Chester County.
JOHN P. LUNDY,
  Rector of Emmanuel Church, Holmesburg.
R. HEBER NEWTON,
  Deacon, Church of the Epiphany.
GEORGE A. CROOKE,
  Rector of St. John's, Northern Liberties.
J. ISIDOR MOMBERT,
  Rector of St. James' Church, Lancaster.
JOHN G. FUREY,
  Missionary at Milton.
JOHN A. JEROME,
  Chaplain U. S. Hospital, Alexandria, Va.
FRANCIS D. HOSKINS,
  Rector of St. John's, Lancaster.
ROBERT W. OLIVER,
  Rector of St. Luke's Memorial Church, Altoona, Pa.
JOHN H. BABCOCK,
  Principal of Yeates' Institute, Lancaster.
ANSON R. HARD,
  Chester.
GEORGE A. LATIMER,
  Rector of Christ Church, Pottstown.
LEWIS W. GIBSON,
  Rector of St. Mark's, Sunbury.
HENRY BROWN,
  Rector of St. Paul's, Chester.

The clergy of Philadelphia protest the proslavery views of Bishop Hopkins of Vermont, September 1863

TABLE 5.1
Proslavery Arguments on the Negro Past

	WRITERS					
Argument	Early Americans	British and West Indians	Americans, 1800–1831	Northerners, 1831–1861	Northerners in the South	Southerners, 1831–1861
Negro historically in servile condition	2	14	4	5	8	7
All Negro nations remain uncivilized	0	13	4	5	7	7
Freed servile race lapses to barbarism	0	13	4	8	9	9
Free Negroes more degraded than slaves	3	12	4	5	9	10
Negro life in Africa always degraded	3	12	7	5	7	9
Slavery not irksome to men who never knew freedom	2	13	3	5	6	7
Total number of writers	12	18	12	15	12	22
Number not mentioning Negro past	4	3	4	7	1	8

Note: The total number of writers in each category does not equal the number of arguments adduced, because some writers applied more than one argument under the heading.

mention of Negro character in their defenses. Once again West Indian proslavery authors showed a greater tendency to apply racist arguments, particularly in their demand for strict regimentation of Negroes. In striking contrast, all American writers after 1831 attested to the ability of the Negro to enjoy some improvement, even though they did not think he could become the white man's equal. Of all the groups, early American writers mentioned the Negro character less frequently (in part because the available defenses from that period are much briefer). Nevertheless, none of the other groups held a monopoly on the use of racist argumentation.

TABLE 5.2
Proslavery Arguments on the Negro Character

Argument	Early Americans	British and West Indians	Americans, 1800–1831	Northerners, 1831–1861	Northerners in the South	Southerners, 1831–1861
	WRITERS					
Negro incapable of being educated or civilized	0	7	5	4	5	6
Negro dull and lazy, requiring constant supervision	2	14	5	6	4	9
Negro can improve, but not to the level of whites	1	9	5	10	6	13
Negro naturally sensuous and barbarous, needing control	2	12	5	5	3	9
Negro happier enslaved than free	1	7	4	8	5	8
Total number of writers	12	18	12	15	12	22
Number not mentioning Negro character	6	4	4	6	5	8

Note: The total number of writers in each category does not equal the number of arguments adduced, because some writers applied more than one argument under the heading.

Slave Society

Whereas little measurable variation can be detected among the various groups in their application of racist arguments to defend slavery, the distribution of arguments on slave society reflects definite tendencies. Under the heading of social classes all groups stressed the fact that slave society provided the only sure protection of property against the propertyless in the presence of an alien race. All American writers after 1831 contended that slave society is perfectly ordered with each class fulfilling a role or function. But only southerners and northern writers living in the South went on to argue that slave society produces the truest republicanism and liberty for all citizens and that it creates the wisest and best rulers. Furthermore, only in the South (including transplanted northerners) did they make the case that slave society fosters equality and a common interest among nonslaves. But, in view of the nature of these latter arguments, it is possible that their popularity in the South indicated more about southern nationalism than any unique propensity in the defense of slavery.

The other types of arguments on slave society confirm that the South was not alone in its analysis of the relations of capital and labor and of slave and free societies. There existed a universal tendency to idealize the master-slave relationship as the most beneficial and benevolent condition for capital and labor (see table 5.3). It is striking how little time writers spent in demonstrating the cheapness and efficiency of slavery, while few seemed to understand the twin value of the slave as both capital and labor. But all writers knew well and promulgated the theory of comparative political economy regarding the status of peasants and factory workers in other countries. That the picture was an idealized one is indicated clearly by the fact that all fifteen northern writers stressed the protective value of slavery, but none would admit that slave status was higher than that of workers in other societies.

A similar pattern emerges in the distribution of arguments comparing slave and free society. All proslavery writers after about 1800 turned to comparative political economy to bolster their defenses of slavery (see table 5.4). Extending their views on capital and labor, they depicted slave society as a self-contained unit able to handle reforms, deal with social ills, and protect its poorest members. In contrast to arguments on the status and value of slave labor, northern writers shared with southern writers organismic views of slave society for they, too, were intimately involved in stamping out abolitionism as a troublesome reform movement. Whatever their reasons, the widespread adoption of provisions implicit in the political economy of slavery counters any simplistic notion that only in southern slave society could one find the world view associated with the political economy of slavery.[10]

American Slavery

Even though proslavery writers generally agreed on the nature of slave society, when they came to consider the nature of American slavery, significant variations in their arguments began to appear. Those most inti-

TABLE 5.3
Proslavery Arguments on Capital and Labor in Slave Society

	WRITERS					
Argument	Early Americans	British and West Indians	Americans, 1800–1831	Northerners, 1831–1861	Northerners in the South	Southerners, 1831–1861
Labor becomes capital, equalizing interests of master and slave	1	3	6	4	2	8
Labor protected against every contingency of life	5	12	9	15	11	15
Status of labor higher than in any other type of society	1	12	10	5	11	15
Cheapest and most efficient form of labor	2	3	1	0	1	1
Total number of writers	12	18	12	15	12	22
Number not mentioning capital and labor in slave society	6	6	0	0	0	2

Note: The total number of writers in each category does not equal the number of arguments adduced, because some writers applied more than one argument under the heading.

mately involved in slavery were the most vocal in accusing others for introducing slavery to America. All writers believed that colonists in America or the West Indies had little choice in the form of labor adopted. But earlier writers frequently blamed slavery's origin on Africans who fought intertribal wars to enslave other Africans and who sold their captives to slave traders. Yet southerners and northern writers living in the South were quick to point their fingers at British imperial policy or the greed of New England and British merchants. Southern-based proslavery writers also examined colonists' attempts to abolish the slave trade, declaring that the continued practice even after those protests made emancipation impossible. The tendency of southern writers to score Brit-

TABLE 5.4

Proslavery Arguments on the Viability of Slave Society

Argument	WRITERS					
	Early Americans	British and West Indians	Americans, 1800–1831	Northerners, 1831–1861	Northerners in the South	Southerners, 1831–1861
Slave society secured against radical movements	0	6	8	10	10	13
Organism of slave society makes re- form movements unnecessary	1	4	6	6	7	10
Slave society attains all the ends sought by reform	2	10	8	10	8	16
Slave society obverse of laissez faire where weak destroyed	0	4	6	8	11	12
Total number of writers	12	18	12	15	12	22
Number not mentioning the viability of slave society	9	6	2	2	0	2

Note: The total number of writers in each category does not equal the number of arguments adduced, because some writers applied more than one argument under the heading.

ain and New England rather than Africans indicated the pleasure south- erners took in highlighting the moral inconsistencies of the North.

Even greater variation appeared in assessments of the character of American and West Indian slavery. All proslavery writers (see table 5.5) believed the system of slavery they defended to be the mildest in history. Whereas only West Indians argued that slavery was an appropriate prac- tice in a mercantile system, almost all later defenders characterized slav- ery as a missionary institution. However, certain other arguments be- came popular primarily in North America and the Old South. The southern argument that slavery was a divine trust complemented the view that slavery was a missionary institution, while the belief that slavery

TABLE 5.5

Proslavery Arguments on the Character of American Slavery

	WRITERS					
Argument	Early Americans	British and West Indians	Americans, 1800–1831	Northerners, 1831–1861	Northerners in the South	Southerners, 1831–1861
Our system the mildest in history	2	9	7	8	10	12
Ours a missionary institution to civilize and Christianize Africans	4	8	1	9	9	17
An essential ingredient in success of the American experiment	1	0	1	0	1	8
A divine trust given as a legacy to Americans	1	0	0	2	1	8
American slavery same as that of the Bible	0	7	1	0	11	13
Slavery and trade according to other practices of mercantilism	0	4	0	0	0	0
Total number of writers	12	18	12	15	12	22
Number not mentioning the character of American slavery	4	3	2	1	0	2

Note: The total number of writers in each category does not equal the number of arguments adduced, because some writers applied more than one argument under the heading.

was an essential ingredient in the American experiment proceeded from the teachings of political economy that the South provided the lion's share of governmental capital through the massive exportation of cotton.

The universal contention among American proslavery writers and some West Indians that American slavery was the same as that practiced in the Bible testifies to the nature of the slavery debate in its last phases in both Britain and America. Ignoring the teachings of political economy, abolitionists charged that slavery was an immoral, unchristian institution. In response to this attack, proslavery writers turned increasingly from arguments of political economy popular in the 1820s to concepts related to morality and religion. Hence, they characterized slavery as a missionary institution, a divine trust, and a practice encouraged by Scripture. From the perspective of moral science no argument was more important for the proslavery case than proving the biblical authorization for American slavery.

In terms of the history of American slavery, nearly half of the writers in all groups argued that slavery and slave society reached the greatest degree of perfection in America (or the West Indies). They also declared that considerations of public policy and benevolence required the continuation of slavery for the foreseeable future. American writers more than West Indians believed that slavery would come to an end only when the Negro was returned to Africa. Yet, as the Civil War approached, southern-based writers frequently stated that either the United States or the South had a mission to maintain perfected republicanism through the perpetuation of slavery. As in the case of the West Indies, when the crisis grew in intensity, the possible alternatives diminished in number and appeal until proslavery writers could speak only in terms of perpetual slave society.

Slavery in American Government

Although there was some variation in the application of arguments on the abstract nature of American slavery, when proslavery writers discussed the legal and constitutional problems relating to slavery they spoke with one voice (except colonial writers and West Indians who lived in different legal settings). Following the American Revolution, proslavery writers everywhere and at all times argued that bills of rights and the dogma of equalitarianism applied only abstractly to man in nature.

They held that slaves, a species of property, were protected by statute and the Constitution, and that they could not be taken away without the destruction of law and order. These writers also agreed that slaves were chattel protected by the law of property, but subject to laws on persons for their conduct. States could reform circumstantial evils connected with the practice of slavery, but neither the state nor the federal government could remove the institution.

Most proslavery advocates went even further in their legal justifications. In a republican government, they said, slavery was necessary to protect the rights of freemen. In fact, slavery ensured American republicanism by protecting property, fostering equality, and guaranteeing liberty to nonslaves. Therefore, not only did the Constitution permit the continuation of slavery, but it also permitted restrictions on the rights of free Negroes and required the return of fugitive slaves to their masters. Since slavery was demonstrably an essential feature of American republicanism, many proslavery writers argued that no amendment could be added to the Constitution that altered the nature of government or the character of society by abolishing slavery. While proslavery writers did not generally discuss the constitutional question in detail, whenever and wherever they did, they were agreed on these points. Southern-based writers stressed them more often and with greater vehemence. But they were not alone in their contentions.

The Morality of Slavery

Following the rise of abolitionism in the 1830s, the debate focused primarily on the morality of slavery. Despite their previous research into political economy and their desire to sell slavery on the grounds of policy and economy, proslavery writers in antebellum America were forced to confront the morality of their institution. But this shift in focus did not lead to the creation of new arguments. It merely meant that, for the first time since the debate on slavery began in the eighteenth century, every writer who favored its perpetuation found it necessary to discuss the manner in which slavery could be viewed as a moral (at least not immoral) institution.

Scripture proved the most important source for establishing the morality of slavery. Arguments based on Scripture had been an integral feature of proslavery literature in early America, the West Indies, and the United States before 1831 (see table 5.6). It only became more signif-

TABLE 5.6
Proslavery Arguments from Scripture

Argument	WRITERS					
	Early Americans	*British and West Indians*	*Americans, 1800–1831*	*Northerners, 1831–1861*	*Northerners in the South*	*Southerners, 1831–1861*
Old Testament—divine decree (curse on Ham)	3	2	2	5	3	8
Old Testament—divine sanction (allowed among patriarchs by divine law)	7	8	6	12	10	16
Old Testament—negative approval (no condemnation by the prophets)	3	1	3	6	3	7
New Testament—negative approval (no condemnation by Christ)	6	8	5	14	10	11
New Testament—sanction of apostles (taught submission of slaves and return of fugitives)	5	9	4	13	10	16
Curse on Ham fulfilled in subsequent history	2	1	2	5	3	8
Servant in Bible means "slave"	2	1	3	6	3	8
Total number of writers	12	18	12	15	12	22
Number not using Scripture	3	8	5	0	2	4

Note: The total number of writers in each category does not equal the number of arguments adduced, because some writers applied more than one argument under the heading.

icant after 1831. In their use of Scripture to defend slavery, proslavery writers could follow one of several courses. The most positive and racist approach looked upon the curse on Ham as a divine decree that set the Negro race apart as an inferior and servile people. The second most positive approach discovered a divine sanction for slavery (irrespective of the enslaved people) in the Old Testament, a negative approval in the Gospels, and the sanction of the Apostles in the Epistles. And the third least positive approach found no condemnation of slavery in Scripture. These three approaches were represented about equally among all groups. The bulk of writers selected the median position.

From the time of the American Revolution the words *reason, humanity,* and *nature* appeared frequently in proslavery literature and became epistemological tools in religion and philosophy. They also developed into authorities for morality. Although few proslavery writers dwelt on them extensively, almost all at some point affirmed the compatibility of slavery with reason, nature, and humanity (see table 5.7). No group (except perhaps northern writers) stressed the reasonableness and humanity of slavery over any other argument. And in this case, unlike that of Scripture, West Indians were in agreement.

A similar pattern emerged in the use of religious tradition as an authority for the morality of slavery. Whether or not they entered into a detailed examination of the role of slavery in church history, both West Indian and American writers appealed to classical and traditional Christian justifications. Another much older belief accepted by Christians from ancient times centered on the right of the faithful to enslave heathen peoples. Based on tradition, the argument was sometimes used in the nineteenth century to justify the enslavement of heathen Africans. Although few applied it, the argument remained current among all groups (except early American) to some extent.

Proslavery writers also appealed to theology to substantiate the morality of slavery. American writers, in particular, drew upon theological affirmations (see table 5.8). Christian theologians believed that certain institutions—family, government, and the church—had been ordained by God as permanent features of society. In the process of developing images of the slave society, proslavery writers in America often included the relation of master and slave. Many saw slavery as a part of God's historic scheme for bringing all men to salvation and argued negatively that if slavery were indeed evil God would not have given it sanction in Scripture. American writers were more likely to attempt to justify slavery

TABLE 5.7
Proslavery Arguments from Reason

	WRITERS					
Argument	*Early Americans*	*British and West Indians*	*Americans, 1800–1831*	*Northerners, 1831–1861*	*Northerners in the South*	*Southerners, 1831–1861*
Slavery reasonable and humane	4	10	4	14	10	14
Slavery not inconsistent with the law of nature	1	12	5	8	8	13
Total number of writers	12	18	12	15	12	22
Number not mentioning reason	7	5	6	1	2	6

Note: The total number of writers in each category does not equal the number of arguments adduced, because some writers applied more than one argument under the heading.

theologically, but among the various groups of American proslavery thinkers there was little variation.

Moral science developed as a branch of theology and philosophy in the United States during the first half of the nineteenth century. Hence, it was not surprising that Christian proslavery writers should apply the procedures and insights of their ethical thinking to slavery. They unanimously chanted that reason and conscience were inadequate rules for morality and that Scripture or revelation embodied the only plenary rule for man. After investigating their basic authority, American proslavery writers concluded that the slave was an individual with the rights of a human being according to his station in life. But he was by no means entitled to some abstract and unscriptural natural rights. More than half of all proslavery writers after 1800 in the United States easily affirmed this position.

Another source of proslavery argumentation integrally related to the problem of the morality of slavery revolved around the proper place of the church in slave society. Particularly in America where clergymen played a major role in the day-to-day combat over slavery, debates on the functions and powers of the church in dealing with social problems sometimes overshadowed the central question of the morality of slavery.

TABLE 5.8
Proslavery Arguments from Theology

	WRITERS					
Argument	Early Americans	British and West Indians	Americans, 1800–1831	Northerners, 1831–1861	Northerners in the South	Southerners, 1831–1861
Slavery a divinely ordained relation (as that of father and son)	2	2	1	11	10	14
Slavery a divine trust to save heathen	2	5	1	3	3	14
Slavery will end only with the millennium	0	0	1	5	6	6
God would not decree sin into existence	1	1	3	11	7	14
Total number of writers	12	18	12	15	12	22
Number not using theology	7	11	7	0	0	2

Note: The total number of writers in each category does not equal the number of arguments adduced, because some writers applied more than one argument under the heading.

American proslavery writers after 1831 universally placed strictures on the powers of the church to deal with slavery. Moreover, they spoke with a single voice in affirming that the church's function was to perfect not to challenge slave society. While these arguments did not directly justify slavery as a moral practice, they did codify the perpetuation of slavery. And what is more, the unanimity of proslavery writers on this point suggests that proslavery writers, wherever they were located in antebellum America, may have shared other convictions on societal arrangements as they impinged upon the overarching issue of slavery.

Master and Slave

Proslavery writers generally articulated the duty of masters to treat slaves justly, and they frequently urged more particularized obligations relating to the slave's comfort and religious instruction (see table 5.9). More than for early writers and West Indians, religious duties were important to American writers. In terms of reforming slavery, they tended to stress the need to foster and protect marriage and family structures among slaves. Despite the fact that slave codes did not recognize slave marriages and families, after 1831 proslavery writers increasingly called upon masters to institute unwritten laws of their own. Some of them even petitioned legislatures to enact laws barring the separation of slave families.

If they enforced the duties of masters, proslavery writers (at least in America) also expounded the obligations of slaves. More than British and West Indian proslavery thinkers, American writers discussed the social and religious foundations for servile obedience always in the context of their larger defense of slavery. While it is not strange that they should be willing and able to argue the case of slave obedience, it is remarkable

TABLE 5.9
Proslavery Arguments on the Duties of Masters

	WRITERS					
Argument	Early Americans	British and West Indians	Americans, 1800–1831	Northerners, 1831–1861	Northerners in the South	Southerners, 1831–1861
Provide comforts of life	3	0	8	14	9	21
Give just treatment	5	16	10	15	10	21
Protect slave marriages and family	0	0	1	9	7	8
Provide religious instruction	2	1	5	14	9	21
Master must answer to God for his treatment of slaves	2	1	4	14	9	13
Total number of writers	12	18	12	15	12	22
Number not mentioning duties of masters	6	0	1	0	2	1

Note: The total number of writers in each category does not equal the number of arguments adduced, because some writers applied more than one argument under the heading.

that proslavery writers not connected in any way with slavery as an institution should have included such discussions in their defenses. That
they did is suggestive of the socially holistic and prescriptive nature of
proslavery writings wherever they appeared in America. Far from being
mere racist defenses of slavery, proslavery writings generally exhibited
an inclusive system of social thought.

   It can be concluded that proslavery argumentation (the basic arguments and their formulations) remains relatively constant over time and
place. Wherever and whenever one encounters a defense of slavery (assuming that it is more than an isolated thrust), the arguments adduced
will conform with those of proslavery literature in other slave societies
and with those in the same society at other periods of time. Although
there will be variations in the selection of arguments and in the number
and scope of defenses, the species of argumentation will remain largely
unchanged. Depending upon the circumstances and the nature of attacks upon slavery, particular types of arguments may be more frequently employed (such as racist arguments in the West Indies and comparative economy in the United States in the 1820s). But on the whole,
all types of argumentation are available and will be applied at least to
some extent wherever proslavery literature appears. Consequently when
one attempts to understand and assess the history of proslavery thought,
argumentation is not and cannot be used as sole index of change.[11]

   If argumentation remains essentially constant over time and locality,
such demonstrably synthetic delimiters as the positive good argument or
political economy are false indices of variations. Similarly, because of the
universality of arguments on Negro racial inferiority in both slave and
free, American and European societies, any analysis that deals exclusively or even primarily with racist argumentation in proslavery literature and thought will reveal neither the crucial changes in nor the
unique character of proslavery in a particular society. Hence, in examining racist arguments in proslavery literature, one will learn more about
alterations in theories of race than about the nature of proslavery. This is
not to say that proslavery literature is not a repository and thereby an
appropriate body of source material for the study of race and racism.
But it is to say that racist argumentation that seeks to demonstrate that
the Negro was an appropriate subject for enslavement was a constant in
proslavery literature.

   It is clear that to achieve any clear understanding of the warp and
woof of proslavery history or proslavery ideology, one must proceed

from some basis other than that of particular arguments on the viability or desirability of slavery in a particular social setting—no matter how reprehensible the particular arguments employed. While the types of arguments used and the special nuances within each type of argument may serve as an index to the nature of the crises being faced by a society attempting to resolve the issue of slavery, they reveal little about the texture and thrust of proslavery ideology and the development of proslavery thought within the society. The search for useful clues to the distinctive nature of American proslavery history must, therefore, be focused elsewhere than on particular proslavery arguments.

SIX

American Defenders of Slavery, 1790–1865

Among the more pernicious errors of proslavery historiography has been the total identification of proslavery literature and thought with southern Americans. Even though no one has heretofore taken the pains to sift through biographical data for the hundreds of individuals who came to slavery's defense, historians have generally assumed that southerners were the authors of defenses, the fomenters of a proslavery mentality, and the propagandists of slave society. Although one historian has suggested that historians might do well to determine the relationship between proslavery thinkers and southern society, neither he nor anyone else has examined the possibility that proslavery ideology might have been the product of forces and people larger than the mere experience of the Old South.

In the conventional image the typical proslavery thinker is a wealthy planter who doubled as politician. He looked upon his slaves as children in need of guidance and care. At the same time, however, out of economic self-interest and racist predilections, he spun theories about the virtues of slavery. He was also a sectionalist, a state's rightist, and, if the occasion demanded, a fire-eating warmonger. As a result of his love of slavery, he overthrew American democratic values in favor of the values and practices of feudal society. And in the face of freedom-loving northerners, he flaunted his wealth, power, and the threat of slavery expansion.

Against the traditional picture, after examining the careers of a half-dozen important proslavery writers, historian David Donald in 1971 found a different "general pattern." All of his subjects were "unhappy men who had several personal problems relating to their place in southern society." "Though ambitious and hardworking," he continued, "all failed in the paths normally open to the enterprising in the South: planting, practicing law, and politics." Although they derived from illustrious southern families, "few of them had any large personal stake in the system which they defended." In their defenses of slavery, therefore, they "looked back with longing to an earlier day of the Republic when men like themselves—their own ancestors—had been leaders in the South." Basically nostalgic, they defended "an idealized paternalistic society which, as they believed, had formerly flourished in the South before it was undermined by the commercialization of urban life on the one hand and by the increasing democratization and decentralization of the frontier on the other."[1] Two studies by Drew Gilpin Faust of southern intellectuals along the lines suggested by Donald indicated that there may be some truth in his suggestions. A relatively large number of southern intellectuals did indeed use proslavery as a means of drawing attention to their abilities and work.[2]

Although the traditional image of proslavery thinkers as volatile and racist planters and Donald's alternative of frustrated, nostalgic social weaklings certainly describe some of slavery's defenders, neither interpretation can account for the vast majority of proslavery writers. In the first place, a significant portion of them were not natives of the South and fewer yet could be considered slaveholding planters. While some may have been social failures who squandered their family heritage, many others were of humble origins. Moreover, not all of them identified their interests with the South. Even fewer succumbed to the mania of southern sectionalism. Indeed, the views they shared were so complex that no simplistic labels such as *southern, slaveholding, frustrated,* or *nostalgic* can serve to describe even a majority of them. Nothing less than an examination of the background, experiences, and careers of hundreds of proslavery thinkers will make it possible to generalize about who the defenders of slavery actually were.

To learn more about American defenders of slavery a statistically based, composite biography of 275 proslavery writers was formulated as a basis for the present chapter. For the purpose of defining and locating the sample group, only two limiting factors were taken into consideration: (1) each man had to have published at some time in his career a defense of slavery in which he argued that slavery should be maintained indefinitely in the United States; and (2) each had to be an ordained clergyman in one of the recognized religious denominations in the nineteenth century or at least serve the functions of a clergyman either in the service of a church or a group of people, where they might exert significant social or cultural influence.

Once the definitional preliminaries were decided, an attempt was made to discover as many individuals as possible in America before 1865 who might qualify as a proslavery clergyman. After sifting through the vast American literature on slavery and biographical information on the hundreds of persons who published defenses of slavery, 275 individuals were found who fit the requirements. Biographical information was compiled on each, coded, and submitted to computer analysis.[3]

There is more logic than whim in the selection of clergymen as the focus for understanding the social history of proslavery. Perhaps more than any other professional or socially responsible group, clergymen were active in every antebellum American community and assumed a multiplicity of socially valued functions. Although frequently caricatured by twentieth-century historians and novelists as pathetic village parsons or as maniacal hell-fire-and-brimstone evangelists, a close examination of the pre–Civil War clergy reveals a diversity of social roles and powers, abilities and interests, connections and offices that perpetually bursts the confines of any simple categorization. Whether as individuals in local communities, as clergy in America's denominational and religious life, or as figures in national affairs, clergymen could and did place themselves in social (and sometimes political) circumstances that defy any notion that they were captives of society who dutifully appeared as instructed in Sunday-morning pulpits. Even without a national moral dilemma, clergymen as individuals and as a group constituted a crucial elite in American society.

As members of an organized and socially valued group, clergymen (at least the most vocal, top layer of the profession) possessed the power and influence normally associated with the elite in any society. Aside from the roles they may have played as pastors in local communities, they forced themselves prominently into dozens of other social institutions and concerns. As educators they determined the direction of the nation's schools at all levels. As scientists they often led the way in pursuing basic research and in developing theory. As editors of newspapers and learned journals and as frequently published writers, they threatened to control the basic channels of communications. As men of literature and thought they produced the bulk of literature and set the standards for America's rising literary culture. As organizers and reformers they were often leaders in the founding of social institutions, benevolent societies, and social movements. Thus, all of their activities and interests placed them at the center of what might be termed America's antebellum moral elite.

In their roles as preachers, educators, writers, organizers, and even as troublesome taunters of ethical conduct, clergymen dominated the key positions for defining values and institutionalizing them. As village parsons and as the preeminent teachers of antebellum society, clergymen gained the respect of most Americans, particularly the socially significant. Far from being passive and impotent observers of public events, clergymen, endowed with talent, intellect, and frequently wealth, took the lead in influencing and managing society's affairs.

If clergymen dominated the offices and fulfilled the functions of America's larger moral elite before the Civil War, it should not be surprising that when American society confronted the problem of slavery ministers became major spokesmen. Far from being a mere question of morals, slavery was an issue that cut across the entire ethos of American values, beliefs, and aspirations. Although much of the debate centered on the morality of holding Negroes in bondage, the future of slavery and the disposition of the Negro was linked irresistibly to the shape and destiny of America. Hence, whenever a social thinker argued either for or against slavery, his ruminations led him inescapably to considerations of the character of American society and government, the function of social institutions, the proper mechanisms of reform and change, and, indeed, the very place of America in the scheme of history. The more abstract and theoretical the discussion became, the more it fell into the province of theologians and moral philosophers.

There were always the Thomas R. Dews, the John C. Calhouns, the James Henry Hammonds, and the George Fitzhughs from among other professions and social realms to lend their acute analyses of slavery in American society. Yet if one combined the nonclerical proslavery thinkers from all walks of life who publicly expressed their proslavery views, their number would not equal the number of clergymen who did so. And in terms of the quality and sophistication of their thinking, few secular thinkers could equal, and none surpassed, the works of such clergymen as Albert Taylor Bledsoe, John Bachman, Nathan Lord, James Warley Miles, and James H. Thornwell. Nor did anyone except Calhoun gather more popular attention than William Gannaway Brownlow, Leonidas Polk, Basil Manly, Augustus Baldwin Longstreet, or Benjamin Morgan Palmer. If they did not exclusively dominate proslavery liter-

ature and thought in America, they shared heavily in the tasks of producing and disseminating whatever proslavery notions Americans
entertained.[4]

Proslavery clergymen, if colonial defenders be included, were born as
early as 1669 and as late as 1839. If their birth dates are grouped according to frequency distributions, however, the bulk of them fall between
1785 and 1836. For whatever reason, their births were not randomly
distributed over the entire period. Through the peaking and troughs of
births, the group of 275 ministers seems to divide quite logically and
almost evenly into three waves. Before 1800, eighty-two were born; between 1801 and 1815, another eighty-seven; with ninety-three births following between 1816 and 1839. While it is difficult without further evidence to assess the meaning of this tripartite pattern, it seems clear that
there were at least three distinct generations of proslavery clergymen
active between 1820 and the end of the Civil War. The first generation
reached maturity prior to the rise of abolitionism; the second near the
peak of the first abolition crisis of the 1830s; and the third during the
last decade before the Civil War.

The chronological distribution of their births was rivaled by the
equally widespread place of nativity. Proslavery clergymen came from
every American state and almost every European country. As strange as
it may seem, of those who wrote defenses of slavery before the onset of
the Civil War nearly as many were born in Europe (twenty-five) or New
England (twenty-one) as in the upper South (thirty-three) or the lower
South (thirty-two). With a logical weighting toward the South taken into
consideration, the entire group of proslavery clergymen roughly approximated the constituency of the American population in the early
nineteenth century.

If their birthplaces are further divided into individual states and countries and ranked accordingly (see table 6.1), it becomes apparent that
certain of them produced inordinately large numbers of proslavery clergymen. Germany, England, and Ireland loom largest among foreign
countries, while in America almost all of the oldest, largest, and most
influential of the original thirteen states are well represented. Among
the states, South Carolina, Virginia, and Georgia—the chief early plantation states—are predominant; while in the northern states, which
provided crucial leadership and education for much of America in the
nineteenth century, Massachusetts, Pennsylvania, New York, and Connecticut contributed heavily. What is perhaps most surprising about

TABLE 6.1
Birthplaces of Proslavery Clergymen

	AUTHORS OF		
State or Country	*Formal Defenses*	*Proslavery Writings*	*Proslavery and War Sermons*
Connecticut	5	8	9
Georgia	10	17	22
Massachusetts	8	17	18
New York	5	8	12
North Carolina	9	11	15
Pennsylvania	10	15	17
South Carolina	18	23	38
Virginia	19	26	38
England	6	10	11
Germany	3	9	13
Ireland	8	10	10

Note: This table and others of similar format present three separate data counts for (1) authors of formal treatises in defense of slavery (Formal Defenses); (2) authors of other forms of proslavery literature (Proslavery Writings); and (3) an all-inclusive category (Proslavery and War Sermons) that also encompasses the relatively large number of clergymen whose only proslavery writing occurred during the Civil War in support of the Confederate war effort.

the distribution of births is that proslavery clergymen derived from the entirety of America and particularly from those states that gave direction to American life in all realms. Proslavery clergymen as a group were definitely not wholly or even primarily southern-born.

If birthplaces are further refined to examine counties and towns of origin, similar results obtain. The only plantation regions that produced large numbers of proslavery clergymen were in South Carolina and Georgia, where the city and county of Charleston gave birth to fourteen, the town and county of Beaufort to nine, and Liberty County, Georgia (with no large town) to eight. By comparison, Boston and Savannah, Georgia, were native homes for four; Philadelphia, Washington, D.C.,

and Norfolk for three apiece. Apart from major cities and towns, the
ministers came from that inland belt extending from Maine to Georgia
and Alabama not characterized by large-scale agriculture. In all states,
they originated in regions where farming was practiced, but they seem to
have been clustered in those areas near state capitals where they might
have witnessed public life in operation (as in Georgia, Tennessee, North
Carolina, Kentucky, Pennsylvania, New York, and Maine). In any case, as
a rule their births occurred more generally in the midst of forums for
decision making than in areas with large numbers of slaves.

A dramatic pattern emerges, however, if birthplaces are examined
over a period of time. Among the first generation of proslavery clergymen, those born in the North and New England clearly predominated;
among those born before 1800, northerners constituted a substantial
majority, while European-born clergymen were also prominent (see
table 6.2). In the second and third generations the number of European-
born remained practically unchanged, while the number of northern-
born diminished. As southerners came to predominate, the number
from the middle states of New York, New Jersey, and Pennsylvania varied widely. Yet, as time passed the statistical array completely reversed so
that among the last generation those from New England numbered the
least and those from the lower South numbered the most. Thus, it is
apparent that although southerners prevailed by the third generation,
proslavery was in the 1830s a national concern in which New Englanders
overshadowed all others. Nevertheless, even on the eve of the Civil War,
a broad national representation of voices still came to slavery's defense.

Although considerably less data are available on the nativity of the parents of proslavery clergymen, there is enough evidence to indicate that
they could not have generally looked back nostalgically to an idealized
South. The majority of clergymen were born in the same state as their
parents. Virginia and Massachusetts, in particular, produced sons from
long entrenched families. Proslavery clergymen born in South Carolina,
Georgia, Pennsylvania, and New York, however, were more likely than
not to have been the sons of immigrants from Europe, New England, or
the upper South. In terms of frequency fathers came most often from
the following states and countries: Virginia, thirty-eight; South Carolina,
twenty-three; Massachusetts, nineteen; England, seventeen; Germany,
fifteen; Pennsylvania, thirteen; Ireland, thirteen; Georgia, twelve; Connecticut, eleven; and North Carolina, ten. Mothers were born in identical locations in substantially the same proportions, although a slight

TABLE 6.2
Birthplaces of Proslavery Clergymen by Date of Birth

Region	BIRTHDATES		
	1669–1800	*1801–1815*	*1816–1839*
Europe	15	16	13
New England	21	14	6
New York, New Jersey, and Pennsylvania	17	6	10
Middle West	0	0	5
Border States	1	7	3
Upper South	15	20	23
Lower South	12	23	29
West Indies	1	0	3

movement of fathers toward the South to find wives can be detected. Hence, in parentage as in their own nativity, ministers who defended slavery seem to have been part of the general movement of population from Europe to America and from North to South in the early years of the nineteenth century. There is little to suggest that even a majority of them should have looked upon the South as their fatherland.

While proslavery clergymen came from all states and countries and represented a composite of the American population, the status of their families was not always representative of national conditions. If family status can be determined by the father's occupation and attainments, relatively few proslavery clergymen came into the world in a condition of abject want. One-fourth were the sons of clergymen; another fourth were the scions of planters who owned and employed numbers of slaves; one-sixth were reared on small farms; and another sixth were the sons of businessmen. A significant one-tenth had fathers who were involved in politics or some other form of federal or state government work. Altogether four out of five proslavery clergymen grew up in circumstances of relative comfort, while the fifth began life with next to nothing.

Considerably less information could be obtained about the mothers of the ministers. But of the one-third about whom data exists, a striking statistic emerges. Although other occupational categories were about proportional to those of the minister's fathers, 46 percent of the mothers came from planting families, while only 9 percent were daughters of clergymen. If that figure were accurate for the mothers of all the ministers, it would indicate that the fathers of proslavery clergymen in significant numbers followed the marital course to instant wealth that was repeated in the next generation by many of their sons. For both fathers and sons as a whole there was a clearly defined tendency to head from any point of origin toward the South in search of work and wealth.

The occupational status of the ministers' families varied greatly with geography and time. Those born in Europe were more likely than not the sons of merchants or businessmen. New Englanders and natives of the Middle Atlantic states displayed the greatest variety of backgrounds, with ministers' sons slightly outnumbering others. In the upper South a clergyman might be the son of a planter, minister, or small farmer; if born farther south he would more likely be the son of a slaveholding planter. In the lower South planters' sons outnumbered the closest alternative more than two to one. However, even in the lower South more of the clergymen who defended slavery came from backgrounds other than the plantation ideal.

Whereas the first generation of proslavery clergymen displayed the widest variety of backgrounds and status, the third generation emerged from higher levels of attainment. Whereas the sons of small farmers and menial laborers played a significant role in the early years of the response to abolition, by the eve of the Civil War proslavery ministers no longer derived from the lower orders of society. Whereas the numbers of sons of planters, professionals, and politicians remained roughly the same over time, larger numbers of clergymen's sons gradually replaced those with poorer backgrounds. For as years passed, greater recruitment from among the clergy occurred to the exclusion of individuals from other occupational backgrounds.

When proslavery clergymen are categorized according to their first status (the situation in which they found themselves at the moment they reached maturity), it is apparent that between the 1780s and the 1850s the defense of slavery became the pursuit of wealthier and more entrenched clergy-citizens. As the process reached fruition on the eve of the Civil War, a few rags-to-riches clergymen remained among those who defended slavery, but their numbers decreased markedly. Before these opportunities waned, however, the ministry proved for many poverty-stricken young men, particularly European immigrants and a third of all those born in the upper South and the Middle Atlantic states, an enticing route of upward mobility.

If the inherited status of the ministers is broken into more discreet components an even clearer picture of their constituency can be drawn. About 37 percent inherited wealth from their parents and did not need to work to support themselves. Another 39 percent inherited an elevated status with either attendant connections or sufficient education to secure a comfortable living. The remaining third were almost without exception totally self-made men. Only a few were able to obtain support from the wealthy with whom they came into contact. The rest often had to overcome nearly insurmountable obstacles, including primary care for large families of siblings, in their quest for comfort and influence.

In their nativity, family background, or inheritances proslavery clergymen as a group did not resemble either the traditional image or Donald's revisionist interpretation of the typical proslavery thinker. What is most striking about the origins of clerical defenders is their diversity, a factor that challenges any simplistic generalization connecting them with a particular section, type of family, or social class. Aside from this finding, perhaps the most illuminating discovery about the group is that its character and constitution altered significantly with the passage of time. There were three rather distinct generations, each with its own peculiar make-up. The first generation was heavily weighted toward New England and Europe, whereas the third was overbalanced toward the South. The first derived from a wider range of social conditions, the third from wealthier and more professionally inclined families. The implication seems to be that the first generation of proslavery thinkers departed most markedly from the conventional interpretation, while the last one came much closer. But even the third generation, despite its southern origins and apparent inherited wealth, still differed widely from the conventional wisdom.

Data relating to proslavery clergymen's nativity, family, and initial status in the world concern elements over which they had almost no control. They had little more over their early educational experiences and opportunities. Nevertheless, their confrontation with new environments, religious institutions, schools, and teachers constituted a new phase in the formation of their character and perceptions, often foreign to the legacies passed down through their families and native environments. Indeed, through their educational and religious experiences and

the manner in which they occurred, proslavery clergymen were prepared most importantly for their eventual defenses of slavery.

Among the early experiences that impelled proslavery clergymen to
defend slavery, residence in the South was not the most crucial. About 50
percent of all proslavery clergymen were born in the South, while only
47 percent spent their early years there. Nearly 43 percent spent their
entire childhood and adolescence outside the South, while a final 10 percent moved about so constantly that no place could be identified as a
childhood home. If West Indians and immigrants to the South are combined with native southerners, however, approximately 54 percent of
the ministers spent their childhoods in slaveholding areas. About one-
fourth of all the clergymen lived on plantations with slaves in their first
years. Another quarter grew up on small farms or in southern cities and
towns. If the southern-bred are combined with others, more than one-
fourth of the entire group grew up in American cities, another fourth in
small towns, and about 18 percent on farms without slaves. The remaining 15 percent lived outside America in countries without slaves or a
Negro population. Hence, neither early residence in the South nor
childhood impressions of slavery played a role in determining the ministers' later stance toward human bondage.

If social, cultural, and environmental factors were not necessarily
important, childhood religious experiences definitely were. As indicated
in table 6.3, four particular Protestant denominations were heavily represented. In fact, 77 percent of the ministers grew up as Presbyterians,
Episcopalians, Congregationals, or Baptists. More than one-fourth of all
ministers (29 percent) were Presbyterians; over one-half (60.2 percent)
were from the three major Calvinist churches. In view of the Episcopal
church's dominance in the large slaveholding regions of Virginia and
South Carolina, its strong representation is not surprising. However,
popularity of the Baptist church in other parts of the South diminished
the significance of the Episcopal church's large representation. Strangest
of all was the presence of so many Presbyterians, the third largest denomination in America, and Congregationals, a religious tradition almost entirely limited within the confines of New England. Yet, despite
the preponderance of these four denominations, no major religious
body was left unrepresented in the ranks of proslavery clergymen.

The religious data also show that, while 41 or 15.8 percent of the
ministers grew up in the Congregational tradition, only 11 of the 41
entered the Congregational ministry. Whereas all of the other major

TABLE 6.3

Religious Denomination of Proslavery Clergymen

	AUTHORS OF		
Denomination	Formal Defenses	Proslavery Writings	Proslavery and War Sermons
Baptist	24	32	40
Congregational	21	39	41
Episcopalian	16	36	44
German Reformed	1	1	11
Jewish	1	5	11
Lutheran	6	7	8
Methodist	12	16	27
Presbyterian	38	61	75
Quaker	1	1	1
Roman Catholic	9	11	11

Note: This table and others of similar format present three separate data counts for (1) authors of formal treatises in defense of slavery (Formal Defenses); (2) authors of other forms of proslavery literature (Proslavery Writings); and (3) an all-inclusive category (Proslavery and War Sermons) that also encompasses the relatively large number of clergymen whose only proslavery writing occurred during the Civil War in support of the Confederate war effort.

churches increased their numbers, the Congregational total decreased. And the thirty Congregational-bred ministers who pressed into the ranks of other Protestant churches provided these denominations with some of their most influential leaders. Impelled in part by the absence of Congregational pastorates in New England and by the overproduction of ministers in New England colleges, a mass migration of well-educated ministers into the South occurred in the first three decades of the nineteenth century. This migration was perhaps the most effective mechanism through which New England culture invaded the South.

When childhood religious preferences are analyzed with respect to time (see table 6.4) it can be seen that Congregational-born-and-bred clergymen outnumbered all others in the first generation of proslavery

TABLE 6.4
*Childhood Churches of Proslavery Clergymen, Grouped by
Date of Birth*

	BIRTHDATES		
Denomination	*1669–1800*	*1801–1815*	*1816–1839*
Baptist	6	12	18
Congregational	23	12	4
Episcopalian	20	12	11
Jewish	0	5	6
Lutheran	2	2	4
Methodist	5	8	14
Presbyterian	17	25	32
Roman Catholic	4	5	2

ministers. By contrast, among the major religious denominations, Congregationals numbered the fewest in the third generation, while Episcopalian-born clergymen experienced a similar precipitate decline. As the two oldest American churches waned in their production of proslavery clergymen, the younger, more expansive ones took their place. From a rank order of Congregational, Episcopalian, Presbyterian, Baptist, and Methodist in the first generation, the three dissenting Protestant sects moved into first place in the third generation. At the same time, immigrant American churches continued to produce clerical defenders of slavery in an uneven, but persistent pattern.

Particular regions, states, and countries produced ministers with definite denominational leanings. Of forty-two born in New England thirty-two were reared as Congregationals; eighteen of twenty-nine born in the Middle Atlantic states were Presbyterian, fourteen Methodist, thirteen Episcopalian, and eight Baptist, while lower South ministers derived mostly from Baptist (twenty-six) and Presbyterian (eighteen) traditions. Immigrants were divided among all churches with Jews, Episcopalians, and Roman Catholics predominant. Although there was diversity in every region except in the North and New England, one must conclude that there was a direct, causal relationship between New England Congregationals and the rise of proslavery in the nineteenth century. Their predominance in the first generation of proslavery clergymen is too extensive to be overlooked.

If geographical and religious data indicate that New England Congregationalism was a strong but peculiar source for the first generation of proslavery clergymen, information on their educational experiences points in a similar direction. In an age when few Americans benefited from extended educational opportunities, future proslavery clergymen generally enjoyed the maximum afforded by the American system of education. About 89 percent of the ministers attended class through the high school level. Relatively few of them received the personal attention of a tutor or the advantages of a boarding school. Between 40 and 45 percent were educated in public schools, and nearly one-third were trained by clergymen in church academics. Only 10 percent received little or no education at the grammar school level.

While nine of ten proslavery clergymen obtained grammar and secondary school educations, three of four also attended college. Moreover, almost two-thirds of the 275 obtained their training in theology by attending a seminary or by studying privately for a similar period of time. In terms of their educational attainments, America's proslavery clergymen qualified as the elite of the ministry and as the most professional individuals in the church. And irrespective of the other educational endeavors pursued by many of them, proslavery ministers were among the best educated in American society.

What is more important than the extensive nature of the education these ministers received, however, is the type. Wherever they might have been located, clerical defenders of slavery were subjected to perspectives and attitudes as theorized and practiced in New England and the North, particularly as taught at Yale University in Connecticut and the College of New Jersey or Princeton University in New Jersey. Although few American-born clergymen traveled far from home for their early training, their first teachers were more likely than not graduates of one of the Congregational or Presbyterian colleges of New England or the Northeast. And when these same clergymen left high school for college, they did not escape the influence of northern teachers, for most existing theological seminaries were either located in the North or staffed by northerners in the South.

One-fourth of proslavery clergymen entered New England Congregational colleges, while slightly smaller groups matriculated at Presbyterian

TABLE 6.5
Types of Colleges Attended by Proslavery Clergymen

Type of College	AUTHORS OF		
	Formal Defenses	Proslavery Writings	Proslavery and War Sermons
Baptist	4	5	6
European	18	39	33
Methodist	2	2	5
New England Congregational	31	50	53
Presbyterian	21	41	48
Roman Catholic	3	5	6
State and municipal	19	30	45

Note: This table and others of similar format present three separate data counts for (1) authors of formal treatises in defense of slavery (Formal Defenses); (2) authors of other forms of proslavery literature (Proslavery Writings); and (3) an all-inclusive category (Proslavery and War Sermons) that also encompasses the relatively large number of clergymen whose only proslavery writing occurred during the Civil War in support of the Confederate war effort.

schools and state and municipal colleges and universities (see table 6.5). In every category of proslavery writings New England–educated ministers provided more publications than any other group. And if Congregational, Presbyterian, and the largely southern public institutions are combined—the very schools in which northern college graduates exerted their greatest influence—it can be seen that more than half of the ministers experienced similar influences.

New England Congregational institutions were particularly important to the first generation of proslavery clergymen (see table 6.6). Of the fifty-four members of the first generation who attended college, thirty-four entered either New England Congregational or largely northern Presbyterian schools. Although attendance at New England schools remained relatively high even in the third generation, widespread Presbyterian colleges and southern state universities claimed forty-two of the seventy-two college graduates of the third generation. And whereas one of four in the first generation did not attend college, only one of nine did not in the third. Aside from the large numbers who attended

TABLE 6.6

*Types of Colleges Attended by Proslavery Clergymen, Grouped
by Date of Birth*

	BIRTHDATES		
Type of College	1669–1800	1801–1815	1816–1839
Baptist	1	3	2
Methodist	0	1	4
New England Congregational	21	21	11
Presbyterian	13	15	20
Roman Catholic	2	1	2
State and municipal	6	17	22
No college education	18	11	9

Congregational and Presbyterian schools, the other denominational colleges prepared few ministers to defend slavery. As in the case of other data, information on college studies points to the heavy influence of New England and northern educational institutions in shaping the experiences of the early raft of proslavery writers.

The impact of the flow of ideas and individuals from north to south is further revealed in the time sequence for attendance at various types of schools. The ministers graduated from American colleges as early as 1788 and as late as 1863, with the bulk of graduations between 1808 and 1855. The median year for all graduations was 1836, also the year with the largest single graduating class (ten). Graduations peaked at precisely the moment antislavery and anti-abolition mob activity was at its highest point. In that year most of the graduates came from schools in New York, Pennsylvania, New Jersey, and Ohio—those states most affected by anti-abolition mobbism. The second largest graduating class fell in 1822, another year of crisis in South Carolina. But it is doubtful that the threatened Vesey insurrection had any effect on the large New England group of graduates that year. Other peak graduation years included 1828, 1835, 1838, 1840, and 1849.

The median year for graduations from schools located in New England was 1825, for schools in the mid-Atlantic states and in the upper

South 1836, and for those in the lower South 1838. Graduated proslavery clergymen, therefore, moved from north to south, with New England graduates taking the lead in the defense of slavery earliest and low
South graduates arriving on the scene in large numbers more than ten
years later. Except in the case of New England where graduations
peaked in 1825, proslavery clergymen generally completed their education after the onset of the first major abolition crisis of the mid-1830s.
Whereas most proslavery ministers from other regions drew upon
knowledge and concepts popular in the midst of the national debate on
slavery, New Englanders and the New England–educated relied on
learning already a part of their intellectual baggage.

The fact that New Englanders generally finished their collegiate studies more than a decade before all others is especially significant. By the
time the other ministers graduated from college, the New Englanders
had already taken up their places as ministers, teachers, and social
thinkers. Hence, they were able to participate fully in the early response
to abolitionism and help shape the perceptions of their followers. Unlike
other proslavery ministers, the New Englanders had previous experience that prepared them for dealings with abolitionism and slavery that
others could not claim. By virtue of these experiences and their ingrained perceptions, the New Englanders were able to dominate and
define the response of the first generation of proslavery ministers.

The influence of New England and northern Presbyterian colleges
was more than a generational phenomenon. As indicated in table 6.7
those schools were responsible for educating proslavery clergymen from
all sections of the nation. While the New England–born attended almost
solely New England schools, large numbers of ministers from the Mid-
Atlantic states and particularly the lower South also came to New England for their schooling. In the mid-regions of the nation, including the
upper South, most future defenders enrolled in the numerous Presbyterian schools in New Jersey, Pennsylvania, and New York. But further
south one lived the more popular were the state universities. In the
lower South, aside from the substantial number who went to New England schools, almost all others attended southern state universities.
Nevertheless, the most prominent proslavery clergymen in the lower
South were those who graduated from New England schools.[5]

When proslavery clergymen are grouped according to the college
from which they graduated, the influence of certain schools becomes
readily apparent. Although these ministers attended sixty-one different

TABLE 6.7
Types of Colleges Attended by Proslavery Clergymen, Grouped by Native Region

	NATIVE REGION				
Type of College	New England	Mid-Atlantic	Upper South	Lower South	Europe
Baptist	0	0	1	4	1
European	0	0	0	0	31
Methodist	0	0	4	1	0
New England Congregational	26	8	2	15	1
Presbyterian	4	14	19	3	1
Roman Catholic	0	1	0	2	1
State university	3	1	14	25	0

colleges and universities in the United States and others in Europe, two-thirds graduated from a total of eighteen schools (see table 6.8). The school with the largest number of graduates—one-tenth of the total number attending college—was Yale University. But Yale merely stood at the head of ten northern schools that fell in the top eighteen. Those ten included four New England schools, five Presbyterian schools, and the University of Pennsylvania. Among the southern schools headed by South Carolina College were four state universities, the municipal College of Charleston, two Virginia Presbyterian schools, and the tiny Methodist outpost, Randolph-Macon. But the dominance of Yale University over all others, including South Carolina College, further suggests the intimate connection between the development of proslavery thought and peculiar circumstances within New England. With more than twice as many proslavery graduates as Princeton and Harvard—two other major national universities with surprisingly large representations of their own—the severely skewed data cannot be considered coincidental.

Yale made the most significant contribution to the ranks of proslavery clergymen. With graduating classes extending from 1799 to 1845, ten studied at Yale under the administration of the elder Timothy Dwight and all except three had completed their work by 1825. From Moses Stuart (1799) to Christopher E. Gadsden (1804), Gardiner Spring

TABLE 6.8

Colleges Most Frequently Graduating Proslavery Clergymen

College	Number Graduated	College	Number Graduated
Yale University	19	Dickinson College	5
South Carolina College	14	Washington and Jefferson College	5
Princeton University	9	University of Pennsylvania	5
College of Charleston	8	University of Georgia	5
Union University, N.Y.	7	Amherst College	4
Hampden-Sydney College	7	Hamilton College (Colgate)	4
Harvard University	7	Randolph-Macon College	4
Brown University	6	University of Virginia	4
University of North Carolina	6	Washington College, Va.	4

(1805), Calvin Colton (1812), Elisha Mitchell (1813), Theodore Clapp (1814), Joseph Clay Stiles (1814), Nathaniel S. Wheaton (1814), Jared Bell Waterbury (1822), and others, Yale's clerical proslavery graduates were as successful and distinguished as nonclerical alumni, Samuel F. B. Morse and John C. Calhoun. Yale was, in a real sense, the vortex of the swirling currents of thought which revolutionized first New England and then America during the first four decades of the nineteenth century.

If Yale was the center of one face of New England culture at the opening of the nineteenth century, Princeton (or the College of New Jersey) served a similar function in the middle Atlantic and upper South states during the same period. While there were slightly fewer proslavery graduates from Presbyterian colleges than from New England Congregational ones, especially in the first two generations, the Presbyterian influence began to be felt by the third generation. Presbyterian schools educated one-sixth of all proslavery clergymen. And as these schools proliferated throughout America in the early nineteenth century and virtually dominated collegiate-level education in the middle and western regions of the nation, each new school drew upon the "log college" example of early Princeton, the principles of education taught by Samuel Stanhope Smith and Charles Hodge, and the ubiquitousness of the Princeton graduate. In the same way that Yale's influence was felt in every corner of America before the Civil War, Princeton's graduates carried throughout the nation a social philosophy learned in their undergraduate experiences that easily meshed with proslavery. No other schools, not even South Carolina College, exerted the national influence of either Yale or Princeton in the shaping of what would become America's proslavery ideology.[6]

Sixty percent of all proslavery clergymen who graduated from American colleges or universities received their degrees from schools north of Mason and Dixon's Line. The four out of ten who attended southern institutions were generally members of the second and third generations whose contributions to proslavery were much later and of less crucial formative quality than those of their earlier northern-educated counterparts. Few southern schools could claim the colonial heritage of a Princeton or a Yale, and fewer yet possessed or directed the social and religious impulses that turned some northern schools into training camps for legions of benevolent reformers. For example, the College of William and Mary, the South's oldest school and the home of Thomas R. Dew, provided only one proslavery clergyman. The University of Virginia, one of the few southern schools with a distinctive curriculum and purpose, educated only four. Every southern school, including South Carolina College, came under the influence of New England and northern Presbyterian culture and did not produce any proslavery clergymen who did not share with their fellows who went north for schooling a roughly similar corpus of learning. When southern schools, including the state universities, came back into the hands of southerners in the 1850s, it was too late to indoctrinate proslavery thinkers, only soldiers.[7]

Although most nineteenth-century American colleges (including many of the southern state universities) followed the Yale and Princeton models and were thereby designed primarily for the preparation of clergymen, as the ministry became more professionalized in the first thirty years of the nineteenth century, denominational theological seminaries began to appear throughout the country. Reserved particularly for the clerical elite, the burgeoning seminaries drew an unusual number of proslavery clergymen and contributed significantly to the formation of the minds of younger ministers who would one day become active in the defense of slavery. As in almost all other matters relating to social organization and education, New England Congregationals took an early lead in establishing seminaries and were followed closely by Presbyterians. By 1855, after the completion of the first phase of seminary building, Congregationals and Presbyterians claimed nearly half of all such institutions, and the student bodies of all but one represented a national spectrum.[8]

Almost two-thirds of all proslavery clergymen attended either an American or a European theological seminary. Another 10 percent set aside at least a year of full-time study under the tutelage of a prominent minister. Only about one-fourth received no theological training prior to entering the ministry. In terms of the type of seminary attended, one-eighth enrolled in New England Congregational schools, while a remarkable total of 43 percent studied at Presbyterian seminaries. Twice as many attended northern as opposed to southern Presbyterian schools. One-sixth enrolled in Episcopal seminaries, while only 5 percent entered ten different Baptist schools. Among the major kinds of seminary training, there was a greater correspondence between the penning of formal defenses as opposed to other forms of proslavery literature among clergymen trained as Congregationals and least among those trained as Episcopalians.

As indicated above and in table 6.9, Congregational and northern Presbyterian schools exerted an early dominant influence. But by the third generation, the position of the Congregational seminary had diminished substantially while the other schools, including northern and southern Presbyterian, reached the peak of their influence. The continuing predominance of northern Presbyterian seminaries is notable in view of the fact that the South had developed a number of good schools by the end of the 1830s.

In terms of geographical preference, New Englanders most often attended nearby Congregational seminaries, despite the fact that New England also produced the largest number of Episcopal seminarians. Those born in the Middle States overwhelmingly matriculated at northern Presbyterian seminaries. Natives of the upper South were almost evenly divided among three types, northern and southern Presbyterian and Episcopalian seminaries; while natives of the lower South were almost evenly divided among seminaries of all types, from Congregational to Baptist. In terms of wealth, young men without adequate funding usually studied at northern Presbyterian or Episcopalian schools. The

TABLE 6.9
Types of Seminaries Attended by Proslavery Clergymen,
Grouped by Date of Birth

	BIRTHDATES		
Type of Seminary	*1669–1800*	*1801–1815*	*1816–1839*
Baptist	2	2	5
Episcopalian	9	13	10
New England Congregational	11	12	1
Northern Presbyterian	16	14	21
Roman Catholic	5	4	2
Southern Presbyterian	3	8	14

affluent tended to cluster at New England Congregational and southern Presbyterian schools.

As in the case of colleges, proslavery clergymen proceeded most commonly from certain types of schools. Nearly two-thirds of those who attended theological seminaries studied at one of six Protestant schools in the United States (see table 6.10). The remaining third were divided among eighteen other American seminaries and as many European schools.

If Yale and Princeton dominated the collegiate training of proslavery ministers, the seminaries into which these institutions most frequently funneled their students led other professional schools. Princeton Theological Seminary outdistanced all other schools, graduating well over twice the total of the two southern Presbyterian seminaries, Columbia and Union. In fact, Princeton sent forth more than one-tenth of all proslavery clergymen and nearly one-fourth of all who attended seminaries. Andover Theological Seminary, located near Boston and known for its training of New England's Congregational clergymen in the nineteenth century, trailed Princeton in preparing ministers. Among Episcopal seminaries, General in New York overshadowed the production of its counterpart in Virginia. Taken together, the three leading northern seminaries turned out more than twice as many proslavery clergymen as the three leading southern schools.

TABLE 6.10
Theological Seminaries Most Frequently Attended
by Proslavery Clergymen

	AUTHORS OF		
Seminary	Formal Defenses	Proslavery Writings	Proslavery and War Sermons
Andover TS (Congregational)	11	16	19
Columbia TS, S.C. (Presbyterian)	3	7	12
General TS, N.Y. (Episcopalian)	2	5	7
Princeton TS (Presbyterian)	14	27	30
Protestant Episcopal TS, Va.	0	3	5
Union TS, Va. (Presbyterian)	4	8	9

Note: This table and others of similar format present three separate data counts for (1) authors of formal treatises in defense of slavery (Formal Defenses); (2) authors of other forms of proslavery literature (Proslavery Writings); and (3) an all-inclusive category (Proslavery and War Sermons) that also encompasses the relatively large number of clergymen whose only proslavery writing occurred during the Civil War in support of the Confederate war effort.

The priority of the northern seminaries in relation to the proliferation of proslavery clergymen can also be demonstrated in the time sequence of graduations from each school. The median year, 1825, for graduation from Andover was by far the earliest, a statistic already noted in the case of Congregational college graduates. The median for Princeton's graduates followed by ten years, while that for other schools was generally later, particularly in the South: Protestant Episcopal, Virginia, 1837; Union, Virginia, 1838; General, New York, 1838; Columbia, South Carolina, 1841. But the general preponderance of northern Presbyterian seminaries can be seen in the fact that the median year for such schools was precisely the same as that for Columbia Theological Seminary, 1841. Although theological seminaries developed slowly from north to south, influences from the Middle States continued to be felt heavily even in the last generation of proslavery clergymen.

In addition to the theological training received by two-thirds of all proslavery clergymen, a third of them had other educational experiences. About 17 percent had spent at least one year studying law, while smaller percentages spent a year or more in advanced academic studies, medicine, or science. A small group of twelve from poor families learned a skill or trade. Those trained in law, medicine, or science frequently used this knowledge to shape their defenses of slavery. Since proslavery literature included discussions of ethnology and debates on the Constitution, many clergymen were well equipped to delve beyond the usual ken of theology and ethics.

From this profile of proslavery clergymen, there is no evidence to indicate that those who gave up law, medicine, or any other pursuit for the ministry did so out of a sense of frustration. Despite vast alterations in the nation's economy and fluctuating opportunities to establish oneself as a professional or a planter, the number of proslavery clergymen who left legal, academic, medical, or scientific studies to enter the ministry during three generations remained absolutely unchanged. In fact, the only type of individual with prior training who showed any basic change over time was the apprentice. By the third generation, former apprentices no longer became proslavery clergymen. Moreover, those who had previously studied law were well distributed throughout the nation, with twelve from New England, ten from the upper South, seventeen from the lower South, and eight from other areas. Proslavery clergymen seem to have chosen the ministry because they felt called in a religious sense or because they saw in this vocation a greater opportunity to affect the direction of society.

Physical health frequently played a prominent role in the formative experiences of proslavery ministers. Although adequate information on this subject could not be found for all (no comment on general health characteristics could be located for 46.5 percent), an extraordinary number of clergymen who defended slavery seemed to have suffered from a variety of physical disabilities before they reached maturity. With a cutoff age of 40 for the compiling of statistics, nearly one-half (44.7 percent) indicated that they had been seriously ill and nearly died, had received an externally apparent physical impairment, or had contracted a chronic illness that led ultimately to their death. In many cases, early illness was cited as a primary reason for entering the ministry. For others, the ministry seemed to offer the only viable career choice following a disabling illness or physical impairment, while a few noted that they had curtailed an active career as a result of illness.

Of the 143 clergymen for whom definite health-related information was available (the absence of information on most of the others probably indicates generally good health), only about 14 percent appeared to have been in robust health. One-third suffered a near fatal illness and about 6 percent lived most of their lives with a severe physical handicap. The extent of illness among the ministers, despite its remarkable proportions, is difficult to interpret. One cannot, however, overlook as a mere happenstance the fact that nearly half of them lived with excruciating pain or remembered a near-fatal illness. While any answer would necessarily have to be tentative, some insights are provided by a "Secret History" maintained by one of the clergymen, James Beverlin Ramsey.

Born in Maryland and educated at Lafayette College and Princeton Theological Seminary, Ramsey began his career as a Presbyterian clergyman in New York. After five years his health failed and his wife and only child died. With a "broken constitution and debilitated frame" Ramsey began compiling a secret diary of his sufferings. In long confessional entries, he made it clear that he believed his misfortune resulted directly from his personal failures in duty, his hypocrisy, and his lack of religious belief. At nearly the same time, Ramsey began defending slavery, extrapolating from his personal experience the categories of his social views. Slavery was a valid social institution, ideally benevolent and humane, but in practice, due to the failure of masters to fulfill their duties, a horrible evil. Abolitionism originated in the failure of Christian statesmen to stamp out infidelity and moral error. The entire slavery controversy and the Civil War were punishments sent from God because Americans failed in their duties to practice holiness. The South's defeat in the Civil War resulted not from the sinfulness of slavery but from the neglect of slaveholders to establish the Kingdom of God in their hearts and in those of their slaves. As he had told himself in the face of suffering, he reiterated to a congregation in Lynchburg, Virginia, on June 16, 1861, "the stability and prosperity of a nation is conditioned simply on its obedience to God." All scourges, whether personal or social, sprang from the failure of duty.[9]

When the effects of their early circumstances, educational backgrounds, and physical sufferings are combined, one must conclude that as proslavery clergymen prepared to launch their ministerial careers they were still confronted with a dizzying array of experiences and formative influences. Yet, in one way or another most of them had been touched by Calvinist religion and New England culture. Among the few experiences that nearly all of them had shared was a uniform collegiate instruction. Throughout their seminary studies—unless they were enrolled in one of the Virginia schools, which could have been true only in the case of the third generation—they had encountered little that would have exacerbated southern loyalties. Rather they had been exposed to distinct bodies of thought and social philosophies, which, for better or for ill, would shape their views of slavery and of abolition and would dictate the manner in which they would understand American society.

By choosing the ministry as a livelihood and as the principal manner in which they would express themselves as social beings, these 275 clergymen moved into a range of status and instrumentalities that could stretch only as far as their profession would allow. They were not, therefore, strictly speaking free men. Like professionals of all ages, they spoke and acted according to a rather sharply drawn code of ethics. However, they lived in an age when American ministers enjoyed freedom of movement.

The ministers who defended slavery took advantage of every opportunity to foist themselves into comfortable livings and into roles in which their influence could not be ignored. As the majority of proslavery clergymen reached adulthood, the clerical profession was concluding a process of revolutionary reorganization. Many of them had been among the leaders of this movement; others were among the beneficiaries. But whatever their contributions to the reformation of the profession, they lived in the golden age of clerical and ecclesiastical influence when a prominent minister could not easily shunt an issue so socially volatile as that of slavery by declaring it outside the ken of his responsibility. By virtue of their personalities and the roles they assumed as clergymen, they were thrust into the very center of the slavery debate.

Nothing reveals more vividly the aspirations and ambitiousness of proslavery clergymen than their eager pursuit of lucrative marriage alliances. For them, like individuals in other professions, marriage to the proper person was one way of achieving success. Although there is not an abundance of information on the wives of proslavery ministers, there is enough to indicate that many clergymen were interested primarily in women who could bring to the altar money and connections. In search of the ideal partner, many of them headed south where the daughters of wealthy planters became prime targets for poor, cultured young men. The ministers' wives most frequently came from South Carolina, Virginia, Georgia, Massachusetts, and North Carolina. The fact that Alabama was twentieth among all states and countries in producing proslavery clergymen, but eighth in providing wives for slavery's clerical defenders, is indicative of the general influx of these ministers into the

South for the purpose of marriage. In 1823 one southern-born minister who had himself desperately sought a wealthy planter's daughter described the arrival of "fortune hunters" from the North in terms reminiscent of postbellum carpetbaggers: "The Yankees have poured in here from all quarters of the North—and having been accustomed to escape starvation in their land have on accommodating terms taken possession of almost every station."[10]

While the status of the families of only one-fourth of the ministers' wives could be determined with accuracy, the data on that small group is persuasive. Only one wife out of sixty-nine came from what could be described as a poor family; two-fifths were daughters of slaveholding planters; one of eight were daughters of clergymen; and the remaining were offsprings of professionals, politicians, and businessmen. By comparing the inherited status of wives with that of clergymen, it becomes apparent that the one-quarter of clergymen born with neither wealth nor status almost without exception chose partners from without their class. More often than not, those born poor married daughters of planters, merchants, or businessmen. Three-fourths of the ministers born with wealth and/or status selected women from backgrounds similar to their own. Without question marriage was the single most important method whereby a poor or marginally secure young clergyman could improve his prospects.

An attempt has been made to determine the factor that more than any other accounted for whatever change of status each clergyman may have experienced in the course of his life. One-third of all proslavery clergymen, because of their inheritances, experienced no essential alteration in social or economic status. Among the two-thirds whose status changed markedly, marriage and professional competence seem to have been equally important. Other means of advancing socially, while they proved effective in individual cases, were considerably less significant for the total. Moreover, while the age at which important status changes occurred ranged from ten to fifty-five, the median age was twenty-nine, much closer to the age of marriage than to that of professional achievement. For most proslavery clergymen, therefore, social acceptability did not depend directly on their public position on the issue of slavery. On the whole, their standing in society was largely fixed about six years before they began publishing defenses of slavery.

Many proslavery clergymen acquired plantations and slaves as a result of their marriages and found it unnecessary to remain clerics to earn a living. Although reliable information could be obtained on only one-fourth of the wives, more than half of those under study came from slave-owning families. Furthermore, one-fifth of all clergymen who owned slaves obtained them from either the dowries or inheritances of their wives. And if the sources are accurate, wives generally seemed to have shared their husbands' views on slavery. There is only one documented case of a proslavery clergyman's wife opposing slavery although, based on the nature of marriage and the role of women in antebellum society, there could have been many more. But even though many of these ministers' marriages took on the character of business ventures, there is little to suggest that their marriages were not essentially happy ones.

From the launching of their careers until their deaths, proslavery clergymen often found other ways besides marriage to advance their status in society. Because of their educational experiences or the opportunities opened to them as clergymen, well over half of the ministers (with 115 cases undocumented) resumed their pre-ministerial occupations in conjunction with their clerical functions. Nearly one-half with prior work experience had served as schoolteachers; almost one-fourth had practiced law; and about 10 percent had been involved in some form of common labor. But it is significant that only four of the total had been planters utilizing slave labor (see table 6.11). Most of these prior occupations were either way stations on the road to becoming ministers or careers from which they turned, often momentarily, when they decided to become clergymen.

School teaching and tutoring were additional mechanisms that drew proslavery ministers from north to south. The absence of a large corps of well-trained teachers in the South made it possible for many prospective clergymen in need of funds to spend a few years working among southerners. At least ten proslavery ministers spent a period of time as tutors in wealthy southern families. Others earned their livelihood from stints as teachers in field schools, village schools, or church academies which provided the sole means of educating southern children throughout most of the antebellum period.[11]

Almost no proslavery clergyman lived on his pastoral salary alone. Nearly all of them could call upon other sources of income to meet any emergency or desire. For example, in 1848, Moses Drury Hoge, pastor

TABLE 6.11
Other Occupations of Proslavery Clergymen Before Ordination

	AUTHORS OF		
Occupation	*Formal Defenses*	*Proslavery Writings*	*Proslavery and War Sermons*
Teaching, tutoring	44	65	73
Law practice	21	28	36
Common labor, farming	11	14	15
Merchant, business, industry	4	8	9
Medical practice	5	5	8
Military, government	3	6	7
Planting	2	3	4

Note: This table and others of similar format present three separate data counts for (1) authors of formal treatises in defense of slavery (Formal Defenses); (2) authors of other forms of proslavery literature (Proslavery Writings); and (3) an all-inclusive category (Proslavery and War Sermons) that also encompasses the relatively large number of clergymen whose only proslavery writing occurred during the Civil War in support of the Confederate war effort.

of the Second Presbyterian Church in Richmond, built a twenty-three–room house and an adjoining school for girls. He then determined how he would pay for his creation:

> After making the most rigid calculations, I find that I shall expend $9,000, this year. It will require that amount to pay my house rent—servants hire. Teachers salaries & to furnish the rooms. . . .
> Now what have I to meet it?
> If I have 20 boarders, my income from them at $200 each will be 4,000. Suppose $500 of it will never be collected & it stands $3,500.
> If I have 40 day scholars, their tuition with that of the Boarders, will amount to (say $2,400—strike off 400) $2,000. My percentage on the French Music Scholars will be about $1,000 more. Washing will be $400. My salary from the church $1,000. So that my entire income from all sources will probably not exceed $7,900, leaving a balance against me of $1,100.
> So that I do not expect to make my expenses the first year. But if I come within Eleven Hundred dollars of it. I shall do well—because much of my outlay is for furniture, carpets, pianos, which have to be purchased but once.

Against his best expectations, Hoge later revealed that his plan had worked. In the first year he was able to pay off the entire sum of $9,000![12]

Hoge's case was by no means singular. In fact, of the 160 proslavery clergymen for which such information is available, only fourteen (or 8.7 percent) pursued no parallel occupation. More typically, 91 percent of the 160 supplemented their ministerial work with other well-paying occupations. Half of them were planters who used slave labor to earn income from agriculture in the South. Although there were only four who had had experience as planters prior to entering the ministry, a total of eighty-one ministers found the means to set themselves up as slaveholding planters after their ordinations. One-fourth supplemented their income by teaching in schools below the college level or by taking to the lecture route. Despite the large number of clergymen with vested interests in the South's plantation slave system, however, a smaller percentage of them wrote formal defenses of slavery than almost any other group with parallel occupations.

Most planting clergymen came primarily but by no means exclusively from the South. Except for the southern preference for planting, parallel occupations were well distributed among all of the regional groups. The dominance of planting as a parallel occupation for those from the lower South suggests that in that region clergymen helped create the popular planting ideal of success. But it should also be remembered that for clergymen with seasonal obligations agriculture offered perhaps the easiest means of making a significant supplementary income. So successful was one proslavery clergyman at dovetailing agriculture and ministerial responsibilities that a banker once wrote him: "I am well aware of your [*sic*] Having plenty of money at all times in Bank to pay your Debts [which] is one Reason that your Credit is so good and we all so Ready to grant you any request you will make."[13]

In spite of the sometimes wide-ranging financial and social interests of proslavery clergymen, they were above all clergymen. Their fellow men identified and judged them according to their abilities as ministers and as representatives of ecclesiastical institutions. William G. Brownlow, even after he had edited a secular newspaper for thirty years and had become Reconstruction governor of Tennessee, continued to be identified by everyone as "Parson" Brownlow. Thus, while a clergyman might become a respected social being through his marriage, his accumulation

TABLE 6.12
Parallel Occupations of Proslavery Clergymen

	AUTHORS OF		
Occupation	Formal Defenses	Proslavery Writings	Proslavery and War Sermons
Planting	40	70	81
Teaching, lecturing	22	34	37
Business	7	9	11
Editing (secular papers)	2	6	6
Science, medicine	3	4	5
Political office	3	3	4
Law	0	2	2

Note: This table and others of similar format present three separate data counts for (1) authors of formal treatises in defense of slavery (Formal Defenses); (2) authors of other forms of proslavery literature (Proslavery Writings); and (3) an all-inclusive category (Proslavery and War Sermons) that also encompasses the relatively large number of clergymen whose only proslavery writing occurred during the Civil War in support of the Confederate war effort.

of wealth, or his success in secular occupations, his influence was always measured against the image he cast as a significant ecclesiastical figure.

Because of the admission of very young men into the clergy of the evangelical churches, the average age at which American clergymen were ordained before the Civil War was usually twenty-two or twenty-three. However, the mean age of ordination for proslavery clergy due to their superior training and their frequent dabbling in other occupations was 26.4 years. Proslavery ministers were generally more accomplished, better educated, and more mature than many of their fellow ordinands when they entered church service. But because the ministry was a means for poor young men to accumulate wealth and influence, proslavery clergymen from poor backgrounds generally submitted to ordination at an earlier age than others with relatively secure inheritances. Depending upon social, psychological, and personal circumstances, a proslavery clergyman might have entered the ministry as early as age sixteen and as late in life as age fifty-five.

Except with one highly significant exception, the churches in which these ministers were ordained and the ones in which they spent their careers were substantially the same as those of their childhood. One-third of all proslavery clergymen were Presbyterians. In descending order about 20 percent were Episcopalian, 18 percent Baptist, and 14 percent Methodist. The remaining 17 percent were spread widely over almost every other church in America in the nineteenth century (see table 6.13). While ministerial affiliation was roughly proportional to childhood religious affiliation in every other instance, in the case of Congregationals the ranking altered from a crucial third behind Presbyterians and Episcopalians to a small fifth. Whereas 15.8 percent of all proslavery ministers grew up in the Congregational tradition, only 5.8 percent were Congregational clergymen. The widespread absorption of Congregationalists into the ministry of other churches provided but another mechanism for the dissemination of New England religion and culture in the nation's ecclesiastical institutions.

The only major shift in denominational affiliation involved the movement of at least twenty-seven individuals bearing the values and outlook of Congregational New England into the ranks of other churches. The new churches they entered were as follows: Presbyterian, fifteen; Episcopal, six; Unitarian, three; Baptist, two; and Universalist, one. While the movement of little more than two dozen clergymen from one religious tradition to another may seem inconsequential in terms of general American social history, those few represented a far larger infiltration of New Englanders into the social institutions of every region of the nation, helped transfer regional peculiarities, and provided a leavening agent to soften the countervailing characteristics of various regions.[14]

Data on the sites of the bulk of their career work illustrates much more strongly the intrepid southward movement. Although about 14 percent or 39 apparently never visited the South, 138 or 50.2 percent of all proslavery clergymen spent their entire careers in the South. A remarkable total of 85.6 percent lived and worked at least sometime in the South (see table 6.14). Hence, southern residence may have been an important factor in impelling many of these ministers to defend slavery. But the mobility of most clergymen as they easily moved from one position to another and from one region to another—even in the nineteenth century—reduces the significance of the data. Moreover, the perplexing one-seventh of the total who never went south further confuses the finding.

Nevertheless, in line with findings that connect the first generation of proslavery ministers more strongly with the North and the third genera-

TABLE 6.13

Denominational Affiliations of Proslavery Clergymen

	AUTHORS OF		
Denomination	*Formal Defenses*	*Proslavery Writings*	*Proslavery and War Sermons*
Baptist	32	40	47
Congregational	11	16	16
Disciples of Christ	0	0	1
Dutch Reformed	1	1	1
Episcopalian	15	41	54
Jewish	2	8	12
Lutheran	3	6	8
Methodist	20	26	38
Presbyterian	39	67	82
Roman Catholic	6	8	8
Unitarian	2	2	2
Universalist	1	1	1

Notes: The Presbyterian total includes three Associate Reformed clergymen; the Methodist total, two Methodist Protestant clergymen; and the Lutheran total, four from the Norwegian Lutheran Church.

This table and others of similar format present three separate data counts for (1) authors of formal treatises in defense of slavery (Formal Defenses); (2) authors of other forms of proslavery literature (Proslavery Writings); and (3) an all-inclusive category (Proslavery and War Sermons) that also encompasses the relatively large number of clergymen whose only proslavery writing occurred during the Civil War in support of the Confederate war effort.

TABLE 6.14

*Percentage of Careers Proslavery Clergymen Spent
in the South*

	AUTHORS OF		
Percentage of Careers	Formal Defenses	Proslavery Writings	Proslavery and War Sermons
0	24	39	39
1–9	3	9	9
10–25	3	7	9
26–50	11	15	20
51–75	14	19	22
76–90	10	15	18
91–99	7	14	15
100	63	102	138

Note: This table and others of similar format present three separate data counts for (1) authors of formal treatises in defense of slavery (Formal Defenses); (2) authors of other forms of proslavery literature (Proslavery Writings); and (3) an all-inclusive category (Proslavery and War Sermons) that also encompasses the relatively large number of clergymen whose only proslavery writing occurred during the Civil War in support of the Confederate war effort.

tion with the South, other data clearly indicate that the later an individual was born the more likely he was to restrict his activities to the South. With the passage of time all regions except the upper and lower South and the Midwest became more infrequent scenes of professional career work. Whereas early proslavery clergymen were widely dispersed in all regions, the career work of the third generation was more nearly, but still not wholly, limited to the South.

Correlations of percentages of careers spent in the South and primary regions of work with place of birth further demonstrate the magnetism that the Old South had for proslavery clergymen. While southern-born clergymen rarely ever went outside the South to work, a majority of all those born in Europe, New England, and the Middle States spent at least a portion of their careers in the South (see table 6.15). For example, fourteen New Englanders did not work in the South, but twenty-eight did; ten from the Middle States did not enter the South, while twenty-

Native Northerners Who Became Proslavery Leaders of Science and Learning in the South

John Bachman, 1790–1874
Naturalist, scientist, pastor of St. John's Lutheran Church, Charleston, South Carolina, 1815–1874

Moses Ashley Curtis, 1808–1872
Botanist, educator, pastor of Episcopal Church, Hillsborough, North Carolina, 1841–1872

Elisha Mitchell, 1793–1857
Mathematician, explorer, Presbyterian clergyman, and professor at the University of North Carolina, 1817–1857

Thomas Smyth, 1808–1873
Naturalist, theorist, pastor of Second Presbyterian Church, Charleston, South Carolina, 1832–1873

TABLE 6.15
Percentage of Careers in the South by Place of Birth

	PERCENTAGE OF CAREERS IN THE SOUTH							
Place of Birth	0	1–9	10–25	26–50	51–75	76–90	91–99	100
Europe and other	13	3	1	7	4	6	6	9
New England	14	2	3	5	3	5	3	7
Mid-Atlantic	10	0	3	3	4	2	2	9
Midwest	0	0	0	1	2	0	0	2
Border states	2	1	1	2	0	1	0	4
Upper South	0	1	1	2	4	3	3	45
Lower South	0	2	0	0	5	1	1	58

three did. About half of all those born outside the South worked at least half of the time in the South, while insignificant numbers of the southern-born spent as much as half of their working years outside the South. In terms of regions, New Englanders were nearly divided between their home states, the Middle States, and the lower South (see table 6.16). Those born in the Middle States dispersed widely into the South; and even those from the upper South joined the ranks of other future proslavery ministers through the migration of more than half of their numbers to the lower South. Europeans tended more often to enter the Middle States and the lower South. But the southern-born from either the upper or the lower South, by contrast, almost always remained entirely in the South.

A further breakdown of those born in New England, the Middle States, and South Carolina reveals the considerable movement of proslavery clergymen into and out of the lower South. Northern-born ministers circulated freely throughout all states, including those of the South. South Carolinians, however, tended to remain either in their home state or to work temporarily in adjoining southern states. Whereas the northern-born might make frequent incursions into the South for temporary employment, South Carolinians did not reciprocate. Furthermore, as indicated by North Carolina, considerably more New Englanders and northerners (fifteen) lived and worked in that state on both

TABLE 6.16
Primary Regions of Career Work by Place of Birth

Place of Birth	PRIMARY REGION OF CAREER WORK				
	New England	Mid-Atlantic	Upper South	Lower South	Europe
New England	13	10	5	13	0
Mid-Atlantic	1	13	9	9	0
Border states	2	2	0	3	0
Upper South	0	1	31	19	0
Lower South	1	0	2	60	0
Europe and other	4	9	8	13	3

a permanent and a temporary basis than South Carolinians (three). New Englanders living in North Carolina on a permanent basis outnumbered South Carolinians three to one.

Even after proslavery clergymen had finished their southward migrations, they were still widely dispersed throughout the nation. Most of the ministers did not necessarily develop sentimental attachments to any one locale in which they may have lived. If a state in which a minister spent 50 percent of his career is deemed a primary state and one in which he spent another 25 percent a secondary state, it is clear that two-thirds of all clergymen moved enough to claim a secondary state. No state or territory that had been in the American empire for any length of time lacked at least one permanent proslavery clergyman.[15] While many of the ministers conducted their ecclesiastical work in the states of the lower South and Virginia, northern states with major metropolitan centers such as New York and Massachusetts had a larger resident proslavery clerical population than such southern states as Alabama, Louisiana, Tennessee, Mississippi, and North Carolina. Maryland was the only border state heavily represented. The Middle States of Pennsylvania and New Jersey fell close behind states of the upper South. As secondary states Pennsylvania, Ohio, and Kentucky ranked high. Thus, despite a marked southern migration, proslavery clergymen remained fairly widely distributed throughout the country.

Notable Leaders Among Proslavery Clergy

George Junkin, 1790–1868
President of several colleges, including Lafayette College, Pennsylvania, and Washington College, Virginia

Augustus Baldwin Longstreet, 1790–1870
President of various colleges, including Emory College, Georgia; University of Mississippi; and South Carolina College

Calvin Henderson Wiley, 1819–1887
First public school superintendent and leading educator in North Carolina

Joseph Ruggles Wilson, 1822–1903
Presbyterian college educator, prominent clergyman, and father of President Woodrow Wilson

For whatever reason they decided to enter the ministry, proslavery clergymen on the whole were among the most successful members of their profession. From the pastorate to college teaching and administration, from mission work to church administration, and from newspaper editing to publishing, proslavery ministers could be found in abundance. They were, in fact, leaders in developing those specialized ministries that enabled American religious institutions to impinge as much as they ever have on the lives of Americans. The ministers who defended slavery rarely remained common pastors for long. Most rose in rapid order through the ranks to the most prominent positions in their profession.

A study of this movement shows that for 72 percent the pastorate was the form of ministry in which they usually remained longest. Of the 275 proslavery clergymen represented in table 6.17, 195 remained longer in the pastoral ministry than in any other. Nevertheless, 11.5 percent or thirty-one entered college teaching or administration almost directly and remained there for the bulk of their careers. Another 10.4 percent or twenty-eight moved immediately into the centers of ecclesiastical power by assuming editorial or administrative posts within churches. Relatively small numbers were contented with teaching in church academies or working as either domestic or foreign missionaries. Despite the seeming preference for the pastoral ministry, however, only 28 percent (a little over one-third of those in the pastorate the longest) of all clergymen actually spent their entire careers in the pastorate. A total of 71.7 percent marked at least a year in some other form of work; almost one-third served in some other capacity for more than half of their ministry. The evidence seems to indicate that most of the ministers could shift from one clerical task to another as easily as they moved about the country.

Although most proslavery clergymen entered church work at the bottom level and served an appropriate time in rural parishes, often combining pastoral work with teaching or farming, few remained long in that condition. In a review of the highest ecclesiastical positions achieved by proslavery ministers before 1861, three-fourths (74.6 percent) of the whole had reached or were on the way to them by the Civil War (see table 6.18). About 16 percent had already secured the highest office in their churches, while another 10 percent were in positions of denominational leadership. Almost 15 percent had assumed faculty or administrative positions at colleges and universities; at least 8 percent had become editors of religious newspapers; and more than one-half had worked their way into influential city pulpits. The statistics also show (even though the

TABLE 6.17
Principal Ecclesiastical Work of Proslavery Clergymen

	AUTHORS OF		
Type of Ministry	Formal Defenses	Proslavery Writings	Proslavery and War Sermons
College administration	9	11	11
College teaching	16	19	20
Church administration	8	13	14
Domestic missions	2	4	5
Editing	10	13	14
Foreign missions	2	4	4
Non-college teaching	6	7	8
Pastoral	80	147	195

Note: This table and others of similar format present three separate data counts for (1) authors of formal treatises in defense of slavery (Formal Defenses); (2) authors of other forms of proslavery literature (Proslavery Writings); and (3) an all-inclusive category (Proslavery and War Sermons) that also encompasses the relatively large number of clergymen whose only proslavery writing occurred during the Civil War in support of the Confederate war effort.

third generation was only coming into maturity) that on the eve of the Civil War only sixty-nine or one-fourth of the entire group was still associated with the common pastorate. What is significant in terms of types of proslavery writings is that the chief authors of those defenses that took the form of crisis or war sermons were clergymen who remained in the pastorate.

Many of the officially designated heads of American churches—bishops, moderators, and others in the national counsels of almost all churches—were proslavery ministers. Among churches with hierarchical structures, they could almost always be found at the top. Some, in fact, were founders of their own national church organizations. Carl F. W. Walther, founder and charismatic president for half a century of what became known as the Missouri Synod Lutheran Church, was in their number. Isaac M. Wise and Isaac Leeser, heads respectively of the two major branches of American Judaism, were proslavery rabbis. Alex-

TABLE 6.18
Highest Ecclesiastical Positions of Proslavery Clergymen
Before 1861

Position	AUTHORS OF		
	Formal Defenses	Proslavery Writings	Proslavery and War Sermons
Bishop, moderator	25	39	44
Synod, convention head	6	9	15
Denominational administrator	4	9	9
College president	18	24	24
College faculty	10	12	16
Editor	18	21	23
Urban church pastor	27	59	72
Common pastor	25	46	69

Note: This table and others of similar format present three separate data counts for (1) authors of formal treatises in defense of slavery (Formal Defenses); (2) authors of other forms of proslavery literature (Proslavery Writings); and (3) an all-inclusive category (Proslavery and War Sermons) that also encompasses the relatively large number of clergymen whose only proslavery writing occurred during the Civil War in support of the Confederate war effort.

ander McCaine was the leading founder and dominant figure in the splinter Methodist Protestant church. Herman A. Preus and Peter L. Larsen headed the organizational structure of Norwegian Lutherans in America. Simon Clough, an early enemy of abolitionists, oversaw the Christian church in New England, a schismatic evangelical sect that separated from Congregationalism in the 1820s. Alexander Newton was the founder and leading light in the United Synod of the Presbyterian church, a new school Calvinist church, which was limited to the South.

If clergymen did not wish to increase their professional status by moving through the ranks of the ecclesiastical hierarchy, there were other ways to enhance their positions and prestige. College presidents and faculty members often rivaled church leaders in income, professional influence, and social esteem. Since college work also offered a stationary position with seasonal work, many proslavery clergymen sought with insatiable avidity the comforts and authority of college teaching and admin-

Immigrant Religious Leaders Who Favored Slavery

Isaac Leeser, 1806–1868
*Prussian-born Jewish leader and
influential Philadelphia rabbi,
1829–1850*

John Mitchel, 1815–1875
*Rebel expatriate of Irish revolution,
Roman Catholic editor, Confederate States
ambassador and spy*

Carl Ferdinand Wilhelm Walther,
1811–1887
*Founder of Missouri Synod Lutheran
Church in the United States*

Peter Laurentius Larsen, 1833–1915
*Chief of Norwegian Lutherans and
president of Luther College, Iowa*

istration. Thirty-nine (14.2 percent) became presidents of educational institutions, while another sixty-eight (24.7 percent) taught on the faculties of colleges, universities, and theological seminaries. Few of them made college teaching or administration a full career. Between 25 and 30 percent in both categories spent more than half of their professional lives following ordination connected to a college or university. But only a few taught or headed such an institution for more than four or five years. For most ministers college work was a reward for outstanding educational and professional achievement, reserved only for those who had demonstrated expertise or who were peculiarly capable of raising funds for financially endangered denominational centers of learning.

The list of colleges and universities over which proslavery clergymen presided as the chief administrators is an effective indication of the success and influence which many of them enjoyed. Proslavery ministers served as presidents of all types of colleges and universities throughout the nation (see table 6.19). They were particularly active as administrators of the newer denominational colleges that appeared in the South during the last two decades before the Civil War. Moreover, on the eve of the conflict, proslavery clergymen controlled more colleges than at any earlier period of time. But as indicated by Nathan Lord's long presidency at Dartmouth and that of Basil Manly at the University of Alabama, their control of America's educational institutions was not always limited in time, space, or areas of influence. And if one adds to the list of schools over which these ministers presided and the schools at which sixty-nine others taught, hardly an important American educational institution was left without the presence of at least one proslavery clergyman.

Through their concerted intervention in the field of education, proslavery clergymen proved their worth and made perhaps their most important long-range contribution to the development of American social thought. But in terms of the more immediate suasion of the great mass of American people, these ministers relied principally upon the religious press. The antebellum period was the golden age of the religious press, when the nation was flooded with tracts, books, and newspapers issued from clergymen's pens. In the lead of those who used and perfected the religious press to dispense news, editorial opinion, and social philosophy stood proslavery clergymen. No less than 101 spent at least part of their careers as editors of various types of newspapers. Most expended only a few years or less than one-half of their work lives in the

TABLE 6.19
College Presidencies of Proslavery Clergymen

College, State	Clergyman	Term
Denominational Colleges (North to South)		
Dartmouth College, N.H.	Nathan Lord	1828–1863
Trinity College, Conn.	Nathaniel S. Wheaton	1831–1837
Dickinson College, Pa.	Samuel B. How	1830–1832
Lafayette College, Pa.	George Junkin	1832–1848
Madison College, Pa.	Henry B. Bascom	1827–1829
Miami University, Ohio	George Junkin	1841–1845
Luther College, Iowa	Peter L. Larsen	1860–1913
Bacon College, Ky.	James Shannon	1840–1849
Concordia College, Mo.	C. F. W. Walther	1850–1887
Hampden-Sydney College, Va.	George A. Baxter	1835–1836
Washington College, Va.	George A. Baxter	1799–1829
Randolph-Macon College, Va.	William A. Smith	1846–1866
Richmond College, Va.	Basil Manly, Jr.	1854–1858
Davidson College, N.C.	Drury Lacy	1855–1860
Furman University, S.C.	James C. Furman	1859–1879
Wofford College, S.C.	William M. Wightman	1854–1859
Emory College, Ga.	Augustus B. Longstreet	1839–1848
Emory College, Ga.	George F. Pierce	1848–1854
Wesleyan College, Ga.	George F. Pierce	1838–1840
Mercer University, Ga.	John L. Dagg	1844–1854
Mercer University, Ga.	Nathaniel M. Crawford	1854–1865
Oglethorpe University, Ga.	Samuel K. Talmage	1840–1865
LaGrange College, Ga.	Richard H. Rivers	1854–1861

(Continued)

TABLE 6.19 (*Continued*)

College, State	Clergyman	Term
Howard College, Ala.	Henry H. Talbird	1853–1861
Southern University, Ala.	William M. Wightman	1859–1866
Semple Broaddus College, Miss.	William C. Crane	1851–1857?
Oakland College, Miss.	William D. Moore	1855–1858
Centenary College, La.	Thomas C. Thornton	1837–1844
Centenary College, La.	Augustus B. Longstreet	1849
Centenary College, La.	Richard H. Rivers	1849–1852
Mt. Lebanon College, La.	William C. Crane	1859–1861?
Austin College, Texas	Rufus W. Bailey	1858–1860
State-Supported Schools (North to South)		
Transylvania University, Ky.	Henry B. Bascom	1842–1849
University of Missouri	James Shannon	1849–1856
College of Charleston	William T. Brantly	1837–1844
University of South Carolina	James H. Thornwell	1852–1855
University of South Carolina	Augustus B. Longstreet	1857–1865
University of Georgia	Andrew A. Lipscomb	1860–1874
University of Alabama	Basil Manly, Sr.	1837–1855
University of Mississippi	Augustus B. Longstreet	1849–1856

office, yet, they produced an extremely high proportion of formal defenses written by proslavery clergymen. Perhaps as a result of the need of regular comment on public issues, these clergymen were more prone than other professionals to contribute formal defenses through their editorials.

Altogether proslavery clergymen sat in the editor's chair of at least 121 separate periodicals or newspapers. In table 6.20 the papers are divided as to type (one paper for each who served as editor); more than two-thirds of all the papers emanated from the South. About 57 percent of all the newspapers were official church organs either for whole de-

TABLE 6.20
Types of Periodicals Edited by Proslavery Clergymen

	AUTHORS OF		
Type of Periodical	Formal Defenses	Proslavery Writings	Proslavery and War Sermons
South—official church	33	41	45
South—religious	9	11	12
South—secular	10	12	14
North—official church	9	13	13
North—religious	5	10	10
North—secular	2	3	3
Other	2	3	3
Single purpose—proslavery	2	2	2

Note: This table and others of similar format present three separate data counts for (1) authors of formal treatises in defense of slavery (Formal Defenses); (2) authors of other forms of proslavery literature (Proslavery Writings); and (3) an all-inclusive category (Proslavery and War Sermons) that also encompasses the relatively large number of clergymen whose only proslavery writing occurred during the Civil War in support of the Confederate war effort.

nominations or for regional subdivisions thereof. Over three-fourths of the papers were primarily religiously oriented. However, proslavery clergymen issued at least nineteen secular newspapers, two of which were devoted entirely to the forwarding of proslavery thought. Location and purpose had little effect on the production of formal defenses, except that those without any official ecclesiastical connection tended slightly toward more formalized proslavery productions.

Despite the fact that more than two-thirds of their papers were located in the South, considerably less than two-thirds of all proslavery editors came from the South. A total of forty-three of 102 editors were born outside slaveholding regions, most frequently in Europe or New England. Of those who edited periodicals in the South, nineteen of seventy-one came from nonslaveholding regions, while of twenty-six in the North only five proslavery editors came from the South. Unlike in other categories, proslavery clerical editors worked primarily in their own regions. In addition, foreign immigrants participated frequently in the proslavery religious journalism of both the North and the South. An important conclusion, therefore, is the fact that proslavery clergymen apparently generally dominated the nation's religious press.

Proslavery clergymen were also widely published authors. About 74 percent of them published books, tracts, or pamphlets other than or in addition to one piece of proslavery literature. One-fourth of them placed in print at least eight separate publications of all types. Taken together on the basis of figures in the table alone, proslavery ministers accounted for a total of at least 1,124 separate publications (with the actual number obviously much greater). Those clergymen who were the most prolific writers doubled as the most fruitful authors of formal defenses, writers of eight items or more produced 39 percent of all formal defenses.

An analysis of the number and nature of their publications indicates that only a small portion of proslavery clergymen restricted their printed comments to the subject of slavery. Nor were their most common publications necessarily sermonic in nature; less than one-half of all clergymen published this kind of literature exclusively (see table 6.21). Another third spent their time composing some of the major theological, religious, and biblical tracts of the nineteenth century. The major writings of one-fourth of the clergymen fell into categories ranging from legal and political topics to belles-lettres. Those who used their writing talents only to produce sermons were least likely to offer formal defenses, even though a large portion of all formal defenses occurred in published sermons. Rather than being monomaniacal defenders of slavery, most proslavery clergymen sought the assistance of printers and publishers for various kinds of pronouncements, only one of which dealt with slavery.

Despite the fact that slavery was but one public issue that garnered their attention, proslavery clergymen's behavior vis-à-vis the Negro slave sheds some light on their personalities and characters. Those clergymen who defended slavery possessed the prejudices and aspirations of most other Americans. An overwhelming number of the ministers were slaveholders and plantation owners with aspirations to expand their agricultural interests and income. While a few clergymen claimed no desire ever to own a slave and others lived in states where they could not if they wished, it is generally true that any who lived where slaveholding was permitted and who could find the means, irrespective of his background, eventually became a slaveholder.

In a study of southern Methodist clergymen who participated in the

TABLE 6.21
Types of Writings of Proslavery Clergymen

	AUTHORS OF		
Type of Writings	Formal Defenses	Proslavery Writings	Proslavery and War Sermons
Sermonic only	34	74	112
Theological, religious	48	68	73
Biblical studies	8	10	10
Legal, political	20	29	32
Literature	11	14	16
Scientific	3	7	7
School texts	2	4	5
Business, finance	0	4	4

Note: This table and others of similar format present three separate data counts for (1) authors of formal treatises in defense of slavery (Formal Defenses); (2) authors of other forms of proslavery literature (Proslavery Writings); and (3) an all-inclusive category (Proslavery and War Sermons) that also encompasses the relatively large number of clergymen whose only proslavery writing occurred during the Civil War in support of the Confederate war effort.

1844 General Conference that debated slavery and that led to the division of the Methodist Episcopal church, one historian has found that many of the leading southern spokesmen could only be described as "traveling preachers and settled farmers." Of the forty-seven southern delegates, he found that thirty-four owned slaves and farms for a total of at least 422 slaves with a net worth of approximately $200,000. Included in the list were nine proslavery clergymen (also included in this study) who owned a total of ninety-one slaves. After examining the holdings and life styles of eleven of the most prominent ministers, the historian concluded: "It seems clear that the men who gathered [at the conference] . . . were southerners first, farmers with families to support second, and theologically-untrained ministers third."[16]

The findings of this historian seem to apply generally to a majority of proslavery clergymen, with the delimiter that one did not have to be a southerner in either birth or sentiments to share slaveholding and planter characteristics. As shown in table 6.22, which is based on a study

TABLE 6.22
Slaveholding Status of Proslavery Clergymen

	AUTHORS OF		
Slaveholding Status	*Formal Defenses*	*Proslavery Writings*	*Proslavery and War Sermons*
Owned no slaves	36	47	69
1–5 slaves or unknown no.	12	23	27
6–10 slaves	10	18	25
11–20 slaves	7	10	10
21–50 slaves	2	3	3
51–99 slaves	3	7	7
100 or more slaves	8	11	17
Resided outside South	33	55	58
Unknown	25	38	59

Source: Compiled by author from U.S. Census manuscript slaveholding schedules and other biographical data.

This table and others of similar format present three separate data counts for (1) authors of formal treatises in defense of slavery (Formal Defenses); (2) authors of other forms of proslavery literature (Proslavery Writings); and (3) an all-inclusive category (Proslavery and War Sermons) that also encompasses the relatively large number of clergymen whose only proslavery writing occurred during the Civil War in support of the Confederate war effort.

of manuscript slaveholding schedules of the United States Census and biographical information, just over half (141) of all proslavery clergymen are known to have owned slaves.[17] Only a small percentage (6.2 percent) of those living in slaveholding areas are known to have held no slaves. But one-fifth (21.1 percent) always lived in areas where they could not have owned slaves if they had wished. Unfortunately the slaveholding status of a similar number (21.5 percent) could not be determined. As indicated by the ratio between formal defenses and other types of proslavery writings, however, slaveholding was manifestly a negligible factor in determining whether one would pen formal defenses (63.1 percent owned slaves), other proslavery writings (64.1 percent), or primarily war sermons (65.3 percent). The addition of writers of war sermons weights slaveholding overduly, but only slightly.

The 141 clergymen who owned slaves had a vested interest in the perpetuation of slavery. Taken together in the most conservative count possible, they owned a total of 2,466 slaves for an average of 17.5 slaves each.[18] If each slave had been valued at $500, proslavery clergymen would have had a minimum figure of approximately $1,233,000 in slave property. Those whose slaveholdings can be determined had on the average about $9,000 each invested in slave property. Nevertheless, the mean figures for the ministers is increased sharply by the fact that seven of their number had slaveholdings ranging from 101 to about 400. Nearly 60 percent of them owned ten or fewer. In terms of change over time, few significant patterns can be detected. The number of clergymen owning slaves tended to rise slightly as the Civil War approached. At the same time those with huge slaveholdings—most were members of the first or second generations—largely disappeared.

Some very significant patterns arise, however, from a study of the origin of slaveholding ministers (see table 6.23). Two-thirds (ninety-four) of all slaveholders were born in the South, while the remaining third (forty-seven), except for two West Indians, were born outside slaveholding areas. An almost equal number of clergymen who owned slaves came from each of three nonsouthern regions. In the South, the lower South produced the bulk of the slaveholders, and most of those with extremely large slaveholdings came from the South. It is clear that slaveholding depended on no factor except southern residence. The only clergymen who never owned slaves were those who never resided in the South.

Since clergymen could only own slaves if they lived in the South, it is instructive to compare the slaveholdings of various southern residents by their region of origin. Of those ministers who lived and worked primarily in the southern states 125 were born in the South and sixty-eight in other regions, approximately the same ratio as clerical slaveholders. While ninety-four or 75.2 percent of the 125 born in the South are known to have owned slaves, forty-seven or 69.1 percent of the outsiders also owned slaves. In terms of slaveholding by each region of origin, seventeen of twenty New Englanders living in the South had slaves, fourteen of nineteen from the Middle States, sixteen of twenty-five from Europe and other countries, thirty-eight of fifty-seven from the upper South, and fifty-two of sixty-three from the lower South. Thus, New Englanders and natives of the lower South were more likely to own slaves than those from other regions.

If it is taken into consideration that nonsoutherners could not inherit slaves and that they could only become slaveholders by purchase or mar-

TABLE 6.23
Slaveholding Proslavery Clergymen, Grouped by Region of Origin

Slaveholding Status (Number Owned)	New England	Mid-Atlantic	Upper South	Lower South	Europe and Other
1–5	8	9	16	21	10
6–10	3	1	8	13	3
11–20	4	3	7	8	3
21–50	1	1	4	4	0
51–99	0	0	1	2	0
100 or more	1	0	2	4	0
Resided outside South	20	13	2	2	15

riage, these ratios are remarkable. No northern or European-born clergymen could claim, as did many southern-born ministers, that their slaveholdings derived from unwanted inheritances. Nor could they charge that they retained their slaves only because they felt a moral obligation to faithful family servants. As best as can be determined from somewhat meager and sketchy information on 127 of the 141 slaveholding clergymen, about 38 percent obtained the bulk of their slaves by inheritance, while approximately 20 percent obtained their slaves through marriage. Only two ministers are known to have received their slaves as gifts from congregations or friends. By contrast, 41 percent or fifty-two of the slaveholding clergymen apparently purchased their slaves. Therefore, it seems that almost any of them, given the opportunity, gladly assumed whatever responsibilities, burdens, or income that might have derived from owning slaves.

Yet the mere fact of extensive slave ownership among proslavery clergymen may be misleading. Many of them might appear as self-interested conservators in their proslavery views. But, since from one-third to one-half of them owned no slaves, their chief interest may have been in keeping open the channels of aspiration and success. For example, long after he had left North Carolina for Mississippi where he used the ministry to become a wealthy slaveholding planter, James Smylie continued to counsel young ministers late in the antebellum period to follow his course of action. One young idealistic clergyman, to whom Smylie had imparted

the notion of marrying a wealthy planter's daughter, abhorred the idea
of mixing his ministerial duties with the pursuit of wealth:

> I agree with you most cordially that a man must have something to live
> upon, but to make gold & silver & negroes the untiring and incessant ob-
> jects of pursuit, I consider a violation of the Gospel & derogatory to the
> Christian name. . . . That wealth adds dignity & usefulness to the minis-
> terial character & office I cannot for a moment believe, & if! if! this is all that
> a minister has to recommend him, better that a millstone were hanged
> about his neck. . . . Look at Vancourt & Bertron & Hazard[,] men who have
> made wealth the primary object to pursuit & where is their dignity &
> usefulness so highly spoken of! Office bearers in the Church of Jesus Christ
> who if justice should be done them would be deposed from the ministry as
> unholy worshipers of filthy lucre![19]

Yet the overwhelming majority of proslavery clergymen agreed with
Smylie. A study of eight Mississippi counties in 1860 reveals that ministers in those areas were either extremely rich with plenty of land and
slaves or extremely poor with little real or personal property. The
wealthier averaged about fifty-six years of age; the less fortunate averaged about thirty-two years and were often found boarding in families of
successful planters, making preparations to alter their status![20]

The available evidence of their aspirations, habits, careers, and status
leads to the inescapable conclusion that proslavery clergymen were generally bent on accumulating wealth and influence by any means that
could be either grasped or conferred. Neither they nor their laities conceived of them as mere ambassadors of the gospel or as heralds of religion, despite the efforts of rival social leaders to compartmentalize
them as votaries of limpid, religious sacramentalism. For proslavery clergymen and other ministers of the antebellum period religion was both a
means and an end. It was a means of achieving personal fulfillment in
terms of their careers and of recruiting masses of people for projects
and perspectives deemed by clerical leaders as crucial for the building of
a virtuous and secure society. The end, on a personal level, was financial
comfort and the ability to exert influence over increasing numbers of
people. The social end, of course, was the construction of a moral empire in which clergymen served as the arbiters of taste, morals, and style
in government and society.

Although the antebellum period was an era of revivalism, personal
piety, and the search for emotional religious conversion and although

Controversialist Proslavery Clergymen

William Gannaway Brownlow,
1805–1877
*Editor, brawler, public debater, anti-
secessionist, and Reconstruction governor
of Tennessee, 1865–1869*

Jesse Babcock Ferguson, 1819–1870
*Evangelical spiritualist and popular seer,
Nashville, 1845–1860*

Leonidas Polk, 1806–1864
*Episcopal bishop of Louisiana, 1841–
1864, and slain Confederate general*

Thornton Stringfellow, 1788–1869
*Most widely published essayist on the Bible
and slavery*

proslavery clergymen practiced evangelical forms of religion, the diaries, journals, and personal correspondence of ministers who defended slavery hardly reflect these realities. Whereas proslavery clergymen endorsed religious forms and practices publicly from the pulpit, in their private lives they seemed concerned heavily with social and financial success. While one might expect at least an occasional mention of camp meetings and church meetings in their personal papers, there are only discussions of financial and organizational matters. Instead of cases of intense, classic personal struggles for salvation and personal piety, there are constant references to planting, harvests, sales and investments as well as to the need to oil and tune the religious and denominational engines for more effective and inclusive operation.

Judged on the basis of their personal and professional achievements, proslavery clergymen cannot be considered mere servants of a religious public. And even though they endorsed by example the planting ideal of the South, they cannot be seen as mere captives of a society with severe restrictions upon their capacities to exert independent influence. Neither professionalism nor the expectations of the laity encapsulated them in clearly defined social roles. In every sense they were leaders, not followers; innovators, not imitators; thinkers, not mirror reflections of pat models. In terms of the yardsticks of success, they were generally accomplished with little cause for frustration and less for recalling nostalgically a forgotten past. Their careers were so varied, their contributions to society so extensive, and their interests so far-ranging that they cannot be made to conform to any simple mold. In their careers and social status are found all of the characteristics and attributes of America's most important social and political leaders—among whom were the proslavery clergy.

How does one relate the manifest character and careers of proslavery clergymen to proslavery history? There is exceedingly little that even a majority of the ministers who published defenses of slavery held in common. Bare majorities of them were born in the South, enjoyed inherited wealth, identified their interests with the slaveholding South, and owned slaves. More important than the shared characteristics that make them conform to conventional models of proslavery thinkers and writers was the absolute variety of their backgrounds, inheritances, abilities, interests, and attainments. Yet there were crucial qualities that nearly all of them shared. They all had a will to power, an insatiable yearning for the accumulation of wealth and influence. Like social leaders of all ages and countries, they were content with nothing less than the ability and opportunity to shape the destiny of men. In their pursuit of education, a proper marriage, parallel careers, authorship, and clerical office, they displayed an undisguised desire for success. And, except in rare instances, they were on the whole able to achieve a social significance that equalled and sometimes surpassed their fondest dreams.

The fact that they were in general socially ambitious and significant beings explains their public pronouncements on slavery. Social leaders, despite their politic concern for their own futures, are bound in times of social stress to comment on public issues, to take positions, and to discredit their adversaries. For a majority of proslavery clergymen, expressing their views on slavery was as natural as commenting on vice in politics, the evils of war, or desecration of the Sabbath. In view of their status in American society, it would have been perhaps more remarkable if they had not assumed a firm stance on the issue of slaveholding.

But why did they defend slavery? And why did they defend it in the ways they did? Certain clues are suggested by the foregoing profile. More striking than any single characteristic that all proslavery clergymen held in common was the variation between the first and third generations. The marked contrast between the constituency of the two subgroups suggests the outlines of an inquiry into proslavery history that has been missed because of myths about the nature and tendencies of proslavery thought.

Whereas the third generation of proslavery clergymen was heavily southern-born, southern-educated, wealthy, and attached to slavery, the first generation was similarly heavily northern-born, northern-educated, socially successful, and attached to social institutions and ideological priorities not normally associated with the defense of slavery. Particularly prevalent in the first generation were ministers born in New England, educated in the Congregational colleges and seminaries of New England, and reared in Congregational churches. While their numbers decreased in the second and third generations, their crucial presence cannot simply be dismissed. For from among those who framed the initial responses to abolitionism and who established the patterns of proslavery literature in America in the 1830s, their domination was unrivaled and their influence, particularly on other ministers, was incalculable.

Instead of suggesting that all things relating to proslavery literature and proslavery thinkers flowed from the South, the foregoing profile indicates that the formative influences for proslavery may have drifted into the South from many quarters. Many potential proslavery clergymen migrated to the South in search of work, wives, and wealth. And they, like countless others who preceded them, brought along the cultural baggage of their formative years in other locales. The barrage of outside influences on the South in the realms of religion, education, and social reform was so great in the early years of the nineteenth century that it is nearly impossible to find a southern-born proslavery cleric whose thought and values were not deeply affected by his early exposure to extra-southern influences. The evidence is so overwhelming that, at least in the case of proslavery clergymen, it is not possible to isolate any substantial number of ministers who were born in the South, grew up in their homeland, and were nurtured almost wholly in southern institutions. On the contrary, it was not until the maturation of the third generation of clerical defenders of slavery that one could begin speaking sensibly of a uniquely southern proslavery clergy. But even then southern clerics were balanced in great measure by new sympathizers in the North and by the continued activity of older proslavery ministers from the first and second generations.

All of the evidence, therefore, points to a potential massive transference of ideas and values from non-southern sources into the South helping to shape the nature and direction of southern proslavery literature and thought. At the same time whatever may have happened to produce proslavery in whatever shape in the South, it was part of a larger national experience that drew on peoples and traditions from all regions of the nation as well as other nations. In any case the gathered evidence argues strongly against any interpretation of proslavery as deriving from southern culture and influences alone. At least in the case of proslavery clergymen it is impossible to speak of proslavery thought as the product of either the southern mind or of southern minds, but it might not be inaccurate to characterize its origins and influences as an outgrowth and product of some significant part of the American mind.

PART TWO

The Rise of Proslavery Ideology in America

SEVEN

Death of America's Revolutionary Ideology, 1776–1798

During the thirty years prior to the Civil War a new and distinctively different ideological persuasion appeared in and became the dominant characteristic of American proslavery literature. Almost random reference to the myriad proslavery literature of the period reveals that relatively small portions of so-called defenses were actually devoted to arguments in favor of slavery. For example, in one of the most famous brief proslavery statements, *Slavery a Divine Trust* (1860), the author, Benjamin Morgan Palmer, made constant references to themes and phrases that seem in retrospect quite foreign to his central purpose. Speaking just after the election of Abraham Lincoln as president on the eve of the Civil War, Palmer argued that slavery was a gift from God for white Americans to perpetuate and perfect, a thesis widely reiterated in the late 1850s. With his few defensive assertions out of the way, Palmer turned to other topics concerning American society and character. Uttering widely heard phrases, Palmer held that in 1860 America was troubled by sectional divisions, "the jealousy of rival interests," "the lust of political power," "bastard ambition which looks to personal aggrandizement rather than to the public weal," "reckless radicalism which seeks for the subversion of all that is ancient and stable," and "furious fanaticism which drives on to its ill-considered conclusions with utter disregard for the evil it engenders."

As indicated by his biting phraseology, Palmer dwelt much more heavily on the psychology of the crisis that gripped America following the election of Abraham Lincoln than on the presumed merits of slavery. The crisis of the Union raised doubts about the national character and providential future of the United States. Both individuals and masses of

Benjamin Morgan Palmer, 1818–1902
*Controversialist pastor of First Presbyterian Church,
New Orleans, 1856–1902*

men were "strained to their utmost tension," he continued. *Distress, perplexity, fear, dread,* and *doom* were the terms he applied to the seemingly unbearable emotional intensity of the crisis. In such difficult times, he held, men could only "seek after God" for guidance and aid in combating the causes of distress. Perceiving himself to be both a social leader and a voice for God, Palmer was happy to tread longest and hardest on the "furious fanaticism" that had ultimately precipitated the crisis. In terms which harked back to another age, he argued that abolitionism was but another term for the infidelity and atheism that had infected the Western world since the days of the French Revolution. It was the same "demon which erected its throne upon the guillotine in the days of Robespierre and Marot." Abolition societies, like Jacobin clubs, strike "at God by striking at all subordination and law, enthralling weak consciences in the meshes of its treachery." From all quarters he seemed to hear the abolitionists' banner-cry, " 'liberty, equality, fraternity,' which simply interpreted, means bondage, confiscation and massacre." "With its [abolition's] tricolor waving in the breeze," he concluded, "it waits to inaugurate its reign of terror."[1]

Despite the dramatic pitch Palmer's pulpit oratory lent to the occasion and the topic, neither his deft handling of the psychology of crisis, his eager plunge into social criticism, nor his identification of abolitionism with French revolutionaries was an isolated phenomenon. He merely reenacted, in fact, a dramatic role that was repeated on hundreds of other platforms throughout America that same thanksgiving day and on thousands of others during the preceding thirty years. Palmer's act, although sometimes seen as the most extreme fire-eating statement of a southern clergyman,[2] was actually only the ritualistic incantation of a scene whose lines and movement had long since been encrusted in the minds of Americans. The keys to the ritual were the references to crisis, the scoring of subversion, and the identification of subversive forces with the French Revolution. With pompous sounding titles ranging from *The Character and Influence of Abolitionism* to *Causes and Remedies of Impending National Calamities* and from *Dangers and Duties of the Present Crisis* to *Cause and Remedies of the Present Convulsions,* clergymen and orators throughout the nation preached the message of impending doom.[3]

Although the crisis of the Union was perhaps the most intense emotional experience in the nation's history, the fiery incantations of Palmer and his fellow clergymen were not necessarily a by-product of Civil War brinkmanship. Indeed, the crisis sermon as a tool of proslavery clergymen was as old as attempts to squelch abolitionism. During the mid-1830s when abolitionists first raised menacing banners against slaveholders, anti-abolitionists inflamed the minds of Americans with sermons and discourses picturing would-be emancipators as monsters without religion or morals who would not be content until they had toppled the very moorings of American society. Abolitionists, they argued, were conspirators against American republicanism employing the tactics of French revolutionaries to spread infidelity and anarchy. By the time the anti-abolitionists of the 1830s had finished their work, no leaf was left unturned for the likes of Benjamin M. Palmer.

But 1835 was not 1860. There were fundamental differences between the crisis mongers of the two periods. Whereas in 1860 the rhetoric of crisis, subversion, and impending revolution could be heard from the lips of all manner of men in all sections, in 1835 almost all of those who participated in the battering of abolitionism and in the launching of a national campaign to uphold slavery shared one important characteristic. Nearly all of the early articulate critics of abolitionists were scions of New England and of that section's peculiar religious and political traditions. More likely than not, those who publicly opposed the aims of abolitionists in the 1830s were natives of New England, sons of staunch Federalists, and the products of Congregational religious training. Contrary to impressions long held by historians, the bulk of early opposition to abolitionism came from those nurtured in New England and the North—and not the South.

Beginning with the tentative criticisms of two giants of Congregationalism, Leonard Bacon and Joseph Tracy, in 1833,[4] the type of perspective heretofore associated by historians only with southerners quickly spread to other New Englanders scattered throughout the nation. What was only barely apparent in the early writings of Bacon and Tracy soon appeared in ever more recognizable forms in the sermons and pamphlets of Simon Clough, Simeon Doggett, and Charles Farley, all natives of Massachusetts. A Congregational Christian clergyman at Fall River, Massachusetts, Clough expressed his notions in a heated *Candid Appeal to the Citizens of the United States* (1834). The following year, Doggett and Farley, both of whom were converts from Congregationalism to Unitarianism, issued strident defenses of slavery, Doggett from his pulpit in Raynham, Massachusetts, and Farley from Richmond, Virginia, where he served an interim pastorate. As the crisis of the thirties deepened, other sons of New England and Congregationalism registered similar sentiments in all corners of the nation. Theophilus Fisk, originally of Massachusetts, told South Carolinians how to combat abolitionism in a discourse entitled *The Bulwark of Freedom* at Fort Moultrie in 1836. The Massachusetts-born brothers George and Frederick Freeman, both of whom converted to Episcopalianism after traveling extensively in North Carolina, lectured both Carolinians and residents of their native state in the evils of abolitionism.

Another New Englander who migrated southward, Rufus William Bailey, followed a similar pattern as he sent back to the North from South Carolina an early important proslavery book entitled *The Issue*. At the same time from New Orleans, Theodore Clapp, another Massachusetts-born defector to Unitarianism, challenged abolitionists severely in a lengthy sermon-essay entitled *Slavery*. Meanwhile, back in Massachusetts, two other stalwarts of the Congregational establishment, George Washington Blagden, pastor of Old South in Boston, and Moses Stuart, professor of biblical studies at Andover Seminary, sermonized the virtues of slavery as opposed to the horrors of abolition. Perhaps none of the New England–born and Congregational-bred early critics of abolitionism exceeded the audacity of one of their fellows, Daniel K. Whitaker. At the height of the crisis in 1836 Whitaker presumed to lecture the South's greatest early proslavery thinker, William Harper, for the latter's failure to denominate abolition the worst evil in the history of man.[5]

The first massive outpouring of anti-abolitionist proslavery literature on the part of clergymen with firm roots in New England came to a conclusion by 1839 with a small book by another of their number. Calvin Colton, who afterward became a Protestant Episcopal clergyman and a Whig pamphleteer, subsumed all of the major ideas of his fellow clergy under one cover with the revealing title *Abolition a Sedition*. In a phrase that aptly symbolized the entire thrust of the early critics of abolitionism, Colton pushed it to its limits in a systematic presentation of the notions that had become current in briefer tirades against the abolitionists. But in addition to labeling abolitionists with blackened epitaphs in the vein of his contemporaries, Colton went on to analyze the place of abolitionists and of slavery in the structure of American society and polity. In brief, Colton's exposé of the abolitionists and slavery served as the definitive statement of the largest and most articulate group of proslavery writers that had yet appeared on the scene of American history. Moreover, one can see in the electrically charged words of Colton's essay a deftly drawn summary of what was already becoming a national proslavery ideology.

The notions of Colton and his immediate forerunners hinged on the perception of abolition as a radical un-American movement and on a reinterpretation of the ideology of the American Revolution. Colton characterized abolitionism as "a foreign power that has stolen a march on the territories of the Republic, obtained a footing, and gained an alarming ascendancy, before the public were apprized of the fact, or had any true knowledge of the character of the invaders." The very sudden-ness with which abolitionism appeared had served to becloud the sedi-tious origins and purposes of the movement. If permitted to go un-checked, it would "revolutionize the Government and divide the Union." Bearing the cloak and dagger of true religion and operating behind the scenes as an engine of political intrigue, abolitionism had violated all of the rules of organized religion and politics pursuing a path that would in the end make a mockery of American liberties and law. Although aboli-tionists feigned to be emancipators of the Negro slave, the incendiary nature of their doctrines and organization shunted aside the problem of slavery and posed the far more fundamental problem of law and order. The central question for Colton became "whether the political fabric of the country . . . shall give way to violence." "The claim of the slave to his freedom," he asserted, "will never be listened to, till that is settled."

Colton's precise position on slavery was characteristic of that of his fellows. Claiming neither to apologize for slavery nor to hold that slavery was other than evil, Colton proceeded to adduce nearly every traditional proslavery argument in the vast arsenal of proslavery thinkers. In a cri-tique of Revolutionary ideology, Colton argued, "there is no such thing as equality among men, nor can there be." Negroes could never attain the social level of American whites; American whites would never stand for an immediate elevation of blacks: "The dangers would be too ob-vious and too imminent to admit of parley." In a comparison of the con-dition of American slaves with laboring classes in other countries and with native Africans, Colton verged on a positive good assertion. Negro slaves "have not been injured, but benefitted, by the position which they now occupy, not only in comparison with the history of the race to which they belong, but also in comparison with the common history of other tribes and nations." No people had ever been brought so quickly, "risen so much, or been improved so much, as a body, in their actual condition, social character, privileges, relations, and prospects, for time and for eternity, as that portion of the African race now to be found in the United States of North America."[6]

From their characterizations of abolitionists as foreign-inspired radicals to their willing buttressing of slavery, Colton and the other New England divines were in remarkable accord. Nearly all of them saw abolition as an infidel movement at variance with true religion and the Bible.[7] With false pretensions and anarchical principles the abolitionists had caused the nation to lurch into a panic of frenzied excitement which could, if continued, they believed, only result in social chaos and civil war.[8] In arguing the merits of slavery, the clergymen were as resourceful as the proslavery heritage of the Western world permitted. They found slavery to be a natural condition of society.[9] They found in the Bible ample evidence of God's favor on the institution, as well as proof for a widely held Hamitic curse on the Negro race.[10] They battered down all notions that men are created equally and are thereby entitled to equal rights.[11] They further held that the Negro was a degraded being incapable of enjoying the fruits of liberty and was, indeed, a very present threat to the perpetuation of freedom.[12]

While nearly all of them admitted that slavery harbored either real or potential evils, they minced no words in their efforts to reveal the beneficial aspects of the institution. Simeon Doggett asked, "Where on earth, could a moral picture be filled with a richer array of human excellence, than the tenure of slavery is capable of exhibiting?" Theophilus Fisk, seeing slavery as an institution created and sanctioned by God, asserted, "it may be an evil to the country, and to the owner—but it is a blessing to the slave." George Freeman saw it as a *"merciful Providence"* that Negroes had been transported from barbarous Africa *"into this land of peace, of security, of abundance, of civilization, and of christian light."* Even though Rufus W. Bailey supported colonization (as did some of the others), he remarked that if he were a slaveholder, "I have no morality and no religion, which would require or permit me, absolutely and without regard to circumstances, to give him [the slave] his freedom." Theodore Clapp measured his agreement by asserting that after years of doubt and personal involvement in emancipation schemes, "we are [now] fully convinced of the rectitude of slavery."[13]

In terms of traditional proslavery history, the arguments used by the New England–born divines to uphold slavery were far from unique. They were neither more nor less positive in their assessments of the values of slavery than either their southern contemporaries or the dozens of defenders who preceded them in the early years of the nineteenth century. They did not develop new arguments in defense of slavery. Nor did they disavow particular arguments as seeming reprehensible. Indeed, from the perspective of the established parameters of proslavery argumentation in the English-speaking world, there was nothing that set them apart from either the proslavery past or its future.

From another perspective, however, the proslavery writings of the New England divines were unique. For the first time in proslavery history on the North American continent they united with defensive argumentation a set of assumptions and a body of principles never before associated with the defense of slavery. Believing that abolition had fallen into the hands of a band of radicals who seemed devoted to the destruction of American society and of the Christian religion, the New England–born divines led the way in altering the entire framework in which discussions of slavery in the United States could occur. And therein lay the most important epoch-making transition in American proslavery history. The change occurred, it is important to note, not in the realm of argumentation, but rather in the arena of ideology.

From 1776 until the 1830s (despite the multiplicity of concerns with which proslavery thought had been joined) there had been only one basic conceptual framework in which to discuss slavery. From the flurry of debate that occurred in the northern colonies on the eve of the Revolution until the climax of the neglected period, the one benchmark against which proslavery writers measured their perceptions of slavery was the heritage of the American Revolution. Wherever their investigations of slavery might lead them, spokesmen for slavery could never escape the judgment that the institution simply did not square with the equalitarian ideals and republican principles of the founding fathers. So long as Americans venerated the principles of the American Revolution, they could never uphold slavery as a fully beneficial institution. The heritage of the American Revolution provided an ideological straitjacket that no publicly articulate American could or would overlook.

In the 1830s, however, the opportunity finally came for a vast alteration in American proslavery history. In the course of that decade when emancipationism became radicalized by a band of dauntless reformers, the time grew ripe for a sweeping change of direction in the moorings of American social thought. At the opening of the decade Americans North and South still generally venerated at least in spirit the heritage of the Revolution, still boasted the revolutionary ideals of Jefferson, and still promulgated the republicanism of Adams, Madison, and other founding fathers. By the end of the decade, however, American social thinkers sounded far different. By 1840 they were far less concerned with the lessons of the American Revolution than with those of the French Revolution. They spoke more frequently of the warnings of Edmund Burke than of the ideals of Jefferson. And when they discoursed on republicanism, they thought much more often about the classical republics of Rome and Greece than about the experimental one launched by American revolutionaries. While they continued to spout some of the rhetoric so essential to American social and political life, their words were charged with new meaning derived from sources quite independent of the American Revolutionary heritage. In brief, an ideological revolution whose influence was decisive for the shape of proslavery thought in the antebellum period transpired in the decade between 1830 and 1840. The stratum of ideology is therefore not only the key to proslavery history, but also the missing link that has beclouded traditional interpretations of proslavery in antebellum America.

The twin observations that ideology is the key to proslavery history and that the chief ideological shift on nineteenth-century proslavery history began with New England–born clergymen are tantalizing assertions. Since fundamental ideological shifts in a society do not merely happen without reference to historical events, one must seek the roots of that configuration of thought in American social experience. Because New England–born clergy seem to have been the first to weld an alternate form of ideology to traditional proslavery thought, the search may begin with those factors in their background that caused them to respond to radical abolitionism with the unanimity that characterized their public statements in the 1830s. Since the heart of their thought consisted of a departure from the ideology of the American Revolution, it is probable that the roots of their strange behavior lay somewhere in that period of time following the American Revolution when some Americans began to question values and ideals espoused by American Revolutionaries. It was in fact in the stress-laden decade of the 1790s and in the peculiarly disturbed towns and villages of New England that changes began to occur that would one day make a revolution in American proslavery thought possible.

The reaction of New England–born clergymen to abolition was first and foremost an instance of countersubversion, an attempt to destroy or discredit a movement viewed as conspiratorial. Abolitionism, however, was hardly the first social current to be labeled subversive by the leading lights of New England culture. From the early days of the Massachusetts Bay Colony to the menacing appearance of the Bavarian Illuminati and Jeffersonian Democracy, witches and fanatics seem perpetually to have bedeviled the bastions of Puritanism. The perception of conspiracy on the part of enemies both external and internal seems to have been one of the perennial characteristics of whatever might be labeled the *New England mind*. Although historians often have minimized such occurrences as little more than a series of aberrations, serious questions may be asked regarding the social and intellectual consequences of a recurrent fear of conspiracy in New England and American culture.

While one might find traces of thought forms that contributed to the New England response to abolitionism in Puritanism and in the peculiar colonial experience of New Englanders, it is not necessary to delve that deeply into the recesses of history. One can begin instead with the event that did most to shape interpretations of slavery during the first half-century of American independence, the American Revolution. The American Revolution was the first grand intercolonial forum for shaping American notions of servitude and of national social ideals. It was also, not without reason, the first national movement to curtail perceived social subversion. As an instance of countersubversion and as a watershed in the making of a national social and political ideology, the Revolution is the crucial starting point for understanding the history of America's distinctive proslavery ideology.[14]

Historian Bernard Bailyn has examined in detail the long and complex career of perhaps the most important countersubversive movement in American history—the American Revolution. His treatment of the Revolution offers both a valuable model and a crucial starting point for understanding the ideological history of America. The ideology of the American war for independence, according to Bailyn, sprang from the political culture of early eighteenth-century England where a small cluster of dissenting politicians verbally lampooned the established order of English government. During a period of otherwise quiet and orderly government, the "opposition press" developed an antigovernment ideology that dwelt upon conspiratorial combinations of men to deprive political minorities of constitutionally guaranteed rights. Having read the compelling notions of the opposition press for several decades, American colonials easily responded to their problems after 1763 in a like manner. In one of the greatest outpourings of pamphlets in American history, the colonial malcontents found at every turn evidences of a well-conceived plot on the part of British cabinet ministers to undermine the long-established rights and liberties of British subjects throughout the empire. The continued perception of a vast conspiracy, reinforced daily by new and ever more compelling occurrences of burgeoning tyranny, gave an irrefutable logic to colonial rebellion.[15]

The American Revolution Bailyn would argue was a vast countersubversive movement that sought to strike down a conspiracy whether the enemy was real or imagined. In the case of the Revolution, anticonspiratorial ideology and rhetoric fostered a transformation in American politics that led eventually to the institutionalization of Revolutionary ideology in novel forms of government and to an infectious desire to follow the logic of the ideology to near-revolutionary social consequences. In the case of Revolutionary ideology, a "contagion of liberty" was unleashed to challenge the illogical perpetuation of Negro slavery, of established religion, of undemocratic governmental forms, and of anachronistic patterns of deferential society. In the best sense of the term, countersubversionary tactics launched a massive reformation, a positive reinterpretation and reorganization of American social life.[16]

In the context of the American Revolution, therefore, an incalculably far-reaching social reformation grew out of a countersubversive movement. Out of the anticonspiratorial literature of the Revolutionary era emerged a full-fledged social and political ideology that served as the meaningful and emotionally loaded symbol-system of the first generation of independent Americans. Since variations of the original ideology continued to energize much of American thought during two centuries of independent existence, the American Revolution must be considered one of the most remarkable ideological movements in the modern world. Whether one chooses to adjudge the ideology truly revolutionary makes little difference. The fact that an ideological system emerged from the colonial crisis and that it persisted indelibly in the minds of a people makes the movement a historical landmark.

Beyond charting the immediate contagion of Revolutionary ideology, Bailyn provides little guide to the future course of American social and political philosophy. One of his students, Gordon S. Wood, has, however, argued that Revolutionary ideology reached a hiatus and suffered a subtle reorientation only a decade after the onset of the Revolution. In the Constitutional Convention of 1787–1788 aristocratic and well-meaning

Federalists employed Revolutionary rhetoric as a weapon to better republican Antifederalists and to alter the direction of the Revolution. The Federalists used "the most popular and democratic rhetoric available"—that of the Revolution—to popularize and defend an aristocratic system of social and governmental polity. They blunted the proliferation and institutionalization of Revolutionary ideology and the social forces released by the Revolution by appealing to the most intense fears of Whig ideologists. The Federalist reaction of the 1780s was, in Wood's words, the "end of American ideology" in that it robbed political ideology of the ability to represent differing social interests.[17]

Although Wood pronounced the death of Revolutionary ideology in 1788 as a viable political force, there is little to suggest that the philosophy of the Revolution was robbed of its social influence at the same time. Surely the Federalists had in mind the buttressing of their own peculiar social system and the halting of democratizing tendencies in American society in the 1780s. And certainly Federalist philosophers and statesmen made thrusts at revaluing the ideological heritage of the Revolution. But their furtive efforts did not stop the process of slave emancipation, at least in the northern states, released by the contagion of liberty. Nor did it stop the disestablishment of churches, the extension of voting rights, and the widening of economic opportunities. Even the voluntary association of men to produce countervailing political organizations did not fall sway to the unitary political aims of the Federalists. Hence, while the Federalist reaction of the 1780s marked the beginning of a change in social thinking, the full revolution in values across wide sectors of the American populace awaited another crisis no less fearful than that of the Revolutionary struggle.

The Bailyn-Wood treatment of the Revolutionary era constitutes the portrayal of a complete ideological cycle in American history, one that stemmed originally from a subversive crisis situation. The perception of conspiracy had drawn colonial social leaders from the comfortable and secure corners of the British Empire to fashion a countersubversive ideology that expressed the beliefs and aspirations of Americans. Until social realities began to place stress on Revolutionary thought in the 1780s, it served as the nationalizing and reforming symbol system of Americans. Although the Federalist creators of the American Constitution sought to defuse the ideology politically and socially to the point of establishing a hierarchical republican society with power in the hands of established leaders, their efforts encountered staunch resistance from

Antifederalists who sought to guard the gains of 1776 and to protect the purity of the Revolution. The Federalists won the battle for a new constitution because of the practical necessities for a more centralized government. They did not, however, win the struggle to refashion the ideology of the Revolution until another national crisis fostered the creation of a new, countervailing ideology.

If American countersubversives in the Revolutionary era created a distinctive American ideology and gave birth to an entire cycle of ideology formation, systematization, institutionalization, and ultimate encrustation, it is likely that other anticonspiratorial movements in America may have fostered successive cycles of ideology. Indeed, there have been ample opportunities for Americans to undergo ideological reorientation in the midst of anticonspiratorial campaigns. One need only to be reminded of the Populist revolt to free silver from the hands of international bankers, of the Red Scare of 1919–1920, of McCarthyism of the 1950s, and a hundred other prophecies of impending doom to enforce the point that countersubversion can and has resulted in pivotal shifts in American thinking. While historians and sociologists are apt to see in countersubversion the "end of ideology," the rejection of utopian schemes, and the reassertion of rigid traditionalism,[18] it is mistaken to assume that social and political reactionaries are bereft of ideology or that they do not deal in the fashioning and unleashing of sometimes startling and revolutionary ideologies.[19]

On the contrary, countersubversion may be a distinctively American mode of creating meaningful social symbols and of making social realities conform to projected ideals. From the Revolution to the Civil War, at least, countersubversionary movements seem to have served as electrifying mechanisms for establishing and transmuting various forms of ideology. Revolutionary ideology, in its pristine form, seems now to have been only the first in a series of reworked symbol-systems that would elicit the emotional approval of a large body of Americans. And while elements of Revolutionary thought remained permanently valuable, other attitudes and beliefs slowly impinged on the ideological system as a whole to produce new amalgams of symbols and newer ideological systems.

In terms of those nationally recognized symbols that continued to attract the allegiance of Americans, however, Revolutionary thought held sway until well into the nineteenth century. And in terms of the ideological framework of public discussions of slavery, Revolutionary thought reigned supreme—except in isolated instances—until the 1830s and the appearance of abolitionism. Nevertheless, important ideological shifts began occurring as early as the Constitutional Convention of 1787, continued apace most significantly in the 1790s in connection with American reaction to the French Revolution, flowered in the midst and wake of the War of 1812, and reached fruition in the first abolition crisis of the 1830s. Every shift, while it usually affected slavery only indirectly at the moment, contributed directly to the process that would ultimately dictate the shape and intensity of proslavery ideology. For in a fundamental sense the rise of proslavery as an ideological system was the story of the failure of Revolutionary ideology to persist as the social and political norm of Americans.

The roots of those ideological shifts that ultimately made America's proslavery ideology possible lay in the first efforts of Federalist politicians to circumvent the logical consequences of Revolutionary ideology. The Constitutional Convention of 1787 was but the first glimmering, outward signal that a shift away from Revolutionary thought was getting under way in America. In a sense, that convention, which drew together troubled leaders from thirteen barely aligned nation-states, represented a mere working out of antediluvian principles of national polity badly disregarded in the less leisurely days of the war. If America were to be a nation rather than a collection of ill-fitting republics, the belts of government had to be tightened. Since the need for national governmental institutions was widely recognized, the transition from Confederation to Constitution did not result in the type of social convulsion that greeted other changes in America. Once the Antifederalists, the "men of little faith," were assured of the continued enjoyment and protection of certain rights and liberties for the states and for local polities, the Federalist revolution—decidedly a revolution in statecraft and not ideology—was complete. Although such threats as Shays's rebellion certainly engendered some fears, the era of the Confederation was never so much a "critical period" as it was a logical transition in nation making.

Irrespective of the rhetoric of Federalists in the 1780s, the constitutional crisis of America stood as a mere headache in comparison with the social and political convulsions of the 1790s. The latter phenomenon was probably much more crucial in determining the shape of the American sociocultural system and in establishing the permanent ideological loyalties of the American people. In terms of the patterns of thought that eventually coalesced in proslavery ideology, the primacy of the 1790s was absolute. As the perception of one conspiracy had helped launch the American Revolution in the 1760s, another vision of subversion in the 1790s helped ignite the forces that would eventually result in a cultural transformation of America by the end of the 1830s. Since the experiences of the frequently overlooked 1790s were so crucial to the future of American history, the period is in need of thorough reevaluation. The roots of a fundamental shift in American social and political beliefs and values during the 1790s cannot be found by merely looking at particular events during the decade that may have affected the practice and perpetuation of slavery at that moment in time.[20]

In the 1790s the American people were at once attempting to create the machinery of a viable national government and seeking to deal with a series of threats to external and internal security. From an uneasy rapprochement with Britain to an undeclared war with France and from furtive social and political reorganization to the crystallization of national political factions, the years of Federalist rule were taut with rapid change, torrid emotionalism, and intense social strain. Religious emotionalism and fanaticism, not seen since the days of the Great Awakening, began to appear in a second great outburst of revivalism and evangelical expansion. Democratic-Republican societies formed to applaud the French Revolution and Jeffersonian alternatives to Federalism. Conditions were so uneasy, in fact, that Americans became for the first time since the 1760s susceptible to all manner of social movements.

The extent of the uneasiness in the 1790s as compared with previous decades may be gauged in some measure by reference to the publication of fitful social and political sermons on the occasion of fast and thanksgiving days. Since such sermons were printed and distributed widely only in connection with important national events and in the midst of crises throughout the eighteenth and much of the nineteenth centuries, they are a remarkable measure of discontent from the Revolution to the Civil War. Table 7.1 indicates the number of published sermons on the occasion of national fast or thanksgiving days from the first such day established by the Continental Congress in 1775 through the War of 1812. Fast days were normally set at the onset of national crises, while thanksgiving days followed an apparent deliverance from danger. Hence, fast day in 1775 followed closely upon the beginning of battle in the American Revolution, while thanksgiving day in 1783 marked the

TABLE 7.1

Sermons Published on National Fast and Thanksgiving Days, 1775–1815

Date	Occasion	Number of Sermons	Date	Occasion	Number of Sermons
1775 July 20	Fast	10	1782 Nov. 28	Thanksgiving	0
1776 May 17	Fast	1	1783 Dec. 11	Thanksgiving	14
1777 Dec. 18	Thanksgiving	3	1784 Oct. 19	Thanksgiving	0
1778 Apr. 22	Fast	0	1789 Nov. 26	Thanksgiving	2
1778 Dec. 30	Thanksgiving	0	1795 Feb. 19	Thanksgiving	33
1779 May 6	Fast	0	1798 May 9	Fast	20
1779 Dec. 9	Thanksgiving	0	1799 Apr. 25	Fast	17
1780 Apr. 26	Fast	0	1812 Aug. 20	Fast	37[a]
1780 Dec. 7	Thanksgiving	1	1813 Sept. 9	Fast	5
1781 May 3	Fast	2	1815 Jan. 12	Fast	9
1781 Dec. 13	Thanksgiving	5	1815 Apr. 13	Thanksgiving	23
1782 Apr. 25	Fast	0			

Source: "Calendar" and Bibliography in Love, *Fast and Thanksgiving Days of New England,* pp. 502–14, 547–98.
[a]Because of personal religious convictions and ideological purposes, President Thomas Jefferson refused to order either national fast or thanksgiving days. James Madison, despite scruples, renewed the custom at the onset of the War of 1812. See Perry Miller, "From the Covenant to the Revival," in Jamison, *Shaping of American Religion,* pp. 357–58.

achievement of peace. The same pattern was followed in the case of the War of 1812, the war-launching fast of August 20, 1812, and the victory thanksgiving on April 13, 1815.

Due to the fine interplay between minister, congregation, and community in the publication of particularly effective or popular fast and thanksgiving sermons, the appearance of such sermons was an indication of social uneasiness in both the eighteenth and nineteenth centuries. Far from being a routine or automatic affair, sermons were put into print extensively on only the most auspicious occasions, hence the vast outpourings at the termini of wars. In the midst of America's wars from the Revolution through the Civil War, numbers of published sermons followed the course of battle from apprehensions of defeat to the exultation of accomplishment in battle. Since social anxiety naturally expands and contracts with the trauma of war, the widespread publication of such sermons should not be surprising. Similarly, extensive publication in seasons of peace is another matter, an indication of anxiety that the social historian cannot overlook.

In such a scale of values, the two special days called by Pres. George Washington in 1789 and 1795 show marked contrast. His call for a thanksgiving celebration on the launching of the new Constitutional government engendered only a trifling interest, despite the fact that Antifederalists in North Carolina had only just been silenced in a second state ratifying convention. The second of Washington's thanksgiving days was far different. The nation had recently experienced the splintering of public men into feuding political factions, the machinations of Citizen Genêt, the threat of renewed war, and a disconcerting uprising of whiskey-producing farmers. Democratic societies were banding together to bedevil Federalist authority. From November 20, 1794, when David Osgood and other Massachusetts clergymen and politicians suggested that a French-American conspiracy might be in the making to undermine Federalist rule, the fear of subversion crescendoed. Washington lent his support to the growing mania by scoring the "self-created" Democratic societies as the agents of American discontent in both his annual message to Congress and in his proclamation declaring February 19, 1795, a day of thanksgiving. The widespread outpouring of sermons on that day reflected the mounting wave of social anxiety that was gripping the nation.[21]

The cudgeling of Democratic societies in 1795 did not diminish the perception of a vast and growing French conspiracy. Subversion mania grew unabated over the next five years reaching new peaks of intensity concurrent with national fast days proclaimed by Pres. John Adams in 1798 and 1799. The XYZ Affair, cracks in the facade of Federalist political unity, and the onset of an undeclared naval war with France moved Adams to point out the "hazardous and afflictive position" of America in proclaiming his first day of fasting. On that day New England clergymen commenced with increased vigor and startling new disclosures their attack upon the great conspiracy confronting America. Drawing upon an obscure reference to the Bavarian Illuminati in a sermon by Yale's president Timothy Dwight nearly a year earlier, Jedidiah Morse, arch-Federalist clergyman, laid bare on May 9, 1798, the entire Illuminati conspiracy. The Bavarian Illuminati was a supposed super-secret organization in central Europe which had fostered the French Revolution. While Morse took his cue from Dwight's earlier, less sensational charges, his detailed information about the inner workings of the Illuminati came from a book by John Robison, professor of natural philosophy at the University of Edinburgh, entitled *Proofs of a Conspiracy Against all the Religions and Governments of Europe* (1797). Applying Robison's arguments to America, Morse revealed that the Illuminati aimed "to root out and abolish Christianity, and overthrow all civil government" by infiltrating civil, social, and cultural institutions.[22]

Fears of a French-inspired conspiracy reached an emotional peak on fast day in 1798. Morse's revelations were repeated for months by clergymen in the churches and colleges of New England, including David Tappan at Harvard and Timothy Dwight at Yale. On the Massachusetts thanksgiving day the following November, Morse returned to the same subject by presenting "proofs of the early existence, progress, and deleterious effects of French intrigue and influence in the United States." John Adams unwittingly bolstered the charges of New England clergy when he called a second national fast for April 25, 1799. In his proclamation, Adams pointed to the "insidious acts" of French agents who disseminated in America principles "subversive of the Foundations of all religious, moral, and social obligations." On the fast day, while other clergymen re-echoed their stale claims of a conspiracy, Morse startled New England with documentary proof of Illuminist operations in America. Publishing a letter connecting a mother agency in France with local agencies in Virginia, St. Domingo, and New York City and claiming that the letter unveiled preparations for a French invasion of America with armies of blacks from St. Domingo, Morse believed he had finally discovered the nature of the Illuminist conspiracy to destroy America. Much to his personal chagrin and that of his fellow clergy, however, he had merely interloped in the secret correspondence of the respected Order of Free Masons.[23] Discredited by the constant trumping up of unfounded evidence of an anti-American conspiracy, the Illuminati scare had run its course by the fall of 1799. A tide of reaction rose in defiance of such ill-advised countersubversive tactics and helped to carry Thomas Jefferson into the presidency in 1800.

Despite the seemingly groundless nature of the fears, however, the five-year-long panic should not be dismissed as an aberrant social event, as a social frenzy induced by clergymen attempting to recoup lost status, or as a typical response of Protestant orthodoxy to creeping rationalism and atheism.[24] Neither dismissal nor a reduction to simplicity can account for and explain what surely must have been one of the great emotional crises in American history. Historians have learned well in recent years that hardly any event can be dismissed out of hand as a freakish occurrence bereft of meaning and significance. Indeed, aberrant social behavior has been demonstrated often to serve highly important social and psychological functions and to indicate the existence of profound tensions within a particular society. Accordingly, in assessing the significance of the five-year campaign against Illuminism and French political intrigue, one must consider the possibility that the event was an outward manifestation of profound social and psychological changes at work among Americans.[25]

Fundamental to the inquiry is the observation that the entire crisis was of internal origin, only barely related to events occurring in Europe. The course of the greatest anti-French campaigner of them all, Jedidiah Morse, is suggestive. Despite massacres, the execution of Louis XVI, rampant anticlericalism, and the Reign of Terror, Morse long remained a champion of the French Revolution. Through even the most repugnant phases of the Revolution, Morse and his fellow clergy continued to believe and to express the view that in the end a free government would evolve in France. As late as the opening months of 1795, Morse and others persisted in their happy comparison of the French and American revolutions. Yet, by the summer of 1795 many of New England's Congregational clergy had changed from condoners of French excesses to Jeremiahs proclaiming that the French Revolution would bring national and international doom. The timing of the shift suggests that the perception of conspiracy among Americans was independent of events in France and that American countersubversion was launched in the wake of internal, not external developments.[26]

Not only were New England clergymen strangely late in condemning French excesses, but they also saved their oratorical barbs largely for American enemies of religious, social, and political orthodoxy. When they spoke of French infidelity, anarchism, and revolutionary bloodletting, they acted less as moral arbiters of events in a transatlantic nation than as critics of currents criss-crossing American society. What disturbed them most was not the irreligion and barbarity of the French people, but rather the perception that something had suddenly unleashed in American society the same detestable forces that had become a commonplace in France. When the Whiskey Rebellion, Jay's Treaty, and Antifederalist political activity coincided with the machinations of Citizen Genêt, the arrival of Thomas Paine's *Age of Reason,* and the formation of Democratic-Republican societies, social and political disorder momentarily took on the cast of insurrection and anarchy. Anti-French slogans borrowed from scathing British attacks on the French Revolution (such as Burke's *Reflections on the Revolution in France*) just as quickly became weapons in the hands of frightened and enraged men to strike down their enemies.[27]

Of equal importance is the fact that the fears of conspiracy were highly localized. Whereas during the American Revolution sermons preached on fast and thanksgiving days proceeded widely and evenly from New England and the middle colonies, during the anti-French campaign of the 1790s those barometers of social pressure appeared heavily in only one state—Massachusetts. On each of the three nationally proclaimed holy days of the 1790s published sermons from Massachusetts outnumbered those from the rest of the nation from two or three to one. Hence, even though as far away as North Carolina and Virginia clergymen might occasionally refer to a French conspiracy, only in New England and specifically Massachusetts did the social trauma attain frightening proportions. For all practical purposes, most of the Middle States and all of the southern states were spared from the emotional panic that seized New England.[28]

All of the evidence seems to point in a single direction: the anti-French and anti-Illuminist campaign of the 1790s was primarily an internal campaign to discredit and disarm opponents of America's social tranquility and the nation's first constitutional government. At the same time national political alliances were coalescing into Federalist and Republican poles, anticonspiratorial rhetoric and tactics were employed to rout the opposition and to consolidate the ascendancy of Federalist leaders. Since Federalism was rapidly becoming synonymous with New England and the North and since Federalism found its strongest, undivided support in the villages and towns of New England, it was perhaps only natural that images of subversion should appear in their starkest forms in the minds and oratory of New Englanders. The fear of an Illuminist conspiracy and of the subversion of American religious, social, and political life was a New England perception—perhaps even more strictly a New England Federalist and Congregational one—not shared in any similar degree by any other region or group in America. It was largely a New England phenomenon from beginning to end. Only there were the social tensions such that good and well-placed men could conceive that a plot had been set afoot to destroy American society. Only there did social strain reach a boiling point.

And only in New England was a train of events set in motion that would over the next generation work a thoroughgoing reorientation of American social and political ideology and a wholesale reorganization of American social and institutional life. While the preparations for a second great ideological shift in American thought began with the movement to provide the nation a new constitution, no grand change occurred in American social and political thought until the crises of the 1790s. Even then, only one geographical area was affected and largely one class of individuals. But they were touched so deeply, shaken so severely, and reoriented so thoroughly by the experiences of their confrontation with Illuminism, infidelity, and anarchy that they launched an ideological revolution that would alter the course of American social thought, deal the final death blow to the nation's pristine Revolutionary ideology, and provide a new framework for the discussion of such knotty problems as the institution of slavery. Little did they know that their furtive efforts to redefine American social values and ideals would one day provide the heart and soul of a national proslavery ideology.

EIGHT

Launching the Conservative Counterrevolution, 1795–1816

The ideological revolution that would cast such great influence on the shape and tone of American society in the nineteenth century began simultaneously with New England's reaction to the French Revolution and the Illuminist scare. As the tide of reaction against Britain in the 1760s had fostered an ideological revolution that eventuated in an independent American republic, the crisis of the 1790s launched and paved the way for a new ideological revolution. And in the same sense that the former movement was the outgrowth of decades of development in America's colonial political culture, the latter was a product of decades of experience with the American republic itself. In comparative terms the 1790s corresponded strikingly with the 1760s as a period during which older conceptions of nationhood and of society were discarded for what seemed at the moment a more desirable set of ideals, more workable social and political goals. What began in the 1760s did not reach fruition until the 1770s and 1780s; what got under way in the 1790s did not have its ultimate national impact until the 1830s, although large segments of the American people were won over to the new principles of governance long before.

At stake in the 1790s were the venerated principles of the American Revolution themselves. Americans had made such a moral commitment to those early ideals that only a generation of concerted reeducation on the forge of experience where revolutionary notions proved unworkable could bring the ideological transformation that got under way in the days of the French Revolution. While many may have come face to face with situations where the demands of American governance and social development did not square entirely with the tenets of the Revolution, few had the foresight, the strength of intellect, and the force of will to forge a new direction for the nation. Only a small band of ideologues envisioned the building of a new philosophy that could supplant that of the Revolution. The groundwork for change was quietly laid by such men as Timothy Dwight, the Connecticut clergyman-scholar, for the development and ultimate nationalization of an ideological system that replaced the symbols and values of America's revolutionary heritage.[1]

At the beginning of his career in the 1770s, Timothy Dwight was an ardent American revolutionary. At the conclusion of his career in 1817, Dwight was as ardently a proponent of America's second great ideological revolution. In the center of his public life there came a crucial turning point when the American Revolution largely lost its meaning and the process got under way for the development of a viable alternative. That historic juncture occurred simultaneously with the outpouring of protest against the French Revolution and the imagination of an Illuminati conspiracy. The crossroad for Dwight seems to have been July 1798 when he published a sermon entitled *The Duty of Americans at the Present Crisis,* a proscription of Illuminism combined with a novel prescription for the solution of America's social ills. While other orators and clergymen would soon be undergoing a similar process behind such titles as "the danger and duty of Americans," "national sins," or "signs of the times," Dwight's *Duty of Americans* seems to have opened the floodgate.

After describing the rise of infidelity and Illuminism in Europe and America and arguing that both were foretold in New Testament prophecy, Dwight shifted from proscription to prescription. The prescriptive portions of his sermon contained the kernel of a new system of thought. From doom-saying prophetic utterances, Dwight entered into a catalogue of necessary social obligations in a stable republican society. In his view, "personal obedience and reformation is the foundation, and the sum, of all national worth and prosperity." Hand in hand with the performance of social obligations went religious duties. For example, "every man . . . who loves his country, or his religion, ought to feel, that he serves, or injures, both, as he celebrates, or neglects, the Sabbath." Religion and liberty in society stood or fell as a unity: "If our religion were gone, our state of society would perish with it; and nothing would be left, which would be worth defending." Political duties flowed inextricably from the needs of society and religion. Infidelity and anarchism bred

Timothy Dwight, 1752–1817
*"Pope Timothy," president of Yale University, 1795–1817, central figure in
America's conservative counterrevolution*

faction, rebellion, the ruin of peace, and the loss of property. Hence, faithful men had to separate themselves entirely from the enemies of republicanism, that is, the irreligious political opposition.

In the face of social, religious, and political subversion, good men needed, Dwight argued, to unite themselves in concurrence with the present conduct of government. Particularly in times of crisis when individuals could not be apprised of the essential information for decision making must men place their confidence in their rulers. The only escape from utter ruin in the face of subversion was "union among ourselves, and unshaken adherence to the existing government." In a final war cry against the enemies of American society Dwight tried to rally his hearers to an "unshaken firmness": the "prime mean of great wealth, learning, wisdom, power and virtue; and without [which] nothing noble or useful is usually accomplished." As if he believed that the Bavarian Illuminati would incite real war, Dwight noted the "great sacrifices of property, of peace, and of life, we may be called to make." He also detailed the misery and affliction that might usher in the reign of the earthly "antichristian empire" that seemed imminent—all to ensure the obedience, the unity, and invincible firmness of Americans in the most alarming state of human affairs "since the deluge."[2]

Far from clerical ranting or the mere drivel of religious reactionism, Dwight's sermon was a profound, if popular, statement of social philosophy. What he was seeking was a new form of social obligation, a new glue for the body politic. Out of religious (that is, social) duty Americans would henceforth place their faith in their chosen rulers, buoy up the republican form of government, and spurn anything that threatened existing governance as infidelity. The corollaries of Dwight's reactionary doctrine were far-reaching and manifold. They were antidemocratic, antirevolutionary, and they grated against the young heritage of the American Revolution. While Dwight did not reveal in any detail the momentous implications of his new philosophy, they were certainly there not far beneath the surface. And in successive, ever more vociferous statements in the coming years, Dwight and the hundreds of other thinkers who shared his experiences would give flesh to their basic skeletal belief that Americans must choose and accept a different form of social obligation than that mediated to them by the American Revolution.

To understand the significance of the ideological about-face Dwight underwent in 1798, his peroration on the *Duty of Americans* must be put in the perspective of his career as a whole. Acutely conscious throughout his life of the tendencies and tone of American society, Dwight constantly mirrored the changing views and aspirations of New England's Revolutionary War generation. Born in Massachusetts and educated at Yale, Dwight (1752–1817) reached maturity as the crisis of the Revolution occurred. Already at Yale he exhibited in brief compositions the poetic genius that one contemporary believed would make him "our American poet." Although always delicate in health, he served briefly as a chaplain in the Continental Army during the war. His wartime service was followed by ordination as the Congregational clergyman at Greenfield, Connecticut, where he remained until succeeding Ezra Stiles as president of Yale in 1795. Whereas in his earlier years he could be characterized chiefly as clergyman and poet, after his inauguration at Yale he became a nationally known pundit of religion, society, and politics— "Pope Timothy" some called him. In the combined realms of Congregational religion, New England society, and Federalist politics, Dwight became in the late 1790s one of the most influential men in America.[3]

Dwight's reputation was first fixed soon after the American Revolution as he celebrated the twofold greatness and promise of America in the nation's first epic poem, the *Conquest of Canaan* (begun 1771; published 1785). Already in 1771 he had praised the rise of American liberty in a brief poem, *America*. But it was in the *Conquest,* which in 1778 he decided to dedicate to George Washington, that Dwight revealed a full absorption of Revolutionary ideology. In eleven books and more than three hundred printed pages Dwight emulated Alexander Pope's revival of the Augustan epic poem to praise the Revolutionary achievement of Americans. An allegory of the biblical account of Joshua's conquest of Canaan, Dwight's poem identified Washington as the great American hero who guided colonials to possession of the new Eden in America. Because the poem was begun before the onset of fighting and not completed until after the achievement of independence, the parts reflected various purposes from the defense of rebellion, to the creation of symbols of revolutionary beliefs, and on to the transfixing of historical events into ideological weapons.[4]

In the *Conquest* Dwight revealed unmistakably his fervent faith in the efficacy and desirability of republican revolutions and in the ability of American colonials to create "the last retreat of science, of freedom and of glory" and "the last retreat for poor oppress'd mankind." The Revolution was an act of united will in which men threw off the shackles of custom and authority, donned the garb of liberty, and prepared to reach for social and spiritual perfection. From the vantage of the struggle against British tyranny, Dwight could see only the unity of Americans under a common banner of justice and freedom launched on a glorious pathway toward the creation of an ideal, utopian America. In another poem penned in 1777, Dwight subsumed his faith symbolically in another telling idealistic couplet: "Columbia, Columbia, to glory arise, / The Queen of the world, and child of the skies!" Not until his dying days would Dwight's faith in America rebound to the lofty peak of the 1770s.[5]

From the conclusion of the Revolution to the end of the War of 1812, Dwight found himself in an unhappy cycle of boosting ideals only in turn to destroy them. In the phrase of a biographer, "one moment he was a Babbitt; the next, Jeremiah." Hardly had his ideal American union achieved its independence when Dwight placed himself in the vanguard of those who clamored for a more perfect union. In an address to the Constitutional Convention of 1787 and in a second lengthy poem a year later, Dwight unveiled the first inklings of mistrust, the first signs of a loss of faith in the glorious destiny of America. The *Conquest of Canaan* was followed by the *Triumph of Infidelity,* a less pretentious poem, which commingled withering Revolutionary ideology with a growing sense of alarm at the factionalism, the moral sickness, and splintering of American social life. Well before the achievements of the Revolution, Dwight began foreshadowing the war with Illuminism. Ever sensitive to the slightest alterations in the tone and fabric of society, Dwight in the 1790s already blamed America's troubles on the arrival of religious infidelity from Europe, where Satan's minions—the Tolands, Tindals, and Voltaires—spouted the stuff that could destroy "realms of freedom, peace, and virtue." Whereas he had previously praised the shedding of custom and authority, in 1788 he called for a new reverence for "grey-hair'd rules" as he noted that "Sway, uncoercive, is [merely] the shade of sway."[6]

By 1794 on the eve of the Illuminist crisis, Dwight had already lost the last semblance of faith in America. Whereas his closest associate in the battle against Illuminism, Jedidiah Morse, had not yet suffered the dramatic shock that would send him aimlessly into a head-on confrontation with French infidelity, Dwight was already demonstrating in another lengthy poem *Greenfield Hill* that he could no longer entertain any hope for America. Unable to think further in terms of a glorious American future, Dwight confined himself to the virtues of New England as found in the basic societal organism—the local community. *Greenfield Hill* was the first major poem in America to be directed primarily to a native audience and to develop a uniquely American localist language. Moreover, in creating a new literary technique, Dwight had begun to revalue American society and to establish a new ideal against which one might measure the progress of Americans. Although intensely provincial, his probe into the structures of village society was in reality an intellectual effort to find the principles along which American society might be reformed.[7]

Distraught with the European bombardment of America with utopian schemes and with the inability of Americans to live in factionless peace and quiet, Dwight portrayed the New England village as a frictionless and individualistic haven of republican equality. In the absence of either great wealth or grinding poverty, villagers were sheltered from the temptations of luxury and the meanness of want. The fact that all townsmen owned property in roughly equivalent portions and that all had to work to produce the means of living fostered a respect for property, for law, and the orderly progress of society. Property and individual competence were the links, the very foundations of republican authority and order. As new principles of republicanism emerged and as the foci of Dwight's social thought shifted from equalitarianism to authoritarianism, he began to burst the bounds of Revolutionary ideology and to experiment with a new American system of thought.[8]

Nothing reveals the cracks—indeed, the chasms—that time had wrought in the fabric of Revolutionary ideology any more clearly than Dwight's changing attitude toward slavery. In *Greenfield Hill* Dwight displayed a strangely equivocal position on slavery—one that both affirmed and denied the teachings of the Revolution. At one point he reinvoked the Revolutionary indictment of slavery "alike in church, in state, and household all," calling it variously "thou chief curse, since curses here began," "first infamy of man," and "laurel of the Infernal mind, / Proud Satan's triumph over lost mankind." But such epithets were reserved solely for what Dwight conceived to be the worst system of slavery in the world, that of the West Indies. In American slavery, by contrast, the position of the slave was without moral qualities. American slaves were proverbial black Sambos, free from the scars of cruelty, "kindly fed, and clad, and treated," and enabled to enjoy a life of song and dance. In America "law, from vengeful rage, the slave defends, / And here the gospel peace extends." The slave was an essential part of the household, sharing the master's toil, but also taking "his portion of the common good." The slave was so free from want and care that Dwight imagined "Lost liberty his sole, peculiar ill, / And fix'd submission to another's will."[9] For the first time Dwight conjoined attributes of both evil and good in his description of slavery, a constant juxtaposition that characterized American discussions of slavery from the 1790s until the rise of abolitionism. The commingling of both sides of slavery's character would confuse both contemporaries and historians as to Dwight's real views on human bondage.[10]

Greenfield Hill was but the first and the softest of Dwight's conscious rejections of the heritage of the American Revolution. Once he had believed that the Revolution had ushered in an age of universal improvement. By the late 1790s when it was coupled with the French Revolution, he came to see the American war as the first stroke in the march of man to final doom. Unlike most clergymen who did not become alarmed until the crisis of Illuminism, Dwight had been arguing in sermon and poem since the 1780s that religious infidelity and political democracy were on the verge of wreaking havoc with American society. Religious truth, respect for authority, and political stability were all parts of a whole upon which social order rested: "The same principles which support or destroy Christianity, alike support or destroy political order and government." Hence, in the late nineties when he began to lash out with renewed fervor against "Infidelity" of all sorts, he was not referring narrowly to religious errors, but to any tendency or group of people who threatened social order. His and other clergymen's use of such words as *infidel, libertarian,* and *Jacobin* introduced into American political and social rhetoric epithets that would be used unsparingly throughout the antebellum period.[11]

When Dwight mounted the rostrum to deliver his *Duty of Americans* in 1798, therefore, he had already clearly shifted his loyalties away from the American Revolution. Moreover, he was approaching the end of an intellectual pilgrimage during which he had developed a new system of thought, the basic tenets of which would inform his thoughts and actions for the remainder of his career. Tired of poetics and of the thankless pursuit of an American form of poetry, Dwight turned in the late 1790s to the sermon and to political oratory as the chief tools of alerting Americans to present dangers and of instilling in them his new form of social obligation. The *Duty of Americans* was among the earliest and most influential of his newly fashioned productions. With such other titles as *Vir-*

tuous Rulers a National Blessing, The True Means of Establishing Public Happiness, and *The Nature and Danger of Infidel Philosophy,* Dwight began to enunciate on the platform the essential principles of his new ideology. Every spoken or written pronouncement until his death became an occasion for defining a part of the whole.

At nearly the same time, in 1795, Dwight assumed the presidency of Yale and thereby entered into perhaps the most important and influential work of his career. Guided by his emerging social thought, he reshaped the university, appointed a new faculty, and established new programs that would remain essentially unchanged for half a century. From the platform of the Yale presidency he indoctrinated and sent forth generations of students steeped in his peculiar world view. His students, at first captive audiences to his authoritarian temper and afterward devoted disciples to his religious and social doctrines, migrated to every corner of America bearing Dwight's thought. Until the Civil War they provided America with perhaps its most powerful and cohesive educated elite. Since Yale, along with Princeton, produced a lion's share of America's college teachers and much of the nation's clerical elite in the early nineteenth century, it would be difficult to overestimate the extent of Dwight's personal influence.

From 1795 forward Dwight's moods, rhetoric, and teachings became a part of America's new conservative heritage. When he challenged all forms of infidelity—a constant theme in nearly all of his public pronouncements—he not only helped shape the views of his Connecticut hearers and a group of students, he also wedged into the minds of future generations of American leaders concepts and doctrines that would define their own beliefs and attitudes. When he helped Jedidiah Morse create hysterical fears of the Bavarian Illuminati in 1798, he contributed to the already well-exercised American ability to suspect conspiracies behind every social movement. When he blockaded social and political change, he taught Americans to fear alterations that might bring in their wake a reign of anarchy. Because of his peculiar position in New England, his style of leadership, and the decisiveness of his influence in both church and state, Dwight was charged during his lifetime as being "The Pope of Federalism," the "Monarch" of Connecticut, and "His Holiness Pope Timothy." Long after his death his name remained on the lips of apostles throughout America.[12]

Dwight's disenchantment with America and the nation's polity reached unprecedented nadirs in 1800 and 1812. In 1800 infidelity, libertarianism, Jacobinism, and all of the evil associated with those phenomena captured the nation in the form of Jeffersonian Republicanism. Jefferson's ascent to the presidency would surely, Dwight believed, bring final ruin to the nation. The prophet's worst fears seemed confirmed in 1812 when America stumbled headlong into a senseless war. At the onset of the war, in another of his fast-day proclamations, Dwight yelled his most frightened jeremiad: "At no time, since the deluge, has the situation of the human race been so extraordinary; the world so shaken; or its changes so numerous, sudden, extensive, and ominous." The doomsday he so long predicted had finally arrived. America in the hands of an antirepublican, antireligious, and anti–New England band of politicians reeled into the very clutches of Satan.[13]

Despite his frequent jeremiads of doom and his staunch resistance to the Virginia dynasty of Jefferson and Madison, Dwight found occasion after 1800 to have his hopes for the future buoyed up. Following the defeat of Federalism in 1800 and the transference of the locus of national power to the South, Dwight spoke and thought as the religious and cultural leader of a spurned minority. Despite a concerted program of revitalization among younger Federalists, their party remained a powerless minority until its final death in 1816. A die-hard Federalist, Dwight gave the party his unsparing support down through the Hartford Convention and the elections of 1816 when Connecticut finally turned Republican. The political situation reached its bottom limits during the war of 1812, when Dwight came to affirm that the American union would inevitably rupture and that his beloved New England would be released from bondage to an inimical central government. At least politically, in his last years Dwight was a hopeless sectionalist, an avowed disunionist.[14]

Ironically, however, Dwight's hopes for the future no longer were tied to the coattails of political success. Indeed, following the Federalist electioneering fiascoes of 1800 and 1804, he began to conceive of a well-ordered, purified society in which politicians and all of their ballyhoo counted for little. Why cater to the machinations of politicians, Dwight asked, when there are alternate leaders and institutions that can as effectively order, yes, even govern American society? And in every public lecture, essay, or debate, as well as in the private realm of his dreams for America, Dwight drew up the outlines of a new social organism in which religion and religious institutions provided the glue of social unity and acted as the catalytic agent for social renewal. Dwight was not thereby abandoning Federalism as a lost cause, appropriately entombed forever. Indeed, in the striking words of a biographer, "New England Federalism had become his religion; New Light orthodoxy, his politics." Dwight's new social system centered in the realm of religion. But religion therein was the vehicle for an avowedly political or social end.[15]

Impetus and meaning were given to Dwight's new system of thought by a series of currents that were the first by-products of the ideological revolution of the 1790s. Dwight has long been credited as the fomenter and leader of such disparate religious movements as the Second Great Awakening and the Benevolent Empire. His role was crucial in both instances. Dwight's continued thumping of infidelity and irreligion set in motion in 1802 a religious revival on the Yale campus. That year one-third of the student body reportedly converted to religion. From Yale the new evangelicalism spread like wildfire to the other college campuses and then through the villages and towns of New England. Although he never took credit for launching the Second Great Awakening, both his contemporaries and historians have attributed the movement to his leadership. By the same token, Dwight, along with his confederate Jedidiah Morse and his uncle Jonathan Edwards the younger, prepared the way for the seminal Plan of Union (1801) between Congregational and Presbyterian churches in America. A program that was consciously conceived to unite the "illiberal" and orthodox of both religious communions and to provide orderly religious cultivation of new settlements in the West, the Plan of Union created the organizational skeleton on which the more fleshy Benevolent Empire would grow. Without the close cooperation of Congregationals and Presbyterians, the latter development would have been unthinkable.[16]

Dwight's revivalism at Yale and the unification of orthodox Congregationalists and Presbyterians were nearly reflex actions to a perceived crisis at the turn of the century. The theologizing and institutionalization of his new system of thought in religious and social organizations over the next twenty years combined both reflex and initiative. As a cultural and social spokesman for a minority region, Dwight began the nineteenth century thinking only in terms of saving New England and the northeast from social destruction. After seeing the first phases of the Second Great Awakening turn the heads of countless New Englanders, Dwight wrote Morse, "I think New England will be saved from ruin."[17]

In the pages of the *New England Palladium* and later the *Panoplist,* both edited by Morse, Dwight spelled out ever more expansive systems of social renovation. At first he urged clergymen into politics and the perpetuation of the Congregational church establishment in New England. Clergymen were particularly aware of the need for social stability, for decent manners, and for "a steady course of wise governmental measures." Without proper religion and an adequate ecclesiastical authority, society would lapse into a total morass of irreligion, immorality, injustice, and inevitable anarchy. Clerical power, by the properly educated clergymen, was the key to the future. Despite the fact that Dwight fought valiantly for the continued church establishment, when the end came in Connecticut, he was not alarmed. He had already proceeded to a new social system in which clergymen served as the chief social statesmen in America, quite irrespective of the reigning political order.[18]

If clerical power was the key to a revitalized America, a particular kind of religious order would reign supreme in the new society. Once again in the *Palladium,* the *Panoplist,* and four massive and popular volumes of *Travels; in New England and New York* Dwight detailed the future religious pattern. At first he thought to make Connecticut into a new Zion where the clergy and right religion reigned supreme. If the remainder of America passed into infidelity, at least Connecticut would survive. But as the tempo of the revivals picked up and as the Benevolent Empire began to take shape, Dwight drew plans to "Connecticutize" the world. He came to believe that one found in Connecticut the purest expression of republicanism. The religious and social institutions of Connecticut, he thought, could serve as the models for the rest of New England and, indeed, for all of America. Hence, in the *Travels,* which consumed much of his interest in his final years, Dwight drew up a blueprint for restructuring nearly every village and every town in northeastern America. Well aware that only a small portion of America had yet been settled and that New England might someday be engulfed by an untamed frontier, Dwight mapped out the methods of "settling in the New England manner" and of building towns to "assume the general New-England character."[19]

In the minutiae of Dwight's rambling *Travels,* his sermons and essays, one can discover the unmistakable flanges of certain steadfast social principles. Conservatism became his theology, his social doctrine, and his principle of action. New England would align with Old England to launch a world religious revival. Through religious education Americans would be taught the virtues and powers of microcosmic governments, particularly the family and the village. There were even harmonious manners in which homes and public buildings should be built to symbolize for Americans the multiple needs for order, property, and beauty. Whatever would teach Americans to revere authority, to appreciate stability, to render deference became the object and end of all his thinking and teaching. And his hopes for the successful nurturing of rising generations were bound inextricably with the prosperity of religion and religious institutions.[20]

For a man who projected every emotion and every observation into social teachings and whose hopes and fears were always linked directly to the tone of society, Dwight arrived in his final years at a seemingly paradoxical peace with America. Three separate writings between 1813 and 1816 expressed various facets of the final, most permanent views of Dwight and his generation of New Englanders. In *Decisions of Questions Discussed by the Senior Class in 1813 and 1814* (published 1833) Dwight summarized time and again in open discussions of delicate social and political issues his disenchantment with the results of the American Revolution and the evolution of America as an independent nation. He condemned the notion that America was the last great hope of man, cast aspersions upon the once-honored Continental Army, and dwelt upon his firm conviction that the United States would not long stand as a unity. Civil war among Americans seemed if not imminent, inevitable: "I fear we may not stand long. I shall not see our fall, but you may." He rejected the American Revolution and all of its ideological cant. He no longer believed that America could establish a viable, permanent national government. It seemed only a question of time before the nation would fly apart in civil war.[21]

The same spirit breathed through his *Remarks on the Review of Inchiquin's Letters* (1815), his final defense of the society and manners of New England against critical foreigners and one of the most remarkable written indices of the views of his generation of New England leaders. Whereas once he had written that he was "an American, a republican, and a Presbyterian," in the *Remarks* he declared, "I am a federalist, and a *New Englander; a Yankee.*" Whereas throughout most of his long career he had defended America against critical British writers, in the *Remarks* he aligned himself with Britain against the American government. The war that America was waging against Britain and America's alliance with France were "in my opinion unnatural, impolitic, causless, and unjust." Casting his bitterest aspersions upon Jeffersonian Republicanism and the administration of James Madison, Dwight attempted to prove that New Englanders both in politics and social views were at one with the ultraconservative English governing elite. England was "a barrier against the ruin of the world," the home of pristine anti-Jacobinism, and the launching pad for world religious renewal—in brief, the only proper ally of New England Congregationalism and politics. Having long rejected the social ideology of the American Revolution, in 1815 Dwight seemed ready to forfeit the political outcome of the war he had once described as the "conquest of Canaan."[22]

Dwight's mature social conservatism as expressed in the *Remarks* had a profound effect on his views of Negro slavery. Although he hated the Virginia dynasty and the very society that spewed it forth and although he felt no compulsion any longer to defend anything that was not an ingredient of New England society, the rampaging conservatism that tinctured all of his other views and those of his comrades finally blinded him to the evils of slavery. He still believed the slave trade to be consonant with "infernal avarice" and slave laws "the proper themes of every moralist." But when British writers scored slavery as a fatal defect in American society, Dwight blanched and came back fighting. The fine buildings of Liverpool, the center of the British slave trade, he charged, "were built of human bones, and cemented with human blood." Furthermore, under the very eye of Parliament (that is, in the British West Indies), "slavery exists in forms, and degrees, incomparably more horrid, than in the Southern *American* States." After proving from various reports to Parliament the truth of his contentions, Dwight concluded, "The Southern Planter, who receives slaves from his parents by inheritance, certainly deserves no censure for holding them." Moreover, "If he treats them with humanity, and faithfully endeavours to Christianize them, he fulfills his duty, so long as his present situation continues." Whereas once he had called slavery "thou chief curse, since curses here began," by 1815 Dwight had resigned himself and America to the practice of perpetual servitude.[23]

Judging from the past record of Timothy Dwight's hopes and fears, of cyclical recurrences of optimism and pessimism, his faith in the future of America should have reached an all-time low in 1816 and 1817. Events in Connecticut and New England bore all of the marks of a complete reversal of everything Dwight had sought over the last twenty years of his life. The Hartford Convention had devolved into a miserable, embarrassing failure. For the first time in 1816 Federalists lost control of the Connecticut legislature. A Republican governor committed to the total disestablishment of religion, to the ending of tax support for Congregational churches and clergy, and to the elimination of religious tests for public office entered the statehouse. And what was occurring in Connecticut was only one of the fruits of a national tide that swept Federalism as an organized political force from American political life.

By all rights Dwight should have been prophesying doom again in 1816. Strangely, however, in his last extensive written comments on America that year Dwight revealed greater optimism than at any point in his career since the American Revolution. In a series of articles entitled "Observations on the Present State of Religion in the World," Dwight documented the grounds on which he could rejoice and participate in an era of national good feelings. The devastating defeat handed Federalism and the Congregational establishment seemed to unleash an era of unbounded religious prosperity. The Second Great Awakening seemed to be picking up where it had left off in the early years of the new century. The Benevolent Empire was rapidly extending its influence to every corner of America. With political struggles removed to the caucus room, nothing stood in the way of revived Congregationalism spreading its message throughout America. Dwight's final message, in fact, reinvoked the stirring idealism of the *Conquest of Canaan,* albeit without the political triumph of his youthful vision: "I am constrained to believe a new era in the moral concerns of man to have commenced; and anticipate from this period a new order of things, in the affairs of our world, in which Religion of the Gospel will rise in all its majesty, beneficence, and glory, to the astonished and delighted view of mankind."[24]

Whereas Dwight had once operated as the religious spokesman for a dying, yet tenacious political minority, in 1816 he transferred all of his energies and allegiance to an emerging religious and social network that, properly indoctrinated and effectively controlled, could succeed where politicized Federalism had failed. For the first time since the 1780s and the Constitutional Convention, Dwight could again think in terms of the whole of America. Shedding his recent sectionalism, Dwight suddenly realized that the new religious order he had helped to build since the fateful days of the Bavarian Illuminati might just be capable of reorganizing America, of gluing together a new society about which he had dreamed and spoken all the time he had been helping to prop up a discredited Federalist-Congregational establishment. So recently a secessionist, he now became a most ardent Unionist, a nationalist eager to export his version of the Second Great Awakening, his Yale graduates, his conservative social philosophy, and his vision of Connecticutized society to the rest of America. While he was only one man and merely part of a larger social and ideological process, his contributions to a new America and to a new framework for the discussion of slavery were telling and perhaps unmatched.

Timothy Dwight was only one of the players, albeit a principal one, in the drama that began with Federalist political ascendancy and ended with the creation of a new conservative ideology that would ultimately transform American society and its social institutions. While historians have long portrayed the demise of the Federalist party and the rise of a one-party system as the crucial development in American polity during the first decades of the nineteenth century, a far more important and ultimately much more far-reaching alteration was the psychological and ideological transformation experienced by Timothy Dwight, his compatriots, and their followers. For although America's political future remained in flux from the age of Washington to the age of Jackson, the ideological revolution wrought by some New Englanders and other thoughtful individuals throughout the North grew constantly and feverishly without abatement or significant alteration from the 1790s until the unhappy rendezvous of the nation with abolitionism in the 1830s. While America's politicians were groping toward the nation's eventual modern two-party system, others who had been largely disillusioned by party politics went about the work of teaching a new conservative ideology to a society that had recently refused to adopt a political system that could accommodate social and moral philosophies. And this general process of ideology formation and transference to the general length and breadth of American society might best be denominated America's conservative "counterrevolution."

In a revision of traditional interpretations of Federalism, David Hackett Fischer found ample political ferment among a national cohort of what he termed "young Federalists" to argue that after 1800 Federalism was very nearly translated into a viable, popularly oriented vote-seeking political party. Youthful Federalists shared the principles, if they did not win the undivided support, of their immediate political forebears. That they would sink to the level of using partisan newspapers, secret political societies, and the electioneering techniques of Jeffersonians irritated Federalists of the "old school." A predictable rift resulted between the two generations of Federalists. Except for the "chance coincidence" of the Hartford Convention, the Treaty of Ghent, and the battle of New Orleans—disunity notwithstanding—Fischer suggested, the Federalist party might have been fully revolutionized and might have withstood the stranglehold Jeffersonians held over dissenting politicians.[25]

Although Fischer disclaimed any intention of explaining the ultimate disintegration of the Federalist party, his story of attempts to revolutionize Federalism comprised the last chapter in the efforts of Federalist politicos to regain the prestige and power that had been theirs in the 1790s. Even the youthful Federalists who attempted to cloak elitism with the rhetoric of democracy saw their demagogic tactics only hasten the broadening of political power and bring more representatives from the lower ranks into government. In any case, with little noise and less ceremony, the Federalist party disappeared after 1816 from the realm of organized American politics forever.[26]

It might not be an exaggeration to suggest, however, that the Federalist party died precisely because many former Federalists embraced a new conservative philosophy after 1800 that could not easily be reined in by a popular party. In a society in which political organization drifted increasingly toward electioneering institutions, the only route toward the implementation of broad social principles lay outside the political arena. Federalists of the old school did not cooperate fully with their younger colleagues precisely because the party elders were experimenting with and discovering other avenues through which they could spread their principles in American society without the political baggage they detested. Whereas 1816 should have been a time for mourning the passage of the Federalist party, it was a time of exultation for such men as Timothy Dwight. By that year his conservative counterrevolution broke the bounds of party politics and began a course of rapid expansion, unhampered by the need for expending energy on the winning of elective offices.[27]

While some former Federalist officeholders may have pined for the influence that government positions had once given them, after 1816 other former Federalists—particularly clergymen who severed all ties with the political world—placed all of their hopes in the re-establishment of right religion, the dissemination of correct education, and the creation of a Benevolent Empire.[28] The first phases of social reform that became a hallmark of antebellum American society were actually expressions of their conservative ideology in action finally directed away from politics toward the very sinews of American society. Social and religious reform in the early nineteenth century stemmed directly from the efforts of disillusioned New England conservative clergymen and countless other secular leaders to reassert themselves as the arbiters and their social philosophies as the guiding principles of American society.[29]

While the world of politics remained in flux between 1816 and the 1830s, the new conservatives and their disciples could be seen in all walks of life teaching America an ideological lesson fashioned since the crises of the 1790s. Timothy Dwight's reactions and innovations were but part of the larger experiences of those whom one historian has described as "Federalists in dissent." Those thoughtful Federalists who demurred at Jeffersonian America and its politics shared many beliefs and came with time to espouse jointly a plan of social renovation. More than most Americans they experienced first the thrills and then the disappointments of an ambiguous Revolutionary heritage. The Revolution promised both political independence from the Old World and the opportunity to build a culturally unique society. The promise of an independent America seemed so great that many of them anticipated the onset of an Augustan age that would rival those of Caesar Augustus in Rome and of England under Queen Anne and the first two Georges.[30]

The Augustan dreams of the early 1780s rapidly shattered in a barrage of disappointments ranging from economic depression to constitutional quibbling, from entanglement in the maze of international politics to the threat of subversion from abroad, and from factional politics to an internal partisan revolt. At first sure of their position, these unhappy Federalists sneered at their opponents and placed themselves above the common sort who seemed ever ready to resort to mobbism and violence. Their confidence was finally shaken in the mid-1790s to the point that subversive plots on the part of their enemies seemed not only plausible, but real. When the nation reeled out of their control in 1800, there followed "a social transformation, the extent of which we are only beginning to appreciate," to use the phrases of Linda Kerber, a knowledgeable historian of Federalist thought.[31]

The transformation was radical, taking erstwhile Federalists from full reverence for the American Revolution to a reactionary critique of anything that smacked of being French or Jeffersonian. Insofar as the counterrevolution was philosophical, reactionary Federalists replaced Locke with Edmund Burke. When they spoke about subversion, intrigue, and social anarchy, they invoked Burke's scathing invective against the French Revolution. Although they continued to believe that the Ameri-

can Revolution had been a great achievement in the history of man, they
began to see the French Revolution and Jeffersonian plans for a new
America as pure nonsense. Revolutions and all social experimentation
came to seem visionary, impractical, and anarchical. Man could not re-
make the world; he could only remodel its periphery. Experience in social leadership was the only proper antidote for plagues of ill-advised
experimentation. Little did they realize that in terms of the tendencies
already at work in American society that their rhetoric and visions were
fully as revolutionary, if not more so, than the notions they sought to
combat.[32]

The emerging conservative ideology clashed sharply not only with
Jeffersonian alternatives but also with America's Revolutionary heritage.
Jeffersonian thought and policy were viewed as aberrations of the Revolutionary heritage. Jeffersonian polity equaled democracy, and democracy meant chaos. Jefferson, the conservative Federalists believed, would
lead a revolution against the customs and habits on which social order
and patterned behavior rested. Worst of all, a Jeffersonian revolution
portended a rapid decline of deferential behavior, the disappearance of
those distinctions that made gentlefolk the superiors over lesser sorts. In
theory, if not in practice, Jeffersonian Democrats (never Republicans in
their rhetoric) espoused the completion of revolution in America—the
melting away of social distinctions, the discontinuation of bankrupt
customs, and the widening of political participation. And those were
precisely the new measures that Federalists could not abide.[33]

The longer the conservative counterrevolutionaries pondered threats
to stability after the French Revolution the more they depreciated America's Revolutionary heritage. As they surveyed the uprisings and violence
of the 1790s, they became convinced that Americans had an unquencha-
ble penchant for mob action as a ready instrument with which to register
grievances. Mobs had played an important role in the winning of independence, perhaps the most striking display of violence in early American history. But in the 1790s and afterward the same tools could have
been employed against the nation's governing elite. The fears of mob
violence were heightened by their belief that the numbers of permanently poor, particularly in the cities, grew rapidly with each passing
year. More and more Americans were becoming dependent upon employers for sustenance, shattering the agrarian myth that Jefferson was
simultaneously creating. By combining the natural tendency of Americans toward violence with widespread permanent poverty, they feared

that the nation might be on the verge of a revolution as radical as that of France.[34]

Timothy Dwight vented his view that America could at any moment devolve into a mobocracy in a long satire entitled *Morpheus* in 1801. In a dramatic scene, normally commonsensical people were thrust into mob violence by a philosopher who proposed the destruction of private property and family structures. The philosopher did not goad his listeners nor did he threaten them personally. Rather with unreasonable suddenness the people turned on him, killed him, and dismantled anything that fell in their path. In just such an illogical moment without notice, Dwight and his fellows believed, America could have turned into a sea of seething violence. And the expectation of such an end was perhaps most intense at the moment Dwight wrote, just as America had passed into the hands of men who did not understand the depraved, unreasonable nature of man.[35]

With Jeffersonians in power and the Federalist party bankrupt, the conservative revolutionaries had to develop new means of action that could circumvent Democratic-Republican hegemony but that could promise effective social control in terms of very definite ideological principles. They desperately wanted to achieve the type of Republicanism in America that had been a part of their fondest dreams of an Augustan age. They wanted to promote stability and the respect for order, authority, and property. In brief, they envisioned a virtuous, moral citizenry willing to obey, ready to fulfill social obligations, and eager to extol proper social values. Not strangely, many of them came to the conclusion that they did not need to control the bodies of men to instill virtue and morality.

If they could not control men's politics, they could at least capture those instrumentalities that swayed minds. The press, the pulpit, and the schools were institutions outside the sway of government (at least after 1815). Through the press they could ensure that Americans would read only proper views. With correct views, the pulpit could be used to promote virtue and proper conduct. By means of controlling education from the cradle up, they could create a new generation with all of the knowledge and values of true republicans. In the words of Linda Kerber, they concluded rightly, "Only a virtuous citizenry would sustain a republic and, in a sinful world, a virtuous citizenry was made, not born."[36]

The conservative counterrevolution bore fruit in every arena of the American social system always as a counterpoise to both Jeffersonian

and political alternatives. In the realm of scientific inquiry, the Boston
Academy of Arts and Sciences became the tool of learned conservatives
who wished to rival and outwit the Philadelphia-based, Jeffersonian
American Philosophical Society. The Boston Academy reflected a conservative religious preference for natural philosophy as opposed to the
Jeffersonian love of natural history as the proper mode of inquiry.
Whereas the Jeffersonian body held religious knowledge, particularly
the biblical record, at arm's length and attempted to study revelation
scientifically, the Boston Academy fielded a frontal attack against religious skepticism, upholding the Scriptures as divine truth.[37]

While political Federalists had once been the prime detractors from
the basic American freedoms of the press, untrammeled expression, and
religion, after 1800 they switched roles with Jeffersonians and became
the defenders of such rights. As the party in power Federalists wished to
crush all forms of dissent. As a spurned and jeopardized minority they
upheld the right to dissent and sought to make every newspaper, every
book, and every piece of literature conservative in sentiment. Having
learned in 1800 the power of a united national press behind Jefferson's
victory, conservative former Federalists devoted themselves to a long-
range plan of dominating insofar as possible all the tools of knowledge
and opinion. As Fisher Ames joined Timothy Dwight and Jedidiah
Morse in establishing the pace-setting national Federalist organ the *New
England Palladium* in 1801, he wrote, "let the interest of the country be
explained and asserted by able men who have had a concern in a transac-
tion of affairs, who understand those interests, and who will, and ever
will, when they try to produce a deep national impression."[38]

Conservative leadership in the fonts of knowledge through science
and the printed word actually served as mere adjuncts to the two realms
in which their domination became most complete. In religion and education they found the keys to renovating American society in their own
image. Since Jeffersonians traditionally exercised restraint, if not indifference, toward institutional religion, America's churches remained an
open field for the infiltration of conservative ideology and properly indoctrinated clergymen. The Second Great Awakening and the burgeoning Benevolent Empire offered the occasion and the mechanisms
whereby their ideas and programs could be inserted as seemingly the
natural work of mainstream Protestantism. Through the Plan of Union
and other cooperative projects with Presbyterians, the great bulk of
America's educated, responsible, and socially sensitive clergy were

united in a purposive superstructure, which brought order to the chaotic denominationalism of post-Revolutionary America. With time, the Calvinist conservative phalanx would move into the citadels of evangelical Methodists and Baptists, who were forwarding their own religious awakening, and help shape their outlooks on American society.

The early nineteenth-century contagion of conservative ideology was most notable in the field of education. Through their domination of key centers of learning, conservative educators and their disciples had a far-reaching impact on the content and scope of education at all levels and at all places in American society. At the same time educational institutions were winning the battle for legal independence with a minimum of governmental interference, conservative thought and techniques were making them uniform. They waged war on Jeffersonian proposals to modernize education with the study of practical subjects and modern languages and to democratize educational opportunities. The study of science, without prior indoctrination in natural philosophy, was not only Jeffersonian, but was also subversive of religion. Instruction in French and German could not be accomplished without the seeping in of modern forms of European infidelity. Conservative counterrevolutionaries knew that Noah Webster was correct when he remarked that American colleges were "nurseries of Inequalities, the enemies of liberty." But then they were violently against any further leveling through the Jeffersonian contagion of liberty. And they were as firmly opposed to any sort of national university from which Jeffersonian ideas might radiate throughout the nation.[39]

The cornerstone of their educational program was their conservative ideology. Positively, they proposed a full-scale salvaging of the classical tradition. If a young man were steeped in the philosophy of ancient Greece, the political thought of Greece and Rome, and the classical languages, he would be insulated against all of the booby-traps of modern infidel thought. The preference for classical learning was not mere traditionalism nor the conservative encrustation of threatened patterns of education. Rather their battle to salvage classical thought was an aggressive assault on the foundations of Jeffersonian Republicanism. Conservatives were convinced that Jeffersonianism was democracy and that all forms of modern democracy drew their inspiration from the French Revolution, which, in turn, equated social and political anarchy. The only true republics were those with rigidly structured societies, with clear-cut class differentiation, and with firmly established patterns of au-

thority. Rome and Greece were obviously the foremost examples of republican societies. Hence, the conservative counterrevolutionists fostered a culture in their propaganda and educational programs that
foreshadowed and long dwarfed that of the Old South.[40]

Instead of Jeffersonian Republicanism radiating from a national university after 1800, northern colleges and schools, tightly in the grasp of
conservative ideologues, began exporting graduates fully indoctrinated
with their philosophy. The Congregational colleges of New England and
the Presbyterian schools of the Middle States, united by the conviviality
of sentiments and denominational cooperation, launched a frontal assault on educational institutions and programs at all levels throughout
America. Their graduates taught conservative ideology and preached
religious orthodoxy wherever they went, until they succeeded in dictat-
ing the shape of American education throughout the antebellum period.

The pace-setting schools, not surprisingly, were Yale and Princeton,
the most prolific hotbeds of the conservative counterrevolution. While
Timothy Dwight made Yale the pre-eminent conservative training
school of New England, Samuel Stanhope Smith (1750–1819) made the
Presbyterian College of New Jersey a similar bulwark for the middle and
southern states. As in the case of Dwight, Smith's sermons, lectures, and
pamphlets after 1800 bristled with conservative thought. Unlike Dwight,
however, near the end of his career, Smith transcribed and published his
long-rehearsed *Lectures on Moral and Political Philosophy* (1812), a work
that served as a veritable textbook of conservative ideology for the generation of leaders who ruled antebellum America.[41] If Yale and Princeton trained up new generations of conservative social leaders, Andover
and Princeton theological seminaries, the respective creations of Congregational and Presbyterian orthodoxy, served a similar function for
prospective clergymen.

By 1815 when conservative counterrevolutionaries were in the process
of solidifying their burgeoning control of the press, the pulpit, and the
educational systems of America, their ideological revolution was entering into its heyday in the former Federalist stronghold of New England.
It had its beginnings with the reemergence of a well-exercised fear of
conspiracy in the face of shock waves radiating from revolutionary
France. In one of the two great emotional crises between the Revolution
and the Civil War, conservative former Federalists in the 1790s lurched
from their lingering adherence to the ideals of the American Revolution
and began rallying around a social philosophy as conservatively reaction-

ary as any in American history. From their tilting with largely imaginary emissaries of Illuminism and agents of French intrigue, the new revolutionaries developed a language, an emotion-laden rhetoric, for dealing with real or imagined subversives who threatened the order and stability of American republicanism. Through continued rehearsal and constant application of antisubversive rhetoric to all foes, foreign and domestic, they made anticonspiratorial thought and language essential ingredients in the American social and political consciousness. During the administrations of Jefferson and Madison they added ideological flesh to the reactionary skeleton of thought born in the crises of the 1790s. The impulse to rethink American ideals, to reassess social and cultural values proved so compelling that an ideological counterrevolution was set in motion that clashed sharply with America's Revolutionary heritage and with Jeffersonian alternatives. Conservative ideology absorbed Calvinist theology, Federalist political theory, and conservative social values and then blended those disparate elements into a new amalgam of coherent ideas, forming a new symbol system as a program of action.

The new conservative movement was, moreover, largely non-political—in some cases antipolitical in character. Many of the new conservatives, most notably clergymen, severed all connections with party politics, expressing utter disgust with the office hunting mania that infected Americans. Timothy Dwight spoke the sentiments of most nineteenth century clergymen and many disaffected Federalists when in 1813 he complained that "party-spirit" was one of the greatest crimes of mankind.[42] Hence, few bemoaned the death of the Federalist party. Many former Federalists found happy and prosperous careers in the Republican party until the political system reshuffled in the 1830s. Many others, however, followed once-Federalist clergymen into the realm of nonpolitical social activity, supporting religious, educational, and benevolent reforms with characteristic fervor. But wherever they went, whether into Republican politics or into social reform, they carried along with them the ideology of the conservative counterrevolution.

In assessing the extent of the counterrevolution by 1815, it is important to note that south of New Jersey the movement was almost unknown. Some southern Americans shared the emotional experiences that gave birth to conservative ideology, but their numbers were few. The South was, in fact, largely insulated by the popularity of the Jeffersonians, the ascendancy of Jeffersonian thought, and regional cultural backwardness from any massive ideological shift until well into the nineteenth century. Except for the rather small political and social elites who managed southern affairs, little occurred between 1790 and 1830 to challenge the calm engendered by the rise of Jefferson and other prominent southerners to national power. Although a few historians in recent years have strained diligently to find the seeds of conservative thought in the South during these years, their efforts have yielded only a few tortured examples of elder statesmen rethinking the shape of the national government and state leaders arguing governance of the states. And even though little attention has been given to social and cultural thought in the South during the Federal and Jeffersonian years, it seems clear that no conservative movement was in the making that could compare with the conservative counterrevolution percolating throughout New England.[43]

It seems safe to conclude that insofar as southerners shared public convictions at all, they were rather nominally oriented toward the perpetuation of Revolutionary ideology as rendered to them by the Jeffersonians. It is therefore not strange that long after northern counterrevolutionaries had developed a distinctly conservative ideology and had largely rejected Revolutionary thought, southerners continued to speak and think in terms of the Revolutionary heritage. Southerners were not simply acting the parts of hypocrites when they continued to toast "Liberty and Union, now and forever" well into the antebellum period. They spoke as libertarians because through the first three decades of the nineteenth century nothing had occurred to upset the calm, to force a reevaluation of America's Revolutionary heritage. Until the abolition crises of the 1830s, southerners remained quite happily and unthinkingly imitators of America's Revolutionary ideology.[44]

It is important to note that whatever impact the conservative counterrevolution had on important issues of social thought, especially the subject of slavery, before the 1830s, the influence was limited largely to the North and more particularly New England. However, the conservative counterrevolution forged a new framework for the discussion of slavery and, in fact, eventually provoked a total reassessment of slavery in American polity. But until the rise of abolitionism, except in isolated instances, only northerners and New Englanders fell under the irresistible sway of the counterrevolutionary ideology and its portentous conclusions for the institution of slavery. Conservative thought would eventually penetrate the South and help shape southern perceptions of slavery, but not until after northern conservative ideologues had charted the course.

By gathering several crucial sets of data concerning the conservative former Federalists' views on slavery and the Negro, the question arises in a stark and inescapable form whether they were not actually proponents of slavery. Although historians have long assumed that New England Federalists were the fathers of abolitionism, the assumption cannot be founded on all of the available evidence. From whatever perspective one might choose to look, one is driven to the conclusion that many former Federalists were the fomenters of a new tradition that, if it was not identical with the grosser forms of American proslavery, certainly helped to lay the foundations for America's antebellum proslavery tradition.

In the first place, it is clear that northern conservatives, not southerners, were the first Americans to revive the defense of slavery in public, polemic writings following the American Revolution. The first interrelated and extensive outpouring of defenses of slavery after the Revolution came between 1810 and 1820 in the transatlantic *Inchiquin* controversy.[45] All of the authors of that spate of nationalistic writings (Charles J. Ingersoll, Samuel S. Smith, Timothy Dwight, James Kirke Paulding, and Robert Walsh) began their careers as Federalists. Two of them (Smith and Dwight) were Federalists of the old school and among the first ranks in Federalist leadership and social thought. Two others (Ingersoll and Walsh) ranked as significant "young" Federalists who attempted to revitalize the Federalist party after 1800. Although Paulding's identity with Federalism did not extend beyond his family origins, he bore all of the marks of his upbringing as he entered into public life. The remarkable thing about the five men is that as a group they shared nothing whatsoever in common other than their experience with Federalism. Although Smith and Dwight were much older than the other three, all five experienced the conservative counterrevolution and came to share a common body of thought. Their writings bristled with counterrevolutionary ideology. But only Walsh ventured to carry the new conservative perspective on slavery to its logical end by evaluating American slavery as a positive good.

That northern conservatives should have revived the defense of slavery in the early years of the nineteenth century ought to come as no surprise to anyone who has examined their attitude toward the Negro. If in the course of the conservative counterrevolution they proved themselves no enemies of slavery, neither did they come across as friends of the Negro once their counterrevolution got under way. Although they sometimes feigned enmity for slavery (causing some historians to see some of them as the fathers of antislavery), their animus was actually a hatred of what one of them called the "slave driving nabobs of Virginia," that is, affluent Jeffersonians. In their rhetoric, they were often harshly critical of the effects of slavery on both master and slave. But their contempt for both Virginia slaveholders and the Negro far overshadowed their dislike of slavery. Slave society was aberrant because it produced misguided leaders. Slavery was a military liability because of the constant threat of insurrection, and it gave masters political and economic benefits not enjoyed by slaveless men. The little criticism of slavery that did proceed from conservative Federalist quarters was largely the result of political expediency and not a product of regard for the Negro.[46]

Among the major tenets of the conservative position on slavery were a patent disregard for the effects of slavery on the Negro, an inordinate fear of slave uprisings, and a growing approbation for various schemes of colonization or expulsion. One of the ways in which politicized Federalists combated Jeffersonian equalitarianism was to suggest that Jefferson would extend equal rights not only to white rabble but also to free blacks and eventually to slaves. Moreover, when they argued that the three-fifths clause in the Constitution that gave southerners undue political advantage should be abolished, they wanted an abolition of representation in Congress based on any Negro population and not an emancipation of slaves. When the Gabriel conspiracy and uprising came to light in 1800, Federalists generally expressed little sympathy for southern masters and even less for the "distracted blacks." Although the New England stronghold of conservatism lay well outside the slave South, Conservatives proved that they were a part of American slave society by the frequent expression of fears that a slave uprising in the South might lead to a general social upheaval.[47]

One of the most remarkable facets of Federalist attitudes toward the Negro was the widespread discussion of race and consequent acceptance of colonization as the proper remedy for America's peculiar institution. While considerations of race and debates on colonization may have been of absorbing interest in Virginia alone before 1800, in the Jefferson era Federalists were chief among those concerned with race and slavery as intellectual and social problems. Samuel Stanhope Smith was nearly alone among northerners in 1787 when he read his *Essay on the Causes of the Variety of Complexion and Figure in the Human Species* before the American Philosophical Society. But when he doubled the length of the essay and published it as a book in 1810, he was merely one voice in a chorus of conservative Federalists who attempted to combat Jeffersonian heresy on the question of race. In his *Notes on the State of Virginia,* also published in 1787, Jefferson had cast doubt on the equality of men and thereby on the common origin of the human species. Such notions pandered easily to growing beliefs that Negroes were of an inferior race, a widespread phenomenon in the young American republic. But more importantly from the perspective of religious orthodoxy, suggestions of multiple racial origins disagreed with the biblical account of creation and threatened the entire aura of authority that orthodox Protestants attributed to the Bible.[48]

The conservative counterrevolution adhered strongly to Christian orthodoxy and made the Bible its most authoritative standard. In response to the infidel ideas of Jefferson and others with regard to race, conservative thinkers launched a defense of the racial unity of mankind that persisted doggedly against all detractors until after the Civil War. Samuel Stanhope Smith and his contemporaries relied upon environmental influences as the cause of racial variation in their quest to answer skeptics of Genesis.[49] Later defenders would use evidence from studies in natural science and anthropology to counter an equally adept American School of Ethnology. But throughout the long struggle, the defenders of human unity were animated by the exigencies of ideological consistency and not regard for the plight of the Negro. Hence, irrespective of their views on the proper disposition of American slaves, both the conservatives and their ideological sons were of one mind on the question of race. Both the conservatives and their followers proved that the most avid proponents of the brotherhood of all men were not necessarily the greatest friends of the Negro nor the least tinged with racism.[50]

At only one point did conservative counterrevolutionaries and Jeffersonian attitudes toward the Negro converge. Both factions came to agree that the Negro had no ultimate future in America and that when the republican edifice of the United States was complete, America would be a white man's country. While the scheme of colonizing Negroes outside the United States may have been a dream most popular in Virginia before 1800, in the first decades of the nineteenth century conservative reactionaries gradually became the most vociferous proponents of Negro removal. An occasional conservative writer chided Jeffersonians for their apparent unwillingness to live alongside freed slaves. But for the most part conservatives gravitated toward colonization as a proper national policy. From a hint of Jonathan Edwards the younger in 1792 that the presence of a freed Negro population in America would create "a mungrel breed" to Samuel Stanhope Smith's suggestion in 1810 that freed Negroes should be separated from slaves on western lands, Negro removal became ever more palatable to conservative consciences. By the mid-1820s, colonization became part and parcel of the conservative scheme for reorganizing American society.[51]

It was not merely in the realm of implicit attitudes that conservative counterrevolutionaries established the pattern for the resurgence of proslavery. Some were overt proponents of slavery and were understood by their contemporaries to be nothing less. In the rather infrequent debates on slavery in Congress during the 1790s certain particularly acerbic conservatives established the pattern for anti-emancipationism. William Loughton Smith, a strait-laced conservative Federalist from South Carolina, guarded slavery like a hawk throughout the 1790s, always capable of blurting forth proslavery polemics. When Smith resigned in 1797, his place was taken by the equally vocal John Rutledge, Jr. On certain occasions, Smith and Rutledge found strong support from New England in the persons of Harrison Gray Otis and John Brown. In debate over the acceptance of a strongly worded antislavery petition from the free Negroes of Philadelphia in 1800, Otis of Massachusetts and Brown of Rhode Island buttressed the arguments of Rutledge with tirades against those who would encourage hopes for freedom among black slaves. Brown, a dabbler in the slave trade despite federal and state prohibitions, sneered at emancipationists and even upheld the slave trade as a benefit since it brought Africans to America. Aside from those Federalists only two Georgia Democrats, James Jackson and James Jones, expressed in Congress a similar conservatism on slavery.[52]

That the frequent expression of defenses of slavery by conservative counterrevolutionaries was considered, even at the time, as nothing less than proslavery is confirmed by the evaluations of their contemporaries. An excellent case in point is Samuel Stanhope Smith's *Lectures on the Subjects of Moral and Political Philosophy* "corrected and improved" for publication in 1812 after thirty-three years of rehearsal. In a lecture "On the Relation of Master and Servant" Smith launched into a discussion of slavery with characteristic post-Revolutionary assertions that slavery was inhumane and had "unhappily been suffered to mingle itself with the original institutions of our own country." It seemed equally "barbaric" to drag Africans from their native homes to America and unthinkable that once in America they should be returned. Having scored the twin evils of slavery and colonization, he then asked, "Is slavery on any ground consistent with the natural laws of justice and humanity?" Since historians have usually interpreted Smith's answer to this question as a flat denunciation of slavery with a "glacially conservative" program of action, it is important to note the views of Smith and his chief critic carefully.[53]

Instead of answering his question directly, Smith rushed into a catalogue of argument commonly used to uphold slavery. While servitude was "undoubtedly a hard lot to the sensibilities of freemen," it was not for slaves. Slaves had been "accommodated to it from their infancy." Their condition in America far exceeded what they had known in Africa. From long practice, slavery in America had become an extraordinarily mild institution. While universal emancipation might be "a worthy object of legislation even in America," Smith cautioned that no immediate general emancipation was either possible or desirable. Invoking fears long associated with slaveholders and more recently characteristic of conservative former Federalists, he warned, "great precaution must be used [not] to render their emancipation a worse evil than their servitude." Listing theft, plunder, violence, and idleness as the common behavior of freed Negroes, he continued, "No event can be more dangerous to a community than the sudden introduction into it of vast multitudes of persons, free in their condition, but without property, and possessing only the habits and vices of slavery." The only solution to the American dilemma Smith could see was gradual emancipation in combination with the settlement of free Negroes on the western frontier where they could not associate with and perhaps incite slaves to rebellion.[54]

Although Smith's response to his own crucial question may have seemed ambiguous and contradictory to historians, one of his contemporaries, writing in 1816, concluded that Smith had "involved himself in a labyrinth; from which by no ingenuity, can he be extricated." In the mind of George Bourne, an emancipationist who urged the immediate, universal abolition of slavery long before the rise of abolitionism, "No sophistry can disguise the principle he [Smith] insinuates, [that is,] the innocence of the present Slave-holder—the justice of his claim to the slaves, and the benignity with which they are maintained." Smith's principles, no matter how much they may have been diluted with protestations of antislavery, Bourne concluded, "uphold involuntary servitude." With a rage that would make Bourne chief among the early abolitionists, he asked, "How dare an Expositor of the Book sanction the detention of

men in Slavery?" The example of Smith and his fellow conservative clergymen caused Bourne to charge long before the days of Stephen S. Foster and James G. Birney, "The most obdurate adherents of Slavery are
Preachers of the Gospel and Officers and Members of the church."[55]

If the inherent proslavery perspective of Smith and other conservatives was not missed by rigorous emancipationists, neither was it misunderstood by slaveholders. The proslavery *Inchiquin* writings, particularly Robert Walsh's massive *Appeal from the Judgments of Great Britain*,
circulated throughout the nation and won the praise of slaveholders who
intended to maintain their valuable property in men. At the onset of the
Missouri debates in 1819, the *National Intelligencer* (Washington, D.C.)
received a spate of correspondence that corroborated the proslavery
tendency of Walsh and his predecessors in their attacks on British reviewers. Responding to the same criticisms in the *Edinburgh Review* that
had sent Walsh to his writing desk, "An American" residing in Virginia
applauded Walsh's volume for its utter refutation of the antislavery calumnies radiating from Great Britain. The Virginian wished that he
could make the book required reading for all British reviewers and all
Americans. The writer further adopted Walsh's arguments in his own
series of articles, since Walsh, as a resident of Philadelphia, "may be supposed to be exempt from that bias and prejudice to which, in a more
southern latitude, he might have been exposed."[56]

With the marvelously correct views of both Walsh and "an American"
in hand, another correspondent of the *National Intelligencer* wrote that
southern editors could wisely continue to display their characteristic
"forebearance" against discussions of slavery. Another who called himself "Cato" and who opposed those who would use violent means to abolish slavery thanked Walsh for his recent volume and proceeded to avail
himself "in a great degree, of the labors of this gentleman" to formulate
his own anti-emancipationist tract. After a month of congratulatory letters approving the proslavery sentiments of Walsh, the *National Intelligencer* received an antislavery letter from "Philanthropos" condemning
the disturbing proslavery tendencies of Walsh's volume and recent letters in the newspaper. The editors, sensing a prolonged clash on slavery
in their columns, suddenly decided that "the discussion should terminate." The proslavery nature of the Federalist *Inchiquin* writers' arguments, nevertheless, had already been revealed to the nation at large.[57]

If conservative ideologues were the first to revive the public defense of
slavery in the nineteenth century, if they displayed little sympathy for

the Negro, if their criticisms of slaveholding were largely politically inspired, if they readily espoused the expulsion of freed Negroes from America, and if they were viewed by contemporary slaveholders and emancipationists alike as defenders of slavery, how is it possible that they could have been viewed for generations as the forerunners and inspiriters of abolitionism? Indeed, the conventional wisdom of historians, early and recent, has been that Federalists were fathers of the abolitionists. With assurances that the Federalists' fathership of numerous abolitionist sons could not be "coincidental," historians normally proceed to list the abolitionist scions, including William Cullen Bryant, William Pitt Fessenden, Hannibal Hamlin, James Russell Lowell, Wendell Phillips, Edmund Quincy, Robert Rantoul, Theodore Sedgwick, Jr., Lewis Tappan, and Josiah Quincy. Nor is the fact that William Lloyd Garrison found a replacement for his own absent father in the Federalist Timothy Pickering overlooked. And despite the fact that most recent students of Federalism have recognized that the Federalist position on slavery was a departure from the post-Revolutionary emancipationism of the North, historians continue to connect Federalism with the eventual rise of abolitionism.[58]

Since most of the evidence for connecting Federalism with abolitionism is genealogical rather than ideological, it is instructive to survey the genealogy of proslavery. A study of the membership rolls of the Society for Promoting National Unity, an avowed proslavery organization formed by Samuel F. B. Morse during the secession crisis of 1861, reveals a striking genealogical continuity between former Federalists and proslavery leaders that equals, if it does not overshadow, the abolitionist connection. The society membership reads like an inclusive listing of the long-entrenched governing elite of New England and the North. Among the members—almost five decades after the demise of Federalism—were four long-lived "young" Federalist leaders, not to mention scores of others from families of former Federalist sympathies. The northern membership of the society was so heavily weighted in the direction of early Federalist inspiration, in fact, that descent from a once-Federalist family seems to have been an important prerequisite for membership.[59]

Former Federalists, sons and grandsons of Federalists, were remarkably active in all phases of the response to abolition from the 1810s until the end of the Civil War. When the earliest proslavery responses began appearing in the South in the 1820s, it was not strange that the two most articulate spokesmen should have been former Federalist politicians.[60] During the abolition crisis of the 1830s such Federalist pundits as Harrison Gray Otis, Noah Webster, James Buchanan, Roger B. Taney, and Jacob Burnet were in the vanguard of those who attempted to discredit abolitionists.[61] While proslavery clergymen largely spurned all mention of politics—whether their own or that of their families—at least twenty derived from staunch Federalist families, mostly of New England.[62] Although it would be difficult to quantify Federalist descent for either abolitionists or proslavery men, it seems safe to conclude that at least as large a percentage of the latter could trace their ancestry to former Federalists.

In view of evidence pointing in a revisionist direction, one must conclude that some conservative former Federalists (at least a significant portion of them) were by any measure proslavery in sentiment. But one must quickly add that the conservative counterrevolution was in no sense a proslavery response to attacks on slavery or a mechanism of defense foisted up by slave society. Rather, as a part of the process of developing a new conservative system of social thought, the conservative counterrevolutionaries entered into the defense of slavery by the back door. Therein lies the irony and seeming paradox of connecting the conservative counterrevolution with proslavery. Proslavery for the new conservatives was the end result of a social and ideological process. The defense of slavery was an implication or an outgrowth, not a focal concern of their "conservative" philosophy.

Conservative counterrevolutionaries were not the originators of proslavery or even of America's proslavery ideology. Proslavery thought was a part of the heritage of western man. And what became the peculiarly American proslavery ideology was yet in the future when conservative former Federalist giants walked the earth. But the new conservatives of the period from 1795 to 1816 *did* develop a social philosophy, indeed a distinctive ideology, that would eventually supply the conceptual and linguistic core of America's proslavery ideology. Conservative counterrevolutionaries were the first group of Americans in the young republic to devise an alternative body of social thought that both reshaped and turned the heritage of the American Revolution on its head. From the first experiences of factionalism in the 1790s to the transference of conservative energies to nonpolitical institutions after 1815, the new conservatives participated in the crucial preparation for the eventual appearance of a distinctively American proslavery ideology in the 1830s.

Out of their counterrevolutionary experience came the language, the outlook, the ideology, and the fitful emotions that would characterize the national campaign of antebellum Americans to destroy abolitionism and to perpetuate slavery. In the departure of Americans from the essentially antislavery stance of Revolutionary ideology, the Federalist counterrevolution brought the most sweeping changes in preparation for proslavery of any movement in American experience.

Nearly every development in the conservative experience contributed in some fundamental way to the creation of an America that could almost instinctively reject abolition and abolitionists. In terms of social values the conservative counterrevolutionaries replaced Revolutionary equalitarianism with a decidedly strong preference for a deferential social structure. Any social movement that had as its aim the equalization of condition for all men fell on deaf ears in the case of conservative Federalists once their counterrevolution was under way. Long after equalitarianism became for them a valueless, even dangerous tendency, they could continue to speak of and value liberty, a closely related Revolutionary ideal. But for them liberty did not mean freedom from restraints. Rather it was in the new conservative lexicon a synonym for order or that quality of social existence that permitted a wide range of movement and choice within a carefully limited social structure. In the reshaping of American thought along conservative lines, all movements that sought to melt away social restraints in the name of greater liberty were regarded as dangerous as incipient equalitarianism.

But for the long-term history of proslavery in America, the expression of proslavery views by conservative Federalists was far less important than their conservative counterrevolutionary ideology. As America headed in the 1830s toward its first national crisis over slavery, the fact that Dwight, Ingersoll, Smith, Walsh, and others defended slavery between 1810 and 1820 would be largely forgotten. What would not be forgotten, however, was the fact that these and other conservative thinkers had developed a new structure of thought, a counterrevolutionary ideology, and a language capable of defending slavery on the one hand and of discrediting abolitionists on the other. Moreover, they had launched a movement to foist their notions on American society.

NINE

The Conservative Proslavery Center, 1816–1865

If the ideology of America's conservative counterrevolution found a place for slavery in American polity during the first decades of the nineteenth century, one must ask if there may not have been some integral relationship between that movement and the emergence in the 1830s of a distinctively American proslavery ideology. In an effort to assess the potential ideological and sociological connections between conservatism and proslavery it will be well to bear in mind an observation made by historian Samuel Eliot Morison after a half-century as a student of Federalist conservatism: "Federalist *croyances* were deeply rooted, and although subject to scorn and contumely, they frequently reappear under other names. No series of Democratic victories in state and nation have suppressed the fundamental Federalist creed that liberty is inseparable from union, that men are essentially unequal, that *vox populi* is seldom if ever *vox Dei*, and that sinister outside influences are busy undermining American integrity."[1] While it would be wrong to equate the conservatism that arose from Federalist roots with any of the movements in which its conservative notions reappeared, the fact is that it has reincarnated frequently as the ideological core of a variety of movements. Conservative Federalists articulated a body of ideas that could be borrowed by anyone who found it useful in advancing his particular social or political objectives. All of which is to say that the Federalist conservative experience helped to inspire and establish a vibrant conservative tradition in America, an interpretation that has rarely escaped the attention of historians.[2]

One of the most direct ways of understanding the interconnections between proslavery and the conservative tradition is to trace the career of proslavery through the records of representative individuals who were imbued with conservative doctrines growing out of the Federalist experience. There seems to have been what might be called a "conservative proslavery center" from the earliest rumblings of abolitionists through the period of the Civil War. That center should be understood as the most characteristic stance of proslavery thinkers throughout America who came under the influence of the novel proslavery dispensation of the 1830s. In addition to representing a characteristic or general attitude, the proslavery center should be understood as the cutting edge in terms of typical leadership in the evolution of proslavery thought and policy. The proslavery center was both a cluster of ideas and responses and a sociological fact.

While any number of men could be selected to elucidate the proslavery center in antebellum America, the combined careers of Harrison Gray Otis, Charles Jared Ingersoll, James Kirke Paulding, and Samuel F. B. Morse will serve to illustrate the transmission of conservative ideas from the era of the conservative counterrevolution to the Civil War.[3] Their public careers when combined stretched from the 1790s until Reconstruction. All four qualified as defenders of slavery and as men whose lives were intimately connected with the proliferation of the conservative counterrevolution. Otis, Ingersoll, and Paulding are particularly significant in terms of the continuity between Federalist era conservative thought and proslavery ideology because they were living, active, and vocal during both the heydays of Federalism and of proslavery. By 1815 all three had been active Federalists and had expressed themselves as favoring the perpetuation of slavery. Samuel F. B. Morse is only slightly less important in those respects since all of his experiences and attitudes had been shaped at the feet of his father Jedidiah and of his foremost teacher Timothy Dwight. All four were intimately involved in framing a response to abolition. All four found themselves attracted to Jacksonian Democracy and became full-fledged Democrats (although Otis spent his last days as a Whig due to Andrew Jackson's bank policies). While Otis died in 1848, the careers of Ingersoll (1782–1862), Paulding (1778–1860), and Morse (1791–1872) extended all the way to the Civil War.

All four began their public careers as devoted Federalists. All absorbed the thought of the conservative counterrevolution. While Otis stuck with the Federalist party to its bitter end, the others bolted the party as a protest against Federalist sectionalism. Inside the party, Otis acted as a restraining influence on the radical sectionalism of the Essex Junto. Ingersoll and Paulding proved themselves nationalists both in the *Inchiquin* controversy and in their active support of the War of 1812. Although Ingersoll received the endorsement of Federalists for vice-president in 1812, he proved himself a war hawk in Congressional deliberations leading up to the war. Paulding, in the meantime, took an active role in the war as a major in the New York militia. At the same time, Morse injured the Federalist sensibilities of his father by defending the policies of Madison and the Republicans to hostile Englishmen during an extended visit to Europe. By the end of the war Ingersoll, Paulding, and Morse were steadfast friends of the Jeffersonians. All three later threw in their lots with Jacksonian Democracy, running for or serving in various national offices as Democrats. Only Otis, following a brief courtship with the party of Jackson, ended up in the ranks of the Whig party.[4]

Although three of them were alienated very early from Federalist politics, none of the four ever budged from his devotion to the conservative ideology of his youth. That body of social thought shaped their opinions in nearly all controversies relating to slavery. Otis, Ingersoll, and Paulding were entirely in the counterrevolutionary mold when they expressed their conservative views on slavery long before the rise of abolitionism. While Morse had not publicized his views on slavery as early as the others, he had apparently become resigned to the presence of slavery in American society by the time he spent four years as a painter in Charleston, South Carolina, without registering a single known complaint about human servitude. But their early defenses of slavery were a mere shadow of sentiments more vividly expressed upon the rise of abolitionism in the 1830s. By the time the first great crisis of abolitionism had reached a peak in the summer of 1835, the quartet of renegade Federalists whose career paths rarely ever crossed were already at work condemning immediatism and defending slavery.[5]

From their first contacts with immediatism, in fact, each of the four began expressing attitudes and arguments that were always characteristic of the proslavery center. The experience of Otis beginning in 1829 was typical. Following a number of fires believed to have been set by arsonists in December 1829, city authorities in Savannah, Georgia, discovered sixty copies of David Walker's *Appeal, in Four Articles . . . to the Colored Citizens of the World, but in Particular to Those of the U.S.* which had been printed in Boston that same year. Believing that a connection existed between the circulation of Walker's *Appeal* and the recent incendiarism, the mayor of Savannah appealed to Otis, then the mayor of Boston, to suppress the book and to quiet Walker. Quite willing to honor the request within the limits of the law, Otis sent an emissary with instructions "to obtain from Walker the despised document, if it could be done with his consent." Finding that the pamphlets could not be confiscated without "recourse to artifice," Otis informed Savannah's mayor that although he and other Boston authorities were willing "to avail themselves of any lawful means for preventing this attempt to throw firebrands" into the South, Walker had broken no law. In a similar letter to the governor of Virginia shortly thereafter, Otis further indicated his disposition to suppress pre-abolitionist immediatism: "You may be assured that your good people cannot hold in more absolute detestation the sentiments of the writer than do the people of this city, and, as I verily believe, the mass of the New England population." With the very limited circulation of the book and "the extravagance of his sanguinary fanaticism tending to disgust all persons of common humanity," Otis wrote, Walker need not be feared.[6]

Otis faced a similar situation and registered a like response in October 1831, when the *National Intelligencer* and other correspondents from the South requested him to muzzle William Lloyd Garrison. Two months earlier Nat Turner had led the most disastrous slave insurrection in American history in Southampton County, Virginia. In the wake of the rebellion, copies of Garrison's *Liberator* had been found in the hands of free Negroes and slaves. Connecting Garrison's agitation and the violence in Virginia, such disparate individuals as Nelly Custis, niece of George Washington, Benjamin Faneuil Hunt, a native Bostonian practicing law in Charleston, and Robert Y. Hayne, United States senator from South Carolina, sent frantic appeals to Otis. Hunt sounded like a native southerner when he wrote, "It would be much better that an actual open war were at once declared between the slaveholding states and our brethren at the North, than that . . . such assaults should be made upon our lives and fortunes." "Being aware of your own [Otis'] just & enlightened Views upon this subject [slavery]," however, he felt safe in placing his trust in the Boston mayor to take proper measures against Garrison.[7]

Otis disappointed neither Hunt nor alarmed southerners. He did not suppress Garrison's *Liberator;* but following a covert investigation of Garrison's precarious operation, he assured all concerned that no action was necessary. In a letter to Hunt, Otis expressed the opinion that no respectable citizen of Boston would lend support to Garrison's "new fanaticism." And while Bostonians entertained the same hope as southerners that slavery would some day be extinguished, they felt "less disposition to interfere with the actual relations of master and slave in our sister states, than has been manifested in other places." "I am desirous," he continued, "of leaving the affair of emancipation of your slaves to yourselves, to time, to the Providence of God." Believing that abolitionist excitement would only make slavery harsher, Otis concluded, "I protest with deep horror against all measures of whatever description, tending to endanger their lives or make miserable the tenure of their existence." It was not, therefore, that Otis was unwilling in 1831 to use vigorous measures to quiet abolitionism, but rather that any attempted muzzling would only draw attention and support to an insignificant form of fanaticism. And that sentiment was typical of those men who would constitute the proslavery center before the crisis of 1835.[8]

The willingness of Otis and others to squelch immediatism and to defend slavery in the early 1830s converted into anti-abolitionist activism in 1835. As the crisis of abolitionism reached a peak in the summer of 1835, Otis, Ingersoll, and Paulding rushed to the podium and into print with charges and arguments characteristic of the proslavery center. Otis and Ingersoll made their statements in epoch-making speeches in Massachusetts and Pennsylvania respectively. Paulding put his ideas in the first book-length response to abolitionism published in America. Since Ingersoll's speech was among the earliest anti-abolitionist statements of a political figure in the nation and Otis's the first by a prominent Bostonian, the threesome were also setting the pace for anti-abolitionist responses.

Ingersoll went first in a speech at Bush Hill, Pennsylvania, on July 4, 1835. Billed as a stump speech to encourage the candidacy of Martin Van Buren for the presidency, Ingersoll could not refrain from a telling outburst on the evils of abolitionism. His chief principles were those of liberty, equality, property, the Union, and republicanism. "All that is good in government is republican," he shouted. The independence and union of American states had brought the greatest republicanism yet known to man. All of America shared in the building up and maintenance of that experiment: "Let Old England and New England say what they may of the Plantation States, they are the headquarters of liberty, as the Eastern States are of independence, and the Eastern of equality."

Leading Figures of the Proslavery Center

Harrison Gray Otis, 1765–1848
*Federalist archconservative, congressman,
Boston mayor, anti-abolitionist*

Charles Jared Ingersoll, 1782–1862
*Philadelphia conservative politician,
congressional defender of slavery and
the South*

James Kirke Paulding, 1778–1860
*Novelist, essayist, Navy administrator,
early proponent of slavery*

Samuel Findley Breese Morse,
1791–1872
*Artist, inventor, ultraconservative agitator,
diehard proponent of slavery*

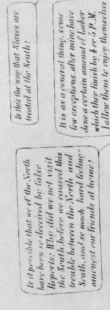

SLAVERY AS IT EXISTS IN AMERICA.

An 1850 Boston print illustrating some of the arguments used by Americans
north and south to uphold slavery

Prefacing his assessment of slavery with the sine qua non of all contemporary comment ("In Pennsylvania we are none of us friends of slavery"), Ingersoll abstracted from the most popular theory of republicanism: "Such men as Montesquieu and Burke have borne their testimony to the fact that the love of freedom is most stubborn and jealous in the Southern masters of slaves." Such was the case in Greece and Rome, "as it is in Virginia and the Carolinas." Burke also condemned the application to society of metaphysical abstractions such as the notion that slavery is deplorable and indefensible. "Slavery in the United States is no more an abstraction than liberty," he continued. "The Union found it in the Union, part and lot of the Union, and was constrained to sanction it as a strand in the bands of the Union, which to take away is to sunder the whole." Despite the objections of many to slavery in the abstract, real slavery as practiced in America was, by implication, perfectly just and defensible.[9]

The crisis had reached even severer proportions by August 21, 1835, when Otis rose to the podium in Faneuil Hall before "the best elements of Boston society." One of a half-dozen prominent speakers, Otis was considered the featured speaker at the meeting. In the opinion of his biographer, Otis delivered one of the most noteworthy speeches of his career, in which he called upon genteel Bostonians to thwart abolitionism before it disrupted American society and caused a severance of the union. The purpose and point of the speech, Otis commented in private a few weeks later, was "to show the south that the general sentiment in the north is correct upon the Slave question, and to endeavor to keep it so." From the speech came Otis's most characteristic and oft-repeated statement on the problem of slavery, "If slavery is a stain, it is one with which the Union was born, and which cannot be removed by our efforts unless by cutting off the limb which wears it."[10]

While Ingersoll and Otis depended on the platform to vent their views on slavery, Paulding began work on his massive *Slavery in the United States,* the first comprehensive critique of abolitionism and the most extensive defense of slavery hitherto published in the United States. By November he had put the finishing touches on the work that he believed would alter the entire course of the slavery debate in America. Although he found that almost every proslavery argument went "directly in the teeth of the fundamental principles of our government," he wrote Martin Van Buren, "I have endeavoured however to get over this difficulty." The peculiar circumstances of the hour seemed to him to justify overt tampering with heretofore sacred principles. As he wrote South Carolina Senator James H. Hammond in early 1836, "Fanaticism indeed seems the characteristic of the age. Mankind have become Fanatics in Religion, morals, politics everything." America was the land of liberty, perhaps beyond the limits of public safety. After counseling Hammond on the proper means of blocking abolition petitions in Congress, Paulding concluded, "We have no right to flatter ourselves that we shall escape the consequences of the excesses of Liberty, any more than other nations have those of Despotism."[11]

Fanaticism as a result of an excess of liberty was the one theme that ran throughout Paulding's *Slavery in the United States*. Contrary to almost everything that had been written on slavery in America, Paulding did not believe slavery to be "an evil of such surpassing enormity as to demand the sacrifice of the harmony and consequent union of the states, followed by civil contention and servile war, to its removal." Although he couched his position in a traditionally negative formula, Paulding went on with a warm defense of slavery. The Bible and religion upheld slavery. The Constitution and laws of property protected slaveholding. Englishmen, not Americans, were responsible for the introduction of slavery in America. The laws of slavery protected slaves from harsh masters. He devoted nearly one-third of the whole to the political economy of slavery, attempting to prove that American slavery was as mild and as beneficial as any other form of labor in the world. After comparing the condition of the slave to that of native Africans, English factory workers, European peasantry, and common laborers in the North, Paulding found that "the bondman of the United States is free from all obligation or anxiety" and that his lot in life was "decidedly preferable" to that of his fellows elsewhere.[12]

Nor did Paulding mind pandering to incipient American racism. On the one hand, Negroes, he wrote, bore the burden of a "natural and incurable inferiority." On the other, they posed threats of amalgamation and racial warfare against white superiors. Universal emancipation would inevitably lead to a "mongrel race," an "inferior mixture" of beings, destroying America's "natural aristocracy of virtue and talent." Civil, social, and racial wars would follow as blacks and those of mixed breeds combined to displace with brute energy the diminishing white race. Blacks were incapable of enjoying the privileges and responsibilities of liberty. Nor could a Negro be educated in the abstract principles of freedom, since such instruction would make him "a libertine in morals and an anarchist in politics." The "woolly-headed race" had never demonstrated any ability to live in freedom under a rule of law. Hence, it was not surprising that "anatomists and physiologists have classed the negro as the lowest in the scale of rational beings."[13]

But all of Paulding's arguments, "racist" and otherwise, were a mere shadow cast by his overarching concern for the maintenance of social stability and republicanism. The theory of natural rights and the Declaration of Independence were false if applied to all human creatures. The bondage of blacks was an "exception" to the general rule recognized by both the founders and all true republicans. Abolitionism is a "holy alliance" of the enemies of liberty in Europe with misguided fanatics in America to destroy American republicanism. Under the guise of philanthropy, fanatical abolitionists would "overturn the whole fabric of human rights, and destroy all personal liberty, [and] all freedom of action or mind." Such fanaticism "has no fireside, no home, no centre." The entire movement to free slaves was the very embodiment of social anarchy.[14]

In the early anti-abolitionist speeches and writings of Otis, Ingersoll, and Paulding can be seen the emergence of a new rationale for the perpetuation of slavery, a novel approach to the problem of slavery, if their statements be placed in the context of the proslavery heritage of the United States. The impulse for their new ideas was the appearance of a new breed of emancipators—the abolitionists. The primary aim of their crusade was the maintenance of the American union and social stability. The informing principles of their onslaught against the disruptive tendencies of immediatism was the revived conservative ideology of their Federalist teachers. Whereas such principles had once been used to slash away at the Illuminati, Jeffersonians, and other enemies of religious and political orthodoxy, Otis, Ingersoll, Paulding, and others of a like constitution dredged up the same arcane rhetoric and tactics to destroy abolitionism. And although these latter-day conservatives perceived the abolitionists as more of a threat to American society than to slavery, they unleashed a pattern and a perspective that would always be characteristic of the proslavery center. The amalgamation of conservative ideology with proslavery was in a sense a by-product of their attempts to deal with a new form of social subversion.

Abolitionism was very different from traditional emancipationism. It was so different, in fact, that it appeared to conservative eyes very much like the reincarnation of the French Revolution. Not only did abolitionism propose the immediate unleashing of America's black population, it also bore all of the marks of a well-organized international conspiracy with huge reserves of men, money, and unblinking audacity. In addition to challenging a firmly fixed national policy against universal emancipation, the abolitionists seemed to dash themselves against all governmental, social, and ecclesiastical authority, every institution, and all order. Paulding asked, "Where shall we look for security to our rights, or stability to our institutions, if they are thus to be sacrificed to a presumptuous interpretation of the law of God and the rights of man?" Because abolitionists seemed to buck against all authority, Paulding could write, "we impeach them as enemies of the law of the land, the constitution of the government, the union of the states, the common courtesies of life, the precepts of religion, and the rights and lives of millions of our countrymen." In the same manner that their fathers, their spiritual forebears, and mentors had been startled by French-inspired conspiracies and had berated all those who sympathized with democratic mobocracy, the anti-abolitionists attempted to discredit and destroy agitators for universal emancipation.[15]

The hallmark of anti-abolition and the conservative proslavery center was an abiding concern for social authority and order. They, like their conservative forebears, favored republicanism over democracy, deferential over leveling behavior, stasis over change. They appealed to the authority of Burke and the Federalist gods as opposed to Jefferson and the French Revolution. They were wont to see at all hands un-American fanaticism, infidelity, and anarchy. So powerful was the influence of the inherited ideology in their thinking and acting that they did not bother with the niceties of developing new rhetoric for their encounter with abolitionism. As if they were still doing battle with the Illuminati, they labeled and believed their enemies to be a reincarnation of French infidelity little different from what had destroyed France during the 1790s. The challenge to America was so persuasively similar to that of the 1790s that they themselves revived for a new encounter that ideology and rhetoric their fathers had created.

The thought and values of the anti-abolitionists conformed more closely with the social ideology than with the political tenets of old Federalists. Unlike those Federalists who lived and died with the party, the anti-abolitionists were staunch, indeed militant unionists. In fact, unionism was more important to them than slavery could ever have been. Paulding declared as his sole aim in defending slavery the determination of "whether THE UNION SHALL LAST ANY LONGER." His only politics was union: "To this Party the writer [Paulding] professes allegiance, and to no other." To the same extent that anti-abolitionists relied upon Burke and conservative philosophy for their social thought, they appealed for union at all costs, for "that union which all good citizens believe to be the great palladium of their present happiness, and that of their posterity."[16] While the old conservatives defended slavery because of the logic of their ideology, the anti-abolitionists defended slavery due to the logic of their unionism.

The fanatical unionism of the anti-abolitionists has perpetually beclouded their decisive contribution to the formation of a national proslavery ideology. Although they set out to preserve the union in their attacks on the abolitionists and in their defenses of slavery, they ended up creating a new proslavery tradition intermingling their learned social principles with traditional thought. And while they thought of themselves primarily as nationalists and not as defenders of slavery, they became America's proslavery center and the nation's leading proslavery ideologists. Even though they perpetually sought to distinguish their attitudes and policies from those of southern slaveholders, they always found themselves out of ideological consistency having to identify themselves with the policies of southerners. From the 1830s until the Civil War their rhetoric and their actions almost always threw them in league with southerners.

No sooner had Otis, Ingersoll, Paulding, and Morse helped launch anti-abolitionism than they were called upon to take sides in a string of sectional issues that arose almost yearly. Paulding had already demonstrated his support for the South in *Slavery in the United States*. By 1839 Otis had come to agree fully with the attempts of southerners to stifle slavery debates in Congress.[17] Between 1835 and 1850 Ingersoll was constantly required to demonstrate his convictions on the question of slavery. Shortly after his Bush Hill speech of July 1835, Ingersoll participated in the Doylestown Convention to shape a new constitution for Pennsylvania. As author of the meeting's address, he penned and defended resolutions for a constitutional amendment that would enlarge white manhood suffrage but that made blacks for the first time legally ineligible to vote. Ingersoll's election to Congress only five years later launched a decade of his crucial involvement in the concerns of Congress with slavery. During the 1840 campaign that brought his election, Ingersoll indicated quite clearly that he considered abolitionists "the worst traitors" ever known in America and that he would do something about them when he arrived in Washington.[18]

As a member of Congress from 1841 to 1849, Ingersoll took what is usually considered a proslavery position on every issue that came before the body. In the renewed gag rule debates of 1841, Ingersoll proved himself one of the most vocal and formidable foes of John Quincy Adams, the great champion of the right of petition. In a series of debates, which continued through four sessions of Congress, Ingersoll carried on an open, verbal warfare with Adams. Ingersoll's sentiments as expressed in one of these speeches, in March 1841, were typical. Indicating that he represented the Middle States, "the great central zone which binds this Union together," Ingersoll treated both slavery and abolition. Slavery was both an evil, albeit a minor one, and a right. The people of Pennsylvania and of the Middle States united with those of the South in upholding the constitutional and social right and the wisdom of retaining slavery until it disappeared spontaneously and naturally. Nothing in slavery failed to conform with both charity and comity.

Abolition, on the other hand, "spurns all—charity, comity, compromise, Constitution, law, order, religion, peace—it tramples down all with an iron hoof of unmerciful fanaticism." Originating in England, abolitionism elicited the support of three types of men who combined in a great "conspiracy" against America: "1st; mere enthusiasts or zealots, who do not pretend to reason, but merely declaim, denounce, and villify. 2d; rational Abolitionists. . . . And 3d; partisans, to whom Abolition is a cloak or disguise by which to impose A or B as a President or member of Congress upon a community, or to prevent their elections, as being favorable or inimical to the abolition of slavery." The first were not to be feared since they discredited themselves by their own behavior. The second were those who attempt to dismember the union: "the law must be enforced against them." The third were most fearful, "the most reprehensible traitors to this country." They covertly used abolition to forward their own ends and would eventually succeed in destroying the Union. These last, not southerners, were the great enemies of American unity.[19]

In addition to upholding slavery and the South, Ingersoll exercised a most telling and crucial practice that characterized anti-abolitionists from the 1830s to the Civil War. He assured southern leaders that the "conservative majority" of the North supported the conduct of the South in both defending slavery and repelling abolitionism. He boomed, "The people of the South may rely upon it, that those of Pennsylvania, and, I believe, of all the free States, are still as averse as ever to such injustice [forced emancipation]." Going far beyond mere assurances, however, Ingersoll, like others, goaded the South into action: "Let me say to the torrid South, that with all its animation, it has never repelled with sufficient vigor this foreign invasion of its rights, and traduction of its character." Moreover, "the policy and duty of the South, instead of the futile expressions of lofty indignation, is [should be] to vindicate themselves [*sic*] by uniting with the North, to repel foreign disparagement, to rouse the enthusiasm of patriotism, to repel that of fanaticism, and thus to put an end to its aggressions."[20]

Ingersoll's assurances extended considerably beyond mere words. He championed and even encouraged what has often been called the slaveholders' war, the Mexican War of 1846–1848. As chairman of the House Committee on Foreign Affairs from 1843 to 1847, Ingersoll had oversight of Congressional moves toward the annexation of Texas and the war of expansion that followed. Beginning in late 1843, Ingersoll undertook a campaign to convince key Congressmen that "it is a great national measure of vital importance" to annex Texas immediately. After a year of maneuvering with a hostile committee that would not approve annexationist reports, Ingersoll succeeded in guiding resolutions for annexation through the House. When war followed, Ingersoll was among the first to urge President Polk to order American troops into Mexico and there "crush the invaders on their own soil." It should go without saying that in the Congressional debates on the disposition of the conquered territories that Ingersoll was among the most vehement opponents of the Wilmot Proviso.[21]

The crisis of the Union in 1850, which followed in the wake of the Mexican War, startled and drew responses from anti-abolitionists no less animated than those they had already registered in the 1830s. Although Otis died in 1848, a firm defender of slavery to the end, and did not live to see the 1850 foretaste of rabid sectionalism, the remaining trio of anti-abolitionists maintained the constant and continuing pattern of the proslavery center. James Kirke Paulding, in comfortable retirement at Hyde Park, New York, roused for another round with abolition. In two public writings, articles in the *Democratic Review,* Paulding reemphasized an old theme, "The Conspiracy of Fanaticism," and expressed his views on a new one, "Fugitive Slaves." Hardly perceiving that the issue of slavery in the territories had considerably altered the continuing debate over slavery, Paulding and other anti-abolitionists lashed out against the new direction taken by the abolitionist conspiracy. Abolitionists had joined forces with politicians, he thought. Fanaticism finally entered the very halls of Congress through such men as Sen. William H. Seward, "one of the most dangerous insects that ever crawled about in the political atmosphere."

Pronouncing himself still a close friend of the Union, Paulding began entertaining fears of its eventual necessary dismemberment. He urged his anti-abolitionist associates of Tammany Hall to help crush abolitionism, "this dangerous spirit that has now got the ascendancy among a portion of the people of the north, and which if not quelled in time will assuredly, if not now, at some future period prove fatal to this Union, against which it has long been waging war." At the same time he applauded the sentiments of John C. Calhoun as expressed in the southerner's last great speech in the Senate: "It gives me great pleasure to see that you take the same ground, with one exception, which I assumed in a pamphlet I had prepared in the same subject [slavery]." Going far beyond mere applause, however, Paulding defended the right of secession and even argued the expediency of armed resistance if political abolitionism were not stopped: "This doctrine [secession] is established beyond controversy, by the unanswered and unanswerable arguments of Sidney and Locke," he told the Southern Rights Association of Charleston, which had already rejected the expediency of such action. He continued, "Were I a citizen of South-Carolina, or any other Southern State, I *trust I should not be found among those, who, after placing themselves in front of the battle* . . . RETIRED FROM THE FIELD, ONLY, IT WOULD SEEM, TO SEE IF THE ENEMY WOULD PURSUE THEM." Whereas Ingersoll had once goaded southerners into greater exertions against abolitionists, Paulding seems to have been reinforcing the growing popularity of secessionism.[22]

Paulding's public proslavery career ended with his last fling at abolitionism in the crisis of 1850. Ingersoll's came to a similar conclusion during the presidential election of 1856, which occurred amidst alarming reports from "bleeding Kansas." Believing that abolitionists had finally resorted to arms to forward their fanatical aims, Ingersoll recoiled with his most extended and articulate defense of slavery, *African Slavery in America*. Using traditional arguments, both racist and nonracist, Ingersoll upheld slavery: "Vouched by irrefutable English and American authority, negro slavery in America may be so vindicated that no American need shrink from its communion. No cause warrants condemnation of the thus far successful American combination of slavery with liberty, the solution of a problem peculiar to these United States." Ingersoll no longer bothered himself with the type of negative evaluation of slavery in the abstract that had characterized his views fifty years earlier.[23]

Instead, Ingersoll continued to dwell most heavily on fanaticism, especially as it had been politicized in the Republican party: "the baneful fanaticism of political abolition . . . has become an intractable distemper, discarding discussion, disregarding facts, ignoring history, however recent and instructive, and substituting shouts of clamorous vituperation, drowning argument and reason." In the recent workings of Congress "a small minority of indefatigably fanatical abolitionists overrode much of the north" with a "reign of terror" like that of "Marat and St. Just in the French Jacobin clubs, reducing a great affrighted majority to the utmost mortification of abject submission." In Congress and elsewhere Ingersoll saw "legions of abolitionists, free-soilers, free-toilers and other adventurers, like Vandals who overran Southern Europe" rallying "to subjugate the Southern states." If southerners did not already know the fate that awaited them, they had only to consult the dire predictions of Charles Jared Ingersoll for enlightenment.[24]

As the ultimate crisis of the Union approached in 1860, the anti-abolitionists of the proslavery center reacted to events in a manner strangely reminiscent to southerners. Paulding had counseled secession in 1850. Morse, when he ran for a seat in Congress in 1854, favored opening the territories for the expansion of slavery and defended slavery as "a social condition ordained from the beginning of the world for the wisest purposes, benevolent and disciplinary, by Divine Wisdom." In 1855 Ingersoll favored the arresting and conviction of any abolitionist who impeded the return of fugitive slaves. Morse reported to his brother privately two years later, "I confess, the more I study the subject [slavery] the more I feel compelled to declare myself on the Southern side of the question." When Lord Brougham affronted a representative of the United States for his racism in 1860, Ingersoll condemned Brougham and berated the American official "for not making on the spot a fitting reply to vindicate the dignity & honor of his country." In the presidential campaign of 1860, in the last public expression of sentiment in his life, Ingersoll urged Pennsylvanians to support John C. Breckinridge, the southern Democratic candidate. A week after the fall of Fort Sumter, Ingersoll's son-in-law, following "a most painful conversation" with the old Federalist warhorse, confided to his diary, "All his party passions are enlisted for the South."[25]

As Paulding and Ingersoll faded from the scene, Samuel F. B. Morse came into his own by upholding the proslavery tradition of his forebears. Anti-abolitionists were crisis-oriented people and Morse was no exception. A longtime opponent of abolition who had adopted a southern position on slavery, Morse reserved his energies for the period of the Civil War. Fearful that southerners would misinterpret the meaning of Lincoln's election in 1860, Morse began pouring letters into the South and uniting the energies of his widespread acquaintanceship with the belief that "if time were taken calmly to ascertain and to prove the real sentiment of the North towards the South, it would be found in indignant rebuke of these troublers of our peace." He praised the efforts of fellow anti-abolitionists North and South who saw correctly that an endorsement of Lincoln was by no means an avowal of abolition. By February 1861, when it became apparent that "we are now the *Untied* and no longer the *United* States," Morse wrote a friend, "I confess that my sympathies are more with the South than the North." In fact,

> Their cause in all that relates to Slavery is intrinsically Sound, and they ought to have trusted in the goodness of their cause for their ultimate triumph which *was*, and I believe, *is* yet to be consummated . . . They have able writers & thinkers, sound logicians, excellent conscientious men, who are writing telling-truths, which must be effective in dispelling this dark cloud of fanaticism, so soon as the party burly [?] created by secession shall have [give?] the clear, truth loving minds of the North an opportunity for calm and dispassionate examination of the question.

Secession, he believed, was a necessary "demonstration" to "convince fanaticism that the south were in earnest." But he continued to hope that southerners would "take counsel of their reason, and not of their passions" and thereby avert war.[26]

Meanwhile, Morse began to exert every energy to ensure that war would not become necessary. After consulting his friends, associates, and fellow anti-abolitionists, he organized the American Society for Promoting National Unity, a combination of men North and South with similar inclinations on the subjects of slavery and abolitionism. Morse was elected president at the society's first meeting on March 6, 1861. On the same occasion those in attendance, characterized by Morse "as warm-hearted, praying, conscientious Christians as ever assembled to devise means for promoting peace," approved a preamble and a constitution written by Morse himself. The preamble expressed all those notions and beliefs that had become characteristic of anti-abolitionists and of the proslavery center. It gave no credence to the "popular declaration that all men are created equal and entitled to liberty" and upheld slavery as an institution that "exists for wise and good ends *by the will of God.*" While the chief aim of the body was the preservation of the Union, Morse indicated that the defending of slavery "will be at present our main topic."[27]

Although the society failed in its purpose of preserving the Union, it did not fail in its aim of defending slavery on a national scale. In 1861 and 1862 the society flooded the North with pamphlets bearing its peculiar philosophy. Among its publications were Bishop John Henry Hopkins's *Bible View of Slavery* and two pamphlets from Morse's own pen, including *The Present Attempt to Dissolve the American Union, a British Aristocratic Plot.* In addition to upholding the right and justice of slaveholding, these and other of the society's publications defended the right of secession. Bishop Hopkins, for example, maintained that since "the political right of the South to the peaceful enjoyment of their domestic institutions, is fully recognized by the Constitution, the laws and the judicial decisions of the United States . . . they have a right to secede." After little more than two months of society activity Morse wrote a southern associate, "My sentiments of friendliness towards, and confidence in the South are so well known here, that the Abolitionists brand me as a Secessionist."[28]

Although Morse and his associates could not restore the Union and the society gradually lost its initial impulse, they were provoked to new exertions in late 1862 and early 1863 by Lincoln's Emancipation Proclamation. Morse's personal reaction to the act was violent in the extreme. Soon after the issuance of the formal proclamation on January 1, 1863, Morse began putting together a second society with "the same general object" as the first. From the first private gathering of influential men at Delmonico's Fifth Avenue Restaurant in New York on February 6, however, it was apparent that the Society for the Diffusion of Political Knowledge would rest on a firmer basis than its predecessor and take more aggressive action. Powerful editors and multimillionaires studded the list of attendants. William Cullen Bryant, who was invited, deigned only to send a reporter who broke the bond of silence imposed by the participants by sensationalizing the new "conspiracy" of millionaires and, revealingly, of New Englanders.[29]

Manton Marble, editor of the *New York World* and originally of Boston, William C. Prime of the *Journal of Commerce* from Connecticut, and James Brooks of the *Express* from Maine represented the New York press. August Belmont, Samuel J. Tilden, and Henry Young, "a Troy millionaire," among others represented the world of business and finance. Morse and his friend George Ticknor Curtis, lawyer in the Dred Scott decision, provided the initial leadership. Once again Morse was elected president. In private letters Morse revealed that this second venture was "backed up by millionaires, so far as funds go who have assured us that funds shall not be wanting for this object." To Amos Kendall he wrote, "It contains intellect, intelligence, and wealth, and with God's blessing we hope to resist the unsanity of the day by a spirit the very reverse of that which is dominant in the ranks of fanaticism." By the end of February cooperating societies were being formed in Boston, Newark, "and in hundreds of other places." To Morse's amazement, "The movement is responded to all over the country, and auxiliaries are organizing everywhere."[30]

Like the earlier organization, the Society for the Diffusion of Political Knowledge undertook a publishing campaign, which continued for two years to express the attitudes of the proslavery center. The twenty-four "Papers" issued by the society stressed defenses of slavery and condemnations of abolitionism. Morse wrote three of the pamphlets, including *An Argument on the Ethical Position of Slavery in the Social System,* his most articulate contribution to proslavery literature. Bishop Hopkins's defense was also reprinted. Other pamphlets written by such men as Samuel J. Tilden, Horatio Seymour, George Ticknor Curtis, Manton Marble, and Thomas P. Kettell stressed new concerns of anti-abolitionists: copperheadism, true loyalty, amalgamation of races, the war debt, and freedom of the press. Begun as an instrument of protest against emancipation, the society became increasingly an instrument of partisan politics in support of Gen. George B. McClellan, the Democratic presidential candidate in 1864.[31]

Morse and the organized members of the proslavery center failed again to stop emancipation or to block Lincoln's bid for reelection. But with each passing event, they moved ever closer to a complete identification with the thinking and interests of the South. They had justly been called secessionists. The Society for the Diffusion of Political Knowledge was scorned by enemies as a tool of the South. Morse and his confederates even came to desire southern victory on the battlefield as the only possible means of vanquishing fanaticism from American life and of restoring social equilibrium. Nor did the eventual military defeat of the South alter their outlook. When Andrew Johnson began blocking radical reconstruction, Morse, speaking for the defeated but ideologically consistent proslavery center, wrote a cousin,

> I did not vote for him, but I am agreeably surprised at his masterly statesmanship, and hope, by his firmness in resisting the extreme radicals, he will preserve the Union against the greatest enemies we have to contend against. I mean those who call themselves Abolitionists. . . . President Johnson deserves the support of all true patriots, and he will have it against all the "traitors" in the country, by whatever soft names of loyalty they endeavor to shield themselves.[32]

In peace as well as in war, in mind as well as opinion, in action as well as thought, anti-abolitionists of Morse's stamp found—as they always had— a strange commonality with southerners and the South.

During the course of the Civil War, Samuel F. B. Morse confronted opponents who charged that he had besmirched the name of his venerable father Jedidiah, the Federalist, Congregational giant who had spent his career swatting infidelity. The critics reminded Morse that his father had openly criticized both slavery and the South. The imperturbable Morse always had a ready reply. To one he wrote in 1861,

> You allude to my honored father, as if he would be opposed to his children. His antislavery feeling was not of the modern sacrilegious type[;] it was the old antislavery feeling of Virginia and the South, well-intentioned, benevolently intended, but even then not soundly based. It had not for its soul, the unscriptural dogma that Slavery is Sin; this monster was born Since his death. He knew nothing of Massachusetts abolitionism. Were he now living, he would not fail to detect in it the logical fruits of that apostacy from the faith against which he battled so nobly during his life. He would see as his children now see, the champions of this error, the Theodore Parkers of the day, the leaders, the fierce supporters of a spurious humanitarianism.[33]

In the mind of Morse and others of his ilk they were waging the same battle that Dwight, Jedidiah Morse, and other conservative Federalists had fought when Illuminists and French infidels walked the earth. Abolitionism was the same social and religious heresy that had beset America since the 1790s. Anti-abolitionism was but a continuation of that staunch orthodoxy of the conservative counterrevolution. And anti-abolitionists constituted the heart and soul of the conservative proslavery center.

As Morse surveyed Civil War America, he found that nearly all of his relatives, friends, and associates who derived from the cradle of Federalism united with him in opposing abolitionism and in upholding slavery and the claims of the South. Hence, when his brother Richard broke the united front in 1864 to support the reelection of Abraham Lincoln, Morse was understandably chagrined. Upon learning of his brother's defection, Morse struck off a letter that reemphasized his most deeply held beliefs:

> I have no reason to change my views respecting abolition. You well know I have ever considered it the logical progeny of Unitarianism and Infidelity. It is characterized by subtlety, hypocrisy and pharisaism, and one of the most melancholy marks of its speciousness is its influence of benumbing the gracious sensibilities of many Christian hearts, and blinding their eyes to their sad defection from the truths of the bible.
>
> I know, indeed, the influences by which you are surrounded, but they are neither stronger nor more artful than those which our brave father manfully withstood in combatting the monster in the cradle. I hope there is enough of father's firmness and courage in battling with error, however specious, to keep you, through God's grace, from falling into the embrace of the body-and-soul-destroying heresy of Abolitionism.[34]

Even though some anti-abolitionists may not have recognized as clearly as did Morse the animating source of their faith and actions, their battle with abolition as well as their ready buttressing of the institution of slavery was a logical extension of the ideological doctrines their fathers had created. More than a mere reaffirmation of those tendencies and principles, anti-abolitionism was a continuation of the conservative counterrevolution.

The anti-abolitionist record of such sons of the conservative tradition as Harrison Gray Otis, Charles Jared Ingersoll, James Kirke Paulding, and Samuel F. B. Morse raises ponderable questions about the nature of proslavery and sectionalism in antebellum America and still more about the terminology and categories traditionally imposed on various types of proslavery literature. The central interpretive problem revolves around the distinction between proslavery and anti-abolition. A close look at the ideas and behavior of such northern-based anti-abolitionists as these four latter-day conservatives shows that typical anti-abolitionists—even with all of their bombast about the Union—were never very far from southern sectionalists either in terms of attitude toward abolition and slavery or on proper policy for the South. In terms of the crisis that abolitionism created for America in the 1830s and beyond, it is wrong to separate anti-abolition and proslavery as sectional and therefore different responses to the same set of circumstances. While there were variations of content and style among respondents according to background and experience, and although one can detect ideological variations among those who sprang to the defense of slavery particularly in the mid-1830s, men in all sections of the nation conformed to the anti-abolitionist pattern almost simultaneously. And in terms of their initial evaluations of slavery, there was very little to distinguish those whom historians have called, on the one hand, anti-abolitionist and, on the other, proslavery.

The conservative proslavery center was actually of a national character. Sociologically speaking, it was neither northern nor southern, for the people who constituted it were scattered throughout America. Ideationally it did not revolve about a particular perspective on the institution of slavery. Rather the proslavery center incorporated men with a wide range of perspectives on slavery, from those who claimed slavery a divine gift to those who believed slavery an abstract evil. What held together the proslavery center was, instead, a commonly held perspective on the shape of American society North and South. At the heart of the proslavery center was a shared ideology that antedated abolitionism and that defined a more basic perspective for dealing with both fanaticism and with inequalities in society. While northern anti-abolitionists and southern proslavery theoreticians might have seemed quite different and might have seemed to be directed toward quite separate social goals, they were united under the banner of one social ideology—that of the conservative counterrevolution.

TEN

Emergence of Proslavery Ideology in the North, 1831–1840

As odd as it may seem, the most important events leading to the final creation of a national proslavery ideology occurred in the North during the decade of the 1830s. Although the South was the primary focus of slaveholding and although slaveholders would have been the greatest losers in any disruption of the institution of slavery, southerners were almost bystanders, albeit very interested observers, as radical abolition emerged in the North only to be discredited by conservative anti-abolitionists. Southerners also watched happily as northern conservatives gave shape to a proslavery ideology that would stand all defenders of slavery in good stead until the Civil War. By the time southerners became generally concerned with the challenge of immediatism, a response to abolitionist proposals and tendencies had already been framed, disseminated, and adopted throughout the North along with a perspective on American society that was almost alien to southern traditions. Because the problems of slavery and abolition became pressing concerns throughout the North several years before they did in the South, one must look to the furtive work of the anti-abolitionists for the actual creation of the amalgam of conservative philosophy and proslavery thought that became America's distinctive contribution to proslavery history.

In examining the circumstances surrounding the final emergence of a viable proslavery ideology, it should be remembered that most proslavery literature written in America in the antebellum years did not consist merely of the definition of arguments favoring slavery. Most proslavery literature whether from northern or southern pens dwelt less on slavery than on the shape and tendencies of American society. Except for a very few studies written by a half-dozen intellectuals mainly in the

1850s, proslavery literature in America displayed little concern for the institution in and of itself. The chief concern of proslavery writers after the appearance of abolitionism, whether in the North or the South, was always the polity and direction of American society. In terms of the development of new theories favoring slavery, the antebellum period in America was nearly barren. The great proslavery revolution that occurred in America during the 1830s was not the development of new proslavery arguments. It was instead the general shift of Americans to a new perspective on their own society that could tolerate the perpetuation of slavery. The real revolution was a national rejection of the libertarian heritage of the American Revolution.

Moreover, although historians have traditionally thought that southerners rose up in defiance of the abolitionists in the mid-1830s and then unleashed a militant new defense of slavery, a survey of the proslavery literature of the 1830s supports neither conclusion. In terms of the number of separate publications on the subject of slavery with the purpose of overturning abolitionism, New Englanders and northerners more than doubled the production of southerners between 1831 and 1840. Of the fifty-five known defenses published during the decade, thirty-seven were written by natives of northern states. In fact, of the twenty-eight residents of the South who published defenses during the 1830s, only eighteen were native southerners. And if the defenses of that decade are classed as either repositories of traditional proslavery arguments or of a new form of proslavery ideology, thirty-five of the fifty-five contain ideological premises that were largely alien to the South before 1835. If one adds the fact that nearly a dozen defenses were published by northern hands before the first southerners got into the act, the importance of examining the North in the years up to and following 1835 becomes much greater.[1] Whereas the South had little need to concern itself with slavery and abolition before 1835, much of the North had already become a battleground between abolitionists and their opponents.

It is fortunate for the work of historians that the nineteenth century was not a period with mass media for the swift dissemination of news and ideas. In a society with mass media, reports of startling events are likely to be coupled with accounts of immediate reaction to the occurrences. If the event is of national or international significance, one might even observe simultaneously similar reactions in a wide variety of locations. Mass media foster a social and cultural unanimity wholly unknown prior to the twentieth century. In the nineteenth century—with a slower and less intensive transmission of news through the printed word—patterns of response to momentous events were much more likely to resemble either chain-linked reactions emanating from the locus of the occurrence or concentrically expanding waves of reactions radiating from a single point. While news items might have been picked up and reprinted by newspapers at a rather rapid tempo, interpretations of the event were likely slow in coming, developing at varied paces in widely separated regions.

In his fascinating study of anti-abolition mobs in the North titled *"Gentlemen of Property and Standing,"* Leonard Richards made much of the sudden national impact of the abolitionists' publishing campaign in the summer of 1835. Although he assumed that southerners had gone to war with abolitionists in 1831 soon after William Lloyd Garrison launched the *Liberator,* Richards found that anti-abolitionists remained nearly undisturbed by the machinations of immediatists until the summer of 1835, at which time abolitionist presses began showering the country with their propaganda. Suddenly Americans learned, Richards argued, that abolitionism was not limited to "a few fiery Boston radicals" and perceived instead "a highly efficient, well-organized propaganda machine" with seemingly inexhaustible reserves of men, money, and schemes of agitation. Momentarily Americans were thrown into a frenzy of fear, which soon translated into violence. Southerners, already laced with anxiety, joined in the reaction with ever more furious responses to the growing storm over slavery.[2]

The summer and fall of 1835 were definitely the point at which resistance to abolition became a national phenomenon, as Richards's graphic documentation of the dramatic upsurge of anti-abolition violence clearly demonstrates. At that moment a national revulsion against abolition occurred, which saw harried old conservatives such as Harrison Gray Otis in Boston and Charles Jared Ingersoll in Philadelphia join grand juries and would-be lynchmen in Alabama and Louisiana in violent denunciations of immediatists. And had there been abolitionists or abolition societies in the South in the summer of 1835, it is likely that southerners would have reenacted the chaotic, sometimes bloody scenes produced by anti-abolition rioters in New York, Philadelphia, Boston, and Utica in August and October of that year. In any case, the first great abolition crisis—perhaps the greatest—occurred in 1835 with almost all Americans joining forces with anti-abolitionists and many elitists, gentlemen of property and standing, taking to the streets to express their disgust.

The formation of street mobs and citizens' meetings, even with the intricate planning that characterized anti-abolition mobs, is one thing; the formation of reasoned thought quite another. While mobbism may be expressive of very definite opinions, the resort to violence by a group of people more likely indicates a momentary level of psychic tensions rather than the development of well-based opinion. The fact that anti-abolition violence occurred within the context of a proportionally similar surge of mobbism unrelated to abolition suggests that an explosive mixture of social tensions converged on Jacksonian Americans. A sudden perception of frustrated hopes, powerlessness, and a seeming legitimation of violence met in a volatile amalgam, sending respectable Jacksonian Americans to the streets in the summer of 1835.[3]

The rioters of 1835 could presumably have turned to mobbism at some other time if the same psychic tensions had combined with other saner expectations. This brief period of national violence followed upon and grew out of a general climate that produced similar, if less dramatic, outbreaks of violent behavior. Abolitionists and blacks had been the objects of attack in the North almost from the beginning of Garrison's campaign. Following Nat Turner's rebellion in Virginia in September 1831, the white citizens of New Haven turned upon abolitionist plans for a Negro college in the town, unanimously denounced Garrisonian tactics, and stoned the home of Arthur Tappan. Between April and September 1833 in nearby Canterbury, Connecticut, other mobs destroyed the schoolhouse and home of Prudence Crandall, a Quaker schoolmistress who sought to open there a school for black girls. The case of Miss Crandall briefly preceded the colonizationist-inspired riot in New York City of October 1833, which sent the city's small band of abolitionists scurrying for safety. The riot of 1833 was only a prelude to the much more extensive anti-abolition rioting that occurred in New York City in July and September 1834, and that followed the pathway of the English abolitionist, George Thompson, from New York throughout New England between September 1834 and his departure for England in November 1835.[4]

Despite the spread of anti-abolition violence from New Haven to the rest of New England and on to New York between 1831 and 1835, Richards concluded that "there was almost no response—either positive or negative—to immediatism until the late summer of 1832, and then only

Some Prominent Northern Proslavery Clergymen

Nehemiah Adams, 1806–1878
*Famous author, traveler, and lifelong
pastor of Essex Street Congregational
Church, Boston, 1834–1878*

John Henry Hopkins, 1792–1868
*Architect, poet, lawyer, and Episcopal
bishop of Vermont, 1832–1868*

Moses Stuart, 1780–1852
*First American biblical scholar and
professor at Andover Seminary,
Massachusetts, 1810–1848*

Nathaniel Sheldon Wheaton,
1792–1862
*Trinity College president, world traveler,
Episcopal clergyman*

a stirring until the summer of 1835" in New England and little more in the rest of the North.[5] And in comparison with the massive outpouring of anti-abolition violence in the summer of 1835, the seemingly disconnected events of the preceding four years appear inconsequential indeed. Nevertheless, there was a steady increase of opposition to abolitionism in those years, so that when the explosion of psychic tensions occurred in 1835 the pattern of violent response to abolition had already been established in New England. Moreover, the modes of reaction adopted in New England were already being exported to other sections of the nation. Indeed, the sudden surge of reaction that gripped the nation as a whole in the summer of 1835 should not overshadow the crucial formative experiences of the years preceding the first national abolition crisis.

If one goes back to the earliest anti-abolitionist responses, it is not strange that Connecticut and the New Haven area should have been the site of the first overt reactions. Nor was it strange that Connecticut should have been the most inhospitable of the New England states to the formation of antislavery societies. The state actually had fewer auxiliaries of the American Anti-Slavery Society per population and more mobs per auxiliary of any state in New England in the 1830s.[6] More than perhaps any other state Connecticut had been thoroughly steeped in the reactionary thought patterns of countersubversive conservatism, particularly Timothy Dwight's variety. Not only were the tactics and rhetoric of abolitionists irresponsible and subversive from the perspective of conservative state leaders, but also the abolitionists' program of immediate universal emancipation and full incorporation of the Negro in American society militated strongly against the accepted policies of former conservative Federalists and their ideological sons. Because of the total suffusion of Connecticut Yankees with the teachings of Dwight and his conservative ideology, Connecticut was prepared, even more than the slaveholders of the South in 1831, to wage battle with abolitionism.

That Connecticut was the first site of anti-abolition violence does not mean other New Englanders did not share the feelings and approve the actions of their neighbors. Historians have made much of the manner in which Harrison Gray Otis dismissed the call of southerners to silence first David Walker in 1829 and then William Lloyd Garrison in 1831. Although Otis rejected both demands, he indicated quite clearly on both occasions that he would have honored the requests by whatever means necessary if he had found either Walker or Garrison to have constituted a threat to peace and order. By 1835 Otis had thrown off the mantel of peacefulness, as he counseled the citizens of Boston to destroy abolitionism.[7]

The steady movement of Otis from a private condemnation of immediatism in 1829 to an open campaign against the movement in 1835 was characteristic of the general tendency of established leadership in church and state in New England during the first years of Garrison's *Liberator.* The case of the New England Congregational clergymen, long considered to have been the major proponents of abolitionism in its early days, is instructive. From the outset the Congregational divine who converted to abolition was an exception rather than the rule. Between 1831 and the onset of the national abolition crisis in the summer of 1835, nearly all leading Congregational clergymen lined up squarely against abolitionism. William Ellery Channing, Lyman Beecher, Justin Edwards, Leonard Bacon, Moses Stuart, Nehemiah Adams, Hubbard Winslow, Ralph Emerson, Josiah Tracy, Parsons Cooke, Nathaniel Taylor, and most other powerful clergymen in the orbit of Yale, Andover, Amherst, and the smaller Congregational colleges had registered their dissent from abolitionism before 1835. All of them were staunch colonizationists and had been numbered among the guiding lights of benevolent reform, including the reform of slavery. Yet, one by one, most of them openly condemned the work of Garrison and began a transition that would, as in the case of Otis, put them in league with the proponents of slavery.[8]

Some of the early Congregational critics of abolition were strongly opposed to slavery. Until their various unhappy encounters with abolition, Lyman Beecher, William E. Channing, and Leonard Bacon could have been considered nothing less than vocal opponents of slavery. They even courted notions of immediatism, hoping in the early years of abolitionism to combine the impulse of immediatism with the ultimate aims of colonization. But by 1833 they knew that Garrison would have nothing to do with colonization, a policy that to them had become an article of orthodox faith. As they rallied to the defense of colonization in the face of Garrison's bitter attacks in 1833, they drew together the machinery of the Benevolent Empire, the moral and social power of orthodox Congregationalism, and their inherited conservative ideology to create a vast bastion against what they already conceived to be a subversive movement against America.[9]

The influential Congregational press, without exception, condemned abolitionism prior to 1835. Bacon himself established in 1834 a paper he called the *Journal of Freedom* to supplement the even more strident anti-abolitionist views of Josiah Tracy, Hubbard Winslow, and Nehemiah Adams, editors of the nationally circulating *Boston Recorder*. Moreover, with iron-fisted tactics, the clerical faculties of Yale, Bowdoin, Amherst, and Andover Seminary prevented in 1833 the type of struggle between student abolitionists and anti-abolitionists that would occur at Lyman Beecher's Lane Seminary in 1834 by ousting antislavery societies in favor of colonization auxiliaries. At Andover, for example, the unheeded warning of Moses Stuart for students not to attend an abolition rally held by George Thompson led to the dismissal of forty theological students in 1835.[10]

By January 1835—fully six months before the peak of the abolition crisis—eight conservative Congregational clergymen, all disenchanted with both colonization and abolition, had altered their direction so far as to form a countersubversive organization, which they named the American Union for the Relief and Improvement of the Colored Race. Intended from the start as a movement to counteract abolitionism by propounding a more vigorous antislavery stance than that of colonization, the American Union soon projected the more conservative views of its founders. In an attempt to circumvent the growing opposition against both colonization and immediatism, the founders preached moderation, gradualism, and greater exertions to elevate slaves toward freedom. The society would use "moral influence to convince all American citizens, that the system of slavery in this country is wrong, and ought to be universally abandoned." Such antislavery statements at the foundation of the American Union understandably elicited, at least initially, the support of abolitionists.[11]

The deep-seated conservatism of the clerical directors, however, soon proved to anger abolitionists and to put the organization in league with slaveholders. By 1836, as it slid increasingly in the direction of a proslavery stance, the American Union had largely recanted its program of moral suasion for a strict policy of noninterference with slave property. In a series of resolutions it pointed to "the ill-success which follows many attempts in this reform [emancipation]" and chose instead to press the Christian gospel upon both master and slave in the hope that Christian principles might influence the attitudes of slaveholders and the character of slaves. One thing was certain, one resolution proclaimed: neither American Union nor the North would ever "attempt to interfere with the slavery of the South, by any other means than by moral influence." After courting moderate emancipationism for the time, the clerical conservatives adopted almost precisely the perspective and program of their southern counterparts—the reform of slavery, not its extinction. With little purpose other than what was already being promoted by other agencies of the Benevolent Empire, the American Union died in 1839, its founders convinced that no separate organization aimed solely at the reform of slavery could ever succeed. But long before that time the founders of the American Union were chanting with single-minded accord the destruction of abolition and the preservation of slavery.[12]

The almost reflexive reaction of latter-day conservative clergymen against abolition produced the earliest comprehensive statements of America's peculiar form of proslavery ideology. Hardly to be considered merely hints and sketches of a future full-blown ideology of proslavery, the clergy of New England launched telling fusillades against abolitionists as early as 1833, which displayed the same rhetoric and body of thought that would eventually flow spontaneously from the lips of southern secessionists on the eve of the Civil War. In 1833 the already apparent disposition of the old Federalists such as Harrison Gray Otis to attack abolition turned into public pronouncements foreshadowing the mammoth outpouring of 1835. The first critiques paraded under the guise of colonization. But once unleashed, the ideas and the rhetoric contained therein were duplicated by imitators in many parts of the North. Before the year was out this initial ideological response to abolitionism had been picked up and restated by such different characters as a physician in New York, a young politician in Philadelphia, and the attorney general of the state of Massachusetts.[13] But it is important to note that the first rumblings of the coming avalanche were heard among the Congregational clergy of New England well before the abolition crisis of 1835.[14]

At least one of the first attacks on abolition, that of Joseph Tracy entitled *Natural Equality* (1833), could easily have served as the textbook for American proslavery writers. Born and reared in Vermont of a family that traced its lineage back to Plymouth Plantation, Tracy graduated from Dartmouth and studied law before entering the Congregational ministry. From 1829 to 1834, Tracy edited the *Vermont Chronicle* and made it the foremost local Congregational newspaper. His brilliant editorial work brought him the co-editorship of the *Boston Recorder* in 1834 and the editorship of the *New York Observer* afterward. Unlike some of his fellow clergy who early despaired of colonization, Tracy spent the remainder of his career from the early 1840s until his death in the service

of the American Colonization Society. His pace-setting critique of abolition was published while he edited the *Vermont Chronicle* and was the text
of an address he delivered before the Vermont Colonization Society in
October 1833.

In the address, as suggested by the title, Tracy began his remarks with
a consideration of "the fundamental doctrine" of the Declaration of Independence, the notion that all men are created equally. That doctrine,
Tracy believed, lay "at the foundation of all that is valuable in the political relations of men,—and yet, when misunderstood and misapplied, is
the most powerful of all political doctrines in the destruction of good
and the production of evil." The idea of natural equality was one of the
most dangerous doctrines in the social and political catechisms of modern man and has proved on numerous occasions to war against the very
sinews of government and social order. Citing aberrant applications of
the theory from Revolutionary France, from England, and from nearby
New York, Tracy argued that with the full implementation of the theory
of natural rights, "it is plain, there can be no government at all." All
rights of property would be "reasoned away." Criminal jurisprudence
would be annihilated. Law would be abolished. Women would wrest the
monopoly of legal authority from men.[15]

In an attempt to redefine a hallowed doctrine of the American Revolution, Tracy claimed that natural equality did not extend beyond the
physical sameness of all men who enter life as infants. In terms of claims
upon society, all men from birth have an equal right to physical and
mental nurture from older and wiser men who can instruct them in
"that government, that restraint and coercion, without which not one of
them in twenty would ever live to be a man." The right of proper nurture did not mean that all men should be protected by the same laws or
that they should be given the same instruction. Any man who has not
been fitted for freedom cannot claim the rights of freemen. While in a
perfect state of society all men should be prepared for freedom, there
are always some who are incapable of enjoying the fruits of liberty. To
unleash such men on society on the sole basis of "the naked doctrine of
the equal rights of all men" is to war against all government.[16]

The proposal of abolitionists to emancipate all slaves immediately was
just such a revolutionary and irresponsible misinterpretation of the doctrine of natural rights. Tracy was quick to identify the source of such
misguided fanaticism: "This is not the American interpretation. It is that
of French Jacobinism." Never in the annals of history—neither in the

most massive nor in the most limited releases of slaves—had a nation or state opted for the immediate, wholesale emancipation of thousands, not to mention millions, of slaves. Immediatism, a scheme "at variance with all the dictates of common sense," was propounded by infidels and Jacobins "merely for the sake of producing excitement" or for fomenting revolution. Only French rebels were capable of such aims, inspired by a frightening doctrine of the rights of man that went far beyond anything ever conceived in America. At great pains to distinguish between American and French interpretations of natural rights, Tracy argued that the founders of the American republic understood the limits of the theory and "built up this republic—the joy and wonder of the world." A few years later, "the Jacobins misunderstood it; and, misled by their own false theory, they deluged France in blood, and whelmed Europe in tears."[17]

Having countered the doctrine of natural equality and having identified abolitionists as misguided French revolutionaries, Tracy outlined his own version of the proper future for America's slave population. Slavery, he believed, should be made into a preparatory school for freedom. Slaves should be instructed in the proper knowledge that would make them responsible, dutiful freemen. Far from espousing the education of slaves for full-fledged citizenship, Tracy only wanted to "furnish them with the ends and objects of human life, and of the duties of man to his fellow man, and establish in their minds such principles for government of their own conduct, as will make them safe citizens." Safe citizens did not necessarily need to learn the arts of reading and writing. Oral instruction would be fully adequate for a people in whose hands certain books might prove "unsafe instruments." Slaves should be taught obedience, industry, faithfulness, sobriety, reverence for God, and respect for men and the property of men. As a model for his moral renovation of slaves, Tracy pointed to the work of the slave missionary, Charles Colcock Jones, and the Liberty County (Georgia) Association for the Instruction of Negroes. Although his plan would take generations and perhaps centuries to prepare every slave for freedom, Tracy thought glacial gradualism the only ultimate solution to America's dilemma. Coupled with gradualism as well was the understanding that any slave who passed muster in America's preparatory school for freedom would savor liberty not in the United States, but rather in one of the states of Africa.[18]

Tracy's address on natural equality was an earthshaking statement in the history of proslavery in America. By denying the theory and practice of equalitarianism, by scoring abolitionism as a revolutionary movement against American republicanism, and by proposing the transformation of slavery into a school of moral training, Tracy brought into focus for the first time three of the most characteristic themes that would appear time and again in proslavery literature. Those three themes formed the heart of the first and ultimately the most lasting body of thought in the arsenal of proslavery writers. Drawn almost directly from the thought and experience of conservatives since the 1790s, Tracy and other early New England critics of abolitionism foisted upon Jacksonian America a set of notions around which Americans could rally. Each flange of the critique derived from and was a reassertion of lessons well-learned during the generation-long struggle of conservative counterrevolutionaries to transform American society. Despite the fact that Tracy was attempting to put his well-rehearsed conservative values in the service of colonization, he couched his arguments in such a framework that they could be appropriated quite directly by those who would afterward support the indefinite perpetuation of slavery. Perhaps most important, however, was the fact that Tracy had put the vast body of conservative thought directly in the service of those who opposed the abolition of slavery.

Before the explosion of 1835 such effusions as Tracy's were restricted largely to men who defended colonization as an alternate mode of abolishing slavery. Nevertheless, an easily perceptible expansion of the geographic occurrence and the scope of the perspective took place. Following Tracy's pace-setting pronouncement of October 1833, Leonard Bacon, Congregational clergyman in New Haven always closely allied with Yale, broadened the scope of the new approach by demonstrating the variance between abolitionism and Scripture and between immediatism and true philanthropy. In 1834, at Fall River, Massachusetts, Simon Clough, another clergyman, reviewed the first report of the American Anti-Slavery Society and, following the patterns of Tracy and Bacon, attempted to show that the doctrines of abolitionism "are wholly inconsistent with the doctrine and teachings of the Bible on this subject [slavery], and that no Minister of the Gospel can consistently become a member of that Society, or advocate its measures." In Clough's estimate the Bible upheld the claims of slaveholders, while the doctrines of abolitionism "lead directly on to a civil war." In nearby Andover, Massachusetts, another giant of Congregationalism with far-ranging influence, Moses Stuart, began lecturing to Congregational seminarians on slavery and the Bible. The Bible, Stuart argued, upheld slavery as just for the

Hebrews and for early Christians. While the Bible could not be used to support American slavery, he added, neither did it lend credence to immediatism. And within the confines of the leadership of the Unitarian establishment in Boston, conservative resistance to abolitionist proposals and demands quickly transformed into open condemnation of the abolitionists and their tactics.[19]

In the wake of the early New England critique of abolition, other colonization writers in New York and Pennsylvania were encouraged to adopt similar tactics in replies to abolition. David M. Reese, a physician in New York, reviewed the Declaration of Sentiments of the American Anti-Slavery Society sentence by sentence to show the "political heresies," "delusion," and "fanaticism" of abolitionists. Threatening abolitionists with greater calamities than they had yet experienced if they continued to preach their "irrational effervescence among the ignorant and depraved," Reese labeled immediatism anti-American, irreligious, and amalgamationist before reviewing ten conclusions wholly consistent with the earlier statements of Tracy and Bacon. In addition to warring against American society, Christianity, and colonization, the American Anti-Slavery Society harbored foreign emissaries and rebels whose work would, in the end, result in servile wars, the hardening of slavery, and the destruction of benevolent reform. In Reese's view a "crisis" was already at hand in which the "whole community" of the North should rise up to reject abolitionism. While Reese ranted about abolition in New York, Job Roberts Tyson, a Philadelphia colonizationist, reiterated in only slightly less frantic language what was apparently a growing consensus among the citizens of his own city.[20]

On the eve of the first great abolition crisis in the summer of 1835, therefore, a vast and growing critique of abolitionism had gotten under way. It had begun in Connecticut and Massachusetts among men who sought to protect colonization as the only sane method of dealing with the twin evils of slavery and the Negro. It had spread throughout the ranks of the Congregational clergy, become a concern to benevolent reformers who wished to protect essential efforts to colonize free blacks and to instruct slaves in Christianity, and won the support of clergymen-educators who sought to protect their colleges and schools from divisiveness and student radicalism. Already a host of old Federalists such as Harrison Gray Otis and Charles Jared Ingersoll had stamped abolition a dangerous subversive movement akin to the Bavarian Illuminati and French infidelity. The critique of abolitionism had in addition already spread beyond Massachusetts and Connecticut to Vermont, to New York, and to Philadelphia. In each instance new critics built upon a perspective that was beginning to snowball throughout the North. And most importantly, despite the fact that nearly all of the early critics of abolition saw themselves as anti-abolitionists and not as proponents of slavery, their combination of conservative social thought with a host of traditional proslavery arguments and with a total reevaluation of America's equalitarian heritage with respect to slavery provided a rationale that could easily fit into the arsenal of proslavery thinkers.

The dangerously swelling waters of early anti-abolition became a flood in the midst of the crisis of 1835. From mid-1835 forward the ideological effusions of conservative anti-abolitionists developed a new intensity of language, a rhetoric of crisis, which paralleled and replayed the violent antisubversive passions of Federalists against the Bavarian Illuminati in 1797 and following. Each new installment from the pens of anti-abolitionists reflected a growing perception of social chaos and the identification of abolitionism as both a cause and a symptom of pervasive disorder. Not since the 1790s had men been as sensitive to disruptive forces pushing society toward an imminent cataclysm. As in other historical moments of social crisis, both popular literature and comment on American society became replete with allusions to apocalyptic interruptions in the history of man. The fear of conspiracy, the perception of a sudden rent in the fabric of society, and the belief that man was on the verge of a historical cataclysm in the eyes of anti-abolitionists set the 1830s apart as perhaps the greatest period of social crisis between similar upheavals in the 1790s and the 1850s.

The crisis turned normally sane social conservatives into witch-hunters and prophets of doom. The widespread and repeated occurrence of mob violence convinced many that the rule of law in America had been abandoned. Not merely in response to abolition, mobbism of all sorts increased dramatically in the 1830s throughout America. In terms of anti-abolition mobbism, however, it is notable that, like the proliferation of ideological responses to abolition, the mobbing of immediatists began in New England and spread southward and to the west, eventually encompassing the entire North. From New Haven and Providence in 1831 to Canterbury, Connecticut, and New York City in 1833, from a long series of destructive scuffles in New York and on the trail of the English abolitionist George Thompson in New York and New England in 1834 to vicious mobbism in Boston, Philadelphia, and Utica in 1835, and from

Cincinnati in 1836 to Alton, Illinois, in 1837, gentlemanly Negro-haters dogged the trail of abolitionism.[21]

In addition to the continued outbreak of violence, in the summer of 1835 a series of theretofore undisclosed revelations about abolitionism persuaded Americans that immediatists, until then discounted as a group of fringe radicals, posed a startlingly formidable threat to the nation. The drenching of every part of the nation with propagandistic literature bearing the name of the American Anti-Slavery Society would seemingly have required the support of thousands, of unlimited financing, and of countless agents. The mass of literature paralleled the rapid expansion of abolition societies in every corner of the North. In August 1835, Harrison Gray Otis told his audience in Boston that the abolitionists were trying

> to erect themselves into a *revolutionary society*—combined and affiliated with auxiliary and ancillary societies, in every state and community, large or small, in the eastern and western states. All men are invited to join in this holy crusade. The ladies are invoked to turn their sewing parties into abolition clubs, and the little children when they meet to eat sugar plumbs [*sic*] or at the Sunday Schools are to be taught that A B stands for abolition:— Sir, I do not exaggerate . . . all I assert is in substance; men, women, and children are stimulated, flattered and frightened in order to swell their numbers.

Moreover, the national society had established open links with British abolitionists who had recently succeeded in loosing the bonds of slavery in the West Indies. Perhaps worst of all from anti-abolitionist eyes, on the eve of the abolition crisis, a number of highly respected individuals had been seduced into openly approving the principle, if not the methods, of immediatism. The defection from the camp of colonization and of anti-abolition of William Jay, William Ellery Channing, and Francis Wayland, among others, was particularly galling, despite the fact that none of the men of their stamp could ever wholeheartedly support abolitionism.[22]

As the crisis deepened in the summer and fall of 1835, articulate anti-abolitionists began to rally around the Federalist-inspired notions of Joseph Tracy and other conservative thinkers. Whereas those ideas had been drawn together to support colonization and to discredit the early fringe radicals who called themselves abolitionists, anti-abolitionists now used them to discredit the highly respected defectors. David Reese, who had recently condemned the proceedings of the American Anti-Slavery

Society, answered William Jay's attack on the American Colonization Society with a book of letters characterizing Jay's views as unadulterated "fanaticism." Completed on the very eve of the crisis, Reese asked, "Under what other influence save that of pure fanaticism, could an intelligent, virtuous, and respectable citizen, gravely affix his name to a book containing such perversions of facts?" James Trecothick Austin, attorney general of Massachusetts, similarly questioned the novel view of slavery recently expounded by William Ellery Channing. Austin initially discounted Channing as a quack moral scientist: "From a refined and elaborate metaphysical subtlety wholly incomprehensible to a great part of mankind—from new light in the recesses of his study, from some double distillation which by a novel process of alchemy he has been able to effect the dry bones of ancient morality." One of the early vigorous defenders of slavery who knew how to adduce all of the traditional proslavery arguments as well as the conservative ideology, Austin charged that moral scientists like Channing dangerously reinforced the fanaticism of immediatist agitators.[23]

As the tensions peaked in 1835, anti-abolitionist rhetoric reached a level of intensity similar to the anti-Illuminist outpouring of 1797–1798. Northern presses poured forth a variety of social criticism, of apocalypticism, and other forms of comment that appear only at moments of the most straitened social circumstances. Thomas Man, clergyman in Rhode Island, wrote *A Picture of Woonsocket, or the Truth in Its Nudity,* a peculiar compilation of translations of modern European poetry and essays and brief anti-abolitionist excoriations of Man's own composition. In one entitled "Order and White Man Contrasted," Man saw abolitionists as anti-Christian fanatics prophesied in Scripture and told his readers, "Let the people of the North enlist themselves under the Banner of Negro-Slavery." In a similar writing by a New Yorker entitled *The Enemies of the Constitution Discovered, or, an Inquiry into the Origin and Tendency of Popular Violence,* William Thomas saw the spread of abolitionism and of countersubversive mobbism as indications of the demise of America.[24]

In New York, where abolitionism threatened to take on the cast of another holy crusade, ideologized anti-abolitionists found their most persuasive evidence of social disruption. In 1836 New York anti-abolitionists gathered at Albany in a conference to frame resolutions against men they viewed as seditious "disturbers of the public peace." Indicating that "we consider discussions which, from their nature, tend to inflame the public mind, and put in jeopardy the lives and property of our fellow-citizens, at war with every rule of moral duty, and every suggestion of humanity," the enemies of abolition promised that "we will, by all constitutional means, exert our influence to arrest the progress of measures tending to loosen the bonds of union." In an added statement that became characteristic of anti-abolitionist tracts and books, the Albany anti-subversives lent support to southerners: "We do not hesitate to assure them that the great body of the northern people entertain opinions similar to those expressed in these resolutions."[25]

Northern anti-abolitionists associated abolition with all of the other forms of novel, even radical experimentation that made New York's famous "burnt-over" district unique. In a book-length tirade against what he considered to be radical popular delusions in science, philosophy, and religion, David Reese catalogued abolitionism among the other *Humbugs of New York* (1838). Treating only "the most mischievous among the reigning impostures," Reese classed devotion to either animal magnetism, phrenology, homeopathy, medical quackery, ultratemperance, ultraabolitionism, ultra-Protestantism, or ultrasectarianism as humbugs promoted by a similarly inclined array of fanatics. All such popular movements were engendered by men at war with Christianity and American society using Americans as dupes for their subversive schemes. Among the misguided fanatics who paraded their impostures before innocent citizens, however, the abolitionists were by far the greatest sinners and abolitionism the roots from which other quack movements grew.[26]

The force of anti-abolitionist logic drove toward the conclusion drawn by Calvin Colton in 1839 that abolition was a sedition against religion, republicanism, harmony, deference, and benevolence—in brief, all those values held precious by conservatives. The encompassing reaffirmation of values and symbols that had given meaning to counterrevolutionary conservatism since the 1790s drew the undivided support of benevolent reformers and old-line conservatives wherever they lived. Such widely separated individuals as Simeon Doggett, Unitarian clergyman of Raynham, Massachusetts; George Washington Blagden, pastor of Old South Church in Boston; Charles Hodge, professor in Princeton Theological Seminary; and Joshua Lacy Wilson, pastor of First Presbyterian Church in Cincinnati came to embrace the perspective and ideological teachings of anti-abolitionists.[27]

While many anti-abolitionists obtained their willing acceptance of conservative ideology from nurture in or long association with the culture of

New England, Charles Hodge and Joshua Lacy Wilson arrived at the perspective of anti-abolitionism by widely varied routes indicating the processes whereby northern social leaders eventually became a united front against abolition. Born in Pennsylvania and educated at Princeton under Samuel Stanhope Smith and Archibald Alexander, two towering Presbyterian Federalists, Hodge became for fifty years the dominant figure at Princeton Theological Seminary and a nationally known leader among Old School Presbyterians. By education, theology, and inclination, Hodge was prepared in the mid-1830s to applaud anti-abolitionist rhetoric and to write one of the most persuasive statements of anti-abolition ideology. In essay after essay throughout the antebellum period, Hodge published in the *Princeton Review* and in separate pamphlets perhaps the most important and instructive contributions toward the formation of a national proslavery ideology of any nineteenth-century American. In fact, when on the eve of the Civil War southerners began publishing in vast volumes the most important proslavery writings in America, Hodge was the only author to have two essays included in the most popular of such volumes, *Cotton is King, and Proslavery Arguments* (1860).[28]

From his first condemnation of abolitionists in 1836 until his essays on wartime America, Hodge reflected in more intellectualized form the attitudes of Otis, Ingersoll, and other latter-day conservatives. In his first essay in 1836, simply entitled *Slavery*, Hodge reacted against abolitionism and the untimely writings of Jay, Channing, and Wayland with some of the characteristic chants of other anti-abolitionists. Abolitionists were deluded, reckless, infatuated, and irrational. Having dismissed abolitionists as fringe radicals of the most dangerous sort in a republic, Hodge drove on to an examination of the morality of slavery. Admitting no source of authority except the Bible, Hodge proved to his own satisfaction that slavery was not necessarily sinful. In fact, "as it appears to us too clear to admit of either denial or doubt, the Scriptures do sanction slaveholding . . . to be consistent with the Christian character and profession . . . [and] to declare it to be a heinous crime, is a direct impeachment of the word of God." Although he was not the first, Hodge was among the most forceful of anti-abolitionists from an unmistakably conservative background to lock in with condemnations of abolition quite vigorous direct defenses of slavery.[29]

Joshua Lacy Wilson came from a very different background but ended up becoming one of Hodge's closest allies in making Old School Presbyterianism an anti-abolitionist religious force. Born in Virginia and reared in Kentucky, Wilson became pastor of Cincinnati's First Presbyterian Church in 1808. Over the next four decades Wilson lost nearly all traces of his southern origin and absorbed ever larger doses of the New England culture, which was being transferred to Ohio in the early years of the nineteenth century. Originally a doctrinaire Jeffersonian, Wilson continually compromised his early beliefs and moved gradually into the camp of latter-day conservatism. In the 1820s he opposed colonization because it did not move energetically enough against slavery and because it aimed to deprive freed blacks of American citizenship. Nevertheless, in 1832, after actively opposing the work of the American Colonization Society for a number of years, Wilson joined the society, arguing in a letter to his son that the Society offered the best means of evangelizing Africa and of ultimately liberating slaves without the bloodshed or amalgamation of races that would follow upon immediate abolition.[30]

Wilson's contradictory course on the subject of slavery won him the enmity of abolitionists and anti-abolitionists alike in 1835. In December of that year in the pages of the newspaper he edited, Wilson condemned both movements for their "uncalled for and improper" hostility toward each other and for the mobbism they engendered. Four years later, however, while visiting relatives in Kentucky, Wilson, in an unguarded moment, admitted that "I cannot deny the lawfulness of the relation between Servant and Master as taught in the Bible." When an Ohio abolitionist learned about Wilson's private comment, the Presbyterian clergyman became known as a "minister of slavery," an epithet that, while initially unfair, increasingly described the direction of Wilson's public and private course. Angered by the half-truths eagerly publicized by abolitionists and exasperated by their tactics, Wilson became a full-fledged anti-abolitionist. He published a few months later a scathing indictment of abolitionists entitled the *Relation and Duties of Servants and Masters*. Both a critique of abolitionists and a vigorous defense of slavery, Wilson patterned his response after the writings of earlier anti-abolitionists, particularly those of Charles Hodge.[31]

Conversion from antislavery to anti-abolition and finally to proslavery became the standard pattern for latter-day conservatives and benevolent reformers in the midst of the 1830s. For example, Nathan Lord, president of Dartmouth College, made every effort to protect the rights and privileges of one of his students who promoted abolition among the

*Some Early Northern
Proslavery Ideologists*

Nathan Lord, 1793–1870
*President of Dartmouth College, 1828–
1863, and perpetual proponent of slavery*

Charles Hodge, 1797–1878
*Famous proslavery theologian and
professor at Princeton University,
1828–1878*

George Washington Blagden,
1802–1884
*Pastor of Old South Congregational
Church, Boston, 1836–1884, and
frequent apologist for slavery*

school's undergraduates in 1835. Despite the fact that Lord disliked some of the sentiments of Stephen S. Foster, a most unusual sophomore, Lord upheld Foster's freedom to preach immediatism. In 1838, however, soon after Foster's graduation, Lord became increasingly disturbed by unauthorized abolitionist meetings in the nearby village of Hanover and by the antireligious sentiments of leading abolitionists. Three years later when Foster returned to Hanover bringing Parker Pillsbury and Henry C. Wright to hold a series of meetings, Lord authorized and promoted the movement that ended in Foster's expulsion from the college church. Thereafter Lord became one of the most vigorous defenders of slavery in New England.[32]

By the end of the 1830s most anti-abolitionists who had originally been impelled into the discussion of slavery as a result of their fears of social anarchy at the hands of radical abolitionists were making the transition to hard-core proslavery. In the same manner in which Harrison Gray Otis, Charles Jared Ingersoll, James Kirke Paulding, and Samuel F. B. Morse became perpetually representative of an American national proslavery center, the northern anti-abolitionists of the 1830s who helped to define a response to the challenge of abolitionism took up places among the leaders of the proslavery front throughout the antebellum period. Although Joseph Tracy and Leonard Bacon continued throughout their careers to wend a middle course between abolition and proslavery by continuously endorsing colonization and Job R. Tyson lost interest in the public debate, all of the remaining anti-abolitionist pamphleteers of the 1830s continued to endorse slavery in ever more precise terms.[33]

James T. Austin became a lifelong enemy of abolitionism and a firm Massachusetts-based friend of slavery. Among his notable acts was his widely popularized comparison of the mob that killed Elijah Lovejoy in Alton, Illinois, with the hallowed heroes of the Boston Tea Party. Simeon Doggett, although very old and removed from public life, continued to defend the rights of slaveholders whenever he could. Calvin Colton, who popularized the image of abolition as sedition, carried his proslavery notions into new posts as political pamphleteer for the Whig party and as a political economist at Trinity College in Hartford, Connecticut. While Hubbard Winslow did little writing precisely on the subject of slavery in later years, during the Civil War he became one of the closest associates of Samuel F. B. Morse in the creation of the American Society for Promoting National Unity and the Society for the Diffusion of Political Knowledge. He served as a corresponding secretary of both organizations. Even though Joshua Lacy Wilson died in 1846, he lived long enough to publish another pamphlet endorsing "African servitude" and to become totally enmeshed in bringing Old School Presbyterians over to a virtual proslavery position.[34]

Other northern anti-abolitionists of the 1830s made great new contributions to the corpus of proslavery literature in the following years. Charles Hodge became one of the most formidable and prolific proslavery writers through the pages of the *Princeton Review*, which he edited throughout the antebellum period. In 1847 George Washington Blagden, pastor of Old South Church in Boston from 1836 until his death in 1884, delivered an important sermon that he later published as *Remarks, and a Discourse on Slavery*. The sermon was typical of the efforts of New England divines to prove that slavery was not at odds with Christian traditions and values. Three years later Moses Stuart of Andover Theological Seminary published his *Conscience and the Constitution* (1850), his most lengthy and important contribution to proslavery literature. The book became an instant source of national controversy because it was a detailed analysis of biblical testimony in favor of slavery by America's foremost nineteenth-century biblical scholar.[35]

Two of the anti-abolitionists remained to the end of the Civil War extraordinarily firm friends of both slavery and the South. Nehemiah Adams, pastor of the Essex Street Congregational Church in Boston, became one of the most controversial men in America when he published his *South-Side View of Slavery*, a report on a three-month journey in the South in 1854. Not daunted by the hostile criticism of his proslavery views, Adams came back with *The Sable Cloud* (1861) and a host of proslavery sermons, one of which approved of southern secession in 1861. As a result of Adams's long defense of slavery and the South, he was one of the few northerners who could be invited to visit and speak in the South following the Civil War. The record of Nathan Lord was just as vigorously inclined toward slavery and the South. The president of Dartmouth College until forced to resign in 1863 for his continuing outspoken defense of slavery and the South, Lord became just as well-known as Stuart and Adams in the late 1850s with his publication of two letters from "a Northern Presbyter" in 1850 and 1855. Wholly absorbed with the defense of slavery, Lord spent the last fifteen years of his life— even after the Civil War—thinking and writing about slavery.[36]

By the conclusion of the 1830s as the first great abolition crisis waned in its intensity, a transition in thought and values had come to fruition in the antebellum North. In response to the various challenges posed by abolitionism a movement grew up that, while it initially sought to halt social subversion, ended up ideologizing the North in the rudiments of a new form of proslavery ideology. In the same manner that New England conservative Federalists had to refashion their social and political values in the 1790s, the North as a section had to come to grips with social subversion and the problem of slavery in the 1830s. In the same manner that disenchanted New England Federalists developed a body of social thought and the mechanisms of applying their beliefs to New England society in the early 1800s, the North as a section seems to have come to a new understanding of its values and place in American society.

The parallel of the Federalist experience between 1790 and 1815 and the anti-abolitionist experience of the 1830s is so strikingly similar and so interrelated that one can learn much by comparing and interconnecting the two movements. Both Federalist conservatism and anti-abolitionism were largely negative responses to perceived conspiratorial phenomena. In both cases enlightened spokesmen spent so much of their time scoring what they opposed that they developed little that was positive. Yet in both cases an ideology—a comprehensive definition of beliefs and values and an ideational springboard for action—emerged. In both cases, in fact, their spokesmen were negative to the point that they made reactionary vigilance and an ingrained fear of conspiracy a primary ingredient in their total program of action. While there were certainly many positive attitudes and beliefs in both the conservative ideology of Federalism and in the conservatism of the anti-abolitionists, both sets of thinkers were always more sure of what they did not want than of what they wished to become a reality.

Both movements progressed from the formation of pure to the adoption of practical ideologies. In the first phase both were largely negative reactions to disturbing social situations. As both movements got into the realm of attempting to solve the problems of social disruption and disorganization, they had to become concerned about more positive proposals for American society. The practical ideology of Federalist conservatism was an emergent body of ideas that overturned the principles of the American Revolution, substituting classical republicanism for democratic conceptions of American polity, a deferential society for equalitarianism, religious orthodoxy for evangelical and experimental Christianity, and classical learning for modern infidelity. The mechanisms of social action for the Federalist counterrevolutionaries were a conservative press, educational system, and Benevolent Empire.

With the anti-abolitionists the case was different. Almost all of them were born into and grew up in the northern conservative tradition. Almost all of them were part and parcel of the ongoing conservative phalanx before the rise of abolitionism. Almost all of them were already well versed in a body of thought that could, if the occasion required, accept the most grinding social condition, even enslavement, as a perfectly legitimate feature of American polity. And yet, on the eve of the abolitionist crisis, most of them were committed to the gradual removal of slavery and the Negro by way of African colonization and to reformation of slavery through the moral instruction of both masters and slaves. Before the appearance of abolition, in fact, it may be said that emancipation, gradual and orderly, was the ideal of most of the northern conservatives who would rise up to strike down abolitionism.

When the crisis came, the anti-abolitionists, unlike their Federalist forebears, did not find it necessary to come up with a wholly new American ideology. The conservative counterrevolutionary tradition was fully capable of dealing with subversion, with inequality, and with social disorganization. Indeed, for them conservatism was a living tradition that helped them to see abolitionism as fanaticism, as social subversion, and as a movement that seemed as irreligious as the French Revolution. Quite naturally, then, they appropriated the ideology, the rhetoric, and the mechanisms of conservative counterrevolutionaries directly for use in combating a new form of subversion. They did not at first similarly appropriate either traditional proslavery arguments or the proslavery tendencies of their fathers. Until the crisis became most severe in the summer of 1835, most of them attempted to maintain the colonization ideal that had grown up since the War of 1812. At first attempting to appear more emancipationist than their ideological scruples would permit, by 1835 they began to react against all emancipationist proposals whatsoever. The closer the combat with abolitionists became, the more they were inclined to admit that there was nothing in their scheme of values that prohibited the practice of slavery.

By the time the smoke had cleared at the end of 1835, the anti-abolitionists had generally already given up on their earlier emancipationist ideals. They began at a faster and faster pace to pick up traditional proslavery arguments. By the end of the 1830s many of them had made the transition to proslavery. For many of them it was a difficult transition. In addition to relinquishing their early emancipationist ideals, they had to admit more openly than any conservative Federalist had ever found necessary that the American Revolution was a dead tradition. They were also put in unhappy league with southerners who it seemed were bent on resectionalizing the nation. For all their qualms about the consequences of endorsing slavery, they nevertheless became part and parcel of America's proslavery center and the primary exponents of America's new form of proslavery ideology.

The new ideology of proslavery was first and foremost an amalgam of conservative social thought with traditional proslavery arguments. The basic structure of their ideology, however, was always more conservative than it was proslavery. Instead of bringing conservative ideology into the van of proslavery thought, the anti-abolitionists superadded proslavery thought to their adopted social outlook. In their proslavery literature and, indeed, in that of most American proslavery writers, more emphasis would always be placed on instilling the outlook and values of conservative republicanism than in arguing the merits of slavery. While the anti-abolitionists inherited a world view that would abide slaveholding, they became aligned with proslavery primarily because they wished to maintain American republicanism, because they wanted to destroy all forms of subversion, because they held orthodoxy in religion a necessity, and because they valued union and social solidarity much more than individual liberty.

The irony of the history of anti-abolitionism is that while most anti-abolitionists neither sought nor wanted to be aligned with proslavery men in the South, they ended up defining America's most central proslavery tradition. Partly because the South did not have its own antilibertarian tradition, they ended up creating a proslavery ideology that would well serve the South and southern slaveholders. For the anti-abolitionists not only won over the North to their point of view in the 1830s, they also infiltrated the South and unleashed there the same set of notions, the same body of rhetoric, and the same mechanisms that had enabled proslavery to be embraced by the growing American conservative tradition.

ELEVEN

Proliferation of Conservative Ideas in the South, 1815–1835

Despite the attempts of historians traditionally to find the seeds of America's peculiar antebellum proslavery tradition in the South of the 1820s and early 1830s, there is little to suggest that the South underwent a wholesale reorganization of values on either the libertarian heritage of the American Revolution or the institution of slavery prior to the national crisis of abolitionism in 1835. Neither the Missouri debates of 1819–1820, the Denmark Vesey conspiracy of 1822, an agricultural depression in South Carolina, nor even the nullification controversy of the early 1830s engendered in southerners the kind of ideological shift that would allow social theorists to proclaim unblinkingly that slavery was an acceptable feature of American republicanism. On the contrary, all of the available evidence suggests that southerners were very late in developing a system of values that could interpret the institution of slavery—in terms of American polity—as other than an incongruous though necessary evil.

In terms of ideological and social values the inheritors of the New England conservative tradition and southerners stood poles apart. While New England and much of the North had experienced an ideological counterrevolution that had turned Revolutionary ideology on its head, southerners, irrespective of their practices with regard to slavery, had remained largely consistent at least in their public veneration of Revolutionary ideals. With only relatively minor Jeffersonian interpolations and redefinitions having been added to the Revolutionary heritage, southerners had continued constant in their glorification of the Revolution even if they had been demonstrably lax in adopting its social teachings. Whereas Fourth of July celebrations in New England had long since devolved into occasions for jeremiads on the political and social sins of Americans, southerners could still eagerly celebrate the day as the anniversary of the arrival of freedom for Americans. As late as the early 1830s, nothing in the southern experience had yet done violence to the Revolutionary heritage. Nothing had yet caused southerners, despite their social practices, to reject either the values or the ideals of the Revolution they celebrated.

Part of the explanation for the longevity of Revolutionary thought as the ideological undergirding of southern society was the fact that the contagion of liberty that grew out of the Revolution had little impact on the South. While southerners shared in the growth of political freedom, the Revolution had done little to alter the shape of southern society, nor had southerners suffered the kind of crisis situation that might have caused them to reshape their ideological beliefs. The French Revolution had not been for them a particularly disturbing event. They found no reason to fear the infiltration of America by anything like the Bavarian Illuminati. While there were Federalists in the South speaking and writing in the same veins as Timothy Dwight and Harrison Gray Otis, they were few in number and had almost no lasting impact on southern thought. And despite the presence of some of America's great intellectuals seeking to address major philosophical and political issues in the form of John Taylor, John Randolph, and Nathaniel Macon, their rambling musings and sporadic writings had little general or lasting impact on the shape of southern society. The War of 1812 was neither socially nor politically a very trying time for southerners. With Jeffersonians in power from 1800 until the mid-1820s, with the southern economy generally booming through most of the period, and with an absence of troublesome social movements, southerners experienced throughout the period of the northern conservative counterrevolution perhaps the most blissful interregnum they would ever know. And neither the rise of colonization, the brief national debate on slavery in the territories, nor the occurrence of two slave uprisings interceded to disturb the general peacefulness of the period. In each of those situations southern slaveholders acted as any set of slaveholders would to protect their immediate pecuniary interest.

Historians have been so certain that a new wave of proslavery sprang forth from the South during the 1820s or 1830s that every discussion of slavery by any southerner or in any event occurring in the South affecting slavery has been subjected to microscopic investigation and interpreta-

tion. The favorite subjects of study have been changes in latter-day
Jeffersonian Virginia and particularly the slavery debates there in 1831–
1832 and the great nullification movement in South Carolina. Both
arenas and the streams of events in both states have been seen as the
formative causes of the type of new conservatism that emerged in the
South that could defend slavery as a beneficial and necessary institution
in American society.

The events in Virginia antedate the nullification controversy by several
years and have been the subject of greatest attention and interpretation in
recent years. Given the living presence of Thomas Jefferson from the
Revolution until 1826 and his abundant expressions of opinion, historians have insisted on finding in Jefferson's frequent comments about
government, the Negro, slavery, and sectionalism the beginnings of a new
conservative philosophy that could undergird proslavery and southern
sectionalism. Some have argued that such thinking can be found in Jefferson's last letters and articles for the public presses. Moreover, in a recent
detailed study of the Virginia Constitutional Convention of 1829–1830,
Dickson Bruce finds that a new rhetoric of conservatism was present in
the deliberations of the convention and that the themes enunciated there
became the core conservative principles that later emerged in southern
proslavery literature and thought. From his perspective, Thomas R. Dew,
in his *Review of the Debates* published in 1832, extracted from the convention the articulated conservative principles and amalgamated them with
proslavery. Dew's essay gave "this proslavery framework its fullest expression" and was the "link between the conservatism of the early national
period and the rhetoric of proslavery that would grow in the South in the
years leading up to the Civil War."[1]

An even more detailed and thorough study of the Virginia slavery
debates of 1831–1832 by Alison Goodyear Freehling comes to a fundamentally different conclusion. In *Drift Toward Dissolution* she portrays the
debates as indecisive. Many participants were fundamentally opposed to
slavery. Most seemed to feel that if slavery were abolished it should be in
association with colonization. The result of the convention was to connect Virginia more clearly with later free soil notions than with the permanent practice of slavery. Thomas Dew's *Review*, far from foreshadowing later proslavery literature and thought, was an effective antidote to
colonization and a strong articulation of free soilism. Freehling found a
continuing ambivalence about slavery in Virginia all the way to the Civil
War. While antislavery and proslavery Virginians joined hands in con-

demnation of the abolitionists, there was never any unanimity in Virginia that slavery must be maintained as a critical ingredient of Virginia society.[2]

Freehling's view of Virginia on the eve of abolitionism in this respect is quite correct. There was not in the Jeffersonian tradition or in the various debates about Virginia government or even slavery up through 1832 any semblance of a conservative ideology or counterrevolutionary movement that could deal with the challenge of perceived subversion in American society. While it is clear that in his latter years Jefferson expressed many concerns about the direction of American government and the difficulties of dealing with the presence of the Negro in American society, his concern was always on the side of ensuring that government did not tyrannize over the rights of freemen and that no governmental instrument be created that would undermine the equality of freemen. His concern was never with the type of social subversion that was represented by the arrival of abolitionism or any socially subversive movement. And the same was true of the two Virginia conventions. In both, Virginians were still arguing about the rights of man in the Revolutionary and Jeffersonian traditions; in neither had they yet become aware that subversion could come as an ingredient of a free society and not from the tyranny of government. As a consequence, the bits and pieces of conservatism observable in Virginia prior to the onset of abolitionism as a threatening force in 1835 were feeble indeed and could not possibly have provided the foundations for the conservative counter-revolution that would undergird America's proslavery ideology.

In contrast to Virginians were the men of South Carolina and Massachusetts who, if they shared a common experience before the rise of abolition, found it in the perception of becoming aggrieved, impotent minorities. Massachusetts had lost its once prominent position in the national counsels with the election of Jefferson in 1800 and the onset of Republican rule. Disturbing events preceding the transition and the shock of loss of power combined to launch a process that in the following decades brought the conservative counterrevolution in Massachusetts. In an uncanny, but nevertheless similar string of events in the late 1820s, South Carolina—more singly than in the earlier case of Massachusetts—experienced a series of unnerving reversals that ended in an equally decisive loss of ability to shape national policy. The end to a generation of southern peace and prosperity came when South Carolina nullifiers broke ranks with Andrew Jackson and tried to win with threats of secession what they had failed to achieve in Congress. It is in the complex history of South Carolina nullification, then, that one might expect to find the first indications of a major shift in southern thought.

William W. Freehling, in his *Prelude to Civil War*, the only thorough examination of the entire nullification controversy, found at the heart of the South Carolinians' impulse toward nullification "a morbid sensitivity to the beginnings of the antislavery campaign." Nullification of the 1828 "tariff of abominations" was but the crowning event in the gradual shift of South Carolina's ruling elite from eager nationalism in 1816 to intense sectionalism by 1836. Despite the focus of South Carolinians on a truly hurtful tariff, Freehling found that slavery was never far beneath the surface. While South Carolina moved toward nullification, it marched with an even, rapid stride toward the open defense of slavery. In fact, Freehling concluded, "the nullification crusade had been, in part, an attempt to check the abolitionists without debating slavery." With the failure of nullification, however, a "Great Reaction" occurred in which South Carolinians used their newly found "conservative philosophy" and "repressive policies" in an open defense of slavery.

Between 1834 and 1836, Freehling continued, South Carolina planters shifted from their previous arguments that "slavery was evil because it fulfilled practical needs" to assertions that as slavery was the least defective of all systems of labor it could be considered a positive blessing. Turning against natural rights theory and Jeffersonian doctrines as "a pack of pernicious abstractions," proslavery theorists rejected the Age of Reason and "retreated to the medieval, Aristotelian concepts of hierarchy, rank, and order." In a sweeping reversal of inherited values, they scored democracy as mobbism or the despotism of the multitude and opted for the rule of gentlemen with "a stake in society." They also imagined that a new breed of politicos or spoilsmen had seized the reins of government from America's natural elite by appealing to the passions of the democratic rabble. The spoilsmen, with no appreciation of republican order, threatened to dismantle what was left of a stable society. The end result of the Great Reaction and of proslavery theory, then, was "to make explicit and theoretical their eighteenth-century passion for an aristocratic republic."[3]

There are many interpretive difficulties connected with Freehling's argument, if it is to be taken as an explanation of the rise of a new perspective on slavery either in the South as a whole or in South Carolina in particular. It cannot be denied that the nullification campaign at least prepared South Carolinians (but few others) for the bitter display of sectionalism that accompanied the South's response to abolitionism. Nor can it be argued that the nullification experience did not contribute to the peculiarly virulent and widespread reaction of South Carolinians to the first abolition crisis of the mid-1830s. But from the national pro-slavery response to abolitionism it seems clear that a new approach to the problem of slavery arose independently of nullification. Neither the pro-slavery response of the South nor that of the nation, at least initially, resulted from the rampant sectionalism that appeared in South Carolina in the late 1820s and early 1830s. While nullification was a campaign restricted almost entirely to South Carolina, the proslavery response to abolition was a widespread, nearly simultaneous phenomenon shouted by men with little knowledge and less interest in the special economic and status problems of South Carolinians. Even in South Carolina practically the only thing that distinguished the proslavery responses of nullifiers and antinullifiers was the manifestly sectional interpretations the former applied to abolitionism. Moreover, of all those who came to the defense of slavery—even in South Carolina—very few had any sympathy with nullification. Finally, as will be seen, most nullifiers eventually came to share intensely nonsectional views on proslavery.

The great progenitors of a new proslavery ideology in the South were in fact the very men who were most opposed to nullification, to sectionalism, and to all of the things for which nullifiers stood. The creators of a new proslavery ideology for the South were those men who were most in tune with nationalism and with the warp and woof of national thought. In a sense, the groundwork for the creation of a new proslavery ideology in the South was laid without the knowledge of southern sectionalists and caught men such as the nullifiers almost by surprise. And in terms of the pace with which southerners picked up the new perspective on slavery and put it to use in propagandizing America, southern sectionalists and the nullifiers in particular were among the last to arrive. They were the last, but eventually the most eager, to fall under the sway of America's conservative counterrevolution.

Long before the crisis of abolitionism that saw southerners eagerly take up conservative social ideology as mediated to them by the anti-abolitionists, conservative ideas were slowly working their way into southern society. Moreover, scores of men who had come under the influence of what was once a distinctively New England world view were quietly applying the principles and policies of America's first counterrevolutionary movement to the institution of slavery. Almost all of them were clergymen. All of them were either born in the North or had been nurtured under the influence of conservative countersubversives. All of them came up in one way or another in the same mold as the early anti-abolitionists of the North. All of them were connected in some way with the organizations and purposes of the Benevolent Empire, that informal machine to use religion to rebuild American society along conservative lines. The most important characteristic they shared in common was the fact that with the rise of abolitionism they came to the defense of slavery in the same manner as did the anti-abolitionists.

As a group they reflected the tendencies and concerns of pre-abolition America. They absorbed themselves in the wide-ranging work of the Benevolent Empire, promoted religious institutions, and carefully steered clear of politics. If they found occasion to take a position on slavery—and they did only rarely—they were with strikingly few exceptions always on the side of moderate emancipationism whether by colonization or through individual manumission. They saw themselves as reformers in everything they did. And they were guided by a set of principles that were shared by all men who came under the sway of the conservative counterrevolution. More than most others in the South, they were attuned to national concerns generally outside the political realm.

Whether the field of endeavor involved the distribution of Bibles, the posting of foreign and domestic missionaries, the education of Indians, the promotion of peace, the organization of Sunday schools, the printing of religious tracts, the fostering of educational institutions, or the general formation of benevolent societies, these future defenders of slavery could be found among the directors, agents, or correspondents of the appropriate national society for this purpose. While most of them were in the nature of conservative reformers, some of their fellows who had not yet arrived from Europe paraded as revolutionaries in their native lands.[4] But most future proslavery clergymen adopted the conservative aims and exciting stimuli of the Benevolent Empire as their own. As early as 1816 in a sermon entitled *Signs of the Times,* Benjamin M. Palmer, a southern Congregational clergyman in Charleston, applauded the new spirit of association in purposive societies that came to characterize American and southern religion. By 1834 benevolent societies had penetrated even to the backwoods of forbidding east Tennessee where William G. Brownlow found Presbyterians forming auxiliaries of every conceivable national society and some not known outside Tennessee.[5]

In the years just prior to the rise of abolition, northern-inspired institutions in the form of benevolent societies spread across the South at a startling pace. Scores of future proslavery clergymen enlisted as missionaries, both foreign and domestic, to carry a newly exciting Christian gospel to heathen lands and to the unchurched at home. Whether in the service of the American Board of Commissioners for Foreign Missions or one of the denominational mission agencies, the late 1820s and early 1830s were years of excitement and purpose for fledgling young men who had not yet discovered that they would one day be numbered among the defenders of slavery.[6] At the Presbyterian Theological Seminary in Columbia, South Carolina, in 1833, George Howe, recently from New England and a professorship at Dartmouth College, urged his southern students "to evangelize the benighted tribes of the earth." In response to his call three of the five graduating seniors became foreign missionaries, among them, John Leighton Wilson, a southern apostle to Africa for more than twenty years.[7]

The same spirit that made missionaries of southern candidates for the ministry caused others to promote in various ways the religious instruction of slaves. The desire of clergymen to carry both religious experience and religious knowledge to slaves has often been seen by historians as a moderate form of antislavery activity—particularly before the rise of abolition. Frequent references to slavery as "a putrid carcass," "a millstone hanging about the neck of our society," and other damaging epithets by ministers involved in slave instruction convinced slaveholders that clergymen could not always be trusted with the souls of slaves. While some staunchly religious masters welcomed missionaries to their slaves, others resisted eager clergymen who they thought might engender unrest or encroach upon the prerogatives and powers of masters. The reaction of some slaveholders against the intermeddling of ministers has often been seen as part of the pattern of resistance against abolitionism. If ministers truly wanted to teach slaves the values of religion, they had to conform to stipulations dictated by slaveholders.[8]

It would be wrong to interpret the rise of concern among clergymen for the religious instruction of slaves in the 1820s and 1830s as part of the impulse that led to abolitionism. While some of the clergymen who participated in fostering missions to slaves may have entertained doubts about the advisability of owning slaves and might even have desired to see an end to slavery in America, their views were entirely consistent with those held by a majority of Americans before the rise of abolition.

And although some slaveholders initially resisted the access of missionaries to slaves, such measures were in no way comparable to the frenzied revulsion they would display against abolitionism. At the heart of the movement to instruct slaves was the impulse toward benevolence—that conservative aim of taking right religion and social practice to all men. When slaveholders stiffened their guards against the armies of missionaries, they were actually reacting to the arrival, at long last, of the Benevolent Empire in the South.

Until the rise of benevolence there had been little impulse in America to give special consideration to the religious wants of slaves. While Thomas Bacon in Maryland and other Anglican clergy and missionaries in Virginia and South Carolina had established model programs of religious instruction in colonial America, from the Revolution to the War of 1812, there is little evidence to suggest that any church or group of clergymen promoted the religious education of slaves. Following the pattern of segregation in the North, some separate churches for free Negroes and slaves sprang up in the South and some blacks (both slave and free) were permitted, particularly by Methodists and Baptists, to minister to their brothers. For the most part, however, slaves attended the churches of their masters and were consigned to separate pews or galleries. The very paucity of literature designed specifically for the instruction of slaves indicated the lack of interest in the religious welfare of slaves. From 1763, when the last of Thomas Bacon's pamphlets with sermons for slaves appeared, until 1813, when William Meade reprinted a collection of Bacon's sermons, no known literature specifically for slaves appeared in print.[9] The lack of concern with the religion of slaves went hand-in-hand with the philosophical indifference or outright hostility toward all things religious that characterized the Jeffersonian South.

Not even the rampant revivalism that crossed and recrossed the frontier South after 1800 could shake the southern image of the social irrelevance of religion. Not until the arrival of the agents of benevolent societies after the War of 1812 did some southerners begin to reckon with the social significance of religious institutions in creating order and obedience among men. Far from being the locus of perennial religious fundamentalism, the South had not yet turned to the abject biblicism that would characterize its religious outlook in the last half of the nineteenth and early twentieth centuries. Biblicism, fundamentalism, and social piety were learned traits that cropped up in the same process that gave rise to proslavery ideology. Hence, it was not strange that slaveholders should look askance upon eager missionaries who demanded access to the minds and hearts of slaves. Clergymen had often proved to be emancipationists in disguise. But also southern religion had always been either socially irrelevant or else perceived as sickly fanatical as in the case of many southern Methodists and Baptists.[10]

The benevolent spirit that spread from North to South during the 1820s slowly revolutionized attitudes toward the religious instruction of slaves. The revolution reached full tide between 1829 and 1835.[11] Beginning rather suddenly in 1822 and continuing throughout the 1820s, various southern clergymen supplied the want for instructional literature for slaves and set about calling masters to their duties. In Virginia, John Mines, a minister, wrote the first catechism for slaves "with a new method of instructing those who cannot read." In South Carolina, Benjamin M. Palmer wrote another "designed chiefly for the benefit of colored persons." In the tiny town of Salem, North Carolina, pietistic Moravians, communal-living Hussites, formed a society, a church, and a school for educating the community's black population. A year later, in 1823, Presbyterian John Holt Rice in Virginia, Episcopalian Frederick Dalcho, and Baptist Richard Furman—the latter two of Charleston—registered in common a plea for both ministers and masters to undertake religious instruction as a chief duty of Christians to both man and God. By 1828 Palmer had printed a second, more usable edition of his catechism, the standard and most commonly used version until the mid-1830s. Finally, in 1829, one prominent layman with vast slaveholdings who had been caught up in the expanding religious revival of the South, Charles Cotesworth Pinckney, published a glowing approval of religious instruction and asked South Carolina Methodists to send missionaries to his plantations.[12]

What had been only a gradual movement in the 1820s became a flood in the early 1830s. Under the auspices of a missionary society connected with South Carolina Methodists and directed by William Capers, clergyman and slaveholder, domestic missionaries were sent to tidewater plantations in South Carolina. Wealthy planters in St. Luke's Parish formed an association among themselves for religious instruction in 1831 to "do something for the thousands of immortal souls who are perishing for the lack of knowledge." A year earlier in the coastal Georgia counties of McIntosh and Liberty, clergymen who doubled as wealthy planters formed similar associations. By 1833 church conferences, presbyteries, and synods were actively debating policies and procedures for

Southern Benevolent Reformers of Slavery

William Capers, 1790–1855
*Methodist bishop, 1846–1855, and
founder of home missions to slaves*

Charles Colcock Jones, Sr.,
1804–1863
*Lifelong Presbyterian missionary to slaves
in Liberty County, Georgia*

Nathaniel Bowen, 1779–1839
*Episcopal bishop of South Carolina,
1818–1839, and promoter of
slave instruction*

William Meade, 1789–1862
*Episcopal bishop of Virginia, 1841–
1862, and author of literature for slaves*

blanketing the South with missionaries to slaves. The ferment of association engendered widespread newspaper comment and discussion in the Episcopal *Gospel Messenger,* the Presbyterian *Charleston Observer,* the Baptist *Christian Index,* the Methodist *Southern Christian Advocate,* and a host of other religious papers strongly endorsing growing efforts for religious instruction.[13]

The intensity of the revolution can be gauged by the appearance of unprecedented numbers of sermons, essays, and instructional material on slave education and the duties of masters. The Liberty County Association for the Religious Instruction of Negroes began publishing annual reports and sermons on slave instruction in 1833 and continued the program until 1848. The guiding figure behind the Association, Charles Colcock Jones, a Presbyterian minister afterward known as "Apostle to the Slaves," had already published in 1832 in four rapid editions a sermon entitled *Religious Instruction of the Negroes.* William Meade, Episcopal bishop of Virginia, followed in 1834 with a *Pastoral Letter* on the same subject "to the ministers, members, and Friends" of the church in Virginia. Nathaniel Bowen, Meade's fellow bishop in South Carolina, followed the Virginia ecclesiastic in a similar *Pastoral Letter* a year later. The numbers of new catechisms, instructional material, and plans of instruction increased as dramatically. Capers published a catechism "for the use of the Methodist missionaries in their Godly work of instructing the Negroes" in 1832 and one of his missionaries, Samuel J. Bryan, published two others in 1833 and 1834. Charles C. Jones issued one of his own as well in the latter year. Edward R. Laurens, a South Carolina planter, and Thomas S. Clay, a slaveholder of Georgia, published plans for systematic instruction in 1832 and 1833. Mrs. Horace S. Pratt, wife of a Presbyterian clergyman, wrote a volume with biographies of exemplary slaves in 1834.[14]

While some men wrote, others took to the field. Jones, Capers, Bryan, Meade, and Bowen were all involved directly or indirectly with the opening of missions to slaves. Despite his wealth, education, and stature, Jones spent nearly all of his waking hours from 1832 until 1848 as a missionary and as the dominant force behind the Liberty County Association. Capers single-handedly directed the mission work of Methodists in the South. Bryan worked as missionary or superintendent of missions to slaves in South Carolina, Georgia, and Florida until too old for the work. Bowen and Meade directed missions from afar at the top of the ecclesiastical ladder. They nevertheless traveled widely to meet missionaries in the field and to study various mission programs. Bowen visited the Moravians in Salem, North Carolina, to investigate their model program. Meade visited South Carolina to see the work of Alexander Glennie, a Cambridge-educated Englishman, who devoted his life from 1832 to 1866 to ministering to the blacks of All Saint's Parish, Waccamaw, South Carolina, and that of Christopher E. Gadsden, afterward bishop of the state. Numerous nonsoutherners were also prominent in the fostering of new missions, including George Howe, the Massachusetts-born professor in Columbia's Presbyterian seminary, who recruited missionaries; and New Yorker John Bachman who pressed Lutheran ministrations to slaves from Charleston. Such crusty southerners as Basil Manly of Charleston, Iveson Brookes of Edgefield, James Smylie of Mississippi, and Joseph C. Stiles of Georgia—all clergymen of wealth and stature—devoted themselves full-time to slave instruction as well in the early 1830s.[15]

The remarkable aspect of the sudden waxing of interest in the instruction of slaves is that it occurred prior and without reference to any acknowledged threat of abolitionism. Far from being the appendage to proslavery that it would afterward become, the movement to give slaves the essence of Christian knowledge seems clearly to have been an outgrowth of benevolence as it bubbled up through the placid surface of pre-abolitionist southern culture. Instead of couching their pleas in the form of resistance to antislavery influences, those clergymen and planters who promoted slave instruction in the early 1830s believed that they were undertaking a social and religious reform in the best interests of benevolence and true religion. Whereas they would later pursue slave instruction as a means toward removing the basis for one of the most severe abolitionist complaints—the absence of the knowledge of religion among slaves—in the early 1830s they spoke only in terms of religious and social duty to what they considered a miserable set of human beings.[16]

While in both their pleas to masters and in instructional matter for slaves they taught the abject subordination and submissiveness of servants, the religious duty of obedience to the master's will, and the hope for heavenly if not earthly bliss as in the case of post-abolition writings, they unmistakably characterized slavery as an evil someday to be removed. The Presbyterian Synod of South Carolina and Georgia, after investigating religious instruction in 1833, wrote, "We are chained to a putrid carcass; it sickens and destroys us. We have a millstone hanging about the neck of our society, to sink us deep in the sea of vice." William Meade counted himself among those in 1834 "who are prone to indulge in fruitless lamentations over the condition of these, our unfortunate fellowbeings; and in heavy condemnations of our forefathers' folly in bringing this evil upon us." Nathaniel Bowen in 1835 saw slavery as a condition of "moral hopelessness, to which not even the roamer of the wilderness, and the tenant of the forest are consigned." A few years earlier while he yet contemplated a career of instructing slaves, Charles C. Jones wrote privately a clear indictment of slavery: "The more I look at it, the more enormous does it appear a violation of all the laws of God and man at once. A complete annihilation of justice. An inhuman abuse of power."[17]

It should not be regarded as strange that the early promoters of slave instruction should speak in such unequivocal terms. They were partakers of and participants in the benevolent reform of slavery that proceeded irresistibly and logically from the same conservative social ideology that undergirded the thought and actions of benevolent reformers throughout the nation. Almost to a man they had been exposed by upbringing or educational experience to the teachings of ideologized New England conservatives. Some got it by direct involvement in Federalist politics or the inheritance of Federalist counterrevolutionary principles (Furman, Dalcho, Pinckney, Capers, and the Gadsdens); others by family connections in New England or educational experiences at Yale, Andover, or Princeton (Bowen, Bachman, Rice, Palmer, Jones, Howe, Stiles); others by the extensions of the Congregational-Presbyterian phalanx into the South (Clay, Palmer, Rice, Smylie, Brookes); and still others by intimate association with benevolent societies (Meade, Manly). Nearly every early proponent of slave instruction participated in the transference of conservative values from North to South under the guise of benevolent reform.

The form in which the benevolent reformers cast their new concern for the instruction of slaves, in fact, attests to the growing influence of New England customs and thought over southern society on the eve of abolitionism. The chief instructional tool, never before used with slaves, was the catechism designed for oral instruction. While historians have often deprecated the growth of oral instruction through catechisms as a form of brainwashing, which circumvented laws against teaching slaves to read, the practice of catechising was in actuality a benign appropriation of one of the most powerful institutions of New England culture. From 1641 when the Massachusetts General Court called for the writing of a catechism designed for the needs of the Puritan children of New

England until 1886 when the last one for widespread use was printed, hundreds or perhaps thousands of variant editions of catechisms or "primers" were published in New England. In its most popular and widely used form alone, that of the *New England Primer,* at least three million copies were printed and sold between 1700 and 1849. Although after 1800 the *Primer* was to some extent secularized, it continued to contain various catechisms. One separate catechism prepared by the Worcester Association of Ministers in 1822 went through fifteen large editions by 1849.[18]

The function of the catechism was to train children in the mold of their parents, to inculcate shared values, and to teach the convictions necessary for right religion. The catechism taught elementary knowledge, theology, social values, moral obligation—all that was necessary for one to assume his place as a virtuous, industrious citizen. Although many churches used catechisms to teach religion, none approached the unique reliance upon it of New England Puritans. Cotton Mather had early realized that fact when he wrote that "few Pastors of Mankind ever took such pains at *Catechising* as have been taken by our New English Divines: Now, let any Man living read the most judicious and elaborate Catechisms published . . . ; and say whether true Divinity were ever better handled." Mather could have added as well, true social ideology, for from the beginning catechisms propagandized children in social values. For example, one in 1679 was designed "*to Create* in them [children] an Abhorrence of Romish *Idolatry at the same time, which being inspired in their green and tender years, may leave an Impression in their Minds to the End of their Lives.*" With similar purposes of indoctrination in mind, in the late eighteenth and early nineteenth centuries, New England catechisms and the Primer were exported, particularly by agencies of the Benevolent Empire, throughout America.[19]

Benevolent reformers bent on instructing slaves appropriated not only the form and purpose of the New England catechisms, they also adopted the New England mode of instruction. In the mid-nineteenth century many aged benevolent reformers recalled the terrors and demands of both the instructional material and the method of teaching. Heman Humphrey, president of Amherst College, recalled in 1850 that apple-stealing children were offered the choice between imprisonment and recitation of the entirety of the catechism before the town magistrate. By the age of four a child was expected to have memorized and to be able to repeat with absolute verbal correctness the entire catechism, whether or not he understood the contents. At church, at school, and at home children were drilled unsparingly until they had perfected every word. Parents lax in their duties were described by Mather as little better than "*Sea-Monstors . . . who will not be moved . . . to Draw out the Breasts* of the Catechism, unto their *Young Ones!*" Another who remembered the instructional techniques of New England in the early nineteenth century might have easily described a catechist instructing slaves. The minister,

> standing in the pulpit, put out the questions to the children in order; and each one, when the question came to him, was expected to wheel out of the line, *a la militaire*, into the broad aisle, and face the minister, and make his very best obeisance, and answer the question put to him without the slightest mistake. To be *told*, that is, to be prompted or corrected by the minister, was not a thing to be permitted by any child, who expected thereafter to have any reputation in that town for good scholarship . . . and many are the persons who recollect, and will long recollect, the palpitating heart, the tremulous voice, the quivering frame, with which for several years, they went through that terrible ordeal.

The same impact, the same terror, and similar lessons dealt their children by the sons of New England were in the 1820s and 1830s directed toward the slaves of the South.[20]

On the eve of the first abolitionist crisis at least those southerners who had become involved in the reform of slavery thought and acted in much the same channels as their northern compatriots. As yet, however, such thinking was limited precisely to those absorbed in some way with benevolent reform. Impelled as they were by the limited, though stridently sought aims of conservative reform, they could on occasion sound and act like eager emancipationists or consecrated agitators bent on reshaping the world. They were, until faced with the threat of abolitionism, among the most hopeful and confident men in America.

In his commencement address at the University of North Carolina in 1819, for example, Iveson Brookes, afterward a southern sectionalist and bitter enemy of abolition, reflected the influence of Elisha Mitchell, a New Englander of the Timothy Dwight mold and of the strongly Presbyterian faculty of the university. Discoursing on the query, "Is the State of the World Better in the Present Age Than at Any Former Period?" Brookes affirmed that "the present age surpasses any former period both in philosophical knowledge and moral excellence." Despite an abundance of infidelity and profligation, moral exertions and true knowledge, he thought, were tipping the scales in favor of "a state of progressive improvement." Many years later upon meeting one of his former classmates, James K. Polk, Brookes recalled his youthful idealism in a letter: "You perhaps remember what an Antislavery fellow I was at Chapel Hill. I wrote several speeches & compositions against slavery, being about as ignorant on the subject as most of the Northern abolitionists now are."[21]

Two years after Brookes vented his youthful moral fervor in Chapel Hill, Basil Manly, later one of Brookes's closest associates in the Baptist ministry, in his own commencement address at the University of South Carolina proved that similar sentiments could be entertained in South Carolina. Speaking "On the Emancipation of Slaves," Manly quickly scored slavery "as an evil under which this country has long groaned." It was evil, he believed, because it caused contention between men, parties, religions, and states. Moreover, it was "utterly repugnant to the spirit of our republican Institutions," a denial of the principle that all men are naturally free and equal. The rapid growth of the slave population posed another threat "to the lives and liberties of the people of this country." Justice to the slave, the expansion of freedom, and the demands for public safety "demonstrate the necessity of an immediate provision against it." Whether by colonization, manumission, or gradual emancipation, the time was near when the federal government "may with propriety declare herself the friend of universal emancipation; when all America shall lift an united voice over the abodes of slavery and wretchedness, and proclaim an eternal jubilee."[22]

Although Manly remained throughout his speech within the basic limits of Jeffersonian thought on slavery, when he broached the topic of methods of emancipation he suggested that the government might "encourage the formation of benevolent societies which have in view the grand object [of emancipation]." For him, Brookes, and other reformers in the 1820s, the conservative-inspired Benevolent Empire held out the only hope for a sane, orderly solution to the problem of slavery. It was, therefore, not strange that many of them should have placed their greatest hopes in the scheme of colonization nor that on the subject of colonization they should express their fondest dreams of eventual universal emancipation. And among those who were driven to free their own slaves, including William Meade and John Leighton Wilson, colonization in Africa seemed as well the best solution to their personal dilemma.

A host of benevolent reformers who afterward played important roles in building up a national proslavery ideology were very active in prompting colonization and the works of the American Colonization Society. William Meade of Virginia, William T. Hamilton of New Jersey (afterward of Alabama), R. B. C. Howell of Tennessee, Henry B. Bascom of Pennsylvania (afterward of Kentucky), Rufus William Bailey of Maine (later in South Carolina and Texas), John Hughes of New York (long in Maryland), Samuel Seabury of Connecticut, and Simeon Doggett of Massachusetts—all active and vocal supporters of colonization before the rise of abolition—proved that regardless of section or religious denomination, most future proslavery writers who took a position on the fate of slavery in the 1820s and early 1830s favored the route of colonization. None, not even Richard Furman, Frederick Dalcho, and other similar writers in South Carolina who are usually credited with getting a southern proslavery response under way, felt that slavery should be continued perpetually without any possibility of an eventual end. Until the bursting of the bubble of colonization by both abolitionists and political economists in the early 1830s, reform-minded Americans pursued colonization as a most desirable social and religious ideal.

The moral fervor that these benevolent reformers often brought to colonization can be perceived in such writings as William T. Hamilton's *A Word for the African* preached in New Jersey in 1825, in Henry B. Bascom's *Claims of Africa* as rehearsed over and over again by the Methodist clergyman throughout America in 1832 and 1833, or in R. B. C. Howell's plea of 1833 in Virginia for "Colonization or the Conversion of Africa." Hamilton deplored slavery as a "horrible crime" against "an entire people, who, though dwelling in the cradle of liberty, are shackeld in the cruel bonds of slavery. This is darkness—horrible darkness, in the midst of light!" John Hughes, afterward Roman Catholic archbishop of New York and an unblinking enemy of abolition, had expressed similar sentiments in the mid-1820s in a widely republished poem entitled "The Slave." In the poem a slave wept,

> Hail Columbia, happy land!
> Where Freedom waves her golden wand,
>   Where equal justice reigns.
> But ah! Columbia great and free
> Has not a boon for mine and me,
>   But slavery and chains.
> Oh! once I had a soothing joy,
>   The hope of other years,
> That free Columbia would destroy

> The source of these my tears.
>   But pining, declining,
> I still drag to the grave,
>   Doomed to sigh till I die,
> Free Columbia's slave.

"Because my hand is black," Hughes's slave continued, he had to suffer injustice and bondage. Only emancipation coupled with colonization, Hughes believed, could remove the blot on America.[23]

Some of the benevolent reformers who afterward blasted abolition and upheld slavery reserved their most radical views for use in their private dealings with others or even for personal contemplation. William Winans of Mississippi was a case in point. Although himself a slaveholder by marriage and a proponent of slaveholding by Christians in later years, the Pennsylvania-born Winans remained a lifelong supporter of manumission coupled with colonization. Even though never an official agent of the American Colonization Society, Winans organized and headed the Mississippi Colonization Society and remained a constant correspondent of Robert R. Gurley and other colonization leaders.[24]

In letters to the parent society extending from the 1820s until his death, Winans maintained an alarming enmity for slavery that caused Mississippians to doubt his devotion to the South. Winans's views in fact so startled his closest friend and appointed biographer, William Watkins, that Watkins could never in good conscience publish his extensive writings on Winans. In 1826, in reference to slaves—"this unfortunate portion of our *hapless* Southern population"—Winans wrote Gurley, "I most decidedly believe that no event, since the promulgation of the Gospel, was ever more important to humanity than those which are contemplated by your society. May the God of *Israel* give success to your benevolent exertions!" After nearly twenty years of battle with abolition near the end of his life, Winans could still write the parent society that there had been no diminution in the "deep interest which for twenty-eight years, I have felt in this important enterprise."[25]

At least one of the benevolent reformers who afterward defended slavery was so intense in this opposition to slavery that he criticized and withdrew his support from the American Colonization Society in the 1820s. Joshua Lacy Wilson, pastor of First Presbyterian Church in Cincinnati, refused to endorse the society in 1826 because it "openly and unblushingly acknowledges the *constitutional* and *legitimate* existence of *slavery*." In an open letter to the governor of Ohio, Wilson argued, "I believe *liberty* to be one of the *unalienable* rights of man . . . one which cannot be transferred." "If liberty be an unalienable right," he continued, "it belongs to the black man as well as the white. No human enactors can make involuntary hereditary slavery lawful." Although he supported other benevolent reforms quite actively, Wilson could not count the Colonization Society among them. The Society hypocritically feigned benevolence, on the one hand, to gain the support of New England and clergymen, and non-interference with slavery, on the other, to win the favor of slaveholders. "Were I a friend to Slavery," he added, "I would patronize it too." But colonization was "bottomed upon an unrighteous determination": "White men will not to do justice to the blacks." As a genuine reformer in the 1820s, Wilson could not accept the moral ends of colonization.[26]

Like the abolitionists who succeeded them as the most vigorous champions of emancipation, the benevolent reformers of the 1820s, especially in the South, could and did experience the frustrations of attempting to root out or correct an intractable social evil. None felt more deeply nor revealed more poignantly the immovability of slavery than Basil Manly while he served as pastor of First Baptist Church of Charleston from 1826 to 1837. During the first three years of his pastorate Manly kept a private "Church Journal" of his work as minister to a large urban congregation consisting of both blacks and whites, slave and free. Nearly half of his extensive journal dealt with free blacks and slaves and his efforts to bring them fully into the fellowship of the church. He attempted to overcome the normally chaotic state of black church membership by enrolling all regular attendants at religious services as full members of the church. He then tried to "establish a system of government and discipline for them." His system was not, however, a tool whereby whites monitored blacks. Instead, he placed the task of discipline fully in the hands of blacks. He also licensed black preachers to oversee the plan and to take charge of the entire black church membership.[27]

In addition to revealing himself to be a conscientious minister and teacher of blacks, Manly had frequent occasion to counsel slaves. Most came to him to discuss their religious faith. One woman, however, confronted Manly with perhaps the greatest moral dilemma of his life. The woman confided that "her master *compels* her to live in constant adultery with him." A church member, she would not take communion for fear of God's punishment for the sin. Manly advised her "to remonstrate kindly with her master, and firmly and decidedly to tell him that she could not consent to sin if he would not hear her mild remonstrance." The master would not listen. Rather than taking it upon himself to talk with the man, Manly told the woman in stronger terms that "it is better for her to die, than to sin—that she simply can prevent the evil if she be resolute and firm—and that God will not hold her guiltless while any possible means of preventing it, even to the risk of life itself, remains untried." Unable for fear of severe recrimination upon the woman to intervene on her behalf or to find a workable solution to the relation between one master and one slave, Manly finally chose the only course left open. After four years of fruitless counsel he purchased the woman and made her "our worthy and respected old nurse." Conscience, desire for just treatment, a personal impulse for the rooting out of sin devolved for Manly into slave ownership as the only possible solution to a moral dilemma.[28]

For southern benevolent reformers at work before the rise of abolition, slavery was in every way a dilemma. Slavery was immoral because it was filled with injustices for the bondsman. But it was also immoral in that it threatened to break down the moral fiber of whites. It was a social and cultural dilemma because it made tyrants of men who valued freedom and because it contradicted protestations of liberty. But even without the aid of abolitionism the benevolent reformers of the South always bore in mind that emancipation carried with it a host of tangles, of unknown traps perhaps better left alone. Immediate and universal emancipation was an unthinkable alternative to the dilemma. Hence, instead of dealing root and branch with the problem of slavery, the benevolent reformers chose all those moderate ends consistent with their growing conservative philosophy. Colonization, gradual emancipation, slave instruction, the calling of masters to their duties—all were half measures guaranteed to perpetuate social order, deference, and harmony, even if they did not put an end to the dilemma. Nevertheless, they believed in the inevitable progress of man and continued to hope that the dilemma could eventually be resolved.[29]

More important than all of the feelings of a moral dilemma among southern benevolent reformers before 1835 was the fact that by participating in the national movement toward benevolence they were quietly helping to transfer to the South a set of values and a perspective on American society that was not native to the South. By whatever mechanism they came into contact with the philosophy of benevolence, they had begun to absorb principles and rhetoric that drew them closer to the conservative movement in the North than to the rising rampant sectionalism of the South. Quite unconsciously they were absorbing ideas that would cause them to respond to abolitionism and to all radical reforms in a manner more characteristic of the anti-abolitionists of the North than of the nullifiers and other sectionalists of the South. Because of their more fundamental connection with the national impulse toward benevolence, and thereby their greater absorption of conservative ideology, they would in fact become, on the one hand, the greatest enemies of nullification and, on the other, the most important progenitors of a national proslavery ideology in the South.

TWELVE

Absence of a Southern Ideology for Proslavery, 1831–1835

One of the more remarkable facts in the history of proslavery in America is that until the crisis of 1835 hardly any southerner bothered to pen a defense of slavery or to launch a systematic critique of abolitionism. Despite the fact that the Garrisonian campaign against slavery had gotten under way in 1831 and despite the fact that the cities of the North were the scenes of bloody confrontations between abolitionists and anti-abolitionists by 1833, southerners generally overlooked and neglected the coming storm. Although a few isolated voices were heard in the South in the winter of 1834–1835, no concerted attempt was made by southerners to answer abolitionist charges until the summer of 1835. The old wisdom that southerners rose up in unison in 1831 after a decade of preparation in the tenets of proslavery is patently an erroneous interpretation. Since no response can be detected either in the Virginia slavery debates of 1831–1832 or in the early nullification movement, one can only conclude that the South was virtually silent until abolitionism emerged starkly in the South. Moreover, in the few responses that can be detected before 1835, there is no evidence of the presence of proslavery ideology, conservative philosophy, or any articulation of ideas to deal with a subversive movement.

Judging from the character and content of early proslavery literature written by native southerners, they were truly taken by surprise by the abolitionists' postal campaign of 1835. They were no less alarmed by the sudden advance of abolitionists from near obscurity to national prominence than were the anti-abolitionists of the North. Unlike northern anti-abolitionists brought up in the school of New England conservatism, however, southerners hardly knew what to say. Some of them—es-

pecially those who had recently been involved in South Carolina's nullification campaign—leaped headlong into new fits of sectionalism,
drawing lurid pictures of an abolition-infested North. These men attempted to unite southerners against abolitionists in the same manner
that they had tried to array the South solidly against Andrew Jackson.
Others merely reiterated the same traditional proslavery arguments that
any southerner, or for that matter any American, could have adduced as
easily in 1800 as in 1835. Still others threw up their hands, admitting
that slavery was an evil, but one that would have to be endured to avert
greater evils. From a survey of the evidence one cannot escape the conclusion that in the early 1830s and even in 1835 few southerners were
aware of or were able to launch the type of countersubversive campaign
at which the anti-abolitionists were already masters. The South, even as
it attempted to frame a response to abolitionism, was void of the basic
tools for mounting an ideological counterattack against antislavery radicalism.

If there was almost a total absence of proslavery literature in the South
from the first appearance of immediatism until late 1834, one must turn
to the newspaper and manuscript literature to tap southern reactions to
abolition. Even in those sources there is little to suggest that the men who
would leap to the defense of slavery after 1835 were overly concerned
with or threatened by the words and writings of abolitionists. Whereas
historians have generally assumed from the paucity of responses that
southerners maintained a conspiracy of silence against all public discussions of slavery in the 1820s and early 1830s, actually most future defenders of slavery rarely mentioned slavery, much less abolitionism, except
in the course of promoting benevolent reforms or the religious instruction of slaves. Except for northern anti-abolitionists who could not abide
the tendencies of abolition and for a handful of nullifiers in South Carolina, America's future proslavery thinkers largely dismissed the growth
of abolition in both their private and public writings.[1]

From an examination of the content of six typical southern religious
newspapers either edited by southerners or published in the South by
immigrants from the North during the period from 1831 to 1835,[2] it is
clear that despite frequent references to slavery and to the struggles of
abolitionists and anti-abolitionists, southern editors were reticent either
to attack abolitionists or to defend slavery. On the contrary, the six papers were filled with news on colonization, on efforts toward the religious instruction of slaves, and with exhortations for masters to fulfill all

duties toward their slaves.[3] Whenever any of the editors stated their own positions on slavery before the spring of 1835, they took the side of gradual emancipation, usually by means of colonization. As an example, in March 1831, after attacking New England for its continuing involvement in the West Indian trade in rum and slaves, William T. Brantly, a thoroughly sectionalized southerner operating in Philadelphia, commented that ill-treated slaves repaid Yankee captors by producing cane for rum, which in turn consumed "the property, the intelligence, the morals, the piety, and the peace of New England." Similarly, in October 1834, Thomas Meredith, a firm friend of the South who was born and grew up in Pennsylvania and was working in New Bern, North Carolina, after seeing that abolitionists received harsh treatment in the streets of New York, wrote, "It is not to be inferred from this [approval], however, that we are the advocates of slavery in any of its forms or under any circumstances." "We believe," added Meredith, "that the interests of the country, as well as those of humanity, require an eventual, and, as far as practicable, a speedy emancipation."[4]

At the same time southern editors and the immigrant editors of southern religious newspapers continued to support the benevolent reform of slavery, colonization, and gradual emancipation, they began to take notice of northern struggles between abolitionists and anti-abolitionists. Less than a month after noticing the Nat Turner insurrection as a "horrible massacre" by "run-away slaves," William Brantly reprinted an article describing the October 1831 "New Haven excitement" engendered by the attempts of abolitionists to establish a Negro college. Commenting on the event, Brantly noted the surprise of the abolitionists "to find that the people of Connecticut are so sensitive on the subject here brought to view." It went to prove, Brantly continued, "that the blacks as a *caste* and a separate order of society, are considered in the non-slaveholding states to be as much degraded, if not more so, than in those states where slavery exists." Two weeks later Brantly received news of the bloodshed between black and white sailors in Providence with similar comments.[5]

In 1832 after they read and compared the writings of abolitionists and transcripts of the debates on slavery in the Virginia Legislature, three of the six editors indicated that while northern abolitionists were making impossible proposals, the citizens of Virginia were moving toward emancipation. One of them wrote, "we know of no newspaper or journal in Virginia, opposed to measures of this character," that is, "the adoption of wise, discreet and efficient measures for the gradual, systematic and cer-

Southern Editors Who Faced Abolitionism

Thomas Meredith, 1795–1850
*Transplanted Pennsylvanian, Baptist editor,
and promoter of anti-abolitionism in
North Carolina*

William Henry Brisbane, 1803–1878
*Native South Carolinian and Baptist editor
who defended slavery and attacked
abolitionism, then embraced antislavery and
became an abolitionist*

tain removal of the tremendous evil which paralizes the energies of our State." Another wrote that every citizen of Virginia knew that *"its removal is practicable."*[6] As the Virginia debates were followed by the nullification campaign of South Carolina, only one editor who recently had come from a long sojourn in low country South Carolina rose to the defense of that state's nullifiers. All of the other editors, as did almost all clergymen, strongly condemned sectionalism. None of them, not even the lone sympathizer, saw nullification as an occasion to come to the defense of slavery.[7]

Persistently faithful to the Union, to gradualism, and to benevolence, the editors continued to note the movements of abolitionists and their northern enemies almost without comment. One of them reprinted approvingly the anti-abolitionist comments of Ebenezer Porter, president of the Congregational seminary at Andover, Massachusetts, in August 1833, wherein Porter claimed that immediate abolition was "not inexpedient merely, but impossible." When, in October 1834, anti-abolitionists took to the streets of New York, the same editor, after reaffirming his endorsement of gradual emancipation and condemning street violence, concluded that the example of the northern cities "shows that the public will tolerate neither their [abolitionists'] principles nor their practice." One of the editors who brought his conservative sympathies from North to South added that abolitionism was "a system of policy as quixotic in itself, as it is incompatible with Christian meekness and social order."[8]

Of the six editors, the first to condemn abolitionism openly without the catalyst of a particular anti-abolitionist act or writing from the North was Richard Gladney of the *Southern Christian Herald,* published at Columbia, South Carolina. In July 1834, Gladney penned an article entitled "The Abolitionists" and called for all southern editors to rise up in condemnation of the principles and purposes of immediatism. From his fellow editors, Gladney drew nothing but scorn for picturing a few isolated and spurned radicals as a threat. One of them wrote, in derision of Gladney's over-extended imagination, "The truth is, the abolitionists are few in number, and public meetings 'got up' in many places to enlist recruits, have added but few to their ranks." Despite Gladney's warnings none of the editors saw abolitionism as a threat to either the South or slavery until 1835.[9]

None of the editors except Gladney openly and eagerly attacked abolition. Neither did they pen defenses of slavery before the summer of 1835. Only one of them attempted to write a defense before the national abolition crisis—and he did so only under the most unusual and reveal-ing circumstances. The innocence and gullibility of some southerners in 1834 on the eve of the postal campaign of immediatists appear in the experience of William Henry Brisbane, editor of the *Southern Baptist and General Intelligencer* in 1835 and afterward an abolitionist of some note. For some reason, unexplained either in his public statements or in his extensive private diary, near the end of 1834 Brisbane wrote an essay entitled "Has Man a Right to Hold Property in Man?" for the *Charleston Mercury*. Apparently guilt-ridden by the fact that he himself was a large slaveholder, Brisbane followed the recent pattern of anti-abolitionist writers by turning to the Bible for an answer. Quite predictably, he found there "a sanction for slavery" and concluded "*that man's* mind must be awfully perverted by prejudice, who does not see" it.[10]

His first defense of slavery in 1834 seems to have resulted from his personal travail with slavery. But Brisbane then followed up his early defense in the first months of 1835 in the *Southern Baptist and General Intelligencer* with some taunting words for abolitionists. Taking the for-mation of the conservative American Union for the Relief and Improve-ment of the Colored Race at Boston to be a newly emerging abolitionist organization, Brisbane invited all abolitionists to come South and pur-chase the freedom of slaves. None would object, he continued, to such sales and none would deny that "our slaves like the poor of other coun-tries are often ground to the dust, and are shamefully abused and ill treated." Nevertheless, he thought that the South's return to prosperity and the furthering of slaveholders' plans for the reform of slavery would eventually remove the objectionable features often adduced by aboli-tionists and benevolent reformers. Again in March and May 1835 Bris-bane argued that immediate emancipation would be ruinous, still prom-ising that "when we can better the condition of slaves, it will be our duty to do so, if by their emancipation we can increase the sum of human happiness, we hope the South will not be reluctant to act in the spirit of true Christian benevolence."[11]

On July 10, still three weeks before the arrival of abolitionist literature in Charleston, Brisbane issued a challenge to northern newspapers. He wanted someone to show him any moral precept in the Bible that for-bade slaveholding. "When it comes," he promised, "we will bow both with submission to the will of God, and twenty-eight slaves shall be im-mediately emancipated." Brisbane certainly wrote those words before July 8, for on that day he read an article by Francis Wayland, the conser-

vative antislavery president of Brown University. Brisbane found Wayland's antislavery arguments unanswerable. In the confidence of his diary, Brisbane recorded his futile attempts to answer Wayland's scriptural
arguments against slavery and his private decision to uphold the terms
of his public challenge by freeing his slaves.[12]

Brisbane's conversion to antislavery occurred at a most unpropitious
moment. In the very issue of his paper in which he announced his
change of heart, he also published the news that on July 29 the steam
packet *Columbia* arrived in Charleston bearing abolitionist publications.
Both items appeared in adjoining articles, one declaring that Wayland's
notions were "the first good arguments we have met with on that side of
the question," the other announcing that "the Southern people *will protect themselves from further aggression*" on the part of abolitionists. In one
Brisbane indicated that he had offered his slaves "full and free permis-
sion to go whenever they please to Liberia or any other place where the
laws of the land will allow them to enjoy their freedom." In the other, he
noted that serious southerners had "come forward on this occasion with
a resolution and firmness that nothing can shake." In one article he expressed the opinion that most slaveholders would be ready to free their
slaves if they could recover from philanthropists or others "half the value of their slaves in executing such a scheme." In the other, Brisbane
indicated that only the efforts of northerners "to arrest these misguided
fanatics and consign them and their works to the contempt and shame
and obscurity which they deserve" could save the union from a bloody
civil and servile war.[13]

Brisbane was not speaking out of both sides of his mouth. Despite the
fact that his conversion to antislavery eventually led him into financial
ruin, engendered the fear and enmity of fellow South Carolinians, and
caused him, after a period of three years, to sell his slaves and head North,
for a space of five years he illustrated the fact that one could be simultaneously both antislavery and anti-abolitionist. Not until January 1840
did he finally come to the conclusion that "to the principles of the Abolitionists . . . can we alone look with any hope of success to put down the
'horrible' system of human robbery & oppression." For three years after
his 1835 conversion Brisbane continued to live in the South and to oppose
slavery while claiming both publicly and in his diary, "I am no Abolitionist." In fact, for a year after his change, he remained editor of the *Southern
Baptist* and therein witnessed to both his dislike of slavery and his hatred
for abolitionists. And whether he included himself or not, by November

1835 he could generalize that "in South Carolina, the discussion on the subject of slavery has established those, who before had doubts, in the firm belief that slavery has the sanction of religion, and is a blessing to our country—our whole country, the North and the South."[14]

Although Brisbane's course was exceptional in the annals of pro-slavery writers, his case is revealing for the development of proslavery. On the eve of the national crisis over abolition and although the editor of a prominent newspaper, Brisbane was innocent about proslavery and uneasy about owning slaves. In an attempt to satisfy his conscience, in late 1834 he penned a defense that was informed by the earlier defenses of anti-abolitionists and by the ready penchant of defenders to turn to the Bible for proslavery arguments. Still uneasy, for six months Brisbane defended slavery and attacked abolitionists, albeit without the vigor and the logic of the anti-abolitionists whose writings he reproduced. In the eleventh hour before the July postal campaign he was won over to anti-slavery by the searing arguments of a nationally prominent conservative anti-abolitionist, not by those of the abolitionists. In the moment of crisis he could consistently continue to oppose slavery in the abstract, defend it on the grounds of necessity, and carry on a vigorous campaign against abolitionists. And that was the standard pattern for southerners in 1835.[15]

Irrespective of his later activities as an abolitionist, what Brisbane discovered and attempted to maintain as long as he lived in South Carolina was the mission and message of benevolence, of anti-abolitionism, and of appropriated conservative ideology. His course from 1834 to 1838 was dictated by the absorption of principles and sentiments that were largely alien to the South before the rise of abolition and the education of America in the tenets of conservative countersubversion by anti-abolitionists. Brisbane's example indicates, moreover, that the travail of slavery for many southerners sprang both from guilt in holding slaves and from an inability to defend an institution, which, from the continuing influence of revolutionary ideology in the South, they felt to be wrong. To establish a rationale for his own distinctive antislavery and anti-abolitionist course, Brisbane relied heavily upon the conservative views of Wayland, Harrison Gray Otis, and other anti-abolitionists. That he later moved on to abolitionism seems to have been the result of personal influences on his behavior having little to do with his views on slavery.

What Brisbane discovered with such personal force in early July 1835, other southerners learned less dramatically and more gradually in the course of the months and years thereafter. While southerners, from two centuries of contact with the Negro, were disposed to set blacks off as an inferior caste and to uphold on the most practical grounds perpetual enslavement, they knew not how to deal logically with the inconsistencies between inherited equalitarian thought and slaveholding. Nor were there categories built into the body of southern thought to deal with perceived widespread subversion. Abolitionism posed both social and ideological problems with which southerners could not contend in the summer of 1835. Through the process of education in the values and beliefs of counterrevolutionary conservatism, however, in the years after 1835 southerners absorbed the ideological tools for dealing with both the psychological and social threats of abolitionism. Out of the confusion and uncertainty revealed in southern newspapers in 1835 there eventually came a South ideologically united with northern conservatives.

Aside from the newspaper literature, which revealed a slowly growing awareness of abolitionism and a related reluctance to defend slavery, there is little to suggest that southerners were preparing to do battle with abolitionism before the spring and summer of 1835. While anti-abolitionists in the North were battering immediatists, the general peace and quiet enjoyed by the South continued almost uninterruptedly until the arrival of the steam packet *Columbia*. In 1834 two southerners finally broke the silence to reassert those values that had been stated in the sprinkling of southern proslavery literature in the 1820s and in Thomas R. Dew's anti-colonization tract in 1832. Both of them recipients of Federalist-styled educations in northern colleges and inclined toward nullification in South Carolina politics, they registered the first formal comments by South Carolinians on slavery since the rise of abolitionism.

Whitemarsh Seabrook, South Carolinian and graduate of Princeton, and Alexander D. Sims, Virginian and graduate of Union College, New York, were both lawyers and politicians in South Carolina from the 1820s forward. Seabrook was a Low Country planter who, as longtime president of the Agricultural Society of South Carolina, promoted scientific methods for southern agriculture. Sims, on the other hand, was an Upcountry lawyer and schoolteacher located at Darlington. As early as 1825, feeling the economic pinch on cotton production, Seabrook had been impelled to defend slavery as an economic benefit to the South and the nation. Sims had not previously published on the subject of slavery. In spite of their desire to uphold slavery, neither man reflected an awareness of either the great dangers of abolitionism or the types of argument that were being used by anti-abolitionists to counter immedi-atism.

Seabrook, in particular, was cemented to the concerns of southerners in the 1820s. One of the two pamphlets written by Seabrook in 1834, *An Essay on the Management of Slaves,* was directed not against abolitionists but against the overly eager benevolent reformers who continually ap-peared in the South. Citing the published writings of reform-minded southern Presbyterians from Charles C. Jones to Thomas Clay, from the Presbytery of Bryan County, Georgia, to the Synod of South Carolina and Georgia, Seabrook reiterated a notion more closely connected with the ideology of the American Revolution than that of proslavery south-erners. Reinvoking the religious deism of southern founders of the na-tion, Seabrook argued that clergymen were dangerous characters un-controlled by the public and abstractionists without any knowledge of or value for real property. Unaware that all of those whose writings he crit-icized were themselves slaveholders bent on reforming slavery, Seabrook displayed a monumental ignorance of the currents that had been seep-ing into the South since the end of the War of 1812 and a resistance to religious reform carried over from the eighteenth century.[16]

Having not even mentioned the word *abolitionist* in his first pamphlet, Seabrook near the end of 1834 published another pamphlet, which, with Sims's similar writing, constituted the entirety of the southern response to abolitionism prior to the crisis of 1835. Still not clear on who the abolitionists really were, Seabrook coupled southern benevolent reform-ers with immediatists in replying to "the open denunciations from abroad, and the foul insinuations at home." Noting that abolitionist no-tions had been carried from the press of the North to the pulpit of the South, Seabrook thought that while in the North they had been hushed by the action of mobs, abolitionists had gone totally unanswered in the South. Relying on the writings of Robert Walsh, Thomas R. Dew, and various hints from the anti-abolitionist press of the North, Seabrook launched into a defense of slavery remarkable only for its reiteration of traditional proslavery wisdom.[17]

Beginning with the oldest and most widely cited defensive argument known to Americans—the witness of Scripture—the anticlerical Sea-brook proceeded to the assertion, which, following the course of Robert Walsh's *Appeal* (1819), placed all blame for American slavery upon the shoulders of British and New England slave traders. In the process Sea-brook made admissions that would become increasingly difficult for southerners after 1835. He admitted that while Scriptures upheld the practice of slaveholding, "slavery is against the spirit of Christianity." At another point he wrote that slavery was an "evil . . . forced upon us, not by ourselves, but by foreigners—by Europeans generally, and by our Northern and Eastern brethren, in particular." "No people," he continued, "have more regretted the existence of such a condition of things than the people of Carolina." Seabrook concluded his defense by relying upon the teaching of political economists from Jones to Pinckney to Dew that the condition of the slave was no worse than that of the northern free black or the poor of any other country. By long quotations from the legislature of Connecticut and from Dew, Seabrook concluded that no plan had yet been devised—whether by emancipators or by colonizationists—that could safely and quickly remove the evil of slavery from America.[18]

In neither of their pamphlets did either Seabrook or Sims display a critical awareness of abolitionism as a distinct and formidable threat to either slavery or American society. Despite their common experience of education at schools dominated by conservative moralists, they were so enmeshed in the peculiar concerns of southern nullifiers that they were not yet prepared to adopt the ideological teachings of their early years as a tool for both defending slavery and halting the growth of abolitionism. Unlike such thinkers as Joseph Tracy, Leonard Bacon, and David Reese in the North whose views were already in the press, Seabrook and Sims were content to rely upon the most traditional foci in the proslavery catechism of arguments. Not even in their comments on the theory of natural rights did they call up the position of their conservative teachers. Instead of arguing like his mentors that equalitarianism did not apply to certain classes of men or that in a civil polity some men must have their rights removed for the sake of society, Seabrook could only say that "in the battles of our revolution they [Negro slaves] formed no part of the enrollment of our armies;—[and] that both before and after our independence, they were considered as mere property." Before 1835, despite the presence of conservative notions in the lives and experiences of Seabrook and Sims, their identification with the revolutionary heritage of the South was more overpowering. They could not, therefore, as had Joseph Tracy in 1833, argue that Negro slaves were by the nature of society, instead of custom, deprived of their natural rights.[19]

It was not that Seabrook or Sims lacked assertiveness in their defenses of slavery. Neither they nor other southerners were meek proslavery men. They merely lacked the logic and ideas that had enabled northern anti-abolitionists long since to launch well-aimed and deadly arrows at the tendencies of immediatism. Furthermore, Seabrook and Sims did not share with anti-abolitionists before 1835 the frightening perception that, if not halted forthrightly, abolitionism would destroy the foundations on which American society rested. Before the summer of 1835 when they began spouting the rhetoric and ideology of anti-abolitionists, no southerner perceived abolitionists as French Revolutionaries, as antireligious, anti-republican malcontents whose course was subversive and seditious. Nor did they think of slave society in terms of the hierarchic, organismic society associated in the minds of northern conservatives with the republicanism of ancient Greece and Rome. Like other slaveholders of their time, particularly in the West Indies, they evaluated slavery as a necessity both economically and racially as taught them by political economists and by their common experience of racial fears with the rest of America.

The lethargy and indecision of the early thirties turned into a concerted corporate attempt to justify slavery after July 1835. But even in the most lengthy and solidly argued early southern responses to the postal campaign, any clearly discernible ideological response to abolitionism was still absent. The South experienced the moment of terror wrought by the postal campaign of the American Anti-slavery Society along with other sections of America. Not having perceived abolitionism as a serious threat before that time, however, southerners were suddenly thrown into a panic from which nothing in their experience could remove them. Prior to 1835 a recurring dream reported by the nullifying clergyman, Iveson Brookes, would have been unthinkable. Writing his wife from one of his three plantations in Georgia, Brookes described in February 1836 what he thought was a "plausible dream":

> The substance of it that in some twenty or thirty years a division of the Northern & Southern States will be produced by the Abolitionists and then a war will issue between the Yankees & slave-holders—that the Army of Yankees will be at once joined by the N[egroe]s who will shew more savage cruelty than the blood thirsty Indians—and that Southerners with gratitude for having escaped alive will gladly leave their splendid houses & farms to be occupied by by [*sic*] those who once served them.—This all looks so plausible that I have been made to conclude that all who act with judicious

foresight should within two years sell every [?] of a negro & land & vest the money in Western lands—so as to have a home and valuable possessions to flee to in time of danger.[20]

In all of his voluminous writings and correspondence on the South, society, and nullification prior to 1835, Brookes never revealed any concern for the future of his property in the face of abolitionists or any other external threatening force. Beginning in 1835, however, his correspondence filled with the anguished outcries of a man distraught by a dreaded sudden collapse of society.

Brookes's anguished state was shared by most southerners in the summer and fall of 1835. Close upon the initial shock induced by apparent abolitionist power, southerners in town meetings and moblike gatherings from Richmond to Mobile adopted resolutions and encouraged responses to abolitionism that were expressive of a sudden fit of corporate rage. Out of such meetings and excited circumstances that surrounded them came a flurry of pamphlets, which, perhaps understandably, displayed more rage than sense in their evaluations of slavery and the threat of abolition. Unlike the initial outpourings of anti-abolitionists such as Harrison Gray Otis or Charles Jared Ingersoll in the North, early southern writers could only threaten the application of lynch law to the cases of antislavery incendiaries.[21]

Such was the message of one statement written in the fall of 1835 by Edmund Bellinger, Jr., originally *A Speech on the Subject of Slavery* presented to a public meeting of frightened citizens in Barnwell District, South Carolina on September 7. Written by open admission only for the consumption of southerners concerned about slavery, Bellinger presented his speech in one of those meetings that adopted heated anti-abolitionist resolutions. In thundering oratory Bellinger, a diehard nullifier, spewed forth proslavery arguments and scorching epithets against abolitionists. Abolitionists were *"impudent pretenders* to Humanity and Religion—the *infamous wretches—the dastardly miscreants—the vile instigators of villainous cut-throats"* whose aim was "to deprive us of our Rights—to disturb our repose—to alarm and distract the minds of those who are near to us in blood and dearer in affection—to render our slaves wretched and miserable—to plunge our happy land into a servile war, and cover it with desolation." Without pronouncing slavery an unmixed blessing, Bellinger contorted any movement toward emancipation in the South into a faithless and traitorous act against the rights and privileges of slaveholders. Making the appearance of abolitionism an occasion for reiterating the constitutional arguments and battle cries of nullification, Bellinger attempted to prove that neither abolitionists, the federal government, nor sister states could legally interfere with slavery in the South. If anyone should, Bellinger warned, the Union would be immediately dissolved.[22]

Bellinger witnessed to the penchant of some southerners in the wake of nullification to find constitutional ground for any favorite cause. That tendency was further amplified in a pamphlet attributed to another nullifier, William Rice, entitled *Vindex: On the Liability of the Abolitionists to Criminal Punishment*. Whereas Bellinger contented himself with demonstrating the constitutional guarantees for slave property, Rice, with almost no reference to slavery, sought to indicate legal instrumentalities whereby southerners in concert with anti-abolitionists in the North could bring abolitionists to justice and prevent them from further "endangering the permanency of our glorious Union, and weakening the last bright hope of regulated liberty, and popular government, on earth." Without uttering a single traditional proslavery argument, Rice demonstrated to his satisfaction that state governments had a right "to suppress, by law, these unauthorized attacks upon the rights of the slaveholding States, these pregnant sources of danger to the harmony, if not to the existence of the Union." As in the case of Bellinger, Rice's *Vindex* was less a defense of slavery than a revivification of the principles of nullification.[23]

Crisis often breeds peculiar notions from strange quarters. The abolition crisis of 1835 in the South was no exception. From Georgia came a raft of pamphlets from the confused mind of John Jacobus Flournoy, a wealthy social outcast, whose peculiar notions were derided by everyone, but whose writings received as wide a circulation as those of most other southern writers on slavery. Becoming both deaf and mute while a student at the University of Georgia in the early 1830s, Flournoy receded into a private world of contemplation and writing made possible by a considerable inheritance. Relying upon his own funds for both printing and circulation, Flournoy published five separate blatantly racist and openly anti-abolitionist pamphlets between 1835 and 1838. While he was impelled into writing by the sudden appearance of abolitionism, Flournoy was no friend of perpetual slavery. His one doctrine was the expulsion of the Negro race by any means whatsoever from America, a policy that he pursued against the criticisms of abolitionists and slaveholders alike.[24] While Flournoy's peculiar views were a rarity in the South of 1835, his strange notions demonstrate once again the fact that in the face of the great and celebrated confrontation of the South with abolitionism, no united ideological response was current in the minds and writings of southerners.

The South was not, therefore, prepared either psychologically or intellectually for the appearance of abolitionism in the mid-1830s. Except in newspaper literature there was in fact a very limited southern response either during the early 1830s or during the crisis of 1835. What is perhaps more remarkable than the paucity of the response was the abject confusion displayed. While most southerners merely overlooked the rise of abolitionism, the few who saw in it a threat could not distinguish between the emancipationism of abolitionists and that of more traditional emancipationists such as benevolent reformers. When the critical distinction was finally made, the charges against abolitionism were as varied and as different as the number of men who launched the attack. Whether in the newspaper literature or in the half-dozen pamphlets that appeared before the end of 1835, no pattern of ideas and no common mode of response emerged as a distinctively southern proslavery witness. Despite all of the heat generated by enraged southerners in the wake of the abolitionists' postal campaign, it cannot be said that southerners as late as the end of 1835 had developed an ideology of proslavery or even a pattern of defensive arguments that differed significantly from the traditional notions that had grown up over two centuries of contact with the Negro. And in spite of the penchant of former nullifiers to attack abolitionism with the same principles that they had recently applied to the federal government, it cannot be said that all early southern respondents to abolitionism saw immediatism as a threat to the Union. As late as the winter of 1835, the emergence of a southern ideology of proslavery was still on the horizon.

THIRTEEN

The South Becomes Ideologized,
1835–1840

One of the most troublesome problems in interpreting the history of proslavery has always been the near simultaneity of the emergence of abolitionism and South Carolina nullification. Because both movements contained the seeds of potential sectionalism and because former nullifiers quickly became some of the severest critics of immediatists, historians have assumed a direct connection between the two phenomena. The fact that debate over slavery eventuated in a sectional war in 1861 would seem to seal the case. Hand in glove with the assumption that nullifiers framed the initial response of the South to abolitionism is the notion that the debate over slavery was a sectional cleavage with the strongest defenses of slavery and the most inimical critiques of abolitionism emanating from the South. A final assumption held in common with the others is that the emergence of abolitionism as a threat in the mid-1830s was merely the occasion of the final, full revelation of an already well-developed southern proslavery ideology.

A close reading of the sources reveals that none of these traditional assumptions is correct. The response to abolitionism was not a sectional phenomenon. Since it was limited largely to one state, nullification was also not a sectional movement. While nullifiers were among the first southerners to respond to abolitionism, their response was insignificant in comparison to the entire body of anti-abolitionist literature that emanated from the South. A close study of the writings of leading nullifiers in the wake of the abolition crisis of 1835 shows, in fact, that nullifiers and southern sectionalists were overwhelmed by both the weight and the logic of a form of proslavery response that originated in other quarters and that proved so persuasive that by the end of the 1830s most old nullifiers and other southern sectionalists were won over to a form of proslavery thought that was wholly uncharacteristic of the South. Through the energetic efforts of anti-abolitionists in the North and others transplanted in the South and of a host of resident benevolent reformers in the South, by the end of the 1830s nullifiers and other southern sectionalists were themselves ideologized in the tenets of America's conservative counterrevolution.

Nullifiers and other southern sectionalists were among the last residents of the South to frame systematic responses to abolitionism. They were beaten to the punch both chronologically and intellectually by transplanted northerners and by southern benevolent reformers. At nearly the same time anti-abolitionists in New England and the North rose up with a united voice to use their reactionary principles to beat back abolitionists and uphold slavery, a number of very similar individuals in the South began chanting the same message. Indeed, many of the early reactions to abolition often associated with the South were actually the products of the same cultural forces that caused New Englanders and other northerners to reject abolitionism. In 1835, for example, the first year during which southerners began publishing open condemnations of abolitionists, three of the seven separate defenses of slavery published in the South were written by nonsoutherners who had developed their outlooks on American society before migrating to the South. During the 1830s as a whole more than one-third of all defenses of slavery published in the South were penned by immigrants from New England and the North. A significant portion of the remainder was written by people more closely identified with the cause of benevolent reform than with southern sectionalism.[1]

While southern-based anti-abolitionists were as fully absorbed by the values of conservatism as their northern counterparts, they were slower to react to the threat of abolition. Not until the postal campaign of July 1835 did they invoke the invective and begin the journey toward proslavery already completed by northerners of the same complexion. Even then, those who appealed most strongly to anti-abolitionist rhetoric as bludgeons against abolitionists were men who came to the South fresh from recent encounters with abolitionism in New England. For example, on August 30, 1835, before any southerner had been able to put together a formal critique of abolitionists in the wake of the postal campaign, Charles Farley, a Unitarian clergyman just arrived from Boston for a brief visit in Richmond, presented in the Unitarian church of that city one of the most devastating critiques of abolitionism heard in the South during the 1830s. Similarly, on June 28, 1836, Theophilus Fisk, just having left the pastorate of a Universalist Church in Suffolk County, Massachusetts, presented an oration condemning abolition and defending slavery at Fort Moultrie in Charleston harbor.[2]

Most ideologized anti-abolitionists, however, had been in the South considerably longer. William J. Hobby came from Connecticut as a young man and made his fortune as editor of the Augusta *Chronicle* in Georgia. Nevertheless, his rootage in an ancient New England family and his Connecticut education were revealed in 1835 when he became one of the first men in the South to condemn the massive abolitionist propaganda campaign with *Remarks upon Slavery, Occasioned by Attempts Made to Circulate Improper Publications in the Southern States.* Daniel K. Whitaker, one of the first to apply conservative notions of hierarchical society to the defense of slavery in 1836, was born in Massachusetts the son of a Congregational clergyman. Educated at Harvard, he too was ordained a Congregational minister before coming to South Carolina in 1823 to assume the management of a rice plantation. Perennially editor of some of the South's most important literary magazines, Whitaker dared in 1836, in a pamphlet entitled *Reflections on Domestic Slavery,* to chide one of South Carolina's earliest and most astute proslavery writers, Chancellor William Harper, for timidity in meeting abolitionists head on. "The time has arrived," he wrote, "for the South, not only to deliberate, but to be up and operating some effective measures for its own salvation."[3]

Three other New England clergymen in various areas of the South helped to alert southerners to the perils of abolitionism. In November 1836 George Washington Freeman, a native of Sandwich, Massachusetts, and a recent immigrant to the South, published the first and one of the very few defenses of slavery ever produced by a resident of North Carolina. Rector of Christ Episcopal Church in Raleigh, Freeman adopted the format, though not the traditional message, of benevolent reformers by sermonizing on the *Rights and Duties of Slaveholders.* While he did exhort masters to their duties, his primary aim was the upholding of masters' rights in the face of abolition. A year later Rufus William Bailey, a Congregational clergyman from Maine and Massachusetts educated at Dartmouth, published two important books on the subject of slavery from his parish in South Carolina. In *The Issue,* a series of letters republished in newspapers throughout America, Bailey defended slavery

Transplanted Imparters of Proslavery Conservative Republicanism

Frederick Freeman, 1800–1883

George Washington Freeman,
1789–1858

The Freeman brothers of Sandwich, Massachusetts, who taught proslavery republicanism to North Carolinians during the 1830s with vibrant attacks on abolitionism after 1835

Rufus William Bailey, 1793–1863
New Englander located in South Carolina who published the first full defense of slavery in the South after abolitionism appeared

Theodore Clapp, 1792–1866
Harvard-trained Congregational from Massachusetts who adopted Unitarianism and proslavery in New Orleans, 1822–1857

against abolitionists with all of the vehemence of a native southerner: "The principles of the abolitionists, *can never prevail here. That interposition will never be permitted—that emancipation cannot now be effected.*" Yet in both *The Issue* and his other volume, *The Family Preacher; or, Domestic Duties,* Bailey dwelt heavily upon conservative thought as it applied to slavery and slave society. The latter work was, in fact, one of the early great applications of New England conservative ideology to a positive image of the ideal slave society.[4]

Two other inveterate haters of abolitionists whose writings produced the first and most influential responses to abolitionism in the states of Mississippi and Louisiana shared the northern background of other ideologized anti-abolitionists in the South. William Winans was born and reared in Pennsylvania and Ohio before coming to Mississippi at the age of twenty-two as a Methodist clergyman. Poorly educated in his youth, Winans absorbed the values of conservative reform through his long contact and energetic work with the Benevolent Empire, especially in the American Colonization Society. A diehard colonizationist, Winans reacted strongly to abolitionism in public prints as early as December 1835 when he published his first major critique of abolition—only the first of dozens to come from his pen over the following twenty years. Meanwhile, in New Orleans, Theodore Clapp, a native of Massachusetts and a graduate of Yale and Andover, delivered a sermon that in published form presented perhaps the most extended, closely argued, anti-abolitionist statement produced in the South in the 1830s. Simply entitled *Slavery,* Clapp, pastor of the Congregational church in New Orleans, summarized for southerners—in a statement as significant for its insights and influence as those of Charles Hodge and Calvin Colton—the ideological message of a decade-long struggle between anti-abolitionists and abolitionists.[5]

While all of the northern-born anti-abolitionists wrote and spoke as residents of the South, none of them could be considered in any manner southern sectionalists. While they warned fellow northerners that immediatism was a dangerous quantity in terms of the South, they bore no notions that the South ought to consider severing the Union. When they spoke of the disastrous results that might proceed from the introduction of abolitionism in the South, they thought not in terms of what the South might do as a section, but rather in terms of a disruption of American society in the face of radicalism. Like their anti-abolitionist fellows in the North they valued the Union, order, and stability above all else. Intellectually, socially, and purposively they were, therefore, almost identical with the anti-abolitionists of the North who preceded them, despite the fact that they defended slavery as a moral social institution much more strongly. While it might be argued that theirs should not be considered a part of the southern response to abolitionism, as time passed their countersubversive message on the subjects of slavery and abolition became increasingly synonymous with the prevalent patterns of the South.

The anti-abolitionist response of native northerners living in the South was only the beginning of the influences that helped alter the force of nullification and shape a southern ideology of proslavery. The rather large coterie of clergymen and benevolent reformers who had been active in the causes of the Benevolent Empire during the 1820s and early 1830s easily fell into line with the pattern of anti-abolitionists after the appearance of immediatism in 1835. Following the lead of such immigrant clerical agents of New England culture as Farley, Fisk, Whitaker, Freeman, Bailey, and Clapp, southern clergymen with prior connections to benevolent enterprises were among the first native southerners to condemn abolitionism as social rather than sectional fanaticism and to apply the insights of conservative thought to a new southern understanding of the problem of slavery. The appearance of abolitionism, instead of throwing them into the camp of southern sectionalism, caused them to proceed with greater speed in their already well-developed program to reshape American society along the lines of conservative ideology.

In 1836 and 1837 three southern-born clergymen contributed substantial writings to the growing list of literature bearing the marks of an emergent national proslavery ideology. George Baxter and James Smylie, Presbyterian ministers in Virginia and Mississippi respectively, and Gabriel Capers, a local Methodist clergyman in South Carolina—all three slaveholding clerics—added to the concert of anti-abolitionism. Baxter was the preeminent figure of the three. President in 1836 of Hampden-Sydney College and professor of theology in Virginia's Union Theological Seminary, Baxter had always been heavily influenced by the theological and social thought of the Princeton faculty. From the 1790s when he studied under William Graham, a Princetonian, into the nineteenth century when he emulated the policies of Samuel Stanhope Smith as president of Liberty Hall (Washington & Lee University), until the 1820s when he absorbed the benevolent spirit of John Holt Rice, Baxter became ever more closely associated with the proliferation of conservative ideological influence.

James Smylie and Gabriel Capers had been infected by the benevolent spirit prior to 1835. Smylie, a native of North Carolina, had been educated at the Log College of Princetonian David Caldwell in Guilford County before migrating in 1811 to Amite County, Mississippi, to become the first Presbyterian clergyman in Mississippi Territory. Inspired by the growth of benevolence, in the early 1830s Smylie began devoting much of his time to the religious instruction of slaves in Mississippi. Before the rise of abolition, he had prepared a catechism, one of the first, for the purpose. Capers, as a brother of the Methodist bishop, William Capers, absorbed much of the spirit that had caused William in the late 1820s to establish a far-ranging missionary program to the slaves of Methodists in South Carolina and Georgia. Less committed to a religious vocation than his brother, however, in the late 1830s Gabriel Capers moved to Louisiana where he spent the rest of his life as a planter.[6]

Baxter's *Essay on the Abolition of Slavery* written in 1836 was a remarkable example of the persistence of the principles of benevolence, in spite of the tendency for all antislavery dissent to be gagged in the South in the wake of abolitionism. Whereas most ideologized anti-abolitionists dwelt upon the errancy of abolition and the correctness of conservative republicanism, Baxter emphasized the duty of southerners to find the quickest and most practicable means of abolishing slavery. Arguing the necessity of slavery until Negroes were educated in the values of freedom, Baxter believed that "as soon as the slaves generally are prepared for emancipation, it will not be difficult to obtain the consent of their masters." In the meantime, slavery could be defended as lawful and proper so long as masters made every effort to uplift their slaves. Admitting that "free labor is better [cheaper] than slave labor" and that slavery could not be perpetual in America (agreeing with the position of Francis Wayland), Baxter joined other anti-abolitionist and proslavery conservatives in promoting the moral and social renovation of America. Yet, Baxter fearlessly added even in the midst of the abolition crisis, "we trust that the application of Christian principles to both master and slave, will hasten the day of general emancipation."[7]

Smylie was less kind to either emancipationism or abolitionism. In a lengthy review of an abolitionist letter from the Presbytery of Chillicothe, Ohio, to the Presbytery of Mississippi, Smylie waxed hot on the perversions of abolition. Depending heavily on David Reese's letters to William Jay, Smylie dwelt endlessly on the infidelity and fanaticism of abolition. Having learned well from anti-abolitionists of the North and basing most of his arguments on a detailed examination of scriptural testimony, Smylie came to a conclusion shared increasingly by most rising proslavery spokesmen that "the evils of slavery, like the evils of matrimony, may be traced to the neglect of the duties incumbent upon the individuals sustaining the relation." Like Baxter, Smylie endorsed every plan that sought the amelioration of the condition of slaves but none that sought immediate abolition.[8] In the vein of Smylie, following a detailed examination of Scripture, Gabriel Capers proclaimed slavery essentially a moral institution, since it conformed to the imperfect nature of man and society. Capers, as well, urged both masters and slaves to fulfill the duties of their respective stations in life.[9]

The emphasis of Baxter, Smylie, and Capers on the fulfillment of social duty derived directly from the positive impulse toward reform that was an essential ingredient of conservative ideology as it was translated into proslavery thought. There was a natural tendency for ideologized anti-abolitionists to move logically from condemnation of abolitionists to some sort of defense of slavery and from the defense of slavery on to prescriptions for the attainment of a moral, reformed society. In the first instance they scourged social fanaticism, in the second they framed their conservative social principles, and in the third they set down the guidelines of conservative reform. A technique and a message in America,as old as the anti-Illuminist writings of Timothy Dwight and Jedidiah Morse, the anti-abolitionists and southern benevolent reformers—all of whom became proslavery nationalists—perfected the practice in a wide range of literary forms, each with its particular social function.

The same impulse that shaped the anti-abolitionist responses of southern clergymen wrought remarkable changes in the outlook and purposes of those benevolent reformers who had been at work since the 1820s reforming slavery. Seemingly undaunted by the presence of abolitionists, those clergymen who had long promoted the religious instruction of slaves and who had been wont to prick the consciences of undutiful masters produced the greatest mass of instructional literature and hortatory calls to duty in the late 1830s that had yet been seen in American history. In actuality, however, they openly resisted abolitionism by putting the benevolent reform of slavery in the service of rising proslavery nationalism.

The immediacy with which benevolent reformers responded to the abolition crisis is clearly evident in the course of Nathaniel Bowen, the Massachusetts-born Episcopalian bishop of South Carolina. Having been asked by the Episcopal state convention in 1834 to create a mechanism for religious instruction of slaves in South Carolina, Bowen proceeded with fear and trepidation in addressing South Carolinians a year later. Whereas a year before it had been easy to talk of reforming slavery, by 1835 it was a subject of great "delicacy": "it is in consequence of an ill-informed, unwise, and even a reckless philanthropy, affecting it, in other parts of our union, surrounded with so much sensibility of alarm and offence . . . that the Ministers of religion cannot approach it, with too great caution and circumspection."[10]

Whereas a year earlier Bowen had been able to speak only of taking the "glad tidings of salvation" to the slaves and of urging masters to their duties, a year later the force of circumstances caused Bowen to become an open defender of slavery. True philanthropy and wise policy, Bowen continued, demanded the retention of slavery and the performance of duty. At that point religious instruction was transformed from an end of benevolent reform to a mechanism of social control. Bowen argued, "even were the *duty* not imperative, it would be sound *policy* in the planter to use every exertion—to employ every lawful means, to furnish his slaves with proper religious instruction." Under new circumstances by pursuing religious instruction, "we may feel that our Christian duty with respect to them is fulfilled, and the happiness and comfort at once of themselves, and of the community, secured." A year later Bowen published a catechism embodying the principles of duty and control necessitated by the perceived social crisis.[11]

As indicated by Bowen's course, the ideological conservatism that went into the formation of a national proslavery ideology could, depending upon the circumstances, parade either as reform or reaction. While benevolent reform intended to improve society, improvement consisted in building up the foundations of order and stability, dutifulness, and obedience. In the absence of revolutionary forces benevolence seemed aggressive and bent on change. In the presence of revolutionary tendencies such as abolitionism, it became reactionary, countersubversive, and aggressively conservative. In both instances, however, benevolence could and did display the qualities of energy, organization, and movement, which made it a powerful national influence. It was the amazing reactionary force of benevolence in 1835 and following that became the crucial vehicle for building up a national proslavery ideology by converting the South to receive conservative thought.

Before 1835 such southern reformers as Charles Colcock Jones and his colleagues in the Association for the Religious Instruction of Negroes in Liberty County, Georgia, seemed eager to alter the practice of slave-holding in the South. Their open criticisms of slavery and of unkind masters as well as their demands for the religious instruction and just treatment of slaves gave all of the appearance of a veiled antislavery movement among the slaveholders of the South. They disliked slave pa-trols. They protested against the separation of slave families. They re-garded masters as sinful who mistreated or otherwise took advantage of helpless slaves. They condemned laws that forbade the instruction of slaves. They seemed, in brief, opposed to any force which impeded the gradual uplifting of slaves for eventual emancipation.[12]

The genuine reformism of the early thirties easily and logically be-came reaction in 1835. After three years of criticising slaveholders, in 1835 Jones and the association he represented showed its true fabric. In the midst of a report that year that generally reflected the concerns of the past, the association inserted a brief note that most benevolent re-formers North and South would have endorsed in the face of the aboli-tionist crisis. Calling abolitionism an irresponsible fanaticism, the sons of New England who populated Liberty County and the Congregational community of Midway said,

> As a community we have been but of one mind touching the fanatical and incendiary movements which have occasioned the excitement, and have therefore refrained and judiciously refrained from any participation in it. And true to the religion which we profess, to the principles which we advo-cate, and to the standing reputation of this Country, we trust we have main-tained our interest in the best good of the Negroes, as well as our confi-dence in the means of promoting that good.

On the basis of the anti-abolition reaction that had already occurred in the North, they concluded that it would be unnecessary and unwise to disturb American liberties by either lynching abolitionists or suppressing their right of free expression. "To the judicious and enlightened of the North," the association wrote, "let us leave the Abolitionists; we trust, that their false principles and improper measures will be exposed and put down, that they will abandon their fanaticism and take juster views of the whole subject."[13]

Having declared common cause with anti-abolitionists throughout America, the association went on to express the duty of southerners in the present crisis. Southerners should burn neither abolitionists nor abolition literature: "No, there is an open, fearless, liberal, Christian course to be pursued which we should understand and adopt. We should protect ourselves *by Law*, as far as possible, from the Circulation of Incendiary publications, and from the teachings of incendiary agents; and then should we look at home, and enter upon such a discharge of our Duty to the Negroes, as will meet the approbation of God and our consciences, and commend ourselves to the consciences of other men." The way to stop fanaticism, association leaders said, was to pursue the same ends they had been promoting for more than three years. They would make reformism the engine of reaction. And for another fifteen years they went on promoting those "reforms" begun before the days of reaction, that is, religious intelligence among slaves, the conversion of slaves' holidays into holy days, the condemnation of criminal neglect of duties by masters toward their slaves, the physical and mental improvement of slaves, and the preservation of nuclear slave families. Along with the continuing reformism went reaction. For example, in 1841, the association amended its constitution to alter its name in a significant detail to maintain the confidence of southerners: "the real name of the Association is, 'The Liberty County Association for the Religious Instruction, *orally*, of the Colored Population.' "[14]

The well-entrenched tradition of benevolent reform represented by Baxter, Smylie, Capers, Bowen, Jones, and the Liberty County Association provided one of the crucial mechanisms for translating the ideology of conservatism into a systematic response to abolitionism and into an ideology of proslavery for the South. Innumerable southern clergymen were already well-versed in the ideology of benevolence before the rise of abolition and thereby in the structure of conservative social thought. In the absence of radicalism on the subject of slavery, southern benevolent spokesmen proved reformers; in the presence of radicalism, they proved reactionaries. With the addition of the impulse of immediatism, they became quite easily the crucial spokesmen for southern culture as they translated both conservative thought and the rhetoric of northern anti-abolitionism into a southern version of anti-abolitionism and of what was becoming a national proslavery ideology. In unison with the anti-abolitionists of the North and countless others speaking the same language in the South, they succeeded in drowning out any sectionalized proslavery ideology that might have grown up in the South.

If anti-abolitionists North and South and benevolent reformers of the South were not entirely successful in putting a halt to abolition, they were able to win the war with southern sectionalism—at least during the 1830s. At the same time they were building up an ideological response to abolitionism on the skeleton of conservative thought, they waged a battle on another front to stamp out the rise of a sectionalized interpretation of the abolition crisis threatening to emerge in the South. By the force of their logic, through the weight of their inspired rhetoric, they succeeded by the end of the 1830s in stamping out any sectionalized version of proslavery ideology and in making their ideas the core of a national ideology of proslavery. The field of their greatest battle was South Carolina and their primary opponent the reservoir of sectionalism engendered by nullification. By 1840, nevertheless, they had succeeded in ideologizing most nullifiers in the tenets of proslavery nationalism.

Of all the early southern respondents to abolitionism only the nullifiers of South Carolina brought to the war on immediatism a sectionalized body of thought that vied for preeminence as a southern version of proslavery ideology. Through their recent conflict with the federal government on the subject of tariffs, they had built up a set of notions largely legal and constitutional on the rights and powers of states to conserve their own institutions and on the duty of states to deal with social miscreants. Given the nature of the nullification controversy and the fact that slavery was largely restricted to the states of the South, it was only natural that former nullifiers should in 1835 transfer the theory and rhetoric of nullification to the problems of abolition and slavery.

The fact that South Carolina's nullifiers shifted the focus of their attacks quite easily from tariffs to abolitionists does not mean that southern proslavery thinkers in the 1830s were primarily old nullifiers, that proslavery men were essentially sectionalists, or even that nullification was a necessary and logical prelude to an open battle with abolitionists. In the first place, only a few of the South's proslavery writers in 1835 and the years that followed had been active nullifiers, and few agreed with the sectionalism of the nullification campaign. Indeed, most of the South's early defenders of slavery—even in South Carolina—had been openly critical of nullification and sectionalism both in 1833 and after 1835, when old nullifiers broached disunion again. Despite the fact that one historian has argued that "the nullification crusade had been, in part, an attempt to check the abolitionists without debating slavery," it does not seem likely that even the nullifiers saw any direct connection between nullification and the campaign against abolitionists other than the fact that the same constitutional arguments could be applied to outside attempts to coerce either economic or social policy.[15]

Not only did the nullifiers not take notice of abolitionists before 1835, during the summer of 1835 they also openly admitted that there was no connection between the impulses that caused nullification and abolitionism. For example, Edmund Bellinger, whose avowal of nullification continued up to and beyond the abolition crisis of 1835, admitted that while he called for disunion in both 1832 and 1835, his sectionalism in each instance proceeded from different causes. In his speech of September 1835 he shouted, "I have said to day *no more* than what I would have said in 1832, had this subject [slavery] been then in agitation; and I said in 1832 what I would have repeated to day had the occasion been similar." "*Those political principles,*" that is, state's rights, he continued, "important 'tis true to none but myself, *have undergone no change.*" Pleased that abolitionism provided the opportunity for him to continue his agitation of state's rights sectionalism, Bellinger concluded, "not even the dread of the charge of political inconsistency could have deterred me from going with you *hand and heart for Southern rights and Southern interests.* Happily for myself, *no such sacrifice is required.*"[16]

While the special interests of southern states had been a problem from the Revolution forward, southern sectionalism had its greatest formal beginning in nullification. After the ignominious failure of 1833, sectionalism was easily transferred to the South's efforts to maintain slavery. Even though most southern proslavery writers from the 1830s to the eve of the Civil War discounted sectionalism and disunion as a viable or wise alternative policy and spurned southern fire-eaters as heatedly as they did abolitionists, South Carolina's fire-eating nullifiers continued to agitate for southern nationhood until 1860, when through a series of peculiar events, their program won the acceptance of many southerners and resulted in secession and war. While the fire-eating sectionalists won new adherents along the way and while some defenders of slavery increasingly saw a sectionalizing of the slavery issue, from the 1820s to the Civil War sectionalism and proslavery followed variant courses, intersecting at moments of crisis when proslavery nationalism seemed inadequate, but retaining a separate character even in the midst of war.

While sectionalism played a role in nearly every southerner's comments on slavery, few avowed sectionalists made substantive contributions to the growing stock of proslavery literature until the crisis of 1850.

And the few who did quickly found that sectionalism alone was an insufficient basis on which to build an ideology of proslavery. Between the shock of 1835 and 1840, only three individuals attempted to couch their sectionalism in proslavery literature. They were Chancellor William Harper, Henry L. Pinckney, and Robert Barnwell Rhett, all of South Carolina. While the writings of James Henry Hammond were eventually among the most influential of those penned by latter-day nullifiers, his *Letters on Slavery in the United States* were not published until 1845. Few others followed before 1850. In the meantime, Harper, Pinckney, and Rhett carried the banners of southern sectionalism and made the only formal attempts outside the realm of political oratory in Congress to systematize proslavery sectionalism. And one of them, in the end, decided to abandon sectionalism entirely.[17]

Of the three former nullifiers who published proslavery writings in the 1830s, only the writings of Chancellor Harper were of lasting significance. Two of Pinckney's three anti-abolition pamphlets, published in 1836, were printed for the purposes of defending his betrayal of southern sectionalists in Congress in the spring of 1836 by promoting a compromise in gag rule debates. Only in the *Spirit of the Age,* an address presented at the University of North Carolina in August 1836, did Pinckney deviate momentarily from his political course to consider more calmly the meaning of contemporary history. Indicating that the age was one of science, liberal principles, and free inquiry, Pinckney slipped into a discussion of the ongoing crisis besetting slavery. Perhaps as a result of his recent attempts to compromise the differences between southern sectionalists and the federal government or as a consequence of the struggle in which he was engaged for his political life, Pinckney expressed in his first calm utterance on slavery and abolition attitudes strange on the lips of a nullifier.[18]

Although in the vein of a state's rights sectionalist he told his student audience at Chapel Hill that they should make themselves "thoroughly conversant *with the true character, and legitimate functions of our federative system,*" Pinckney quickly added that "the language of *disunion* has become too *common.*" Time and events had so "diminished the offensiveness" of threats of disunion that the beating of sectional drums was no longer a wise or effective policy. In one of the most telling comments by a former diehard nullifier, Pinckney proclaimed:

> Cherish, then an ardent devotion to our happy forms of government, both State and Federal. Sustain *the States, to the full extent of their reserved authorities,*

William Winans, 1788–1857
Mississippi Methodist, radical anti-
abolitionist, staunch colonizationist

Whitemarsh Benjamin Seabrook,
1792–1855
Agronomist, nullifier, radical reactionary,
eventual South Carolina governor,
1848–1850

William Harper, 1790–1847
South Carolina chancellor, ideologized
proslavery theorist promoting union and
conservative republicanism

William Gilmore Simms, 1806–1870
Southern author, poet, novelist,
ideologized proslavery writer

and restrain the Federal Legislature within its constitutional sphere. But cultivate, also, an expanded patriotism, and a generous attachment *to every portion of the Union.* Never suffer your country to be sacrificed to faction, nor your judgment to be blinded by local prejudices, but, rising above all sectional and contracted views, remember that you are American citizens, as well as citizens of States, and that he who is false to our common country, can never be faithful to his native State.[19]

In the mind of at least one nullifier, therefore, the doctrine of nullification was a dead letter.

After declaring a newfound devotion to the Union that took him from the opposite pole of his pre-abolition nullification views, Pinckney went on to establish some of the new principles by which he would be guided in his future attempts to uphold the peculiar institution of the South. As if he had recently read the anti-abolitionist views of northerners David Reese, James T. Austin, or James Kirke Paulding, Pinckney began describing "the spirit of mobocracy [that] has crossed the Atlantic, and burst forth, in this land of law, in all its hideous deformity, and atrocious violence." If mobocracy continued to grow in America, "anarchy will usurp the place of law, and our country will become the theatre of many a bloody and disgraceful scene." The whole movement rested upon "that revolting doctrine that would array the poor against the rich . . . under the specious appellation of an equality of rights." Glancing at history, Pinckney found instances in the history of Greece and Rome when the same doctrines turned republics into anarchy. Also "this same doctrine was interwoven with the French Revolution, and caused many of the horrors of that memorable drama. And now we have it in America." While radical equalitarianism had thus far been confined to the cities of the North in America, "like the spirit of mobocracy, it is contagious in its character, and therefore cannot be too solemnly deprecated, or too earnestly resisted." Warning the students, like an old Federalist, to be wary of "the excesses of party spirit" and the enervating effects of petty factionalism, Pinckney counseled that every Christian American should place his trust in principles and ideals, not in the power of men.[20]

Since the summer of 1835, in the space of only one year of abolitionist excitement, Pinckney had undergone a dramatic shift of loyalties, of values, and of principles that was indicative of the process whereby American leaders were drawn to and united behind a national body of symbols dealing with abolitionism and slavery. Only a year earlier considered one of the most radical nullifiers in South Carolina, Pinckney reversed his values in a manner that, at least for the moment, affected the course of American history. Not only did his change of direction result in a Congressional compromise ending the gag rule debates and abating national tensions, but he also charted a new course of nationalism that other southern leaders could follow. In a courageous move away from the tradition of state's rights sectionalism, he discarded for the most part all of the legal and constitutional baggage that unnecessarily encumbered the South's response to abolitionism. Rejecting the complex and hopelessly confused rhetoric of South Carolina's nullifying lawyers and politicians, Pinckney opted for the simpler and ultimately more persuasive ideology of the anti-abolitionists.[21]

Among those nullifiers who underwent an alteration of values and perspective from sectionalism to a new version of proslavery nationalism, Pinckney was hardly alone. Indeed, the man who has often been considered one of the chief intellectual architects of both nullification and southern proslavery theory displayed a similar change in the wake of the abolition crisis of 1835. William Harper, a native of Antigua, the son of a Methodist clergyman, and among the first graduates of South Carolina College in 1808, practiced law and entered politics in South Carolina during the 1820s. Once a nationalist, Harper in 1828 became a radical nullifier whose extensive writings and political activity helped shape the legal and ideological basis of the movement. As chancellor of the state of South Carolina almost continuously from 1830 until his death in 1847, Harper took his place as one of the most influential and brilliant leaders in the antebellum history of the state. In 1837 he published his lengthy and influential *Memoir on Slavery*, the most extensive and systematic defense of slavery written by a South Carolinian, let alone a nullifier, in the 1830s.

A deeply thoughtful man whose writings reveal none of the hasty composition of many proslavery tracts, Harper waited until December 1835 before announcing his opinions on abolition and slavery. And then, in a searching oration before the South Carolina Society for the Advancement of Learning, Harper indicated to his hearers' surprise that as a result of recent events he could not claim a single settled opinion on the subject that threatened to destroy America. Instead of tossing out half-formed opinions and popular cries for the punishment of abolitionists, Harper suggested that southerners and members of the society undertake a long-postponed investigation of the institution of slavery: "Nothing . . . can be more interesting to us, than that the nature of this

institution, in reference to its moral and political, as well as its eco-
nomical character and effects, should be thoroughly understood; and no
duty more sacred and imperative devolves on this society, than the full
and thorough investigation of the whole subject, in all its bearings and
relations. I suggest this as the first business of the society." Certain that
southerners were not yet ready to overthrow slavery, Harper merely
called for slaveholders to reevaluate and "thoroughly understand its
character."[22]

In the rest of his oration Harper suggested the directions any wholesale reassessment of slavery might take. Southerners needed to restudy
the doctrine of natural rights, remembering that "the whole of existence
is but a choice between evils" and that "natural equality and universal
freedom never did and never can exist." "We are lovers of liberty, and
republicans," Harper continued. But Americans should not attempt to
hide the fact that their republicanism actually developed into aristocracy
"as all the great and successful republics of the world have been aristoc-
racies." For an aristocratic republic to survive "there must exist the consideration, deference, respect and influence which are yielded to superior worth, to virtue, talent and public service." Upon the shoulders of
republican aristocrats rested the "protection of property, law, justice,
order, religion and true liberty, when the rest of the world shall be involved in the wildest anarchy or subjected to the sternest despotism."
Indeed, they could parade as missionaries and reformers: "we by our
position are *conservatives;* and it is our business to show that conservatives
are the truest reformers. We will not overturn the fundamental institutions of society; but we will improve them to the utmost where they are
capable of improvement—supply their deficiencies, and remedy their
abuses." Conservative, aristocratic republicans needed to take upon
themselves the responsibility for reforming the world.[23]

Harper was precise enough in his outline for the future of America to
indicate those sources from which slaveholders might draw inspirations
and wisdom for the task ahead. They should refer to the patterns of
Greece and Rome: "I may observe that the history of these great republics, from which the rest of the world learns wisdom, may be studied
with double advantage and instruction by us." He also recommended the
politics of Aristotle: "Little of what is just or profound on the principles
of government has appeared since, of which the traces may not be found
there." Slaveholders should also consult Montesquieu and Madame de
Staël's reflections on the French Revolution. "But above all," Harper as-

serted, "I would recommend the speeches and political writings of Burke." As if he had suddenly discovered something that should have been obvious all along, Harper declared Edmund Burke "the great political philosopher of modern times" whose writings "comprehend the profoundest wisdom of the noblest eloquence." "And great as may be the influence which he has exercised on the affairs of the world, and much as his name has been in the mouths of men," Harper concluded, "I venture to predict that he has not yet begun to gather his fame."[24] Never before had Burke drawn the undivided and unstinting praise of such a southerner.

Although Harper had not yet systematized the ideas that would make him known as one of the savants of proslavery history, he had discovered since July 1835 the body of ideas and the peculiar values that would inform his proslavery argumentation. In an intellectual shift no less dramatic than the defection of Henry L. Pinckney from the camp of southern sectionalism, Harper swung away from the legalistic cant of his nullification years toward that body of ideological thought that underlay forty years of American conservatism. As Burke had been the single most influential source for New England's violent rejection of the French Revolution in the 1790s, Burke would now become the chief source for a southern disavowal of latter-day French infidelity in the form of abolitionism. As conservative values became the rallying point for a Federalist countersubversive campaign to reform society in the image of aristocratic republicanism, a similar conservatism would impel southerners to reshape the South into a like ideal society. As conservative republicanism informed the ideology of New England reformers from the 1790s into the mid-nineteenth century, it would now form the basis of southerners' proslavery ideology. While Harper was perceptive enough to discover the values of Burkean conservatism for the defense of slaveholding society, he probably did not perceive that the ideas and values that would form the basis of his proslavery thinking were mediated to him through the persistence of conservatism in the speeches and writings of northern anti-abolitionists in the months and years preceding and following the abolition crisis of 1835.

Having rejected nullifying sectionalism as a proper or usable foundation on which to build the South's proslavery assault on the modern world, having locked into the ongoing heritage of conservative ideology, and having denoted the latter as the appropriate basis for proslavery thought, Harper two years later fashioned his *Memoir on Slavery* out of the growing American ideological consensus. Noting that Thomas R. Dew's massive *Review of the Debate in the Virginia Legislature*, "perhaps the most profound, original, and truly philosophical treatise, which has appeared within the time of my recollection," had made little dent in the disposition of Americans to attack slavery, Harper proposed the creation of a new line of defense made possible by his new appreciation for Burkean conservatism. Relying heavily upon the writings of Burke, those of James Kirke Paulding in his recent anti-abolitionist volume *Slavery in America*, and a newly published evaluation of English and American society by Edward Gibbon Wakefield,[25] Harper proceeded to systematize in the service of perpetual slavery the values and beliefs that had long guided New England conservatives.

After admitting that it was possible for one to hold quite logically the opinion that "it is better it [slavery] should not exist" in any society, Harper arrived at the heart of the South's moral and ideological dilemma. Slave labor was obviously more expensive and burdensome than free labor. Slavery brought in its van great evils and abuses both for the slave and for the master. Slaves were also unkindly deprived of any form of social, economic, or educational betterment. Nevertheless, after comparing the condition of the slave with that of the poor in the North and in England, Harper found that of all the circumstances in which the world's poor had to live, slavery was the least evil, the least reprehensible of all. The real problem for Americans and for southerners was not that their poor folk lived in harsh circumstances but that the poor of the South were separated from all others by the term *slave:* "There is something in this word *Slavery* which seems to partake of the qualities of the insane root, and distempers the minds of men."[26]

Americans because of the Declaration of Independence and the rhetoric of the American Revolution, Harper argued, had developed a moral and social astigmatism that blurred any appreciation of the real essence of slavery. Clearly evidencing that southerners had only recently begun the intellectual process long since completed by northern counterrevolutionaries and their followers, Harper described the recent revulsion against revolutionary thought in the South: "the truth is, that, until very lately, since circumstances have compelled us to think for ourselves, we took our opinions on this subject, as on every other, ready formed from the country of our origin [U.S.]. And so deeply rooted were they, that we adhered to them, as most men will do to deeply rooted opinions, even against the evidence of our own observation, and our own senses."

Southerners had remained subservient to a set of values that did not conform to reality: "It is not long since a great majority of our free population, servile to the opinions of those whose opinions they had been accustomed to follow, would have admitted Slavery to be a great evil, unjust and indefensible in principle, and only to be vindicated by the stern necessity which was imposed upon us."[27]

Released from bondage to an outmoded and unworkable liberalism too long blindly accepted by southerners, the South could rise up in defiance against abolitionists and direct the nation toward the establishment of a modern aristocratic republic. To save the nation from fanaticism and kakistocracy, southern republicans would cultivate the values of conservatives, particularly those of Burke. They would replace infidelity with religion, fanaticism with calm deliberation, and mobbism with law and order. Most importantly they would instruct the world in the important lessons to be gained from Burke and the examples of the ancient republics: "They teach us that slavery is compatible with freedom, stability, and long duration of civil government, with denseness of population, great power, and the highest civilization." As true, responsible reformers, southern conservatives would eventually build a model civilization for the admiration of all men.[28]

Although Harper persisted in thinking in terms of the South alone and although other nullifiers such as Robert Barnwell Rhett resisted any thoughts of foregoing sectionalism for a reideologizing of the South,[29] thoughtful southerners after 1835 absorbed and began to transmit values and beliefs that had been alien to their minds a few short years earlier. Until the 1850s, however, fire-eaters such as Rhett were the exception among proslavery men, being spurned alike by the nation as a whole and by responsible southern leaders. Most assumed the stance of Harper, wishing to rebuild the South ideologically and structurally into a conservative republican edifice. Most proslavery men also took the compromising nonsectional position of Pinckney. On the battleground of post-nullification South Carolina, Pinckney suffered a stinging defeat for his betrayal of southern sectionalists; however, elsewhere in the South social leaders and thinkers found it easier to rally around the proslavery nationalism being given expression by conservative thinkers, benevolent reformers, and anti-abolitionists in every corner of America. By 1840 the ideas of South Carolina's nullifiers were playing little or no role in the South's newly adopted proslavery ideology.

If southern sectionalists generally fell under the sway of rising proslavery nationalism, it should not be surprising to learn that southern opponents of nullification—the unionists of 1832 and 1833 in South Carolina and elsewhere—generally subscribed to proslavery nationalism as soon as they were alerted to the ideology and rhetoric of anti-abolitionism. The revolution of values that can only be dimly perceived in the case of former nullifiers was with unionists an openly admitted fact. For example, in *The South Vindicated from the Treason and Fanaticism of the Northern Abolitionists,* a long and hastily written book usually attributed to William Drayton,[30] a leading antinullification nationalist, nearly all of the arguments were drawn directly from the vast literature of conservatively ideologized anti-abolitionists. Appealing to the passions and perceptions that anti-abolitionists shared in 1835, the author described abolitionists as "the misbegotten and dangerous brood," "incendiaries," and reckless destroyers of families who "by maudlin verses and lying pictures, essay not only to rouse the passions of the slave, but to excite the prejudices of the ignorant and unreflecting of our citizens." Reviewing the history of slavery in America from the writings of Robert Walsh, outlining the foundations on which to build a Burkean national republic, and calling for a national countersubversionary movement to overthrow the conspiracy of abolitionists, the author reflected a heightened awareness of the principles and writings of prominent anti-abolitionists without any corresponding appreciation of the sectional outbursts of South Carolina's nullifiers.[31]

Particularly notable among antinullifiers whose early proslavery writings displayed an absorption of anti-abolitionist ideology was William Gilmore Simms, a crucial figure in the history of southern sectionalism. Even though Simms, one of the leading creative writers of the antebellum South, later became the chief symbolic leader of southern sectionalism in literature, in the 1830s he endorsed the flowering proslavery nationalism of anti-abolitionists and benevolent reformers. In an article reviewing Harriet Martineau's *Society in America* in 1837, Simms reacted strongly to the English woman's comments on South Carolina. After correcting some of her glaring errors that had resulted from misleading information, Simms entered into a discussion of slavery. Admitting the factual basis for many of Miss Martineau's references to abuses of slaveholders, Simms, like Harper and Pinckney before him, called for a reform of slavery under the aegis of a new understanding of slavery and society. Following the lead of conservatives and anti-abolitionists in denying the validity of the doctrine of equalitarianism, Simms rejected the words of the Declaration of Independence for those of "a greater philosopher than Thomas Jefferson." Finding in the writings of William Shakespeare support for the growing emphasis on order, stability, and harmony, Simms wrote, "Democracy is not leveling—it is, properly defined, the harmony of the moral world. It insists upon inequalities, as its law declares, that all men should hold the place to which they are properly entitled."[32]

From a devotion to rights, Simms saw the moral and social world moving toward the doctrine of duty. *"The truth is,"* he continued, *"that our rights depend entirely upon the degree of obedience which we pay to the laws of our creation. All our rights whether from nature or from society . . . result from the performance of our duties."* Some must rule out of duty to society; others must follow, performing their own appointed tasks. Slaveholders were bound to fulfill duties toward the slaves as dictated by society, including kind treatment, comfortable livings, and moral instruction. The slaveholder was forced to fulfill his moral obligations "in compliance with what he should consider a sacred duty, undertaken to God and man alike." "Indeed," Simms concluded, paraphrasing both Harper and benevolent reformers, "the slaveholders of the south . . . are the great moral conservators, in one powerful interest, of the entire world." While Simms wrote providentially of the future course of slaveholders, he sounded the constant refrain of proslavery nationalism.[33]

Fifteen years later, in 1852, when Simms revised his article on Miss Martineau's *Society in America* for inclusion in a large volume entitled *The Pro-Slavery Argument,* he had largely succumbed to southern sectionalism. Still unaware that in 1837 he had imbibed sentiments on the nature of society that were only then becoming national, he was not unaware that the South had undergone an ideological revolution in the mid-1830s. Before 1835, he wrote, "few persons in the South undertook to justify Negro Slavery, except on the score of necessity." It had not been easy "to eradicate" from the minds of southerners a "falsehood" that "had been the growth of prescription and a habit of thought, of phrase and formula, for a hundred years." In the moment of crisis, southerners had experienced "a morbid feeling of weakness in respect to the moral of our claim." Simms had been among the very few who took what he called "other and higher grounds" in the defense of slavery.[34]

Unaware that he may have absorbed in the heat of crisis an entirely new perspective on the nature of man and society, he could not appreciate the fact that the higher ground he had assumed with respect to slavery flowed logically and inevitably from a proslavery nationalism that neither he nor other southerners had been responsible in the first instance for creating. The higher ground was not some conscious decision to stop calling slavery a "necessity" and start labeling it a "positive good." Rather it was the absorption and adoption of a body of thought transported by New England conservatives, benevolent reformers, and anti-abolitionists into the South that made slavery seem a natural and inevitable institution in republican society. While Simms and other knowledgeable southerners already knew from researches in political economy that slavery could be socially beneficial in a free economy, it was only from the rhetoric and ideology of counterrevolutionary respondents to abolitionism that they learned the lesson that slavery could conform with republicanism and that even in America where men lived in the shadow of a republican Revolution slavery could indeed be defended on higher grounds. But once proslavery southerners learned the lessons of their adopted conservative ideology, they began trumpeting its most disturbing message and carried America's distinctive proslavery ideology to its logical conclusion.

FOURTEEN

Proslavery Republicanism

As late as 1830 there was nothing that could be understood as an American variety of proslavery ideology. There was nothing in the history of proslavery in the confines of the United States that would set it apart from proslavery as it had occurred in other parts of the world. While many Americans could and did defend slavery from time to time on various grounds of necessity, most Americans believed slavery to be some manner of evil that ought to be removed as soon as possible. That was the teaching of the Revolutionary heritage. And even in areas of the North where doughty conservative Federalists had revived the notions of ranks and orders in society and in regions of the South where slave holders had become resigned to perpetual slavery, hardly anyone challenged the belief that slavery would one day, with great benefit, be wiped from the face of the earth. In fact, despite the varied experiences of diehard Federalists in the North and the great slaveholders of the South and despite the fact of sometimes rancorous debate over various aspects of the problem of slavery, the period from the Revolution to the rise of abolitionism was largely uneventful in terms of the formal shape of proslavery history. Defenses of slavery written in the South of the 1820s looked and read little differently from those penned in the North forty years earlier. All of them were written under the dispensation of Revolutionary thought.

Abolitionism changed everything. From the first moment Americans perceived immediatism as a threat to American society, their ideas about slavery began undergoing a dramatic change. In the face of supposed legions of radicals who seemed to care not a whit for the union of the states, for orthodoxy in religion, or for peace and order in society, Americans changed their minds about the future of slavery almost overnight. From the Revolutionary doctrine that slavery had no place in republican society, they leaped to a diametrically opposed notion that slavery had

347

been and indeed could be an essential ingredient in a republic. From the perspective of those who underwent the transformation, the latter idea came to seem as logical and as consistent with American values as the former had been for half a century. In that stark and amazing transformation America's first, most pervasive, and distinctive proslavery ideology emerged.

While it is difficult to generalize in any study of American history about what the majority of Americans believed or experienced at any particular time, it seems likely during the decade of the 1830s that many, if not most, Americans in the North and South who had not already done so fell sway to what, in American experience, can only be characterized as the nation's conservative counterrevolution. They became part of what both conservative ideologues and proslavery writers constantly referred to as the *conservative majority*. Fashioned to deal with crisis, to maintain social hierarchy, to generate respect for law and order, and to promote a renovation of society, it was perhaps only logical that Federalist era counterrevolutionary thought should have been adopted as the primary intellectual and popular framework for proslavery. America's conservative thought and values had been forged on an anvil so similar to the crisis of abolitionism that many of the old Federalists and their conservative offspring who had lived through the turmoil of the French Revolution and Jeffersonian Democracy challenged the abolitionists in a manner that suggested the stream of French infidels, Illuminati, and Democrats had not ended in the decades between the 1790s and 1830s. Because such conservative reactionaries were so effective in their portrayals of abolitionists as the direct descendants of French revolutionaries and because through the conservative counterrevolution after 1815 they had drawn so many crucial people—particularly clergymen—into their pattern of thought, they were able during the 1830s to transport conservative thought fully into the South and to make it the ideological core for an ideology of proslavery. They were so successful initially, in fact, that they ended up creating an approach to slavery and to abolitionism that can only be characterized as *proslavery republicanism*.[1]

One might well ask just what were the principles of America's conservative counterrevolution that appealed so strongly to anti-abolitionists, benevolent reformers, and defenders of slavery and made it possible for them to develop a form of proslavery ideology distinctively American. Fortunately for the historian latter-day conservatives who doubled as defenders of slavery expounded their principles with great regularity and comprehensiveness. One of the most concise and systematic presentations of conservative ideology as it was shaped on the heels of abolitionism was given by Hubbard Winslow of Boston on July 4, 1838, in an oration entitled *The Means of the Perpetuity and Prosperity of Our Republic.* Winslow prepared the address at the behest of the mayor and other municipal authorities of Boston both to celebrate the anniversary of American independence and to inculcate in the citizens of Boston principles whereby they might withstand abolitionism. The oration as republished was intended as a popular textbook of accepted conservative principles. The mayor and city council were so pleased with the resultant document that they had it printed and distributed at city expense. The oration could as easily have been a textbook of America's proslavery republicanism, for it contained in a systematic format all of the basic social principles that would be harangued by anti-abolitionists and proslavery thinkers for a generation to come. Hence, in detailing the conservative principles of Hubbard Winslow as of 1838, one is also describing the essence or the ideological core of America's most distinctive and enduring form of proslavery ideology—proslavery republicanism.[2]

Winslow divided his oration into four major concerns, as follows: civil government, pure religion, human rights and liberties, and "correct views respecting what constitutes the essential strength and glory of a nation." In each of the four divisions he set forth the principles of conservatism, explained very carefully how those principles related to the American crisis over slavery, and outlined prescriptively the things needed to be done to ensure that America should become a conservative republic. While much conservative and proslavery literature consisted of negatives and criticisms of obstacles to the creation of such a republic or the perpetuation of slavery, Winslow succeeded in establishing the positive, prescriptive programs that underlay the work of anti-abolitionists, benevolent reformers, and proslavery republicans.

Under the heading of civil government, Winslow began with a truism always upheld by both conservatives and proslavery thinkers: "one of the greatest earthly blessings, and that on which all others depend, is a *good civil government.*" In a sense everything else flowed from the social prerequisite of a sound and orderly government. Without decent government, Winslow continued, "Factions, riots, frauds, confiscations, impostures, murders—every description of crime and cruelty—unite to worry and devour their unhappy victims, and to blight the last blossoms of hope which survived the ruins of Eden." Actually few people had ever enjoyed the privilege of living under a good civil government: "What a frightful book is the history of mankind!" Rare indeed could one find the converse, "A whole nation of human beings, at once perfectly free and perfectly governed, having their separate and their associate interests well defined and equally protected; mutually pledged to resist oppression, rebuke injustice, secure equity, and promote the true ends of human existence." But Winslow made clear that the conservative ideal was not perfect; rather, it harnessed freedom.[3]

Good civil government depended partly on the form of government employed. Winslow admitted that "a monarchical government" was the best form but that good governance depended more on the "wisdom and fidelity in the presiding powers." Hence, a republic could work "*provided the appropriate means are employed.*" Winslow, despite his preference for a monarchy, approved heartily "this Federal Republic" whose anniversary he celebrated. Yet, like most of his conservative forebears, he was skeptical about its ultimate success: "it cannot fail to appear that the great experiment is but begun, and that its final result is, to human view, highly problematical." Its longevity and its success depended upon "*the diffusion of the essential elements of intelligent and virtuous power among all classes of citizens.*" It also hinged upon the extent to which Americans adopted the prescriptive principles and policies he and other like-minded men held essential.[4]

The first and most essential element in the maintenance of good government was the adoption and perpetuation of "enlightened and pure religion." Few conservatives and even fewer proslavery advocates after 1835 doubted the necessity of a pure and undefiled orthodoxy in religion as a primary ingredient in the foisting up of an orderly society. Winslow, along with his reactionary forebears, believed strongly that "the *actual service* of God was an essential means of sustaining civil liberty." Moreover, they held "firmly to the Sacred Scriptures, as an infallible utterance of the Divine Mind for our standard of moral truth and duty." The belief in the necessity of religion was so strong, in fact, that Winslow argued that a removal of religious institutions, veneration for Scripture, and moral duty "would prove [this] the last celebration of our nation's freedom."[5]

One had only to look at "the sanguinary history of atheistic France" to get an idea of the consequences of a nation devoted both to liberty and to atheism. The consequence for America would be that "the sun of this nation would be turned to darkness and its moon to blood." Whenever any nation resorted to disbelief or to experimentation in religion, it "has ever resulted, and ever must result, in that general prostration of soul and character, which leads directly, by the bloody steps of anarchy and revolution, to enslaving credulity and despotic power." In obvious reference to the supposed principles of abolitionists, Winslow charged, "Adversaries of human accountability to God, are therefore enemies to our republic." "No republican government could be possibly sustained by a community of such men," he concluded. Nevertheless, call it what one will—atheism, enthusiasm, or orthodoxy—men will have some kind of religion. For Winslow and his compatriots, "The only question is, whether they shall have religion pure or corrupted." In his mind every patriot should "be commissioned, as set forth and sanctioned in the sacred scriptures, to enlighten the understandings, invigorate the intellects, elevate the aims, inspire the hearts, and control the wills, of both subjects and magistrates [so that] to the end of time may our free institutions stand, firm as mountains of brass."[6]

Second only to the maintenance of orthodoxy in religion for Winslow was the necessity of inculcating in Americans "just and temperate views respecting human rights and liberties." As had become common quite early to conservative Federalists, later to the benevolent reformers, and finally to the proslavery men of the South, Winslow did not hesitate to strike down any notion of an equality of rights for Americans. "The spirit of liberty," Winslow held, "has ever carried along with it a strong tendency to excess and anarchy." The love of freedom, as grand as it sounded in the abstract and as noble as it seemed "needs to be enlightened, tempered, guided and restrained, or it will rush headlong to its own destruction." Nor did the love of freedom confer anything approaching equal social rights: "Mere *humanity* confers neither equality of rights nor ability for self-protection." In a long passage notable for the lack of a reference to slavery, Winslow argued the cornerstone doctrine of conservatism and proslavery republicanism: "It is the right and the duty of the sane to take care of the insane, of the virtuous to restrain the vicious, of the learned to instruct the ignorant, of the wise to guide the simple, of the strong to protect the weak, of the aged to counsel the young;—and if it is the duty of some to do these things, it is the duty of those for whom they are needed to consent to have them done." In fact, all rights and duties "are ultimately to be determined, not by each individual for himself, but by the society or government of which he is a member."[7]

About one item, Winslow was adamant. A proper perspective on liberty and equality in America had nothing whatsoever to do with "leveling." He found the theory of leveling to be "against all the analogies of nature and providence." Inequality was ordained by God: "that there should be inequality in the conditions of men, as there is in all the other works of providence, is clearly a wise and benevolent ordinance of heaven." Citing one of the famous aphorisms of the god of both conservatism and proslavery, Edmund Burke, Winslow wrote, "Those who attempt to level never equalize." "So far from levelling," Winslow continued, "it [radicalism] ultimately renders society more uneven, and that too in a way disastrous to all classes."[8]

"What then *is* the true republican doctrine of equal rights and liberties?" Winslow asked: "I conceive it to be summarily this, that all men have by nature the same right, and should have equal liberty, to serve their Maker with all their powers, in the way most conducive to their own welfare and to that of their fellow beings." After extending his summary view to include personal, moral, religious, civil, and political liberties, Winslow concluded that "Republican liberty" was the aggregate of all of them and could be "measured by no abstract theory." Rather, liberty was a relative matter dependent entirely upon the good of society. And "in a republic of intelligent and good citizens, every man will increase his rights and liberties, *just in the degree that he increases his merits*." By Winslow's definition and that of other conservatives and proslavery republicans, a man had essentially no rights that were not conferred upon him by the whim of society.[9]

Following another outpouring on the sins of abolitionists, Winslow proceeded to his third main necessity for the maintenance of the conservative republic, "correct views respecting what constitutes the essential strength and glory of a nation." This was Winslow's catchall section, which enabled him to expound upon a long series of favorite conservative themes and principles. Eschewing the practice of statesmen who concerned themselves with political economy, Winslow argued that "the true strength and glory of a republic lie *in the intelligence, the genius, the integrity, the industry, the patriotism, the intellectual and moral worth of the people*." In his mind there were a number of "essential virtues" and beliefs that had to be taught throughout the nation if the republic were to survive.[10]

Children had to be taught "true republican doctrine" by which he meant correct conservatism. They must be taught the importance of union, or "that state of the republic in which harmony of views, feelings, and interests prevail between the various classes and members of society and the different sections of the country." Newspapers must be made "eminently republican." They, as "the most constant companions and teachers of the people," needed to be saved from "perversion" and disseminated as widely as possible. Academies and colleges should be built and endowed with true republicanism "to train for public service the best minds from all the ranks and conditions of society." All of the professions of jurisprudence, law, medicine, theology, and teaching should be made "branches of one and the same universal science" to build up and improve republican government. Farms and villages should be made training schools in virtue, piety, industry, and efficiency. Every institution in the land, in brief, must be turned into moral and social training centers for the promotion of true republicanism.[11]

Winslow had a number of quite special comments regarding leadership and governance. It was a duty of all citizens to elevate only the wisest and most faithful conservatives into public office. In fact, Winslow would have nothing to do with any rags-to-riches mentality in America. Paraphrasing more words from Burke, he wrote, "I do not hesitate to say, that the road to eminence and power from obscure condition, ought not to be made too easy, nor a thing too much of course." And once solid republicans were installed in office, they ought to be given the unstinting devotion of all citizens: "Few earthly affections are stronger or more sacred, than those which ought to exist between republican citizens and the men who sustain to them the relations of faithful magistrates and protectors, physicians, pastors, and teachers. Guardians of their individual and social rights, of their health and life, of their morals and religion, of the education of their children, they should deserve and receive their highest love and esteem." At the same time, it was the duty of public officials not to resort to "innovations" and "experiments" in legislation. Legislative enactments "should never be an experiment, but the *results* of all experiments from the beginning of time." Experience not experimentation, moderation not extravagance, and devotion to duty not innovation were the principles proclaimed by conservative republicans and proslavery men alike.[12]

There were several evils that Winslow thought had become all too prevalent in American society, each of which he thought ought to be curbed. "The community has been pushing and scrambling with all its might for money" to the point of warping society. "Wealth thus sought and thus idolized," he thought, "will open a short and sure way through enervation and profligacy to ruin." In addition to the worship of money, too many young, ill-educated, and misguided men were taking the road to demagoguery. In the name of reform, many were being "raised up and sustained . . . to mislead the people and foment discords." Such people had to be turned aside from their dangerous course, their motives disclosed, and their careers ended. Along with money worship and demagoguery went one of the most alarming tendencies of all—the elevation of women "out of their own sphere." The movement resulted from "the extravagant movements of a few eccentric minds." Winslow believed that the values of republicanism should be imparted to "our daughters as to our sons" and "the peculiar virtues of sex, and the qualifications for their appropriate sphere, should be neither impaired nor neglected." A woman could best serve the republic by sitting "as a queen in robes of purity and light . . . for the admiration, delight and example of the whole world."[13]

When Winslow finally arrived in his catalogue of "correct views" at the proper content of American culture and learning, he reverted to a lecture on the virtues of classicism. Americans, in order to avert the perversions of the modern world, needed to develop a full range of classical tastes in art, music, architecture, and even horticulture. Classical learning should become the standard fare in all academies and colleges in the land. Americans needed to study the classical empires of Greece and Rome to learn what made them great and the causes of their ultimate demise. "What was it," Winslow asked, "that placed Egypt, Syria, Greece, and Rome, so high in greatness and influence over all the world, while so many nations, great, populous, warlike, flushed in their brief day with numerous and mighty conquests, passed immediately away to oblivion?" Americans needed to know and to rely on the classical patterns for their very style of life.[14]

But in Winslow's mind the classical font of culture and learning needed one great supplement, the addition of the British example. "No intellect," he claimed, "surpasses British intellect." Britain took classical learning, improved upon it, and developed through its many great savants a new venerable style for republicanism. As a result, "Britain holds ascendency over all other nations of the Old World." In fact, "the greatness of her intellectual power, the sound learning and pure religion wrought for ages into her character and institutions, are, in the present improved state of the world, pledges that her national existence and glory will last till the end of time." The British pattern was the one that Americans needed most badly to take to heart. Americans, by following the British example, could develop their own republican edifice which would also last throughout the ages.[15]

Winslow's emphasis on classicism and on the British model was but one avenue of getting to what he considered the most essential guide for future American thought and attempts to perpetuate the conservative republic. American thinkers and leaders needed to make Edmund Burke and his writings practically their sole guide in the building up of a good republic. Winslow parroted conservatives and proslavery men alike when he stated flatly that "Burke rose highest of all mortals in majesty, splendor and power of intellect." Winslow's praise for Burke was unlimited:

> Edmund Burke was the first and the greatest of the few "enlightened men" . . . who foresaw and predicted the result of those principles which produced the French Revolution. Standing forth strong and clear upon the conservative side, amidst the prevailing tendencies of his age to revolution, by the soundness of his wisdom, the integrity of his politics, the invincibleness of his arguments, and the subduing power of his eloquence, he did more than perhaps any other man to save Britain and the other civilized nations from plunging into the gulph of anarchy, and into another long and dreary night of dark ages. His writings should be in the hands of all American citizens. A firm friend of rational liberty and human rights, a christian, a patriot, a scholar, an orator, of the soundest and most finished order, he can be read by no American citizen without intense interest and true profit.

Winslow was himself so enamored with Burke's thought that in writing his own textbook for American republicanism Burke proved to be nearly his only cited authority. Moreover, in the midst of his otherwise closely argued *Oration,* Winslow devoted more than three pages to discussing the splendor and wisdom of Burke's views. While Winslow paid strict attention to separating Burke's writings from his own, dozens of other conservatives and proslavery writers after 1835 cited Burke's famous observations with abandon, rarely noting from whence they came. With his elegy to Edmund Burke, Winslow's treatise on conservative republicanism came to an end.[16]

Winslow's system of conservative ideology as of 1838 was not only a remarkably cogent treatment of latter-day conservative beliefs, values, and policies. It was also quite directly a logical and consistent rendering of the beliefs, values, and policies of the vast majority of all respondents throughout America to the threat of abolitionism after the summer of 1835. Due to the presence in America of a host of articulate individuals who had been brought up on the tenets of counterrevolutionary conservatism during 1835 and the immediate years of crisis thereafter, conservative republicanism was adopted body and soul as the basic ideology of proslavery. From 1835 onward whenever men took up the cudgels of proslavery, they not only rehearsed arguments that had been used to defend slavery for centuries past, but they also hoisted the banner of conservative republicanism, making it the very foundation upon which they spun their web of proslavery logic.

In 1835 and for a generation to come there was an equation between conservative ideology and that body of thought that undergirded proslavery. That is not to say that dozens of proslavery writers did not go on developing and refining what can only be considered proslavery arguments. By the 1850s clergymen and biblical scholars had examined every possible passage of Scripture that would be used as a support for slavery. By that time the Constitution had been wrenched in every conceivable direction to provide legal guarantees for the maintenance of slavery. Philosophers and moralists had examined every system of thought from both the ancient and the modern world for any logical defense of slaveholding. Racists and ethnologists had conducted scientific studies of fauna, genera, and species in the hope of providing a rational basis for the domination of one race by another. And last, but certainly not least, statesmen and political economists had examined various systems of free and slave labor, feudal and capitalist economies, and free and slave societies through observation, the compilation of statistics, and the study of history in order to prove that slavery was a benevolent and profitable base on which to construct a modern society. But no matter where the defenders of slavery went in quest of the argument that would clinch the case for slavery, they almost never departed from the system of symbols and the body of ideas that made conservative republicanism the core ideology of proslavery.

There were many reasons why conservative republicanism remained the ideological core of proslavery to the eve and even into the period of the Civil War. Most of them involved unconscious decisions on the part of proslavery writers. The structure of Revolutionary and Jeffersonian thought provided little basis for the mounting of an ideology of proslavery. So long as one clung to the libertarian ideals of either the Revolution or Jefferson, one could not find a tenable ground on which to

"A Family Quarrel"
Cartoon from *Punch, or the London Charivari*, September 28, 1861

defend slavery. The only possible ground of defense under those systems of thought was the route selected by nullifiers and sectionalists: slavery, whatever its nature, was protected by law, and the states had the ultimate authority to maintain the law even against contrary actions of the federal government.

In the face of the sectionalizing tendencies of nullification, most proslavery writers chose to endorse the nationalizing tendencies of conservative republicanism. It provided both the logic and the rationale for maintaining ranks and orders in society. Far from endorsing any libertarian ideals, it could easily be used to maintain the status quo, however severe the condition of some classes of men might be. Proslavery writers would not only uphold the perpetuation of enslavement; they could also discredit sectionalism and parade, with great applause from all quarters, as nationalists in love with the Union, in love with law and order, and in love with the perpetuation of a well-integrated society. By embracing conservatism, since its tenets were widely held by so many people in New England, the Middle States, and the Midwest, they drove proslavery toward the mainstream of American thought. By making conservative ideology the basis for proslavery ideology, proslavery writers won the undivided support of what they perpetually understood to be the vast "conservative majority" of the American body politic.

In adopting the route of conservatism, proslavery thinkers, secondly, took full advantage of perhaps the most highly developed system of embattled rhetoric that had yet surfaced in American social and political parlance. Along with conservative doctrine came a highly structured and universally understood language, which, when employed in popular oratory and pamphleteering, gave proslavery thinkers an advantage their abolitionist opponents did not enjoy. The words *infidel, libertarian, enthusiast,* and scores of others were emotionally laden terms that gave to the user an automatic superiority. They dredged up associations and meanings that had become intrinsically attached to American social rhetoric. Their use in opposition to abolitionism immediately put the detractor of immediatism in league with religious orthodoxy, political conservatism, and social responsibility—not to mention the highly approved causes of benevolence, industriousness, and piety. The adoption of the rhetoric of conservatism ensured that proslavery could become not only national, but also socially and morally acceptable.

A third valuable asset that accrued to proslavery thought by the adoption of conservatism was the right to use a proven method of undermin-

"'Caesar Imperator!' or, The American Gladiators"
Cartoon from *Punch, or the London Charivari,* May 18, 1861

ing and destroying any movement that could be construed as socially
subversive. American conservatism had its birth as a countersubversionary movement and, as long as its ideology remained intact, enjoyed its
finest hours only when its proponents could identify a real or imagined
enemy. Beginning with French infidels and the Bavarian Illuminati, conservatives sedulously searched for real or imaginary enemies of the republic. Basically a force of reaction from the beginning, conservatism
could not thrive without an enemy. By taking on the countersubversionary methods of conservative counterrevolutionaries in their dealings
with abolitionists, proslavery thinkers and activists were easily able to
portray themselves as the friends of American liberty, the upholders of
the constitutional form of government, and the dutiful protectors of the
rights of all men. Their vivid portrayals of abolitionists as the enemies of
order, as the friends of subversion, and as the abettors of anarchy won
them an acceptance that could only come to successful countersubversives.

The fourth and most important asset that proslavery writers derived
from conservative thought was a singular characteristic perennially lacking in proslavery thought in other nations—a positive program of social
renovation. By becoming proponents of purity in religion, of devotion to
civil rulers and the state, of personal industry and virtue, of education
for all (including the slave), of classical learning, of the program of benevolence, of chastity and purity among women, and of Burkean conservatism, proslavery writers latched onto perhaps the strongest single organized force in nineteenth-century American society—the urge to
purify and upgrade the nation. From the moment proslavery ideology
became one with latter-day conservatism, proslavery became associated
with and integrated into a program of social uplift that had long since
gained the hearty approval of a majority of Americans. Whereas in all
other places and nations proslavery resembled always a last-ditch attempt of the old guard to protect its economic interests, the association
of proslavery with the positive program and aspirations of conservative
republicanism made American proslavery a movement of moral and social renovation.

America, therefore, did indeed have an ideology of proslavery best
known as proslavery republicanism. In terms of the general history of
proslavery in the Western world it was unique. While the word *republicanism* only describes its direction and scope, it was much more than
a mere endorsement of government and nation. It was a nationally held

system of symbols and beliefs that, despite all of the appearances of the mood and direction of antebellum America, seems to have won the adherence and endorsement of a vast number of Americans both in the North and in the South. And despite the fact that the Union smashed on the rocks of disunion and engaged in a ferociously fought Civil War, the happy acceptance by so many Americans of the values and principles of proslavery republicanism probably postponed for a quarter-century a war that seemed inevitable. What is even more important to recognize is that proslavery republicanism was always much more than a mere endorsement of slavery and its indefinite perpetuation. It was a system of values and beliefs that reconciled for Americans the inevitable conflict between the nation's Revolutionary ideals and the facts of enslavement. It was a system of countersubversion that provided the means for discrediting and allaying the influence of abolitionism. It was most importantly a system of positive prescription with a generally acceptable plan for the total renovation of American society as a great conservative republic.

Proslavery republicanism from its emergence and nationalization in the 1830s provided the basis for the bulk of American proslavery writings through the period of the Civil War. That the South accepted those conservative prescriptions, as did hosts of thinkers and leaders in other sections of the nation thereby making counterrevolutionary conservatism the core of a distinctively American proslavery ideology, is a significant development for any future assessments of the antebellum South or of the causes of the Civil War. From the history of proslavery in America, it seems clear that the South underwent a cultural transformation as it entered into the general defense of slavery, just as historians have always argued. But from the perspective of proslavery history it appears that the cultural transformation did not occur fully until after 1835, that it was spurred by impulses from outside the South, and that nonsoutherners as well as nonsouthern ideas were chiefly responsible for the transformation.

Strangest of all is the observation that instead of setting off on its own independent, sectional course, the South in its cultural transformation was brought into America's lively conservative counterrevolutionary tradition and thereby into the mainstream of American history. The adoption of a proslavery ideology by the South in the 1830s marked, not a departure from the rest of the nation either ideologically or psychically, but rather a full adoption of what may have been at the time America's strongest sociopolitical and cultural philosophy and tradition. As to the causes of the Civil War, historians will have to look elsewhere than proslavery, for the South's basic proslavery ideology was wholly American and nationalistic. Proslavery republicanism was the creation of Americans, not southerners alone, and it expressed both ideologically and believably what were at the time the attitudes, values, and beliefs of a vast number of Americans—North and South.

APPENDIX ONE

Proslavery Clergymen

There follows a complete listing of all those clergymen whose biographical data have been included in the biographical profile portion of the Proslavery Ideography as explained in appendix 2. The statistical evaluation of the following 275 men formed the basis for chapter 6. In order to be included in the study, each man had to be ordained in one of the recognized religious denominations in America before or during the Civil War or to serve the functions of a clergyman in one of them. Each also had to publish either in a book, a pamphlet, or a periodical article a defense of slavery which argued in favor of the indefinite perpetuation of servitude. While an attempt was made to include every clergyman who qualified under those criteria, no pretension is made that the following list is inclusive of all such men.

Nehemiah Adams
John Bailey Adger
Samuel James Pierce Anderson
James Osgood Andrew
George Dodd Armstrong
Joseph Mayo Atkinson
Thomas Atkinson
Isaac Stockton Keith Axson
John Bachman
Thomas Bacon
Rufus William Bailey
Robert Baird
Samuel John Baird
Joseph S. Baker
Samuel Davies Baldwin
William Barlow
William Hazzard Barnwell
Otto Sievers Barten
Henry Biddleman Bascom

Archibald John Battle
George Addison Baxter
Samuel Benedict
Philip Berry
Daniel Perrin Bestor, Sr.
George Washington Blagden
Albert Taylor Bledsoe
Seth Bliss
Joseph Luke Blitch
Jonas Bondi
Jonathan Boucher
Nathaniel Bowen
James Pettigru Boyce
Ebenezer Boyden
William Theophilus Brantly
William Tomlinson Brantly
William Henry Brisbane
Iveson Lewis Brookes
David Brown

William Gannaway Brownlow
Samuel J. Bryan
William Calmes Buck
John Lansing Burrows
William C. Butler
Gabriel Capers
William Capers
Theodore Clapp
Simon Clough
John Calkins Coit
Calvin Colton
Amasa Converse
Moncure Daniel Conway
William Carey Crane
Nathaniel Macon Crawford
Moses Ashley Curtis
Lucius Cuthbert, Jr.
Robert Lewis Dabney
John Leadley Dagg
Frederick Dalcho
William Tucker Dickinson Dalzell
William C. Dana
Amos Cooper Dayton
Thomas Lockwood DeVeaux
Andrew Flinn Dickson
David Seth Doggett
Simeon Doggett
Daniel Isaiah Dreher
John Dubose
Thomas Sanford Dunaway
James Alexander Duncan
Samuel Dunwoody
William Woodward Eells
James Habersham Elliott
Stephen Elliott
John England
Charles Andrews Farley
Benedict Joseph Fenwick
Jesse Babcock Ferguson
Isham Randolph Finley
Theophilus Fisk(e)
Robert Fleming

Frederick Freeman
George Washington Freeman
Richard Fuller
John Fulton
James Clement Furman
Richard Furman
Christopher Edwards Gadsden
Christopher P. Gadsden
John Lafayette Girardeau
Richard S. Gladney
Alexander Glennie
William Graham
William Henry Green
Alexander Gregg
James K. Gutheim
William T. Hamilton
Charles Hodge
John F. Hoff
Jonathan M. Hoffmeister
Moses Drury Hoge
William James Hoge
Adam Tunno Holmes
John Henry Hopkins
Samuel Blanchard How
George Howe
William Bell White Howe
Robert Boyte Crawford Howell
John Hughes
Bernard Illowy
Ferdinand Jacobs
George Jacobs
Henry Jacobs
Devereux Jarratt
Jeremiah Bell Jeter
Charles Colcock Jones, Sr.
Hugh Jones
John Jones
George Junkin
Henry Keeling
James Ryland Kendrick
Francis Patrick Kenrick
Leander Ker(r)

William Knox
Ulrick Vilhelm Koren
John Michael Krebs
Drury Lacy
James Sanford Lamar
Sylvanus Landrum
Peter Laurentius Larsen
Joseph Spry Law
William T. Leacock
P. R. Leatherman
Hanson Lee
Leroy Madison Lee
Isaac Leeser
Edwin Leigh
Max Lilienthal
Andrew Agate Lipscomb
Augustus Baldwin Longstreet
John Chase Lord
Nathan Lord
William Wilberforce Lord
James Adair Lyon
Alexander McCaine
John B. McFerrin
William Henry McIntosh
James Alphonsus McMaster
Samuel Brown McPheeters
Holland Nimmons McTyeire
David Magie
Charles Dutton Mallory
Adolphus Williamson Mangum
Basil Manly, Jr.
Basil Manly, Sr.
Auguste Marie Martin
William Meade
Thomas Francis Meagher
Patrick Hues Mell
Alexander Gardiner Mercer
Thomas Meredith
Maximillian J. Michelbacher
James Warley Miles
Charles Frederic Ernest Minnigerode
John Mitchel

Arthur Mitchell
Elisha Mitchell
James Cake Mitchell
   (born James Mitchell Cake)
Thomas Vernor Moore
Philip P. Neely
Alexander Newton
William Norwood
Jacob Aall Ottesen
Benjamin Morgan Palmer
Benjamin Morgan Palmer
   (nephew of above)
John Paris
Joel Parker
George Patterson
Thomas Ephraim Peck
Napoleon Joseph Perche
George Foster Pierce
Henry Niles Pierce
Charles Cotesworth Pinckney
William Swan Plumer
Leonidas Polk
Edward Albert Pollard
Abner A. Porter
Rufus Kilpatrick Porter
Jehu G. Postell
Nathaniel Alpheus Pratt
William Otis Prentiss
Herman Amborg Preus
Josiah Priest
Robert Quartermann
James Beverlin Ramsey
Alfred Magill Randolph
Morris Jacob Raphall
Edward Reed
William Rees
John Jefferson DeYampert Renfroe
Nathan Lewis Rice
Richard Henderson Rivers
John Robinson
Stuart Robinson
Frederick Augustus Ross

William Henry Ruffner
John Andrew Scott, Sr.
William Anderson Scott
Samuel Seabury
William H. Seat
James Shannon
Wilhelm Sihler
Alexander Sinclair
Philip Slaughter
Robert Newton Sledd
James A. Sloan
Jacob Henry Smith
Whitefoord Smith
William Andrew Smith
James Smylie
Thomas Smyth
Ichabod Smith Spencer
Urbane C. Spencer
Gardiner Spring
Edward Josiah Stearns
John Steele
Joseph Clay Stiles
Thornton Stringfellow
Moses Stuart
C. F. Sturgis
Thomas Osmond Summers
Henry H. Talbird
Samuel Kennedy Talmage
J. A. W. Thomas
Thomas Thompson
Thomas C. Thornton
James Henley Thornwell
Isaac Taylor Tichenor
Henry Holcombe Tucker

Joel W. Tucker
Henry Allen Tupper
Simon Tuska
Henry Jackson Van Dyke
Charles Stuart Vedder
William H. Vernor
Augustin Verot
Francis Vinton
Carl Ferdinand Wilhelm Walther
Ebenezer Willis Warren
Jared Bell Waterbury
William Hamilton Watkins
Benjamin Joseph Webb
Judah Wechsler
Nathaniel Sheldon Wheaton
William Wheelwright
William Spotswood White
George Whitefield
John Thomas Wightman
William May Wightman
Calvin Henderson Wiley
Albert Williams
J. D. Williams
Richard Hooker Wilmer
John Leighton Wilson
Joseph Ruggles Wilson
Joshua Lacy Wilson
Samuel Ramsey Wilson
William Winans
Edwin Theodore Winkler
Thomas Sumner Winn
Hubbard Winslow
Isaac Mayer Wise

Proslavery Ideography Codebook

The Proslavery Ideography, as used in the foregoing study, includes several types of data for each of the individuals chosen for inclusion in the composite study: (1) biographical data; (2) data regarding the nature and appearance of each individual's slavery-related writings; and (3) data on the content of each individual's most prominent proslavery writing. The "codebook" is a systematic arrangement of the data into manageable variables which can be statistically analyzed. The resultant calculations on the biographical data were used as the basis for the biographical profile in chapter 6, on content data for argument analyses in chapter 5, and on slavery writings data for various tabular presentations throughout the study.

I. Biographical variables
1. Person's name
2. Date of birth
3. Father's place of birth
4. Father's occupation/status
5. Father's slave ownership
6. Mother's place of birth
7. Mother's father's status
8. First status (ages 15–20)
9. Wife's place of birth
10. Wife's father's status
11. Wife's slave ownership
12. Childhood place
13. Childhood church affiliation
14. Childhood environment
15. Education, grammar school
16. Education, secondary school
17. Education, college (name of school)
18. Education, college (type of school)

19. Education, theological education (school)
20. Education, theological education (type of school)
21. Physical health
22. Death (year)
23. Other occupations (before ordination)
24. Ordination age
25. Ordination church affiliation
26. Type of ministry of longest duration
27. Pastoral ministry, percentage of career
28. Primary state of labor
29. Secondary state of labor (25 percent or more of career)
30. Years in South (percentage of career)
31. College teaching, percentage of career
32. College teaching, school (name)
33. College teaching, school (type)
34. College teaching, subject taught
35. College presidency, percentage of career
36. College presidency, school (name)
37. College presidency, school (type)
38. Editorial work, percentage of career
39. Editorial work, periodical (name)
40. Editorial work, periodical (type)
41. Parallel occupations
42. Publications, number
43. Publications, type
44. Theological position (within church)
45. Highest ecclesiastical position attained
46. Highest secular position attained
47. Age of greatest change in status
48. Cause of greatest change in status
49. Slave ownership, greatest number owned
50. Slave ownership, source of slaves owned
51. Professional contact with slaves
52. Civil War activity, occupation in 1861
53. Civil War activity, location in 1861
54. Civil War activity, position on secession
55. Civil War activity, 1861–1865
56. Number of connections with proslavery men
II. Variables on slavery-related writings
   1. Writings on slavery, number
   2. Nature of most prominent writing
   3. Antislavery, year

   4. Antislavery, age
   5. Colonization, year
   6. Colonization, age
   7. Colonization, place of writing
   8. Anti-abolition, year
   9. Anti-abolition, age
  10. Anti-abolition, place
  11. Slave literature, year
  12. Slave literature, age
  13. Duties of masters, type
  14. Duties of masters, year
  15. Duties of masters, age
  16. Ethnology, year
  17. Ethnology, age
  18. Crisis or war sermon, year
  19. Crisis or war sermon, occasion
  20. Crisis or war sermon, age
  21. Formal defense, year
  22. Formal defense, age
  23. Most prominent defense, type
  24. Most prominent defense, length in pages
  25. Most prominent defense, year
  26. Most prominent defense, age
  27. Most prominent defense, location
  28. Most prominent defense, occupation/status
  29. Most prominent defense, stated cause for writing
  30. Position on slavery
  31. Degree of militancy
III. Argument analysis variables
  A. The institution
    1. Nature of slavery (definition)
    2. Origin of slavery
    3. Legal foundation for slavery
    4. Future of slavery in America
  B. The Negro
    5. Negro physiology
    6. Negro past
    7. Negro character
    8. Ethnology of racial diversity
    9. Ethnology of racial unity
  C. Slave society
    10. Social classes

NOTES

Preface

1. *The Random House Dictionary of the English Language* (New York: Random House, 1967), p. 1154.

2. The most successful ideological studies of topics in American history have centered on the American Revolution and antebellum politics and social philosophy: Bailyn, *Ideological Origins of the American Revolution* (1967); Wood, *Creation of the American Republic* (1969). In the antebellum period Eugene D. Genovese's two books, *The Political Economy of Slavery* (1965) and *World the Slaveholders Made* (1969) have been important, along with Eric Foner, *Free Soil, Free Labor, Free Men* (1970).

3. The quotations and references above are from Clifford Geertz, "Ideology as a Cultural System," in a notable book on the sociology of ideology, David E. Apter, ed., *Ideology and Discontent* (1964), pp. 47–76. I have, however, altered Geertz's analysis to suit my own purposes.

4. The suggestive model for my distinction between pure and practical ideologies is derived from Franz Schurmann, *Ideology and Organization in Communist China*, 2d ed. (1968), pp. 18–23.

5. Clergymen probably wrote well over half of all defenses. The conclusion mentioned above is based upon an examination of the vocations of the authors of the 279 proslavery writings listed in the bibliography of William S. Jenkins's *Pro-slavery Thought in the Old South*, pp. 313–53, the most complete listing available. At least 130 of the publications there listed, and perhaps more, were definitely the products of clergymen.

Chapter One

1. See Freehling, *Prelude to Civil War*, p. 329 and n. 48. The writing to which Freehling referred appeared twice, once anonymously and another time under the name of Daniel Kimball Whitaker (1801–81), a native of Sharon, Mass., and

son of a Congregational clergyman. After receiving the B.A. and M.A. degrees at Harvard and entering the ministry, Whitaker's health failed causing him to move to South Carolina where he became a planter. Chiefly known as the founder and editor of several influential southern literary journals, Whitaker became one of the great writers of the Old South. Freehling apparently knew only of the anonymous version of "Reflections on Domestic Slavery, Elicited by Judge Harper's Anniversary Oration, Delivered before the South Carolina Society for the Advancement of Learning, 7th December, 1835," as it appeared in Whitaker's *Southern Literary Journal and Monthly Magazine* 2 (July 1836): 375–92. Later, in the same year, the article was issued at Charleston as a pamphlet under Whitaker's name.

2. I refer here to William Sumner Jenkins, *Pro-slavery Thought in the Old South*, the general history, and to Genovese, *World the Slaveholders Made*. For a comprehensive assessment of the historiography of proslavery, see Larry E. Tise, "Proslavery Ideology: A Social and Intellectual History of the Defense of Slavery, 1790–1840" (Ph.D. dissertation, University of North Carolina at Chapel Hill, 1974), esp. pp. 8–46.

3. Jenkins, *Pro-slavery Thought in the Old South*, pp. 75–78, passim. Historians have taken Jenkins to mean that the pamphlets by E. C. Holland (1822), Frederick Dalcho (1823), Richard Furman (1823), Whitemarsh B. Seabrook (1825), Edward Brown (1826), and Thomas Cooper (1826) were repositories of the positive good argument. Instead, his limited evidence for the theory derived from statements by C. C. Pinckney and Gov. Stephen D. Miller in 1829, the Charleston *Courier* and the Charleston *Mercury* in 1833, and Gov. George McDuffie in 1835.

4. Hofstadter, "U. B. Phillips and the Plantation Legend" (1944), pp. 109–24. Stampp, *The Peculiar Institution* (1956). On liberal historians of the 1930s see Elkins, *Slavery: A Problem in American Institutional and Intellectual Life* (1959), pp. 17–18, 20–23; Stanton, *The Leopard's Spots* (1960), pp. 54–58, 192–95; Fredrickson, *Black Image in the White Mind* (1971), pp. 43–70, passim; Jordan, *White Over Black* (1968), pp. 199–200, 304–8, 325–30, 569. Jordan saw early American proslavery statements as merely the premonition of the avalanche that would occur in the South in the 1820s.

5. Dumond, *Antislavery Origins of the Civil War* (1939), pp. 16, 44; and *Antislavery: The Crusade for Freedom in America* (1961), pp. 87–88. Franklin, *From Slavery to Freedom: A History of Negro Americans*, 3d ed. (1967), pp. 260–62. See also Fawn Brodie's praise for Dumond with a similar approach in "Who Defends the Abolitionist?" in Duberman, *The Antislavery Vanguard* (1965), pp. 52–67. Also Gilbert Hobbs Barnes, *The Anti-slavery Impulse, 1830–1844* (1933).

6. Tannenbaum, *Slave and Citizen: The Negro in the Americas* (1946), pp. 106–10. Elkins, *Slavery,* pp. 63–64. Genovese, *World the Slaveholders Made,* pp. 98–101, 131, 132–36, where he states that "the Old South alone developed a serious positive-good proslavery argument." Carl N. Degler, *Neither Black Nor*

White (1971), pp. xi, 82–88. Degler thought the positive good argument was "a full-blown racial defense of slavery" and that it was not "a natural consequence of a slave society."

7. Litwack, *North of Slavery* (1961), esp. pp. 263–64. Berwanger, *The Frontier Against Slavery* (1967). Ratner, "Northern Concern for Social Order as a Cause of Rejecting Anti-Slavery, 1831–1840" (1965), pp. 1–18, and *Powder Keg* (1968). Richards, *"Gentlemen of Property* and *Standing"* (1970). Zilversmit, *The First Emancipation* (1967), see pp. 59–60, 95, 115–16, 131–32, 134–35, 143–44, 178, 197–98. Robinson, *Slavery in the Structure of American Politics* (1971), pp. 301, 306–9, 330–31, 410–11.

8. Cash, *The Mind of the South* (1941), pp. 62–63, 85–89. Eaton, *Freedom of Thought in the Old South* (1940). Sellers, "The Travail of Slavery," in Sellers, *The Southerner as American* (1960), pp. 40–71. Woodward, *The Burden of Southern History* (1960), pp. vii–xi, 3–25. Morrow, "The Proslavery Argument Revisited" (1961), pp. 79–94. Freehling, *Prelude to Civil War,* esp. pp. ix–xi, 79–82, 327–33.

9. Genovese, *World the Slaveholders Made,* pp. 118–244, passim. But also see Wish, *George Fitzhugh, Propagandist of the Old South* (1943), and Fitzhugh, *Cannibals All! or Slaves Without Masters* (reprint, 1960). For an evaluation of the Genovese approach see Fredrickson, *Black Image in the White Mind,* esp. pp. 64–68.

10. David Donald, "The Proslavery Argument Reconsidered" (1971), pp. 3–18. Also Shalhope, "Race, Class, Slavery, and the Antebellum Southern Mind" (1971), pp. 557–74.

11. Faust, *A Sacred Circle,* esp. pp. 1–6. Faust, "A Southern Stewardship" (1979), pp. 63–80. Wyatt-Brown, "Proslavery and Antislavery Intellectuals" in Perry and Fellman, eds., *Antislavery Reconsidered* (1979), pp. 308–36. On the southern clergy, see Maddex, "Proslavery Millennialism" (1979), pp. 46–62. Oakes, *Ruling Race* (1982), esp. pp. 127–50. Several individuals have been examined in some detail as well: Faust, *J. H. Hammond and the Old South* (1982). Blesser, ed., *Hammonds of Redcliffe* (1981). Byrne, "Charles C. Jones and Intellectual Crisis of the Antebellum South" (1980), pp. 274–85. May, "John A. Quitman and His Slaves" (1980), pp. 551–70.

12. Two excellent articles on Unitarians expand the focus in one small arena to a national level, Stange, "Abolitionism as Maleficence" (1978), pp. 146–71 and Stange, "Abolitionism as Treason" (1980), pp. 152–70. But cf. Tise, "Interregional Appeal of Proslavery Thought" (1979), pp. 58–72.

13. Morgan, *American Slavery, American Freedom* (1975), esp. pp. 363–87. Shalhope, "Thomas Jefferson's Republicanism" (1976), pp. 529–56. Bruce, *Rhetoric of Conservatism* (1982). Alison Freehling, *Drift Toward Dissolution* (1982).

14. Schmidt and Wilhelm, "Early Proslavery Petitions in Virginia" (1973), pp. 133–46. Robson, "Important Question Answered: William Graham's Defense of Slavery" (1980), pp. 644–52. Shaffer, "Between Two Worlds: David Ramsay and the Politics of Slavery" (1984), pp. 175–96. Burke, "Proslavery Argument and

the First Congress" (1969), pp. 3–15. Ohline, "Slavery, Economics, and Congressional Politics, 1790" (1980), pp. 335–60. Morrison, "Nearer to the Brute Creation" (1980), pp. 228–42. Loveland, "Richard Furman's 'Questions on Slavery' " (1975), pp. 177–81. Streifford, "American Colonization Society: Application of Republican Ideology" (1979), pp. 201–20.

15. MacLeod, *Slavery, Race and the American Revolution* (1974), esp. pp. 8, 61, 92–94, 183–84. Morgan, *American Slavery, American Freedom*, pp. 380–81.

16. In addition to the Bruce and Freehling volumes mentioned above are the following: Dawson, "Puritan and Cavalier" (1978), pp. 597–614. Faust, ed., *Ideology of Slavery* (1981). Greenberg, "Revolutionary Ideology and the Proslavery Argument" (1976), pp. 365–84. Maddex, " 'The Southern Apostasy' Revisited" (1979), pp. 132–41. Mathews, *Religion in the Old South* (1977), pp. 136–84.

17. Kolchin, "In Defense of Servitude: American Proslavery and Russian Proserfdom Arguments, 1760–1860" (1980), pp. 809–27.

18. In view of the significant recent ferment in the study of proslavery, it is disappointing that the latest efforts to reinterpret southern political history reflect little awareness of the fact. See for example, Cooper, *South and the Politics of Slavery* (1978) with little discussion of even proslavery political literature. Also McCardell, *Idea of a Southern Nation* (1979), esp. pp. 55ff., still with the notion that proslavery underwent some radical change in the South in the 1820s.

19. Simpson, *Dispossessed Garden* (1975), esp. chaps. 1–2. I am most grateful for the assistance and advice provided by Eugene D. Genovese, including copies of each of the following: Fox-Genovese and Genovese, *Fruits of Merchant Capital* (1983), esp. pp. 16–17, 23, 178, 257–60, 391–411; Genovese, "Slavery Ordained of God" (1985), pp. 7–11, 17, 21–23; Genovese, "Western Civilization Through Slaveholding Eyes" (1986), pp. 1–26. Greenberg, *Masters and Statesmen* (1985), esp. pp. 85–103.

Chapter Two

1. Jordan, *White Over Black*, p. vii, and for his rather brief discussion of the meaning of proslavery, pp. 304–8, 325–30, and other random references.

2. For a fuller explanation and documentation of my belief that argumentation was essentially constant throughout proslavery history, see chap. 5.

3. The best discussion of the inherited concepts of slavery brought to America is that of Davis, *The Problem of Slavery in Western Culture*, esp. chaps. 2–4. Also see Edmund Morgan's excellent analysis for Virginia, *American Slavery, American Freedom*, esp. chaps. 15–18.

4. For instances of local debates on slavery in the eighteenth century, see Zilversmit, *First Emancipation*, pp. 59–60, 92, 95, 115–16, 130, 131–32, 142–46, 177–78, 179, 186–87, 197–98. See Morgan, *American Slavery, American Freedom*, pp. 369–87.

5. Samuel Sewall, *The Selling of Joseph: A Memorial.* John Saffin, *A Brief and Candid Answer to a Late Printed Sheet.* While no complete copy of Saffin's pamphlet remains, parts of it were published in George H. Moore, *Notes on the History of Slavery in Massachusetts* (New York: D. Appleton & Co., 1866), pp. 251–56, and in Abner C. Godell, "John Saffin and His Slave Adam," pp. 103–12. For information on the court case and events leading up to it, see ibid. and see also Towner, "The Sewall-Saffin Dialogue on Slavery," pp. 40–52.

6. Saffin, *Brief and Candid Answer to a Late Printed Sheet,* as reprinted in Moore, *Notes on the History of Slavery in Massachusetts,* pp. 251–56.

7. Ibid.

8. Ibid. Reference is here made to a speech delivered in Congress by John C. Calhoun in 1839, cited by William S. Jenkins as an excellent elaboration of the positive good theory. In the speech Calhoun claimed, "We now believe it [slavery] has been a great blessing to both of the races—the European and African, which, by a mysterious Providence, have been brought together in the Southern Section of this Union. That one has greatly improved, and the other has not deteriorated." See Jenkins, *Pro-slavery Thought in the Old South,* p. 80. Statements by other nineteenth-century defenders, not mentioned by Jenkins, more closely approximate the precise wording of Saffin.

9. Moore, *Notes on the History of Slavery in Massachusetts,* p. 256.

10. For an explanation of the basis for this conclusion, refer to the statistical study in chap. 5. Quite obviously, Saffin merely touched on arguments in some of the areas with very little elaboration. Areas untouched by him included legal and constitutional arguments and observations on the nature of slave society.

11. Towner, "Sewall-Saffin Dialogue," pp. 51–52.

12. Jones, *The Present State of Virginia,* pp. 52–53, 75–79, 93, 99, 111, 116, 130, 131, 149. Beginning with an ethnological discussion on the three races that inhabited Virginia, Jones easily slipped into a discussion of and an apology for slavery in Virginia. In the colonial period, Jones's variety of promotional work constituted one of the few instances in which colonials reflected upon the nature of their slave society—an important process in the fostering of certain types of proslavery notions.

13. Godwyn, *The Negro's & Indians [sic] Advocate,* pp. 1–8, 106–12. Davis, *Problem of Slavery in Western Culture,* pp. 204–6, 339–40, 342–48.

14. Hales, *A Sermon Preach'd before the Trustees for Establishing the Colony of Georgia in America,* pp. 11–16.

15. Bacon published a large body of useful literature all of which was frequently republished in various shapes and forms in both the eighteenth and nineteenth century. He issued four basic sets of sermons: (1) A set of *Two Sermons Preached to a Congregation of Black Slaves at the Parish of St. Peter in the Province of Maryland* (1749; reprint, 1782). These were also reprinted in 1753 and 1783. (2) A set of four sermons to both masters and slaves, *Four Sermons upon the Great*

Indispensable Duty of All Christian Masters and Mistresses to Bring up Their Negro Slaves in the Knowledge and Fear of God (1750). This was reprinted in 1813 by Bishop William Meade of Virginia in *Sermons Addressed to Masters and Servants, and Published in the year 1743, by the Rev. Thomas Bacon* (Winchester, Va.: John Heiskell, Printer [1813]), pp. 1–81. The year 1743 in Meade's edition seems to have been in error, since Bacon was not yet in Maryland at that time. The original edition was selected for distribution by the Society for Promoting Christian Knowledge. (3) *Four Sermons, Preached in the Parish Church of St. Peter, in Talbot County, in the Province of Maryland* (1753). This tract was reprinted by an Anglican clergyman in 1783 "for the purpose of distributing, gratis, through such channels as may coincide with the plan originally proposed." (4) A series of six sermons on the duties of slaves published in 1751 reprinted in 1763 and the 1830s by the Society for the Advancement of Christianity in South Carolina as *Sermons by Rev. Thomas Bacon, of Maryland, First Published in 1763, on the Duties of Servants* (ca. 1835). The society was busy reprinting proslavery tracts by Richard Furman, George W. Freeman, and others in the mid-1830s.

For the quotations above, see Bacon, *Four Sermons, Preached at the Parish Church* (1783 ed.), pp. 4–5, 182.

For further on the charity school and the opposition it stirred up, see Thomas Bacon to William Dawson, 24 July, 12 Sept. 1753; Edwin Long to William Dawson, 3 March 1758, William Dawson Papers.

16. For background on the operations of the Trustees and their position on slavery, see Clark-Kennedy, *Stephen Hales*, pp. 185–86. Also see Davis, *Problem of Slavery in Western Culture*, pp. 144–50. [Stephens and Everhard], *Brief Account of Causes that Have Retarded the Progress of the Colony of Georgia*, p. 8.

17. Whitefield, *Three Letters from the Reverend Mr. G. Whitefield*, pp. 13–16; *The Works of the Reverend George Whitefield*, 2:90, 208–9, 404–5. See also Henry, *George Whitefield*, pp. 115–16.

18. [Knox], *Three Tracts Respecting the Conversion and Instruction of the Free Indians, and Negro Slaves in the Colonies*, esp. pp. 28–30, with Knox's outline of perfected slave society, pp. 31–41. For other information on Whitefield, Habersham, Knox, and other evangelicals, see Bellot, "Evangelicals and the Defense of Slavery in Britain's Old Colonial Empire," pp. 19–40. Knox believed that the British government should insure the preservation of slavery and at the same time limit the power of slaveholders. Interestingly Knox in his positive view of slave society proposed the writing of a catechism for use by clergymen in teaching slaves "a very short summary of religion" emphasizing that God "punishes all roguery, mischief, and lying, either before death or after it" and "the doctrine of satisfaction" with one's condition in life (Knox, *Three Tracts*, pp. 39–41). In the United States catechisms were not employed for religious instruction of slaves until the 1820s when, under the influence of the ancient New England practice of catechising, benevolent reformers began compiling catechisms specifically for

slaves. While catechising was a system of indoctrination, it was the product of conservative reform.

19. For a brief account of early antislavery, see Dumond, *Antislavery,* pp. 16–25. Essential for understanding slavery debates in the era of the American Revolution are David B. Davis, *Problem of Slavery in the Age of Revolution,* esp. pp. 255–342, and MacLeod, *Slavery, Race, and the American Revolution,* esp. pp. 14–61. Both outline the limits of Revolutionary ideology to affect the future of slavery in America.

20. Boucher, *A View of the Causes and Consequences of the American Revolution,* pp. 38–42. Although students of Boucher have claimed that he heavily doctored his early American discourses before publishing them near the end of his life, his criticisms of Lee's antislavery views were probably original. For evaluations of Lee, see Jordan, *White Over Black,* pp. 309–10; and Davis, *Problem of Slavery in Western Culture,* pp. 440–41. But the immediate impulse for Boucher's outpouring was several articles printed by Lee in the *Virginia Gazette* (Jenkins, *Pro-slavery Thought in Old South,* pp. 28–29). For Boucher's political and social views, see Zimmer and Kelly, "Jonathan Boucher: Constitutional Conservative," pp. 897–922. While Zimmer and Kelly portrayed Boucher as a tentative defender of slavery and argue that "on the subject of black racial equality Boucher . . . is simply silent," the above quotations clearly reveal the racist basis of Boucher's defense. It is also unlikely that he wrote this particular section of *View of the Causes and Consequences* a decade after his *Reminiscences* (1786), as they claim. In fact, in Jonathan Boucher, ed., *Reminiscences, of an American Loyalist, 1738–1789* (1925), he presented an even more sophisticated defense of slavery (pp. 96–100), which more clearly reflected the Burkean bent of his later thought. Adopting a perspective that would become the standard line of nineteenth-century American conservatives, Boucher argued in his reminiscences that slavery or de facto slavery was the circumstance of "the lower classes of mankind everywhere." Yet, harsh circumstances did not keep them from experiencing happiness. As for Negro slavery in Virginia, the Negroes were better cared for and "not upon the whole worse off nor less happy than the labouring poor in Great Britain." And in a comparative analysis of various systems of servitude, the Virginia model ranked at the top. In Virginia, the total population "was a motley mixture [*sic*]" that could "never thoroughly coalesce" without firm controls over the inferior sorts. Hence, under the influence of Burke and other conservative political thinkers in England, Boucher headed directly toward the type of proslavery that would characterize nineteenth-century American proslavery ideologists.

21. Thompson, *The African Trade for Negro Slaves,* p. 9. Granville Sharpe's reply was *An Essay on Slavery.* Benezet's contempt was revealed in his extended private comments written in the margins and at the end of his own copy of Thompson's exceedingly rare pamphlet now owned by Rutgers University Library, New Brunswick, N.J. Thompson's fame rested on the publication of two

volumes describing his missionary work in America and in Africa as follows: [Thompson], *A Letter from New Jersey, in America* (1756); Thompson, *An Account of Two Missionary Voyages* (1758), pp. 1–6, 11–14, 18, 22–24, 26–30, 34–35, 37, 53, 57, 65, 68, for Thompson's impression of Africans.

22. Thompson, *African Trade*, pp. 7–31, passim. Anthony Benezet, in his marginal annotations, apparently did not take Thompson's arguments very seriously. At one point Benezet scribbled that proponents of the slave trade could only vindicate it "by asserting falshood." When Thompson discounted without refutation arguments that the slave trade was contrary to religion, Benezet commented, "The Author does not seem to consider the weight of *this part* of his own argument—which cannot be ballanced by all his *subsequent sophistry.*" He also objected to Thompson's inferences from Scripture, particularly his equation of scriptural and natural law. When Thompson admitted that the evils of slavery derived from the abuse of power, Benezet added, "Therefore no man should be allowed such powers." Aside from his comments on Thompson's conception of natural law, Benezet's most penetrating rebuttal followed Thompson's assertion that absolute freedom is incompatible with civil establishments: "*Absolute Freedom is not incompatible with civil establishments: because absolute freedom can only consist in restraining Evil Doers* by just & equitable *Laws,* that the *Weak & Poor,* may be *as free to do good* according to their ability; & if they are *not free to do evil,* it is not to be account'd a restraint upon *liberty;* but a restraint only upon Tyranny; so that the author has manifestly confounded the law [one?] for the other." Although taken lightly by Benezet, it was obvious that Thompson's remarks posed problems for the equalitarian. See Thompson, *African Trade*, pp. 8, 11, 15, 16, 18, 22–23, 30, 31–32. Rutgers University Library.

23. [Nisbet], *Slavery Not Forbidden by Scripture*, pp. i–iii, 1–30, passim. For the little information known about Nisbet, see Jordan, *White Over Black*, p. 306 and n. 73. Sixteen years later Nisbet published a much more favorable estimate of the Negro, *The Capacity of Negroes for Religious and Moral Improvement Considered* (1789).

24. *Personal Slavery Established*, pp. 3, 5–7. In terms of American proslavery ideology, it should be noted that the term *infidel* and its cognates are conspicuously absent from the author's catalogue of epithets.

25. Romans, *A Concise Natural History of East and West Florida* (1775), pp. 103–11. For Romans's brief tenure in New York and Philadelphia, see Rembert W. Patrick, "Introductory," in Romans, *A Concise Natural History* (facsimile reprint; Gainesville: University of Florida Press, 1962), pp. xi–xix.

26. In his opening statement Pearson said directly to Parsons, "if I rightly remember, I have sometimes heard you express a very different sentiment [about slavery]." See [Parsons and Pearson], *A Forensic Dispute on the Legality of Enslaving the Africans*, p. 4. For circumstances leading up to the debate, see Theodore Parsons, Diary, 1772–1773, Harvard Archives, Harvard University Library,

28 May, 19 June, 15 July, 12 August 1773. For biographical information on Parsons see Sibley's Manuscript Collections, 2:642, Theodore Parsons File, Harvard

Archives, Harvard University Library. For his father's slaveholding and the church dispute, see Theophilus Parsons, [Jr.], *Memoir of Theophilus Parsons, Chief Justice of the Supreme Judicial Court of Massachusetts* (1859), pp. 7, 9, 12, 14–15, 16–19. The deacon later admitted to Parsons's church that he had "urged his arguments against the slavery of the Africans with excessive vehemence and asperity, without showing a due concern for his [the elder Parsons's] character and usefulness as an elder, or for the peace and edification of the church." The elder Parsons continued to hold his slaves, two men and a woman, until forced by Massachusetts law to set them free.

27. [Parsons and Pearson], *A Forensic Dispute,* pp. 6–9.

28. Ibid., pp. 9–16, 21–31. Strangely, while Parsons attempted to refute the theory of natural rights, Pearson did not seek to uphold it. As a defender of the ideology of the Revolution, Pearson was a miserable failure (see Jordan, *White Over Black,* p. 308).

29. This is the label given the period in the book of that title by Arthur Zilversmit. A variety of proslavery statements and minidebates in Congress and state legislatures have been documented in recent years. Worthy of note are Schmidt and Wilhelm, "Early Proslavery Petitions in Virginia," pp. 133–46, primarily responses to the antislavery activities of Methodist clergy Thomas Coke and Francis Asbury; Robson, "Important Question Answered: William Graham's Defense of Slavery," pp. 644–52, the lectures on slavery of the president of Liberty Hall in the early 1790s; Shaffer, "Between Two Worlds: David Ramsay and the Politics of Slavery," pp. 175–96, especially Ramsay's attitudes on slavery in his history of the American Revolution; and Morrison, "Nearer to the Brute Creation: Scientific Defense of American Slavery before 1830," pp. 228–42, with numerous essays between the Revolution and 1808.

30. It cannot, of course, be denied that the issue of slavery was debated indirectly on numerous occasions. For the best catalogue of such debates and their political ramifications, see Robinson, *Slavery in the Structure of American Politics.* Two articles on the Congressional debates that occurred during the first session of 1790, without affecting the future course of slavery, are outlined in Burke, "Proslavery Argument and the First Congress," pp. 3–15, and Ohline, "Slavery Economics, and Congressional Politics, 1790," pp. 335–60. Ohline's article is particularly instructive and conscious of the larger context in which the first Congressional debates occurred.

31. *Pennsylvania Journal,* 31 January, 5, 21 February 1781; *New Jersey Gazette,* 8 November 1780, 10 January, 14 February 1781; *New Jersey Journal,* 29 November, 27 December 1780, 17, 24, 31 January, 7, 28 February 1781, as summarized and quoted by Zilversmit, *The First Emancipation,* pp. 129–35, 142–46. One of the New Jersey writers claimed as did Nisbet and others that Negro slaves were

"better off than the generality of the white poor." Another on the theory of natural rights as expressed in the Declaration of Independence wrote, "arguments drawn from this topic prove too much; and therefore nothing." For more extensive newspaper debate in this period see Jordan, *White Over Black*, pp. 307–8. Also Jordan, "An Antislavery Proslavery Document?" pp. 54–56.

32. *Boston Evening-Post*, 3 May 1783; *New York Argus*, 23 January 1796; *American Minerva*, 8 February 1796, as summarized and quoted by Zilversmit, *The First Emancipation*, pp. 115–16, 178, 179; also pp. 186–88, 197–98.

33. The best study of southern opinion on slavery during the period of the first emancipation is that of McColley, *Slavery and Jeffersonian Virginia*, see pp. 115–16, 119. Despite a diligent investigation of Virginia newspapers during the period, McColley found little evidence of any public discussion of slavery. Edmund Morgan, *American Slavery, American Freedom*, pp. 361–87, and Duncan MacLeod, *Slavery, Race, and the American Revolution*, passim, argue that southerners, at least Virginians, thought about slavery enough during these years to determine how it fit into their polity and system of society. Both feel that an accommodation between slavery and Virginians' idea of republicanism had been forged to the point that they saw slavery as an important foundation for the republic and equality among all freemen therein. However, so little is written about slavery during this period of time elsewhere in the South (and actually quite little in Virginia) that it is speculative to suggest any common attitude about slavery and its defense. Much more is said about the evils of slavery on all hands than on any of its virtues.

34. Boucher, *Causes and Consequences of the American Revolution*, p. 39. [Parsons and Pearson], *A Forensic Dispute on the Legality of Enslaving the Africans*, p. 27. For the clustering of Harper with Fitzhugh and other southerners in the development of the positive good argument see Genovese, *World the Slaveholders Made*, pp. 134–35. William Harper, "Memoir on Slavery," in *The Pro-Slavery Argument*, p. 9. Fitzhugh, *Cannibals All! or Slaves Without Masters*, pp. 7, 21.

35. An alternate explanation of the use of the term *evil* in transitional proslavery literature is that of Daniel Boorstin as explained in *The Lost World of Thomas Jefferson*, pp. 148–51. From Boorstin's perspective on Jeffersonian thought, one might argue that southerners perceived their slave population as a possible source of social evil, whether as an emancipated, uncontrolled horde or as a discontented labor force. "When the Jeffersonian came upon the concept of evil in theology or moral philosophy," Boorstin explains, "he naturalized it into just another bodily disease." When encountered in the social realm, Boorstin continued, "The Jeffersonian explained evil, not as intended to magnify good, but as designed indirectly to promote activity." In the wake of the Revolution rather than rationalize the evil of slavery in some equation with a countervailing good, southerners who cared sat about their parlors dreaming up schemes of action that would tear out the disease root and branch. Gradual emancipation was one

possibility southerners considered. The diffusion of slavery and thereby of the Negro throughout the American continent was another. Colonization of the Negro outside America or in some forsaken corner of the continent was another. In the end colonization outside America came to seem the only ultimate solution. When southerners finally moved from scheming to action, colonization was the direction in which their consciences, their minds, and their reading of Revolutionary ideology and American social needs caused them to proceed. As they groped toward colonization and even after they became proponents of that policy, their outlook on slavery became that of a necessary evil—an evil to be maintained until the ultimate evacuation of the Negro. For documentation of southern consideration of the foregoing schemes, see McColley, *Slavery and Jeffersonian Virginia*, pp. 129–38, 174–75; Jordan, *White Over Black*, pp. 542–69.

36. Letter, Devereux Jarratt to Edward Dromgoole, 22 March 1788, Edward Dromgoole Papers. For background on Jarratt and his confrontation with Coke, see Jarratt, *Life of Devereux Jarratt*, pp. 183–89. Matlack, *The History of American Slavery and Methodism*, p. 15. Thomas Coke, "The Journal of Thomas Coke, Bishop of the Methodist Episcopal Church, 18 September 1784 to 3 June 1785," *Arminian Magazine* [American] (1789) 1:341, 392.

37. Devereux Jarratt, *Thoughts on Some Important Subjects in Divinity in a Series of Letters to a Friend*, pp. 75–82. Jarratt's views on slavery are contained in two letters dated 15 April and 31 August 1790.

38. The chief instances in which historians have been deceived into interpreting proslavery negativism as antislavery have been in their views of conservative Federalists and anti-abolitionists as will become clear in later pages. For some examples, see Winthrop Jordan's estimate of Samuel Stanhope Smith's views on slavery in Smith, *An Essay on the Causes of the Variety of Complexion and Figure in the Human Species*, ed. by Winthrop D. Jordan (1965), pp. xvii–1. Banner, *To the Hartford Convention*, pp. 104–9. Kerber, *Federalists in Dissent*, pp. 58–66.

39. See n. 32 above.

40. Drayton, *A View of South Carolina, as Respects Her Natural and Civil Concerns*, pp. 144–49. For Drayton's comments on Smith's erroneous suppositions on race, see pp. 222ff.

41. For Furman's career and leadership of southern Baptists, see Cook, *A Biography of Richard Furman*, esp. pp. 2–10. For various decisions of the Charleston Baptist Association on slavery and Furman's circular letters on the same, see *Minutes of the Charleston Baptist Association* (annual; various imprints, 1775–present), 1779, p. 2; 1800, pp. 5–7; 1801, pp. 1, 3; 1802, p. 1; 1806, p. 2. For his private correspondence on various aspects of slavery, see Richard Furman to Oliver Hart, 16 July 1785, 4 July 1788, 25 July 1789, 23 September 1793; Oliver Hart to Richard Furman, 30 May 1793; William Mussell to Richard Furman, 28 October 1805, Richard Furman Correspondence, Furman University.

42. For an account of the antislavery proceedings of the Methodist General

Conference of 1800 and the reception of its emancipationist address in Charleston, see Mathews, *Slavery and Methodism*, pp. 20–22.

43. The defense that appeared in Savannah in 1800 was written by one "W. Jno. Beck" and was mentioned in a letter, Henry Holcombe to Richard Furman, 16 July 1800, Richard Furman Correspondence, Furman University. Exhaustive efforts to locate the defense mentioned by Holcombe have yielded nothing. Beck's identity likewise remains a mystery. The defense did not appear in either of the Savannah newspapers known to have been published during 1800, the *Columbian Museum* or the *Georgia Gazette*. For Furman's opinions during the same year, see *Minutes of the Charleston Baptist Association*, 1800, pp. 5–7.

44. Richard Furman to Dear Sir [Rev. W. Mg. (?)], 29 June [1807], Richard Furman Correspondence, Furman University. This letter presents a number of insoluble problems as to dating the circumstances that called it forth. Only two things are absolutely certain: it was written by Furman (it is signed "R. F."), and it was written on 29 June 1807 (the year determined from internal evidence referring to the Congressional enactment banning the slave trade on 2 March 1807 and other references to the fact that the ban had not yet taken effect). At the beginning of the letter Furman indicated that he was replying to the assailant's arguments made at the last association meeting and also a letter written by the same person in July 180— (the last digit is faded and could either be a 0 or a 6). Although he nowhere identifies his correspondent directly, in one portion of the letter he constructs a parabolic example to make a point in which the principal actors are "Dr. F." and "Rev. W. Mg." However, no person with these initials was listed as present at the meeting that year and there is no letter in Furman's correspondence from a man with similar initials. For another interpretation of the origins and significance of this unpublished item, see Loveland, "Richard Furman's 'Questions on Slavery,'" pp. 177–81.

Chapter Three

1. Adams, *The Neglected Period of Anti-Slavery in America*, p. 249.

2. It is this book's contention, as will become clear, that proslavery ideology was part and parcel of a general social reorientation experienced by Americans between the 1790s and the 1830s. Mention of the process at this point is merely for the purpose of emphasizing the overarching significance of that which follows.

3. [Ingersoll], *Inchiquin, The Jesuit's Letters*, pp. iii, 106–7, 110, 120.

4. Anonymous review of *Inchiquen* [sic], *The Jesuit's Letters*, in London *Quarterly Review*, pp. 494–539, esp. 513, 518–20. The writer called particular attention to the inconsistency between the words and personal behavior of Thomas Jefferson in condemning, yet practicing slavery.

5. [Dwight], *Remarks on the Review of Inchiquin's Letters,* pp. 14–15, 80–86. See also the excellent commentary on Dwight's disenchantment with America in Silverman, *Timothy Dwight,* pp. 141–49.

6. [Paulding], *The United States and England,* pp. [3], 46–48, 72–74.

7. [Paulding], *Letters from the South.* The edition used here is the reprint in *Paulding's Works,* 13 vols. (New York: Harper & Brothers, 1835), 5:29–30, 96–98. Paulding had already been attracted to the habits and values of southerners before entering the *Inchiquin* controversy as revealed in a letter to a New York Federalist congressman in 1813. Describing an all-night drinking party given in Washington by the Republican editor of the *National Intelligencer,* Joseph Gales, Paulding wrote, "Truly I say again Morris, these *Suthrons* are a set of bitter Lads. Yet do I like them, for there is a great generosity, gallantry, and frankness in their dispositions, and they have not that mean hypocrisy, and narrow selfishness which I beg leave to say is one of the precious 'Steady Habits' of New England. In truth my Dear friend the people of this Country are deplorably ignorant of each other, and filled with sad prejudices arising from various Causes. A native of New England Knows nothing of a native of the South, but what he learns from, a Travelling Tinman, a Captain of a Skipper, or from the misrepresentations of Dr. [Jedidiah] Morse" (see Aderman, *Letters of James Kirke Paulding,* pp. 33–36).

8. [Paulding], *Letters from the South,* in *Paulding's Works,* 5:172–73; but see also his larger treatment of disunifying factors, pp. 161–84. The reference to 1836 is to Paulding's *Slavery in the United States,* a massive and early reaction to radical abolitionism at the height of the crisis of the mid-1830s. The latter work won the admiration and appreciation of southern proslavery writers. See, for example, Harper, "Memoir on Slavery," in *Pro-Slavery Argument,* p. 3.

9. [Paulding], *A Sketch of Old England,* particularly his discussion of poor houses and penitentiaries (1:78–94), the low estate of the Welsh (1:iii–14, 131–37), crime and poverty (1:254–66), and English abolitionism (1:227–54). An indication of Paulding's absorption with the defense of slavery in his *Sketch of Old England* was his choice of epigrams for inclusion on the title page. All four referred not to Britons, but to Americans. Three of the four (from the *Quarterly Review, Blackwood's Magazine,* and the *Edinburgh Review*) contained references to American slaveholders and slavery. One called American republicanism "negro-driving"; a second described the cursing and beating of slaves as the popular pastime in South Carolina; the last called Americans "scourgers and murderers of slaves." Judging from these, Paulding's central purpose in the work must have been to defend American slavery and slaveholders.

10. Robert Walsh, *An Appeal from the Judgments of Great Britain.* For Paulding's charge, see Aderman, *Letters of James Kirke Paulding,* pp. 424–27. The reactions of Madison, Jefferson, and Adams, as well as that of American journals and newspapers, are quoted extensively in Lochemes, *Robert Walsh: His Story,* pp. 96–106. Madison called the book "a triumphant vindication of our Country against the

libels which have been lavished on it." Jefferson wrote, "Your work will furnish the first volume of every future American history." Adams even suggested that the book "is worthy to be translated into the Modern Languages and dispersed in all the Courts and Nations in Europe, at our National Expense." Walsh had corresponded with all three in preparation of the volume and with Madison and Jefferson, in particular, on the subject of slavery.

11. Walsh, *Appeal from the Judgments*, pp. ii, v, 306–85, passim, 387–88.

12. Ibid., pp. 388–95, 398, 401, 402–4.

13. Ibid., pp. 404–24, passim. Walsh offered extensive quotations from the British reviews both in the text and in appended notes. Notes W through Z, pp. 483–512, relate to his defense of slavery.

14. It should be noted that the *Inchiquin* controversy did not by any means end with Walsh's *Appeal*. His criticism of British reviewers was answered by Francis Jeffrey in an extended review article in the May 1820 *Edinburgh Review*, pp. 395–431. The same reviews that irritated Walsh were refuted by "An American," "To the Edinburgh Reviewers," *National Intelligencer*, 18, 20, 23, 25 November 1819. The letters were later printed separately as *Letter to the Edinburgh Reviewers: by "An American." First Published in the National Intelligencer of November 16 [sic], 1819* (n.p.:1819). "An American" was then answered by Wright, *A Refutation of the Sophisms* (1820).

15. Smith, *Lectures, Corrected and Improved*, 2:159–79, passim.

16. Saffin, *Brief and Candid Answer to a Late Printed Sheet*, in Moore, *Notes on the History of Slavery in Massachusetts*, pp. 252–53. Saffin wrote that if the slaves of Massachusetts were freed "then the Negroes must be all sent out of the Country, or else the remedy would be worse than the Disease; and it is to be feared that those Negroes that are free, if there be not some strict course taken with them by Authority, they will be a plague to this Country" (Jordan, *White Over Black*, pp. 544–51). See also Boucher, *Causes and Consequences of the American Revolution*, pp. 39–40. Zilversmit, *First Emancipation*, pp. 134–35. For the colonization proposals of one West Indian, see Francklyn, *Answer to the Rev. Mr. Clarkson's Essay on the Slavery and Commerce of the Human Species*, pp. 207–10. Even Benjamin Morgan Palmer, who declared slavery a "divine trust" from God in 1860, argued that, if slaves were freed, they would have to be removed. "Their residence here," Palmer said, "in the presence of the vigorous Saxon race, would be but the signal for their rapid extermination before they had time to waste away through listlessness, filth and vice." Colonization would be the only mode of "disposal"; but that too would "be but the most refined cruelty." See Palmer and Leacock, *Rights of the South Defended in the Pulpits*, p. 5. For the other extreme that colonization would be the means of civilizing and Christianizing Africa at the same time slavery continued in America, one should consult the extensive late antebellum writings of Calvin H. Wiley and James A. Lyon. Two good articles to be consulted on the American colonization movement are Friedman, "Purifying the White Man's

Country," pp. 1–24, and Streifford, "The American Colonization Society: An Application of Republican Ideology to Early Antebellum Reform," pp. 201–20. Streifford's article is a nicely developed analysis of the ideological ingredients I have identified as laying the groundwork for proslavery ideology.

17. Walsh, *Appeal from the Judgments of Great Britain*, pp. 392, 398. The latter quotation is from [Holland], *Refutation of the Calumnies Circulated Against the Southern & Western States*, pp. 35–36. In 1812 Samuel Stanhope Smith had argued that Negroes should be colonized on the western frontier where they could not associate with and perhaps incite remaining slaves to rebellion (see Smith, *Lectures on the Subjects of Moral and Political Philosophy*, pp. 175–79).

18. Staudenraus, *The African Colonization Movement*, pp. 19–21, 28–32, 51–52.

19. Ibid., pp. 77, 85, 97–103, 104–5, 117, 135, 169–74. For the general acceptance of colonization among Congregational clergymen, students, and faculties see Senior, "New England Congregationalists and the Anti-Slavery Movement," pp. 22–41. For treatments of the Benevolent Empire, see Foster, *Errand of Mercy*, and Griffin, *Their Brothers' Keepers*.

20. Meade's address was extracted in *African Repository, and Colonial Journal* 1 (July 1825), 146–50. Hamilton, *A Plea for the African*, pp. 17, 19, 23–25. [Worcester], *Essays on Slavery* (1826). Debates in the last three newspapers are noted in *Controversy Between Caius Gracchus and Opimius, in Reference to the American Society for Colonizing the Free People of Colour of the United States* (1827). The letters of Caius Gracchus were but the first barrage of the systematic disengagement of proslavery colonizationists from the whole colonization program. Caius Gracchus argued that the removal of the entire Negro population of the United States was both visionary and impossible, that the desire of colonizationists to abolish slavery would cause unrest among slaves and foster a campaign of fanatical philanthropy, and that since the scheme was utterly impossible it could lead to nothing except evil consequences to American society. He compared colonization to the medieval Crusades: "The God of Nature has fixed his seal upon destiny; and all the feeble efforts of man, in opposition to its laws, will only serve to swell the list of human miseries. Prompted by the goadings of a blind fanaticism, which seems already to have placed itself in close alliance with you, this, which is a sheer political question, may be tortured into a theme for pulpit declamation. Once let it obtain a place there, and the Christian religion . . . will be made the medium of one of the severest scourges of the American people" (pp. 5–6, 20–21). Hence, like Paulding and Seabrook, among others, Caius Gracchus revealed an expectancy that a national campaign against slavery was getting under way. Critiques of colonization would later reach the fullest and most incisive form in the writings of Thomas R. Dew and William Lloyd Garrison.

21. Seabrook, *A Concise View of the Critical Situation, and Future Prospects of the Slave-holding States*, pp. 3–30, passim. Seabrook acknowledged (p. 15 and n) that he was impelled to print by the aforementioned newspaper writings. Seabrook

expressed similar views two years later in *An Address, Delivered at the First Anniversary Meeting of the United Agricultural Society of South Carolina*, pp. 37–38.

22. For further information on the rejection of colonization from both angles, see the discussion of Garrison and Dew below.

23. See particularly Glover Moore's detailed study, *The Missouri Controversy.* MacLeod, *Slavery, Race, and the American Revolution*, pp. 46–47, 105–8, obviously attaches considerably greater importance to the debates than indicated here.

24. For an extensive survey of the struggle over slavery in the Old Northwest from the eighteenth century forward, see Berwanger, *The Frontier Against Slavery*, pp. 7–18, passim. For similar debates in Tennessee and Kentucky, see William Warren Sweet, ed., *Religion on the American Frontier: The Presbyterians* (Chicago: University of Chicago Press, 1936), pp. 129, 147, 163, 169, 170, 173–79, 182–83, 189, 222, 244, 382. Also, see Sweet, ed., *Religion on the American Frontier: The Baptists, 1783–1830* (Chicago: University of Chicago Press, 1931), pp. 77–88.

25. Steele, *The Substance of an Address*, pp. 3–43, passim. Steele wrote and spoke in answer to an attack on slavery in the *Christian Intelligencer*, the official paper of his church.

26. For the most rancorous attack by a southern congressman on free soilers in 1819 see the speech of William Smith in the Senate in January 1820, *Annals of Congress of the United States*, 16th Cong., 1st sess., 1820, 1:259–75, which William W. Freehling adjudged "the only *unqualified* proslavery argument developed by a South Carolinian in the 1820s" (see Freehling, *Prelude to Civil War*, p. 82n). One historian who successfully dissociates the free soilers of 1819 from antislavery is Dangerfield, *Awakening of American Nationalism*, pp. 97–140. For racism, colonization, and proslavery of the South in Republican ideology, see Foner, *Free Soil, Free Labor, Free Men*, pp. 261–317.

27. Walsh, *Free Remarks on the Spirit of the Federal Constitution*, pp. 4, 5, 9. For his correspondence with Madison and Jefferson, see Lochemes, *Robert Walsh*, pp. 109–17.

28. For actual details of the acts of British commanders and the Gabriel plotters, see Franklin, *From Slavery to Freedom*, pp. 131–38, 210–11. For the connection with Quakers, Methodists, and Frenchmen, see Jordan, *White Over Black*, pp. 393–95 and n. 28. For the inordinate fears of Federalists stemming from the 1790s and continuing throughout the neglected period, see Kerber, *Federalists in Dissent*, pp. 40–52. For the reaction in Charleston, S.C., see Mathews, *Slavery and Methodism*, pp. 21–22.

29. Charleston *Southern Intelligencer* (weekly), 16 November 1822, p. 183; 23 November 1822, p. 188. The *Southern Intelligencer* and other Charleston newspapers in 1822, instead of squelching all discussion of slavery as argued by Jenkins and others, particularly William Freehling, actually were quite open in their printing of articles about all facets of slavery, including many critical of slaveholding. In the first five months of 1822, the paper published weekly arti-

cles on colonization, slavery reform, and emancipation. After a brief interruption following the intended insurrection, the paper took up a course vigorously pro-colonizationist. See especially 12 January 1822, p. 1; 26 January 1822, p. 4; 2 February 1822, p. 3; 25 May 1822, p. 84; 22 June 1822, pp. 92–93; 17 August 1822, p. 131; 24 August 1822, p. 135.

30. [Holland], *A Refutation of the Calumnies Circulated Against the Southern & Western States*, pp. v–vi, 7–15, 60–61, 77–78, 82–87. The sections of the pamphlet which Holland took directly from Walsh were a history of the slave trade and American attempts to close it off (pp. 16–46) and a history of American insurrections (pp. 62–79).

31. Furman, *Exposition of the Views of the Baptists*, pp. 3–19, passim. Furman capped his *Exposition* with a report of a committee of the Massachusetts House of Representatives recommending the adoption of laws forbidding the immigration of free Negroes into the state (pp. 21–24). Believing that the New England state was as concerned with a large Negro population as South Carolina, Furman wrote, "From the following declaration it appears that our fellow citizens of Massachusetts do not differ from the people of South Carolina, as to the pernicious tendency of a free colored population—nor do they differ as to the right and propriety of adopting measures to arrest and remove the evil."

32. [Dalcho], *Practical Considerations Founded on the Scriptures*, pp. 3–10, 20–23, 26, 27, 31–38.

33. Cooper, *Lectures on the Elements of Political Economy*, pp. 106–7. Cooper, *Two Essays*, pp. 44–49. On Cooper's early estimate of Walsh, see Lochemes, *Robert Walsh*, p. 114.

34. Edward Brown, *Notes on the Origin and Necessity of Slavery*, pp. 5–38, passim.

35. In any case it should be noted that one cannot compare and contrast numbers of items without using comparative and superlative terminology. Pinckney, *An Address Delivered in Charleston, Before the Agricultural Society of South Carolina*, pp. 3–4. This document is often attributed to the elder Charles Cotesworth Pinckney, who in the 1820s became a disgruntled colonizationist. However, the distinguished statesman died in 1825. The author of the present address was the father of the Episcopal clergyman of the same name and nephew of the former Federalist presidential contender. See Webber, "The Thomas Pinckney Family of South Carolina," pp. 15–35. Jenkins, *Pro-slavery Thought in the Old South*, p. 76, was of course responsible first for calling Pinckney's statement "a positive good argument."

36. [Kingsley], *A Treatise on the Patriarchal, or Co-operative System of Society*, pp. ii–iii, 5–10. Kingsley published his *Treatise* in four editions between 1828 and 1834. For Kingsley's peculiar career and views on race see May, "Zephaniah Kingsley, Nonconformist, 1765–1843," pp. 145–59. In an appendix to the *Treatise*, Kingsley spelled out in some detail the integrated society of blacks and whites he envisioned and the manner in which the patriarchal system of slavery

should be continued. Slavery would always be present, he believed, whether the poor were legally free or not. He also thought that the Christian religion did nothing but corrupt Negroes. They should be permitted to practice their African religion and customs as freely as they wished, he believed (pp. 11–16).

37. Raymond, *Prize Essay, on the Comparative Economy of Free and Slave Labour, in Agriculture*, pp. 3, 16.

38. Jones, *An Address on the Progress of Manufactures and Internal Improvement, in the United States*, pp. 1–18, passim. The extent to which political economy was becoming an absorbing and respected discipline was indicated by Jones when he admitted that he had little knowledge of political economy and did not know how his notions would fare in the theories of political economists. He continued, "I have very slender claims to knowledge upon this subject; in fact, I can scarcely say, that I have formed a theory for myself; although I, of necessity, entertain opinions which appear to me to have their foundation in practical truth, which is my only guide" (p. 18).

39. Garrison, *Thoughts on African Colonization*, p. iv. Dew, *Review of the Debate in the Virginia Legislature of 1831 and 1832*. Cf. Garrison's views on the effect of colonization in increasing the value of slaves (Garrison, *Thoughts on African Colonization*, pp. 74–78), on colonization being nourished by fear (pp. 95–110), on the economic unfeasibility of colonization (pp. 151–58) with Dew's treatment of the same subjects in the reprint of his volume, "Professor Dew on Slavery," *Pro-Slavery Argument*, pp. 357–70, 420–23, 462–72.

40. Jenkins, *Pro-slavery Thought in the Old South*, pp. 87–89, believed Dew's essay brought Virginia to the extreme proslavery position already adopted in the lower South: "From now on the South as a whole became united in the active defense of its institution." Eugene Genovese, in *World the Slaveholders Made*, pp. 129–30, thought Dew a necessary step toward the interpretation of slavery as a question of class relations. But Genovese also considered Thomas Cooper's clearly neutral or even negative statement of only a few pages of equal importance. George Fredrickson termed Dew's *Review* definitely "transitional," setting forth "the most thorough and comprehensive justification of the institution that the South had yet produced" (see Fredrickson, *Black Image in the White Mind*, pp. 44–46). For a more balanced if overstated account of Dew's significance, see Kenneth Stampp, "An Analysis of T. R. Dew's *Review of the Debates in the Virginia Legislature*," pp. 380–87. Others who continue to laud the *Review* as the fundamental turning point in proslavery history include the following: Faust, *Ideology of Proslavery*, pp. 8–9; McCardell, *Idea of a Southern Nation*, pp. 53–60; Bruce, *Rhetoric of Conservatism*, pp. 179–88. Despite the importance of these various studies in the interpretation and teaching of proslavery history, none recognized Dew's specialized work as primarily an effort to demolish colonization. One exception is Alison G. Freehling. In *Drift toward Dissolution*, pp. 202–8, she writes, "Despite a more positive tone, Dew did not present a consistent proslavery ide-

ology. More momentous, even as he decried *legislative* emancipation, Dew linked Virginia's destiny to the free-soil North, not to the slaveholding South" (p. 203).

41. On the protectionist–free trade debate, see William Appleman Williams, *The Contours of American History,* pp. 207–15. Later southern political economists, according to Eugene Genovese, thought in terms of southern autarky (*World the Slaveholders Made,* pp. 165–66).

42. Dew, "Professor Dew on Slavery," in *Pro-Slavery Argument,* pp. 294–355, passim, with quotations from pp. 292, 325. Eugene Genovese, "Western Civilization Through Slaveholding Eyes" (1986), takes a very different view of the ideas and influence of Dew. However, I can only conclude that Genovese seems to read Dew's later ideas into this relatively early stage of his career and of the defense of slavery in the South.

43. Ibid., pp. 365–80, 392–417.

44. Ibid., pp. 433, 437, 451, 489.

45. Harper, "Memoir on Slavery," in *Pro-Slavery Argument,* p. 88. But Harper (pp. 2–3) was also one of those who later believed, as indicated below, that Dew had written in opposition to abolitionism.

Chapter Four

1. Degler, *Neither Black Nor White,* p. xi. Genovese, *World the Slaveholders Made,* p. 131. Peter Kolchin's "In Defense of Servitude: American Proslavery and Russian Proserfdom Arguments, 1760–1860," pp. 809–27, is just the type of comparative study needed. David Brion Davis, *Slavery and Human Progress,* pp. 193ff. has helped to put West Indian proslavery in some historical context.

2. [Long], *The History of Jamaica,* as cited and discussed in Davis, *Problem of Slavery in Western Culture,* pp. 459–64; and Jordan, *White Over Black,* pp. 491–94.

3. As will become clear in this and following chapters, the form of argumentation identified by Eugene Genovese as distinctively southern was in actuality part and parcel of American social thought. Any proslavery writer who was conversant with the most informed social and political literature of the period could have easily and quite logically parroted the same line of argumentation.

4. For the bare outlines of the British antislavery movement, see Coupland, *The British Anti-Slavery Movement,* esp. pp. 36–56, 86–91, 112–50. For a slightly more detailed account, see Frank J. Klingberg, *The Anti-Slavery Movement in England.*

5. Harris, *Scriptural Researches on the Licitness of the Slave-Trade,* pp. v–vii, 9–11, 13, 20, 36, 50, 51n, 60, 75–77. Also, like American proslavery clergymen, Harris intended to write a separate section on the duties of masters to be united with his pamphlet (p. [78]). For the interesting background on Harris (Hormaza), see Davis, *Problem of Slavery in Age of Revolution,* pp. 442–51.

6. Holder, *A Short Essay on the Subject of Negro Slavery,* pp. iii–v, 7–10, 16, 24, 28, 36, 40–44.

7. Francklyn, *Answer to the Rev. Mr. Clarkson's Essay on the Slavery and Commerce of the Human Species,* pp. 1–10, 11–14, 18, 31, 44, 46–52, 56–60, 87, 95, 104, 137, 147, 153, 159–84, 189–204, 211–24, 225, 229, 242–43.

8. [Knox], *A Letter from W. K. Esq. to W. Wilberforce, Esq.,* pp. 15–16, as cited and discussed in Bellot, "Evangelicals and Defense of Slavery," pp. 34–35.

9. Foot, *A Defence of the Planters in the West Indies,* pp. 1–26, 46–66, 76, 101.

10. Ibid., p. iii.

11. Tobin, *A Farwel Address to the Rev. Mr. James Ramsay,* pp. 1–6, 10–14, 20, with a list of Tobin's other replies to Ramsay on the back cover. Tobin included as appendices (pp. 21–36) the letter of Burton published in Knox, *Three Tracts,* pp. 28–30, and a translation of the French declaration of 9 August 1777, providing for the deportation of any Negro entering France.

12. [McCarty], *An Appeal to the Candour and Justice of England,* pp. 8, 14–18, 21, 33, 46, 111, 118.

13. *A Country Gentleman's Reasons for Voting Against Mr. Wilberforce's Motion,* pp. 1–15. See also Coupland, *British Anti-Slavery Movement,* pp. 95–99.

14. Edwards, *The History, Civil and Commercial, of the British Colonies in the West Indies.* Jordan, *White Over Black,* pp. 237, 590.

15. Brougham, *An Inquiry into the Colonial Policy of the European Powers,* 2:5–7, 67–68, 74, 76, 119–20, 135, 144, 147, 401–7, 412–19, 432, 478–97.

16. [Francis Jeffrey], Review of *An Appeal from the Judgments of Great Britain Respecting the United States of America,* by Robert Walsh, *Edinburgh Review* 66 (May 1820):420–21.

17. Among the numerous British and West Indian proslavery writings not considered in the text were the following from this period: Sir Henry William Martin, *A Counter Appeal, in Answer to "an Appeal" from William Wilberforce, Designed to Prove that the Emancipation of the Negroes in the West Indies by a Legislative Enactment, Without the Consent of the Planters Would Be a Flagrant Breach of National Honour, Hostile to the Principles of Religion, Justice, and Humanity, and Highly Injurious to the Planter and to the Slave* (London: C. & J. Rivington, 1823). Nathaniel Sotham, *Plain Facts; or, Circumstances as They Really Are; Being an Impartial and Unprejudiced Account of the State of the Black Population in the Isle of Jamaica* (London: J. M. Richardson, 1824). Alexander MacDonnell, *Considerations on Negro Slavery . . .* (London: Longman, Hurst, Rees, Orme, Brown and Green, 1825). Henry Peter Brougham, *Opinions of Henry Brougham, Esq., on Negro Slavery: With Remarks* (London: Whitmore and Fenn, 1826), a printing of extracts from Brougham's *Inquiry into Colonial Policy* resurrected by his enemies to haunt him. Joseph Clayton Jennyns, *An Appeal to the Earl Bathurst, When Colonial Minister, on the Unconstitutional Continuance of Foreign Laws in the Colonies Ceded to Great Britain . . .* (London: Sams, 1828). Alexander MacDonnell, *An Address to the Members*

of Both Houses of Parliament on the West India Question, 2nd ed. (London: J. Ridgway, 1830). Henry Duncan, *A Presbyter's Letters on the West India Question; Addressed to the Right and Honourable Sir George Murray* . . . (London: T. and G. Underwood, 1830). Sir John Gladstone, *Facts Relating to Slavery in the West Indies and America, Contained in a Letter Addressed to the Right Hon. Sir Robert Peel, Bart.,* 2nd ed. (London: Baldwin and Cradock, 1830). *A Reply to Mr. Jeremie's Pamphlet. By an Inhabitant of St. Lucia* . . . (London: E. Wilson, 1832). *The Condition of the West India Slave Contrasted with That of the Slave in Our English Factories* (London: W. Kidd, [1833]).

18. Bridges, *A Voice from Jamaica, in Reply to William Wilberforce,* pp. 5–6, 8–13, 30, 36–41, 48.

19. Hurd, *A Letter to the Right Honourable the Earl of Liverpool,* pp. 1–18, passim. This is not to suggest that either Fitzhugh or Hughes read proslavery literature from the West Indies, but rather that certain views and concepts were endemic to the defense of slavery.

20. MacQueen, *The West India Colonies,* pp. vi–x, 245.

21. Ibid., pp. 335–36. For a somewhat earlier view of British abolition as subversion, see Bridges, *A Voice from Jamaica,* pp. 36–41, 48. At one point Bridges wrote rhetorically to William Wilberforce, "you are, in fact, the tame abettor of a party spirit, the tool of designing men, who labour under the popular mask of philanthropy, to bring down destruction and ruin on our West Indian Colonies, and complete the dreadful tragedy which was unhappily acted in a neighboring island." MacQueen, *West India Colonies,* pp. 324–30, employed another tactic frequently used by Americans who looked down their noses at West Indian slaveholding society. Somewhere he found that American writers admitted that slavery in the United States was much harsher than that in the West Indies. And he found that free Negroes were barely able to subsist in Connecticut, most of them being sent eventually to the South for reenslavement.

22. Barclay, *A Practical View of the Present State of Slavery in the West Indies,* pp. vi–vii, xvi–xvii, xix, 1, 62, 245, 250, 335–55. For anyone who believes that the Old South developed the patriarchal image of slavery, the following passage from Barclay's *Practical View* should prove enlightening: If one follows the West Indian master in his daily routine, "you will regard him rather as the father of a family; you will see him attending to the comforts and the wants of his people, with a degree of kindness and solicitude, which it would be vain and unreasonable in English labourers to expect from masters, who have no further interest in their welfare than the services of the passing day" (pp. 205–6).

23. [Long], *Negro Emancipation No Philanthropy,* pp. 1–6, 25–29, 38.

24. Bayley, *Four Years' Residence in the West Indies,* pp. vii, 364–75, 379, 401ff., 409ff., 440–43.

25. *The Condition of the West India Slave Contrasted with That of the Slave in Our English Factories,* pp. 1–37, passim.

26. Wilkinson, *Thoughts on Negro Slavery,* pp. 1–16, passim.

27. Among the several proslavery pieces that emanated from England during the Civil War was a very notable one that was picked up by the violently racist New York publisher John Van Evrie: Dr. James Hunt, *The Negro's Place in Nature; a Paper Read Before the London Anthropological Society* (New York: Van Evrie, Horton & Co., 1864).

28. For example, Thomas R. Dew in his *Review of the Debate in the Virginia Legislature of 1831 and 1832,* in addition to his primary reliance upon the philosophers Blackstone, Adam Smith, Malthus, Hume, and Burke, frequently drew upon the proslavery writings of Henry Brougham, Gilbert Francklyn, Bryan Edwards, and the Frenchman Pierre Malouet. Harper, in his *Memoir on Slavery,* used fewer sources but similarly relied on British sources, including an anonymous writing entitled *England and America* and various travel accounts of Britons to Africa, the West Indies, and South America. Both men, of course, found Robert Walsh's *Appeal* their most useful American source. Until the rise of abolition, the latter work was probably the most widely cited authority in American proslavery literature.

29. It has not been possible in the limited space that can be devoted here to comparative proslavery to analyze defenses of slavery proceeding from other slave societies. However, a brief survey of both primary and secondary sources from other countries demonstrates the accuracy of these conclusions. The British proslavery writers always conceived of their French counterparts as even more insistent defenders of slavery. An examination of the following French proslavery writers seems to bear them out: J. Bellon de Saint Quentin, *Dissertation sur la traite et le commerce des Negres* ([Paris]: n.p., 1764). Pierre Victor Malouet, *Memoire sur l'esclavage des Negres . . .* ([Toulon?]: A. Neufchatel, 1788). [Jacques François Begouen], *Precis sur l'importance des colonies, et sur la servitude des noirs . . .* ([Versailles]: Imprimerie de Ph. D. Pierres, 1790). F. R. de Tussac, *Cri des colons contre un ouvrage de M. l'eveque et senateur Gregorie, avant pour titre de la litterature des Negres . . .* (Paris: Delaunay, libraire, 1810). [Huc], *L'emancipation de la race africaine, consideree sous le rapport religieux* (Paris: Deuvin et Fontaine, 1840). Charles Louis Levavasseur, *Esclavage de la race noir aux colonies francaises* (Paris: Imprimerie de C. Bajat, 1840). Adolphe Jollivet, *L'Emancipation Anglaise Jigee par ses resultats . . .* (Paris: Imprimerie de Moquet et Hauquelin, 1842). Petit de Baroncourt, *Sur l'emancipation des noirs . . .* (Paris: Amyot, 1845). French proslavery writings even followed the pattern of timing already noted in the cases of Britain and America, i.e., strictly on the heels of antislavery attacks.

The experience of the Spanish in the West Indies may have been similar. A comparison of slave societies in St. Domingo and Cuba by Gwendolyn Midlo Hall, *Slave Control in Slave Plantation Societies: A Comparison of St. Domingue and Cuba* (1971), pp. 24–26, 136–39, suggests at least some parallels in racial ideology with British and American proslavery. Arthur F. Corwin in his *Spain and the Abolition of Slavery in Cuba, 1817–1886* (1967), pp. 24, 36–38, 70–73, 100–1,

163–65, 170–71, 174, 178, 194–95, 207–9, 220–21, 257, 305, found many similar arguments in Cuba and Spain. Corwin also (pp. 164–65) pointed out one
Spanish defense written by the influential historian and nobleman Jose Ferrer de
Condo. During the Civil War Ferrer served as the editor of *La Cronica*, a pro-
Spanish and anti-Cuban exile paper in New York City. Deeply affected by the
American war—a war he conceived of as the result of irresponsible and subversive abolitionism—Ferrer published in 1864, in both Spanish and English, an
anti-abolitionist defense with a scope and intensity rarely approached in American proslavery literature (Spanish title: *Los negros in sus diversos estados y condiciones; tales como son como se supone que son y como deben ser;* English title: *Enough of
War! The Question of Slavery Conclusively and Satisfactorily Solved, as Regards Humanity at Large and the Permanent Interests of Present Owners* [Eng. and Sp. eds.: New
York: S. Hallet, Printer, 1864]). Ferrer intended to treat "the great and momentous question which has divided the people of a great nation into two different sections and arrayed them in arms one against the other, viz: *the civil status of
the Negro in America.*" His purpose was not to give just another defense of slavery,
but rather "to expose a very great evil and to point out the most certain remedy."
The evil, in his view, was abolitionism, which threatened all organized labor in
the Western Hemisphere. His remedy consisted of a combination of peace treaties, of altering laws to establish a system of warranteeism, and of African colonization. Before he got to proposing his remedy, which he believed would "impose silence on the philanthropic abolitionists since it deprives them of all reason
to continue their clamor," he traced the entire history of slavery in the Western
world and adduced every imaginable argument in favor of the institution, including a history of slavery and the Civil War in the United States (Eng. ed.: pp.
5–13, 245–98).

Chapter Five

1. Jenkins, *Pro-slavery Thought in the Old South*, see pp. 65, 73, 76–81, 87–89.
The efforts of historians to figure out what made the Old South's positive good
argument distinctive continue apace. According to Dickson Bruce, "Racial Fear
and the Proslavery Argument," pp. 461–78, the positive good formulations of
the Old South's proslavery literature became a conventional rhetorical formula
intended to overcome internal questioning and racial fear within southern
culture. According to Kenneth Greenberg, "Revolutionary Ideology and the
Proslavery Argument," pp. 365–84, on the other hand, the positive good element resulted from the fact that southerners, when they concluded that they
could not or would not emancipate their slaves, chose to emancipate them in
theory if not in fact by portraying slavery as a perfected institution and way of
life for the enslaved. Jack Maddex, " 'Southern Apostasy' Revisited," pp. 132–41,

saw that positive good notions derived from the fact that southerners did indeed adopt a class ideology and departed fully from the libertarian traditions of the Revolution thereby transmuting the meaning of such terms as good and beneficial. These interpretations, of course, overlook the fact that proslavery was a national and multinational phenomenon. Only Peter Kolchin in his article "In Defense of Servitude: American Proslavery and Russian Proserfdom Arguments," pp. 809–27, has suggested in writing there could be similar phenomena wherever proslavery literature and thought appear.

2. Jenkins, *Pro-Slavery Thought*, p. 76. Nisbet, *Slavery Not Forbidden by Scripture*, pp. 27, 29; McCarty, *Appeal to the Candour and Justice*, p. 21; Walsh, *Appeal from the Judgments of Great Britain*, p. 409.

3. Freehling, *Prelude to Civil War*, pp. 81–82.

4. Jenkins, *Pro-slavery Thought in the Old South*, pp. 76–77. Francklyn, *Answer to the Rev. Mr. Clarkson's Essay*, pp. 11, 14. Ingersoll, *Inchiquin, the Jesuit's Letters*, pp. 107, 120.

5. Jenkins, *Pro-slavery Thought in the Old South*, pp. 86–87; Foot, *Defense of the Planters in the West Indies*, p. 27; Ingersoll, *Inchiquin, the Jesuit's Letters*, p. 106; Walsh, *Appeal from the Judgments of Great Britain*, p. 404.

6. Jenkins, *Pro-slavery Thought in the Old South*, p. 80; Parsons and Pearson, *Forensic Dispute*, p. 31; *Personal Slavery Established*, p. 3; Holder, *Short Essay on the Subject of Negro Slavery*, p. 16.

7. A complete listing of defenses included in the argument analysis appears in the bibliography of Tise, "Proslavery Ideology," under the heading of Proslavery Literature. Each defense included is there marked with an asterisk (*).

8. For a complete listing of headings in the argument analysis refer to appendix 2, "Proslavery Ideography Codebook."

9. As is the case in many quantitative studies, it is neither possible nor desirable to present every table. Hence, many assertions in this chapter are supported by statistical evidence not presented.

10. These conclusions and the statistics in tables 5.3 and 5.4 argue most heavily, of course, against any thesis that only the Old South produced a world view critical of capitalism and free society. On the contrary, given a basic familiarity with political economy, the statistics above would suggest that such views were inherent in any proslavery formulations whether from writers in a slave society or not.

11. For a quite similar conclusion in the case of proserfdom literature in Russia, see Kolchin, "In Defense of Servitude," pp. 809–16.

Chapter Six

1. Donald, "The Proslavery Argument Reconsidered," pp. 3–18, is the lone historian who has suggested the need to study "southern" proslavery thinkers.

2. See Faust's excellent and suggestive article, "A Southern Stewardship: The Intellectual and the Proslavery Argument," pp. 63–80. Her much larger work, *A Sacred Circle*, see pp. 1–6, focuses particularly on Edmund Ruffin, James Henry Hammond, William Gilmore Simms, George Frederick Holmes, and Nathaniel Beverly Tucker. Unfortunately, by the selection of a group of would-be intellectual leaders to ask questions about proslavery, her findings on their role in southern society predictably mirrored those emotional qualities suggested by Donald. Whether or not the intellectual defended slavery, there simply was no place in southern society for cultural professionals.

3. For a complete list of individuals included in the analysis, see appendix 1, "Proslavery Clergymen." For a complete outline of the codebook format employed, see appendix 2, "Proslavery Ideography Codebook." It has been possible in the text of this study to present in capsule form only some of the most relevant findings from a much larger analysis. Except where it seems necessary, an attempt has been made to refrain from presenting bulky and space-consuming tables.

4. In the absence of any study that purports to analyze and interpret the clergy, or for that matter any other profession, as a significant social elite, the reader will have to accept the foregoing generalizations as hypotheses that will have to be documented in other contexts. Most are ideas expounded by Donald G. Mathews in a tentative study entitled "The Southern Clergy as a Strategic Elite, 1780–1870." Those tentative ideas were subsequently included in his *Religion in the Old South* (1977), see esp. pp. 83–97. Donald Scott, *From Office to Profession*, esp. pp. 52–75 and throughout his book identifies the changing role of clergymen in American society. Although his focus was New England, and some of the traditions there never appeared elsewhere in America, his basic ideas on the role of clergy as a profession fit American society generally. Two other studies that portray clergymen in southern society are Anne C. Loveland, *Southern Evangelicals and the Social Order, 1800–1860*, esp. pp. 30–64, with a view of clergymen as being somewhat dependent beings, and Holifield, *Gentlemen Theologians*, pp. 3–4, 13, 149, 154, with the view that the southern clergy made itself both a social and a moral elite of considerable force and power.

5. Among the southern-born graduates of New England Congregational schools were the following: Christopher E. Gadsden, Augustus B. Longstreet, Stephen Elliott, Richard Fuller, Charles Colcock Jones, Patrick Hues Mell, Benjamin Morgan Palmer, Andrew F. Dickson, and Joseph C. Stiles. Actually three others were graduates of another significant college, Brown University. They were James Petigru Boyce, William T. Brantly, Jr., and Edwin T. Winkler.

6. Cf. the comments of Rudolph, *American College and University*, p. 131, on the influence of Yale and Princeton to the exclusion of other major universities.

7. The control of southern schools by Congregational and Presbyterian conservative clergymen from the North was one of the most important mechanisms for the transfer of New England and northern conservative social philosophy to

the South. For example, South Carolina College, which produced a large number of the South's proslavery thinkers, was under the control of a New England diehard Federalist clergyman during its important first sixteen years. Jonathan Maxcy, although a Baptist and former president of Brown University and Union College, New York, combined the social and religious conscience of New Englanders described elsewhere in this study. Upon his arrival at South Carolina College in 1804, Maxcy greeted an entering class that long relied upon his teachings and that was indicative of the influence that one ideologized clergyman might have had over southern thinkers. In that first class were three influential future proslavery clergymen: William Capers, William T. Brantly, Sr., and Thornton Stringfellow. And among the nonclerical students were five men who took leading roles in developing the South's proslavery and sectional stance: John Murphy, future governor of Alabama; William Harper, chancellor and senator of South Carolina who wrote the crucial *Memoir on Slavery* (1836); Stephen D. Miller, governor of South Carolina during the nullification era; and William J. Grayson, the South's greatest proslavery novelist. One of them who always remained close to Maxcy and who worshiped him as a man "of talent and excellence seldom equalled" later wrote that one could hardly "appreciate the influence which Dr. Maxcy exerted over the minds of men." For the extensive correspondence between Maxcy and Richard Furman, which led to Maxcy's appointment as president of the college, see Richard Furman Correspondence, Furman University. For Maxcy's first students, see Maximilian LaBorde, *History of South Carolina College*, pp. 438–39. For Brantly's memories of Maxcy, see [Taylor], *A Brief Memoir of the Rev. William T. Brantly*, pp. 7–9. For comments of another, see Wightman, *Life of William Capers*, pp. 47–49, 59–62. Although South Carolina College came from 1820 to 1834 under the influence of Thomas Cooper, political economist, Jeffersonian, and former revolutionary, from 1835 until the Civil War it remained largely in the hands of ideologized proslavery clergymen including James H. Thornwell, Robert Henry, and Augustus B. Longstreet.

A similar influx of New England influence can be seen in the case of other southern universities during the periods in which proslavery thinkers were in attendance. The exceedingly strong personality at the University of North Carolina was Elisha Mitchell, a former student of Dwight at Yale and a Congregational-turned-Presbyterian clergyman. For Mitchell's assessment of his position in Chapel Hill, see letters, Elisha Mitchell to My M. [Maria North], 11 February 1818; Elisha Mitchell to Dr. J. J. Summerell, 26 January 1857, Elisha Mitchell Papers. For the reaction to Mitchell of one future proslavery minister, see letter, Iveson Brookes to Jonathan Brookes, 13 February 1818, Iveson L. Brookes Papers, Southern Historical Collection, University of North Carolina at Chapel Hill. See also Phillips, *A Memoir of the Rev. Elisha Mitchell*, p. 9. Mitchell was the dominant figure at the university from his arrival in 1818 until his accidental death in 1857.

Among the proslavery men educated by Mitchell were Leonidas Polk, Iveson Brookes, Calvin H. Wiley, William Norwood, Samuel Brown McPheeters, and George Patterson, not to mention future president James Knox Polk, Mitchell's prize-winning mathematics student in 1818.

At the University of Georgia, Moses Waddel, a North Carolina–born Presbyterian clergyman, served as president from 1819 to 1829. Waddel came to the university from an academy at Willington, S.C., where he had educated such southern luminaries as John C. Calhoun, William H. Crawford, Hugh S. Legare, George McDuffie, Augustus B. Longstreet, and James L. Petigru. Waddel, however, was succeeded in 1829 by Alonzo Church, a Vermonter and graduate of Middlebury College, who headed the university until the eve of the Civil War in 1859. For the impact of Church on one future proslavery clergyman, see Johnson, *Life and Letters of Benjamin Morgan Palmer,* pp. 57–60.

Although the College of Charleston, second only to South Carolina College among southern schools in the production of proslavery clergymen, had no dominant figure to compare with Maxcy, Mitchell, or Church, it did have a long string of similarly inclined faculty and presidents, including Nathaniel Bowen, the Boston-born Episcopal bishop of South Carolina; Jasper Adams, an Episcopal clergyman from Massachusetts, nephew of John Adams, and cousin of John Quincy Adams; and John Bachman, a New York–born Lutheran clergyman in Charleston. See Easterby, *A History of the College of Charleston,* pp. 74–89. See also Norton, *Life of Bishop Bowen,* pp. 21–24, 26.

It would not be an exaggeration to claim that only in Virginia was there any semblance of a distinctively southern pattern of college-level education. Both state-supported and private institutions in Virginia charted, in varying degrees, a course independent of the Yale and Princeton inspired mode of education that characterized most nineteenth-century American schools. The College of William & Mary was distinctive because it catered to the planting elite of Virginia. The University of Virginia, designed by Jefferson with the avowed purpose of erecting an alternative to the New England and Princeton models, followed a peculiar course but exerted a negligible influence on the shape of American and southern educational institutions and on the course of proslavery. And although Hampden-Sydney and Washington College, two Virginia Presbyterian schools, drew inspiration from Princeton, they tried whenever possible to use only Virginia–born and –educated ministers on their faculties. Largely as the result of the influence of John Holt Rice and George A. Baxter the two schools remained independent producers of graduates for the South. Washington College, however, finally succumbed to the overwhelming northern influence when it hired as president in 1848 a Pennsylvanian named George Junkin. Virginia's other important school, Randolph-Macon, after a brief period with a Vermonter and graduate of Middlebury as its president, followed the independent southern course of the state's older educational institutions. For information on the purposes and records of Virginia's

schools, see Rudolph, *American College and University,* pp. 68–69, 93, 125–28, 131–
33, 157–58, 170. Adrienne Koch, *Jefferson & Madison: The Great Collaboration* (New
York: Oxford University Press, 1964), pp. 260–80. For the reaction of one proslavery clergyman to the un-American nature of the University of Virginia, see
letters, Robert L. Dabney to Charles W. Dabney, 20 February 1837, 15 June 1841,
Dabney Family Papers, University of Virginia. Johnson, *Life and Letters of Robert
Lewis Dabney,* p. 55. See also Morrison, *College of Hampden-Sydney: Dictionary of
Biography,* pp. 65–67, 104–6, 137–40, 254–60. Smith, *Presbyterian Ministry in American Culture,* pp. 166–68. Irby, *History of Randolph-Macon College,* pp. 35–44, 60–
63, 102–7.

8. Baird, *Religion in America,* pp. 149–53.

9. James B. Ramsey, Secret History, 1 January, 20 May 1850; 1, 5 January, 17
July 1851; 17 July 1852; 1 January 1862; 20 May 1868; also sermons, "The
Church's Mission & the World's Only Hope," 16 June 1861; "Thanksgiving for
the Victory of Manassas," 28 July 1861; "The Word of the Lord Is Tried," 31 May
1863; "Fear Ye the Rod, and Who Hath Appointed It," 10 March 1865; "Revelation 1:6," 16 April 1865, James B. and George Junkin Ramsey Papers. See also
Ramsey's published sermons, *God's Way in the Sanctuary Remembered,* and *True Eminence Founded on Holiness,* in the latter of which Ramsey argued that Jackson had
been one of the few men who had achieved holiness by fulfilling all the duties of
man (pp. 14, 19)!

10. The rankled southerner was Iveson Brookes, who had just completed a
successful wife-hunting jaunt into Georgia. See Iveson Brookes to William
Brookes, 9 October 1823, Iveson Brookes Papers, Southern Historical Collection. Just before the above-quoted passage, Brookes had told his envious cousin,
"There are many fine women in Georgia it is true—but so many have been
imposed on by fortune hunters that all prudent girls are cautious of strangers—
a young man to marry to advantage *viz.* commonly [?] a girl of fortune possessing fair character & personal accomplishments—must come to her & her friends
highly recommended & conduct himself with much circumspection. If you have
a predilection for old maids & such as have not much [money] they are tolerably
numerous & quite comestable if I may coin a word."

11. Among those northern-born proslavery ministers who worked as tutors in
southern families were the following: Simeon Doggett, Charles S. Vedder, Theodore Clapp, and Moses Ashley Curtis. Curtis was the proverbial fortune-seeking
Yankee. He married one of his students, the daughter of a wealthy North Carolinian. See Moses Ashley Curtis, Diary, vol. 6, 5 and 21 October 1830, 9–24 September 1831, Moses Ashley Curtis Papers. Among the nonsouthern clergymen
who served as teachers were the following: Frederick and George Washington
Freeman, Nathaniel S. Wheaton, Gardiner Spring, Alexander Glennie, William
T. Leacock, and James Shannon.

12. Letter, Moses Drury Hoge to Drury Lacy, 18 September 1848; 27 April 1849, Moses Drury Hoge Letters.

13. Letter, J. W. Broadnax to Iveson Brookes, 20 February 1856, Iveson Brookes Papers, Southern Historical Collection.

14. Among the Congregational-born who affiliated with other denominations and who spent most of their careers in the South were the following: Presbyterians—John C. Coit, William C. Dana, William W. Eells, Elisha Mitchell, Nathaniel A. Pratt, Joseph C. Stiles, and Charles S. Vedder; Episcopalians—Nathaniel Bowen, Moses A. Curtis, George W. Freeman, William W. Lord, and Edward J. Stearns; Baptists—Daniel P. Bestor and Charles D. Mallary; Unitarian—Charles A. Farley and Theodore Clapp; Universalist—Theophilus Fisk.

15. State totals where clergymen spent 50 percent or more of their careers were as follows: South Carolina, 42; Virginia, 39; Georgia, 31; New York, 19; Alabama, 18; Louisiana, 12; Massachusetts, 12; Tennessee, 11; Maryland, 10; Mississippi, 10; North Carolina, 10; Pennsylvania, 9; New Jersey, 8; Ohio, 6; Kentucky, 5; Missouri, 5; Connecticut, 4; Wisconsin, 3; Texas, 3; Florida, 2; Vermont, 2; Maine, 1; New Hampshire, 1; Rhode Island, 1; Indiana, 1; Illinois, 1; Minnesota, 1; Iowa, 1; Arkansas, 1.

16. Mitchell, "Traveling Preacher and Settled Farmer," pp. 3–14. Mitchell's ranking of characteristics is debatable. In view of the nature of proslavery and the character of proslavery clergymen, the ministers' southernism was probably last as a defining characteristic.

17. Statistics on the slaveholding of proslavery clergymen have been taken whenever possible from the Slaveholding Schedule, U.S. Census, 1850 and 1860. Where clergymen could not be located in the manuscript census lists statements of slave ownership have been culled from biographies or other sources. In some cases very precise listings of slaves were obtained from tax lists in personal papers. In cases where slave ownership was established in biographies, the clergymen were placed in the 1–5 category, except where biographical information was quite precise. Where I have indicated that a clergyman owned no slaves, that fact was established from biographical sources, manuscript materials, or a definite absence from census reports. There are perils in the use of the manuscript census schedules, since there were wide disparities in methods of reporting and glaring inaccuracies in the attribution of ownership of slaves because of widespread slave rental and absentee ownership. Hence, table 6.22 represents a conservative estimate of the proportions of slaveownership by proslavery clergymen in either 1850 or 1860.

18. This is an extremely conservative total based on actual count for those whose precise number of slaves could be determined. About 35 of those numbered in the 1–5 category definitely owned slaves, but a precise number could not be found in the census or manuscript sources. Hence, their holdings were

counted as one. If their actual holdings approximated the average ownership of those known, the total number would increase to approximately 3,000. That still leaves 59 whose status could not be determined due to imprecise information on their whereabouts in the census years or the fact that they died before the census figures were compiled.

19. Letters, Mat Bolls to James Smylie, 27 March 1837; Samuel Montgomery to Joseph A. Montgomery, 2 May 1839, Montgomery Family Papers.

20. These statistics are based on a survey of all clergymen, including their property values and slaveholdings in the United States Census, Manuscripts Schedules 1 and 2, 7th Census, 1860, for the following Mississippi counties: Adams, Amite, Attala, Bolivar, Lafayette, Marshall, Wilkinson, and Winston.

Chapter Seven

1. Palmer, *Thanksgiving Sermon, November 29, 1860*, pp. 1–11, passim.

2. Silver, *Confederate Morale & Church Propaganda*, pp. 16ff. Silver believed that Palmer's statements put him in league with other fire-eaters of the South such as Robert Barnwell Rhett and William Lowndes Yancey. What made his sermon radical, however, was his endorsement of secession, not any particularly advanced view of slavery.

3. Among the more vociferous statements of the theme were the following sermons from all corners of the nation: Van Dyke, *Character and Influence of Abolition*. Samuel R. Wilson, *The Causes and Remedies of Impending National Calamities*. Anderson, *Dangers and Duties of the Present Crisis*. Baird, *Southern Rights and Northern Duties in the Present Crisis*. John Chase Lord, *Cause and Remedies of the Present Convulsions*. Mercer, *American Citizenship*.

4. Bacon, *Slavery Discussed in Occasional Essays*. Tracy, *Natural Equality*. Despite all of the study of proslavery in recent years, still very few historians have tried to figure out the ideological and logical relationship between what has long been denominated anti-abolition literature and proslavery literature. The only historian who has made the connection is Douglas C. Stange in two fascinating articles about Unitarian clergy North and South who attacked abolitionism and ended up defending slavery. See Stange, "Abolitionism as Maleficence: Southern Unitarians versus Puritan Fanaticism, 1831–1860," pp. 146–71 and "Abolitionism as Treason: The Unitarian Elite Defends Law, Order, and the Union," pp. 152–70. The only other historian who has struggled with similar issues but who came to very different conclusions is David Streifford, "American Colonization Society," pp. 201–20.

5. See Clough, *Candid Appeal*. Doggett, *Two Discourses on the Subject of Slavery*. Farley, *Slavery; a Discourse*. Fisk, *Bulwark of Freedom*. Freeman, *Rights and Duties of Slaveholders*. Frederick Freeman, *A Plea for Africa*. Bailey, *The Issue*. Clapp, *Slavery:*

A Sermon. Blagden, *The Principles on Which a Preacher of the Gospel Should Condemn Sin.* Birney, *American Churches the Bulwarks of American Slavery,* pp. 46–48. Whitaker, *Reflections on Domestic Slavery.*

6. [Colton], *Abolition a Sedition,* pp. vi–vii, 31, 79, 102, 125–26, 141, 167–69, 185.

7. Clough, *Candid Appeal,* pp. 5, 38–39. Blagden, *Principles on which a Preacher Should Condemn Sin,* pp. 26–30. Farley, *Slavery,* p. 6. Fisk, *Bulwark of Freedom,* p. 12. Clapp, *Slavery,* p. 65.

8. Doggett, *Two Discourses on Slavery,* pp. 4, 21–24, 28. Clough, *Candid Appeal,* p. 38. Farley, *Slavery,* p. 15. Fisk, *Bulwark of Freedom,* p. 15. Bailey, *The Issue,* p. 103.

9. Clough, *Candid Appeal,* pp. 6–15. Doggett, *Two Discourses on Slavery,* pp. 5–6.

10. Clough, *Candid Appeal,* pp. 18–38. Doggett, *Two Discourses on Slavery,* pp. 6ff. Farley, *Slavery,* pp. 7ff., 17. Freeman, *Rights and Duties of Slaveholders,* pp. 6ff. Clapp, *Slavery,* pp. 81ff.

11. Farley, *Slavery,* pp. 12–14. Clapp, *Slavery,* pp. 35–37.

12. Doggett, *Two Discourses on Slavery,* p. 23. Farley, *Slavery,* pp. 15ff. Clapp, *Slavery,* pp. 44–46. Freeman, *Plea for Africa,* pp. 168–75.

13. It should be noted that these quotations are positive good statements in the sense in which that misnomer long existed in historical literature. Doggett, *Two Discourses on Slavery,* pp. 10, 12. Fisk, *Bulwark of Freedom,* pp. 15, 19. Freeman, *Rights and Duties of Masters,* pp. 17–19. Bailey, *The Issue,* pp. 19, 47. Clapp, *Slavery,* pp. 34, 55. Blagden, *Principles on Which a Preacher Should Condemn Sin,* p. 26.

14. During the 1960s a number of distinguished historians, including Richard Hofstadter, Bernard Bailyn, and David Brion Davis, discussed a phenomenon variously described as "the paranoid style," the "fear of conspiracy," or "counter-subversion" as it had occurred in American history. Their combined notions inform my interpretation of a conservative counterrevolution in America. For Hofstadter's important essay, "The Paranoid Style in American Politics," and for Davis's early article, "Some Themes of Countersubversion: An Analysis of Anti-Masonic, Anti-Catholic, and Anti-Mormon Literature," see Davis, *Fear of Conspiracy,* pp. 2–22.

15. Bailyn's arguments and conclusions are documented in two books, *Origins of American Politics,* esp. pp. 3–58, and *Ideological Origins of the American Revolution,* esp. pp. 22–54, 94–123, and "A Note on Conspiracy," pp. 144–59.

16. The working out of the revolutionary consequences of American counter-subversion can be traced in Bailyn's discussions of "Transformation" and "The Contagion of Liberty," in *Ideological Origins of the American Revolution,* pp. 160–229, 230–319.

17. Wood, *Creation of the American Republic,* esp. pp. 471–99, 519–24, 562–64.

18. The reference here is to consensus historians who assumed that because the American political system is generally devoid of ideological factions and parties in the sense of European political systems that the American political and

social world is thereby devoid of ideology; and more particularly to such productions of the 1950s and following as Daniel Bell's *The End of Ideology: On the Exhaustion of Political Ideas in the Fifties* (1960).

19. That is, they are revolutionary if revolution is understood as a radical
departure from present circumstances and not as a sudden turn to a leftist pole
in the political and social spectrum.

20. A number of historians have searched for indications that philosophical
and ideological shifts had occurred or were occurring during the 1780s and
1790s making it possible for southerners, particularly Virginians, to defend slavery. Among those are Schmidt and Wilhelm, "Early Proslavery Petitions in Virginia," pp. 133–46; Robson, "Important Question Answered: William Graham's
Defense of Slavery," pp. 644–52; Shaffer, "Between Two Worlds: David Ramsey
and the Politics of Slavery," pp. 175–96; Burke, "Proslavery Argument and the
First Congress," pp. 3–15; Ohline, "Slavery, Economics, and Congressional Politics, 1790," pp. 335–60. The most articulate uses that have been made of this
and other evidence are Duncan MacLeod, *Slavery, Race, and the American Revolution* and David Brion Davis, *Problem of Slavery in Age of Revolution*. MacLeod particularly documents the limits of the Revolution's ideological impact on slavery in
the South. While the Revolution forced people to think about slavery, it did not
solve the problem. While the Revolution's impact in the North may have led to
the extinction of slavery, in the South the rhetoric of the Revolution was viewed
as political and not social, reinforcing equality among free men but not necessarily meaning that more men should be freed. Americans were so busy setting
up their new government and all of its systems that the resolution of conflict
between the implicit ideology of the Revolution and the continued existence of
slavery was postponed. See esp. pp. 78–81, 94, 126ff.

21. Love, *Fast and Thanksgiving Days of New England*, pp. 364–70. Miller,
Federalist Era, pp. 160–62. For the famous sermon charging the existence of a
French conspiracy that went rapidly through six editions, see David Osgood, *The
Wonderful Works of God Are to Be Remembered. A Sermon Delivered on the Day of Annual Thanksgiving, November 20, 1794* (1794). Two-thirds of the published sermons on Thanksgiving Day were the products of Massachusetts clergymen. For a
complete listing of the sermons, see Love, *Fast and Thanksgiving Days of New England*, pp. 558–62.

22. Morse, *Jedidiah Morse: A Champion of New England Orthodoxy*, pp. 51–56.
Stauffer, *New England and the Bavarian Illuminati*, pp. 229–38. Love, *Fast and
Thanksgiving Days of New England*, pp. 373–75. See also Jedidiah Morse, *A Sermon,
Delivered at the New North Church in Boston, May 9, 1798*.

23. Morse, *A Sermon Preached at Charlestown, November 29, 1798*. Morse, *A Sermon Exhibiting the Present Dangers, and Consequent Duties of the Citizens of the United
States of America*. See also the commentary and analysis of Stauffer, *New England*

and the Bavarian Illuminati, pp. 261–302. Love, *Fast and Thanksgiving Days of New England,* pp. 375–78.

24. These are cited as standard interpretations by David Brion Davis, *Fear of Conspiracy,* pp. 35–37. See also Banner, *To the Hartford Convention,* pp. 154–56, and Stauffer, *New England and the Bavarian Illuminati,* pp. 302–60, passim.

25. Especial reference should be made to studies of violence and various types of aberrant social behavior. See for example, Kai T. Ericson, *Wayward Puritans: A Study in the Sociology of Deviance* (1966).

26. This is the thesis of Nash, "American Clergy and the French Revolution," pp. 392–99. Despite his interpretation that the anti-French campaign of clergymen was independent of foreign events, Nash continued to ascribe the creation of the crisis to "real" causes (those factors which can directly precipitate an event) rather than to largely imagined threats.

27. Ibid., pp. 399–412.

28. The total number of fast and Thanksgiving sermons on nationally proclaimed days from 20 July 1775 to 11 December 1783 were as follows for each state: New Hampshire, 1; Vermont, 1; Massachusetts, 8; Connecticut, 8; New York, 1; New Jersey, 2; Pennsylvania, 12; Delaware, 2; Virginia, 1. On 19 February 1795, Massachusetts sermons outnumbered all others 23 to 10; on 9 May 1798, 12 to 8; and on 25 April 1799, 13 to 4. For the three days Massachusetts produced 48 published sermons, while other state totals were as follows: New Hampshire, 2; Maine, 3; Connecticut, 1; New York, 5; New Jersey, 1; Pennsylvania, 6; Virginia, 2; and North Carolina, 2. Compiled from Love, *Fast and Thanksgiving Days of New England,* pp. 547–72.

Chapter Eight

1. The interpretive framework for much of the following is an amalgam of reflections suggested by the theses and arguments presented primarily in three books: Fischer, *Revolution of American Conservatism;* Banner, *To the Hartford Convention;* and Kerber, *Federalists in Dissent.*

2. Dwight, *Duty of Americans at the Present Crisis,* pp. 4–32, passim.

3. The most extensive biographical study of Dwight is that of Cunningham, *Timothy Dwight, 1752–1817.* However, in terms of interpretation, the most incisive and informative study is that of Silverman, *Dwight,* pp. 13–15, for a sketch of Dwight's career and p. 111 for the designation of Dwight as "Pope."

4. Silverman, *Dwight,* pp. 22–31.

5. Ibid., pp. 35–41.

6. Ibid., pp. 21, 47–51. Dwight, *Triumph of Infidelity,* pp. 5–6, 16–18.

7. Silverman, *Dwight,* pp. 52–63.

8. Ibid., pp. 63–69.

9. Dwight, *Greenfield Hill*, pp. 36–40.

10. See chaps. 2–3 for references to proslavery negativism as a constant in proslavery literature from the Revolution to the 1830s. That Dwight's views on slavery could cause confusion even to the present is evident in James D. Essig's *Bonds of Wickedness* (1982), esp. pp. 101–2, 115, 126–28, where Dwight is found to be an antislavery leader up until the turn of the century. In fact Dwight was on the verge of becoming quite comfortable with slavery. Although Essig does find that Dwight thought slavery in Connecticut was the mildest in America, he concludes that Dwight and the other evangelicals simply turned their attention to other causes following the conclusion of the slave trade. He also argues that the Morse and Dwight tilt with Illuminism was parallel with their antislavery work and that one reinforced the other.

11. Silverman, *Dwight*, pp. 79, 87.

12. Ibid., p. 101.

13. Ibid., pp. 103, 137.

14. Ibid., pp. 138–41.

15. Ibid., p. 106.

16. Cunningham, *Dwight*, pp. 125–30. Morse, *Jedidiah Morse*, pp. 59–81, with Morse's use of the term *illiberal*, p. 60. Smith, Handy, and Loetscher, *American Christianity*, 1:520–23. Silverman, *Dwight*, pp. 111–12.

17. Quoted in Silverman, *Dwight*, p. 103.

18. Ibid., pp. 104–5, 125, 149. Morse, *Jedidiah Morse*, pp. 75–81.

19. Silverman, *Dwight*, pp. 106, 113, 114–22, 127, 131–35.

20. Ibid., pp. 112, 119, 129, 131.

21. Theodore Dwight, Jr., *President Dwight's Decisions of Questions*, pp. 1–348, passim. Among Dwight's telling comments were some of the following: On the question "Ought the Clergy to be Supported by Law?" he said, "No free government has ever existed without religion. But one attempt was ever made to establish such a government without it: that was made in France . . . [and] it was worse than an irruption of Goths and Vandals" (ibid., p. 83). On "Would a Division of the Union be Beneficial?" he commented, "I think it is time for the old 'Tree of Liberty' [the U.S.] to die: we have heard enough about it" (ibid., p. 97). On party-spirit, he stated, "I consider party-spirit one of the greatest crimes mankind are ever guilty of. . . . If we could ship off a few of our office-hunters it might be for benefit, especially if another brood did not spring up. . . . I cannot see how a republic can live with parties" (ibid., pp. 139–40). See also Silverman, *Dwight*, pp. 139–41.

22. [Dwight], *Remarks on the Review of Inchiquin's Letters*, pp. iii–v, 14–15. Silverman, *Dwight*, pp. 141–43.

23. [Dwight], *Remarks on the Review of Inchiquin's Letters*, pp. 80–86, 81n.

24. Silverman, *Dwight*, pp. 149–51, quoting from Timothy Dwight, "Observa-

tions on the Present State of Religion in the World," *Religious Intelligencer* (August–September 1816).

25. Fischer, *Revolution of American Conservatism*, esp. pp. xviii–xx.

26. Ibid., pp. xx, 197–99. See Livermore, *Twilight of Federalism;* also Moore, *Missouri Controversy.*

27. Most explanations of the demise of the Federalist party are cast in terms of the failures of party structure, with former Federalists grieving the loss of their rightful public offices. See Livermore, *Twilight of Federalism,* pp. 266–68. Also, Paul Goodman, "The First American Party System," in *The American Party Systems: Stages of Political Development,* ed. William Nisbet Chambers and Walter Dean Burnham (New York: Oxford University Press, 1967), pp. 85–89.

28. Fischer, *Revolution of American Conservatism,* pp. 47–49, noted the movement of even Federalist politics toward religious and educational reform as part of the Young Federalists' transition from "open" to "covert" elitism. In his estimation they returned to Christianity "with an evangelical enthusiasm." One of them noted in 1814 the "great change respecting the truth of Christianity which has taken place of late years in the minds of the educated classes, and especially among public men." Nevertheless, Fischer suggests that they found in religion a spiritual solace, not a new form for the assertion of authority. In the realm of education, however, he thought that Federalists saw schooling as the proper means "to control the common man, not to liberate him."

29. This argument is an appropriation of the findings of a host of historians who have examined the impulses that led to the formation of the Benevolent Empire and the social ideas of representative leaders. See Cole, *Social Ideas of the Northern Evangelists;* Bodo, *Protestant Clergy and Public Issues;* Foster, *Errand of Mercy;* Griffin, *Their Brothers Keepers.* This study disagrees, however, with the commonly held view that such theological developments as Samuel Hopkins's (1721–1803) doctrine of "Disinterested Benevolence" did more than provide a retrospective rationale for social reform and that such tenets offered little initial impetus for the creation of the Benevolent Empire.

30. The only historian who has examined in detail Federalist thought in the period after 1800 has been Linda Kerber in her *Federalists in Dissent,* on which much of the following discussion of Federalist ideology is based; see esp. pp. vii–ix, 1–4.

31. Ibid., pp. viii–ix.

32. Ibid., pp. 21–22.

33. Ibid., pp. 173–78.

34. Ibid., pp. 182–93.

35. Ibid., pp. 179–81.

36. Ibid., pp. 206–12.

37. See Ibid., pp. 67–94.

38. Fischer, *Revolution of American Conservatism,* pp. 129–49, passim; 167–69.

39. Kerber, *Federalists in Dissent,* pp. 95–98, 106–8, 109, 115.

40. Ibid., pp. 122–23, 126, 129–30, 131, 134.

41. Fischer, *Revolution of American Conservatism,* p. 326.

42. Dwight, ed., *President Dwight's Decisions,* p. 139.

43. For the experiences and fortunes of southern Federalists, see Rose, *Prologue to Democracy,* pp. 109–10, 161–66, 167–68, 173, 179, 194–95. Also, see Broussard, "Federalist Party in the South Atlantic States," pp. 362–66, 417, arguing that Federalism lived on in the South after 1800 to the extent that Federalist leaders could engender fears of revolutionary France. The efforts to find in Jeffersonian thought and Jeffersonian Virginia the seeds of conservative social principles later appearing in proslavery literature have been extensive. Among the most suggestive studies are these: Duncan MacLeod, *Slavery, Race, and the American Revolution,* pp. 94ff., 126ff., wherein MacLeod sees the acceptance of slavery as a permanent feature of southern life developing in parallel fashion with Jeffersonian theories. Robert Shalhope, "Thomas Jefferson's Republicanism and Antebellum Southern Thought," pp. 529–56, tries to make the elder Jefferson the author of proslavery by depicting Jefferson's doubts about the sanity of northerners and the benevolent movement and his conviction that the South would have to protect the integrity of the republic as indications that Jefferson was laying the groundwork for proslavery in the South. Jefferson's latter day ruminations, however, do not suggest a concerted conservative movement was afoot. Much the same must be said of Dickson Bruce's portrayal of the Virginia constitutional convention of 1829–1830 in *Rhetoric of Conservatism,* esp. pp. 7, 90, 166, 169, 175–79. The extensive debates about the proper shape of state government and fears about who will control government were but the same issues that had been argued since the time of the American Revolution. There were no clear indications of antisubversive rhetoric or social philosophy such as was already universally accepted in New England. True conservative thought would have dealt with all elements of society and not just with the shape of government.

44. Persistent liberalism in the face of the contradiction of slavery in the South has bothered many historians, particularly the expositors of the "travail of slavery" thesis. See Charles G. Sellers, "The Travail of Slavery," in Sellers, *Southerner as American,* esp. pp. 40–51. If southerners had experienced an ideological shift as did New Englanders, they would have developed the conceptual categories and the rhetoric to appear other than liberal. From the perspective of America's ideological history, it seems clear that they did not until well into the antebellum period.

45. See chap. 3.

46. Fischer, *Revolution of American Conservatism,* pp. 159–60, 167. Kerber, *Federalists in Dissent,* pp. 23–26, 31, 39–40, 44, 50–52. Kerber sees Federalist "political abolitionism" (opposition to slavery out of political expediency) as the root cause or even a source of "humanitarian abolitionism" (Garrisonian). Such sons

of Federalist politicians as Edmund Quincy, James Russell Lowell, Wendell Phillips, Theodore Sedgwick, Jr., and a cultural son, William Lloyd Garrison, drew their inspiration for abolitionism when "they took their fathers at their word" (*Federalists,* pp. 59–66). It is the contention of this study, however, that for many young Federalists the more natural continuum proceeded from Federalism to colonization to anti-abolition to possible proslavery, than from Federalism to abolitionism. An example of how historians continue to misconstrue the Federalists' views on slavery is Essig, *Bonds of Wickedness,* who views Dwight and other Federalist conservatives as antislavery and as paving the way for abolitionism in the future (esp. pp. 107–13).

47. Fischer, *Revolution of American Conservatism,* pp. 160, 165–67. Kerber, *Federalists in Dissent,* pp. 50–51. Frederickson, *Black Image in the White Mind,* pp. 4–5.

48. On both Smith's *Essay* and Jefferson's *Notes,* see Jordan, *White Over Black,* pp. 429–81, 486–90; also Morrison, "Nearer to the Brute Creation," pp. 228–42.

49. See Samuel Stanhope Smith, *An Essay on the Causes of the Variety of Complexion and Figure in the Human Species,* pp. xiv–xvi, 23–31. Timothy Dwight was in complete agreement with Smith; see Cuningham, *Timothy Dwight,* pp. 310–13. For Dwight's most concise statement of the environmentalist principle, see Dwight, *President Dwight's Decisions,* pp. 117–28. Another Federalist clergyman who challenged Jefferson's views directly was Clement Clark Moore, *Observations upon Certain Passages in Mr. Jefferson's Notes on Virginia,* quoted in Kerber, *Federalists in Dissent,* pp. 53–55. For others involved in the early ethnological debate, see Jordan, *White Over Black,* pp. 440–57. According to Kerber, *Federalists in Dissent,* p. 53, Moore's exposition of the unity argument was standard Federalist fare. However, she labels it as "a quasi-abolitionist position."

50. The fullest account of the later ethnological debate is Stanton, *The Leopard's Spots.* It is my contention that later southern opponents of theories of diverse origins were inheritors of conservative ideological emphases, including the Christian case for Genesis. Hence, those southern clergymen of the 1840s and 1850s such as Moses A. Curtis, John Bachman, William T. Hamilton, and Thomas Smyth, whom Stanton identified as biblicist anti-intellectuals, drew the impetus for their views from sources other than southern religious fundamentalism (see Stanton, *Leopard's Spots,* pp. 192–95).

51. Samuel Stanhope Smith, *Lectures, Corrected and Improved,* 2:176. Jordan, *White Over Black,* pp. 543–44. For the involvement of Congregational clergy and Federalists in the early years of the American Colonization Society, see Staudenraus, *American Colonization Movement,* esp. pp. 77–79, 85, 86, 124, 132–35. See also Senior, "New England Congregationalists and the Anti-Slavery Movement," pp. 24–41, 54–61, 73, 79–81, 84, 112. Both Staudenraus and Senior document very carefully the full-scale swing of conservatives to active participation in colonization between 1822 and 1825. By 1830 the identification of colonization with

the Benevolent Empire and thereby with conservative counterrevolution was complete. See David Streifford's "American Colonization Society," pp. 203–4, arguing this precise point.

52. Jordan, *White Over Black*, pp. 325–31. The bill to end the slave trade engendered little debate on the merits of slavery, more on the proper means of enforcement. In those debates, three Democrats, Peter Early of Georgia, John Randolph of Virginia, and James Holland of North Carolina were said to have expressed "ominous" opinions, though they did not defend slavery (ibid., p. 331).

53. Smith, *Lectures on the Subjects of Moral and Political Philosophy*, pp. 159–79, passim. For a typical evaluation of Smith's views as antislavery in nature, see Winthrop Jordan, "Introduction," in Smith, *Essay on the Causes of the Variety of Complexion and Figure in the Human Species*, p. xiix.

54. Smith, *Lectures on the Subjects of Moral and Political Philosophy*, pp. 159–79, passim.

55. Bourne, *The Book and Slavery Irreconcilable*, reprinted in Christie and Dumond, *George Bourne and the Book and Slavery Irreconcilable*, pp. 108–9, 197, 199–200, 202–3, 205–6.

56. "An American," "To the Edinburgh Reviewers," *National Intelligencer*, 18, 20, 23, 25 November 1819. These letters were later printed separately as *Letter to the Edinburgh Reviewers: by "An American." First Published in the National Intelligencer of November 16 [sic], 1819.* Another who saw the writings of Walsh and An American as proslavery in nature was Wright, *Refutation of the Sophisms*.

57. *National Intelligencer*, 25, 27, 30 November, 2, 7 December 1819. Among the correspondents was Benjamin Rush, who, although usually considered an enemy of slavery, approved Walsh's attribution for the guilt of American slavery to British merchants and rulers (ibid., 25 November 1819). It hardly needs to be added that the editors of the *Edinburgh Review*, against whom Walsh had ranted, saw the Walsh volume as a "jaundiced" defense of slavery (see *Edinburgh Review* 66 [May 1820]: 395–431, esp. 420–21).

58. Among the historians who carry on the argument with lists of Federally inspired abolitionists are Banner, *To the Hartford Convention*, pp. 99–109, with the listing, pp. 108–9 n. 5, and Kerber, *Federalists in Dissent*, pp. 59–66.

59. The "young" Federalists were James Buchanan, Gulion Crommelin Verplanck, Peter Dumont Vroom, and Roger Brooke Taney. Others descended from Federalist leaders were the three Morses—Samuel F. B., Sidney E., and Richard C.—William and William H. Appleton, Green C. Bronson, Frederick and Edwin Croswell, Pliny and William W. Cutler, William Wolcott Ellsworth, William Marcellus Goodrich, Francis Granger, James Harper, Benjamin Chew Howard, Ashel Huntington, Amos Kendall, John McKeon, Alfred Osborne Pope Nicholson, Joel Parker, Watts Sherman, William Sprague, Robert Field Stockton, Martin Van Buren, and others who were clergymen (listed in n. 62 with others).

60. Frederick Dalcho and Richard Furman. Dalcho served as coeditor of the most important Federalist newspaper in the South, the *Charleston Courier,* from 1806 until 1813 (Williams, *Rev. Frederick Dalcho,* p. 3). Furman had long been involved in politics from the Revolution to membership in the constitutional convention of South Carolina in 1790. His involvement continued after 1800 through close association with the Pinckneys and Henry De Saussure.

61. These are among the leading anti-abolitionists mentioned by Richards, *Gentlemen of Property and Standing,* pp. 21, 37–38, 50, 54, 58–59, 94.

62. Northern-born proslavery clergymen from acknowledged Federalist backgrounds were Nehemiah Adams, Rufus William Bailey, Robert Baird, John C. Coit, Calvin Colton, William C. Dana, Amos C. Dayton, Nathan Lord, John C. Lord, William Wilberforce Lord, Joel Parker, Gardiner Spring, Moses Stuart, Isaac T. Tichenor, and Nathaniel S. Wheaton. Descendants of southern Federalists were William H. Barnwell, James C. Furman, Christopher E. and Christopher P. Gadsden, Charles Cotesworth Pinckney, and Leonidas Polk.

Chapter Nine

1. Morison, *Harrison Gray Otis,* p. x, with a statement on the failure of twentieth-century historians to appreciate the abiding influence of Federalism. Compare the interpretation of some of the same individuals mentioned here in Streifford, "American Colonization Society: An Application of Republican Ideology to Early Antebellum Reform," pp. 201–10.

2. Rossiter, *Conservatism in America,* pp. 106–27, connecting both Federalists and southern proslavery thinkers in the conservative tradition.

3. Many other names (e.g., Nathan Lord, Moses Stuart, Gardiner Spring, Nehemiah Adams, and a host of southerners) could be added to this list. They are mentioned at this point only because, while it has long been recognized that most of them defended slavery, they have normally been treated by historians as aberrant northerners and not as crucial formulators of proslavery thought.

4. Ingersoll first broke with the Federalism of his father and that which he learned under Samuel Stanhope Smith at Princeton when he ran for the Pennsylvania State Assembly in 1811. Nevertheless he continued to be considered a moderate Federalist until he turned against the Second Bank of the United States in 1832. He served in Congress as a Democrat from 1841 to 1849 and earlier as a Republican from 1813 to 1815. See Meigs, *Life of Charles Jared Ingersoll,* pp. 31–44, 48, 62, 166–84. See also Fisher, *Philadelphia Perspective,* p. 20. Paulding served in the Madison and Monroe administrations on the figurehead Board of Navy Commissioners, 1815–1823, Navy Agent for New York, 1824–1838, and Secretary of the Navy in the Van Buren administration, 1838–1841.

See Aderman, ed., *Letters of Paulding*, pp. xvi–xxiii. On Morse's rebellion from Federalism, see Mabee, *American Leonardo*, pp. 31–38, 169–72, 176–78, 343–45. Morse ran for mayor of New York City in 1836 and 1841 as a Nativist Democrat and for Congress from New York in 1854. He was unsuccessful on each occasion. For the political leanings of Otis, see Morison, *Harrison Gray Otis*, pp. 88–89, 246–48, 480.

5. Mabee, *American Leonardo*, pp. 342–43. Leonard Richards, *Gentlemen of Property and Standing*, pp. 10–19, has charted the rise of anti-abolitionism in the North in terms of mobs with the peak of excitement occurring in August 1835. Richards, however, assumed that southerners began demanding the silencing of Garrison's *Liberator* following the Nat Turner insurrection in Virginia in August 1831, an assumption that seems to be unfounded. While southern newspapers did take notice of immediatism well before the summer of 1835, abolitionism did not become the occasion of a massive crisis of fear and demands for action a moment before the peaking of anti-abolitionism in the North in the summer of 1835. If anything, as will be seen, the southern crisis followed that of the North. See Richards, *Gentlemen of Property and Standing*, pp. 16–17, 21, 37, 52–58.

6. Morison, *Life and Letters of Harrison Gray Otis*, 2:257–58. See also Howard, "Georgia Reaction to David Walker's *Appeal*," pp. 34–38.

7. Morison, *Life and Letters of Otis*, 2:259–61, 276–81.

8. Ibid., pp. 262–64. The notion that Otis was totally unaware of Garrison and the *Liberator* until the *National Intelligencer* called attention to them is based on an unreliable letter written by Otis in his eighty-third year less than a month before his death. In the letter, as noted by Morison, Otis thoroughly confused the Walker and Garrison episodes. See ibid., pp. 261 and n. 7, 262 and n. 8.

9. Meigs, *Life of Ingersoll*, pp. 189–94. The speech was published in the *Pennsylvanian*, 29 July 1835, and the *Washington Globe*, 12 August 1835. For the early reaction of Morse to abolitionism, see Mabee, *American Leonardo*, p. 342.

10. Morison, *Life and Letters of Otis*, 2:270–75.

11. James K. Paulding to Martin Van Buren, 16 December 1835; Paulding to James H. Hammond, 8 March 1836, in Aderman, ed., *Letters of Paulding*, pp. 172–73, 176–77.

12. Paulding, *Slavery in the United States*, pp. 5–11, 263–64, and chaps. 1, 6, 7, 8, 9 (pp. 174–280, entirely on political economy).

13. Ibid., pp. 90, 270–80, and chaps. 4, 5.

14. Ibid., pp. 37–47, 109–11, 281–312.

15. Ibid., pp. 302–3.

16. Ibid., pp. 6–7.

17. Morison, *Life and Letters of Otis*, 2:274–75, citing "Mr. Otis's Letter" to the Rhode Island legislature in 1839.

18. Meigs, *Life of Ingersoll*, pp. 195–96, 222–23.

19. Ibid., pp. 238–46, 252–53.

20. Ibid., pp. 239–40. For Paulding's support of Ingersoll in his debates with Adams, see James K. Paulding to Charles J. Ingersoll, 22 June 1841, in Aderman, ed., *Letters of Paulding*, pp. 308–9.

21. Meigs, *Life of Ingersoll*, pp. 256–70.

22. James K. Paulding to Robert J. Dillon, James T. Brady, Daniel Sickles, Augustus Schell, and Edward C. West, 14 March 1850; Paulding to John C. Calhoun, 19 March 1850; Paulding to Henry S. Foote, 3 June 1850; Paulding to F. D. Richardson, H. H. Raymond and W. H. Peronneau, 6 September 1851, in Aderman, ed., *Letters of Paulding*, pp. 508–18, 521–27.

23. Ingersoll, *African Slavery in America*, pp. 4, 5–15, 37.

24. Ibid., pp. 3, 55–56.

25. Morse, *Samuel F. B. Morse*, 2:331–34, 389–90. Mabee, *American Leonardo*, p. 344. Meigs, *Life of Ingersoll*, pp. 331–32. Fisher, *A Philadelphia Perspective*, pp. 250, 359–60, 386. Just before Ingersoll's death in May, 1862, Fisher, himself a very strident defender of slavery, but not of the South, found that Ingersoll had succeeded in convincing the entire Ingersoll clan to "sympathize with the rebellion" (ibid., p. 424).

26. Samuel F. B. Morse to George L. Douglas, 29 December 1860; Morse to Rev. Henry J. Vandyke, 2 January 1861; Morse to Hon. William Bigler, 6 February 1861; Morse to ?, 11 February 1861; Morse to Amos Kendall, 15 February 1861, Morse Papers.

27. Samuel F. B. Morse to Hon. Charles Mason, 25 March 1861; Morse to Rev. H. G. Ludlow, 10, 13 May 1861, Morse Papers. Mabee, *American Leonardo*, p. 346. Morse, *Samuel F. B. Morse*, 2:415–19. *American Society for Promoting National Unity*, pp. 3–8.

28. Hopkins, *Bible View of Slavery*, pp. 10–11. Cf. Samuel F. B. Morse, *Present Attempt to Dissolve the American Nation*. Samuel F. Morse to George L. Douglas, 21 April 1861, Morse Papers.

29. Samuel F. B. Morse to Hubbard Winslow, 21 February 1863, Morse Papers. Mabee, *American Leonardo*, pp. 347–48.

30. Mabee, *American Leonardo*, pp. 347–49. Samuel F. B. Morse to "My dear Cousin," 9 February 1863; Morse to Amos Kendall, 14 February 1863; Morse to Jacob P. Jewett, Esq., 28 February 1863, Morse Papers. *Papers from the Society for the Diffusion of Political Knowledge, No. 1: The Constitution* (1863), pp. 1–2.

31. *Papers from the Society for the Diffusion of Political Knowledge*, nos. 1–24 (New York: Various imprints, 1863–1864). Mabee, *American Leonardo*, pp. 349–50.

32. Morse, *Samuel F. B. Morse*, 2:430–31, 446. For a satire on the southern sentiments of the latter society, see the spurious pamphlet, *Society for the Diffusion of Political Knowledge, Delmonico's, Feb. 14, 1863: To Churchmen* (New York: Society for the Diffusion of Political Knowledge, 1863).

33. Samuel F. B. Morse to Rev. H. G. Ludlow, 13 May 1861, Morse Papers.

34. Morse, *Samuel F. B. Morse*, 2:429–30.

Chapter Ten

1. The men who wrote defenses that contained the ingredients of a new proslavery ideology were as follows: Leonard Bacon, Joseph Tracy, Job Roberts
Tyson, David Reese, Simon Clough, Simeon Doggett, Thomas Man, James T.
Austin, James K. Paulding, William Thomas, Charles Hodge, Frederick Freeman, George W. Freeman, Daniel K. Whitaker, George W. Blagden, Calvin Colton, William J. Hobby, Charles A. Farley, Theophilus Fisk, Theodore Clapp,
William Winans, Rufus W. Bailey—all native northerners—and two native
southerners, Joshua Lacy Wilson, a Presbyterian clergyman in Cincinnati, and
George A. Baxter, a Presbyterian clergyman in Virginia closely aligned with
Princeton conservatives. Although many historians have tried to find the roots of
a new direction in proslavery in the South before 1835, there is no basis for such
a premise.

2. Richards, *Gentlemen of Property and Standing,* pp. 48–49. Despite his great
interest in the timing of anti-abolition mobbism and the unleashing of social stimuli, Richards is vague about the relationship between anti-abolition and southern
responses to abolitionism.

3. For anti-abolition and other nonrelated violence in the mid-1830s, see ibid.,
pp. 10–19. Cf. *Report of the National Advisory Commission on Civil Disorders* (New
York: New York Times Company, 1968), pp. 203–6.

4. All of these riots and mob activities are described in varying detail in Richards, *Gentlemen of Property and Standing,* pp. 26–30, 37–40, 113–22.

5. Ibid., pp. 15, 37.

6. Ibid., pp. 37, 40.

7. See chap. 9.

8. For a detailed account of the anti-abolition witness of each of the above-
mentioned clergymen, see Senior, "New England Congregationalists and the
Antislavery Movement, 1830–1860," pp. 54–117, passim.

9. For Beecher and Bacon's early approval and subsequent disenchantment
with abolitionism, see ibid., pp. 57–61.

10. Ibid., pp. 74–86.

11. Ibid., pp. 85–86, 87.

12. Ibid., pp. 86–89.

13. See the writings of David Reese, Job Roberts Tyson, and James Trecothick
Austin examined below.

14. Among those who contributed to the early attack on abolition among the
clergy of New England were Leonard Bacon, *Slavery Discussed in Occasional Essays,* pp. 13–56, 57–79; Joseph Tracy, *Natural Equality* (1833); Clough, *Candid
Appeal to the Citizens of the United States* (1834); Simeon Doggett, *Two Discourses on
the Subject of Slavery* (1835); Thomas Russell Sullivan, *Letters Against the Immediate
Abolition of Slavery* (1835). Compare the treatment of these types by Streifford,

"American Colonization Society: An Application of Republican Ideology to Early Antebellum Reform," pp. 201–20.

15. Tracy, *Natural Equality,* pp. 3–8.

16. Ibid., pp. 9–11.

17. Ibid., pp. 11–14, 21–22. Tracy cited documents from the French Revolution to prove that the European revolutionaries consciously went far beyond the American theory of natural equality (see notes A, B, ibid., pp. 21–22).

18. Ibid., pp. 14–19.

19. Bacon, *Slavery Discussed in Occasional Essays,* pp. 13–56, 57–79 (two articles reprinted from the *Quarterly Christian Spectator,* 1833 and 1834). Clough, *Candid Appeal to the Citizens of the United States,* pp. 5, 38. Moses Stuart, Abstract of Lecture on Slavery, 1834 [dated from references to "Notes on Lecture on Biblical View of Slavery, 1834, 1835, 1836," in Stuart's "Expression of My Desire as to the Disposal of My Manuscripts," 21 April 1837], Moses Stuart Papers. For Unitarian response in the North see Stange, "Abolitionism as Treason," pp. 152–70. Among Unitarian anti-abolitionists were Edward Everett, Simeon Doggett, Nathaniel L. Frothingham, Francis Parkman, George Putnam, Ephraim Peabody, and Henry Bellows.

20. Reese, *A Brief Review of the "First Annual Report of the American Anti-Slavery Society,"* pp. 3–5, 8–9, 13, 40–41, 42–45. Tyson, *Discourse before the Young Men's Colonization Society,* esp. pp. 39–48.

21. Although Leonard Richards, *Gentlemen of Property and Standing,* details the character and causes of anti-abolition mobs, he nowhere made mention of the striking spread of such mobbism from New England outward. In his scheme of interpretation, mobbism followed closely upon the heels of the appearance of new abolition societies in any particular locality. However, the peculiar timing of such mobs as those of New York in 1834, Boston in 1835, and Cincinnati in 1836 indicates that other factors may well have been at work, perhaps in some cases the expansion of anti-abolition thought.

22. See ibid., pp. 47–81, passim. Parts of Otis's speech at Faneuil Hall, Boston, 22 August 1835, are reprinted in Davis, *Fear of Conspiracy,* pp. 138–39.

23. Reese, *Letters to the Hon. William Jay,* pp. v–viii, 16–18, 68–69. [Austin], *Remarks on Dr. Channing's Slavery,* pp. 3–4, 17, 24, 44–45.

24. Man, *Picture of Woonsocket,* pp. 3–4, 23–32. Thomas, *Enemies of the Constitution Discovered,* pp. iii–viii.

25. *Northern Sentiments Upon the Movements of the Abolitionists. Proceedings of the Anti-abolitionist Meeting at Albany* (1836), pp. 1–3.

26. Reese, *Humbugs of New-York,* pp. iii–viii, 148–49, 160–64.

27. Doggett, *Two Discourses on the Subject of Slavery;* Blagden, *Principles on Which a Preacher of the Gospel Should Condemn Sin.* For the writings of Hodge and Wilson, see below.

28. For a listing of Hodge's essays as they originally appeared in the *Princeton*

Review, see Danhof, *Charles Hodge as a Dogmatician,* pp. 271–320. For Hodge's two most popular proslavery essays, "The Fugitive Slave Law" and "The Bible Argument on Slavery," see Elliott, *Cotton Is King,* pp. 809–40, 841–77.

29. Charles Hodge, "Slavery," from the *Princeton Review* (1836), reprinted in Hodge, *Essays and Reviews,* pp. 473–512.

30. Joshua L. Wilson to Jeremiah Morrow, Esqr., ca. 1826; Joshua L. Wilson to Samuel R. Wilson, 10 February 1832, Wilson Family Papers.

31. Cincinnati *Standard,* 19 November 1835, p. 214; 10 December 1835, p. 217. For the circumstances leading up to Wilson's anti-abolitionist tirade, see Dr. G. Bailey to Joshua L. Wilson, 1 February 1839; Joshua L. Wilson to Dr. G. Bailey, 2 February 1839; Joshua L. Wilson to Samuel R. Wilson, 27 March, 18 April 1839; Joshua L. Wilson to Miss Rebecca C. Clopper, 23 May 1839, Wilson Family Papers. Wilson, *Relation and Duties of Servants and Masters,* esp. pp. 3–4, 5, 32–33.

32. John King Lord, *History of Dartmouth College,* 2:252–55. Alpheus Crosby, *Eulogy Commemorative of the Life and Character of Nathan Lord,* pp. 16–22. Crosby and Lord disagree slightly on the dating of Lord's conversion to proslavery.

33. Two prominent anti-abolitionists mentioned in foregoing pages, David Reese and Simon Clough, virtually disappeared from historical records.

34. On Austin, see Richards, *Gentlemen of Property and Standing,* p. 69. Brigham, *Biographical Sketch of Rev. Simeon Doggett,* pp. 37–38. For Winslow as officer in the Morse organizations, see *American Society for Promoting National Unity,* p. 2; Samuel F. B. Morse to Rev. Hubbard Winslow, 21 February 1863, Morse Papers, Library of Congress. Joshua Lacy Wilson to Samuel Ramsay Wilson, 27 March, 18 April 1839; Joshua Lacy Wilson to Miss Rebecca C. Clopper, 23 May 1839; Joshua Lacy Wilson to William M. Eagles, 17 September 1845, Wilson Family Papers.

35. On Hodge's numerous proslavery essays, see n. 28 above. Blagden, *Remarks, and a Discourse on Slavery.* Stuart, *Conscience and the Constitution.*

36. Adams, *South Side View of Slavery.* See also Adams, *Sable Cloud.* For Adams's admission that the South was justified in secession, see "The Re-Union of the States. A Sermon Preached at Boston, Mass., Sept. 26, 1861," in Moore, *Spirit of the Pulpit,* pp. 78–84. For Adams's triumphant visit to Charleston after the war, see Adams, *At Eventide,* esp. pp. iv–ix. For his precise position on slavery in the 1830s, see Nehemiah Adams to Charles T. Torrey, 13 November 1837, Torrey Papers. For Lord's unusual proslavery views, see *Letter of Inquiry to Ministers of the Gospel;* and Lord, *Northern Presbyter's Second Letter to Ministers of the Gospel.* For his wartime opinions, see Lord, *True Pictures of Abolition.* Lord left a number of lengthy, but unfinished manuscripts on slavery, several begun after the Civil War. For one of the more readable proslavery manuscripts, see Nathan Lord to Rev. Mr. Campbell, December 1864, Nathan Lord Papers.

Chapter Eleven

1. The seeds of the notion that Jeffersonian Virginia may have produced useful conservative or republican ideas that later affected proslavery were planted by MacLeod, *Slavery, Race, and the American Revolution,* pp. 94ff. and 126ff., and by Morgan, *American Slavery, American Freedom,* pp. 363–87. The best article and most effective analysis of Jefferson's potential influence on later conservative republicanism and proslavery in the South is that of Robert Shalhope, "Thomas Jefferson's Republicanism and Antebellum Southern Thought," pp. 529–56, esp. 552–55. For Dickson Bruce's interpretation, see *Rhetoric of Conservatism,* esp. pp. 175–93.

2. Freehling, *Drift Toward Dissolution,* esp. pp. 168, 185, 195, 203, 228, 230, 248, 257.

3. Freehling, *Prelude to Civil War,* pp. x–xi, 327–33.

4. Among those who served in official capacities in various national benevolent societies before the mid-1830s were the following: William C. Buck, Jared Bell Waterbury, William H. Brisbane, Nehemiah Adams, David Magie, Phillip Berry, Robert Baird, William Barlow, Seth Bliss, William S. White, Joshua L. Wilson, John Leighton Wilson, Joel Parker, George Junkin, John B. Adger, Benjamin M. Palmer (elder), William S. Plumer, William A. Scott, Joseph C. Stiles, Samuel K. Talmage, George W. Freeman, and Thomas Meredith, not to mention those involved in educational institutions and the American Colonization Society. Among those considered to be reformers in various European countries were John England, Bernard Illowy, Max Lilienthal, and Isaac M. Wise. Among those forcibly expelled from European countries for revolutionary activities were John Mitchel and Thomas F. Meagher (Ire.), Bernard Illowy (France and Austria), and Charles Minnigerode (Prussia).

5. Palmer, *Signs of the Times Discerned.* Coulter, *William G. Brownlow,* pp. 32–34. Several historians have outlined in similar terms much of the following story of the rise of benevolence and benevolent institutions in the South: Mathews, *Religion in the Old South,* passim; Loveland, *Southern Evangelicals and the Social Order,* esp. pp. 159–85; and Holifield, *Gentlemen Theologians,* esp. pp. 149–54. However, none of these emphasizes the direct influence of the northern benevolent movement.

6. Foreign and domestic missionaries from among future proslavery clergymen in the 1820s and early 1830s included John Leighton Wilson, John B. Adger, William Capers, Amasa Converse, Moses A. Curtis, George W. Freeman, Drury Lacy, John B. McFerrin, William S. Plumer, William A. Scott, Joseph C. Stiles, Samuel K. Talmage, Rufus W. Bailey, and Iveson Brookes.

7. John L. Girardeau, "Eulogy on Professor George Howe, D.D., LL.D., Delivered before the Alumni Association of Columbia Theological Seminary, May 9,

1883," in *Memorial Volume on the Semi-Centennial of the Theological Seminary at Co-lumbia*, pp. 404–5. DuBose, *Memoirs of Rev. John Leighton Wilson*, pp. 36–40.

8. William W. Freehling, in *Prelude to Civil War*, pp. 72–76, 335–39, saw minis-ters in the 1820s as covert abolitionists. After the "Great Reaction," however, "ministers, like everyone else, conformed to the massive orthodoxy, and a new era in slave religion commenced." Donald G. Mathews, in "Methodist Mission to the Slaves, 1829–1844," pp. 615–31, believed, however, that at least Methodists began as moderate opponents of slavery and continued their mission to the slaves as the only possible witness against slavery in what became a proslavery culture. Ministers only joined in the defense of slavery, he believed, as a means of retaining access to slaves. On the rise of religious instruction see Raboteau, *Slave Religion*, pp. 125–26 and passim.

9. Meade, *Sermons Addressed to Masters and Servants, and Published in the Year 1743, by the Rev. Thomas Bacon.* Charles Colcock Jones, who searched out almost exhaustively every reference to the religious instruction of slaves, found little to record for the period from 1790 to 1820 and concluded that religious "instruc-tion was extensively and most seriously neglected." See Jones, *The Religious In-struction of the Negroes in the United States*, pp. 47–64.

10. This periodization conforms to that indicated by Jones, *Religious Instruc-tion of the Negroes*, pp. 96–97. However, Jones thought that the revolution con-tinued unchanged until 1842.

11. For examples of opposition to the religious instruction of slaves, see Freehling, *Prelude to Civil War*, pp. 72–76.

12. The catechism of Mines, Palmer's first edition, and Rice's sermon are men-tioned in Jones, *Religious Instruction of the Negroes*, pp. 65–70. Dalcho, Furman, and Pinckney's pamphlets are normally viewed as early defenses of slavery, de-spite the fact that most of their contents were devoted to religious instruction. See Dalcho, *Practical Considerations Founded on the Scriptures*, pp. 21–38; Furman, *Exposition of the Views of the Baptists*, pp. 16–19; Pinckney, *Address Delivered in Charleston, Before the Agricultural Society of South Carolina*, pp. 3–24, passim. Pal-mer, *Plain and Easy Catechism.* Mathews, *Slavery and Methodism*, pp. 68–72. See Mathews, *Religion in the Old South*, pp. 137–49.

13. Mathews, "Methodist Mission to the Slaves, 1829–1844," pp. 618–30. Freehling, *Prelude to Civil War*, pp. 74–76. Jones, *Religious Instruction of the Negroes*, pp. 72–75.

14. Association for the Religious Instruction of the Negroes in Liberty County, Georgia, *Annual Reports* (various imprints, 1833–1848). Charles Colcock Jones, *Religious Instruction of the Negroes. A Sermon.* Meade, *Pastoral Letter of the Right Rever-end William Meade.* Bowen, *Pastoral Letter, on the Religious Instruction of the Slaves.* Clay, *Detail of a Plan for the Moral Improvement of Negroes on Plantations.* The exceed-ingly rare works of Capers, Bryan, Jones, Laurens, and Mrs. Pratt are mentioned

in Jones, *Religious Instruction of the Negroes*, pp. 72, 75, 79, 80. For further on Jones, see Byrne, "Charles C. Jones and Intellectual Crisis of the South," pp. 274–85.

15. Myers, *Children of Pride*, pp. 14–16. Mathews, "Methodist Mission to the Slaves, 1829–1844," pp. 618–19. Information on Bryan compiled from Methodist Episcopal Church, *Minutes of the Annual Conferences*, 1817–1844. Bryan was superannuated in 1841. For Bowen's visit to Salem, see Adelaide L. Fries, et al., eds., *Records of the Moravians in North Carolina*, 11 vols. (Raleigh: North Carolina Department of Archives and History, 1920–1969), 8:3922–23, 16 July 1830. Two of Meade's visits to South Carolina to study slave missions are described in Norton, *Life of Bishop Gadsden*, pp. 57–59, 100–111, along with the work of Gadsden and Glennie. See also Christopher E. Gadsden to John W. Mitchell, 8 December 1835; and John H. Tucker to T. D. Grimke, ca. 13 April 1818, Miscellaneous Manuscripts, South Carolina Historical Society. Giradeau, "Eulogy on Prof. George Howe," pp. 404–5. [Catherine C. Bachman], *John Bachman, the Pastor of St. John's Lutheran Church*, pp. 354–55, 359. Norton, *Life of Bishop Bowen*, pp. 133–39. Basil Manly, Church Journal, numerous entries, 21 March 1828–2 January 1829, Basil Manly, Sr., Sermons and Papers, Furman University Library. James Smylie, Biography File, Historical Foundation, Montreat, N.C. *In Memoriam—Rev. Joseph C. Stiles*, pp. 11–13, 29–30.

16. Such strongly worded reform-minded pleas were characteristic of the following writings: Palmer, *Plain and Easy Catechism*, p. [3], an "Advertisement" written for those "who have in any way the charge of the hundreds of thousands of immortal souls in our region." Jones, *Religious Instruction of the Slaves. A Sermon*, p. 34, "Every owner of slaves has an account to render to God for his treatment of them [slaves]." Clay, *Detail of a Plan*, p. 22, for "those anxious to improve the moral condition of the negroes." Meade, *Pastoral Letter*, p. 23, "*A public sentiment on this subject has now begun its existence. It must become as universal as that on Temperance, or any other work of philanthrophy [sic] and Christian benevolence. It must live.*"

17. Freehling, *Prelude to Civil War*, p. 75. Meade, *Pastoral Letter*, p. 5. Bowen, *Pastoral Letter*, p. 6. Charles Colcock Jones to Mary Jones, 8 September 1829, Charles Colcock Jones Papers, Tulane University, quoted in Mathews, "Southern Clergy as a Strategic Elite, 1780–1870."

18. The best treatment of catechisms as used in the popular New England Primer is Ford, *The New-England Primer*, pp. 22, 43, 45. For a critical listing of New England catechisms from their beginnings to 1800, see Eames, "Early New England Catechisms," esp. pp. 170–71 and nn. 1–2.

19. Ford, *New England Primer*, pp. 6–7, 20, 23–26, 34–35, 44–45.

20. Ibid., pp. 80–85. Eames, "Early New England Catechisms," pp. 172–74. When the Episcopal Bishop of Ohio, Philander Chase, visited Alexander Glennie, pastor of hundreds of slaves at Waccamaw, S.C., in 1840, he was astounded

to find that Glennie catechised and taught slave children in the same manner as he himself had been taught the catechism during his childhood in Cornish, New Hampshire. Following one catechising session, Chase wrote, "After dinner the chapel bell rang for the colored children to attend catechism. There the Rev. Mr. Glennie, in the presence of all the white people, taught them in many questions from the catechism prepared by our Church for the colored people of South Carolina. Their answers, for correctness and promptitude, were far better than I expected. The black children of a South Carolina planter know more of Christianity than thousands of white children in Illinois!" Of one slave master and his family, Chase later wrote, "They are all pious people, and are instructing their colored people, as they should do. Of these they have several hundred. Mr. Weston [the master] himself teaches." See Norton, *Life of Bishop Gadsden,* pp. 100–7. A comparison of one of the popular New England catechisms of the early nineteenth century with one of the so-called catechisms for slaves reveals an extraordinary similarity of content. Both teach from the same scriptural authorities the student's heinousness of sin, the absolute severity of man's judgment by God, contentment with poverty and straitened circumstances, the equality of all men in the sight of God, absolute obedience to laws and superiors, strict observance of the ten commandments, proper respect for civil and social authority, the duty of hard work without the necessity of supervision, frugality with one's own and others' property, the necessity of punishment for wrongs, the religious nature of morality and social duties, admonitions against coveting and stealing, and the promise of rewards for faithfulness and virtue in heaven if not on earth—all teachings sometimes regarded as perversions of religion for the benefit of masters. Cf. Bowen, *Catechism to Be Used by the Teachers in the Religious Instruction of Persons of Colour,* pp. 8, 12, 14–15, 27, 53–54, 59–66, 71–72, 74, 78–79, 81ff., 94ff.; and *A Scripture Catechism . . . By a Clergyman of Massachusetts,* pp. 13, 17, 20–21, 26, 27–29, 32, 35, 36, 39, 41, 43–44, 45–50, 52, 53, 55, 56–60, 61–62, 64, 65–66, 68–69, 71–72, 74–78, 82–84, 88–90, 94, 102ff. It seems apparent that slaves were taught the same message through similar mechanisms used in the case of children who anywhere came under the influence of the conservative ideology of benevolence as it was disseminated by Congregationals, Presbyterians, Baptists, Methodists, and Episcopalians.

21. Iveson Brookes, "Commencement Address, Quer: Is the State of the World Better in the Present Age Than at Any Former Period?" 21 May 1819; Iveson Brookes to Thomas B. Slade, 20 March 1849, Iveson Brookes Papers, Southern Historical Collection, University of North Carolina.

22. Basil Manly, "On the Emancipation of Slaves," April 1821; also the manuscript notes of Basil Manly, Jr., "Fifty Years with Southern Baptists; or the Life and Times of Basil Manly, Senior," Basil Manly, Sr., Sermons and Papers, Furman University Library.

23. Hamilton, *A Word for the African,* p. 17. Henry B. Bascom, "Claims of Af-

rica; or an Address in Behalf of the American Colonization Society," in Ralston, *Posthumous Works of the Rev. Henry B. Bascom,* 2:249–90. John Hughes, "The Slave," reprinted in Hassard, *Life of John Hughes,* pp. 42–44. R. B. C. Howell, "Colonization, or the Conversion of Africa," 4 July 1833, Manuscript Notes to Sermons, Howell Family Papers.

24. See Mathews, *Slavery and Methodism,* pp. 45–46, 93, 94, 95, 97.

25. William Winans to R. R. Gurley, 20 June 1826; Winans to Messrs. Directors American Colonization Society, 30 March 1852, William Winans Papers.

26. Joshua L. Wilson to Jeremiah Morrow, Esqr., late Governor of the State of Ohio, ca. 1826, Wilson Family Papers. Wilson later became a vigorous supporter of colonization in the face of the alternative of abolition.

27. Basil Manly, Church Journal, 20, 25 December 1828; 3 August, 3 October 1829, Basil Manly, Sr., Sermons and Papers, Furman University.

28. Ibid., 21 March, 29 April, 20 December 1828; for the story of Lydie Frierson, 22 June 1829, with an appended note dated December 1833.

29. Several recent historians have carried this interpretation even further by indicating that southern evangelicals, hampered in dealing with slavery as an institution, chose to reform slavery by reforming each individual in slave society—slaveholder, slave, nonslaveholder. See Mathews, *Religion in the Old South,* pp. 137, 149, 180; Loveland, *Southern Evangelicals and the Social Order,* pp. 159–62. While that may have been the effect of their methods, the benevolent reformers in the South believed that institutions could be built by those reformed and devoted themselves to institutional development as well as individual preaching. James Essig, *Bonds of Wickedness,* pp. 35–40, carries the same interpretation back to the eighteenth century where it seems more appropriate.

Chapter Twelve

1. It can safely be said that none of the 275 clergymen who published defenses of slavery after the 1820s, except the anti-abolitionists already considered, paid any great attention to the rise of abolitionism, if their manuscript papers are an indication. Unless one of them happened to be a student in a northern school where abolitionists collided with latter-day conservatives, as in the cases of William C. Crane, Benjamin M. Palmer, Stuart Robinson, and Patrick H. Mell, there is no reference to abolition in their private papers before 1835. See William Carey Crane, Diary, 24, 26, 27, 29 July 1833, William Carey Crane Papers. Hickey, "Benjamin Morgan Palmer," pp. 12–15. Saunders, *Memorial upon the Life of Rev. Stuart Robinson,* pp. 19–20. Mell, *Life of Patrick Mell,* pp. 16–26.

2. The six newspapers, all nonpolitical weeklies, were located in North Carolina, Virginia, Pennsylvania, and Ohio, as follows: *Baptist Interpreter,* January 1833–December 1834 (Edenton and New Bern, N.C.) and *Biblical Recorder* (New

Bern, N.C.), January 1835–December 1837, both edited by Thomas Meredith, a native of Pennsylvania; *Christian Index and Baptist Miscellany* (also entitled *Columbian Star;* Philadelphia), January 1831–June 1833, edited by William T. Brantly, a native of North Carolina who had become closely associated with South Carolina; *Southern Baptist and General Intelligencer* (Charleston, S.C.), January 1835–June 1836, edited by William H. Brisbane of South Carolina, afterward an abolitionist; *Southern Christian Herald* (Columbia, S.C.), March 1834–March 1839, edited by Richard S. Gladney, a South Carolinian; *The Standard* (Cincinnati, Ohio), January–December 1835, edited by Joshua L. Wilson, a Virginian who spent his early years in Kentucky and who was concerned with the problem of slavery by the mid-1820s; *Visitor & Telegraph* (Richmond, Va.), February 1833–December 1835, edited by Amasa Converse, a native of New Hampshire.

3. For the extensive publication of such material, see, for example, the *Christian Index*, 19 March 1831, p. 192; 26 March 1831, pp. 196, 197, 207; 9 April 1831, p. 238; 24 December 1831, pp. 410–11; 23 February 1833, pp. 113f.; 29 June 1833, pp. 408–9. See also, *Visitor & Telegraph*, 15 March 1833, p. 42; 5 July 1833, p. 106; 16 August 1833, p. 130; 14 March 1834, p. 43; 25 April 1834, p. 66; 9 May 1834, p. 76; 30 May 1834, p. 88; 20 June 1834, pp. 97, 100; 18 July 1834, p. 115; 18 August 1834, p. 126; 15 [*sic*, 25] August 1834, pp. 130, 132; 26 September 1834, pp. 154, 156.

4. *Christian Index*, 19 March 1831, p. 192. *Baptist Interpreter*, 4 October 1834, pp. 233–34. For similar expressions of continuing antislavery sentiment, see the following: *Visitor & Telegraph*, 13 February 1833, p. 26, where Amasa Converse asserted that Virginians were increasingly detesting slavery because it "paralized [*sic*] the arm of industry, repressed the energies of the spirit of enterprise, retarded the progress of intellectual and moral improvement, enervated all classes, [and] impeded the growth of this fair portion of our country." *Southern Baptist and General Intelligencer*, 7 August 1835, pp. 89–90, where William Brisbane indicated that he had offered his slaves their freedom and encouraged other slaveholders to follow suit.

5. *Christian Index*, 3 September 1831, p. 154; 1 October 1831, p. 220; 15 October 1831, pp. 249–50.

6. Ibid., 11 February 1832, p. 90. *Visitor & Telegraph*, 13 February 1832, p. 26. *Baptist Interpreter*, 17 January 1833, pp. 20–21.

7. William Brantly, editor of the *Christian Index*, pastor of churches in Beaufort, S.C., and Augusta, Ga., from 1811 to 1826 before coming to Philadelphia, was the lone exception among the editors. See *Christian Index*, 5 January 1833, pp. 1–2; 12 January 1833, p. 28; 26 January 1833, p. 64; 2 February 1833, p. 78; 16 February 1833, pp. 99–101. Because of his support for nullification, and not his defense of slavery as is sometimes assumed (he had not yet written a defense of slavery), Brantly was forced in June 1833 to remove the *Christian Index* from

Philadelphia to Georgia, giving up its editorship in the process. He himself remained in Philadelphia as pastor of the First Baptist Church until 1837. See ibid., 29 June 1833, p. 416. For the alternate view, see Stroupe, *Religious Press in the South Atlantic States*, pp. 13–14, 59. For antinullification views, see *Baptist Interpreter*, 17 January 1833, pp. 20–21; *Visitor & Telegraph*, 13 February 1833, p. 27; 5 July 1833, p. 106. Of the 275 clergymen studied, only three are known to have supported nullification, while hosts of others proved themselves staunch enemies of the nullifiers. The supporters, in addition to Brantly, were Augustus B. Longstreet (see Wade, *Augustus Baldwin Longstreet*, pp. 121–32) and Iveson Brookes. To forward his views Longstreet founded a nullification newspaper at Augusta, Ga., called the *State Rights Sentinel* (January 1834–July 1836). Brookes was made a Minuteman by the governor of South Carolina. See Iveson Brookes to Virgil H. Walker, 24 January 1833, Iveson Brookes Papers, Duke University. For typical antinullifiers in 1833, see the stances of Basil Manly (Boyce, *Life and Death the Christian's Portion*, p. 47), William G. Brownlow (Coulter, *William G. Brownlow*, p. 24), and John Bachman (Bachman, *John Bachman*, p. 75).

8. *Baptist Interpreter*, August 1833, pp. 176–77; 4 October 1834, pp. 233–34. For other similar comments on the work of anti-abolitionists and remarks about mobocracy, see *Southern Baptist and General Intelligencer*, 25 September 1835, pp. 199–203; 30 October 1835, pp. 284, 285. *Standard*, 19 November 1835, p. 214.

9. *Southern Christian Herald*, 11 July 1834, pp. 216–27. In the last issue of the *Herald* under his editorship in March 1836, Gladney tried to avenge himself for the scorn he had received in 1834: "Even those that accused us of exaggeration, following after us, are compelled to admit what was then denied" (20 March 1836, p. 3). For opposition from several papers to Gladney's early views, see the *Visitor & Telegraph*, 18 July 1834, p. 114; 13 [*sic*, 25] August 1834, p. 129. It is interesting in this connection that although William Freehling saw nullification as a double response to protective tariffs and slavery agitation, he did not adduce sources that related the economic crisis of South Carolina to a growing perception of threats by abolitionists. Although the constitutional issues of nullification were portentous for continued state control over slaves as the nullifiers contended, they did not in any sense perceive abolitionists as the enemies in their struggle. See Freehling, *Prelude to Civil War*, pp. 255–59. In fact, if one carefully scrutinizes Freehling's sources for the "Great Reaction," which focused on abolitionists, it can be seen that South Carolina's criticism of abolitionism as opposed to the power of the federal government came in every case *after* July 1835. In addition, when Freehling quotes pre-1835 statements as indications of anti-abolitionist sentiments, he adds in the word *abolitionist*, a term that does not seem to have appeared in the writings and speeches of nullifiers before 1835. See, for example, the McDuffie statement at the Nullification Convention in March 1833 (ibid., p. 322), and that of Duff Green in January 1833 (ibid., p. 328). On the basis

of such intermixing of nullifying and anti-abolitionist sources, one might conclude that the so-called Great Reaction of South Carolina to abolitionism occurred after July 1835, the same time as that of the rest of the nation.

10. To prove later that he was not an abolitionist, Brisbane reprinted the 1834
essay in the *Southern Baptist and General Intelligencer,* 17 April 1835, pp. 247–49.

11. Ibid., 20 February 1835, p. 121; 13 March 1835, pp. 169–70; 22 May
1835, pp. 328–29.

12. Ibid., 10 July 1835, p. 18. William Brisbane, Diary, 8, 14, 17, 18 July 1835,
Brisbane Papers. Even after the awakening, however, on 18 July Brisbane could
write, "I am no Abolitionist."

13. *Southern Baptist and General Intelligencer,* 7 August 1835, pp. 89–90.

14. Both in his diary and in the *Southern Baptist* Brisbane recorded the problems that his conversion to antislavery caused him. Most of his family and friends
thought him deluded, although he found both encouragement and sympathy
from a surprising number of individuals. While he was never threatened by
anyone, he was generally snubbed by old friends and acquaintances. He seems to
have recanted his intentions to free his slaves and in the *Southern Baptist* returned
to rather profuse defenses of slavery. By April 1836, he found himself in financial difficulty and had to sell five of his slaves for $2,000. Not as a result of
proslavery pressure, but because of the loss of time and his own money, Brisbane
resigned from the editorship of the paper in April 1836. Still bothered by slavery
the following June, Brisbane traveled to Providence where he spent a few days
with Wayland. Writing as if he no longer opposed slavery, Brisbane confided to
his diary, "We are very much pleased with this worthy man, notwithstanding our
difference of opinion on the subject of slavery." Though he had taken up the
study of medicine in Charleston, as a new profession, his absence from the plantation and impulsive waste of money caused his financial woes to increase. By
December 1837, he was beset by financial crisis so that he had to find remunera-
tive work immediately or lose the remainder of his inherited fortune. In January
1838, having failed to secure a stable income in South Carolina, Brisbane sold
the rest of his property—both land and slaves—reserving one slave family "to
wait upon us." In February he, his family, and the remaining slaves moved to
Cincinnati. In Cincinnati Brisbane frittered away the rest of his fortune. Never
able to secure a continuing and secure income, he leaped from one scheme to
another losing money with each venture. Nearly penniless, in January 1840,
Brisbane decided to become an abolitionist and seek income from speaking tours
in behalf of abolition. Despite continuing financial straits, by December 1841
Brisbane succeeded in buying back and emancipating all but three of his former
slaves. See William Brisbane, Diary, 23 August 1835–19 December 1841, passim,
William Henry Brisbane Papers. Brisbane's record of antislavery statements, attacks on abolition, defenses of slavery, and troubles with proslavery people—on

a public level—may be followed in the *Southern Baptist and General Intelligencer,* 21 August 1835, pp. 119–20; 4 September 1835, pp. 152–53; 11 September 1835, pp. 168–69; 18 September 1835, pp. 179–81 (consisting of Brisbane's defense against Wayland's views which had been responsible for his original conversion); 25 September 1835, pp. 196, 199–203 (the speech of Harrison Gray Otis at Faneuil Hall with appropriate comments); 2 October 1835, p. 240; 30 October 1835, pp. 274, 284, 285; 6 November 1835, p. 290; 13 November 1835, p. 314.

15. This is the way Brisbane described his position and subsequent activity in one of the first of his speeches as an abolitionist in 1840. See Brisbane, *Speech of the Rev. Wm. H. Brisbane,* pp. 3–8.

16. Seabrook, *Essay on the Management of Slaves,* pp. 3–24, passim, with Seabrook's own limited plan of religious instruction on pp. 25–26.

17. [Seabrook], *Appeal to the People of the Northern and Eastern States,* p. 3. Sims, *A View of Slavery.*

18. [Seabrook], *Appeal to the People of the Northern and Eastern States,* pp. 3–23, passim.

19. Ibid., pp. 20–21.

20. Iveson Brookes to Sarah J. Brookes, 25 February 1836, Iveson Brookes Papers, Duke University.

21. See examples cited by Richards, *Gentlemen of Property and Standing,* pp. 16–17, 55–58.

22. Bellinger, *Speech on the Subject of Slavery,* pp. 12–15, 25–27, 32–33, 35.

23. [Rice], *Vindex: On the Liability of the Abolitionists to Criminal Punishment,* pp. 3, 15, 26–27.

24. Flournoy, *Essay on the Origin, Habits, &c. of the African Race.* For Flournoy's other writings and a sympathetic portrayal of his strange life, see Coulter, *John Jacobus Flournoy,* esp. pp. 102–4.

Chapter Thirteen

1. These figures are based on the number of books or pamphlets, not newspaper writings, that have been gleaned from known sources. There are doubtless others not yet discovered.

2. Farley, *Slavery; a Discourse in the Unitarian Church.* Robbins, "Charles A. Farley, Messenger of Liberalism," pp. 1–12. Fisk, *The Bulwark of Freedom.* Notes in Universalist Register, Universalist Historical Society, Tufts University.

3. *Biographical Souvenir of the States of Georgia and Florida* (Chicago: F. A. Battey & Company, 1889), p. 412. Whitaker, *Reflections on Domestic Slavery,* reprinted from the *Southern Literary Journal and Monthly Magazine* 2 (July 1836): 375–92, esp. 376 [misnumbered 276].

4. Freeman, *Rights and Duties of Slaveholders,* esp. pp. 5–20. Bailey, *The Issue, Presented in a Series of Letters on Slavery,* pp. 3, 10. Bailey, *The Family Preacher,* pp. 119–58.

5. The newspaper texts of Winans's anti-abolition essays, which were published in a wide variety of places between December 1835 and 1857 were collected in a Scrapbook of Newspaper Clippings, William Winans Papers, Millsaps College. Clapp, *Slavery,* esp. pp. 3–6, 35–38, 60–67. Clapp soon became a Unitarian and was merely one of a number of transplanted Unitarians living in the South who defended slavery. See Stange, "Abolitionism as Maleficence," pp. 146–71.

6. James Smylie, Biographical File, Presbyterian Historical Foundation, Montreat, N.C. Salley, "Captain William Capers and Some of His Descendants," 2:283. Baxter's primary teachers Smith and Graham, of course, both taught proslavery principles along with conservatism at the turn of the century. See Robson, "Important Question Answered: William Graham's Defense of Slavery," pp. 644–52.

7. Baxter, *Essay on the Abolition of Slavery,* pp. 5–6, 16, 18–23.

8. Smylie, *Review of a Letter from the Presbytery of Chillicothe,* pp. 3–5, 12–16, 69–74.

9. [Capers], *Bondage a Moral Institution,* esp. pp. 18, 23–31, 62–63.

10. Bowen, *Pastoral Letter on the Religious Instruction of the Slaves,* p. 9.

11. Ibid., pp. 14, 21–24. Bowen, *Catechism to Be Used by Teachers in the Religious Instruction of Persons of Colour,* esp. pp. 14–17.

12. All of these were common concerns of Jones and other benevolent reformers before 1835.

13. Association for the Religious Instruction of Slaves in Liberty County, Georgia, *Third Annual Report,* pp. 18–19.

14. Ibid., *Sixth Annual Report* through *Thirteenth Annual Report,* passim, and *Seventh Annual Report,* p. 22.

15. See Freehling, *Prelude to Civil War,* passim, and p. 327.

16. Bellinger, *Speech on the Subject of Slavery,* pp. 39–40.

17. There are doubtless others whose writings could have been included in this list if other yardsticks were used. However, Harper, Pinckney, Rhett, and Hammond are the sectionalists most often mentioned by historians as having fostered southern proslavery thought. Pinckney, as explained below, decided to abandon his own sectional witness.

18. See the openly political pamphlets as follows: Henry L. Pinckney, *Remarks on the Resolution Offered by Him Relative to the Abolition of Slavery.* Henry L. Pinckney, *Address to the Electors of Charleston District.* Pinckney was defeated for reelection to Congress in the fall of 1836 as a result of his compromise measures.

19. Henry L. Pinckney, *"Spirit of the Age,"* pp. 9, 14, 25–26.

20. Ibid., pp. 26–30.

21. For Pinckney's radical nullification views and his efforts to compromise the combatants in the gag-rule debate, see Freehling, *Prelude to Civil War,* pp. 255–56, 351–55.

22. William Harper, *Anniversary Oration, Dec. 9, 1835,* pp. 6–7.

23. Ibid., pp. 7, 9–11.

24. Ibid., pp. 14–17. Southerners and southern proslavery writers had rarely used Burke in their writings on slavery. Perhaps the first reference to Burke in a defense of slavery by a southerner (there were constant references to him in those of anti-abolitionists) was a brief mention by Thomas R. Dew of Burke's famous statement that slavery in the southern United States fostered republicanism and liberty. Whereas Dew merely mentioned the statement in passing, Harper based his entire view of slavery upon it. See Dew, "Review of the Debate in the Virginia Legislature," in *Pro-slavery Argument,* pp. 461–62.

25. [Wakefield], *England and America.* Although Wakefield proposed the ultimate removal of slavery from America, his volume was filled with reflections and information which, to Harper's mind, proved the inferiority of English free society to the slave society of the South. Harper, "Memoir on Slavery," in *Pro-slavery Argument,* pp. 2–4, 19.

26. Harper, "Memoir on Slavery," in *Pro-slavery Argument,* pp. 18–19, 25–26, 28, 35, 51.

27. Ibid., pp. 58–59, 77.

28. Ibid., p. 71, but the principles here enunciated run throughout Harper's *Memoir.*

29. Rhett, *Address to the People of Beaufort and Colleton Districts, upon the Subject of Abolition, January 15, 1838,* pp. 5–7. There Rhett claimed exaggeratedly that all Americans outside the South "are abolitionists in principle and feeling." Yet, even Rhett had learned to use the rhetoric, if he could not adopt the perspective, of ideologized anti-abolitionism, as indicated by his comments on abolitionism: "Born in atheism, and baptized in the blood of revolutionary France, it accomplished its purpose there. In England, it has sprung up under the guise of religion, and it has accomplished its purpose there. It has never yet failed, and never will fail, in accomplishing its purpose, *where the slave-holder does not control his own destinies.* It is now flaming in the United States, and extending its number with a rapidity far surpassing the operation of the gospel itself, in bringing converts to its cause" (ibid., pp. 6–7). He also learned to speak of republicanism in the vein of Burke: *"Let it be remembered, that no republic has yet been long maintained without the institution of slavery"* (ibid., p. 9).

30. [William Drayton], *The South Vindicated from the Treason and Fanaticism of the Northern Abolitionists.* It is by no means certain that Drayton or any other southerner wrote this volume often cited as a peculiarly clear statement of southern

anti-abolitionism. For example, in the introduction there is a personal reference to the author that reads, "We do not, at the North, claim a right so to discuss this subject as to disturb or agitate the South" (p. xvii).

31. Ibid., particularly the author's chapters on slavery and civilization and on the character and policy of abolitionists, pp. 100–122, 150–56, 157–71, 172–88.

32. Simms, "Miss Martineau on Slavery," pp. 641–46, passim, 647, 652–53.

33. Ibid., pp. 654, 656–57.

34. See Simms, "The Morals of Slavery," in *Pro-slavery Argument*, pp. 175–80.

Chapter Fourteen

1. The extent to which conservative principles became attached to proslavery and vice versa can be gauged by reference to the extensive anti-abolitionist and proslavery writings in America from the 1830s through the Civil War. For an analysis of the conservative ideological content of such writings, see Tise, "Proslavery Ideology," pp. 634–38, 655–69 and the accompanying charts and tables.

2. Winslow, *Means of the Perpetuity and Prosperity of Our Republic*. For the background of the oration, see p. [3].

3. Ibid., pp. 5–7.

4. Ibid., pp. 8–9.

5. Ibid., pp. 9–11.

6. Ibid., pp. 11–12.

7. Ibid., pp. 12–16.

8. Ibid., pp. 16–17.

9. Ibid., pp. 17–18.

10. Ibid., pp. 19–22.

11. Ibid., pp. 22–26.

12. Ibid., pp. 31–35.

13. Ibid., pp. 44–48.

14. Ibid., pp. 35–40.

15. Ibid., pp. 40–43.

16. Ibid., pp. 17 n., 41 and n. (41–44).

BIBLIOGRAPHY

In a study like the foregoing, it is not possible to list all works consulted. Considerations of length make it unwise even to list all sources cited (for example, all sources of biographical information for the 275 individuals in the biographical profile). The present listing includes those works that influenced interpretation or provided crucial documentation. Those essential to the argument analysis in chapter 5 are included and noted as well. Since the study depended on three distinct types of sources, the bibliography is divided into three major sections with appropriate subdivisions as follows:

Primary Sources
    Manuscripts
    Official and Governmental Records
    Periodicals
    American Proslavery Literature
    Non-American Proslavery Literature
    Other Printed Sources
Biographical Sources
    Biographical Reference Works
    Biographies, Autobiographies, and Biographical Studies
Secondary Sources
    Articles
    Unpublished Studies
    Books

Further explanation of the contents of each major section and their subdivisions is provided with explanatory notes where needed, at the beginning of each division.

Primary Sources

Manuscripts

Papers which provided crucial interpretive insights or extensive documentation have been included. Those which proved most helpful in understanding the social history of proslavery are marked with an asterisk (*).

American Jewish Archives. Cincinnati.
  James Koppel Gutheim Papers.
  *Maximilian J. Michelbacher Papers.
  Morris Jacob Raphall Correspondence.
American Jewish Historical Society. Waltham, Mass.
  *Isaac Leeser Papers.
Andover-Newton Theological Seminary. Andover, Mass.
  *Moses Stuart Papers.
Baylor University. Texas Collection. Waco, Texas.
  William Carey Crane Papers.
Columbia University. Library. New York, N.Y.
  *William Wilberforce Lord Papers.
  Mitchel Family Papers.
Congregational Library. Boston.
  Charles Turner Torrey Papers.
Dartmouth College. Archives. Hanover, N.H.
  *Nathan Lord Papers.
Duke University. Perkins Library. Durham, N.C.
  *Iveson Brookes Papers.
  Eugene R. Hendrix Papers.
  *George F. Holmes Letterbook.
  *James Warley Miles Papers.
  *James B. and George Junkin Ramsey Papers.
  Whitefoord Smith Papers.
Emory University. Library. Atlanta, Ga.
  Methodist Leaders Papers.
Essex Institute. Salem, Mass.
  Adams Family Papers.
Filson Club Library. Louisville, Ky.
  Robert J. Breckinridge Papers.
  William Calmes Buck Papers.
Furman University. Library. Greenville, S.C.
  *Richard Furman Correspondence.
  *Manly Family Correspondence.
  *Basil Manly, Sr., Sermons and Papers.
General Theological Seminary. New York, N.Y.
  *Samuel Seabury Papers.
Harvard University. Archives. Boston.
  Theodore Parsons Diary.
  John Langdon Sibley Collections.
Historical Foundation of the Presbyterian and Reformed Churches. Montreat,
  N.C.

Rufus William Bailey Papers.
*Biographical Files.
Benjamin Morgan Palmer Papers.
Stuart Robinson Scrapbooks.
*Henry Ruffner Papers.
Joint University Libraries. Nashville, Tenn.
John James Tigert Papers.
Knoxville Public Library. McClung Collection. Knoxville, Tenn.
*T. A. R. Nelson Papers.
Frederick A. Ross Scrapbooks.
Library of Congress. Manuscript Division. Washington, D.C.
*Samuel John Baird Papers.
William Dawson Papers.
*Samuel F. B. Morse Papers.
Thomas DeWitt Talmage Papers.
Methodist Publishing House. Library. Nashville, Tenn.
Henry Biddleman Bascom Letters.
Millsaps College. Library. Jackson, Miss.
*William Winans Papers.
Mississippi Department of Archives and History. Jackson, Miss.
*James A. Lyon Diary.
New York Public Library. New York, N.Y.
Jane Vernor Mitchel Letters.
North Carolina Division of Archives and History. Raleigh, N.C.
Calvin Henderson Wiley Papers.
Rutgers University. Library. New Brunswick, N.J.
Anthony Benezet Marginal Annotations in Thomas Thompson, *African Trade for Negro Slaves.*
*How Family Papers.
South Carolina Historical Society. Charleston, S.C.
James Adger Papers.
Bowen-Cooke Papers.
Brisbane Family Notes.
Family Account Books.
Miscellaneous Manuscripts.
New England Society of Charleston Records.
State Historical Society of Wisconsin. Madison, Wis.
*William Henry Brisbane Papers.
Tennessee State Library and Archives. Nashville, Tenn.
William G. Brownlow Papers.
*Howell Family Papers.
Morton Boyte Howell Family Papers.

Trinity College. Archives. Hartford, Conn.
 *Nathaniel S. Wheaton Papers.
Union Theological Seminary. Richmond, Va.
 George Dodd Armstrong Scrapbook.
 *Robert L. Dabney Papers.
 *Moses Drury Hoge Letters.
 Drury Lacy Papers.
Universalist Historical Society. Medford, Mass.
 Universalist Register.
University of Alabama. Library. Tuscaloosa, Ala.
 *Iveson L. Brookes Papers.
 *Manly Family Papers.
University of Georgia. Library. Athens, Ga.
 Howell Cobb Papers.
 *Charles Colcock Jones Papers.
 Andrew Agate Lipscomb Papers.
 Patrick Hues Mell Papers.
University of Kentucky. Library. Lexington, Ky.
 *Wilson Family Papers.
University of North Carolina. Southern Historical Collection. Chapel Hill,
 N.C.
 *Iveson L. Brookes Papers.
 *Moses Ashley Curtis Papers.
 *Dabney Family Papers.
 Edward Dromgoole Papers.
 Mangum Family Papers.
 *Elisha Mitchell Papers.
 *John Paris Papers.
 Margaret Junkin Preston Papers.
 *Calvin Henderson Wiley Papers.
University of South Carolina. South Caroliniana Library. Columbia, S.C.
 *Iveson L. Brookes Papers.
 Charles W. Hutson Papers.
 Augustus Baldwin Longstreet Papers.
 Pinckney Family Papers.
 *James Henley Thornwell Papers.
University of Virginia. Alderman Library. Charlottesville, Va.
 *Dabney Family Papers.
 George Junkin Letters.
Washington and Lee University. Library. Lexington, Va.
 *George A. Baxter Papers.

Official and Governmental Records

Association for the Religious Instruction of the Negroes in Liberty County, Georgia. Annual Reports, 1835–1848.
Charleston Baptist Association. Minutes, 1775–1845.
Society for the Diffusion of Political Knowledge. Papers, 1863–1864.
United States Bureau of the Census. Manuscript Census Reports, 1790–1860.

Periodicals

African Repository, and Colonial Journal, 1825–1826. Washington, D.C.
American Israelite, 1854–1856. Cincinnati.
Baptist Banner & Western Pioneer, 1834–1836. Louisville, Ky.
Baptist Interpreter, 1833–1834. Edenton and New Bern, N.C.
Biblical Recorder, 1835–1837. New Bern, N.C.
Christian Index and Baptist Miscellany, 1831–1833. Philadelphia, Pa.
Edinburgh Review, 1810–1820. Edinburgh.
The National Crisis, 1860. Washington, D.C.
National Intelligencer, 1819. Washington, D.C.
Patriarch, or Family Library Magazine, 1841–1842. New York, N.Y.
Presbyterial Critic & Monthly Review, 1855–1856. Baltimore, Md.
Southern Baptist and General Intelligencer, 1835–1836. Charleston, S.C.
Southern Christian Herald, 1834–1836. Columbia, S.C.
Southern Intelligencer, 1822. Charleston, S.C.
The Standard, 1835. Cincinnati, Ohio.
Visitor & Telegraph, 1833–1835. Richmond, Va.

American Proslavery Literature

Included in the following are all forms of proslavery literature (anti-abolitionist writings, formal defenses, literature for slaves, crisis and war sermons). All known defenses are included up to 1840. After 1840, only the most important for understanding proslavery history are included. Those used in the argument analysis of chapter 5 are marked with an asterisk (*).

Adams, Nehemiah. *A South-side View of Slavery; or Three Months at the South, in 1854*. Boston: T. R. Marvin, 1854.
———. *The Sable Cloud: A Southern Tale, with Northern Comments*. Boston: Ticknor and Fields, 1861.
Adger, John B. *The Christian Doctrine of Human Rights and of Slavery, in Two Articles, from the "Southern Presbyterian Review" for March, MDCCCXLIX*. Columbia, S.C.: I. C. Morgan, 1849.

———. *The Religious Instruction of the Colored Population. A Sermon Preached by the Rev. John B. Adger, in the Second Presbyterian Church, Charleston, S.C., May 9, 1847.* Charleston: T. W. Hayes, 1847.

American, An. *Letter to the Edinburgh Reviewers: by "An American." First Published in the "National Intelligencer" of November 16, 1819.* N.p.: 1819.

American Society for Promoting National Unity. Society Rooms: Bible House, Astor Place, New York. New York: John F. Trow, Printer, 1861.

Anderson, Samuel James Pierce. *The Dangers and Duties of the Present Crisis: A Discourse Delivered in the Union Church, St. Louis, Mo., Jan. 4, 1861.* St. Louis: Schenck & Co., 1861.

Andrew, James Osgood. *Family Government. A Treatise on Conjugal, Parental, Filial and Other Duties.* 3d ed. Richmond, Va.: John Early, 1852.

Armstrong, George Dodd. *The Christian Doctrine of Slavery.* New York: Charles Scribner, 1857.

———. *A Discussion on Slaveholding. Three Letters to a Conservative.* Philadelphia: Joseph M. Wilson, 1858.

———. *Politics and the Pulpit: A Discourse Preached in the Presbyterian Church, Norfolk, Va., on Thursday, November 27, 1856.* Norfolk, Va.: J. D. Ghiselin, Jr., 1856.

Atkinson, Thomas. "The Unity of the Races." *North Carolina University Magazine* 7 (April 1858): 349–69.

Austin, James Trecothick. *Remarks on Dr. Channing's Slavery. By a Citizen of Massachusetts.* Boston: Russell, Shattuck and Co., and John H. Eastburn, 1835.

Bachman, John. *A Notice of the "Types of Mankind," with an Examination of the Charges Contained in the Biography of Dr. Morton, Published by Nott and Gliddon.* Charleston: James, Williams and Gitsinger, 1854.

———. *An Examination of Professor Agassiz's Sketch of the Natural Provinces of the Animal World and Their Relation to the Different Types of Man.* Charleston: James, Williams and Gitsinger, 1855.

———. *The Doctrine of the Unity of the Human Race—Examined on the Principles of Science.* Charleston: C. Canning, 1850.

———. *Unity of the Human Race. A Refutation of the Theory of Dr. Morton, Professor Agassiz, and Dr. Nott, on the Characteristics of Genera and Species.* Nashville: A. H. Redford, 1857.

Bacon, Leonard. *Slavery Discussed in Occasional Essays from 1833–1846.* New York: Baker and Scribner, 1846.

Bacon, Thomas. *Four Sermons, Preached at the Parish Church of St. Peter, in Talbot County, in the Province of Maryland, by the Rev. Thomas Bacon, Rector of the Said Parish. Two Sermons to Black Slaves, and Two Sermons for the Benefit of a Charity Working-School, in the above Parish, for the Maintenance and Education of Orphans and Poor Children, and Negroes.* London: Printed by John Oliver, 1753.

*———. Four Sermons upon the Great Indispensable Duty of All Christian Masters and

Mistresses to Bring up Their Negro Slaves in the Knowledge and Fear of God. London: Printed by J. Oliver, 1750.

————. *Sermons Addressed to Masters and Servants, and Published in the Year 1743* [*sic*—1753?], *by the Rev. Thomas Bacon, Minister of the Protestant Episcopal Church in Maryland. Now Republished with Other Tracts and Dialogues on the Same Subject, and Recommended to All Masters and Mistresses To Be Used in Their Families by the Rev. William Meade*. Winchester, Va.: John Heiskell, [1813].

————. *Sermons by the Rev. Thomas Bacon, of Maryland, First Published in 1763, on the Duties of Servants. Reprinted for the "Society for the Advancement of Christianity in South-Carolina."* 2d ed. N.p.: [ca. 1830].

————. *Six Sermons on the Several Duties of Masters, Mistresses, Slaves, etc. Preached at the Parish Church of St. Peter, in Talbot County in the Province of Maryland*. London: Printed by J. Oliver; and Sold by B. Dod, Bookseller to the Society for Promoting Christian Knowledge, 1751.

————. *Two Sermons Preached to a Congregation of Black Slaves, at the Parish Church of St. Peter in the Province of Maryland*. London: n.p., 1749.

————. *Two Sermons, Preached to a Congregation of Black Slaves, at the Parish Church of S.P. in the Province of Maryland*. London: Printed by John Rivington, Jun., for John Francis, and Charles Rivington, 1782.

Bailey, Rufus William. *The Family Preacher; or, Domestic Duties Illustrated and Enforced in Eight Discourses*. New York: John S. Taylor, 1837.

————. *The Issue, Presented in a Series of Letters on Slavery.* New York: John S. Taylor, 1837.

Baird, Samuel John. *Southern Rights and Northern Duties in the Present Crisis. A Letter to Hon. William Pennington*. Philadelphia: Lindsay & Blakiston; Smith, English & Co. and Other Booksellers, 1861.

Baldwin, Samuel Davies. *Dominion; or, the Unity and Trinity of the Human Race; with the Divine Political Constitution of the World, and the Divine Rights of Shem, Ham, and Japheth*. Nashville: E. Stevenson & F. A. Owen, 1858.

Barnwell, William Hazzard. *The Divine Government. A Sermon, for the Day of Thanksgiving, Humiliation & Prayer, Appointed by the Governor of South-Carolina, November 21, 1851*. Charleston: Edward C. Councell, 1851.

————. *Views Upon the Present Crisis: A Discourse Delivered in St. Peter's Church, Charleston, on the 6th of December, 1850, the Day of Fasting, Humiliation, and Prayer*. Charleston: Letter-Press of E. C. Councell, 1850.

Bascom, Henry Biddleman. *Methodism and Slavery: with Other Matters in Controversy Between the North and the South; Being a Review of the Manifesto of the Majority, in Reply to the Protest of the Minority, of the Late General Conference of the Methodist E. Church, in the Case of Bishop Andrew*. Frankfort, Ky.: Hodges, Todd & Pruett, 1845.

*Baxter, George Addison. *An Essay on the Abolition of Slavery.* Richmond, Va.: T. W. White, 1836.

Bellinger, Edmund, Jr. *A Speech on the Subject of Slavery; Delivered 7th of September, 1835, at a Public Meeting of the Citizens of Barnwell District, South Carolina.* Charleston: Dan J. Dowling, 1835.

Berry, Philip. *A Review of the Bishop of Oxford's Counsel to the American Clergy, with Reference to the Institution of Slavery.* Washington, D.C.: William A. Morrison, 1848.

*Blagden, George Washington. *The Principles on Which a Preacher of the Gospel Should Condemn Sin: With Some Reference to Existing Evils.* Boston: Crocker & Brewster, 1837.

*———. *Remarks, and a Discourse on Slavery.* Boston: Ticknor, Reed, and Fields, 1854.

Bledsoe, Albert Taylor. *An Essay on Liberty and Slavery.* Philadelphia: J. B. Lippincott & Co., 1856.

*Boucher, Jonathan. *Causes and Consequences of the American Revolution; in Thirteen Discourses Preached in North America between the Years of 1763 and 1775.* London: G. G. and J. Robinson, 1797.

Bowen, Nathaniel, ed. *A Catechism to Be Used by the Teachers in the Religious Instruction of Persons of Colour.* Charleston: A. E. Miller, 1837.

———. *A Pastoral Letter, on the Religious Instruction of the Slaves of Members of the Protestant Episcopal Church in the State of South Carolina, Prepared at the Request of the Convention of Churches of the Diocese.* Charleston: A. E. Miller, 1835.

Boyden, Ebenezer. *The Epidemic of the Nineteenth Century.* Richmond, Va.: Chas. H. Wynne, 1860.

*Brookes, Iveson Lewis. *A Defense of the South Against the Reproaches and Incroachments of the North: In which Slavery Is Shown to Be an Institution of God Intended to Form the Basis of the Best Social State and the Only Safeguard to the Permanence of a Republican Government.* Hamburg, S.C.: Republican Office, 1850.

———. *A Defence of Southern Slavery Against the Attacks of Henry Clay and Alexander Campbell. In Which Much of the False Philanthropy and Mawkish Sentimentalism of the Abolitionists Is Met and Refuted.* Hamburg, S.C.: Robinson and Carlisle, 1851.

[Brown, David]. *The Planter: Or Thirteen Years in the South. By a Northern Man.* Philadelphia: H. Hooker, 1853.

*Brown, Edward. *Notes on the Origin and Necessity of Slavery.* Charleston: A. E. Miller, 1826.

*Brownlow, William Gannaway. *A Sermon on Slavery; a Vindication of the Methodist Church, South: Her Position Stated. Delivered in Temperance Hall, in Knoxville, on Sabbath, August 9th, 1857, to the Delegates and Others in Attendance at the Southern Commercial Convention.* Knoxville, Tenn.: Kinsloe & Rice, 1857.

Brownlow, William Gannaway, and Pryne, A. *Ought American Slavery to Be Perpetuated? A Debate between Rev. W. G. Brownlow and Rev. A. Pryne. Held at Philadelphia, September, 1858.* Philadelphia: J. B. Lippincott & Co., 1858.

*Buck, William Calmes. *The Slavery Question*. Louisville, Ky.: Harney, Hughes & Hughes, 1849.

[Capers, Gabriel]. *Bondage a Moral Institution, Sanctioned by the Scriptures of the Old and New Testaments, and the Preaching and Practice of the Saviour and His Apostles*. Macon, Ga.: Griffin & Purse, 1837.

Capers, William. *A Catechism, for the Use of the Methodist Missionaries in Their Godly Work of Instructing the Negroes*. Charleston: B. B. Hussey, 1836.

*Clapp, Theodore. *Slavery: A Sermon, Delivered in the First Congregational Church in New Orleans, April 15, 1838*. New Orleans: John Gibson, 1838.

Clay, Thomas S. *Detail of a Plan for the Moral Improvement of Negroes on Plantations. Read Before the Georgia Presbytery*. N.p.: Printed at the Request of the Presbytery, 1833.

*Clough, Simon. *A Candid Appeal to the Citizens of the United States, Proving That the Doctrines Advanced and the Measures Pursued by the Abolitionists, Relative to the Subject of Emancipation, Are Inconsistent with the Teachings and Directions of the Bible, and That Those Clergymen Engaged in the Dissemination of These Principles Should Be Immediately Dismissed by Their Respective Congregations, as False Teachers*. New York: A. K. Bertron, 1834.

Cobb, Howell. *A Scriptural Examination of the Institution of Slavery in the United States; with Its Objects and Purposes*. [Perry, Ga.]: Printed for the Author, 1856.

Coit, John Calkins. *An Address Delivered to the Freemen of Chesterfield District, on Tuesday, Second Day of Court Week, March, 1851*. Columbia, S.C.: From the Steam-Power Press of I. C. Morgan, 1851.

———. *A Discourse Upon Governments Divine and Human, Prepared by Appointment of the Presbytery of Harmony, and Delivered before That Body During its Sessions in Indiantown Church, Williamsburg District, S.C., April, 1853*. Columbia: T. F. Greneker, 1853.

Colfax, Richard H. *Evidence against the Views of the Abolitionists, Consisting of Physical and Moral Proofs of the Natural Inferiority of Negroes*. New York: James T. M. Bleakley, 1833.

[Colton, Calvin]. *Abolition a Sedition. By a Northern Man*. Philadelphia: Geo. W. Donohue, 1839.

———. *Colonization and Abolition Contrasted*. Philadelphia: Herman Hooker, [1839].

*Cooper, Thomas. *Two Essays 1. On the Foundation of Civil Government: 2. On the Constitution of the United States*. Columbia, S.C.: D. & J. Faust, 1826.

The Crisis: Being, an Inquiry into the Measures Proper to Be Adopted by the Southern States, in Reference to the Proceedings of the Abolitionists. Charleston: Dan J. Dowling, 1835.

Curtis, Moses Ashley. "Unity of the Races." *Southern Quarterly Review* 7 (April 1845): 372–448.

Dabney, Robert Lewis. *A Defense of Virginia (and Through Her of the South) in Recent and Pending Contests against the Sectional Party.* New York: E. J. Hale & Son, 1867.

Dagg, John Leadley. *The Elements of Moral Science.* New York: Sheldon & Company, 1860.

*[Dalcho, Frederick]. *Practical Considerations Founded on the Scriptures, Relative to the Slave Population of South Carolina. Respectfully Dedicated to "The South Carolina Association." By a South Carolinian.* Charleston: A. E. Miller, 1823.

Dew, Thomas Roderick. *Review of the Debate in the Virginia Legislature of 1831 and 1832.* Richmond: T. W. White, 1832.

*Doggett, Simeon. *Two Discourses on the Subject of Slavery.* Boston: Minot Pratt, 1835.

*Drayton, John. *A View of South Carolina, as Respects Her Natural and Civil Concerns.* Charleston: W. P. Young, 1802.

[Drayton, William Henry (?)]. *The South Vindicated from the Treason and Fanaticism of the Northern Abolitionists.* Philadelphia: H. Manly, 1836.

*Dunwody, Samuel. *A Sermon upon the Subject of Slavery.* Columbia, S.C.: S. Weir, 1837.

Dwight, Timothy. *Remarks on the Review of Inchiquin's Letters.* Boston: Samuel T. Armstrong, 1815.

Eells, William Woodward. *Gratitude for Individual and National Blessings. A Discourse, Preached in the Second Presbyterian Church, Newburyport, Thanksgiving Day, November 28, 1850.* Newburyport: Moses H. Sargent, 1850.

Elliott, Ebenezer Newton, ed. *Cotton Is King, and Pro-slavery Arguments: Comprising the Writings of Hammond, Harper, Christy, Stringfellow, Hodge, Bledsoe, and Cartwright, on This Important Subject.* Augusta, Ga.: Pritchard, Abbott & Loomis, 1860.

England, John. *Letters of the Late Bishop England to the Hon. John Forsyth, on the Subject of Domestic Slavery.* Baltimore: John Murphy, 1844.

*Farley, Charles Andrews. *Slavery; a Discourse Delivered in the Unitarian Church, Richmond, Va., Sunday, August 30, 1835.* Richmond: James C. Walker, 1835.

*Ferguson, Jesse Babcock. *Address on the History, Authority and Influence of Slavery Delivered in the First Presbyterian Church, Nashville, Tenn., 21st of November, 1850.* Nashville: John T. S. Fall, 1850.

*Fisk, Theophilus. *The Bulwark of Freedom: An Oration Delivered at the Universalist Church, in the City of Charleston, S.C., June 28, 1836, on the Anniversary of the Glorious Victory at Fort Moultrie, June 28, 1776.* Charleston: Printed for the Publishers at the Office of the Southern Evangelist, 1836.

Flournoy, John Jacobus. *An Essay on the Origin, Habits, &c. of the African Race: Incidental to the Propriety of Having Nothing to Do with Negroes: Addressed to the Good People of the United States.* New York: n.p., 1835.

Freeman, Frederick. *A Plea for Africa, Being Familiar Conversations on the Subject of*

Slavery and Colonization. 3d ed. Philadelphia: Printed by William Stavely for the Proprietor, 1838.

*Freeman, George Washington. *The Rights and Duties of Slaveholders. Two Discourses Delivered on Sunday, November 27, 1836, in Christ Church, Raleigh, North Carolina.* Raleigh: J. Gales & Son, 1836.

Fuller, Richard, and Wayland, Francis. *Domestic Slavery Considered as a Scriptural Institution: In a Correspondence between the Rev. Richard Fuller of Beaufort, S.C., and the Rev. Francis Wayland of Providence, R.I.* New York: Lewis Colby, 1845.

*Furman, Richard. *Rev. Dr. Richard Furman's Exposition of the Views of the Baptists, Relative to the Coloured Population of the United States in a Communication to the Governor of South Carolina.* Charleston: A. E. Miller, 1823.

Girardeau, John Lafayette. *Conscience and Civil Government. An Oration Delivered before the Society of Alumni of the College of Charleston, on Commencement Day, March 27th, 1860.* Charleston: Evans & Cogswell, 1860.

Godwyn, Morgan. *The Negro's and Indians [sic] Advocate, Suing for Their Admission into the Church: or, a Persuasive to the Instructing and Baptizing of the Negro's [sic] and Indians in Our Plantations.* London: Printed for the Author by J. O., 1680.

*Graham, William. *The Contrast, or the Bible and Abolitionism: An Exegetical Argument.* Cincinnati: Printed at the *Daily Cincinnati Atlas* Office, 1844.

*Hales, Stephen. *A Sermon Preach'd before the Trustees for Establishing the Colony of Georgia in America; and before the Associates of the Late Rev. Dr. Thomas Bray, for Converting the Negroes in the British Plantations, and for Other Good Purposes; at Their Meeting in the Parish Church of St. Brides, Fleet Street, on Thursday, March 21, 1734.* London: T. Woodward, 1734.

*Hamilton, William T. *The Duties of Masters and Slaves Respectively: or, Domestic Servitude as Sanctioned by the Bible: A Discourse Delivered in the Government-Street Church, Mobile, Alabama, on Sunday Night, December 15, 1844.* Mobile: F. H. Brooks, 1845.

———. *The "Friend of Moses"; or, A Defense of the Pentateuch as the Production of Moses and an Inspired Document, against the Objections of Modern Skepticism.* New York: M. W. Dodd, 1852.

Harper, William. *Anniversary Oration; Delivered by the Hon. William Harper, in the Representative Hall, Columbia, S.C., Dec. 9, 1835.* Washington, D.C.: Duff Green, 1836.

[Hobby, William J.]. *Remarks upon Slavery; Occasioned by Attempts Made to Circulate Improper Publications in the Southern States. By a Citizen of Georgia.* Augusta: Printed at the S. R. Sentinel Office, 1835.

*Hodge, Charles. *Essays and Reviews Selected from the "Princeton Review."* New York: Robert Carter & Brothers, 1857.

*[Holland, Edwin Clifford]. *A Refutation of the Calumnies Circulated against the Southern & Western States, Respecting the Institution and Existence of Slavery Among Them.* Charleston: A. E. Miller, 1822.

Hopkins, John Henry. *The American Citizen: His Rights and Duties, According to the Spirit of the Constitution of the United States.* New York: Pudney & Russell, 1857.

*———. *Bible View of Slavery.* N.p.: 1861.

———. *Scriptural, Ecclesiastical, and Historical View of Slavery, from the Days of the Patriarch Abraham to the 19th Century. Addressed to the Right Reverend Alonzo Potter, D.D., Bishop of the Prot. Epis. Church, in the Diocese of Pennsylvania.* New York: W. I. Pooley & Co., 1864.

How, Samuel Blanchard. *Slaveholding Not Sinful. Slavery, the Punishment of Man's Sin, Its Remedy, the Gospel of Christ. An Argument before the General Synod of the Reformed Protestant Dutch Church, October, 1855.* 2d ed. New Brunswick, N.J.: J. Terhune's Press, 1856.

Howe, George. "The Raid of John Brown and the Progress of Abolition." *Southern Presbyterian Review* 12 (January 1860): 784–815.

Ingersoll, Charles Jared. *African Slavery in America.* Philadelphia: T. K. and P. G. Collins, 1856.

[———]. *Inchiquin, the Jesuit's Letters, During a Late Residence in the United States of America: Being a Fragment of a Private Correspondence, Accidentally Discovered in Europe.* New York: I. Riley, 1810.

*Jarratt, Devereux. *Thoughts on Some Important Subjects in Divinity; in a Series of Letters to a Friend, by the Rev. Devereux Jarratt, Rector of Bath Parish, in Dinwiddie County, Virginia.* Baltimore: Warner & Hanna, 1806.

Johnson, S. M. [John Fulton.] *The Dual Revolutions. Anti-slavery and Pro-slavery.* Baltimore: W. M. Innes, 1863.

Jones, Charles Colcock. *A Catechism of Scripture Doctrine and Practice, for Families and Sabbath Schools, Designed also, for the Oral Instruction of Colored Persons.* 3d ed. Savannah, Ga.: T. Purse & Co., 1844.

———. *The Religious Instruction of the Negroes. A Sermon Delivered before the Associations of Planters in Liberty and M'Intosh Counties, Georgia.* 4th ed. Princeton, N.J.: D'Hart & Connolly, 1832.

———. *The Religious Instruction of the Negroes in the United States.* Savannah, Ga.: Thomas Purse, 1842.

*Jones, Hugh. *The Present State of Virginia from Whence Is Inferred a Short View of Maryland and North Carolina.* Edited by Richard L. Morton. Chapel Hill: University of North Carolina Press for the Virginia Historical Society, 1956.

Jones, Thomas P. *An Address on the Progress of Manufacturers and Internal Improvement, in the United States; and Particularly, on the Advantages to be Derived from the Employment of Slaves in the Manufacturing of Cotton and Other Goods. Delivered in the Hall of the Franklin Institute, November 6, 1827.* Philadelphia: Published by Judah Dodson; Jesper Harding, Printer, 1827.

Jordan, Winthrop. "An Antislavery Proslavery Document?" *Journal of Negro History* 47 (January 1962): 54–56.

Junkin, George. *The Integrity of Our National Union vs. Abolitionism: An Argument from the Bible.* Cincinnati: R. P. Donogh, 1843.

Kenrick, Francis Patrick. *Theologia Moralis.* 3 vols. Philadelphia: Eugene Cummiskey, 1840–1843.

Ker, Leander. *Slavery Consistent with Christianity, with an Introduction, Embracing a Notice of the "Uncle Tom's Cabin" Movement in England.* Weston, Mo.: Finch & O'Gorman, 1853.

*———. *Slavery Consistent with Christianity.* Baltimore: Sherwood & Co., 1840.

*Kingsley, Zephaniah. *A Treatise on the Patriarchal, or Co-operative System of Society as It Exists in Some Governments, and Colonies in America, and in the United States, under the Name of Slavery, with Its Necessity and Advantages.* 2d ed. N.p.: 1829.

*[Knox, William]. *Three Tracts Respecting the Conversion and Instruction of the Free Indians, and Negro Slaves in the Colonies. Addressed to the Venerable Society for the Propagation of the Gospel in Foreign Parts.* London: n.p., 1768.

Krebs, John Michael. *The American Citizen. A Discourse on the Nature and Extent of Our Religious Subjection to the Government under Which We Live.* New York: Charles Scribner, 1851.

Lacon. [Richard S. Gladney.] *The Devil in America: A Dramatic Satire.* Philadelphia: J. B. Lippincott & Co., 1860.

Lacy, Drury. *A Thanksgiving Discourse, Delivered in the Presbyterian Church, Raleigh, N.C., on Thursday, the 27th of November, 1851.* Raleigh, N.C.: Seaton Gales, 1851.

Leatherman, P. R. *Elements of Moral Science.* Philadelphia: James Challen & Son, 1860.

*Lipscomb, Andrew Agate. *North and South. Impressions of Northern Society upon a Southerner.* Mobile, Ala.: Carver & Ryland, 1853.

*Longstreet, Augustus Baldwin. *Letters on the Epistle of Paul to Philemon, or the Connection of Apostolical Christianity with Slavery.* Charleston, S.C.: B. Jenkins, 1845.

———. *A Voice from the South: Comprising Letters from Georgia to Massachusetts, and to the Southern States.* Baltimore: Samuel E. Smith, 1848.

Lord, John Chase. *The Cause and Remedies of the Present Convulsions. A Discourse Delivered on the Day of Fasting, Humiliation and Prayer, Appointed by the President of the United States, January 4, 1861.* N.p.: 1861.

*———. *"The Higher Law," in Its Application to the Fugitive Slave Bill. A Sermon on the Duties Men Owe to God and to Governments. Delivered at the Central Presbyterian Church, Buffalo, on Thanksgiving-Day.* New York: Published by Order of the "Union Safety Committee," 1851.

[Lord, Nathan]. *A Letter of Inquiry to Ministers of the Gospel of All Denominations, on Slavery. By a Northern Presbyter.* Boston: Little, Brown, and Company, 1854.

———. *A Letter to J. M. Conrad, Esq., on Slavery.* Hanover, N.H.: Dartmouth Press, 1860.

*————. *A Northern Presbyter's Second Letter to Ministers of the Gospel of All Denomina-tions on Slavery.* Boston: Little, Brown and Company, 1855.

————. *A True Picture of Abolition.* Boston: Daily Courier, 1863.

*McCaine, Alexander. *Slavery Defended from Scripture, against the Attacks of the Abo-litionists in a Speech Delivered before the General Conference of the Methodist Protes-tant Church, in Baltimore, 1842.* Baltimore: Wm. Wooddy, 1842.

Man, Thomas. *A Picture of Woonsocket, or, the Truth in Its Nudity; to which Are Added Translations from the Best French, Spanish and Italian Writers.* N.p.: Printed for the Author, 1835.

Meade, William. *Pastoral Letter of the Right Reverend William Meade, Assistant Bishop of Virginia, to the Ministers, Members, and Friends, of the Protestant Episcopal Church in the Diocese of Virginia, on the Duty of Affording Religious Instruction to Those in Bondage.* Alexandria, D.C.: *Gazette* Office, 1834.

*[Mell, Patrick Hues]. *Slavery. A Treatise, Showing that Slavery Is Neither a Moral, Political nor Social Evil.* Penfield, Ga.: Benj. Brantly, 1844.

Mercer, Alexander G. *American Citizenship, Its Faults and Their Remedies. A Sermon for the Day of National Fast, January 4, 1861.* Boston: Little, Brown and Com-pany, 1861.

Meredith, Thomas. *Christianity and Slavery. Strictures on Rev. William Hague's Re-view of Doctors Fuller and Wayland on Domestic Slavery.* Boston: Gould, Kendall and Lincoln, 1847.

Michelbacher, Maximilian J. *A Sermon Delivered on the Day of Prayer, Recommended by the President of the C. S. of A. the 27th of March, 1863, at the German Hebrew Synagogue, "BAYTH AHABAH."* Richmond, Va.: Macfarlane & Fergusson, 1863.

Miles, James Warley. *God in History. A Discourse Delivered before the Graduating Class of the College of Charleston on Sunday Evening, March 29, 1863.* Charleston: Evans & Cogswell, 1863.

*[Mitchell, Elisha]. *The Other Leaf of the Book of Nature and the Word of God.* N.p.: 1948 [*sic*—1848].

Morse, Samuel F. B. *The Present Attempt to Dissolve the American Union, A British Aristocratic Plot.* New York: J. F. Trow, 1862.

Newton, Alexander. *Dr. Newton's Columns on the Position of the Old School Pres-byterian Assembly on the Subject of Slavery.* Jackson, Miss.: Purdom & Brother, 1859.

*[Nisbet, Richard]. *Slavery not Forbidden by Scripture. Or a Defence of the West-India Planters, from the Aspersions Thrown out against Them, by the Author of a Pamphlet entitled, "An Address to the Inhabitants of the British Settlements in America, upon Slave-keeping." By a West-Indian.* Philadelphia: n.p., 1773.

Northern Sentiments upon the Movements of the Abolitionists. Proceedings of the Anti-abolitionist Meeting at Albany. N.p.: [1836].

[Palmer, Benjamin Morgan]. *A Plain and Easy Catechism, Designed Chiefly for the*

Benefit of Coloured Persons. To Which Are Annexed Suitable Prayers and Hymns. Charleston: Observer Office Press, 1828.

*Palmer, Benjamin Morgan [nephew of foregoing]. *The South: Her Peril, and Her Duty. A Discourse Delivered in the First Presbyterian Church, New Orleans, on Thursday, November 29, 1860.* New Orleans: Office of the True Witness and Sentinel, 1860.

Parker, Joel, and Rood, A. *The Discussion between Rev. Joel Parker, and Rev. A. Rood, on the Question "What Are the Evils Inseparable from Slavery," which Was Referred to by Mrs. Stowe, in "Uncle Tom's Cabin."* New York: S. W. Benedict, 1852.

*[Parsons, Theodore, and Pearson, Eliphalet]. *A Forensic Dispute on the Legality of Enslaving the Africans. Held at the Public Commencement in Cambridge, New England, July 21st, 1773. By Two Candidates for the Bachelor's Degree.* Boston: Printed by John Boyle for Thomas Leverett, 1773.

[Patterson, George]. *The Scripture Doctrine with Regard to Slavery.* 2d ed. Pottsville, Pa.: Printed by Benj. Bannan for the Author, 1856.

[Paulding, James Kirke]. *A Sketch of Old England, by a New-England Man.* 2 vols. New York: Charles Wiley, 1822.

[————]. *Letters from the South. By a Northern Man.* New York: James Eastburn & Co., 1817.

————. *Slavery in the United States.* New York: Harper & Brothers, 1836.

[————]. *The United States and England: Being a Reply to the Criticism on Inchiquin's Letters, Contained in the Quarterly Review for January, 1814.* New York: A. H. Inskeep, 1815.

Personal Slavery Established, by the Suffrages of Custom and Right Reason. Being a Full Answer to the Gloomy and Visionary Reveries, of All the Fanatical and Enthusiastical Writers on that Subject. Philadelphia: John Dunlap, 1773.

Pinckney, Charles Cotesworth. *An Address Delivered in Charleston before the Agricultural Society of South-Carolina, at Its Anniversary Meeting, on Tuesday, the 18th of August, 1829.* Charleston: A. E. Miller, 1829.

Pinckney, Henry Laurens. *An Address to the Electors of Charleston District.* Charleston: Burges & Honour, 1836.

————. *Remarks of the Hon. H. L. Pinckney, of South Carolina, on the Resolution Offered by Him Relative to the Abolition of Slavery: Delivered in the House of Representatives, Monday, February 8, 1836.* Washington, D.C.: Gales and Seaton, 1836.

————. *"The Spirit of the Age." An Address Delivered before Two Literary Societies of the University of North Carolina.* Raleigh: J. Gales & Son, 1836.

Pollard, Edward Alfred. *Black Diamonds Gathered in the Darkey Homes of the South.* New York: Pudney & Russell, 1859.

Porter, Abner A. *Our Danger and Our Duty. A Discourse Delivered in the Glebe-Street Presbyterian Church, on Friday, December 6th, 1850.* Charleston: Letter-Press of E. C. Councell, 1850.

Pratt, Nathaniel Alpheus. *Perils of a Dissolution of the Union; a Discourse Delivered in* the Presbyterian Church, of Roswell, on the Day of Public Thanksgiving, November 20, 1856. Atlanta: C. R. Hanleiter & Co., 1856.

Priest, Josiah. *Slavery, as It Relates to the Negro, or African Race, Examined in the Light of Circumstances, History and the Holy Scriptures.* Albany, N.Y.: C. Van Benthuysen and Co., 1843.

The Pro-slavery Argument: as Maintained by the Most Distinguished Writers of the Southern States, Containing the Several Essays, on the Subject, of Chancellor Harper, Governor Hammond, Dr. Simms, and Professor Dew. Charleston: Walker, Richards & Co., 1852.

Ramsey, James Beverlin. *God's Way in the Sanctuary Remembered. A Sermon Preached December 23d, 1860, before the Congregations of the 1st and 2d Presbyterian Churches of Lynchburg, Assembled Together, in Commemoration of the First Meeting of the General Assembly of the Church of Scotland, on December 20th, 1860.* Lynchburg, Va.: J. C. Johnson, 1861.

———. *True Eminence Founded on Holiness: A Discourse Occasioned by the Death of Lieut. T. J. Jackson. Preached in the First Presby. Ch. of Lynchburg, May 24, 1863.* Lynchburg: Virginian "Water-Power Presses" Print, 1863.

*Raphall, Morris Jacob. *Bible View of Slavery. A Discourse Delivered at the Jewish Synagogue, "B'NAI JESHURUM," New York, on the Day of the National Fast, January 4, 1861.* New York: Rudd & Carleton, 1861.

Reese, David M. *A Brief Review of the "First Annual Report of the American Antislavery Society, with the Speeches Delivered at the Antislavery Meeting, May 6, 1834." Addressed to the People of the United States.* New York: Howe & Bates, 1834.

———. *Humbugs of New York: Being a Remonstrance against Popular Delusion: Whether in Science, Philosophy, or Religion.* New York: John S. Taylor, 1838.

———. *Letters to the Hon. William Jay, Being a Reply to His "Inquiry into the American Colonization and American Anti-slavery Societies."* New York: Leavitt, Lord & Co., 1835.

Rhett, Robert Barnwell. *Address to the People of Beaufort and Colleton Districts, upon the Subject of Abolition, January 15, 1838.* N.p.: 1838.

Rice, Nathan Lewis, and Blanchard, Jonathan. *A Debate on Slavery: Held in the City of Cincinnati, on the First, Second, Third, and Sixth Days of October, 1845, upon the Question: Is Slaveholding in Itself Sinful, and the Relation between Master and Slave, a Sinful Relation?* Cincinnati: Wm. H. Moore & Co., 1846.

*Rice, Nathan Lewis. *Lectures on Slavery; Delivered in the First Presbyterian Church, Cincinnati, July First and Third, 1845.* Cincinnati: J. A. James, 1845.

———. *Lectures on Slavery: Delivered in the North Presbyterian Church, Chicago.* Chicago: Daily Democrat Print, 1860.

———. *Ten Letters on the Subject of Slavery: Addressed to the Delegates from the Congregational Associations to the Last General Assembly of the Presbyterian Church.* 2d ed. St. Louis: Keith, Woods & Co., 1856.

[Rice, W.] *Vindex: On the Liability of the Abolitionists to Criminal Punishment, and on the*

Duty of the Non-slaveholding States to Suppress Their Efforts. Charleston: A. E. Miller, 1835.

Rivers, Richard Henderson. *Elements of Moral Philosophy.* Edited by Thomas O. Summers. Nashville: Southern Methodist Publishing House, 1860.

Robinson, John. *The Testimony and Practice of the Presbyterian Church in Reference to American Slavery.* Cincinnati: John D. Thorpe, 1852.

Robinson, Stuart. *Slavery as Recognized in the Mosaic Civil Law, Recognized also, and Allowed, in the Abrahamic, Mosaic, and Christian Church, Being One of a Series of Sabbath Evening Discourses on the Laws of Moses.* Toronto: Rollo & Adam, 1865.

Romans, Bernard. *A Concise Natural History of East and West Florida.* New York: Printed for the Author, 1775.

Ross, Frederick Augustus. *Slavery Ordained of God.* Philadelphia: J. B. Lippincott & Co., 1857.

Ross, Frederick Augustus, and Colenso, John William. *Dr. Ross and Bishop Colenso: or, the Truth Restored in Regard to Polygamy and Slavery.* Philadelphia: Henry B. Ashmead, 1857.

Ruffner, William Henry, ed. *Lectures on the Evidences of Christianity, Delivered at the University of Virginia, During the Session of 1850–1.* New York: Robert Carter & Brothers, 1856.

*Saffin, John. *A Brief and Candid Answer to a Late Printed Sheet, Entituled the Selling of Joseph Whereunto Is Vindication of the Author's Dealing with and Prosecution of His Negro Man Servant for His Vile and Exhorbitant Behavior towards His Master and His Tenant, Thomas Shepard; which Hath Been Wrongfully Represented to Their Prejudice and Defamation.* Boston: n.p., 1701.

[Scott, John]. *The Lost Principle; or the Sectional Equilibrium: How It Was Created—How Destroyed—How It May Be Restored.* Richmond, Va.: James Woodhouse & Co., 1860.

Seabrook, Whitemarsh B. *An Address, Delivered at the First Anniversary Meeting of the United Agricultural Society of South-Carolina, 6th Dec. 1827.* Charleston: A. E. Miller, 1828.

[————]. *An Appeal to the People of the Northern and Eastern States, on the Subject of Negro Slavery in South Carolina. By a South Carolinian.* New York: n.p., 1834.

*————. *A Concise View of the Critical Situation, and Future Prospects of the Slaveholding States, in Relation to Their Coloured Population. Read before the "Agricultucal [sic] Society of St. John's Colleton," on the 14th of September, 1825, and Published at Their Request.* 2d ed. Charleston: A. E. Miller, 1825.

————. *An Essay on the Management of Slaves, and Especially, on Their Religious Instruction; Read before the Agricultucal [sic] Society of St. John's Colleton.* Charleston: A. E. Miller, 1834.

Seabury, Samuel. *American Slavery Distinguished from the Slavery of English Theorists, and Justified by the Law of Nature.* New York: Mason Brothers, 1861.

Seat, William H. *The Confederate States of America in Prophecy.* Nashville: Printed for the Author at the Southern Methodist Publishing House, 1861.

*Shannon, James. *An Address Delivered before the Pro-slavery Convention of the State of Missouri, Held in Lexington, July 13, 1855: On Domestic Slavery, as Examined in the Light of Scripture, of Natural Rights of Civil Government, and the Constitutional Power of Congress.* St. Louis: Republican Book and Job Office, 1855.

*————. *The Philosophy of Slavery, as Identified with the Philosophy of Human Happiness. An Essay.* Frankfort, Ky.: A. G. Hodges & Co., 1849.

Simms, William Gilmore. "Miss Martineau on Slavery." *Southern Literary Messenger* 3 (November 1837): 641–57.

Sims, Alexander Dromgoole. *A View of Slavery, Moral and Political.* Charleston: A. E. Miller, 1834.

Sloan, James A. *Great Question Answered, or, Is Slavery a Sin in Itself (Per Se) Answered According to the Teaching of the Scriptures.* Memphis: Printed at the Avalanche Southern Book and Job Office by Hutton, Gallaway & Co., 1857.

Smith, Samuel Stanhope. *The Lectures, Corrected and Improved, which Have Been Delivered for a Series of Years, in the College of New Jersey; on the Subjects of Moral and Political Philosophy.* 2 vols. Trenton, N.J.: Published by Daniel Fenton for the Author, 1812.

Smith, Whitefoord. *God, the Refuge of His People. A Sermon, General Assembly of S.C., on Fri. Dec. 6, 1850, Being a Day of Fasting, Humiliation, & Prayer.* Columbia: A. S. Johnston, 1850.

*————. *The Inequalities of Life as Illustrating the Wisdom and Goodness of God.* N.p.: n.d.

————. *National Sins: A Call to Repentance. A Sermon Preached on the National Fast, August 3, 1849, in Cumberland Church, Charleston, S.C.* Charleston: Office of the Southern Christian Advocate, 1849.

Smith, William Andrew. *Lectures on the Philosophy & Practice of Slavery, as Exhibited in the Institution of Domestic Slavery in the United States; with the Duties of Masters to Slaves.* Nashville: Stevenson and Evans, 1856.

*Smylie, James. *A Review of a Letter, from the Presbytery of Chillicothe, to the Presbytery of Mississippi, on the Subject of Slavery.* Woodville, Miss.: Wm. A. Norris and Co., 1836.

Smyth, Thomas. *The Unity of the Human Races; Proved to Be the Doctrine of Scripture, Reason, and Science. With a Review of the Present Position and Theory of Professor Agassiz.* New York: George P. Putnam, 1850.

Society for the Diffusion of Political Knowledge. To Churchmen. New York: Society for the Diffusion of Political Knowledge, 1863.

Spencer, Ichabod Smith. *Fugitive Slave Law. The Religious Duty of Obedience to Law: A Sermon Preached in the Second Presbyterian Church in Brooklyn, November 24, 1850.* New York: M. W. Dodd, 1850.

Stearns, Edward Josiah. *Notes on Uncle Tom's Cabin: Being a Logical Answer to Its*

Allegations and Inferences Against Slavery as an Institution, with a Supplementary Note on the Key. Philadelphia: Lippincott, Grambo & Co., 1853.

――――. *A Platform for All Parties.* Baltimore: J. P. Des Forges, 1860.

*Steele, John. *The Substance of an Address, Delivered by Rev. J. Steele in the Associate Reformed Synod of the West, at Their Meeting in Steubenville, on the Evening of October 16, 1829, on the Question of Making the Holding of Slaves a Term of Communion in the Church.* Washington, Guernsey Co., Ohio: Hamilton Robb, 1830.

*[Stephens, Thomas]. *Brief Account of Causes That Have Retarded the Progress of the Colony of Georgia, in America.* London: n.p., 1743.

Stiles, Joseph Clay. *Modern Reform Examined; or, the Union of the North and South on the Subject of Slavery.* Philadelphia: J. B. Lippincott & Co., Publishers, 1857.

*――――. *Speech on the Slavery Resolutions, Delivered in the General Assembly which Met in Detroit in May Last.* Washington: Jno. T. Towers, 1850.

*Stringfellow, Thornton. *A Brief Examination of Scripture Testimony on the Institution of Slavery, in an Essay, First Published in the "Religious Herald."* Washington, Congressional Globe Office, 1850.

――――. *Scriptural and Statistical Views in Favor of Slavery.* 4th ed. Richmond, Va.: J. W. Randolph, 1856.

Stuart, Moses. *Conscience and the Constitution with Remarks on the Recent Speech of the Hon. Daniel Webster in the Senate of the United States on the Subject of Slavery.* Boston: Crocker & Brewster, 1850.

Sullivan, Thomas Russell. *Letters against the Immediate Abolition of Slavery; Addressed to the Free Blacks of the Non-slaveholding States.* Boston: Hilliard, Gray and Co., 1835.

Summers, Thomas Osmond. *Christian Patriotism: A Sermon Preached in Cumberland St. M. E. Church, Charleston, S.C. on Friday, Dec. 6, 1850.* Charleston: C. Canning, 1850.

Talmage, Samuel K. *Thanksgiving Discourse, Delivered before the Governor, State House Officers, and Legislature of Georgia, and the Churches of Milledgeville, at the Request of a Joint Committee of the Two Houses, on the 24th of November, 1853.* N.p.: 1853.

[Thomas, William]. *The Enemies of the Constitution Discovered, or, an Inquiry into the Origin and Tendency of Popular Violence.* New York: Leavitt, Lord, & Co., 1835.

Thompson, Thomas. *The African Slave Trade for Negro Slaves, Shewn to Be Consistent with Principles of Humanity, and With the Laws of Revealed Religion.* Canterbury, England: Simons and Kirkby, [1772].

Thornton, Thomas C. *An Inquiry into the History of Slavery; Its Introduction into the United States; Causes of Its Continuance; and Remarks upon the Abolition Tracts of William E. Channing.* Washington, D.C.: William M. Morrison, 1841.

*Thornwell, James Henley. *The Rights and the Duties of Masters. A Sermon Preached at the Dedication of a Church Erected in Charleston, South Carolina, for the Benefit and Instruction of the Coloured Population.* Charleston: Walker & James, 1850.

*――――. *Report on the Subject of Slavery, Presented to the Synod of South Carolina, at

Their Sessions in Winnsborough, November 6, 1851, Adopted by Them, and Published by Their Order. Columbia: A. S. Johnson, 1852.

Tracy, Joseph. *Natural Equality: A Sermon before the Vermont Colonization Society of Pennsylvania, Delivered October 17, 1833.* Windsor, Vt.: Chronicle Press, 1833.

Tyson, Job Roberts. *A Discourse before the Young Men's Colonization Society of Pennsylvania, Delivered October 24, 1834, in St. Paul's Church, Philadelphia.* Philadelphia: Printed for the Society, 1834.

*Van Dyke, Henry Jackson. *The Character and Influence of Abolitionism. Extracts from a Sermon.* Charleston: Evans & Cogswell, 1860.

*Walsh, Robert. *An Appeal from the Judgments of Great Britain Respecting the United States of America.* Philadelphia: Published by Mitchell, Ames, and White; William Brown, Printer, 1819.

*Wheaton, Nathaniel S. *St. Paul's Epistle to Philemon—Exhibiting the Duty of Citizens of the Northern States in Regard to the Institution of Slavery, December 22, 1850.* Hartford, Conn.: Press of Chase Tiffany & Company, 1851.

Whitaker, Daniel Kimball. *Reflections on Domestic Slavery, Elicited by Judge Harper's Anniversary Oration, Delivered before the South Carolina Society for the Advancement of Learning, 7th December, 1835.* Charleston: n.p., 1836.

Wiley, Calvin Henderson. *Scriptural Views of National Trials: Or the True Road to the Independence and Peace of the Confederate States of America.* Greensboro, N.C.: Sterling, Campbell & Albright, 1863.

*[———]. *A Sober View of the Slavery Question. By a Citizen of the South.* N.p.: [1849].

*Wilson, Joshua Lacy. *Relation and Duties of Servants and Masters.* Cincinnati: Isaac Hefley & Co., 1839.

*Wilson, Samuel Ramsey. *The Causes and Remedies of Impending National Calamities. An Address by Samuel R. Wilson, Pastor of the First Presbyterian Church, Cincinnati.* Cincinnati: J. B. Elliott, 1860.

*Winans, William. *Report on Abolition, Mississippi Annual Conference, Methodist Episcopal Church, December 2, 1835.* N.p.: 1835.

Winslow, Hubbard. *Elements of Moral Philosophy; Analytical, Synthetical, and Practical.* New York: D. Appleton and Company, 1856.

Non-American Proslavery Literature

Only sources that have provided crucial evidence or insights are included. Those used in the argument analysis of chap. 5 are marked with an asterisk (*).

*Barclay, Alexander. *A Practical View of the Present State of Slavery in the West Indies; or, an Examination of Mr. Stephen's "Slavery of the British West India Colonies."* 3d ed. London: Smith, Elder & Co., 1828.

*Bayley, F. W. N. *Four Years' Residence in the West Indies, During the Years 1826, 7, 8, and 9.* London: William Kidd, 1832.

*Bridges, George Wilson. *A Voice from Jamaica; in Reply to William Wilberforce.* 2d ed. London: Longman, Hurst, Rees, Orme, Brown and Green, 1823.

*Brougham, Henry Peter. *An Inquiry into the Colonial Policy of the European Powers.* 2 vols. Edinburgh: D. Willison, 1803.

———. *Opinions of Henry Brougham, Esq., on Negro Slavery: With Remarks.* London: Whitmore and Fenn, 1826.

The Condition of the West India Slave Contrasted with That of the Slave in Our English Factories. London: William Kidd, [1833].

A Country Gentleman's Reasons for Voting against Mr. Wilberforce's Motion for a Bill to Prohibit the Importation of African Negroes into the Colonies. London: J. Debrett, 1792.

Duncan, Henry. *A Presbyter's Letters on the West India Question; Addressed to the Right Honourable Sir George Murray.* London: T. and G. Underwood, 1830.

Edwards, Bryan. *The History, Civil and Commercial, of the British Colonies in the West Indies.* 3 vols. London: John Stockdale, 1793–1801.

Epping, Johann Peter Martin. *The Civil War and Negro Slavery in the United States of America.* Gothenburg: Office of the Handelstiduingens Bolag, 1862.

Ferrer de Condo, Jose. *Enough of War! The Question of Slavery Conclusively and Satisfactorily Solved, as Regards Humanity at Large and the Permanent Interests of Present Owners.* New York: S. Hallet, 1864.

*Foot, Jesse. *A Defence of the Planters in the West-Indies; Comprised in Four Arguments. I. On Comparative Humanity, II. On Comparative Slavery, III. On the African Slave Trade and IV. On the Condition of Negroes in the West Indies.* 2d ed. London: J. Debrett, 1792.

*Francklyn, Gilbert. *Answer to the Rev. Mr. Clarkson's Essay on the Slavery and Commerce of the Human Species; Particularly the African; in a Series of Letters from a Gentleman in Jamaica, to His Friend in London.* London: Logographic Press, 1789.

Gladstone, Sir John. *Facts Relating to Slavery in the West Indies and America, Contained in a Letter Addressed to the Right Hon. Sir Robert Peel, Bart.* 2d ed. London: Baldwin and Cradock, 1830.

*Harris, Raymund. *Scriptural Researches on the Licitness of the Slavetrade, Shewing Its Conformity with the Principles of Natural and Revealed Religion, Delineated in the Sacred Writings of the Word of God.* London: John Stockdale, 1788.

*Holder, Henry Evans. *A Short Essay on the Subject of Negro Slavery, with a Particular Reference to the Island of Barbadoes.* London: Printed by Couchman and Fry, for Charles Dilly, 1788.

Hunt, James. *The Negro's Place in Nature; a Paper Read before the London Anthropological Society.* New York: Van Evrie, Horton & Co., 1864.

*Hurd, S. P. *A Letter to the Right Honourable the Earl of Liverpool, K.G., on the Claims of the West India Proprietors.* London: Simpkin and Marshall, 1823.

[Jeffrey, Francis]. "Review of An Appeal from the Judgments of Great Britain

Respecting the United States of America, by Robert Walsh." *Edinburgh Review* 66 (May 1820): 395–431.

Jennyns, Joseph Clayton. *An Appeal to the Earle Bathurst, when Colonial Minister, on the Unconstitutional Continuance of Foreign Laws in the Colonies Ceded to Great Britain*. London: Sams, 1828.

[Knox, William]. *A Letter from W. K., Esq., to W. Wilberforce, Esq.* [London]: n.p., 1790.

*Long, Charles E. *Negro Emancipation no Philanthropy: A Letter to the Duke of Wellington*. London: James Ridgway, 1830.

Long, Edward. *The History of Jamaica: Or, General Survey of the Antient and Modern State of that Island: With Reflections on Its Situation, Settlements, Inhabitants, Climate, Products, Commerce, Laws, and Government*. 3 vols. London: T. Lowndes, 1774.

*[McCarty, Captain]. *An Appeal to the Candour and Justice of the People of England, in Behalf of the West India Merchants and Planters, Founded on Plain Facts and Incontrovertible Arguments*. London: J. Debrett, 1792.

MacDonnell, Alexander. *An Address to the Members of Both Houses of Parliament on the West India Question*. 2d ed. London: J. Ridgway, 1830.

———. *Considerations on Negro Slavery*. London: Longman, Hurst, Rees, Orme, Brown and Green, 1825.

*MacQueen, James. *The West India Colonies; the Calumnies and Misrepresentations Circulated against Them by the Edinburgh Review, Mr. Clarkson, Mr. Cropper, &c, Examined and Refuted*. London: Longman, Hurst & Co., 1825.

Martin, Sir William. *A Counter Appeal, in Answer to "An Appeal" from William Wilberforce, Designed to Prove that the Emancipation of the Negroes in the West Indies by a Legislative Enactment, without the Consent of the Planters Would be a Flagrant Breach of National Honour, Hostile to the Principles of Religion, Justice, and Humanity, and Highly Injurious to the Planter and to the Slave*. London: C. & J. Rivington, 1823.

A Reply to Mr. Jeremie's Pamphlet. By an Inhabitant of St. Lucia. London: E. Wilson, 1832.

Sotham, Nathaniel. *Plain Facts; or, Circumstances as They Really Are; Being an Impartial and Unprejudiced Account of the State of the Black Population in the Isle of Jamaica*. London: J. M. Richardson, 1824.

*Tobin, James. *A Farwel Address to the Rev. Mr. James Ramsay: From James Tobin, Esq.* London: G. and T. Wilkie, 1788.

*Wilkinson, J. W. *Thoughts on Negro Slavery*. London: James Ridgway, 1833.

Other Printed Sources

Adams, Nehemiah. *At Eventide. Discourses by Nehemiah Adams*. Boston: D. Lothrop and Company, 1877.

Aderman, Ralph M., ed. *The Letters of James Kirke Paulding*. Madison: University of Wisconsin Press, 1962.

Bascom, Henry B. *Claims of Africa; or an Address in Behalf of the American Colonization Society.* Vol. 2, *Posthumous Works of the Rev. Henry B. Bascom,* edited by Thomas N. Ralston, 249–90. Nashville: E. Stevenson & F. A. Owen, 1856.

Birney, James G. *The American Churches the Bulwarks of American Slavery.* 3d ed. Newburyport, Mass.: Charles Whipple, 1842.

Bourne, George. *The Book and Slavery Irreconcilable. With Animadversions upon Dr. Smith's Philosophy.* Philadelphia: J. M. Sanderson & Co., 1816.

Brisbane, William Henry. *Speech of the Rev. Wm. H. Brisbane, Lately a Slaveholder in South Carolina.* Cincinnati: Samuel A. Alley, 1840.

Controversy between Caius Gracchus and Opimius; in Reference to the American Society for Colonizing the Free People of Colour of the United States. Georgetown, D.C.: James C. Dunn, 1827.

Cooper, Thomas. *Lectures on the Elements of Political Economy.* 2d ed. Columbia, S.C.: M'Morris & Wilson Printers, 1830.

Dwight, Theodore, Jun., ed. *President Dwight's Decisions of Questions Discussed by the Senior Class in Yale College, in 1813 and 1814.* New York: Jonathan Leavitt, 1833.

Dwight, Timothy. *The Duty of Americans, at the Present Crisis, Illustrated in a Discourse, Preached on the Fourth of July, 1798.* New Haven, Conn.: Thomas and Samuel Green, 1798.

———. *Greenfield Hill: A Poem in Seven Parts.* New York: Childs and Swaine, 1794.

———. *The Triumph of Infidelity: A Poem.* N.p.: Printed in the World, 1788.

Fast Day Sermons: or, the Pulpit on the State of the Country. New York: Rudd & Carlton, 1861.

Fisher, Sidney George. *A Philadelphia Perspective: The Diary of Sidney George Fisher Covering the Years 1834–1871.* Edited by Nicholas B. Wainright. Philadelphia: Historical Society of Pennsylvania, 1967.

Garrison, William Lloyd. *Thoughts on African Colonization: or, an Impartial Exhibition of the Doctrines, Principles and Purposes of the American Colonization Society.* Boston: Garrison and Knapp, 1832.

Hamilton, William T. *A Word for the African. A Sermon for the Benefit of the American Colonization Society, Delivered in the Second Presbyterian Church, Newark, July 24, 1825.* Newark, N.J.: W. Tuttle & Co., 1825.

*Hepburn, John. *The American Defense of the Christian Golden Rule, or, An Essay to Prove the Unlawfulness of Making Slaves of Men.* London: n.p., 1715.

"Inchiquen the Jesuit's Letters." Review of *Inchiquin, The Jesuit's Letters, During A Late Residence In The United States of America,* by Charles Jared Ingersoll. *London Quarterly Review* 10 (January 1814): 494–539.

Moore, Clement Clark. *Observations upon Certain Passages in Mr. Jefferson's Notes on Virginia, which Appear to Have a Tendency to Subvert Religion, and Establish a False Philosophy.* New York: n.p., 1804.

Moore, Frank, ed. *Spirit of the Pulpit, with Reference to the Present Crisis: A Collection of Sermons by Distinguished Divines, North and South.* New York: G. P. Putnam, 1861.

Morse, Jedidiah. *A Sermon, Delivered at the New North Church in Boston, in the Morning, and in the Afternoon at Charlestown, May 9, 1798.* Boston: Samuel Hall, 1798.

———. *A Sermon Exhibiting the Present Dangers, and Consequent Duties of the Citizens of the United States of America. Delivered at Charlestown, April 25, 1799, the Day of National Fast.* Charlestown: Samuel Ethridge, 1799.

———. *A Sermon, Preached at Charlestown, November 29, 1798, on the Anniversary Thanksgiving in Massachusetts.* Boston: Samuel Hall, 1798.

Myers, Robert Manson, ed. *The Children of Pride: A True Story of Georgia and the Civil War.* New Haven, Conn.: Yale University Press, 1972.

The New England Primer: Twentieth Century Reprint. Boston: Ginn and Company, n.d.

Osgood, David. *The Wonderful Works of God Are to Be Remembered. A Sermon Delivered on the Day of Annual Thanksgiving, November 20, 1794.* Boston: Samuel Hall, 1794.

Palmer, Benjamin Morgan. *The Signs of the Times Discerned and Improved, in Two Sermons, Delivered in the Independent or Congregational Church, Charleston, S.C.* Charleston, S.C.: J. Hoff, 1846 [*sic*—1816].

Raymond, James. *Prize Essay, on the Comparative Economy of Free and Slave Labour, in Agriculture.* Frederick, Md.: John P. Thomson, 1827.

Rice, John Holt. *A Sermon on the Duties of a Minister of the Gospel Preached at the Opening of the Presbytery of Hanover, October 11, 1809.* Philadelphia: William W. Woodward, 1810.

Robson, David W. "An Important Question Answered: William Graham's Defense of Slavery in Post-Revolutionary Virginia." *William and Mary Quarterly,* 3d ser., vol. 37 (October 1980): 644–52.

Schmidt, Frederika Teute, and Wilhelm, Barbara Ripel. "Early Proslavery Petitions in Virginia." *William and Mary Quarterly,* 3d ser., vol. 30 (January 1973): 133–46.

A Scripture Catechism: or, System of Religious Instruction in the Words of Scripture. By a Clergyman of Massachusetts. Cambridge, Mass.: William Hilliard, 1804.

Sewall, Samuel. *The Selling of Joseph: A Memorial.* Boston: Bartholomew Green and John Allen, June 24, 1700.

Sharpe, Granville. *An Essay on Slavery, Proving from Scripture Its Inconsistency with Humanity and Religion; in Answer to a Late Publication, Entitled, "The African Trade for Negro Slaves Shewn to Be Consistent with Principles of Humanity, and with the Laws of Revealed Religion."* Burlington, England: Isaac Collins, 1773.

Smith, Samuel Stanhope. *An Essay on the Causes of the Variety of Complexion and Figure in the Human Species.* Edited by Winthrop Jordan. Cambridge, Mass.: Belknap Press of Harvard University Press, 1965.

Spring, Gardiner. *The Power of the Pulpit; or, Thoughts Addressed to Christian Ministers and Those Who Hear Them.* New York: Baker and Scribner, 1848.

[Thompson, Thomas]. *A Letter from New Jersey, in America, Giving Some Account and Description of That Province. By a Gentleman, late of Christ College, Cambridge.* London: M. Cooper in Paternoster-row, 1756.

[Wakefield, Edward Gibbon]. *England and America. A Comparison of the Social and Political State of Both Nations.* New York: Harper & Brothers, 1834.

Walsh, Robert. *Free Remarks on the Spirit of the Federal Constitution, the Practice of the Federal Government, and the Obligations of the Union, Respecting the Exclusion of Slavery from the Territories and New States.* Philadelphia: A. Finley, 1819.

Whitefield, George. *Three Letters from the Reverend Mr. G. Whitefield: viz. Letter I. To a Friend in London, Concerning Archbishop Tillotson. Letter II. To the Same, on the Same Subject. Letter III, To the Inhabitants of Maryland, Virginia, North and South-Carolina, Concerning Their Negroes.* Philadelphia: B. Franklin, 1740.

———. *The Works of the Reverend George Whitefield.* 6 vols. London: Edward and Charles Dilly, and Messrs. Kincaid and Bell, 1771–1772.

Winslow, Hubbard. *The Means of the Perpetuity and Prosperity of Our Republic, An Oration, Delivered by Request of the Municipal Authorities, of the City of Boston, July 4, 1838, in the Old South Church, in Celebration of American Independence.* Boston: John H. Eastburn, 1838.

[Worcester, Samuel Melancthon], ed. *Essays on Slavery; Re-published from the "Boston Recorder & Telegraph" for 1825. By Vigornius, and Others.* Amherst, Mass.: Published by Mark H. Newman; Carter and Adams, Printers, 1826.

Wright, John. *A Refutation of the Sophisms, Gross Misrepresentations and Erroneous Quotations Contained in "An American's" "Letter to the Edinburgh Reviewers"; or, Slavery Inimical to the Character of the Great Father of All, Unsupported by Divine Revelation, a Violation of Natural Justice, and Hostile to the Fundamental Principles of American Independence.* Washington, D.C.: Printed for the Author, 1820.

Biographical Sources

Since a major feature of this study is biographical and is based in part on a biographical profile of 275 men, materials depicting the lives and characters of proslavery men have constituted a major focus of research. The following list includes only the most significant sources used.

Biographical Reference Works

The American Church Clergy and Parish Directory: A Treasury of Information about the American Church for the Clergy and Laity. Edited by Frederic E. Lloyd. Cleveland: Frederic E. J. Lloyd, 1898–1913.

Appleton's Cyclopedia of American Biography. Edited by James Grant Wilson and John Fiske. 7 vols. New York: D. Appleton and Company, 1887–1900.

Biographical Souvenir of the States of Georgia and Florida. Chicago: F. A. Battey & Company, 1889.

Bodensieck, Julius, ed. *The Encyclopedia of the Lutheran Church.* 3 vols. Minneapolis: Augsburg Publishing House, 1965.

Carter, Hodding, and Carter, Betty Werlein. *So Great a Good: A History of the Episcopal Church in Louisiana and of Christ Church Cathedral, 1805–1955.* Sewanee, Tenn.: University Press, 1955.

Cathcart, William, ed. *The Baptist Encyclopedia: A Dictionary of the Doctrines, Ordinances, Usages, Confessions of Faith, Sufferings, Labors, and Successes, and of the General History of the Baptist Denominations in All Lands.* Philadelphia: Louis H. Everts, 1881.

Delaney, John J., and Tobin, James Edward, eds. *Dictionary of Catholic Biography.* Garden City, N.Y.: Doubleday & Company, Inc., 1962.

Dictionary of American Biography. Edited by Allen Johnson and Dumas Malone. 20 vols. New York: Charles Scribner's Sons, 1928–1937.

Dictionary of National Biography. Edited by Leslie Stephen and Sidney Lee. 63 vols. London: Oxford University Press, 1885–1901.

Encyclopedia of Southern Baptists. 2 vols. Nashville: Broadman Press, 1958.

Fowler, Henry. *The American Pulpit; Sketches, Biographical and Descriptive, of Living American Preachers, and of the Religious Movements and Distinctive Ideas which They Represent.* New York: J. M. Fairchild & Co., 1856.

Landman, Isaac, ed. *The Universal Jewish Encyclopedia.* 10 vols. New York: Universal Jewish Encyclopedia, 1943.

Living Church Quarterly: Containing an Almanac and Calendar for the Year of Our Lord 1891. Milwaukee: Young Churchman Company, 1890.

Lueker, Erwin L., ed. *Lutheran Cyclopedia.* St. Louis: Concordia Publishing House, 1954.

Lutheran Church in America, North Carolina Synod. *Life Sketches of Lutheran Ministers, North Carolina and Tennessee Synods, 1773–1965.* Columbia, S.C.: n.p., 1966.

Methodist Episcopal Church. *Minutes of the Annual Conferences, 1784–1844.* Various Imprints.

Methodist Episcopal Church, South. *Minutes of the Annual Conferences, 1845–1890.* Various Imprints.

National Cyclopedia of American Biography. 51 vols. New York: James T. White & Company, 1892——.

Nevin, Alfred, ed. *Encyclopedia of the Presbyterian Church in the United States of America: Including the Northern and Southern Assemblies.* Philadelphia: Presbyterian Encyclopedia Publishing Co., 1884.

Pittfield, R. H. *Biographical History of Primitive or Old School Baptist Ministers of the United States.* Anderson, Ind.: Herald Publishing Co., 1909.

Scott, E. C., comp. *Ministerial Directory of the Presbyterian Church, U.S., 1861–1941.* Austin, Tex.: Order of the General Assembly, 1942.

Simpson, Matthew, ed. *Cyclopedia of Methodism, Embracing Sketches of Its Rise, Progress and Present Condition, with Biographical Notices and Numerous Illustrations.* 4th ed. Philadelphia: Louis H. Everts, 1881.

Sprague, William Buell. *Annals of the American Pulpit; or, Commemorative Notices of Distinguished American Clergymen of Various Denominations, from the Early Settlement of the Country to the Close of the Year Eighteen Hundred and Fifty-five.* 9 vols. New York: Robert Carter & Brothers, 1857–1869.

Biographies, Autobiographies, and Biographical Studies

Adger, John Bailey. *My Life and Times, 1810–1899.* Richmond, Va.: Presbyterian Committee of Publications, [1899].

[Bachman, Catherine C.]. *John Bachman, D.D., LL.D., Ph.D., the Pastor of St. John's Lutheran Church, Charleston.* Charleston: Walker, Evans & Cogswell Co., 1888.

Barbee, David Rankin. "Lincoln, Chase, and the Rev. Dr. Richard Fuller." *Maryland Historical Magazine* 46 (June 1951): 108–23.

Bennett, John Boyce. "Albert Taylor Bledsoe: Social and Religious Controversialist of the Old South." Ph.D. dissertation, Duke University, 1942.

Blackburn, George A. *The Life Work of John L. Girardeau, D.D., LL.D., Late Professor in the Presbyterian Theological Seminary, Columbia, S.C.* Columbia: State Company, 1916.

Bleser, Carol, ed. *The Hammonds of Redcliffe.* New York: Oxford University Press, 1981.

Bost, Raymond Morris. "The Reverend John Bachman and the Development of Southern Lutheranism." Ph.D. dissertation, Yale University, 1963.

Boucher, Jonathan, ed. *Reminiscences, of an American Loyalist, 1738–1789: Being the Autobiography of the Revd. Jonathan Boucher, Rector of Annapolis in Maryland and Afterwards Vicar of Epsom, Surrey, England.* Boston: Houghton Mifflin Company, 1925.

Boyce, James P. *Life and Death the Christian's Portion. A Discourse Occasioned by the Funeral Services of the Rev. Basil Manly, D.D., at Greenville, S.C., December 22, 1868.* New York: Sheldon & Co., 1869.

Braverman, Howard. "Calvin Henderson Wiley, North Carolina Educator and Writer." Ph.D. dissertation, Duke University, 1950.

Brigham, Charles H. *Biographical Sketch of Rev. Simeon Doggett, Pastor of the Second Congregational Church in Raynham.* Boston: Crosby, Nichols, and Company, 1852.

Brokhage, Joseph D. *Francis Patrick Kenrick's Opinion on Slavery.* Washington, D.C.: Catholic University of America Press, 1955.

Byrne, Barbara Anne. "Charles C. Jones and the Intellectual Crisis of the Antebellum South." *Southern Studies* 19 (Fall 1980): 274–85.

Celebration of the Fiftieth Anniversary of the Appointment of Professor William Henry Green as an Instructor in Princeton Theological Seminary, May 5, 1896. New York: Charles Scribner's Sons, 1896.

Church of the Redeemer. *A Tribute of Respect Paid to the Memory of the Late Reverend Charles Cotesworth Pinckney, D.D., LL.D.* N.p.: n.d.

Clapp, Theodore. *Autobiographical Sketches and Recollections, During a Thirty-five Years' Residence in New Orleans.* Boston: Phillips, Sampson & Company, 1857.

Clark-Kennedy, A. E. *Stephen Hales, D.D., F.R.S.: An Eighteenth Century Biography.* Cambridge, England: Cambridge University Press, 1929.

Cook, Harvey Toliver. *The Life Work of James Clement Furman.* Greenville, S.C.: Alester G. Furman, 1926.

―――, ed. *A Biography of Richard Furman.* Greenville, S.C.: Baptist Courier Job Rooms, 1913.

Coulter, Ellis Merton. *John Jacobus Flournoy: Champion of the Common Man in the Antebellum South.* Savannah: Georgia Historical Society, 1942.

―――. *William G. Brownlow, Fighting Parson of the Southern Highlands.* Chapel Hill: University of North Carolina Press, 1937.

Crosby, Alpheus Benning. *A Eulogy Commemorative of the Life and Character of Nathan Lord, D.D., LL.D., President of Dartmouth College. Delivered before the Association of the Alumni of Dartmouth College, at the Annual Commencement, June, 1872.* Hanover, N.H.: J. B. Parker, 1872.

Cunningham, Charles E. *Timothy Dwight, 1752–1817: A Biography.* New York: Macmillan Company, 1942.

Dagg, John Leadley. *Autobiography of Rev. John L. Dagg, D.D. Written by Request, for the Perusal of His Family, and not for Publication.* Rome, Ga.: J. F. Shanklin, 1886.

Danhof, Ralph John. *Charles Hodge as a Dogmatician.* Goes, Netherlands: Oosterbaan & Le Cointre, [1930].

Dill, J. S. *Isaac Taylor Tichenor: The Home Mission Statesman.* Nashville: Sunday School Board, Southern Baptist Convention, 1908.

Dillon, William. *Life of John Mitchel.* 2 vols. London: Kegan Paul, Trench & Co., 1888.

Doggett, David Seth. *Sermons, by the Late Rev. David Seth Doggett, D.D., One of the Bishops of the Methodist Episcopal Church, South, with a Biographical Sketch of the Author, by the Rev. John E. Edwards, D.D.* Nashville: Southern Methodist Publishing House, 1882.

Drury, Clifford Merrill. *William Anderson Scott: "No Ordinary Man."* Glendale, Calif.: Arthur H. Clark Company, 1967.

DuBose, Hampden C. *Memoirs of Rev. John Leighton Wilson, D.D., Missionary to Africa, and Secretary of Foreign Missions.* Richmond, Va.: Presbyterian Committee of Publication, 1895.

Dunaway, Thomas Sanford. *Personal Memoirs, Sermons and Addresses.* Lynchburg, Va.: J. P. Bell Company, 1900.

Elliott, James H., comp. *In Memoriam. Tributes to the Memory of the Rev. C. P. Gadsden, Late Rector of St. Luke's Church, Charleston, S.C.* Charleston: Fogarties Book Depository, 1872.

Faust, Drew Gilpin. *James Henry Hammond and the Old South: A Design for Mastery.* Baton Rouge: Louisiana State University Press, 1982.

First Baptist Church, Richmond, Va. *Dr. John Lansing Burrows, 1814–1893, Died in Stellaville, Ga., January 2, 1893; Buried in Richmond, Va., January 5, 1893, Age Seventy-nine.* Richmond: E. T. Walthall, 1893.

Fitzgerald, O. P. *John B. McFerrin: A Biography.* Nashville: Publishing House of the M.E. Church, South, 1888.

Ford, Paul M. "Calvin H. Wiley and the Common Schools of North Carolina, 1850–1869." Unpublished D.Ed. thesis, Harvard University, 1960.

———. "Calvin H. Wiley's View of the Negro." *North Carolina Historical Review* 41 (January 1964): 1–20.

Gannon, Michael V. *Rebel Bishop: The Life and Era of Augustin Verot.* Milwaukee: Bruce Publishing Company, 1964.

Garber, Paul Leslie. "The Religious Thought of James Henley Thornwell." Ph.D. dissertation, Duke University, 1939.

Gardner, Robert G. "John Leadley Dagg: Pioneer American Baptist Theologian." Ph.D. dissertation, Duke University, 1957.

Genovese, Eugene D. "Western Civilization Through Slaveholding Eyes: The Social and Historical Thought of Thomas Roderick Dew." Unpublished article supplied by author, 1986.

Giles, Joseph Lafayette. "An Analysis of Thomas Meredith's Views Concerning Slavery as Expressed in the Biblical Recorder, 1835." Th.M. thesis, Southeastern Baptist Theological Seminary, 1964.

Girardeau, John Lafayette. *"Eulogy on Professor George Howe, D.D., LL.D., Delivered before the Alumni Association of Columbia Theological Seminary, May 9, 1883." Memorial Volume of the Semi-Centennial of the Theological Seminary at Columbia, South Carolina.* Columbia: Presbyterian Publishing House, 1884.

Goodell, Abner C. "John Saffin and His Slave Adam." *Colonial Society of Massachusetts Publications* 1 (1895): 85–112.

Graham, William. *The Cause and Manner of the Trial and Suspension of the Rev. William Graham, by the New School Synod of Cincinnati.* N.p.: [1845].

Gregg, Wilson. *Alexander Gregg: First Bishop of Texas.* Edited by Arthur Howard Noll. Sewanee, Tenn.: University Press at the University of the South, 1912.

Guilday, Peter. *The Life and Times of John England: First Bishop of Charleston (1786–1842).* 2 vols. New York: America Press, 1927.

Hassard, John R. G. *Life of John Hughes, First Archbishop of New York.* New York: D. Appleton and Company, 1866.

Haywood, Marshall DeLancey. "Thomas Atkinson, Third Bishop of North Carolina." Marshall DeLancey Haywood, ed., *Lives of the Bishops of North Carolina from the Establishment of the Episcopate in that State Down to the Division of the Diocese.* Raleigh, N.C.: Alfred Williams & Company, 1910.

Heller, James Gutheim. *Isaac M. Wise: His Life, Work and Thought.* New York: Union of American Hebrew Congregations, 1965.

Henry, Stuart C. *George Whitefield: Wayfaring Witness.* New York: Abingdon Press, 1957.

Henry Jackson Van Dyke. New York: Anson D. F. Randolph & Company, 1892.

Hickey, Doralyn Joanne. "Benjamin Morgan Palmer: Churchman of the Old South." Ph.D. dissertation, Duke University, 1962.

Hodge, Archibald Alexander. *The Life of Charles Hodge, D.D., LL.D., Professor in the Theological Seminary, Princeton, N.J.* New York: Charles Scribner's Sons, 1880.

Holder, Ray. *William Winans: Methodist Leader in Antebellum Mississippi.* Jackson: University Press of Mississippi, 1977.

Hopkins, John Henry. *Autobiography in Verse: Dedicated to My Children.* Cambridge, Mass.: Riverside Press, [1866].

Hopkins, John Henry, Jr. *The Life of the Late Right Reverend John Henry Hopkins, First Bishop of Vermont, and Seventh Presiding Bishop.* 2d ed. New York: F. J. Huntingdon and Co., 1875.

Hoyt, William Russell, III. "The Religious Thought of Gardiner Spring with Particular Reference to His Doctrine of Sin and Salvation." Ph.D. dissertation, Duke University, 1962.

Illoway, Henry. SEFER MILHAMOTH ELOHIM: *Being the Controversial Letters and the Casuistic Decisions of the Late Rabbi Bernard Illowy, Ph.D., with a Short History of His Life and Activities.* Berlin: M. Poppelauer, 1914.

In Memoriam. Rev. I. S. K. Axson, D.D., Oct. 3, 1813–March 31, 1891. Savannah, Ga.: Morning Newsprint, 1891.

In Memoriam. Rev. J. Henry Smith, D.D. Born in Lexington, Va., August 13, 1820. Died in Greensboro, N.C., November 22, 1897. Baltimore: John Murphy Co., 1900.

In Memoriam—Rev. Joseph Clay Stiles. N.p.: [1876].

Jarratt, Devereux. *The Life of Devereux Jarratt, Rector of Bath Parish, Dinwiddie County, Virginia, Written by Himself in a Series of Letters Addressed to the Rev. John Coleman.* Baltimore: Warner & Hanna, 1806.

Jeter, Jeremiah Bell. *The Recollections of a Long Life.* Richmond: Religious Herald Co., 1891.

Johnson, Thomas Cary. *The Life and Letters of Benjamin Morgan Palmer.* Richmond: Presbyterian Committee of Publication, 1906.

Junkin, D. X. *The Reverend George Junkin, D.D., LL.D.: A Historical Biography.* Philadelphia: J. B. Lippincott & Co., 1871.

Kwitchen, Mary Augustine, Sister. *James Alphonsus McMaster: A Study in American Thought.* Washington, D.C.: Catholic University of America Press, 1949.

Korn, Bertram Wallace. "Isaac Leeser: Centennial Reflections." *American Jewish Archives* 19 (November 1967): 127–41.

Lamar, James S. *Recollections of Pioneer Days in Georgia.* N.p.: n.d.

Larsen, Karen. *Laur. Larsen: Pioneer College President.* Northfield, Minn.: Norwegian-American Historical Association, 1936.

Lochemes, M. Frederick, Sister. *Robert Walsh: His Story.* Washington, D.C.: Catholic University of America Press, 1941.

Lord, William W., Jr. "A Child at the Siege of Vicksburg." *Harper's Monthly Magazine* 117 (December 1908): 44–53.

Loveland, Anne C. "Richard Furman's 'Questions on Slavery'." *Baptist History and Heritage* 10 (July 1975): 177–81.

Mabee, Carleton. *The American Leonardo: A Life of Samuel F. B. Morse.* New York: Alfred A. Knopf, 1943.

Mallard, Robert Q. *Montevideo—Maybank: Some Memoirs of a Southern Christian Household in the Olden Time; or, the Family Life of the Rev. Charles Colcock Jones, D.D., of Liberty County, Ga.* Richmond, Va.: Presbyterian Committee of Publications, 1898.

Martin, Albert William, Jr. "Holland Nimmons McTyeire and the Negro." M.A. thesis, Vanderbilt University, 1961.

May, Philip S. "Zephaniah Kingsley, Nonconformist, 1765–1843." *Florida Historical Quarterly* 23 (January 1945): 145–59.

Meigs, William M. *The Life of Charles Jared Ingersoll.* Philadelphia: J. B. Lippincott Company, 1897.

Mell, Patrick Hues, Jr. *Life of Patrick Hues Mell, by His Son.* Louisville, Ky.: Baptist Book Concern, 1895.

Mellen, T. L., ed. *In Memoriam: Life and Labors of the Rev. William Hamilton Watkins, D.D., Late a Member of the Mississippi Conference, M.E. Church, South, and One Time President of Centenary College.* Nashville: Southern Methodist Publishing House, 1886.

Memoir of John C. Lord, D.D., Pastor of the Central Presbyterian Church for Thirty-eight Years. Buffalo: Courier Company, 1878.

Memorial Volume by the Essex Street Church and Society Boston to Commemorate the Twenty-fifth Anniversary of the Installation of Their Pastor, Nehemiah Adams, D.D. Boston: Printed for the Use of the Members, 1860.

[Minnigerode, Charles]. *To the Memory of Rev. Wm. Norwood, D.D., First Rector, St. Paul's Church, Richmond, Va.* N.p.: By the Vestry, n.d.

Montgomery, Horace. "The Two Howell Cobbs: A Case of Mistaken Identity." *Journal of Southern History* 28 (August 1962): 348–55.

Morison, Samuel Eliot. *Harrison Gray Otis, 1765–1848: The Urbane Federalist.* Boston: Houghton Mifflin Company, 1969.

———. *The Life and Letters of Harrison Gray Otis, Federalist, 1765–1848.* 2 vols. Boston and New York: Houghton Mifflin Company, 1913.

Morse, Edward Lind, ed. *Samuel F. B. Morse: His Letters and Journals.* 2 vols. Boston and New York: Houghton Mifflin Company, 1914.

Morse, James King. *Jedidiah Morse: A Champion of New England Orthodoxy.* New York: Columbia University Press, 1939.

Neely, Philip P. *Discourses by the Rev. Philip P. Neely, D.D., First Series.* New York: S. H. Goetzel & Co., 1857.

Nichols, Thomas L. *Supramundane Facts in the Life of Rev. Jesse Babcock Ferguson, A.M., LL.D., Including Twenty Years' Observation of Preternatural Phenomena.* London: F. Pitman, 1865.

Norton, John N. *The Life of Bishop Bowen, of South Carolina.* New York: General Protestant Episcopal S. School Union and Church Book Society, 1859.

———. *Life of Bishop Freeman, of Arkansas.* New York: General Protestant Episcopal S. School Union and Church Book Society, 1867.

———. *Life of Bishop Gadsden, of South Carolina.* New York: General Protestant Episcopal S. School Union and Church Book Society, 1858.

Owens, Hubert B. *Georgia's Planting Prelate, Including an Address on Horticulture at Macon, Georgia, in 1851.* Athens: University of Georgia Press, 1945.

Palmer, Benjamin M. *The Life and Letters of James Henley Thornwell, D.D., LL.D., Ex-President of the South Carolina College, Late Professor of Theology in the Theological Seminary at Columbia, South Carolina.* Richmond, Va.: Whittet & Shepperson, 1875.

Park, Edwards A. *A Discourse Delivered at the Funeral of Professor Moses Stuart.* Boston: Tappan & Whittemore, 1852.

Parks, Joseph H. *General Leonidas Polk, C. S. A.: The Fighting Bishop.* Baton Rouge: Louisiana State University Press, 1962.

Parsons, Theophilus, Jr. *Memoir of Theophilus Parsons, Chief Justice of the Supreme Judicial Court of Massachusetts.* Boston: Ticknor and Fields, 1859.

Philipson, David. *Max Lilienthal: American Rabbi, Life and Writings.* New York: Bloch Publishing Co., 1915.

Phillips, Charles, ed. *A Memoir of the Rev. Elisha Mitchell, D.D., Late Professor of Chemistry, Mineralogy & Geology in the University of North Carolina.* Chapel Hill: J. M. Henderson, Printer to the University, 1858.

Pierce, George Foster. *Incidents of Western Travel: In a Series of Letters.* Nashville: E. Stevenson & F. A. Owen, for the Methodist Episcopal Church South, 1857.

Pierson, David H. *Memorial of David Magie, D.D., Late Pastor of the Second Presbyterian Church of Elizabeth, N.J.* N.p.: Francis Hart & Company, 1865.

Pinckney, Charles Cotesworth. *A Faithful Pastor. The Character and Career of the Rev. James H. Elliott, D.D.* Charleston: Lucas & Richardson, Steam Job Print, 1878.

Polk, William H. *Leonidas Polk: Bishop and General.* 2 vols. New York: Longmans, Green, and Co., 1915.

Poole, Charles Harold. "Thomas O. Summers: A Biographical Study." M.A. thesis, Vanderbilt University, 1958.

Robbins, Wallace J. "Charles A. Farley, Messenger of Liberalism." *Proceedings of the Unitarian Historical Society* 6 (1938): 1–12.

Ross, Charles C., ed. *The Story of Rotherwood from the Autobiography of Rev. Frederick A. Ross, D.D., in Letters Addressed to a Lady of Knoxville, Tennessee, Mrs. Juliet Park White.* Knoxville: Bean, Warters & Co., 1923.

Salley, A. S., Jr. "Captain William Capers and Some of His Descendants." *South Carolina Historical and Genealogical Magazine* 2 (October 1901): 273–98.

Saunders, J. N. *Memorial upon the Life of Rev. Stuart Robinson.* Richmond, Va.: Presbyterian Committee of Publication, 1883.

Shaffer, Arthur H. "Between Two Worlds: David Ramsay and the Politics of Slavery." *Journal of Southern History* 50 (May 1984): 175–96.

Silverman, Kenneth. *Timothy Dwight.* New York: Twayne Publishers, 1969.

Slaughter, Philip. *Views from Cedar Mountain. Present, Retrospective, and Prospective.* N.p.: [1884].

Smith, George C. *The Life and Letters of James Osgood Andrew, Bishop of the Methodist Episcopal Church, South.* Nashville: Southern Methodist Pub. House, 1883.

———. *The Life and Times of George Foster Pierce, D.D., LL.D., Bishop of the Methodist Episcopal Church, South.* Sparta, Ga.: Hancock Publishing Company, 1888.

Smithson, William T. *In Memoriam: Rev. Bishop James Osgood Andrew, D.D., Rev. Augustus B. Longstreet, D.D., LL.D., Rev. William A. Smith, D.D.* New York: Wm. T. Smithson, 1871.

Smyth, Thomas. *Autobiographical Notes, Letters and Reflections.* Edited by Louisa Cheves Stoney. Charleston: Walker, Evans & Cogswell, 1914.

Spitz, Lewis William. *Life in Two Worlds: Biography of William Sihler.* St. Louis: Concordia Publishing House, 1968.

Spitz, Lewis W., Sr. *The Life of Dr. C. F. W. Walther.* St. Louis: Concordia Publishing House, 1961.

Spring, Gardiner. *Personal Reminiscences of the Life and Times of Gardiner Spring, Pastor of the Brick Presbyterian Church in the City of New York.* 2 vols. New York: Charles Scribner & Co., 1866.

Steffens, D. H. *Doctor Carl Ferdinand Wilhelm Walther.* Philadelphia: Lutheran Publication Society, 1917.

[Taylor, Charles E.]. *A Brief Memoir of the Rev. William T. Brantly, D.D.* Boston: William S. Damrell, 1846.

Thompson, Thomas. *An Account of Two Missionary Voyages by the Appointment of the Society for the Propagation of the Gospel in Foreign Parts. The One to New Jersey in North America, the Other from America to the Coast of Guiney.* London: Printed for Benj. Dod at the Bible and Key, 1753.

Tigert, John J., IV. *Bishop Holland Nimmons McTyeire: Ecclesiastical and Educational Architect.* Nashville: Vanderbilt University Press, 1955.

Vinton, John Adams. *The Vinton Memorial, Comprising a Genealogy of the Descendants of John Vinton of Lynn, 1648.* Boston: S. K. Whipple and Company, 1858.

Webber, Mabel C., comp. "The Thomas Pinckney Family of South Carolina." *South Carolina Historical and Genealogical Magazine* 29 (January 1938): 15–35.

Wheaton, Nathaniel Sheldon. *A Journal of a Residence of Several Months in London; Including Excursions through Various Parts of England; and a Short Tour in France and Scotland in the Years 1823 and 1824.* Hartford, Conn.: H. & F. J. Huntingdon, 1830.

Whitaker, Walter C. *Richard Hooker Wilmer, Second Bishop of Alabama: A Biography.* Philadelphia: George W. Jacobs & Co., 1907.

White, William S. *Rev. William S. White, D.D., and His Time, 1800–1873: An Autobiography.* Edited by H. M. White. Richmond, Va.: Presbyterian Committee of Publications, 1891.

Wiley, Bell Irvin. "The Movement to Humanize the Institution of Slavery during the Confederacy." *Emory University Quarterly* 5 (December 1949): 207–20.

William T. Brantly, D.D. A Memorial. Baltimore: Printed for private distribution only, 1883.

Williams, George W. *The Rev. Frederick Dalcho, M.D. An Address Delivered before the Dalcho Historical Society, January 20, 1953.* Charleston: Dalcho Historical Society, 1960.

Wilmer, Richard H. *In Memoriam. A Sermon in Commemoration of the Life and Labors of the Rt. Rev. Stephen Elliott, D.D. (Late Bishop of Georgia), Delivered in Christ Church, Savannah, Ga., on Sunday, January 27, 1867.* Mobile, Ala.: Farrow & Dennett, 1867.

Wilson, Harold. "Basil Manly, Apologist for Slavocracy." *Alabama Review* 15 (January 1962): 38–53.

Wish, Harvey. *George Fitzhugh, Propagandist of the Old South.* Baton Rouge: Louisiana State University Press, 1943.

Yager, Arthur. *Sketch of the Life of William Calmes Buck.* N.p.: C. T. Dearing Printing Company, n.d.

Zimmer, Anne Young, and Kelly, Alfred H. "Jonathan Boucher: Constitutional Conservative." *Journal of American History* 58 (March 1972): 897–922.

Secondary Sources

The following list is restricted to assessments of proslavery, of topics dealing with slavery, and of specialized topics dealing with proslavery history.

Articles

Allen, Cuthbert Edward. "The Slavery Question in Catholic Newspapers, 1850–1865." *Historical Records and Studies* 26 (1936): 99–167.

Bellot, Leland J. "Evangelicals and the Defense of Slavery in Britain's Old Colonial Empire." *Journal of Southern History* 37 (February 1971): 19–40.

Bruce, Dickson D. "Racial Fear and the Proslavery Argument: A Rhetorical Approach." *Mississippi Quarterly* 33 (Fall 1980): 461–78.

Burke, Joseph C. "The Proslavery Argument and the First Congress." *Duquesne Review* 14 (Spring 1969): 3–15.

Carsel, Wilfred. "The Slaveholders' Indictment of Northern Wage Slavery." *Journal of Southern History* 6 (August 1940): 504–20.

Dawson, Jan C. "The Puritan and the Cavalier: The South's Perception of Contrasting Traditions." *Journal of Southern History* 44 (November 1978): 597–614.

Deschamps, Margaret Burr. "Union or Division? South Atlantic Presbyterians and Southern Nationalism, 1820–1861." *Journal of Southern History* 22 (November 1954): 484–89.

Donald, David. "The Proslavery Argument Reconsidered." *Journal of Southern History* 37 (February 1971): 3–18.

Dowty, Alan. "Urban Slavery in Pro-southern Fiction of the 1850's." *Journal of Southern History* 32 (February 1966): 25–41.

Eames, Wilberforce. "Early New England Catechisms." *Proceedings of the American Antiquarian Society* n.s. 12 (October 1897–1898): 76–182.

Faust, Drew Gilpin. "A Southern Stewardship: The Intellectual and the Proslavery Argument." *American Quarterly* 31 (Spring 1979): 63–80.

Franklin, John Hope. "The North, the South, and the American Revolution." *Journal of American History* 62 (June 1975): 5–23.

Friedman, Lawrence J. "Purifying the White Man's Country: The American Colonization Society Reconsidered, 1816–1840." *Societas* 6 (Winter 1976): 1–24.

Genovese, Eugene D. "'Slavery Ordained of God': The Southern Slaveholders' View of Biblical History and Modern Politics." Fortenbaugh Memorial Lecture, Gettysburg College, 1985.

Gerster, Patrick and Nicholas Cords. "The Northern Origins of Southern Mythology." *Journal of Southern History* 43 (November 1977): 567–82.

Gravely, William B. "Methodist Preachers, Slavery, and Caste: Types of Social Concern in Antebellum America." *Duke Divinity School Review* 34 (Autumn 1969): 209–29.

Greenberg, Kenneth S. "Revolutionary Ideology and the Proslavery Argument: The Abolition of Slavery in Antebellum South Carolina." *Journal of Southern History* 42 (August 1976): 365–84.

Hesseltine, William B. "Some New Aspects of the Pro-slavery Argument." *Journal of Negro History* 21 (January 1936): 1–15.

Hofstadter, Richard. "U. B. Phillips and the Plantation Legend." *Journal of Negro History* 29 (April 1944): 109–24.

Hubbart, Henry Clyde. "Pro-southern Influence in the Free West, 1840–1865." *Mississippi Valley Historical Review* 20 (June 1933): 45–62.

Kolchin, Peter. "In Defense of Servitude: American Proslavery and Russian Proserfdom Arguments, 1760–1860." *American Historical Review* 85 (October 1980): 809–27.

Lyons, Adelaide Avery. "Religious Defense of Slavery in the North." *Trinity College Historical Society, Historical Papers* 13 (1919): 5–34.

Maddex, Jack P., Jr. "Proslavery Millennialism: Social Eschatology in Antebellum Southern Calvinism." *American Quarterly* 31 (Spring 1979): 46–62.

———. " 'The Southern Apostasy' Revisited: The Significance of Proslavery Christianity." *Marxist Perspectives* 2 (Fall 1979): 132–41.

Mathews, Donald G. "The Methodist Mission to the Slaves, 1829–1844." *Journal of American History* 51 (March 1965): 615–31.

———. "The Second Great Awakening as an Organizing Process, 1780–1830: An Hypothesis." *American Quarterly* 21 (Winter 1969): 23–43.

May, Robert E. "John A. Quitman and His Slaves: Reconciling Slave Resistance with the Proslavery Defense." *Journal of Southern History* 46 (November 1980): 551–70.

Mitchell, Joseph. "Traveling Preacher and Settled Farmer." *Methodist History* 5 (July 1967): 3–14.

Morrison, Larry R. "Nearer to the Brute Creation: The Scientific Defense of American Slavery before 1830." *Southern Studies* 19 (Fall 1980): 228–42.

Morrow, Ralph E. "The Proslavery Argument Revisited." *Mississippi Valley Historical Review* 47 (June 1961): 79–93.

Murphy, Robert Joseph. "The Catholic Church in the United States during the Civil War Period (1852–1866)." *Records of the American Catholic Historical Society* 39 (December 1928): 272–346.

Ohline, Howard A. "Slavery, Economics, and Congressional Politics, 1790." *Journal of Southern History* 46 (August 1980): 335–60.

Perkins, Howard C. "The Defense of Slavery in the Northern Press on the Eve of the Civil War." *Journal of Southern History* 9 (November 1943): 501–31.

Purifoy, Lewis M. "The Southern Methodist and the Proslavery Arguments." *Journal of Southern History* 32 (August 1966): 325–41.

Ratner, Lorman A. "Northern Concern for Social Order as Cause of Rejecting Anti-slavery, 1831–1840." *Historian* 28 (November 1965): 1–18.

Sellers, Charles G., Jr. "The Travail of Slavery." In *The Southerner as American*, edited by Charles G. Sellers, Jr. Chapel Hill: University of North Carolina Press, 1960.

Shalhope, Robert E. "Race, Class, Slavery, and the Antebellum Southern Mind." *Journal of Southern History* 37 (November 1971): 557–74.

———. "Thomas Jefferson's Republicanism and Antebellum Southern Thought." *Journal of Southern History* 42 (November 1976): 529–56.

Silbey, Joel H. "Pro-slavery Sentiment in Iowa, 1838–1861." *Iowa Journal of History and Politics* 55 (October 1957): 289–318.

Stampp, Kenneth M. "An Analysis of T. R. Dew's Review of the Debates in the Virginia Legislature." *Journal of Negro History* 27 (October 1942): 380–87.

Stange, Douglas C. "Abolitionism as Maleficence: Southern Unitarians versus Puritan Fanaticism, 1831–1860." *Harvard Library Bulletin* 26 (April 1978): 146–71.

———. "Abolitionism as Treason: The Unitarian Elite Defends Law, Order, and the Union." *Harvard Library Bulletin* 28 (April 1980): 152–70.

Streifford, David M. "The American Colonization Society: An Application of Republican Ideology to Early Antebellum Reform." *Journal of Southern History* 45 (May 1979): 201–20.

Tandy, Jeannette R. "Pro-slavery Propaganda in American Fiction of the Fifties." *South Atlantic Quarterly* 21 (January and April 1922): 41–50, 170–78.

Tise, Larry Edward. "The Interregional Appeal of Proslavery Thought: An Ideological Profile of the Antebellum American Clergy." *Plantation Society* 1 (February 1979): 58–72.

Towner, Lawrence W. "The Sewall-Saffin Dialogue on Slavery." *William and Mary Quarterly,* 3d ser., vol. 21 (January 1964): 40–52.

Wyatt-Brown, Bertram. "Prelude to Abolitionism: Sabbatarian Politics and the Rise of the Second Party System." *Journal of American History* 58 (September 1971): 316–41.

———. "Proslavery and Antislavery Intellectuals: Class Concepts and Polemical Struggle." In *Antislavery Reconsidered: New Perspectives on the Abolitionists,* edited by Lewis Perry and Michael Fellman. Baton Rouge: Louisiana State University Press, 1979.

Unpublished Studies

Broussard, James Hugh. "The Federalist Party in the South Atlantic States, 1800–1812." Ph.D. diss., Duke University, 1968.

Crook, Roger H. "The Ethical Emphases of the Editors of Baptist Journals Published in the Southeastern Region of the United States up to 1865." Ph.D. diss., Southern Baptist Theological Seminary, 1947.

Howard, Elizabeth Cary. "The Georgia Reaction to David Walker's Appeal." M.A. thesis, University of Georgia, 1968.

Mathews, Donald G. "Southern Clergy as a Strategic Elite, 1780–1870." Chapel Hill, N.C., 1972. (Mimeographed.)

Senior, Robert C. "New England Congregationalists and the Anti-slavery Movement, 1830–1860." Ph.D. diss., Yale University, 1954.

Shuck, Emerson Clayton. "Clergymen in Representative American Fiction,

1830–1930: A Study in Attitudes Toward Religion." Ph.D. diss., University of Wisconsin, 1943.

Taylor, Hubert Vance. "Slavery and the Deliberations of the Presbyterian General Assembly, 1833–1838." Ph.D. diss., Northwestern University, 1964.

Tise, Larry Edward. "Proslavery Ideology: A Social and Intellectual History of the Defense of Slavery in America, 1790–1840." Ph.D. diss., University of North Carolina at Chapel Hill, 1974.

Books

Adams, Alice Dana. *The Neglected Period of Anti-slavery in America, 1808–1831.* Boston and London: Ginn and Company, 1908.

Apter, David E., ed. *Ideology and Discontent.* New York: Free Press of Glencoe, 1964.

Auer, J. Jeffrey, ed. *Antislavery and Disunion, 1858–1861: Studies in the Rhetoric of Compromise and Conflict.* New York: Harper and Row, 1963.

Bailyn, Bernard. *The Ideological Origins of the American Revolution.* Cambridge: Harvard University Press, 1967.

———. *The Origin of American Politics.* New York: Alfred A. Knopf, 1968.

Baird, Robert. *Religion in America; or, an Account of the Origin, Relation to the State, and Present Condition of the Evangelical Churches in the United States with Notices of the Unevangelical Denominations.* New York: Harper and Brothers, 1856.

Banner, James M., Jr. *To the Hartford Convention: The Federalists and the Origins of Party Politics in Massachusetts, 1789–1815.* New York: Alfred A. Knopf, 1970.

Barnes, Gilbert Hobbs. *The Antislavery Impulse, 1830–1844.* New York: D. Appleton-Century Co., 1933.

Bell, Daniel. *The End of Ideology: On the Exhaustion of Political Ideas in the Fifties.* New York: Free Press, 1960.

Berwanger, Eugene H. *The Frontier against Slavery: Western Anti-Negro Prejudice and the Slavery Extension Controversy.* Urbana: University of Illinois Press, 1967.

Blied, Benjamin J. *Catholics and the Civil War.* Milwaukee: By the Author, 1945.

Bodo, John R. *The Protestant Clergy and Public Issues, 1812–1848.* Princeton, N.J.: Princeton University Press, 1954.

Boorstin, Daniel J. *The Lost World of Thomas Jefferson.* New York: Henry Holt and Company, 1948.

Bruce, Dickson D. *The Rhetoric of Conservatism: The Virginia Convention of 1829–30 and the Conservative Tradition in the South.* San Marino, Calif.: Huntingdon Library, 1982.

———. *Violence and Culture in the Antebellum South.* Austin: University of Texas Press, 1979.

Calhoun, Daniel H. *Professional Lives in America: Structure and Aspiration, 1750–1850.* Cambridge: Harvard University Press, 1965.

Campbell, Stanley W. *The Slave Catchers: Enforcement of the Fugitive Slave Law, 1850–1860.* Chapel Hill: University of North Carolina Press, 1970.

Cash, Wilbur J. *The Mind of the South.* New York: Alfred A. Knopf, 1941.

Christie, John W., and Dumond, Dwight L. *George Bourne and the Book and Slavery Irreconcilable.* Wilmington, Del., and Philadelphia: Historical Society of Delaware and Presbyterian Historical Society, 1969.

Cole, Charles C., Jr. *The Social Ideas of the Northern Evangelists, 1826–1860.* New York: Columbia University Press, 1954.

Cooper, William J., Jr. *The South and the Politics of Slavery, 1828–1856.* Baton Rouge: Louisiana State University Press, 1978.

Corwin, Arthur F. *Spain and the Abolition of Slavery in Cuba, 1817–1886.* Austin: Published for the Institute of Latin American Studies by the University of Texas Press, 1967.

Coupland, Reginald, Sir. *The British Anti-slavery Movement.* New York: Barnes & Noble, 1964.

Craven, Avery. *The Coming of the Civil War.* New York: Charles Scribner's Sons, 1942.

Dangerfield, George. *The Awakening of American Nationalism, 1815–1828.* New York: Harper & Row, 1965.

Davis, David Brion, ed. *The Fear of Conspiracy: Images of Un-American Subversion from the Revolution to the Present.* Ithaca: Cornell University Press, 1971.

Davis, David Brion. *The Problem of Slavery in the Age of Revolution, 1770–1823.* Ithaca: Cornell University Press, 1975.

———. *The Problem of Slavery in Western Culture.* Ithaca: Cornell University Press, 1966.

———. *Slavery and Human Progress.* New York: Oxford University Press, 1984.

Degler, Carl N. *Neither Black nor White: Slavery and Race Relations in Brazil and the United States.* New York: Macmillan Company, 1971.

Duberman, Martin, ed. *The Antislavery Vanguard: New Essays on the Abolitionists.* Princeton, N.J.: Princeton University Press, 1965.

Dumond, Dwight Lowell. *Antislavery Origins of the Civil War in the United States.* Ann Arbor: University of Michigan Press, 1961.

———. *Antislavery: The Crusade for Freedom in America.* Ann Arbor: University of Michigan Press, 1961.

———, comp. *A Bibliography of Antislavery in America.* Ann Arbor: University of Michigan Press, 1961.

Dunham, Chester Forrester. *The Attitude of the Northern Clergy Toward the South, 1860–1865.* Toledo, Ohio: Gray Company, 1942.

Easterby, J. H. *A History of the College of Charleston: Founded 1770.* N.p.: Trustees of the College of Charleston by the Scribner Press, 1935.

Eaton, Clement. *The Freedom-of-Thought Struggle in the Old South.* New York: Harper & Row, 1964.

Elkins, Stanley M. *Slavery: A Problem in American Institutional and Intellectual Life.* Chicago: University of Chicago Press, 1959.

Ericson, Kai T. *Wayward Puritans: A Study in the Sociology of Deviance.* New York: John Wiley & Sons, 1966.

Essig, James D. *The Bonds of Wickedness: American Evangelicals Against Slavery, 1770–1808.* Philadelphia: Temple University Press, 1982.

Ezekiel, Herbert T. *The Jews of Richmond During the Civil War.* Richmond, Va.: Press of Herbert T. Ezekiel, 1915.

Faust, Drew Gilpin, ed. *The Ideology of Slavery: Proslavery Thought in the Antebellum South, 1830–1860.* Baton Rouge: Louisiana State University Press, 1981.

————. *A Sacred Circle: The Dilemma of the Intellectual in the Old South, 1840–1860.* Baltimore: Johns Hopkins University Press, 1977.

Finley, Moses I. *Ancient Slavery and Modern Ideology.* New York: Viking Press, 1980.

Fischer, David Hackett. *The Revolution of American Conservatism: The Federalist Party in the Era of Jeffersonian Democracy.* New York: Harper & Row, 1965.

Foner, Eric. *Free Soil, Free Labor, Free Men: The Ideology of the Republican Party before the Civil War.* London: Oxford University Press, 1970.

Foner, Philip S. *Frederick Douglass.* New York: Citadel Press, 1964.

Ford, Paul Leicester, ed. *The New-England Primer.* New York: Dodd, Mead and Company, 1899.

Foster, Charles I. *An Errand of Mercy: The Evangelical United Front, 1790–1837.* Chapel Hill: University of North Carolina Press, 1960.

Fox-Genovese, Elizabeth, and Genovese, Eugene D. *Fruits of Merchant Capital: Slavery and Bourgeois Property in the Rise and Expansion of Capitalism.* Oxford: Oxford University Press, 1983.

Franklin, John Hope. *From Slavery to Freedom: A History of Negro Americans.* 3d ed. New York: Alfred A. Knopf, 1967.

Frederickson, George M. *The Black Image in the White Mind: The Debate on Afro-American Character and Destiny, 1817–1914.* New York: Harper & Row, 1971.

Freehling, Alison Goodyear. *Drift Toward Dissolution: The Virginia Slavery Debate of 1831–1832.* Baton Rouge: Lousiana State University Press, 1982.

Freehling, Alison Goodyear. *Drift Toward Dissolution: The Virginia Slavery Debate of 1831–1832.* Baton Rouge: Louisiana State University Press, 1982.

Genovese, Eugene D. *The Political Economy of Slavery: Studies in the Economy and Society of the Slave South.* New York: Vintage Books, 1965.

————. *Roll, Jordan, Roll: The World the Slaves Made.* New York: Pantheon Books, 1974.

————. *The World the Slaveholders Made: Two Essays in Interpretation.* New York: Pantheon Books, 1969.

Gossett, Thomas F. *Race: The History of an Idea in America.* Dallas: Southern Methodist University Press, 1963.

Greenberg, Kenneth S. *Masters and Statesmen: The Political Culture of American Slavery.* Baltimore: Johns Hopkins University Press, 1985.

Griffin, Clifford S. *Their Brothers' Keepers: Moral Stewardship in the United States, 1800–1865.* New Brunswick, N.J.: Rutgers University Press, 1960.

Hall, Gwendolyn Midlo. *Slave Control in Slave Plantation Societies: A Comparison of St. Domingue and Cuba.* Baltimore: Johns Hopkins University Press, 1971.

Hart, Albert Bushnell. *Slavery and Abolition, 1831–1841.* New York: Harper & Brothers, 1906.

Hofstadter, Richard. *The American Political Tradition and the Men Who Made It.* New York: Alfred A. Knopf, 1948.

Holifield, E. Brooks. *The Gentlemen Theologians: American Theology in Southern Culture, 1795–1860.* Durham, N.C.: Duke University Press, 1978.

Irby, Richard. *History of Randolph-Macon College, Virginia.* Richmond, Va.: Whittet & Shepperson, [ca. 1898].

Jenkins, William Sumner. *Pro-slavery Thought in the Old South.* Chapel Hill: University of North Carolina Press, 1935.

Jordan, Winthrop D. *White over Black: American Attitudes toward the Negro, 1550–1812.* Chapel Hill: University of North Carolina Press for the Institute of Early American History and Culture, 1968.

Keller, Suzanne. *Beyond the Ruling Class: Strategic Elites in Modern Society.* New York: Random House, 1963.

Kerber, Linda K. *Federalists in Dissent: Images and Ideology in Jeffersonian America.* Ithaca: Cornell University Press, 1970.

Klingberg, Frank J. *The Anti-slavery Movement in England.* New Haven, Conn.: Yale University Press, 1926.

Korn, Bertram Wallace. *American Jewry and the Civil War.* Philadelphia: Jewish Publication Society of America, 1951.

———. *Jews and Negro Slavery in the Old South, 1789–1865.* Elkins Park, Pa.: Reform Congregation Keneseth Israel, 1961.

LaBorde, Maximilian. *History of the South Carolina College.* Columbia, S.C.: Peter B. Blass, 1859.

Litwack, Leon F. *North of Slavery: The Negro in the Free States, 1790–1860.* Chicago: University of Chicago Press, 1961.

Livermore, Shaw. *The Twilight of Federalism.* Princeton, N.J.: Princeton University Press, 1962.

Lloyd, Arthur Young. *The Slavery Controversy, 1831–1860.* Chapel Hill: University of North Carolina Press, 1939.

Lord, John King. *A History of Dartmouth College, 1815–1909.* 2 vols. Concord, N.H.: Rumford Press, 1913.

Love, William DeLoss. *The Fast and Thanksgiving Days of New England.* Boston and New York: Houghton, Mifflin and Company, 1895.

Loveland, Anne C. *Southern Evangelicals and the Social Order, 1800–1860*. Baton Rouge: Louisiana State University Press, 1980.

McCardell, John. *The Idea of a Southern Nation: Southern Nationalists and Southern Nationalism, 1830–1860*. New York: W. W. Norton & Co., 1979.

McColley, Robert. *Slavery and Jeffersonian Virginia*. Urbana: University of Illinois Press, 1964.

McKitrick, Eric L., ed. *Slavery Defended: The Views of the Old South*. Englewood Cliffs, N.J.: Prentice-Hall, 1963.

MacLeod, Duncan J. *Slavery, Race, and the American Revolution*. London: Cambridge University Press, 1974.

Mathews, Donald G. *Religion in the Old South*. Chicago: University of Chicago Press, 1977.

———. *Slavery and Methodism: A Chapter in American Morality, 1790–1845*. Princeton, N.J.: Princeton University Press, 1965.

Matlack, Lucius G. *The History of American Slavery and Methodism, from 1780 to 1849; and History of the Wesleyan Methodist Connection of America*. New York: n.p., 1849.

Miller, John C. *The Federalist Era*. New York: Harper & Row, 1960.

Moore, George H. *Notes on the History of Slavery in Massachusetts*. New York: D. Appleton & Co., 1866.

Moore, Glover. *The Missouri Controversy, 1819–1821*. Lexington: University of Kentucky Press, 1953.

Morgan, Edmund S. *American Slavery, American Freedom: The Ordeal of Colonial Virginia*. New York: W. W. Norton & Co., 1975.

Morrison, A. J. *College of Hampden Sidney: Dictionary of Biography, 1776–1825*. Hampden Sidney, Va.: Published by Hampden Sidney College, [ca. 1921].

Murphy, John C. *An Analysis of Attitudes of American Catholics Toward the Immigrant and the Negro, 1825–1925*. Washington, D.C.: Catholic University of America Press, 1940.

Murray, Andrew Evans. *Presbyterians and the Negro: A History*. Philadelphia: Presbyterian Historical Society, 1966.

National Advisory Commission on Civil Disorders. *Report of the National Advisory Commission on Civil Disorders*. New York: New York Times Company, 1968.

Nelson, E. Clifford, and Fevold, Eugene L. *The Lutheran Church Among Norwegian-Americans: A History of the Evangelical Lutheran Church*. Minneapolis: Augsburg Publishing House, 1960.

Oakes, James. *The Ruling Race: A History of American Slaveholders*. New York: Alfred A. Knopf, 1982.

Peterson, Thomas Virgil. *Ham and Japheth: The Mythic World of Whites in the Antebellum South*. Metuchen, N.J.: Scarecrow Press, 1978.

Pressly, Thomas J. *Americans Interpret Their Civil War*. Princeton, N.J.: Princeton University Press, 1954.

Raboteau, Albert J. *Slave Religion: The 'Invisible Institution' in the Antebellum South.* New York: Oxford University Press, 1978.

Ratner, Lorman A. *Powder Keg: Northern Opposition to the Anti-slavery Movement, 1831–1840.* New York: Basic Books, 1968.

Rice, Madeleine Hooke. *American Catholic Opinion in the Slavery Controversy.* New York: Columbia University Press, 1944.

Richards, Leonard L. *"Gentlemen of Property and Standing": Anti-abolition Mobs in Jacksonian America.* London: Oxford University Press, 1970.

Robinson, Donald L. *Slavery in the Structure of American Politics, 1765–1820.* New York: Harcourt Brace Jovanovich, 1971.

Rohne, J. Magnus. *Norwegian American Lutheranism up to 1872.* New York: Macmillan Company, 1926.

Rose, Lisle A. *Prologue to Democracy: The Federalists in the South, 1789–1800.* Lexington: University of Kentucky Press, 1968.

Rossiter, Clinton. *Conservatism in America: The Thankless Persuasion.* 2d ed. New York: Random House, 1962.

Rudolph, Frederick. *The American College and University: A History.* New York: Alfred A. Knopf, 1962.

Schurmann, Franz. *Ideology and Organization in Communist China.* 2d ed. Berkeley: University of California Press, 1968.

Scott, Donald. *From Office to Profession: The New England Ministry, 1750–1850.* Philadelphia: University of Pennsylvania Press, 1978.

Silver, James W. *Confederate Morale and Church Propaganda.* Tuscaloosa, Ala.: Confederate Publishing Company, 1957.

Simpson, Lewis P. *The Dispossessed Garden: Pastoral and History in Southern Literature.* Athens: University of Georgia Press, 1975.

Smith, Elwyn Allen. *The Presbyterian Ministry in American Culture: A Study in Changing Concepts, 1700–1900.* Philadelphia: Westminster Press for the Presbyterian Historical Society, 1962.

Smith, H. Shelton. *In His Image, But . . . : Racism in Southern Religion, 1780–1910.* Durham, N.C.: Duke University Press, 1972.

Smith, James Ward and Jamison, A. Leland, eds. *Religion in American Life. Vol. I: The Shaping of American Religion.* Princeton, N.J.: Princeton University Press, 1961.

Stampp, Kenneth M. *The Peculiar Institution: Slavery in the Antebellum South.* New York: Alfred A. Knopf, 1956.

Stanton, William. *The Leopard's Spots: Scientific Attitudes toward Race in America, 1815–1859.* Chicago: University of Chicago Press, 1960.

Staudenraus, Philip J. *The African Colonization Movement, 1816–1865.* New York: Columbia University Press, 1961.

Stauffer, Vernon. *New England and the Bavarian Illuminati.* New York: Columbia University Press, 1918.

Stroupe, Henry Smith. *The Religious Press in the South Atlantic States, 1802–1865: An Annotated Bibliography with Historical Introduction and Notes.* Durham, N.C.: Duke University Press, 1956.

Sydnor, Charles S. *The Development of Southern Sectionalism.* Baton Rouge: Louisiana State University Press, 1948.

Tannenbaum, Frank. *Slave and Citizen: The Negro in the Americas.* New York: Alfred A. Knopf, 1946.

Thornton, J. Mills. *Politics and Power in a Slave Society: Alabama, 1800–1860.* Baton Rouge: Louisiana State University Press, 1978.

Vander-Velde, Lewis G. *The Presbyterian Churches and the Federal Union, 1861–1869.* Cambridge, Mass.: Harvard University Press, 1932.

Weaver, Glenn. *The History of Trinity College.* Hartford, Conn.: Trinity College Press, 1967.

Wentz, Abdel Ross. *A Basic History of Lutheranism in America.* Rev. ed. Philadelphia: Fortress Press, 1964.

Williams, William Appleman. *The Contours of American History.* Cleveland: World Publishing Company, 1961.

Wood, Gordon S. *The Creation of the American Republic, 1776–1787.* Chapel Hill: University of North Carolina Press for the Institute of Early American History and Culture, 1969.

Woodward, C. Vann. *The Burden of Southern History.* Baton Rouge: Louisiana State University Press, 1960.

Wyatt-Brown, Bertram. *Southern Honor: Ethics and Behavior in the Old South.* New York: Oxford University Press, 1982.

Zilversmit, Arthur. *The First Emancipation: The Abolition of Slavery in the North.* Chicago: University of Chicago Press, 1967.

ILLUSTRATION CREDITS

Facing page 22: George Whitefield, print, 1742, courtesy of Methodist Archives Center, Madison, New Jersey. William Knox, photograph courtesy of William L. Clements Library, Ann Arbor, Michigan. Jonathan Boucher, portrait, ca. 1785, by Daniel Gardner, courtesy of Yale University Art Gallery. John Drayton, portrait, 1801, by William Williams, courtesy of South Caroliniana Library, Columbia, South Carolina.

Following page 25: Pages from *The African Slave Trade*, photograph of Benezet's personal copy, 1772, courtesy of Rutgers University Library.

Facing page 30: Title page from printed public debate on slavery, 1773, photograph courtesy of Houghton Library, Harvard University.

Facing page 45: Cartoon from *Punch, or the London Charivari,* 1847.

Facing page 49: Robert Walsh, undated miniature, after Thomas Sully, courtesy of American Philosophical Society, Philadelphia. Samuel Stanhope Smith, portrait, ca. 1800, by James Sharples, courtesy of the Art Museum, Princeton University.

Facing page 62: Richard Furman, photograph from Cook, *Biography of Richard Furman,* 1913. Frederick Dalcho, miniature, 1823, by Charles Fraser, courtesy of C. R. Banks, St. Matthews, South Carolina. Thomas Cooper, portrait, 1819, by Charles Wilson Peale, courtesy of Mutter Museum, College of Physicians, Philadelphia. Thomas Roderick Dew, portrait, 1846, by G. P. A. Healy, courtesy of Joseph and Margaret Muscarelle Museum of Art, College of William and Mary.

Facing page 87: Cartoon from *The Looking Glass,* 1832.

Following page 87: Frontispiece from Cobden, *The White Slaves of England,* 1853. Illustration from Cobden, *The White Slaves of England,* 1853.

Following page 103: Illustrations, ca. 1860, from author's collection.

Facing page 109: Broadside, 1863, courtesy of Vermont Historical Society, Montpelier.

Facing page 159: John Bachman, portrait, 1840, by Alexander Anderson, courtesy of American Philosophical Society, Philadelphia. Moses Ashley Curtis, photograph courtesy of North Carolina Collection, University of North Carolina Library at Chapel Hill. Elisha Mitchell, photograph courtesy of North Carolina Division of Archives and History, Raleigh. Thomas Smyth, photograph from Smyth's *Autobiographical Notes,* 1914.

Facing page 160: George Junkin, portrait, ca. 1835, by Robert Street, courtesy of Lafayette College Art Collection, Easton, Pennsylvania. Augustus Baldwin Longstreet, photograph courtesy of Methodist Archives Center, Madison, New Jersey. Calvin Henderson Wiley, photograph courtesy of North Carolina Division of Archives and History, Raleigh. Joseph Ruggles Wilson, photograph courtesy of Woodrow Wilson Collection, Firestone Library, Princeton University.

Facing page 164: Isaac Leeser, photograph courtesy of American Jewish Archives, Cincinnati, Ohio. John Mitchel, engraving from Mitchel's *Jail Journal,* 1868. Carl Ferdinand Wilhelm Walther, photograph from Guenther, *Dr. C. F. W. Walther,* 1890. Peter Laurentius Larsen, photograph from Larsen's *Laur. Larsen,* 1936, courtesy of Luther College, Decorah, Iowa.

Facing page 177: William Gannaway Brownlow, engraving from Brownlow, *Sketches of the Rise of Secession,* 1862. Jesse Babcock Ferguson, photograph courtesy of Disciples of Christ Historical Society, Nashville. Leonidas Polk, photograph courtesy of North Carolina Division of Archives and History, Raleigh. Thornton Stringfellow, photograph courtesy of Virginia Baptist Historical Society, Richmond.

Facing page 185: Benjamin Morgan Palmer, photograph courtesy of the Historic New Orleans Collection, New Orleans, Louisiana.

Facing page 207: Timothy Dwight, portrait, 1817, by John Trumbull, courtesy of Yale University Art Gallery.

Facing page 242: Harrison Gray Otis, portrait, 1809, by Gilbert Stuart, courtesy of Society for the Preservation of New England Antiquities, Boston. Charles Jared Ingersoll, photograph from Meigs, *Life of Charles Jared Ingersoll,* 1897. James Kirke Paulding, engraving from author's collection. Samuel Findley Breese Morse, self-portrait, n.d., courtesy of Addison Gallery of American Art, Phillips Academy, Andover, Massachusetts.

Following page 243: Slavery in America print, 1850, by John Haven, Boston, courtesy of the Harry T. Peters America on Stone Lithography Collection, Smithsonian Institution.

Facing page 264: Nehemiah Adams, engraving from Essex St. Church, *Memorial Volume,* 1860. John Henry Hopkins, engraving from Hopkins, *Life of J. H. Hopkins,* 1875. Moses Stuart, portrait, ca. 1841, by Thomas Buchanan Read, courtesy of Yale University Art Gallery. Nathaniel Sheldon Wheaton, undated portrait, courtesy of Trinity College Library, Hartford, Connecticut.

Facing page 281: Charles Hodge, portrait, 1825–1840, by Rembrandt Peale, courtesy of Presbyterian Historical Society, Philadelphia. Nathan Lord, portrait, ca. 1846, by Thomas Bayley Lawson, courtesy of Hood Museum of Art, Dartmouth College, Hanover, New Hampshire. George Washington Blagden, engraving from Hill, *Old South Church,* 1890.

Facing page 297: William Capers, photograph courtesy of Methodist Archives Center, Madison, New Jersey. Charles Colcock Jones, Sr., photograph courtesy of the Georgia Historical Society, Savannah. Nathaniel Bowen, engraving from Norton, *Life of Bishop Bowen,* 1859. William Meade, portrait, ca. 1843, by Edward Dalton Marchant, courtesy of Historical Society of Pennsylvania, Philadelphia.

Facing page 310: Thomas Meredith, photograph courtesy of North Carolina Division of Archives and History, Raleigh. William Henry Brisbane, daguerreotype, courtesy of State Historical Society of Wisconsin, Madison.

Facing page 327: Frederick Freeman, photograph courtesy of Sandwich Historical Society, Sandwich, Massachusetts. George Washington Freeman, engraving from Norton, *Life of Bishop Freeman,* 1867. Rufus William Bailey, photograph from *The Patriarch,* 1841, courtesy of William R. Perkins Library, Duke University. Theodore Clapp, engraving from Clapp, *Autobiographical Sketches,* 1857.

Facing page 336: William Winans, photograph courtesy of Methodist Archives Center, Madison, New Jersey. Whitemarsh Benjamin Seabrook, photograph of miniature, courtesy of South Caroliniana Library, Columbia. William Harper, portrait, n.d., courtesy of South Caroliniana Library, Columbia. William Gilmore Simms, engraving from author's collection.

Facing page 356: "A Family Quarrel," cartoon from *Punch, or the London Charivari,* September 28, 1861.

Facing page 358: "'Caesar Imperator!' or, The American Gladiators," cartoon from *Punch, or the London Charivari,* May 18, 1861.

INDEX